Lecture Notes in Computer Science 9454

Commenced Publication in 1973
Founding and Former Series Editors:
Gerhard Goos, Juris Hartmanis, and Jan van Leeuwen

More information about this series at http://www.springer.com/series/7409

Juan M. García-Chamizo · Giancarlo Fortino
Sergio F. Ochoa (Eds.)

Ubiquitous Computing and Ambient Intelligence

Sensing, Processing, and Using Environmental Information

9th International Conference, UCAmI 2015
Puerto Varas, Chile, December 1–4, 2015
Proceedings

 Springer

Editors
Juan M. García-Chamizo
Universidad de Alicante
Alicante
Spain

Giancarlo Fortino
University of Calabria
Rende
Italy

Sergio F. Ochoa
Universidad de Chile
Santiago
Chile

ISSN 0302-9743   ISSN 1611-3349   (electronic)
Lecture Notes in Computer Science
ISBN 978-3-319-26400-4   ISBN 978-3-319-26401-1   (eBook)
DOI 10.1007/978-3-319-26401-1

Library of Congress Control Number: 2015954580

LNCS Sublibrary: SL3 – Information Systems and Applications, incl. Internet/Web, and HCI

Springer International Publishing AG Switzerland is part of Springer Science+Business Media
(www.springer.com)

Preface

Ambient intelligence (AmI) represents the functionality of environmental systematic and automatic sensing and the corresponding proactive acting. AmI problems belong to the domain of "being Helped": social, psychological, and instrumental disciplines.

Ubiquitous computing (UC) provides the infrastructure to obtain environmental information and its massive processing in a non-limited way. UC is the confluence of computing, communication, and control technologies. It takes place regardless of the place, the time, and all other contextual variables.

The UCAmI Conference brings together AmI with its support, that is, UC. In other words, the UACmI Conference joins UC with its result, that is, AmI. Globally, the essence of the conference is an integral conception that mutually empowers UC and AmI.

Ideally, the recipients within an AmI environment will not be aware of the ambient devices; however, they will obtain benefits from the services that devices could provide. Devices embedded within the environment are aware of the people's presence and subsequently react to their gestures, actions, and context. Recently, interest in AmI has grown considerably owing to new challenges posed by society, demanding highly innovative services such as vehicular ad hoc networks (VANET), ambient-assisted living (AAL), e-health, Internet of Things, and home automation, among others.

We are interested in the sound development of UC and AmI because it is the only way to properly satisfy the expectation around these excitant fields of information, communications, and control technologies. Therefore, the main focus of this edition of the UCAmI Conference was "Ubiquitous Computing and Ambient Intelligence: Conceptual Framework, Methodical Development, and Systematic Innovation".

Self evaluation of expertise grade of each reviewer reaches an average of 3,63 in an up to 5 scale. In our permanent effort to enhance the relevance of the UCAmI Conference — beside the revision process including 74 reviewers from 26 countries — during the conference, each session chair was assisted by two additional session reviewers in order to intensify the discussion with authors during their presentation.

We received 62 submissions for this ninth edition of UCAmI that involved 183 authors from 16 countries. A total of 161 reviews were performed, reaching the high average of 2.60 reviews per submission. The acceptance rate was 58 %.

We would like to thank all the authors who submitted their work for consideration, as well as the reviewers who made the considerable effort of providing detailed and constructive reviews.

Finally, we are very grateful to our colleagues who assisted in the organization of this joint event, to the keynote presenters, and to the speakers who presented their accepted papers. They were the essence of the UCAmI Conference.

December 2015

Sergio F. Ochoa
Giancarlo Fortino
Juan M. García-Chamizo

Organization

General Chair

José Bravo   University of Castilla-La Mancha, Spain

Local Organizing Chair

Sergio F. Ochoa   University of Chile, Chile

Program Committee Chairs

Juan Manuel   University of Alicante, Spain
  García-Chamizo
Giancarlo Fortino   University of Calabria

Publicity Chair

Jesús Fontecha Diezma   University of Castilla-La Mancha, Spain

Webmaster

Iván González Díaz   University of Castilla-La Mancha, Spain

Steering Committee

Xavier Alaman, Spain
José Bravo, Spain
Jesus Favela, Mexico
Juan Manuel García-Chamizo, Spain
Luis Guerrero, Costa Rica
Ramón Hervás, Spain
Rui Jose, Portugal
Diego López-De-Ipiña, Spain
Chris Nugent, UK
Sergio F. Ochoa, Chile
Gabriel Urzáiz, Mexico
Vladimir Villarreal, Panama

Organizing Committee

Nelson Baloian, Chile
Javier Bustos, Chile
Francisco Gutiérrez, Chile
Valeria Herskovic, Chile
José Pino, Chile
Gustavo Zurita, Chile
Tania Mondéjar, Spain
Iván González, Spain
Justyna Kidacka, Spain

Program Committee

Xavier Alamán	UAM, Spain
Jan Alexandersson	DFKI GmbH, Germany
Mohamed Bakhouya	University of technology of Belfort Montbeliard, France
Nelson Baloian	University of Chile, Chile
Jean-Paul Barthes	Université de Technologie de Compiègne, France
Paolo Bellavista	University of Bologna, Italy
Stephane Bouchard	Université du Québec en Outaouais, Canada
Fatima Boujarwah	Kuwait University, USA
José Bravo	Castilla La Mancha University, MAmI Research Lab, Spain
Sophie Chabridon	CNRS UMR SAMOVAR, France
Wei Chen	Eindhoven University of Technology, The Netherlands
Walter Colitti	ModoSmart S.L., Spain
Geoff Coulson	Lancaster University, UK
Boris De Ruyter	Philips Research, The Netherlands
Stefan Decker	DERI Galway, Ireland
Anna Fensel	University of Innsbruck, Austria
Carlo Ferrari	University of Padova, Italy
Giancarlo Fortino	Universidad de Calabria, Italy
Leo Galway	University of Ulster, UK
Juan Manuel García-Chamizo	University of Alicante, Spain
Raffaele Gravina	University of Calabria, Italy
Dan Grigoras	UCC, Ireland
Antonio Guerrieri	University of Calabria, Italy
Bin Guo	Institut Telecom SudParis, France
Chris Guy	University of Reading, UK
Antonio Gómez Skarmeta	University of Murcia, Spain

Jan Havlík	Czech Technical University in Prague, Czech Republic
Ramón Hervás	Castilla La Mancha University, MAmI Research Group, Spain
Jesse Hoey	University of Waterloo, Canada
Alan Jovic	University of Zagreb, Croatia
Wolfgang Kastner	TU Vienna, Austria
Ryzsard Klempous	Wroclaw University of Technology, Poland
Jean-Christophe Lapayre	DISC - Université de Franche-Comté, France
Sungyoung Lee	KyungHee University, Korea
Ernst Leiss	University of Houston, USA
Tun Lu	Fudan University, China
Wolfram Luther	University of Duisburg-Essen, Denmark
Diego López-De-Ipiña	University of Deusto, Spain
Vittorio Miori	Italian National Research Council, Italy
Francisco Moya	University of Castilla La Mancha, Spain
Tatsuo Nakajima	Waseda University, Japan
Sergio F. Ochoa	Universidad de Chile, Chile
Philippe Palanque	University Toulouse 3, France
Till Plumbaum	Technische Universität Berlin, Germany
Jose Antonio Pow-Sang	Pontificia Universidad Católica del Perú, Peru
Uli Sattler	University of Manchester, UK
Markus Schneider	University of Florida, USA
Weiming Shen	National Research Council Canada, Canada
Giandomenico Spezzano	Italian National Research Council, Italy
Chantal Taconet	Télécom SudParis, France
Natalia Villanueva-Rosales	University of Texas at El Paso, USA
Vladimir Villarreal	Technological University of Panama, Panama
Benjamin Weyers	RWTH Aachen, Germany
Erik Wilde	Siemens, USA
Juan Ye	University of St Andrews, UK
Rui Zhang	IBM Research - Almaden, USA
Jing Zhou	Communication University of China, China

Additional Reviewers

Iván González, Spain
Abel Méndez Porras, Costa Rica
Daniel Ruiz Fernández, Spain
Rafael Jesús Valdivieso Sarabia, Spain
Jerónimo Mora Pascual, Spain
Mingyuan Xia, Canada
Francisco Javier Ferrández Pastor, Spain
Freddy Paz, Peru

Jesús Fontecha, Spain
Jan Nikodem, Poland
Óscar Marín Alonso, Spain
Mario Nieto Hidalgo, Spain
Carmelo R. García, Spain

Contents

Ambient Intelligence for Transport

Human Interaction and Ambient Intelligence

ICT Instrumentation and Middleware Support for Smart Environments and Objects

Ambient Intelligence for Urban Areas

Adding Intelligence for Environment Adaptation

MagicFinger: A New Approach to Indoor Localization

Daniel Carrillo, Victoria Moreno$^{(\boxtimes)}$, and Antonio F. Skarmeta

Department of Information and Communications Engineering, University of Murcia,
Campus de Espinardo, 30100 Murcia, Spain
{daniel.carrillo2,mvmoreno,skarmeta}@um.es

Abstract. This paper presents a novel approach for mobile phone centric observation applied to indoor localization. The approach involves a localization fingerprinting methodology that takes advantage of the presence of magnetic field anomalies inside buildings, and uses all three components of the measured magnetic field vectors to improve accuracy. By using adequate soft computing techniques, it is possible to adequately balance the constraints of common solutions. The resulting system does not rely on any infrastructure devices and therefore is easy to manage and deploy. Experimental evaluations carried out in two different buildings confirm the satisfactory performance of indoor localization based on magnetic field vectors. These evaluations provided an error of (11.34 m, 4.78 m) in the (x, y) components of the estimated positions in the first building where experiments were carried out, with a standard deviation of (3.41 m, 4.68 m); and, in the second building, an error of (4 m, 2.98 m) with a deviation of (2.64 m, 2.33 m).

Keywords: Indoor localization · Smartphone · Magnetic field · Fingerprinting

1 Introduction

In indoor environments such as buildings, obtaining precise localization information is still a challenging task. Traditional mechanisms such as GPS [1] are unworkable inside buildings due to the attenuation of satellite signal. This has resulted in the development of alternative indoor localization systems with acceptable results.

As an alternative, the potential use of exploiting mobile phones for sensing and context recognition has recently attracted interest from researchers in both industrial and academic communities. This has resulted in a huge range of new solutions for indoor localization related problems [2]. The ubiquitous and longitudinal data that smartphones can provide are expected to revolutionize technological services and spark a new wave of ubiquitous services.

In this work, we present MagicFinger: a novel approach to indoor localization using the magnetometers that are integrated in common smartphones.

© Springer International Publishing Switzerland 2015
J.M. García-Chamizo et al. (Eds.): UCAmI 2015, LNCS 9454, pp. 3–12, 2015.
DOI: 10.1007/978-3-319-26401-1_1

Unlike most infrastructure-based solutions [3], our system does not rely upon any additional support infrastructure. Our solution only requires a personal smartphone able to sense the magnetic field present inside buildings. The methodology consists of two phases. First, maps containing the magnetic field profile of the building in which the localization problem is to be solved are generated; this constitutes the offline training phase of the system. Then, during the online phase, users supply the system with the magnetic field vectors measured by their phones, and, based on these measurements, the system is able to provide accurate localization data.

The structure of this paper is as follows: Sect. 2 reviews some localization solutions proposed in literature and presents our approach to use magnetic field measurements for solving indoor localization. Section 3 explains the different phases of our indoor localization system, which is based on an off-line phase to generate the localization model, followed by an on-line phase that estimates position in real-time. Section 4 details the scenario where we carry out the tests for the system evaluation, and the experimental results obtained are collated here. Finally, Sect. 5 provides conclusions and future directions of our work.

2 Related Work

Localization proposals based on magnetic field measurements assume that the success in estimating orientation and position is conditioned by the capacity of magnetometers to sense the Earth's magnetic field in environments containing magnetic anomalies. In principle, a non-uniform indoor ambient magnetic field produces different magnetic observations depending on the path taken through it. In other words, static objects or infrastructures inside buildings (such as steel structures, electric power systems and electronic and mechanical appliances) perturb the Earth's magnetic field and can make up a profile of magnetic field values (a map composed of magnetic field fingerprints), which can be used to solve the localization problem. Nevertheless, this magnetic profile must be well characterized and quantified previously at estimation process.

To date, most efforts have been directed at studying the feasibility of using the indoor magnetic field for localization purposes, concluding that it represents a stable and unique solution applicable to this problem as long as the infrastructure of the building remains stable. Two proposals to generate magnetic maps of buildings to be used for indoor localization are [4,5], both of them based on considering only the intensity value of the magnetic field measured inside buildings. Furthermore, the scalability and robustness of localization solutions based on this approach in buildings are open issues that require to be further addressed, especially in buildings where the number of magnetic field perturbation sources is low, or when these sources are of the same nature. Bearing all these aspects in mind, MagicFinger uses the three magnetic field components sensed by smartphone magnetometers to provide a robust and accurate indoor localization system for buildings. This approach is addressed by [6]. Nevertheless, in this last authors only provide experimental results using their methodology to map the magnetic field on the ground's surface in their indoor research facilities, but it is not provided a validated solution in a real building.

3   MagicFinger: An Indoor Localization Mechanism Based on 3D Magnetic Fingerprints

3.1   Offline Training Phase

The aim of this step is to generate 3D magnetic field patterns of buildings. At following, we describe the different actions to be performed to generate such models for indoor localization.

Data Collection. Magnetic field data are gathered using a smartphone with a built-in magnetometer, which allows our system to not depend on any infrastructure. During this first stage, user phone carrying position (where and how user carries the phone) is pre-established to be later considered and associated to the appropriate magnetic field maps generated at the end of the offline training phase of our system.

Considering each one of the pre-established user phone carrying positions, "snapshots" of the magnetic field are collected over short periods of time (less than a minute at each localization Z_q) and throughout the building. These snapshots are taken by rotating the sensor, gathering data every 3 or 4 degrees of rotation at a particular localization Z_q. Such measurements are then associated to the physical localizations $Z_q^{(t)}$ where they were gathered. Several data collection sets are carried out, considering different context conditions such as different levels of occupancy, different times of the day, etc., so that the building models generated are sufficiently representative to cover different contextual conditions of the building.

Pre-Processing. Feature vectors are extracted from the data for use in localization estimation. The different processing techniques applied at this stage are as follows:

1. *Transformation:* The values within the dataset are arranged into windows of between 80 and 100 samples, grouping the values at Z_q—which corresponds to the different orientations at that particular localization, producing a vector containing 27 features.

2. *Filtering:* During this process, a filter is applied to remove features extracted from the training dataset that vary very little or too much.

3. *Normalization:* All values in the dataset are normalized. The resulting values are in the [0,1] range for every feature extracted form the initial dataset.

4. *Feature selection:* the features that have been filtered are ranked through recursive feature elimination by means of a resampling algorithm, as explained in [7]. The model used for measuring performance is *Random Forests* [8]. Finally, different features are used for clustering and for training the classifier and the estimators—particularly, the features that prove to be the most appropriate for each technique.

Clustering. The data gathered are processed to identify zones of the building where the magnetic field distribution presents peaks and similarities that can be used as magnetic field landmarks. These landmarks will be used later to georeference the magnetic field values measured in the building during the online phase of MagicFinger. Thus, the space inside the building is divided according to the distribution of the magnetic field values, and the data collected are grouped according to the clusters identified. This partitioning of the space into zones makes the estimation much more accurate, and also makes the system scalable.

We perform a comparison of the *Expectation Maximisation (EM)* algorithm [9] and the *k-means* technique using the method proposed by *Witten et al.* [10], which selects the best subset of features based on a lasso-type penalty criterion, because we do not know which features could lead to optimum partitioning. We are interested in analyzing the performance of models using only the three components of the magnetic field and also considering more information, extracted in the form of features. Furthermore, each localization $Z_q^{(t)}$ is also used to force the algorithm to group data that are close in space, making the estimation more precise.

After trying with different numbers of clusters and configurations of features for each algorithm, the best clustering method and partitioning are to be selected, which results to be those zones provided by the EM algorithm using intensities, as shown in Sect. 4.

Landmark Classifier. The landmark classifier assigns each new magnetic field measurement to a specific landmark previously determined by the clustering algorithm.

In order to select a suitable classification technique, we analyze the performance of different Classifiers. We first choose a classifier that works with Gaussian processes, based on the assumption that most features can be modelled by a mixture of Gaussian functions, as resulted from an analysis of each feature distribution. As we wish to assess the performance of a range of classifier techniques, four totally different classifiers are added so as to cover diverse approaches. The algorithms selected are the following, and their mathematical foundations can be found in the corresponding references: Gaussian Process with Radial Basis Function Kernel [11]; Single C5.0 Tree [12]; SIMCA [13]; Multi-layer Perceptron with Rprop learning algorithm [14]; and Bagged CART [15].

We assess the performance with the f1-score metric, whose expression is: $F_1 = 2 \cdot \frac{precision \cdot recall}{precision + recall}$, and whose value range is $0 <= F_1 <= 1$. *Precision* is the fraction of retrieved instances that are relevant, and *recall* is the fraction of relevant instances that are retrieved. Even though it does not consider the true negative rate, it is possible to see whether each class (i.e. zone) has been correctly predicted or not with respect to the other classes, but this is underestimated. The best classifier turns out to be the technique that uses Gaussian processes. After classifying the zone of the building for each new measurement, we can focus on the magnetic field characterization of the landmark covering this zone, and ignore the rest of the space to estimate localization.

Localization Estimator. Once the magnetic field measurements are correctly classified according to their associated landmark, the zone of the building to which every measurement belongs can be inferred.

In contrast to other works, we propose to estimate each component at a particular localization. This system is valid for an estimation made at a fixed height from the floor, so it will yield (x, y) position. This estimated localization is referenced to a local coordinate system within the building. Therefore, it is necessary for each particular building to have a specific coordinate system defined. Bearing this in mind, we train different regression algorithms for each zone and coordinate of the 2D position: *Gaussian Process with Radial Basis Function Kernel*, in which we assume that our variables can be modelled by a normal distribution, and *Bayesian regularized neural network*, which fits an artificial neural network consisting of two layers by making use of regularization to optimize the output function [16]. The error is measured in terms of RMSE (*Root-mean-square error*), because it yields the values in the same units as the output of the estimators, i.e. in metres, so the results can be interpreted easily. This measure describes the standard deviation of the residuals, which are the differences between ground truth and predicted data.

At the end of this stage, as many estimators will have been trained as there are magnetic field landmarks (zones) and components (x, y), enabling the optimum regression technique to be determined for each zone within the building.

3.2   Online Localization Phase

After the offline phase, user localization can be estimated using the magnetic field maps generated, and the localization estimator designed for each zone. A schema of the steps followed during the online phase of the MagicFinger system can be seen in Fig. 1. The input data consist of the magnetic field measurements sensed by the user's phone magnetometer. From such measurements, the magnetic field features are extracted in the form of a vector. This feature vector is classified as belonging to a particular landmark cluster. Finally, the user's localization is estimated using the corresponding estimator that has been implemented for each landmark.

4   Evaluation and Result Analysis

In this section, we describe the experiments carried out in two buildings with different infrastructures and activity levels (building A and B), to get the

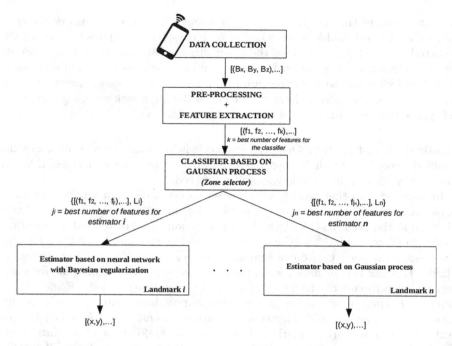

Fig. 1. Building model based on the magnetic field for indoor localization.

optimum parameters for each final selected technique. These experiments are done in order to implement the localization mechanism proposed as well as to validate of the mechanism, using 5-times 10-fold cross validation, or bootstrapping in the case of the estimators due to the size of the set of samples of each particular zone/cluster.

Because a trade-off between the amount of data and the building size needs to be achieved, we decide to collect data every 150 cm, which results in 323 localizations to be measured in building A, and 151 localizations in building B. Data are gathered on different days during a week and at different times of the day, and test data are gathered two weeks after training data are collected.

After data have been pre-processed, the best clustering method and partitioning are to be selected. In the case of k-means, the optimum number of clusters chosen is based on the silhouette coefficient, which measures the quality of the clusters, i.e. how well the data have been grouped. This method divides space into only two regions. With respect to the EM algorithm, the criterion for selecting the optimum k is the Bayesian Information Criterion (BIC) [17]. In all cases except for the configuration with the features *Bx Intensity, By Intensity, Bz Intensity* and *Magnitude of Intensity*, the best partition is also found to be two clusters. If the building was divided in two zones, the estimators would have to predict a huge range of values, so the system would not be scalable or accurate. However, by using only the magnetic field intensities, the EM algorithm recognizes eight zones with different distributions in building A, and seven zones in building B, all corresponding to those that were foreseen. The identified zones are presented in Fig. 2. Therefore, EM algorithm is the most suitable technique for scalability purposes.

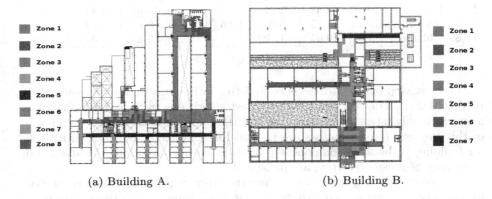

(a) Building A.   (b) Building B.

Fig. 2. Zones identified by the EM algorithm (Color Figure Online).

While performing classification, we discover that the best classifier, the one based on Gaussian Process, can classify only five zones out of eight (building A) or seven (building B) with a f1-score higher than 0.5, which is considered to be the minimum acceptable value of this measure. Thus, the main drawback of MagicFinger is that it is not able to cover the whole building space, although it does cover a significant portion of it. The reason for this may be that those unclassifiable zones have a considerable difference in perturbation, i.e. perturbation is not as stable there as it is in the other areas, so estimators take advantage of this variation whereas classifiers suffer the consequences. Classification results from well-classified zones can be seen in Table 1.

Table 1. f1-score of classification in the zones that can be correctly classified.

(a) Building A.   (b) Building B.

Zone	f1-score
1	0.519
5	0.675
6	0.660
7	0.694
8	0.548

Zone	f1-score
2	0.593
3	0.867
5	0.753
6	0.857
7	0.75

Table 2. RMSE (metres) of estimation in the zones that can be correctly classified.

(a) Building A.

Zone	Surface	$RMSE_x$	$RMSE_y$
1	21 m x 46.5 m	6.04	10.63
5	63 m x 7.5 m	14.05	0.76
6	60 m x 4.5 m	12.33	1.71
7	66.5 m x 28.5 m	14.25	9.06
8	40.5 m x 7.5 m	10.05	1.72

(b) Building B.

Zone	Surface	$RMSE_x$	$RMSE_y$
2	9 m x 9 m	2.45	1.81
3	10.5 m x 7.5 m	2.95	1.54
5	9 m x 34 m	1.44	6.46
6	27 m x 0 m	8.09	-
7	18 m x 9 m	5.04	2.13

The last step of the process is to find the optimum estimator for each well-predicted zone. For this, the two proposed algorithms in Sect. 3 are analyzed, along with only intensities or with the features selected for each zone. As a result of this process, ten estimators are trained for building A and nine estimators for building B, because component y of the zone 6 is constant. In Table 2, the accuracies of these predictors are presented.

Regarding building A, we can see how the error ranges from 6.04 m to 14.25 m in component x, and from 0.76 m to 10.63 m in component y. Although the error obtained seems reasonable—in view of the size of the zones where localization is to be solved—, it is not suitable for fine-grained estimation of the user's localization, but it is suitable for predicting the subzone where the user is. When it comes to results from building B, most zones have errors of less than 5 m, which allows our system to estimate localization fairly accurately. However, some zones lack fine-grained precision, and thus their estimators are only able to estimate the subzone in which the user is.

As conclusions of the analysis presented here, tackling the problem of indoor localization using only the magnetic field and the proposed mechanism is seen to be feasible and to yield reasonably good precision in estimating user's localization, or at least the subzone where the user is located. The results obtained after applying our approach to two different buildings show that, even if the buildings differ in magnetic perturbation and level of activity, the proposed methodology adapts itself to the particular conditions of each building, resulting in a scalable system.

5   Conclusions and Future Work

This paper presents MagicFinger as a novel methodology for solving indoor localization based on 3D magnetic field measurements inside buildings obtained from off-the-shelf smartphones. The use of landmarks derived from magnetic field disturbances for the purpose of indoor localization has one considerable advantage over radio-based localization techniques: no external infrastructure is required. Our experience, presented in this paper, shows that this localization approach is a feasible solution for use in indoor environments.

The experiments, although currently limited to a fixed device height, highlight the potential of MagicFinger to provide a serious low-cost alternative for indoor localization. This is borne out by the fact that it is evaluated in two environments with different conditions, yielding similar and promising results for estimating user localization or the subzone where the user is located. Therefore, MagicFinger represents a novel methodology for indoor localization that optimizes localization accuracy since it is able to adapt to building conditions.

Further work will focus on combining MagicFinger with techniques such as uDirect [18], in order to calibrate magnetic field measurements to a common reference coordinate system. The purpose of this is to make device carrying position irrelevant during the fingerprinting and localization estimation phases. In addition, more exhaustive data collection campaigns should be conducted in order to generate a more complete map of the buildings.

Acknowledgments. This work has been sponsored by European Commission through the FP7-SOCIOTAL-609112 EU Project.

References

1. Misra, P., Enge, P.: Special issue on global positioning system. Proc. IEEE **87**, 3–15 (1999)
2. Lane, N.D., Miluzzo, E., Lu, H., Peebles, D., Choudhury, T., Campbell, A.T.: A survey of mobile phone sensing. IEEE Commun. Mag. **48**, 140–150 (2010)
3. Hightower, J., Borriello, G.: Location systems for ubiquitous computing. Computer **34**, 57–66 (2001)
4. Gozick, B., Subbu, K.P., Dantu, R., Maeshiro, T.: Magnetic maps for indoor navigation. IEEE Trans. Instrum. Measur. **60**, 3883–3891 (2011)
5. Li, B., Gallagher, T., Dempster, A.G., Rizos, C.: How feasible is the use of magnetic field alone for indoor positioning? In: 2012 International Conference on Indoor Positioning and Indoor Navigation (IPIN), pp. 1–9. IEEE (2012)
6. Angermann, M., Frassl, M., Doniec, M., Julian, B.J., Robertson, P.: Characterization of the indoor magnetic field for applications in localization and mapping. In: 2012 International Conference on Indoor Positioning and Indoor Navigation (IPIN), pp. 1–9. IEEE (2012)
7. Kuhn, M., Johnson, K.: Applied Predictive Modeling. Springer, New York (2013)
8. Breiman, L.: Random forests. Mach. Learn. **45**, 5–32 (2001)
9. Fraley, C., Raftery, A.E.: Bayesian regularization for normal mixture estimation and model-based clustering. J. Classif. **24**, 155–181 (2007)
10. Witten, D.M., Tibshirani, R.: A framework for feature selection in clustering. J. Am. Stat. Assoc. **105**, 713–726 (2010)
11. Williams, C.K., Barber, D.: Bayesian classification with gaussian processes. IEEE Trans. Pattern Anal. Mach. Intell. **20**, 1342–1351 (1998)
12. Quinlan, J.R.: C4. 5: Programs for Machine Learning. Elsevier, Amsterdam (2014)
13. Branden, K.V., Hubert, M.: Robust classification in high dimensions based on the simca method. Chemom. Intell. Lab. Syst. **79**, 10–21 (2005)
14. Riedmiller, M., Braun, H.: A direct adaptive method for faster backpropagation learning: the rprop algorithm. In: IEEE International Conference on Neural Networks, pp. 586–591. IEEE (1993)
15. Breiman, L.: Bagging predictors. Mach. Learn. **24**, 123–140 (1996)

16. Foresee, F.D., Hagan, M.T.: Gauss-newton approximation to bayesian learning. In: Proceedings of the 1997 International Joint Conference on Neural Networks, vol. 3, pp. 1930–1935. IEEE, Piscataway (1997)
17. Schwarz, G., et al.: Estimating the dimension of a model. Ann. Stat. **6**, 461–464 (1978)
18. Hoseinitabatabaei, S.A., Gluhak, A., Tafazolli, R.: udirect: A novel approach for pervasive observation of user direction with mobile phones. In: 2011 IEEE International Conference on Pervasive Computing and Communications (PerCom), pp. 74–83. IEEE (2011)

A Mobile Application as an Unobtrusive Tool for Behavioural Mapping in Public Spaces

Alfonso Bahillo[1]([✉]), Barbara Goličnik Marušić[2], and Asier Perallos[1]

[1] Deusto Institute of Technology (DeustoTech), University of Deusto,
48007 Bilbao, Spain
{alfonso.bahillo,perallos}@deusto.es
[2] Urban Planning Institute of the Republic of Slovenia, 1127 Ljubljana, Slovenia
barbara.golicnik-marusic@uirs.si

Abstract. In any man-made environment, discrepancies may exist between the intent of its design and how it is actually used. Behaviour mapping allows researchers to determine how participants use a designed space by recording participant behaviours and/or tracking their movement within the space itself. Not only the participants' movements, other characteristics referring to users (e.g. age, gender, cultural background) and variety of circumstantial factors -including the time of a day, the day of the week, the season or weather conditions - may have a dramatic impact on the types of participant behaviours displayed. This paper highlights a new unobtrusive tool for helping behaviour mapping to easily identify patterns of engagements, gather suggestions and environmental factors within public spaces. The tool mainly consists of a smartphone application (app) and a web service. The app, on one hand tracks the way participants use the space, allowing them to get contextual information, answer contextual questions, and to send augmented reality suggestions or complaints. On the other, the web monitors the way participants use the space allowing to visualize participants' suggestions, answers, or their traces. The tool features and its research ability have been discussed as well as some lessons are expected to be drawn towards building a more participatory and collaborative processes of planning, designing, maintaining and monitoring of urban spaces.

1 Introduction

As part of actual transport and urban development activities, this paper is concerned with a niche addressing development and research of the applicability of ICT tools in public spaces which serve as the interface between the public space and the people. On the one hand, such interfaces could help public space designers and decision-makers to catch the perception, demand, attention or complaints of people using a space. On the other, the people could use these interfaces to enhance their participation in places with contextual information, games or socialising. Addressing various aspects of people-place relations, and focusing on actual uses in real places, the concept of behaviour mapping,

© Springer International Publishing Switzerland 2015
J.M. García-Chamizo et al. (Eds.): UCAmI 2015, LNCS 9454, pp. 13–25, 2015.
DOI: 10.1007/978-3-319-26401-1_2

a method which allows researchers to determine how people use a designed or natural space by recording their behaviours and/or tracking their movement within the space itself, seems relevant. It can be particularly useful to help identifying underlying patterns of users' behaviour within a given environment. In travel behaviour studies most of behaviour mapping methodologies have followed the process individual-centred, i.e. tracing people across times and locations, using various technologies. But, when focusing on one location and variety of users there, the attention is paid to many users at the same time, and in such situation manual mapping is tiring and time-consuming, especially taking into account all further activities concerned with database settings and data analysis and evaluations. However, such approach is unobtrusive (done "at a distance") and often undertaken in public areas, so participant consent may not be required. The purpose of this work is to develop a new fairly unobtrusive ICT tool for helping behaviour mapping to easily identify and automatically track patterns of engagements, gather suggestions and environmental factors within public spaces.

Today, with the advent of global navigation satellite systems (GNSS) global positioning in the earth's surface is a successfully overcome problem. Nonetheless, local positioning in indoor environments is still a matter of active research, since GNSS signals get severely degraded in this type of environments due to multipath and attenuation losses, and thus they cannot be used to track people or objects with acceptable accuracy [24]. Many local positioning systems have been developed during the past two decades based on different technologies that include ultrasound [9,10,20], radio-frequency [1,13,15,22], vision cameras [19,23] and magnetic [2,3], among others. After all this research effort, it is becoming clear that none of these technologies clearly outperforms the others, and it is expected now a new tendency to design systems that combine some of them to benefit from their complementary strengths. The tool described here is based on a localization engine which performs seamless localization estimation of the participant's smartphone in real time by fusing heterogeneous signals. This localization engine would be the ideal platform for location based services (LBS) that provides the participant with context based information [18]. Therefore, this work shows a combination of two original approaches, a seamless localization engine and GIS behaviour mapping [5], both presented within the COST Action TU1306[1], which main objective is to create a research platform on the relationship between ICT and the production of public open spaces, and which offers a frame for a joint further development and improvements of the proposed monitoring tool. This tool, easy to use and unobtrusive, is an attempt to better understand how participants use public open spaces and to investigate the crucial elements to be responded by design, research, and policy-making aiming to produce more responsive, stronger, safer and inclusive cities.

The paper is organized as follow: Sect. 2 introduces the related work with regards to behavioural mapping methodologies, Sect. 3 describes the monitoring tool, Sect. 4 draws the tool features and its research ability, and Sect. 5 summarizes the work and introduces some future work.

---

[1] http://www.cost.eu/COST_Actions/tud/Actions/TU1306.

2 Behavioural Mapping Methodology

Originally, behaviour mapping, grounded and well used in the field of environmental psychology [11], is focused on recording behaviour as it occurs in a designed setting. Chronologically, some of the most common ways, usually applied in indoor spaces, were systematically writing notes and filling formatted tables, mostly having no connection to actual layout of the observed place. The development of photo-video techniques influenced the latter methods of recording and map production. Nowadays ICT development is forthcoming, offering various ways of recording people's engagement with places. Behaviour map is a product of observation and a tool for place analysis and design at the same time, where spatial features and behaviours are linked in both time and space. There are two main approaches to behaviour mapping known: place-centred mapping and individual-centred mapping [17].

In public open space researches (e.g. [6,7]) usually follow the place-centred mapping, a process for recording location-based observations of people activities in places through the annotation of manual or digital maps. It is the approach, where information is recorded on layouts of the settings that reflect physical characteristics of the particular environment. In such approach [8], it is necessary to clearly define the area of observation, the types of activities and details of behaviours to be observed, to schedule specific times and their repetitions for observation, to provide a system for recording, coding, counting and analysing, and an accurate scale map of the area to be observed. Finally, the process, using GIS supported software, provided data organised into thematic layers in which original information collected on the field is listed in the attached table and based on that finally visualised on the map.

The value of behaviour maps for place analysis, design and decision-making is in empirical knowledge about dimensions, spatial requirements of uses and understanding of co-habitation of uses in places.

3 The Monitoring Tool

The main motivation behind the monitoring tool is to get to know how participants use a designed space by recording their behaviours and/or tracking their movement within the space itself. Not only the patterns of participants' movements or other engagements in places, from various passive (e.g. sitting and observing) to active activities (e.g. playing) there, but other factors such as the time of a day, the day of the week, the season, the weather conditions, or even allowing participants to send suggestions, may help urban planners and decision-makers to investigate the crucial elements aiming to produce more responsive, stronger, safer and inclusive cities.

To achieve this goal, this paper highlights a new methodology for behaviour mapping based on a monitoring tool consisting of three main elements: a smartphone application, a set of web services and the cloud (see Fig. 2). The relation among these elements is as follows. The participant's smartphone uses its sensors

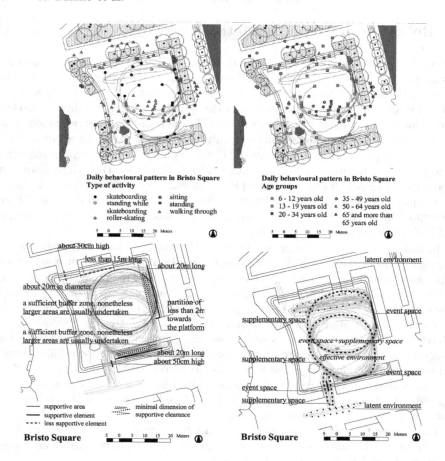

Fig. 1. Examples of behaviour maps and relevant empirical knowledge derived from them.

to collect the so called signals of opportunity (SoOP) which are transmitted for localization or non-localization purposes but may be exploited to this end. The smartphone app is in charge of computing its own position by fusing those SoOP according to a localization engine which is explained below. Also, the smartphone app allows the participants to set their profile, get contextual information, answer contextual questions, and send augmented reality suggestions. All this information -participant profile, position, answers and suggestions- is sent and stored into the cloud. On the other hand, the web services get the information from the cloud allowing to visualize participants' suggestions, answers, weather conditions, real time positions, or the paths filtered by the participants profile characteristics among others. The following subsections discuss the smartphone app, its localization engine, and the web services in more detail.

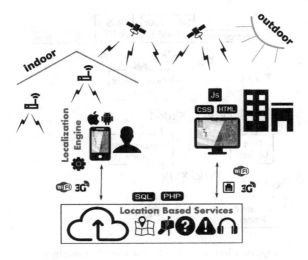

Fig. 2. Logical architecture diagram of the tool.

3.1   The Mobile Application

The core of the mobile application is the localization engine which performs seamless localization estimation of the participant's smartphone in real time by fusing several SoOP. Once the participant's position is estimated, several functionalities based on the context are implemented.

The localization engine is thought as a modular system for commercially available smartphones where SoOP coming from their sensors could be easily fused. Nowadays, the smartphones already integrate a GNSS receiver, a WiFi and Bluetooth adapter, a camera, and shortly, most of them will integrate other sensors such as the barometer, inertial sensors or the proximity contactless technology NFC. Bayesian filters are a theoretically sound way to combine multiple and different SoOP. Bayes filters probabilistically estimate a dynamic system's state from noisy observations. They represent the state at time k by random variables $\mathbf{x}_k$. At each point in time, a probability distribution over $\mathbf{x}_k$, called *belief*, represents the uncertainty. Bayes filters aim to sequentially estimate such beliefs over the state space conditioned on all information contained in the observations [4]. In this paper, the state is the participant's location, $\mathbf{x}_k = [x_k, y_k, z_k]^T$, while the SoOP provide observations about the state. Among the different Bayes filters, Kalman filters are the most widely used. They are optimal estimators, assuming the initial uncertainty is Gaussian, the observation model and system dynamics are linear functions of the state, and the measurement and process noise distributions are Gaussian. However, the lack of linearity in the models that relates most of the SoOP to the participant's location implies the usage of a suboptimal solution, where the most common is to use the EKF. Nevertheless, the unscented Kalman filter (UKF) better captures the higher order moments caused by the non-linear transformation and avoids the computation of Jacobian and Hessian

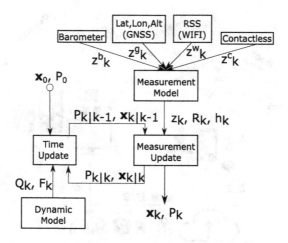

Fig. 3. Flowchart of the localization engine.

matrices [12]. Furthermore, the overall number of computations performed by the UKF are the same order as the EKF, and much lower than solutions such as the particle filter which better represents the belief but needs a number of computations unacceptable for most smartphones. Therefore, in the localizatin engine the SoOP will be fused by means of an UKF.

Consider the following non-linear system, described by the *dynamic* and *measurement* models with additive noise:

$$\mathbf{x}_k = \mathbf{f}(\mathbf{x}_{k-1}) + \mathbf{w}_{k-1} \tag{1}$$

$$\mathbf{z}_k = \mathbf{h}(\mathbf{x}_k) + \mathbf{v}_{k-1} \tag{2}$$

where $\mathbf{w}_k$ and $\mathbf{v}_k$ are the process and observation noise which are both assumed to be zero mean multivariate Gaussian noise with covariance $\mathbf{Q}_k$ and $\mathbf{R}_k$, respectively. The function f can be used to compute the predicted state from the previous estimate and similarly the function h can be used to compute the predicted measurement from the predicted state.

On the one hand, the dynamics of the system can be represented as

$$\mathbf{x}_k = \mathbf{x}_{k-1} + \dot{\mathbf{x}}_{k-1}\Delta t + \mathbf{w}_{k-1} \tag{3}$$

where $\Delta t = (t_k - t_{k-1})$ is the time step and $\dot{\mathbf{x}}_k$ is the first derivative of the state, in this case, the user's velocity. Finally, $\mathbf{w}_k$ is assumed to be a zero-mean Gaussian variable with covariance matrix $\mathbf{Q}_k$. The values of $\mathbf{Q}_k$ depend on the dynamic of the target, in this paper for example, a walking person. In practice, $\mathbf{Q}_k$ is a diagonal matrix whose in-diagonal elements represent the variance of the user's position and velocity [21].

On the other hand, the function h depends on the SoOP. In the GNSS case, the measurement model, called h^g, can be represented as

$$\mathbf{z}_k^g = \mathbf{x}_k + \mathbf{v}_{k-1}^g \tag{4}$$

where $\mathbf{z}_k^g$ is the GNSS position estimation and $\mathbf{v}_k^g$ represents the GNSS noise which can be assumed to be zero-mean Gaussian variable with covariance matrix $\mathbf{R}_k^g$. In practice, $\mathbf{R}_k^g$ is a diagonal matrix whose in-diagonal elements represent the variance of the measurements coming from the satellites, and its value depends on the number of satellites in line-of-sight. The more satellites with good GDOP (Geometric Dilution of Precision), the more reliable the GNSS data. There is a benefit form the GNSS data only in open areas where it accurately reports the participant's position.

In the barometer case, the measurement model, called h^b, can be represented as

$$\mathbf{z}_k^b = p_0 \cdot \left(1 - \frac{\lambda}{T_0}\mathbf{x}_k[3]\right)^{\frac{g}{\lambda R_{air}}} + \mathbf{v}_{k-1}^b \tag{5}$$

where $\mathbf{z}_k^b$ is the air pressure, $\mathbf{x}_k[3]$ is the third element of the state, $T_0 = 288,15$ K is the temperature at sea level, $\lambda = -0.0065\ K/m$ is the temperature gradient, $p_0 = 1013.25\ mbar$ is the pressure at sea level, $R_{air} = 287\ m^2(s^2K)^{-1}$ is the atmosphere gas constant, and $g = 9.8\ m/s^2$ is the earth gravity. $\mathbf{v}_k^b$ represents the air pressure noise which can be assumed to be zero-mean Gaussian variable with covariance matrix $\mathbf{R}_k^b$. This measurement model is not exact because it assumes some variables as constants, and it does not take into account other factors such as humidity, temperature, or the presence of air conditioning systems. However, not the absolute but the relative altitude is used. The estimated relative altitude is used to compensate GNSS errors in altitude.

In the contactless technologies cases, such as NFC tags and QR codes, the measurement model, calle h^c, can be represented as

$$\mathbf{z}_k^c = \mathbf{x}_k + \mathbf{v}_{k-1}^c \tag{6}$$

where $\mathbf{z}_k^c$ is the position of the NFC tag or QR code. $\mathbf{v}_k^c$ represents the observation noise which can be assumed to be zero-mean Gaussian variable with covariance matrix $\mathbf{R}_k^c$. As the SoOP gather by the contactless technologies have to be read at few centimeters from the tag or code, in practice, $\mathbf{R}_k^c$ is a diagonal matrix whose in-diagonal elements are lower than $1\ m$. These proximity contactless technologies work anywhere and they can update the location algorithm with accurate position information.

Finally, in those places where the GNSS signals are blocked -inside buildings or in dense urban environments-, the localization engine could take advantage of WiFi signals which predominate in most cities. In the WiFi (and Bluetooth) case the measurement model, called h^w, can be represented as

$$\mathbf{z}_k^w = \alpha - 10n\log_{10}(||\mathbf{x}_k - \mathbf{AP}||) + \mathbf{v}_{k-1}^w \tag{7}$$

where $\mathbf{z}_k^w$ is the RSS measured value; α is a parameter that remains constant in those scenarios where the antennas gain and the power transmitted from the access points are also constant, a situation typically found in most WiFi WLANs, (in practice, this value can be known beforehand from experimental measurements taken in a generic environment similar to that where the location system

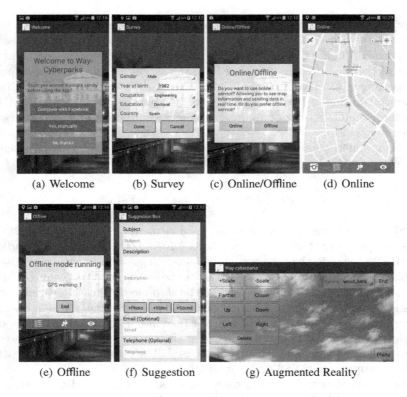

(a) Welcome   (b) Survey   (c) Online/Offline   (d) Online

(e) Offline   (f) Suggestion   (g) Augmented Reality

Fig. 4. Main screenshots of the smartphone application.

is going to operate) [14]; **AP** is the position of the WiFi access point; and n is the path-loss exponent corresponding to the actual propagation environment. In free space $n = 2$, however in practice, depending on the environment the path-loss exponents ranging from 1.5 to 4.5 [14,16]. $\mathbf{v}_k^w$ represents the RSS noise and it can be assumed to be zero-mean Gaussian variable with covariance matrix $\mathbf{R}_k^w$. In practice, there is h_i^w with $i = 1, 2, \ldots M_k$ functions, where M_k is the number of WiFi access points in range at each time step k. Accordingly, $\mathbf{R}_k^w$ is a diagonal matrix whose in-diagonal elements represent the variance of the measurements coming from each WiFi access point.

As shown in Fig. 3, and it is well described in [12], once the dynamic and measurement models, and their noise covariace matrices are described, the UKF is straightforward to implement. Notice that the initial values of the state covariance matrix, P_0, depends on the initial state confidence. UKF main advantage is their computational efficiency (same as EKF and lower than particle filters), better linearization than EKF (accurate in the third-order Taylor series expansion), and derivative-free (no Jacobian and Hessian matrices are needed) [12].

This localization engine would be the ideal platform for LBSs that provides the participant with context based information [18]. Currently, the smartphone app has different functionalities already implemented in Android and iOS mobile based platforms. These are summarized in Fig. 4. At first the app welcomes the participants and invites them to complete a short survey that will define their profile -they could do it typing the answers or it can be filled in automatically by logging to their Facebook account-. After that the app asks the participants to work in online or offline mode. In the online mode the app regularly sends the participant's position through the data communication link (4G, 3G, 2G or WiFi) to the cloud. In the offline mode the app stores all the participant's positions in the smartphone memory card. When finishing the track, the app asks the participant to send all the positions stored together to the cloud. Based on the working mode, the participant could send or save (to be sent later) suggestions to the cloud attaching text, photos, videos and/or audio records. The participant could enhance also the photo to be attached creating a virtual world adding virtual objects using the augmented reality engine. Finally, the participant could get contextual information in diferent formats: text notifications, audio tracks, video files or internet links. All of them are related to the context and based on the participant's position.

3.2 The Web Services

The aim of the web service is to help urban planners, designers or decision-makers to view how participants use the designed space. It is hosted in http://services.cyberparks-project.eu/, and at the moment it provides a few different pilot case studies in Europe. Figure 5 shows a general view of the web service. It consists of three main elements, the main menu on the right, the filter on the left and the map in between.

The filter is used to select the participants' path that one wants to view based on several profile characteristics such as the gender, occupation, education and age. The main menu has the following five sections:

– Current case study: it denotes the case study results one is viewing, and allows to select also other case studies to see the results.
– Positions: it denotes the participants' positions in real or past time, the position of the points of interest, and allows to see the participants' positions in real time or to search for a specific period of past time. It also allows to see the points of interest of the case study on the map.
– User data: it denotes the questions and participants' answers, suggestions and alarms; allowing to see on the map where are the questions related to the case study, their radius of influence and the answers of the participants; where participants' suggestions have been taken including their content -subject, description, photos, videos, audio, email, telephone - and the weather conditions reported by the nearer weather forecast station; and finally, where are the alarm zones, its shape, who enters and when, the time spend inside the alarm zone, and when leaves the zone.
– Edition: it denotes the edition of points of interest, questions, alarm zones, audio tracks and buildings allowing to add/edit/delete points of interest on

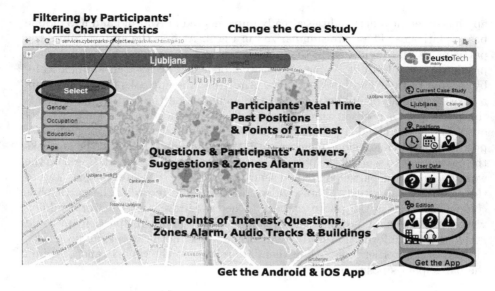

Fig. 5. Location based services and places more crowded.

the map characterized by a name, url and short description; add/edit/delete questions on the map characterized by a radius of influence, a short description of the question and several optional answers; add/edit/delete alarm zones on the map with irregular shapes charaterized by a name and several actions to perform just in case a participant goes into the zone sending email, SMS or activating some sensors; add/edit/delete audio tracks on the map characterized by a radius of influence and the text describing the track that is going to be reproduced when the participant goes into the zone of influence; and finally allowing to add/edit/delete markers inside buildings. If a building plan has been previously loaded in the web service, section edition allows to add/edit/delete contactless technology markers such as NFC or QR characterized by an identifier and a location inside the building; and WiFi and Bluetooth access points characterized by a power of reference, a mac address and a location inside the building.

– Get the app: it allows to get the Android and iOS based smartphone app through Google Play and Apple Store, respectively.

4   Discussion

The last version of the app has been successfully tested in the city of Ljubljana; Slovenia, where various types of public spaces from natural green and hilly areas to paved flat surfaces of various articulation and equipment are at hand in the time distance of 10 minutes. Testing phase paid attention mostly on technical capability of the app. However, having discussions with representatives of various user groups, the app seems interesting to them to get informed about places and to let others know about pleases in relation to their presence there, not only via behavior pattern which occurred running the app, but also via other means of communication the app offers (e.g. photo, video, message etc.). Besides, pilot actions also revealed that quite some effort will have to be made to attract various users to use the app, to finally get a comprehensive picture of dynamic patterns of public spaces of studied cities.

Advantages using the new app as a monitoring tool, discussed in this paper, are in precise and fast data collection, simultaneous and evolving analytics and valorisations. However, one must bear in mind that such app riches only people who are familiar with smartphones and their advanced use, but left aside other users who are not. For this reason, when addressing place occupancies and co-habitation and compatibility of uses and user groups, combinations of methods, from using the proposed app, simulations it offers based on previous empirical knowledge, to traditional field observations would still need to be applied. In this respect, triangulation of such various behavior mapping techniques offers insights into advantages and disadvantages of the tool and opens discussion for possible further development of the tool and its compatibility with other (new coming) tools and approaches.

5   Conclusions

The unobtrusive tool that has been presented in this paper shows a new methodology for helping behaviour mapping to easily identify patterns of engagements, gather suggestions and environmental factors within public spaces. The combination of this localization engine, thought as a modular system for commercial available smartphones where heterogeneous signals can be easily fused, and behaviour mapping provides a powerful tool to support designers with empirical evidence of the relationship between environmental design and use of open space that is presented in a spatial and visual language familiar to designers. Future work goes towards (1) including in the localization engine the difference between the measured GNSS pseudoranges and actual pseudoranges measured at fixed, ground-based reference stations which positions are known. This way the accuracy in open spaces will improve from the 10-m nominal GNSS accuracy to lower than 1 meter, and (2) performing a case study with focused user groups of urban spaces (e.g. skateboarders) to create research and working environment where communication between users and tool developers is easy, to be able to adopt and refine the tool as useful for both, place and app users as well as for spatial planning and design related professionals, who want to understand users relations with places, encourage and produce better places then they would otherwise be produced.

Acknowledgements. This work has been supported by the Spanish Ministry of Economy and Competitiveness under the ESPHIA project (TIN2014-56042-JIN), by Slovenian Research Agency within Programme Spatial Planning (P5-0100), and by the

Cost Action TU1306, called CYBERPARKS, with special thanks to Mrs. Ina Šuklje Erjavec for encouraging the short time scientific mission.

References

1. Bahillo, A., Mazuelas, S., Lorenzo, R.M., Fernández, P., Prieto, J., Durán, R.J., Abril, E.J.: Hybrid RSS-RTT localization scheme for indoor wireless networks. EURASIP J. Adv. Signal Process **2010**, 1–12 (2010)
2. Blankenbach, J., Norrdine, A., Hellmers, H.: Adaptive signal processing for a magnetic indoor positioning system. In: Proceedings of the 2011 International Conference on Indoor Positioning and Indoor Navigation (2011)
3. Chung, J., Donahoe, M., Schmandt, C., Kim, I.J., Razavai, P., Wiseman, M.: Indoor location sensing using geo-magnetism. In: Proceedings of the 9th International Conference on Mobile Systems, Applications and Services (MobiSys 2011), pp. 141–154 (2011)
4. Fox, D., Hightower, J., Liao, L., Schulz, D., Borriello, G.: Bayesian filters for location estimation. IEEE Pervasive Comput. **2**, 24–33 (2003)
5. Goličnik, B., Thompson, C.: People in place: a configuration of physical form and the dynamic patterns of spatial occupancy in urban open public space. Submitted for the Degree of Doctor of Philosophy, B. Goličnik (2005)
6. Goličnik, B., Thompson, C.W.: Emerging relationships between design and use of urban park spaces. Landscape Urban Plan. **94**(1), 38–53 (2010)
7. Goličnik Marušić, B.: Analysis of patterns of spatial occupancy in urban open space using behaviour maps and GIS. Urban Des. Int. **16**, 36–50 (2011)
8. Goličnik Marušić, B., Marušić, D.: Behavioural maps and GIS in place evaluation and design. In: Application of Geographic Information Systems, 31 October 2012
9. González, J.R., Bleakley, C.J.: High-precision robust broadband ultrasonic location and orientation estimation. IEEE J. Sel. Top. Signal Process. **3**(5), 832–844 (2009)
10. Hazas, M., Ward, A.: A novel broadband ultrasonic location system. In: Borriello, G., Holmquist, L.E. (eds.) UbiComp 2002. LNCS, vol. 2498, p. 264. Springer, Heidelberg (2002)
11. Ittelson, W.H., Rivlin, L.G., Proshansky, H.M.: The Use of Behavioral Maps in Environmental Psychology. Holt, Rinehart and Winston, New York (1970)
12. Julier, S., Uhlmann, J.K., Durrant-Whyte, H.F.: A new method for the nonlinear transformation of means and covariances in filters and estimators. IEEE Trans. Automat. Contr. **45**(3), 477–482 (2000)
13. K, A., Adepoju, F.: A model for estimating the real-time positions of a moving object in wireless telemetry applications using RF sensors. In: Proceedings of the IEEE Sensors Applications Symposium (2007)
14. Li, X.: RSS-based location estimation with unknown pathloss model. IEEE Trans. Wireless Commun. **5**(12), 3626–3633 (2006)
15. Mazuelas, S., Bahillo, A., Lorenzo, R.M., Fernández, P., Lago, F., García, E., Blas, J., Abril, E.J.: Robust indoor positioning provided by real-time RSSI values in unmodified WLAN networks. IEEE J. Sel. Top. Signal Process. **3**(5), 821–831 (2009)
16. Pahlavan, K., Levesque, A.H.: Wireless Information Networks. Wiley, New York (1995)
17. Sommer, R., Sommer, B.: A Practical Guide to Behavioural Research. Oxford University Press, New York (2002)

18. Steiniger, S., Neun, M., Alistair, E.: Foundations of Location Based Services. CartouCHe1-Lecture Notes on LBS 1 (2006)
19. Tilch, S., Mautz, R.: Current investigations at the ETH Zurich in optical indoor positioning. In: Proceedings of the 7th Workshop on Positioning Navigation and Communication, vol. 7, pp. 174–178 (2010)
20. Ureña, J., Hernández, A., Villadangos, J.M., Mazo, M., García, J.C., García, J.J., Álvarez, F.J., de Marziani, C., Pérez, M.C., Jiménez, J.A., Jiménez, A., Seco, F.: Advanced sensorial system for an acoustic LPS. Microprocess. Microsyst. **31**, 393–401 (2007)
21. Wakim, C.F., Capperon, S., Oksman, J.: A Markovian model of pedestrian behavior. In: SMC, vol. 4, pp. 4028–4033. IEEE (2004)
22. Whitehouse, K., Karlof, C., Culler, D.: A practical evaluation of radio signal strength for ranging-based localization. ACM SIGMOBILE Mob. Comput. Commun. Rev. **11**(1), 41–52 (2007)
23. Willert, V.: Optical indoor positioning using a camera phone. In: Proceedings of the 2010 International Conference on Indoor Positioning and Indoor Navigation (2010)
24. Zandbergen, P.: Accuracy of iPhone locations: a comparison of assisted GPS, Wifi and cellular positioning. Trans. GIS **13**(s1), 5–25 (2009)

Thought and Life Logging: A Pilot Study

N. Hernández[1]([⊠]), G. Yavuz[2], R. Eşrefoğlu[2], T. Kepez[2],
A. Özdemir[2], B. Demiray[3], H. Alan[2], C. Ersoy[2],
S. Untersander[3], and B. Arnrich[2]

[1] Computer Science Department, CICESE Research Center, Ensenada, Mexico
netzahdzc@cicese.mx
[2] Computer Engineering Department, Boğaziçi University, Istanbul, Turkey
{gokhan.yavuz, mete.esrefoglu, berkant.kepez,
abdulmecit.ozdemir, hasan.alan, ersoy,
bert.arnrich}@boun.edu.tr
[3] Psychology Department, University of Zürich, Zurich, Switzerland
b.demiray@psychologie.uzh.ch,
sarah.untersander@uzh.ch

Abstract. Thought and Life Logging (Tholilo) is an interdisciplinary research project of computer engineers and psychologists. One aspect of Tholilo is to understand how daily context influence our mood and temporal thinking. In this contribution, we present a data collection framework which records sensor data and survey responses from smartphones to infer user's context, user's mood and temporal thinking. In a pilot study, data is collected from two collectives located in Turkey and in Switzerland. We examine correlations between phone data and surveys. As a proof of concept, we show how phone data is correlated with changes in participant's mood. We conclude with lessons learned and future work.

Keywords: Mobile sensing · Lifestyle · Physical activity · Social interaction

1 Introduction

In recent years various application scenarios were presented in which context-aware smartphones play a major role. With context-awareness, we refer to (1) characterizing the situation of the user, e.g. activity, affective state, behavior, (2) persons/objects around, e.g. who is around, how many persons are around, what kind of objects are around and (3) places visited, e.g. place category, ambient temperature/noise. Context-awareness is inferred by relying on the embedded sensor modalities and/or phone usage. Sensor modalities that are available in many modern smartphones consist of accelerometer, gyroscope, compass, light sensor, thermometer, camera, microphone, Bluetooth, GPS, Wi-Fi. An example of a context-aware smartphone application is to automatically characterize visited places into categories (e.g. education, entertainment, restaurant, home, shops, workplace) by opportunistically collecting and processing images, audio recordings, Wi-Fi scans and GPS from smartphone users [1].

In this paper we present a data collection framework which records sensor data and survey responses from smartphones. A dashboard service allows to configure the

© Springer International Publishing Switzerland 2015
J.M. García-Chamizo et al. (Eds.): UCAmI 2015, LNCS 9454, pp. 26–36, 2015.
DOI: 10.1007/978-3-319-26401-1_3

sensor modalities (sampling frequency, duty cycle), to manage surveys, to monitor participant's data completeness, and to send messages to the participants.

In a pilot study, data is collected from two collectives located in Turkey and in Switzerland. The pilot study is part of the interdisciplinary research project Thought and Life Logging (Tholilo) which is conducted by computer engineers and psychologists located in Turkey and Switzerland respectively. One aspect of Tholilo is to understand how daily context influence our mood and temporal thinking [2]. User's context is inferred from smartphone's sensor data and smartphone usage. User's mood and way of thinking is obtained by surveys filled out on the smartphone. In this contribution we examine correlations between phone data and surveys. As a proof of concept, we show how phone data is correlated with changes in participant's mood. We conclude with lessons learned and future work.

2   Related Work

The most widely studied smartphone sensor is the accelerometer [3]. For example, an accelerometer-based smartphone pedometer is studied in [4] by evaluating common walk detection and step counting algorithms applied to smartphone sensor data which was gathered at different smartphone positions. Other sensor modalities and various combinations of sensor readings were investigated as well. One early example is CenceMe, which infers context information from user's mobile phone by applying machine learning techniques to the sensory input from the microphone, the accelerometer, the camera, and the Bluetooth radio [5]. Another example is VibN, which uses accelerometer, audio, and localization sensor data to determine what is happening around the user [6]. In [7], an extended sensor framework for Android smartphones is employed to obtain objective and subjective measures of relevant lifestyle parameters from two very dissimilar environments: the city of Istanbul as one of the largest mega cities worldwide and the rural district of Mersin in the south-eastern part of Turkey. In [8], ANT + and Bluetooth inter-person proximity measures are obtained to identify pilgrim's social networks and apply social network analysis. In [9], it is shown how phone call conversations can be used to objectively predict manic and depressive episodes of bipolar disordered people. In [10], a smartphone app and a signal processing chain is presented for assessing the stress experience of individuals by using features derived from smartphones and wearable ECG chest belts. In [11], smartphones are employed to acquire objective data on team communication and physical activity in an automatic way. In [12, 13], it is shown how smartphone data can be used as a novel outcome measure for surgical pain therapy in daily life. In [14], smartphones are employed to monitor performance indicators of firefighters in real-world missions. In [15], smartphones are employed to sense group proximity dynamics of firefighting teams. In [16], a survey on measuring happiness with smart phones is presented. In [17] it is shown that it is possible to determine the health status of individuals using co-location and communication information gathered from mobile phones. [18] explores the potential of participatory sensing derived from location sharing systems (e.g., Foursquare) to understand human dynamics of cities. [19] uses mobile phones' Bluetooth (as proximity sensor), frequency of applications, and call data records to recognize social patterns in daily user activity, to infer relationships, and to identify socially significant locations. [20] uses physical activity data to model implications between mood regulation and depression level.

3 Tholilo Data Collection Framework

The Tholilo data collection framework is based on the funf open sensing framework [21]. The funf framework was extended to meet the requirements of the Tholilo project. Two main extensions were implemented: privacy-preserving audio recordings on the client side and a dashboard service on the server side. The dashboard allows configuring the sensor modalities to be collected (sampling frequency, duty cycle), to manage surveys, to monitor participant's data completeness, to send messages to the participants and to perform online data analysis.

The overall data collection framework is shown in Fig. 1. Once the sensing application is installed on the mobile phone, data probes are collected in the background. During an adjustable period of time (e.g. between 9am and 6 pm), the user receives surveys at random times. Both sensor data and survey answers are encrypted and temporarily stored on the mobile phone, waiting to be sent opportunistically to the server. The server collects data and stores it into MySQL databases. The dashboard service allows to monitor the gathered data and to provide technical support in case the user experiments a technical miss function on the sensing application. Assistance is offered remotely and in real time.

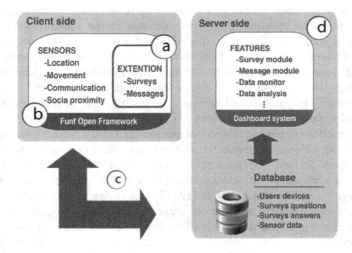

Fig. 1. Tholilo data collection framework.

Framework's Client Side: The Tholilo framework allows to capture audio recordings at random times during a day. On the one side, audio data is a very rich source of information which allows for example to detect whether someone is having a conversation, on the other side most people do not accept audio recordings due to privacy reasons. In order to overcome this tradeoff, a privacy preserving way of audio recording was implemented. As shown in Fig. 2, users can listen to their recordings whenever they want. For each audio recording the user can decide whether the recording is uploaded for further processing or deleted.

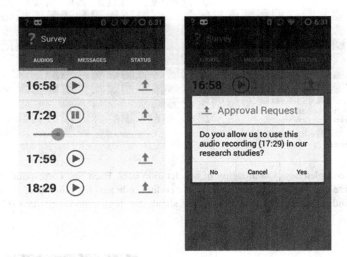

Fig. 2. Privacy-preserving audio recording: users can listen to each audio recording whenever they want. For each audio recording the user can decide whether the recording is uploaded for further processing or deleted.

Tholilo supports two survey mechanisms: (1) experience sampling for gathering responses at random time intervals during a day and (2) daily reconstruction survey for collecting responses at the end of the day after the last survey from the first category. Both survey types can consist of a mixture of input types: check boxes, sliders, free text entry and audio message. Figure 6 shows two exemplary questionnaires from the pilot study.

Framework's Server Side: In order to recognize data collection problems in a timely manner, a dashboard service was implemented to inspect data completeness in real time. In Fig. 3 a data completeness visualization of acceleration sensor data is shown. It can be observed that data collection started in the evening of the first day. In the early morning of the fifth day no acceleration data was collected for a few hours. Afterwards, the data collection problem was solved and similar amounts of data like before were collected.

In case there is a problem during data collection, participants can be informed via a messaging service. Figure 4 shows how a participant is asked to enable GPS on his phone.

The Tholilo data collection framework provides an online data analysis functionality, which enables us to observe event-related changes in the data in real time.

Data Completeness

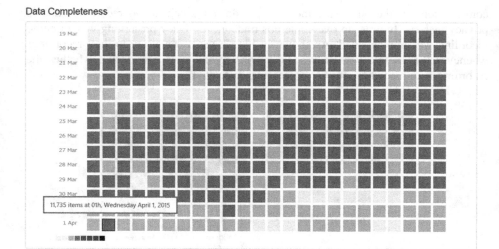

Fig. 3. Data completeness visualization of acceleration data. Each line corresponds to one day and each square corresponds to one hour. Color coding indicates the amount of data collected: bright color indicates no/less data, dark color stands for high amount of data (Color figure online).

Fig. 4. Messaging service via dashboard for informing participants.

In Fig. 5 an exemplary online data analysis function is shown. Similar to the data completeness visualizations, it displays how many unique Bluetooth devices were found within each hour. In this example it can be observed that in the evening of the second and third day the number is increased. The reason behind is that those two days were weekend days and the user went out to see friends.

4 Pilot Data Collection

The Tholilo data collection framework was utilized in a pilot study. Data from two collectives located in Turkey and in Switzerland were collected. Table 1 shows some basic characteristics of both collectives. In order to keep the battery consumption low,

Bluetooth Devices (unique devices)

Fig. 5. Number of unique Bluetooth devices found within each hour. Each line corresponds to one day and each square corresponds to one hour. Color coding indicates the amount of unique devices: bright color indicates few devices, dark color indicates many devices (Color figure online).

sensor data was not collected continuously but in periodic time intervals. The following sensor configuration was employed:

- Bluetooth (scans for devices every 5 min),
- GPS (every 30 min),
- Accelerometer (sample with a frequency according to user's device configuration on intervals of 10 s every 5 min),
- Running apps, and
- Screen on/off states

Each participant was notified 7 times a day at random time points to fill out a survey. Two exemplary questionnaires are shown in Fig. 6. One minute before each notification, a one minute long audio sample was recorded in the privacy-preserving way explained before. Data was collected during a 10-day period.

Table 1. Group characteristics.

	Group A	Group B
No. of participants	6	6
City, Country	Zürich, Switzerland	Istanbul, Turkey
Size of the city	Medium (360 K)	Large (14 M)
Gender	(1 male; 5 female)	(1 male; 5 female)
Average age (S.D.)	33.16 (14.40)	23.33 (1.50)

5 Results of Pilot Data Analysis

A total of 265 surveys were collected during a 10-day period (105 from Group A and 160 from Group B). For both groups, sensor data before the onset of the survey were correlated with the survey answers. We present our results in three sections: one for Group A, a second one for Group B, and a third one in which we merge both groups. For each section, we analyzed sensor data within different time intervals before the onset of the survey. In the following we present the results of 150 and 180 min time

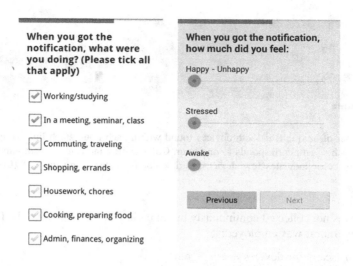

Fig. 6. Exemplary questionnaires from the pilot study.

Table 2. Correlation coefficients between phone data obtained 180 min before the onset of the survey and perceived level of happiness, stress and wakefulness. The first cell (*) represent Group A, the second cell (**) represent Group B, and the third cell (***) represent both groups together.

	150 min data before survey							
	# Bluetooth devices around		# Screen interaction		# Apps		Mean acceleration	
Level of happiness	0.04*	**0.31****	−0.04	0.07	0.19	−0.13	0.06	0.02
	0.21***		0.21		−0.07		0.01	
Level of stress	−0.09	**−0.27**	−0.09	**−0.27**	**−0.32**	−0.11	0.04	−0.02
	−0.23		−0.23		**−0.28**		−0.06	
Level of wakefulness	0.13	0.14	0.13	0.14	**0.28**	−0.22	0.10	−0.01
	0.12		0.12		−0.15		−0.02	

intervals before the onset of the survey. In Tables 2 and 3 the correlation coefficients between phone data before the onset of the survey and perceived level of happiness, stress and wakefulness are shown.

When considering the significant correlations between phone data obtained 150 min before the onset of the survey, we observe the following results for the two groups and all participants together:

Group A: The amount of interaction with applications is positively correlated with level of wakefulness ($r = 0.28$), and negatively correlated with level of stress ($r = -0.32$).

Table 3. Correlation coefficients between phone data obtained 150 min before the onset of the survey and perceived level of happiness, stress and wakefulness. The first cell (*) represent Group A, the second cell (**) represent Group B, and the third cell (***) represent both groups together.

	180 min data before surveys							
	# Bluetooth devices around		# Screen interaction		# Apps		Mean acceleration	
Level of happiness	0.03*	**0.32****	−0.01	0.06	0.22	−0.15	0.10	0.02
	0.21***		−0.00		−0.08		0.03	
Level of stress	−0.11	**−0.26**	−0.14	0.01	**−0.33**	−0.12	−0.03	−0.03
	−0.23		−0.13		**−0.30**		−0.06	
Level of wakefulness	0.12	0.14	0.10	−0.01	**0.28**	−0.24	0.07	−0.01
	0.11		−0.07		−0.16		−0.01	

Group B: The number of unique Bluetooth devices around is positively correlated with level of happiness ($r = 0.31$), and negatively correlated with level of stress ($r = −0.27$).

All: The number of applications used is negatively correlated with level of stress ($r = −0.28$).

When considering the significant correlations between phone data obtained 180 min before the onset of the survey, we observe the following results for the two groups and all participants together:

Group A: The number of applications the user interacts with is positively correlated with level of wakefulness ($r = 0.28$), and negatively correlated with level of stress ($r = −0.33$).

Group B: The number of unique Bluetooth around devices is positively correlated with level of happiness ($r = 0.32$), and negatively correlated with level of stress ($r = −0.26$).

All: The amount of interaction with mobile applications is negatively correlated with level of stress ($r = −0.30$).

6 Conclusion and Discussion

We have presented a smartphone data collection framework, which allowed us to collect sensor data and surveys for investigating how daily context influences our mood and temporal thinking. The framework is based on the funf open sensing framework. It was extended by privacy-preserving audio recordings on the client side and by a dashboard service on the server side. The dashboard allows configuring the sensor modalities to be collected (sampling frequency, duty cycle), to manage surveys, to monitor participant's data completeness, to send messages to the participants and to perform online data analysis. As a proof of concept, we have shown how phone data is correlated with changes in participant's mood.

Data were collected from participants living in Turkey and Switzerland. Based on the presented results and recognizing the limitations of this study in terms of its sample size $(n = 12)$, it is speculated that for some populations such as Turkish people, face-to-face communication affects people's mood in a positive way by making them feel happier and less stressful (as shown for Group B). For Swiss people, mobile phone interaction seems to be a hint for mood changes (Group A). However, since we have not explored all our data yet, we need to be careful in particular when interpreting non-significant correlations, e.g. no correlation between Bluetooth devices and mood changes in Group A does not necessarily mean that Swiss people are not affected by social communication.

We need to further explore other parameters that may influence participants' mood. Given the presented results from the pilot study, we envision to predict people's mood based on user's context derived from phone sensor data and phone usage. In line with the presented correlations, we expect that machine learning algorithms will allow us to predict some mood conditions such as happiness, stress, and wakefulness.

Future Work Our preliminary results of the pilot study show correlations between mobile phone data and mood changes. There are some limitations and challenges we will overcome in our future studies as outlined below.

Surveys: In certain situations some participants refused to fill out the survey. We need to better understand under which circumstances the participants are not willing to fill out the survey. In the pilot study, we already asked the participants to provide us with reasons when they did not fill out a survey. We still need to analyze participant's feedback. In future work we will also investigate correlations between user's context and willingness to fill out surveys. This will allow us to turn off surveys in situations in which participants tend to refuse answering a survey.

Audio: We will consider two alternatives in audio data analysis: (1) manual annotation of speech content if there is any; (2) automatic voice detection and in case there is speech an automatic tense detection (past, present, future) will support the investigation of temporal thinking.

Bluetooth Devices: We have used the number of Bluetooth devices sensors around as a marker of people around. However, individuals might carry multiple Bluetooth devices such as headphones, mobile phone, tablets, and so on, and thus we cannot be sure that each device corresponds to one person.

Accelerometer: We observed a huge variety of accelerometer sampling frequencies due to the usage of different phone models. In the future work, we need to consider the different sampling frequencies in order to achieve sophisticated physical activity recognition.

Acknowledgment. We thank our participants from Turkey and from Switzerland. With your valuable feedback we will start with the second round of data collection in autumn 2015.

This work was partially funded by the Co-Funded Brain Circulation Scheme Project "Pervasive Healthcare: Towards Computational Networked Life Science" (TÜBITAK Co-Circ 2236, Grant agreement number: 112C005) supported by TÜBİTAK and EC FP7 Marie Curie Action COFUND.

References

1. Yohan, C. L., Nicholas, D., Li, F., Cha, H., Zhao, F.: Automatically characterizing places with opportunistic crowdsensing using smartphones. In: Proceedings of the 2012 ACM Conference on Ubiquitous Computing, pp 481–490 (2012)
2. Demiray, B., Mehl, M., Martin, M.: How much do people talk about their future in everyday life? A naturalistic observation study. Poster presented at the International Conference on Prospective Memory, Naples, Italy (2014)
3. Giordano, S., Puccinelli, D.: When sensing goes pervasive. Pervasive Mob. Comput. **17**, 175–183 (2015). Part B
4. Brajdic, A., Harle, R.: Walk detection and step counting on unconstrained smartphones. In: Proceedings of the 2013 ACM International Joint Conference on Pervasive and Ubiquitous Computing, UbiComp 2013 (2013)
5. Miluzzo, E., Lane, N., Fodor, K., Peterson, R., Lu, H., Musolesi, M., Eisenman, S., Zheng, X., Campbell, A.: Sensing meets mobile social networks: the design, implementation and evaluation of the CenceMe application. In: Proceedings of the International Conference on Embedded Networked Sensor Systems, SenSys 2008 (2008)
6. Miluzzo, E., Papandrea, M., Lane, N.D., Sarroff, A.M., Giordano, S., Campbell, A.T.: Tapping into the vibe of the city using vibn, a continuous sensing application for smartphones. In: Proceedings of First International Symposium on Social and Community Intelligence, SCI 2011. Beijing, China (2011)
7. Arnrich, B., Erdem, N.Ş, Alan, H.F., Ersoy, C.: Sensing healthy lifestyle in urban and rural environments. In: 3rd International Conference on Context-Aware Systems and Applications (2014)
8. Muaremi, A., Bexheti, A., Gravenhorst, F., Seiter, J., Feese, S., Arnrich, B., Tröster, G.: Understanding aspects of pilgrimage using social networks derived from smartphones. Pervasive Mob. Comput. **15**, 166–180 (2014)
9. Muaremi, A., Gravenhorst, F., Grünerbl, A., Arnrich, B., Tröster, G.: Assessing bipolar episodes using speech cues derived from phone calls. In: Cipresso, P., Matic, A., Lopez, G. (eds.) MindCare 2014. LNICST, vol. 100, pp. 103–114. Springer, Heidelberg (2014)
10. Muaremi, A., Arnrich, B., Tröster, G.: Towards measuring stress with smartphones and wearable devices during workday and sleep. BioNanoScience **3**(2), 172–183 (2013)
11. Feese, S., Arnrich, B., Rossi, M., Tröster, G., Burtscher, M., Meyer, B., Jonas, K.: Towards monitoring firefighting teams with the smartphone. In: IEEE International Conference on Pervasive Computing and Communications (PERCOM), pp 381–384 (2013)
12. Seiter, J., Macrea, L., Feese, S., Amft, O., Arnrich, B., Maurer, K., Tröster, G.: Activity monitoring in daily life as outcome measure for surgical pain relief intervention using smartphones. In: 17th International Symposium on Wearable Computers (ISWC), pp 127–128 (2013)
13. Seiter, J., Feese, S., Arnrich, B., Tröster, G., Amft, O., Macrea, L., Maurer, K.: Evaluating daily life activity using smartphones as novel outcome measure for surgical pain therapy. In: 8th International Conference on Body Area Networks (BodyNets), pp 153–156 (2013)
14. Feese, S., Arnrich, B., Tröster, G., Burtscher, M., Meyer, B., Jonas, K.: CoenoFire: monitoring performance indicators of firefighters in real-world missions using smartphones. In: ACM International Joint Conference on Pervasive and Ubiquitous Computing (UbiComp 2013), pp 83–92 (2013)
15. Feese, S., Arnrich, B., Tröster, G., Burtscher, M., Meyer, B., Jonas, K.: Sensing group proximity dynamics of firefighting teams using smartphones. In: International Symposium on Wearable Computers (ISWC), pp 97–104 (2013)

16. Muaremi, A., Arnrich, B., Tröster, G.: A survey on measuring happiness with smart phones. In: 6th International Workshop on Ubiquitous Health and Wellness (UbiHealth) (2012)
17. Madan, A., Cebrian, M., Lazer, D., Pentland, A.: Social sensing for epidemiological behavior change, pp. 291–300 (2010)
18. Silva, T.H., de Melo, P.O.S.V., Almeida, J.M., Salles, J., Loureiro, A.A.F.: Revealing the city that we cannot see. ACM Trans. Internet Technol. **14**(4), 1–23 (2014)
19. Eagle, N., Pentland, A.S.: Reality mining: sensing complex social systems. Pers. Ubiquitous Comput. **10**(4), 255–268 (2005)
20. Both, F., Hoogendoorn, M., Klein, M.C.A., Treur, J.: Computational modeling and analysis of the role of physical activity in mood regulation and depression. In: Neural Information Processing: Theory and Algorithm, pp. 270–281 (2010)
21. Aharony, N., Gardner, A., Sumter, C., Pentland, A.: Funf: Open Sensing Framework. http://funf.media.mit.edu (2011)

A Top-Down Design Approach
for an Automated Testing Framework

Abel Méndez-Porras[1,3]($\boxtimes$), Mario Nieto Hidalgo[2],
Juan Manuel García-Chamizo[2], Marcelo Jenkins[3],
and Alexandra Martínez Porras[3]

[1] Department of Computer Science, Costa Rica Institute of Technology,
Cartago, Costa Rica
amendez@itcr.ac.cr
[2] Department of Computer Technology, University of Alicante, Alicante, Spain
{mnieto,juanma}@dtic.ua.es
[3] Center for ICT Research, University of Costa Rica, San Pedro, Costa Rica
{marcelo.jenkins,alexandra.martinez}@ecci.ucr.ac.cr

Abstract. Mobile applications have become popular work tools. Portability and ease of Internet connectivity are characteristics that favor this adoption. However, mobile applications sometimes incorrectly process events associated with the user-interaction features. These features include content presentation or navigation. Rotating the devices, and gestures such as scroll or zoom into screens are some examples. There is a need to assess the quality with which mobile applications are processing these user-interaction features in order to improve their performance. In this paper, we present a top-down design approach for an automated testing framework for mobile applications. Our framework integrates digital image processing, GUI information, and historical bug information to identify new bugs based on user-interaction features. Our framework captures images before and after applying the user-interaction features and uses the SURF algorithm to identify interest points in each image. We compared interest points to note differences on the screens before and after applying the user-interaction features. This differences helps to find bugs in mobile applications. The first results show that it is feasible to identify bugs with user-interaction features using the proposed technique.

Keywords: Top-down design · Automated testing · User-interaction features · Interest points · Historical bug information · Mobile applications

1 Introduction

Mobile applications have evolved from isolated applications running on a device, to applications that offer different services through mobile ecosystems composed of mobile devices, mobile networks and application servers. These components

© Springer International Publishing Switzerland 2015
J.M. García-Chamizo et al. (Eds.): UCAmI 2015, LNCS 9454, pp. 37–49, 2015.
DOI: 10.1007/978-3-319-26401-1_4

exhibit significant changes in their behavior such as loss of network connectivity, bandwidth variability, and network congestion. Applications must be tested against variations exhibited by each of the components mentioned above [1]. Several studies state the importance of the context in which mobile applications are executed to ensure quality [2–4].

Fragmentation is the variety in both mobile devices and operating system versions. Fragmentation in mobile devices is manifested in both hardware and software [5–8]. Mobile applications behave differently on each device affecting the usability and performance. The reuse and maintenance of test cases to expose defects is affected by the diversity of devices and platforms.

According to [6], a mobile application receives user GUI input and environmental context events. User GUI include keyboard events and touch events. Environmental context events include physical context events and social context events. Physical context events are obtained from the built-in GPS receiver, bluetooth chips, accelerometer sensor, humidity sensor, magnetic sensor, and network. Social context events, like nearby MSN friends, the current activity the user is up to, and even the user's mood. In [4], these events are called "context event". The mobile application must accept and react to the changing context events as inputs to produce appropriate outputs. Modeling the context events of mobile applications for automated testing is one of the major challenges currently.

To meet the growing demand for high quality applications, developers must spend more effort and attention on the processes of software development. In particular, software testing and automation play a strategic role in ensuring the quality of mobile applications.

We conducted a systematic mapping and review [9] to provide empirical validation of automated testing of mobile applications. The findings showed open problems regarding the uses of user-interaction features and historical bug information to find bugs in mobile applications. In this paper, we propose the creation of a framework for automated testing of mobile applications that integrates digital image processing, GUI information, and historical bug information to identify new bugs based on user-interaction features. A top-down technological design method is used to design a solution that can be rationally justified. In summary, this work makes the following contributions:

- Uses the top-down technological design method to design the proposed framework.
- Innovatively combines digital imaging processing and GUI information to find bugs in mobile applications generated by user-interaction features.
- Uses historical bug information to improve the selection of sequences of events to be used as test cases (to find bugs in mobile applications).

This paper is organized as follows: Sect. 2 presents the related work, Sect. 3 presents the top-down design approach for the automated testing framework, Sect. 4 describes the component of the automated testing framework, Sect. 5 shows an example of using the proposed automated testing framework, and Sect. 6 presents the conclusions and future works.

2   Related Work

The creation of automated testing tools has been increasing. Here, some tools are described.

Dynodroid [10] uses model learning and random testing techniques for generating inputs to mobile applications. It is based on an "observe-select-execute" principle that efficiently generates a sequence of relevant events. It generates both user interface and system events.

MobiGUITAR [11] uses model learning and model based testing techniques. The application model is created using an automated reverse engineering technique called GUI Ripping. Test cases are generated using the model and test adequacy criteria. These test cases are sequences of events.

A3E [12] uses model based testing techniques. This tool systematically explores applications while they are running on actual phones. A3E uses a static, taint-style, data-flow analysis on the application bytecode in a novel way to construct a high-level control flow graph that captures legal transitions among activities (application screens). It then uses this graph to develop an exploration strategy named Targeted Exploration, and uses a strategy named Depth-first Exploration.

SwiftHand [13] generates sequences of test inputs for Android applications. It uses machine learning to learn a model of the application during testing, uses the learned model to generate user inputs that visit unexplored states of the application, and uses the execution of the applications on the generated inputs to refine the model.

Orbit [14] is based on a grey-box approach for automatically extracting a model of the application being tested. A static analysis of the application source code is used to extract the set of user actions supported by each widget in the GUI. Then, a dynamic crawler is used to reverse engineer a model of the application, by systematically exercising extracted actions on the live application.

The above approaches do not focus on user-interaction features and do not focus on historical bug information to find bugs in mobile applications.

3   Top-Down Design Approach

Our approach is based on the top-down technique for technological design proposed by García-Chamizo and Nieto-Hidalgo [15]. The starting point is the statement of a problem in the version of initial conjecture. This is a hypothesis that consists of an initial phase which is essentially the scope of the problem, and a second phase which is essentially the domain of the solution.

The problem domain phase addresses a technique to express the problem statement with a correct and accurate definition, contextual in a domain of reference that is a model of the problem and based on a predetermined syntactic structure. This phase produces a formal specification of the problem in a logical or mathematical expression that relates the problem to a model that denotes, from external focus to the problem, the objectives that the solution meet.

The solution domain phase gets a structural specification of a solution to the problem, which is a descriptor tree hierarchy of modules, and a graph of relationships between modules, namely the organization of the modules. The foundation of the decision-making process from the top-down technique is to classify the actions that make up the design method and establish a ranking among the classes found.

Our approach divides the problem into smaller problems. We proceed iteratively with the smaller problems until instances of problems can be resolved by specific techniques or whose solution is known.

3.1 Defining Objectives, Threats, Weaknesses and Requirements

Objectives are written as environmental conditions and are established from an external viewpoint. The requirements are derived from the objectives and are established from an internal viewpoint. The system weaknesses and threats were also defined. Objectives are obtained by answering the question of "what for" serves our system.

Once we have the objectives of the system, the utility that provides the outside world, we must define the requirements of the system, internal features to meet the objectives. The requirements are obtained by answering the question of "how to" meet the objectives. Table 1 shows the objectives, the threats, and weaknesses in the proposed framework in the first level.

Table 1. Traceability matrix of first level.

Requirements		1	2	3	4	5	6	7	8	9
Objectives	1. Automated detection of bugs	x	x	x	x				x	x
	2. Re-usability of test cases						x			
	3. System based on user-interaction features	x	x	x						
	4. System based on historical bug information	x	x	x		x				
	5. System based on digital image processing	x			x					x
	6. Metrics							x		
	7. Testing in both actual devices and emulated devices								x	
Threats	1. Fragmentation in both software and hardware								x	
	2. Reduced time for testing								x	
Weaknesses	1. There is not historical bug information at the beginning					x				

To meet the objectives, reduce threats and counter the weaknesses, the following requirements are defined:

1. Automated explorer of applications (meet objective 1).
2. Create testing based on user-interaction features (meet objective 1 and 3).
3. Create testing based on historical bug information (meet objectives 1 and 4).
4. Use digital image processing to find bugs (meet objectives 1 and 5).
5. Storage of historical bug information (meet objective 3, counteract weakness 1).
6. Storage of test cases (meet objective 2).
7. Apply metrics (meet objective 6).
8. Run testing in both actual devices and emulated devices (meet objectives 1 and 7, reduce threats 1 and 2).
9. Analyze bugs based on GUI (meet objective 1).

We created a traceability matrix (Table 1) to facilitate the process of verification of coverage requirements for each objective, threat, and weakness. In this table the objectives, the weaknesses, and the threats were placed in rows, and the requirements were placed in the columns. Each cell that intercepted a requirement with an objective, threat, or weakness was evaluated. If there was a strong relationship between a requirement and an objective, a threat, or a weakness, an indicator was placed in the cell. It was considered a strong relationship if the relationship directly affected the performance of the system. This matrix was useful in verifying if there was a requirement that met an objective, decreased a threat, or countered a weakness. Table 1 shows the traceability matrix to requirements for the first level of the solution proposed.

Furthermore, the traceability matrix is used to create the diagram of the solution. In the creating of the diagram, requirements can be grouped by similitude. The requirements that can be broken down into more than one should be raised as a new problem, and perform the same process described above in this section. Figure 1 shows the hierarchical organization of the system requirements. The requirements have been grouped into 5 nodes, the first level of the tree. Nodes 2 and 4 are atoms, they can not decomposed into sub-problems. Table 2 shows how requirements of nodes 1, 3, and 5 were decomposed into sub-problems. Objectives and new requirements were defined. The new requirements for nodes 1, 3, and 5 should be added to the second level of the tree shown in Figure 1. A traceability matrix was also created for nodes 1, 3, and 5, but is not shown here.

4 Proposed Framework

We now present our approach for creating a framework for automated testing of mobile applications for Android platform. This approach integrates an interest point detector and descriptor, GUI information, and historical bug information to identify new bugs based on user-interaction features. Figure 2 shows an overview of the approach. The framework design was obtained by the top-down

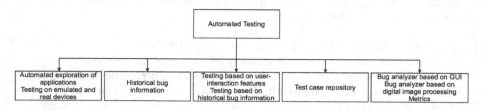

Fig. 1. Hierarchical organization of the system requirements.

Table 2. Objectives and requirements of second level.

First node	
Objective	Requirement
1. Automated explorer of applications	1. Automated explorer technique for mobile applications (meet objective 1)
2. Testing on emulated and real devices	2. Capture images during the application exploration (meet objective 1)
	3. Testing on emulated and real devices (meet objective 2)
Second node	
Objective	Requirement
Historical bug information repository	Storage of historical bug information
Third node	
Objective	Requirement
1. Testing based on user-interaction features	1. Create test cases based on user-interaction features (meet objective 1)
2. Testing based on historical bug information	2. Create test cases based on historical bug information (meet objective 2)
Fourth node	
Objective	Requirement
Test case repository	Storage of test case
Fifth node	
Objective	Requirement
1. Bug analyzer based on digital image processing	1. Analyze bugs based on digital image processing (meet objective 1)
2. Bug analyzer based on GUI	2. Analyze bugs based on GUI (meet objective 1)
3. Metrics	3. Run metrics (meet objective 3)

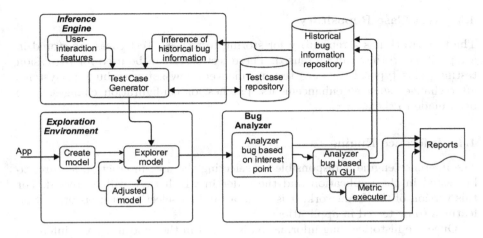

Fig. 2. Overview of automated testing framework.

technological design method. Framework is composed of an exploration environment, an inference engine, a bug analyzer, a bugs repository, and a test cases
repository. These five modules were obtained after to analyzer the hierarchy
organization showed in Fig. 1. The interaction between the different components
of the modules is shown by of lines with arrowheads. The arrowhead shows the
direction of the interaction between two components. In the following sections,
each of the components of the proposed framework are described.

4.1   User-Interaction Features

Mobile applications allow a set of user-interaction features that are independent
of the application logic. Such features include presentation or navigation content
such as turning the device or using various gestures to move or change the size on
screen. Zaeem et al. [16] conducted a bug study and they found that a significant
fraction of bugs in mobile applications can be attributed to user-interaction
features. They defined the following 8 user-interaction features: double rotation,
killing and restarting, pausing and resuming, back button functionality, opening
and closing menus, zoom in, zoom out, and scrolling.

An *activity* is an application component that provides a screen with which
users can interact. The lifecycle of an activity is composed of the following states:
create, start, resume, pause, stop, restart, and destroy. The user-interaction features mentioned above affect the states of the activities. Changes in the activities'
states can generate bugs in the application behavior.

4.2   Bug Repository

The framework has a repository for storing historical bug information. In the
future, the inference engine to create test cases could use historical bug information. Our inference engine, using machine learning, consults this repository and
makes inferences about how and which user-interaction features apply in new
testing.

4.3 Test Case Repository

The framework has a repository for storing test cases. Test cases are stored in a repository so they can be reused. These test cases can be used for regression testing. This type of software testing uncovers new software bugs in systems after changes such as enhancements, patches, or configuration changes, have been made to them.

4.4 Inference Engine

The inference engine is responsible for selecting the user-interaction features to be tested in the application and the order in which they will be tested. For this version of the framework, it is using a random selection of user-interaction features to be tested in applications.

Once the historical bug information is stored in the repository, the inference engine uses this information to select the user-interaction features and the order in which they will be tested in applications.

4.5 Bug Analyzer

The bug analyzer receives information of the activity being explored and two images captured during the uses of user-interaction features. The first image is captured before the applying of a user-interaction feature being tested, and the second image is captured after the applying. We used the interest point detector and descriptor SURF [17] to gets interest points in each image. The interest points with the specifications of GUI are used to determine whether there are bugs produced by the user-interaction feature applied. If bugs are found, they are stored in the repository of historical bug information.

GUI information is used to identify widgets that generated the bug. GUI information is obtained before the incorporation of a user-interaction feature being tested, and GUI informations is obtained after the applying.

4.6 Exploration Environment

The exploration environment is responsible for creating a model of the application. This model is used to explore the application automatically. SwiftHand [13] automatically creates a model and explores the application. We are modifying SwiftHand to allow the inclusion of user-interaction features while it explores the model of the application. In addition, we are adding the functionality to capture images before and after the execution of the user-interaction features. These images are sent to the bug analyzer to find possible bugs in the application.

5 Preliminary Results

We selected the user-interaction feature "Back button functionality" to show the preliminary results obtained with the framework proposed. The back button functionality should return the application to the previous screen. During this process the application may have some bugs with setting data to different application resources. We will simulate a data modification on two text fields and the loss of image by the use of the back button functionality.

5.1   Image Capture

The capture of two screens of an application was developed and used by us for the purpose of testing. Application is in the screen "Add New Product", Fig. 3(a). By pressing the button "Add CATEGORY" the application is changed to the screen to add a new category. By pressing the hardware back button on Android device the applications was returned to the initial state. However, during this process the data of text fields of price and product description are changed, Fig. 3(b).

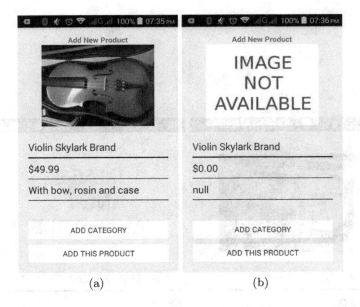

(a)   (b)

Fig. 3. User-interaction feature "Back button functionality".

5.2   Interest Point Detector and Descriptor

The first task was to apply SURF to captured images before and after the back button functionality. The red circles in the images of Fig. 4(a) and (b) represent the interest points detected by SURF. It can be seen that the most points of interest are focused where there are alphanumeric characters.

Fig. 4. Interest point found with SURF.

We obtained the following data by applying the SURF algorithm: interest point in Fig. 4(a) was 535, interest point in Fig. 4(b) was 553, extraction time in milliseconds was 229, amount of similar interest points was 299, and percentage of similarity between images was 55 %. With this information, we can decide whether to do a more thorough review of the images for possible bugs caused by the back button functionality.

The percentage of similarity between Fig. 4(a) and (b) was 55 %. This value suggested important differences between the two images due to bugs in the back button functionality. We focused on different interest points between the two images. Different interest points between the captured image before applying back button functionality and captured image after applying back button functionality are shown in Fig. 4(c) and (d). We found that different interest points are largely concentrated on the characters of the text field and the image space.

5.3   GUI Specifications

Having located the different interest points between the two images, the next step was to identify what controls were found in those coordinates to identify possible changes these controls. To perform these tasks the specifications of the GUI application was used. With the GUI specifications we determined the object type where the bugs were generated. The properties of these objects are analyzed to determine if there are variations in their configurations.

Once we identified bugs, we proceed to store the report in the repository of historical bug information. We saved the sequence of events that was running, the event where the bug was found, the controls that had the problem, and the time until the bug was found.

6   Conclusions and Future Work

This paper describes and proposes a new automated testing framework to detect bugs in mobile applications for the Android platform. The approach is described using a top-down design to provide a rational justification.

The framework proposed integrates an interest point detector and descriptor, GUI information, and historical bug information to identify new bugs based on user-interaction features. This framework uses SURF algorithm to detect interest points in images captured during the exploration of the mobile applications and applying user-interaction features.

Detection and description of interest points combined with GUI specifications allow the identification of bugs effectively.

The detection and description of interest points is a task that introduces computational cost. To solve this problem we are analyzing the possibility of using cloud computing and parallelism.

We are planning to add other user-interaction and environmental features to look for other types of bugs in mobile applications. In addition, we would like to increase the repository of historical bug information to experiment with the generation of sequences of events. The main goal is to minimize the number of sequences of events generated to find bugs and maximize the number of bugs found.

This research was supported by the Costa Rican Ministry of Science, Technology and Telecommunications (MICITT).

References

1. Dhanapal, K., Deepak, K., Sharma, S., Joglekar, S., Narang, A., Vashistha, A., Salunkhe, P., Rai, H., Somasundara, A., Paul, S.: An innovative system for remote and automated testing of mobile phone applications. In: Annual SRII Global Conference, pp. 44–54. SRII (2012)
2. Muccini, H., Di Francesco, A., Esposito, P.: Software testing of mobile applications: challenges and future research directions. In: 2012 7th International Workshop on Automation of Software Test, AST 2012 - Proceedings, pp. 29–35 (2012)
3. Wang, Z., Elbaum, S., Rosenblum, D.: Automated generation of context-aware tests. In: 29th International Conference on Software Engineering, 2007, ICSE 2007, pp. 406–415 (2007)
4. Amalfitano, D., Fasolino, A., Tramontana, P., Amatucci, N.: Considering context events in event-based testing of mobile applications. In: Proceedings - IEEE 6th International Conference on Software Testing, Verification and Validation Workshops, ICSTW 2013, pp. 126–133 (2013)
5. Ham, H.K., Park, Y.B.: Mobile application compatibility test system design for android fragmentation. In: Kim, T., Adeli, H., Kim, H., Kang, H., Kim, K.J., Kiumi, A., Kang, B.-H. (eds.) ASEA 2011. CCIS, vol. 257, pp. 314–320. Springer, Heidelberg (2011)
6. Liu, Z., Gao, X., Long, X.: Adaptive random testing of mobile application. In: ICCET 2010–2010 International Conference on Computer Engineering and Technology, Proceedings, vol. 2, pp. V2297–V2301 (2010)
7. Kaasila, J., Ferreira, D., Kostakos, V., Ojala, T.: Testdroid: automated remote ui testing on android. In: Proceedings of the 11th International Conference on Mobile and Ubiquitous Multimedia, MUM 2012 (2012)
8. Lu, L., Hong, Y., Huang, Y., Su, K., Yan, Y.: Activity page based functional test automation for android application. In: Proceedings of the 2012 3rd World Congress on Software Engineering, WCSE 2012, pp. 37–40 (2012)
9. Méndez-Porras, A., Quesada-López, C., Jenkins, M.: Automated testing of mobile applications: a systematic map and review. In: XVIII Ibero-American Conference on Software Engineering, Lima-Peru, pp. 195–208, April 2015
10. Machiry, A., Tahiliani, R., Naik, M.: Dynodroid: an input generation system for android apps. In: 2013 9th Joint Meeting of the European Software Engineering Conference and the ACM SIGSOFT Symposium on the Foundations of Software Engineering, ESEC/FSE 2013 - Proceedings, pp. 224–234 (2013)
11. Amalfitano, D., Fasolino, A., Tramontana, P., Ta, B., Memon, A.: Mobiguitar - a tool for automated model-based testing of mobile apps **PP**(99), 1 (2014)
12. Azim, T., Neamtiu, I.: Targeted and depth-first exploration for systematic testing of android apps. ACM SIGPLAN Not. **48**(10), 641–660 (2013)
13. Choi, W., Necula, G., Sen, K.: Guided gui testing of android apps with minimal restart and approximate learning. ACM SIGPLAN Not. **48**(10), 623–639 (2013)

14. Yang, W., Prasad, M.R., Xie, T.: A grey-box approach for automated GUI-model generation of mobile applications. In: Cortellessa, V., Varró, D. (eds.) FASE 2013 (ETAPS 2013). LNCS, vol. 7793, pp. 250–265. Springer, Heidelberg (2013)
15. García-Chamizo, J.M., Nieto-Hidalgo, M.: Formalización algebraica del método de arriba hacia abajo de diseño tecnológico. Departamento de Tecnologá Informática y Computación, Universidad de Alicante (2015)
16. Zaeem, R., Prasad, M., Khurshid, S.: Automated generation of oracles for testing user-interaction features of mobile apps. In: Proceedings - IEEE 7th International Conference on Software Testing, Verification and Validation, ICST 2014, pp. 183–192 (2014)
17. Bay, H., Tuytelaars, T., Van Gool, L.: SURF: speeded up robust features. In: Leonardis, A., Bischof, H., Pinz, A. (eds.) ECCV 2006, Part I. LNCS, vol. 3951, pp. 404–417. Springer, Heidelberg (2006)

Parameter Optimization for Online Change Detection in Activity Monitoring Using Multivariate Exponentially Weighted Moving Average (MEWMA)

Naveed Khan[1(✉)], Sally McClean[1], Shuai Zhang[2], and Chris Nugent[2]

[1] School of Computing and Information Engineering,
University of Ulster, Coleraine, UK
khan-n5@email.ulster.ac.uk, si.mcclean@ulster.ac.uk
[2] School of Computing and Mathematics, University of Ulster, Jordanstown, UK
{s.zhang, cd.nugent}@ulster.ac.uk

Abstract. In recent years, body worn sensors have become popular for the purpose of activity recognition. The sensors used to capture a large amount of data in a short period of time which contain meaningful events. The change points in this data can be used to specify transition to a distinct event which can subsequently be used in various scenarios such as to identify changes in patient vital signs in a medical domain or to assist in the process of generating activity labels for the purposes of annotating real-world datasets. A change point can also be used to identify the transition from one activity to another. The multivariate exponentially weighted moving average (MEWMA) algorithm has been proposed to automatically detect such change points for transitions in user activity. The MEWMA approach does not require any assumptions to be made in relation to the underlying distributions to evaluate multivariate data streams and can run in an online scenario. The focus of this paper is to evaluate the performance of the MEWMA approach for change point detection in user activity and to determine the optimal parameter values by tuning and analyzing different parameters of MEWMA. Optimal parameter selection results in an algorithm to detect accurate change points and minimize false alarms. Results are presented and compared based on real world accelerometer data for standard and optimal parameters evaluated using different metrics such as accuracy, precision, G-mean and F-measures.

Keywords: Activity monitoring · Change points · Daily activities · Multivariate exponentially weighted moving average (MEWMA) · Wearable sensors

1 Introduction

In recent years, numerous wearable sensor technologies such as accelerometers, GPS, light sensors and gyroscope have been used to provide support in data collection providing low power communication and fast processing [2]. Activity monitoring empowers novel context aware solicitations in various domains such as industrial, educational and medical areas. For instance, a vigorous depiction of daily activities can

J.M. García-Chamizo et al. (Eds.): UCAmI 2015, LNCS 9454, pp. 50–59, 2015.
DOI: 10.1007/978-3-319-26401-1_5

be valuable in assessing health and wellbeing, in order to care for elderly people and to gain an appreciation of their ability to live independently. The objective of activity monitoring is therefore to automatically detect the activities of daily life. Body movement can be captured through wearable sensors (e.g. accelerometers) to identify different transitions of movement patterns in performing various activities e.g. sitting, walking, and running [1]. The characteristics of such sensors are that they are light-weight, unobtrusive and power efficient. Change point detection is used to identify the transition from one underlying time series generation model to another. The sudden change in mean, variance or both can represent change points in time series data [3]. Change point detection algorithms can be categorized as being online or offline. Online change detection algorithms are used in real time systems to observe, monitor and process data as it becomes available. In the offline scenario, firstly the data is collected and then the change point algorithm is used to collectively process all of the data. Online change point detection is sequential, fast and minimizes false alarms. One of the problems that still has to be addressed within this domain of research is automatic change point detection in user activity when the transition has occurred. This involves selection of an algorithm to form a fundamental component of a real system and accurately detect a change point, which for example solicits autonomously user interaction based on transition within an input stream. Such in time solicitation can be helpful in various situations like annotating activities for making real world annotated data sets or for detecting variation whilst monitoring patient vital signs for example heart rate.

In our proposed framework the Multivariate Exponentially Weighted Moving Average (MEWMA) is proposed as an innovative approach for change point detection. The MEWMA is a statistical method which averages the input data within a data stream and provides a reduced degree of weighting to earlier data points. The primary aim of using MEWMA is to detect small shifts quickly in the data [4].

The aim of this paper is to evaluate MEWMA for online change detection in activity monitoring. The multivariate approach is used due to the nature of accelerometery data being represented in 3 dimensions, which are not independent or each other. Multi-variate analysis is used to measure more than one characteristic of a system and also to evaluate the relationship amongst these characteristics. The standard MEWMA approach [4, 5] has been used in the literature for change point detection in user activity. In our experiments we used the standard MEWMA approach for change point detection and also tune the different parameters such as λ the parameter which weights current and historical data, window size and significance values with the aim to achieve better performance and accurate change point detection. The different metric measures such as accuracy, precision, G-means and F-measure were used to evaluate the change point detection in activity monitoring for the standard MEWMA approach and for the approach when considering the tuning of its parameters. The tuned parameters help to identify optimal values for each activity by achieving better results for different metrics. The remainder of this paper is structured as follows: in Sect. 2 the related work is discussed. In Sect. 3 we provide an overview of MEWMA and the experimental setup with results presented in Sect. 4. Finally, Conclusions and Future Work are presented in Sect. 5.

2 Related Work

The various kinds of activities depend on in-time decisions identified from observed data. The varying nature of input data generates considerable challenges for different learning algorithms. Thus, an accurate and in time detection of change points in data is a very significant issue. In the literature, a number of algorithms have been utilized for change point detection in health related sensor data. The Cumulative Sum Control Chart (CUSUM) has been used for change point detection in cardiovascular events [6]. This technique is more effective for detecting small shifts using the mean of the process. The core methods used were an online activity recognition method, a process control method, a biometric extraction method which has been used to evaluate physiological monitoring module [6]. Sudden shifts in accelerometer data cannot, however, be detected by CUSUM and are therefore ineffective for such changes [7]. An independent random sequence was used to detect changes by a univariate change detection algorithm in [8]. In the first step, the index of the changeover for the most likely point inside the processing window was calculated. Secondly, the hypothesis was verified for the expected change point whether correct or incorrect for the expected change. The algorithm utilizes small memory, is computationally inexpensive and does not require knowledge of the underlying distribution of the data. An activity recognition (AR) module was developed based on mobile data [2] to detect changes in daily life activities. The Gaussian mixture classifier was used to detect changes in current activities of daily life scenarios. Stationery and non-stationary activities were considered such as standing-still and running, respectively. For the activity detection process 3 consecutive windows of 9 s were used by the AR module. Meanwhile, the transition from one activity to another such as stand–still to walking could be detected and labelled simultaneously. The limitation of this technique is the user transition from non-stationary 'walking' to stationary 'stand-still', makes it unsuitable for a real time scenario. Short delays are also a cause for incorrect detection of user activity. An open source programming framework known as signal processing in node environment (SPINE) has been developed for body sensor network applications. The aim of SPINE was to evaluate performance analysis for different sensor platforms [14]. The early drift detection (EED) approach has been used for detecting small and abrupt changes in time series data [9]. In this approach, the distance between two classification errors was used and calculated from the average distance and its standard deviation. If the calculated distance was small, the change was detected otherwise the new point was considered as belonging with the previous points. The exponentially weighted moving average (EWMA) has been used for change point detection in time series data with the same concept as that of EDD mentioned earlier. The additional characteristic of the exponential weighted moving average is to update the estimated error frequently with data. The One-Class Support Vector Machine (OCSVM) has also been used for change detection in human activities [10]. The high dimensional hypersphere was used to model data where the change point detection was evaluated based on the distribution of radi of hypersphere. The high and low values correspond to changes in different activities. The template matching algorithm known as dynamic time warping (DTW) [11] has been developed for gesture detection. For each activity one template is used and the number of templates identifies the processing time for recognition. The support vector change point detection (SVCPD) algorithm has been used [3] to detect change points in a data stream. To detect change points, the algorithm used feature space, hypersphere and hypersphere radius to determine the location of new data points. The SVCPD was also used to evaluate each data point with the current hypersphere model to accurately identify changes occurring in the data stream.

In summary, the analysis of the literature reflects that the current change-point detection methods tend to be more sophisticated in nature. In addition, the pre information is often required about the possible changes and their distribution. This might make the change detection methods implementation more challenging as automatic, online change detection application. The other weakness could be the numerous estimation parameter requirements, several monitoring descriptors and various number of tuning parameters. These issues increase when multivariate time series used simultaneously.

3   Multivariate Exponentially Weighted Moving Average (MEWMA) Change Point Detection Algorithm

MEWMA is a statistical method that averages the input data within a data stream and provides less weight to earlier data points. The primary aim of using MEWMA is to detect small shifts quickly in time series data [4]. The results of the EWMA technique rely on EWMA statistics, which is, an exponentially weighted moving average of all prior data, including historical and current data. The multivariate EWMA is an extension of EWMA for multivariate data [5] in order to monitor and analyse the multivariate process. MEWMA can be defined as:

$$\mathbf{Z}_i = \mathbf{\Lambda}\mathbf{X}_i + (1 - \mathbf{\Lambda})\mathbf{Z}_{i-1} \ i = 1, 2, 3 \ldots n \tag{1}$$

where $\mathbf{Z}_i$ is i^{th} EWMA vector, $\mathbf{\Lambda}$ is the diagonal matrix with elements λ_i for $i = 1, 2, 3 \ldots n$ where p is the number of dimensions and $0 < \lambda_i \leq 1$, and $\mathbf{X}_i$ is the ith observation vector, $i = 1, 2, 3, \ldots n$. The out-of-control signal is given as:

$$\mathbf{T}_i^2 = \mathbf{Z}_i' * \sum_i^{-1} * \mathbf{Z}_i < h \tag{2}$$

where $\sum_i$ is the variance covariance matrix of $\mathbf{Z}_i$ and h (>0), chosen to achieve a specified in-control signal. Multivariate analysis is used to measure more than one characteristic of a system and also evaluate the relationship among these characteristics. In multivariate analysis, the data points $x_1, x_2, x_3 \cdots x_n$ is a subsequence where n is the length of a data stream. Each data point x_i is an element of each n sensor observations. Each data point in the data stream may be of various distributions so, for example, as $x_1, x_2, x_3 \cdots x_{i-1}$ and $x_i, x_{i-1} \cdots x_n$ can be from distributions D1 and D2 respectively. The aim of the algorithm is to determine and classify the position of change points i in data stream. The MEWMA algorithm firstly calculates the exponentially weighted moving average of the multivariate input observations to find the change points. Moreover, the sliding window version of the algorithm is used to analyze the specific number of data points sequentially incremented by 1 within a window. In each window, the index variable, i slides subsequently to determine the global statistics for each index i, $1 < i \leq n$. Each input vector of multivariate data is used to find the MEWMA vector represented by $\mathbf{Z}_i$. In addition, the variance and covariance matrix of $\mathbf{Z}_i$ is calculated recursively and represented by $\sum_i$. Once the T-squared statistic is calculated as shown in (Eq. 2) where, the significance value h is used to identify the confidence of the entire window. If the T-squared value is greater than h, then x_i will be labelled as a change point within a data stream. The accelerometer data analysis identifies the actual values of specific change points which may represent an increase or decrease in the data. Therefore, the sliding window algorithm detects a number of adjacent change points which highlights the significant change point in the data. The adjacent change points can be classified by defining a new parameter k in order to be removed, if representing the same event of the real change in the data stream.

3.1 Experimental Setup

The MEWMA approach was evaluated for change point detection on a real dataset of accelerometer data. The data was captured from two participants wearing the shimmer wireless sensing platform [12]. The shimmer sensor was placed in the middle of the participant's left pectoral and at the mid-point between the thigh and knee on the anterior of the participant's right leg. The sensor placement positions on the subject's body enabled anterior-posterior and lateral movements to be captured effectively [13]. The different activities were performed by two participants involving a set of activities consisting of sit, stand, walk corridor, walk upstairs and walk downstairs. For the static activities such as sit and stand, the participants remained in each state for approximately 30 s and then transitioned to other static activities such as sit to stand and stand to sit [13]. The dynamic activities were measured by accelerometer data where the subject stood for approximately 30 s, followed by an activity performed for 30 s and then transition to standing. In the data collection, the activity execution of accelerometer data was wirelessly streamed to a receiving computer via the IEEE 802.15.1 Bluetooth communications protocol.

4   Results and Discussion

This Section presents the details of the evaluation of the feasibility and performance of the proposed MEWMA on a real dataset for the standard and tuned parameters of MEWMA. The acceleration magnitudes for the multivariate approach calculated from x, y and z axes of the captured data are used as input to the MEWMA algorithm. The MEWMA vector is calculated to detect the change points in the data stream. To analyze our algorithm, we manually labelled the start and end point of each activity in the data set being considered. For evaluation, the standard MEWMA ($\lambda = 0.3$) is used and for optimal parameters such as λ the parameter which weights current and historical data, window size (1 s, 1.5 s, 2 s, 2.5 s, 3 s) and significance values (0.05, 0.025, 0.01, 0.005) are varied in an effort to find better performance and accurate change point detection. Metrics of precision, G-means and F-measure were used to evaluate change point detection in activity monitoring for the standard MEWMA approach and its tuned parameters.

In our experiments we used the standard MEWMA and tuned (optimal) values for change point detection as presented in Fig. 1(A) and (B), respectively. The detected change point is considered true if in the data stream the index i, $i \in \{z - (f/4), \ldots \ldots z - (f/4)\}$ as z indicates the index of manually label change in the data stream and f denotes the sampling frequency in Hz. The target of our algorithm is to detect the primary transitions in high level activities such as stand still – downstairs – stand still and stand still – downstairs, as presented in Fig. 1.

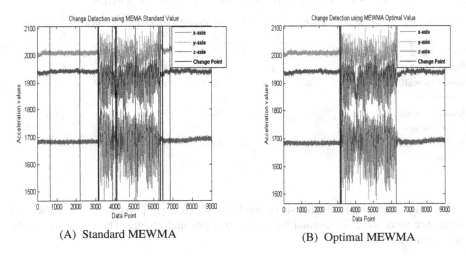

(A) Standard MEWMA

(B) Optimal MEWMA

Fig. 1. Examples of sliding window change detection results for the activity's tand still – walk downstairs - stand still'. (A): The window size was 2 s second with significance $p = 0.005$ and $\lambda = 0.3$ (B): The window size was 1.5 s second with significance $p = 0.005$ and $\lambda = 0.7$

The positive and negative detection cases were defined as, the true positive (TP) representing the correctly identified change points and true negative (TN) denoting the non-transitional points which is not labelled as change. The false positive (FP) is the non-transition point which the algorithm highlighted as a change while false negative (FN) occurs when the algorithm is unable to detect changes in user activity.

The standard MEWMA identified a maximum number of false positives in the real data because of the dynamic and complex nature of the accelerometery data. Figure 1 (A) and (B) used the standard and optimal MEWMA respectively to detect the primary change points in real data. Nevertheless, the non-primary change points were detected by the standard MEWMA approach whereas in Fig. 1(B) only the primary change points were detected using MEWMA tuned with optimal values. A number of false positives were detected in the real data using the standard MEWMA approach as presented in Fig. 1(A) which can minimize the accuracy, precision and F measure.

The results of both approaches when applied to a real dataset for five activities {Sit to Stand, Stand to Sit, Stand to Walk Corridor, Stand to Walk Downstairs and Stand to Walk Upstairs} are presented in Tables 1 and 2. We used standard MEWMA and tuned different parameters for our experiments. Table 1 presents, results for each activity using the standard MEWMA approach ($\lambda = 0.3$) for change point detection. Table 2 represents the experimental results for different values of λ ranging from 0.1 to 0.9 for each activity with corresponding significance values 0.05, 0.01, 0.025, 0.005 and window sizes 1 s, 1.5 s, 2 s, 2.5 s and 3 s.

Table 1. MEWMA Standard Values for 5 different activities.

Activity	Significance value	Win size	λ	Accuracy %	Precision %	G-means %	F-measure %
Sit to stand	0.005	2 s	0.3	99.5	40	70	40
Stand to sit		3 s		99.6	40	70	50
Stand to walk corridor		2.5 s		99.2	40	70	40
Stand to walk downstairs		2 s		98.5	50	70	44.4
Stand to walk upstairs		2 s		97.5	30	70	40

Different performance measures such as accuracy, precision, G-means and F-measure were used for evaluation of the experimental results. The accuracy can be calculated using Eq. 3:

$$\frac{TP + TN}{TP + TN + FP + FN} \tag{3}$$

to find a high number of true negatives in the data. The true positive (TP) representing the correctly identified change points and true negative (TN) denoting the non-transitional points which is not labelled as change. The false positive (FP) is the non-transition point which the algorithm highlighted as a change while false negative (FN) occurs when the algorithm is unable to detect changes in user activity. These results were relatively high about 99.5 % to 99.9 % for optimal parameters and 97.5 % to 99.6 % for standard MEWMA.

The optimal parameters of MEWMA change point detection persistently attained higher precision, G-means and F-measure than standard MEWMA. Precision is evaluated for both standard and optimal value using Eq. 4:

$$\frac{TP}{TP + FP} \tag{4}$$

Table 2. MEWMA optimal parameter selection for 5 different activities.

Activity	Significance value	Win size	λ	Accuracy %	Precision %	G-means %	F-measure %
Sit to stand	0.005	2 s	.1	97.5	20	75	30
	0.005	.5 s	.2	99.6	35	70	35
	0.005	.5 s	.4	99.5	30	70	40
	0.005	.5 s	.5	99.3	50	70	50
	0.005	.5 s	.6	99.2	50	90	66.7
	0.01	**.5 s**	**.7**	**99.9**	**66.7**	**100**	**80**
	0.005	2.5 s	.8	99.8	50	85	57
	0.01	.5 s	.9	99.7	50	90	65
Stand to sit	0.005	2.5 s	.1	99.3	30	80	44.4
	0.01	2.5 s	.2	99.4	30	70	40
	0.005	1.5 s	.4	99.6	50	75	40
	0.005	**2.5 s**	**.5**	**99.9**	**50**	**100**	**66.7**
	0.01	2.5 s	.6	99.4	40	85	57
	0.01	2.5 s	.7	99.6	30	80	44.4
	0.01	.5 s	.8	99.5	40	75	40
	0.005	1 s	.9	99.7	20	70	30
Stand to walk corridor	0.01	3 s	.1	99.2	10	65	20
	0.005	2.5 s	.2	98.5	40	70	30
	0.01	2.5 s	.4	99.1	30	66	40
	0.005	**2 s**	**.5**	**99.9**	**50**	**70**	**50**
	0.01	1.5 s	.6	98.8	40	68	40
	0.01	2 s	.7	98.3	20	60	30
	0.01	2.5 s	.8	99.1	30	68	40
	0.01	1 s	.9	99.4	35	65	40
Stand to walk downstairs	0.005	2.5 s	.1	97.7	30	65	40
	0.01	2.5 s	.2	98.2	40	70	50
	0.01	1.5 s	.4	98.5	20	75	30
	0.005	2 s	.5	99.2	30	80	40
	0.025	1.5 s	.6	99.3	40	70	44.4
	0.01	**1.5 s**	**.7**	**99.9**	**50**	**100**	**66.7**
	0.01	1 s	.8	99.5	20	90	40
	0.005	1 s	.9	99	30	85	50
Stand to walk upstairs	0.005	2.5 s	.1	97.5	10	65	20
	0.005	2.5 s	.2	98	30	60	44.4
	0.005	1 s	.4	99	20	65	30
	0.005	1.5 s	.5	98.5	40	66	44.4
	0.005	**1.5 s**	**.6**	**99.9**	**50**	**70**	**50**
	0.005	2 s	.7	97..9	20	60	30
	0.005	3 s	.8	99.5	30	65	40
	0.005	1.5 s	.9	98.8	20	60	30

The maximum precision for standard MEWMA achieved in the range of 30 % to 50 % with 0.005 significance value and window sizes 2 s to 3 s. For optimal parameters the approach attained figures in the range of 50 % to 66.7 % with λ value (0.5 & 0.7), significance value (0.01 & 0.005) and window sizes (0.5 s to 2.5 s).The higher precision was attained due to the minimum number of false positive detections using optimal parameters.

Likewise, the G-means is the combination of sensitivity and specificity and defined as the ratio of positive accuracy (sensitivity) and the ratio of negative accuracy (specificity) calculated using Eq. 5:

$$\sqrt{\text{sensitivity} \times \text{specificty}} \tag{5}$$

The highest G-means achieved for the optimal parameters ranged from 70 % to 100 % with the same λ, window sizes and significance values discussed earlier and a value of only 70 % was attained for the standard MEWMA approach. Moreover, the F-measure was used to find the overall effectiveness of the activity by combining the precision and recall and can be calculated using Eq. 6:

$$\frac{2 \times \text{Recall} \times \text{Precision}}{(\text{Recall} + \text{Precision})} \tag{6}$$

The best F-measure obtained was between 50 % and 80 % for optimal parameters and 40 % to 50 % for the standard MEWMA approach. The analysis of overall results suggests that optimal parameter selection provides better accuracy than standard parameter values and precision, G-means and F-measure improved by more than 10 % for each activity with optimal parameters of MEWMA.

5 Conclusion and Future Work

The multivariate exponentially weighted moving average (MEWMA) has been used to automatically detect change points corresponding to different transitions in user activity. The different parameters of MEWMA were evaluated to select the optimal parameters. The standard MEWMA and optimal parameters were used to analyse the performance of MEWMA. The optimal parameters of MEWMA outperformed the standard values on real world accelerometer data for accuracy, precision, G-means and F-measure compared with the standard approach. Also, the MEWMA approach achieved low computation costs and can run in the online scenario. A key part of future work will be the automatic optimization of optimal parameter selection in terms of λ, window size and significance value. The synthetic dataset will also be used to determine the impact of parameter choices using MEWMA. Additionally, other multivariate algorithms for change point detection will be used from the state of the art to compare with MEWMA and analyse their performance. Moreover, MEWMA will be incorporated into real world systems such as mobile based applications for collection and active sampling to label data.

References

1. Stikic, M., Larlus, D., Ebert, S., Member, S., Schiele, B.: Weakly supervised recognition of daily life activities with wearable sensors. IEEE Trans. Pattern Anal. Mach. Intell. **33**(12), 2521–2537 (2011)
2. Cleland, I., Han, M., Nugent, C., Lee, H., McClean, S., Zhang, S., Lee, S.: Evaluation of prompted annotation of activity data recorded from a smart phone. Sensors (Basel) **14**(9), 15861–15879 (2014)
3. Camci, F.: Change point detection in time series data using support vectors. Int. J. Pattern Recognit. Artif. Intell. **24**(1), 73–95 (2010)
4. Lucas, J.M., Saccucci, M.S.: Exponentially weighted moving average control schemes: properties and enhancements. Technometrics **32**(1), 1–12 (1990)
5. Khoo, M.B.C.: An extension for the univariate exponentially weighted moving average control chart. Matematika **20**(1), 43–48 (2004)
6. Zhang, S., Galway, L., Mclean, S., Scotney, B., Nugent, C.: Deriving relationships between physiological change and activities of daily living using wearable sensors. Sens. Syst. Softw. **57**, 235–250 (2010)
7. Prajapati, D.R., Mahapatra, P.B.: A new X chart comparable to CUSUM and EWMA charts. Int. J. Product. Qual. Manag. **4**(1), 103–115 (2009)
8. Jain, A., Wang, Y.: A New Framework for On-Line Change Detection. Accsessed http://excelsior.cs.ucsb.edu, pp. 1–36 (2015). http://citeseerx.ist.psu.edu/viewdoc/download?doi=10.1.1.62.5929&rep=rep1&type=pdf. Accessed May 2015
9. Baena-García, M., del Campo-Ávila, J., Fidalgo, R., Bifet, A., Gavaldà, R., Morales-Bueno, R.: Early drift detection method. In: ECML PKDD Workshop on Knowledge Discovery from Data Streams, pp. 1–10 (2006)
10. Vlasveld, R.: Temporal segmentation using support vector machines in the context of human activity recognition. Master degree thesis, p. 1–85, February 2014
11. Murao, K., Terada, T.: A recognition method for combined activities with accelerometers. In: ACM International Joint Conference on Pervasive and Ubiquitous Computing Adjunct Publication - UbiComp, pp. 787–796 (2014)
12. Kuris, B., Dishongh, T.: SHIMMER - sensing health with intelligence, modularity, mobility and experimental reusability - hardware guide. In: IEEE Software (2006)
13. Zhang, S., Galway, L., Mclean, S., Scotney, B., Nugent, C.: A framework for context-aware online physiological monitoring. In: 24th International Symposium on Computer Based Medical System, pp. 1–6 (2011)
14. Fortino, G., Giannantonio, R., Gravina, R., Kuryloski, P., Jafari, R.: Enabling effective programming and flexible management of efficient body sensor network applications. IEEE Trans Hum-Mach Syst. **43**(1), 115–133 (2011)

Generation of a Partitioned Dataset with Single, Interleave and Multioccupancy Daily Living Activities

Francisco J. Quesada[1], Francisco Moya[1], Javier Medina[1], Luis Martínez[1], Chris Nugent[2], and Macarena Espinilla[1(✉)]

[1] Department of Computer Science, University of Jaén, Jaén, Spain
{fqreal,fpmoya,jmquero,martin,mestevez}@ujaen.es
[2] School of Computing and Mathematics, University of Ulster,
Jordanstown BT37 0QB, UK
cd.nugent@ulster.ac.uk

Abstract. The advances in electronic devices have entailed the development of smart environments which have the aim to help and make easy the life of their inhabitants. In this kind of environments, an important task is the process of activity recognition of an inhabitant in the environment in order to anticipate the occupant necessities and to adapt such smart environment. Due to the cost to checking activity recognition approaches in real environments, usually, they use datasets generated from smart environments. Although there are many datasets for activity recognition in smart environments, it is difficult to find single, interleaved or multioccupancy activity datasets, or combinations of these classes of activities according to the researchers' needs. In this work, the design and development of a complete dataset with 14 sensors and 9 different activities daily living is described, being this dataset divided into partitions with different classes of activities.

Keywords: Dataset · Activity recognition · Smart environments · Single activities · Interleave activities · Multioccupancy activities

1 Introduction

The advance in the miniaturization of electronic devices in addition to a reduction in their cost, have created an environment whereby we are surrounded by embedded sensing technology, arising the Ambient Intelligence (AmI) concept [14]. The notion of a smart home follows this vision with an environment of embedded technology and processing sensor data with the ability to ascertain the behaviour of its inhabitants.

This kind of environments can help people, especially people with cognitive diseases, in their daily live. Thus, for example, in a smart home it is possible to prompt inhabitants how to finish a given activity daily living (ADL) action, like preparing a tea, remind them where is a particular object, like the sugar, when

J.M. García-Chamizo et al. (Eds.): UCAmI 2015, LNCS 9454, pp. 60–71, 2015.
DOI: 10.1007/978-3-319-26401-1_6

they have to take their medicines, or when they should move after abnormal periods of inactivity [10].

Nowadays, researchers are focusing on their efforts on the improvement of smart homes, in order to be more helpful. So, there are many researching areas with this aim, being one of the most important the area of activity recognition (AR) [3,8,15].

The process of activity recognition aims to recognize the actions and goals of one or more person within the environment based on a series of observations of actions and environmental conditions [1]. It can, therefore, be deemed as a complex process that involves the following steps: (i) to choose and deploy the appropriate sensors to objects within the environment in order to effectively monitor and capture a user's behavior along with the state change of the environment; (ii) to collect, store and process information and, finally, (iii) to infer/classify activities from sensor data through the use of computational activity models.

There are two categories for activity recognition: Data-Driven Approaches (DDA) and Knowledge-Driven Approaches (KDA). The former, DDA, are based on machine learning techniques in which a preexistent dataset of user behaviors is required. A training process is carried out, usually, to build an activity model which is followed by a testing processes to evaluate the generalization of the model in classifying unseen activities [6,9]. Regarding KDA, an activity model is built through the incorporation of rich prior knowledge gleaned from the application domain, using knowledge engineering and knowledge management techniques [2].

In these approaches, activity models must be trained and tested in order to check their performances. Nevertheless, it is very difficult, expensive and complex to test the performance of them in real environments. Thus, it is a challenge to check the performance of activity models by means of datasets in a more economical and easy way. There are many datasets proposed in the literature in which three classes of activities can distinguish:

- Single activity [4,16] is an activity which has been carried out completely before to start the performance of a new one.
- Interleave activity [12] is an activity which is carried out while another activity is performing at the same time.
- Multioccupancy [13] is a class of activity in which some people are performing their activities simultaneously.

The division in these classes allows researchers to train and test their activity models only in one kind of them, not allowing to combine several classes. Nevertheless, there are some cases that can be interesting to train and test activity models the combination of some activity classes. This is difficult because it is not easy to find datasets with these characteristics.

In this contribution, we present the design and the development of a complete ADL dataset which is partitioned in several subsets depending on the activity class. Thus, the complete dataset has 3 activity classes (single, interleave and multioccupancy) that can be combined in 7 subsets or partitions.

The remainder of the work is structured as follows: in Sect. 2, previous works of datasets that have been developed are reviewed. Section 3 describes, first, the smart environment where the dataset has been developed and the considered ADLs. Then, the generated dataset is described, focusing on their partitions. Finally, in Sect. 4 conclusions and future works are drawn.

2 Related Works

Some datasets have been generated in smart homes or smart environments in order to overcome the difficulties to test and to train activity models in real smart environments. In the literature, some contributions have been presented about the generation of datasets; some of the most important ones are reviewed in this Section.

There are repositories which contain several AmI datasets. One the most well-known repositories is CASAS[1] [4], where there are different datasets developed by Cook et al. and some links to other popular AmI ones. Bellow, some of these datasets are reviewed:

- Tapia et al. [15]. The single activity class dataset is composed of the data collected from 2 apartments inhabited by a man and a woman respectively. The sensor network has 77 sensors in the first apartment and 84 sensors in the second one, gathering data during 14 days. The activities performed during the experiment were labeled by the inhabitants regarding 35 preestablish ADLs like *toileting, grooming, preparing lunch* or *preparing a beverage*.
- Roggen et al. [11] deployed a sensor network with 72 sensors to gather data of 12 common ADLs, performed daily morning, for example, *prepare breakfast*. The single activity class dataset was developed by one person during 25 hours.
- Van Kasteren et. al [16] generated a single activity class dataset locating 14 sensors in an apartment which had an inhabitant during 28 days. The dataset contains 7 ADLs like *prepare breakfast, get drink* or *prepare dinner*.
- Among all of these authors, it is noteworthy the work developed by Cook et al. [4] in the ADL datasets generation. These datasets contain the data that a smart apartment sensor network produces when the inhabitants perform their ADLs. Some of the most representative datasets are the following ones:
  - Cook and Schmitter-Edgecombe [5] developed a single activity class dataset, which was performed by the occupant of an apartment. The sensor network was composed by 37 sensors. In this dataset, there are performed 5 ADLs.
  - Singla et al. [12] developed an interleave activity class dataset. The data was collected from the sensor network, which was composed by 78 sensors, when the participants were performing 8 different ADLs.
  - A multioccupancy class dataset was developed during four months in a student apartment [13]. The data represents two participants in the apartment at the same time performing fifteen ADL activities. The sensor network was composed by 78 sensors, which are the responsible to gather the data.

[1] http://ailab.wsu.edu/casas/datasets/ (last checked on August 27, 2015).

These datasets present the difficulty of combining them in mixed datasets because the structure and the syntax are not the same. Thus, in this work we present the design and development of a complete dataset which has been divided in different partitions which combine activity classes to be used according to the researchers' needs.

3   Dataset Generation

This Section describe the design and development of the partitioned dataset in a smart environment in which daily living activities (single, interleave and multioccupancy) have been carried out. To do so, first, the smart environment, where the dataset has been developed is described and the considered ADLs are indicated. Then, the dataset description is provided, focusing on their partitions.

3.1   Smart Environment and ADLs

Regarding the smart environment, the dataset has been generated in the smart-lab of the University of Ulster that consists of a kitchen and a living room, which is illustrated in Fig. 1.

Fig. 1. Smartlab kitchen and the living room

The ADLs that are considered in the generated dataset are the most popular activities that are presented in the literature in such places. Therefore, the activities that we have considered are: *prepare drink, call by phone, prepare snack, watch TV* and *wash dishes*. Nonetheless, it is usual to prepare drinks and snacks in different ways depending on the kind of drink and snack. Thus, we consider that *prepare drink* can be *drink a glass of water, prepare a tea with the kettle, prepare a hot chocolate in the microwave* or *drink a glass of milk*. On the other hand, the kind of *prepare snack* that are considered in this dataset are *prepare hot snack in the microwave* and *prepare cold snack*. So, the 9 different ADLs, which have been carried out in the smartlab, are described regarding their performance, as follow:

1. **Drink a glass of water**. The inhabitant goes to the kitchen, takes a glass from the glasses cupboard, opens the sink tab and fills the glass with water.

2. **Prepare a tea with the kettle**. The dweller goes to the kitchen, fills the kettle with water and switches it on. After that, he takes the tea bag from the groceries cupboard, the cup from the glasses cupboard and a spoon from the cutlery cupboard. Finally, he puts the tea bag into the cup and pours the hot water from the kettle.

3. **Prepare a hot chocolate in the microwave**. The occupant goes to the kitchen, takes the milk from the fridge and a cup from the glasses cupboard. Later, she pours the milk into the cup and heats it in the microwave. In the meantime, she takes the chocolate from the groceries cupboard and a spoon from the cutlery cupboard. Finally, she puts some chocolate into the cup and saves the resting milk and chocolate in their locations.

4. **Drink a glass of milk**. The resident goes to the kitchen, takes the milk from the fridge and a cup from the glasses cupboard. Later, she pours the milk. Finally, she saves the milk in its location.

5. **Call by phone**. The occupant goes to the living room, picks up the phone and dial. When the call is finished, he hangs up the phone.

6. **Prepare hot snack in the microwave**. The dweller goes to the kitchen, takes a plate from the plates cupboard and the food from the fridge. Afterwards, he heats the food in the microwave and takes the cutlery from the cutlery cupboard.

7. **Prepare cold snack**. The inhabitant goes to the kitchen takes a plate from the plates cupboard and the food from the fridge and the groceries cupboard. After the meal preparation, he saves the remaining food in their locations.

8. **Watch TV**. The resident goes to the living room and switches the TV on. When she finishes, she switches it off.

9. **Washing dishes in the sink**. The occupant goes to the kitchen, open the sink tab and washes all the plates, cutlery, glasses and cups that are dirty. When he has finished, he saves all the tableware in its location.

The sensors' network is composed by contact and pressure sensors. Specifically, we have used Tynetec[2] pressure and contact sensors (see Fig. 2). These sensors use transmit on 169 MHz frequency, and the data is handled by a receiver that is connected to a computer, which saves all the data in an SQL database.

Fig. 2. Pressure and contact sensor

Considering the previous ADLs, several sensors have been located in different places of the smartlab, in order to gather the data from the interactions

[2] www.tynetec.co.uk (last checked on August 27, 2015).

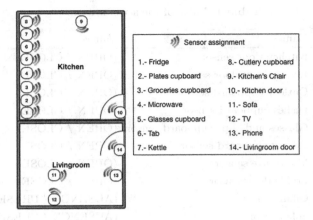

Fig. 3. Sensors' location in the smartlab

between the inhabitants and the environment when they develop the defined ADLs. Therefore, contact sensors have been located on the fridge, the plates cupboard, the groceries cupboard, the microwave, the glasses cupboard, the tab, the kettle, the cutlery cupboard, the kitchen's chair, the kitchen door, the sofa, the TV, the phone and the living room door (see Fig. 3). Furthermore, a couple of pressure sensors has been located on the sofa and the kitchen's chair.

3.2 Dataset Description

The dataset is a CSV file which gather the interactions in the smart environment between the inhabitants and the sensors' network.

Each dataset line is an event that is a state variation in a sensor of the smart environment. Regarding each event, the following information is saved: date, time, sensor identifier and sensor value. Table 1 shows the possible values of each sensor, once the raw sensor data has been processed.

The dataset has been labeled manually with the ADLs that are carried out in order to know in which event an activity begins or ends. The label which marks the beginning is *Begin_[IdActivity]* and the mark which means the end of the activity is *End_[IdActivity]*. Furthermore, in the multioccupancy dataset, it is necessary to indicate the inhabitants labels, *P_[IdOccupant]*.

Depending on each person and his/her culture and experience, it is usual that the same ADL be performed in a different way. Thus, depending on the ADL performance the sensors' interactions can be different. Table 2 shows the sensors that interact during a particular ADL. There are sensors that are compulsory (Y), optional (O) and unnecessary (N). For example, in the *watch TV* ADL, there are compulsory that the *living room door* and the *TV* sensors have been activated, being optional the *sofa* sensor activation.

Regarding the dataset performance, it has been developed by a man during one week. He interacts with the smart environment, carrying out his daily activ-

Table 1. Value of the set of sensors

IdSensor	Name	Values
D01	Kitchen door sensor	(OPEN / CLOSE)
D02	Living room door senor	(OPEN / CLOSE)
D03	Cutlery cupboard sensor	(OPEN / CLOSE)
D04	Dishes cupboard sensor	(OPEN / CLOSE)
D05	Glasses and cups cupboard sensor	(OPEN / CLOSE)
D06	Pantry cupboard sensor	(OPEN / CLOSE)
D07	Microwave sensor	(OPEN / CLOSE)
D08	Frigde door sensor	(OPEN / CLOSE)
M01	Chair sensor	(AUSENCE / PRESENCE)
M02	Sofa sensor	(AUSENCE / PRESENCE)
TV	Television sensor	(ON / OFF)
PH	Phone sensor	(PICK_UP / HANG_UP)
WT1	Water sensor	(OPEN / CLOSE)
KT	Kettle sensor	(ABSENT / PRESENT)

Table 2. Sensors which interact in each activity

Id	Activity	D01	D02	D03	D04	D05	D06	D07	D08	M01	M02	TV	PH	WT1	KT
1	Drink a glass of water	Y	N	N	N	Y	N	N	N	O	N	N	N	Y	N
2	Prepare a tea	Y	N	O	N	Y	N	N	N	O	N	N	N	O	Y
3	Prepare a hot chocolate	Y	N	O	N	Y	Y	Y	Y	O	N	N	N	N	N
4	Drink a glass milk	Y	N	N	N	Y	N	N	Y	O	N	N	N	N	N
5	Call by phone	N	Y	N	N	N	N	N	N	N	O	N	Y	N	N
6	Prepare hot snack	Y	N	O	Y	N	N	Y	Y	O	N	N	N	N	N
7	Prepare cold snack	Y	N	O	Y	N	Y	N	Y	O	N	N	N	N	N
8	Watch TV	N	Y	N	N	N	N	N	N	N	O	Y	N	N	N
9	Washing dishes	Y	N	O	O	O	N	N	N	O	N	N	N	Y	N

ity routines in single and interleave ways. Besides, sometimes a woman interacts with the smart environment at the same time that the man, carrying out some activities simultaneously (multioccupancy). In Fig. 4 is illustrated some events about the three different classes of activities. Then some details about each activity classes are provided.

- **Single activity class**. There are 364 single ADLs, being *drink a glass of water* and *watch TV* the most frequent activities and *prepare hot chocolate* the fewer one. Figure 5 depicts the single activity class distribution.
- **Interleave activity class**. There are 24 interleave ADLs. Some activities that have been performed in a interleave manner are *call by phone* while the occupant is *preparing a hot chocolate* or *drink a glass of water* while the inner is *preparing hot snack*. The interleave activity class distribution is showed in Fig. 6.

Single	Interleave	Multioccupancy
2015-02-20 18:22:32 D01 CLOSE Begin_1	2015-02-26 10:31:25 D01 OPEN Begin_3	2015-02-22 16:58:59 D01 CLOSE Begin_1 P1
2015-02-20 18:22:46 D01 OPEN	2015-02-26 10:31:48 D08 OPEN	2015-02-22 16:59:10 D01 OPEN
2015-02-20 18:22:53 D01 CLOSE	2015-02-26 10:31:53 D05 OPEN	2015-02-22 16:59:23 D01 CLOSE
2015-02-20 18:23:07 D05 OPEN	2015-02-26 10:31:54 D08 CLOSE	2015-02-22 16:59:30 WT1 OPEN
2015-02-20 18:23:20 D05 CLOSE	2015-02-26 10:31:56 D07 OPEN	2015-02-22 16:59:36 D02 OPEN Begin_5 P2
2015-02-20 18:23:27 WT1 OPEN	2015-02-26 10:32:01 D05 CLOSE	2015-02-22 16:59:41 D02 CLOSE
2015-02-20 18:23:36 WT1 CLOSE	2015-02-26 10:32:03 D07 CLOSE	2015-02-22 16:59:45 PH PICK_UP	
2015-02-20 18:24:35 D01 OPEN	2015-02-26 10:32:33 D02 OPEN Begin_5	2015-02-22 17:00:15 D05 OPEN	
2015-02-20 18:24:41 D01 CLOSE End_1	2015-02-26 10:32:54 PH PICK_UP	2015-02-22 17:00:20 WT1 CLOSE
2015-02-20 18:24:50 D02 OPEN Begin_5	2015-02-26 10:33:01 PH HANG_UP	2015-02-22 17:00:22 D05 CLOSE
2015-02-20 18:24:56 D02 CLOSE	2015-02-26 10:33:09 D02 CLOSE End_5	2015-02-22 17:00:26 D01 OPEN
2015-02-20 18:25:10 PH PICK_UP	2015-02-26 10:33:33 D03 OPEN	2015-02-22 17:00:31 D01 CLOSE End_1 P1
2015-02-20 18:26:01 PH HANG_UP	2015-02-26 10:33:36 D07 OPEN	2015-02-22 17:00:45 D01 OPEN Begin_6 P1
2015-02-20 18:26:15 D02 OPEN	2015-02-26 10:33:40 D03 CLOSE	2015-02-22 17:00:51 D01 CLOSE
2015-02-20 18:26:22 D02 CLOSE End_5	2015-02-26 10:33:42 D07 CLOSE	2015-02-22 17:00:54 D04 OPEN
2015-02-20 18:26:32 D01 OPEN Begin_7	2015-02-26 10:33:43 D06 OPEN	2015-02-22 17:00:57 D08 OPEN
2015-02-20 18:26:38 D01 CLOSE	2015-02-26 10:33:48 D08 OPEN	2015-02-22 17:01:01 D04 CLOSE
2015-02-20 18:30:19 D06 OPEN	2015-02-26 10:33:50 D06 CLOSE	2015-02-22 17:01:04 D08 CLOSE
2015-02-20 18:31:03 D06 CLOSE	2015-02-26 10:33:54 D08 CLOSE	2015-02-22 17:01:05 D07 OPEN
2015-02-20 18:31:08 D04 OPEN	2015-02-26 10:33:59 D01 CLOSE End_3	2015-02-22 17:01:10 D03 OPEN
2015-02-20 18:31:18 D04 CLOSE	2015-02-26 10:34:22 D01 OPEN Begin_1	2015-02-22 17:01:12 D07 CLOSE
2015-02-20 18:31:25 D08 OPEN	2015-02-26 10:34:27 D05 OPEN	2015-02-22 17:01:18 D03 CLOSE
2015-02-20 18:31:40 D08 CLOSE	2015-02-26 10:34:30 WT1 OPEN	2015-02-22 17:01:21 PH HANG_UP
2015-02-20 18:32:26 M01 PRESENCE	2015-02-26 10:34:34 D05 CLOSE	2015-02-22 17:01:25 D02 OPEN End_5 P2

Fig. 4. Single, Interleave and Multioccupancy dataset classes

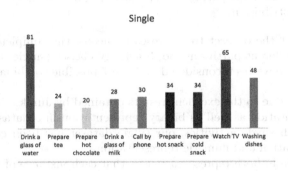

Fig. 5. Single activity distribution

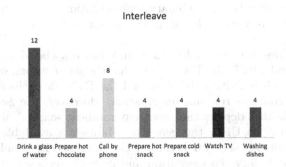

Fig. 6. Interleave activity distribution

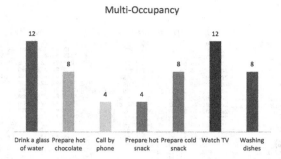

Fig. 7. Multioccupancy distribution

- **Multioccupancy class**. There are 56 ADLs with 36 ones performed in a multioccupancy way. For example, when someone is *drinking a glass of water*, the other one is *calling by phone*. Another example is when someone is *watching TV*, the other one is *preparing a cold snack*. Figure 7 depicts the multioccupancy data distribution.

In order to adapt the dataset to the research needs, the complete dataset has been split into different partitions. So, 3 activity classes (single, interleave and multioccupancy) have been considered and the 7 possible combinations of them have been made.

Furthermore, due to the excellent results obtained by Jurek et al. [7] using a numeric representation as well as binary representation in a dataset of a smart environment with single activities, our single dataset has been converted into binary representation and numeric representation.

The main idea in both representations is that each instance of the dataset is a vector with $n+1$ components, the first n components corresponds to the value of the n sensors involved in the smart environment and the last component, $n+1$ corresponds to the activity performed. In the numeric representation (see Fig. 8), the value of sensor indicates how many times there are a state change of such sensor in the activity. In the binary representation (see Fig. 9), the value of sensor is 1, if there is a state change in the sensor during activity, and 0, if no change.

The dataset files are accessible[3]. Each link has associated a .zip file which contains a CSV and a RTF file. The CSV file has the set of events, where the *begin* and the *end* of each activity is labeled, and the RTF file includes the dataset description that contains relevant information. Moreover, the *Sensors' Layout* link, is a PNG file that depicts the smart environment sensors' distribution.

So, in the previous URL, the generated dataset is available in the seven combinations of classes and, furthermore, the dataset with single activities is available with the binary representation and numeric representation, following the scheme of the web page is presented:

---

[3] http://ceatic.ujaen.es/smartlab (last checked on August 27, 2015).

D01	D02	D03	D04	D05	D06	D07	D08	KT	M01	M02	PH	TV	WT1	Activity
5	0	0	0	2	0	0	0	0	0	0	0	0	2	1
0	4	0	0	0	0	0	0	0	0	0	2	0	0	5
4	0	0	2	0	2	0	2	0	2	0	0	0	0	7
0	4	0	0	0	0	0	0	0	0	3	0	2	0	8
4	0	0	2	2	0	0	0	0	0	0	0	0	1	9
4	0	0	0	2	2	0	0	2	0	0	0	0	4	2
0	4	0	0	0	0	0	0	0	0	0	2	0	0	5
4	0	0	2	0	2	0	2	0	2	0	0	0	0	7
0	4	0	0	0	0	0	0	0	0	3	0	2	0	8

Fig. 8. Numeric representation of the single dataset

D01	D02	D03	D04	D05	D06	D07	D08	KT	M01	M02	PH	TV	WT1	Activity
1	0	0	0	1	0	0	0	0	0	0	0	0	1	1
0	1	0	0	0	0	0	0	0	0	0	1	0	0	5
1	0	0	1	0	1	0	1	0	1	0	0	0	0	7
0	1	0	0	0	0	0	0	0	0	1	0	1	0	8
1	0	0	1	1	0	0	0	0	0	0	0	0	1	9
1	0	0	0	1	1	0	0	1	0	0	0	0	1	2
0	1	0	0	0	0	0	0	0	0	0	1	0	0	5
1	0	0	1	0	1	0	1	0	1	0	0	0	0	7
0	1	0	0	0	0	0	0	0	0	1	0	1	0	8

Fig. 9. Binary representation of the single dataset

– Sensors' Layout
  - *SensorsLayout.png*

1. Single
   – *Single.zip*
     - *DataSingle.csv*
     - *ReadmeSingle.rtf*
   – *SingleNumeric.csv*
   – *SingleBinary.csv*
2. Interleave
   – *Interleave.zip*
     - *DataInterleave.csv*
     - *ReadmeInterleave.rtf*
3. Multioccupancy
   – *Multioccupancy.zip*
     - *DataMultioccupancy.csv*
     - *ReadMultioccupancy.rtf*
4. Single and Interleave
   – *SingleInterleave.zip*
     - *DataSingleInterleave.csv*
     - *ReadmeSingleInterleave.rtf*
5. Single and Multioccupancy
   – *SingleMultioccupancy.zip*
     - *DataSingleMultioccupancy.csv*
     - *ReadmeSingleMultioccupancy.rtf*

6. Interleave and Multioccupancy
   - *Interleave and Multioccupancy.zip*
     - *DataInterleaveMultioccupancy.csv*
     - *ReadmeInterleaveMultioccupancy.rtf*
7. Single, Interleave and Multioccupancy
   - *SingleInterleaveMulti.zip*
     - *DataSingleInterleaveMulti.csv*
     - *ReadmeSingleInterleaveMulti.rtf*

4   Conclusions and Future Works

This contribution has presented the generation of a complete smart home dataset which gather the data from the sensors' network when some of the most common daily living activities are performing. The dataset is divided in 7 partitions that combine three different classes of ADLs: single activity, interleave activities and multioccupancy. These classes can be used individually or together, depending on the researchers' needs. Furthermore, the numeric and binary representation has been used for the single partition. Regarding future works, we are focused on incrementing the number of different dataset activities and the frequency of them. Furthermore, we will address the issue of how the sensor data can be recorded automatically without human interaction using NFC (Near Field Comunication) technology. Finally, we are focused on using the dataset with ambient intelligence algorithms.

Acknowledgments. This contribution was supported by Research Projects TIN-2012-31263, CEATIC-2013-001, UJA2014/06/14 and by the Doctoral School of the University of Jaén. Invest Northern Ireland is acknowledge for partially supporting this project under the Competence Centre Program Grant RD0513853 - Connected Health Innovation Centre.

References

1. Chen, L., Hoey, J., Nugent, C.D., Cook, D.J., Yu, Z.: Sensor-based activity recognition. IEEE Trans. Syst. Man Cybern. Part C Appl. Rev. **42**(6), 790–808 (2012)
2. Chen, L., Nugent, C.: Ontology-based activity recognition in intelligent pervasive environments. Int. J. Web Inf. Syst. **5**(4), 410–430 (2009)
3. Chen, L., Nugent, C.D., Wang, H.: A knowledge-driven approach to activity recognition in smart homes. IEEE Trans. Knowl. Data Eng. **24**(6), 961–974 (2012)
4. Cook, D., Schmitter-Edgecombe, M., Crandall, A., Sanders, C., Thomas, B.: Collecting and disseminating smart home sensor data in the casas project. In: Proceedings of the CHI Workshop on Developing Shared Home Behavior Datasets to Advance HCI and Ubiquitous Computing Research, pp. 1–7 (2009)
5. Cook, D.J., Schmitter-Edgecombe, M., et al.: Assessing the quality of activities in a smart environment. Methods Inf. Med. **48**(5), 480–485 (2009)
6. Gu, T., Wang, L., Wu, Z., Tao, X., Lu, J.: A pattern mining approach to sensor-based human activity recognition. IEEE Trans. Knowl. Data Eng. **23**(9), 1359–1372 (2011)

7. Jurek, A., Nugent, C., Bi, Y., Wu, S.: Clustering-based ensemble learning for activity recognition in smart homes. Sensors **14**(7), 12285–12304 (2014)
8. Lepri, B., Mana, N., Cappelletti, A., Pianesi, F., Zancanaro, M.: What is happening now? detection of activities of daily living from simple visual features. Pers. Ubiquit. Comput. **14**(8), 749–766 (2010)
9. Li, C., Lin, M., Yang, L.T., Ding, C.: Integrating the enriched feature with machine learning algorithms for human movement and fall detection. J. Supercomput. **67**(3), 854–865 (2014)
10. Moshtaghi, M., Zukerman, I., Russell, R.: Statistical models for unobtrusively detecting abnormal periods of inactivity in older adults. User Model. User-Adap. Inter. **25**(3), 231–265 (2015)
11. Roggen, D., Calatroni, A., Rossi, M., Holleczek, T., Forster, K., Troster, G., Lukowicz, P., Bannach, D., Pirkl, G., Ferscha, A., et al.: Collecting complex activity datasets in highly rich networked sensor environments. In: 2010 Seventh International Conference on Networked Sensing Systems (INSS), pp. 233–240. IEEE (2010)
12. Singla, G., Cook, D.J., Schmitter-Edgecombe, M.: Tracking activities in complex settings using smart environment technologies. Int. J. Biosci. Psychiatry Technol. (IJBSPT) **1**(1), 25 (2009)
13. Singla, G., Cook, D.J., Schmitter-Edgecombe, M.: Recognizing independent and joint activities among multiple residents in smart environments. J. Ambient Intell. Humanized Comput. **1**(1), 57–63 (2010)
14. Streitz, N., Nixon, P.: The disappearing computer. Commun. ACM **48**(3), 32–35 (2005)
15. Tapia, E.M., Intille, S.S., Larson, K.: Activity recognition in the home using simple and ubiquitous sensors. In: Ferscha, A., Mattern, F. (eds.) PERVASIVE 2004. LNCS, vol. 3001, pp. 158–175. Springer, Heidelberg (2004)
16. Van Kasteren, T., Noulas, A., Englebienne, G., Kröse, B.: Accurate activity recognition in a home setting. In: Proceedings of the 10th International Conference on Ubiquitous Computing, pp. 1–9. ACM (2008)

Adapting a Bandwidth-Efficient Information Dissemination Scheme for Urban VANETs

Estrella Garcia-Lozano[✉], Celeste Campo, Carlos Garcia-Rubio, and Alicia Rodriguez-Carrion

Department of Telematic Engineering, University Carlos III of Madrid, Leganés, Spain
{emglozan,celeste,cgr,arcarrio}@it.uc3m.es

Abstract. The recent release of standards for vehicular communications will hasten the development of smart cities in the following years. However, the standards do not define efficient schemes for infotainment dissemination over urban networks. These networks present special features and difficulties that may require special measures. In a previous work, we proposed three different schemes. The preliminary results of the three were satisfying but we still had to explore the values for some parameters that affect significantly their behavior. In this article, we tackle this task. Our findings clear up the strengths and weaknesses of each scheme and open the door to new advances.

1 Introduction

The appearance of next generation vehicles will be a key step in creating smart cities. High end cars already carry embedded on-board computers with GPS capability. And with the recent release of vehicular communications standards in Europe, U.S.A. and Japan, they will be able to communicate wirelessly very soon. Though different, these standards are based or contemplate the communication among vehicles (V2V) or between vehicles and infrastructure (V2I) via 802.11p.

This new technology will soon assist in urban everyday-life. For example, a portable sign post can warn about a closed road to vehicles that are in the vicinity. A vehicle can send an alert to others traveling behind it when it brakes suddenly. Or a business can announce daily offers to drivers coming close to its location.

In most cases, like the ones aforementioned, a single-hop broadcast will be insufficient. The transmission range may cover a few hundred meters but the region of interest (ROI) is usually wider. In addition, the abundant presence of buildings and other obstacles blocks the signal and impedes vehicles in the transmission range receiving the message. The problem of message dissemination inside cities arose as of high interest several years ago [7]. The standards contemplate dissemination schemes like ETSI's GeoNetworking [4], but they were in experimental phase until recently. As a consequence, there is still plenty of research being done nowadays [9,10,13].

© Springer International Publishing Switzerland 2015
J.M. García-Chamizo et al. (Eds.): UCAmI 2015, LNCS 9454, pp. 72–83, 2015.
DOI: 10.1007/978-3-319-26401-1_7

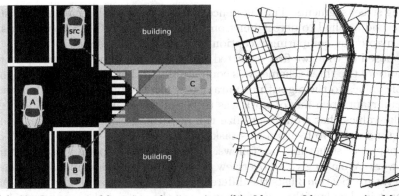

(a) Shadowing problem in urban envi-   (b) 2 km × 2 km area in Madrid,
ronments.   Spain.

Fig. 1. Urban scenario.

We presented a preliminary study on three alternatives for urban message dissemination in [5]. We parted from our solution for message dissemination in roadways [6], that is built upon a distance-based contention. We assume every vehicle knows its own position by means of GPS. They are also able to determine the location of any neighbor from whom it is receiving a message, may it be from information inserted in the message or from previous beacons. Eeach vehicle computes a contention wait, based on the distance to the relay. It will forward the message when the wait expires, unless it hears a duplicate of the same message before that. If the TTL is lower than the stored value, the vehicle aborts the contention because someone else forwarded the message first. The duplicate is ignored only if it comes from a vehicle located over the previous relay, because it belongs to the dissemination in the opposite direction.

In said article, we proposed two variations to take advantage of junctions to spread the message in new ways. In order to understand how buildings and junctions influence the dissemination, we represent a typical situation in an urban scenario in Fig. 1a. Here, vehicle "src" sends a message that needs to be disseminated. We want to reduce the overhead, so the next relay should be vehicle "B" in order to minimize the number of necessary hops. However, due to the shadowing effect of buildings, vehicle "C" will not receive the message from "src" nor from "B". Vehicle "A" is the only one in line-of-sight with "C". Thus, vehicle "A" need be the next relay so that "C" can also receive the message. Of course, not every junction have all right angles, as the real map in Fig. 1b shows. Though there is some variability in the incoming angles and the shadowed areas, there will be similar situations in every layout.

Following this line of thought, we modified our base roadway scheme so that, if a vehicle is inside an intersection, it gets priority for becoming a relay. This way, the forwarded message can be received and relayed by vehicles in any of the converging street segments. The difference between the two alternatives consisted in the method applied to detect junctions – by locating the GPS coordinates in a digital map or by comparing reception angles with a threshold.

As opposed to what we first expected, the preliminary study showed that the performance of the three schemes was comparable. In that work, we had assigned reasonable values to the algorithms parameters like the maximum per-hop wait. So, an important open line of work was to better tune said parameters in order to find the values that would optimize the performance metrics and make one of them stand out. We focus in this task for this article.

The paper is structured as follows. In Sect. 2, we explain how the three schemes work. We also give an overview of similar urban dissemination schemes in the literature. Section 3 lists the different parameters that must be tuned, how they impact in the algorithms performance and the metrics that we use to check the results. Next, in Sect. 4, we detail the software, the configuration and the scenario for the simulations that we have carried during this study. In Sect. 5, we reflect on the results. Finally, we sum up our conclusions and the new open lines of work in Sect. 6.

2   Related Work

First, we explain our previous work [5], base for this paper, and then we mention two solutions in the literature that are similar to our urban adaptations.

2.1   Previous Work

For reference, we succinctly point out the characteristics and equations that define our three variants for multi-hop dissemination. Basically, the map-based and the angle-based modifications of the base roadway scheme only differ in the method applied to decide if a vehicle or another relay are in a junction. The reader can find in [5] further details along with a flow diagram of the adapted urban schemes.

Scheme for Roadways. The base algorithm [6], that is already valid for roadways, relies on a distance-based contention. Whenever a vehicle hears a new message, it waits a short time, W, for simultaneous duplicates of the same message. The distance to the closest relay of the same message is stored as d_{min}. According to this distance, it waits an amount of time, t_w, before forwarding:

$$t_w = T_{max} \times (1 - d_{min}/r). \tag{1}$$

Here, r is the reception range and T_{max} is the configurable maximum wait.

Map-Based Adaptation for Cities. In addition to what was explained above, now a vehicle finds out if it is located in a junction by checking its position in a digital map. If so, it uses its distance to the junction center, d_{center}, to compute a different contention delay:

$$t_j = T_j \times (d_{center}/r_{junction}).$$ (2)

T_j is the maximum wait for vehicles in junctions and $r_{junction}$ is the radius of the given intersection. The purpose is to prioritize the vehicle that is closest to the intersection center, in order to reach as many other vehicles as possible.

The junction contention only affects the vehicles in the same intersection. Conversely, a vehicle located at an intersection will ignore every duplicate except if it comes from the same intersection. This is done by checking the other's location in the map.

Angle-Based Adaptation for Cities. In this variant, a vehicles uses the reception angle to determine if it is in an intersection. Whenever it receives a new message, it pays attention to the angle of the previous relay with respect to its own trajectory. A problem of urban scenarios is that the signal may bounce, so we calculate the angle with the other's reported location and the receiver knowledge of its own trajectory. We use two threshold angles, α_{min} and α_{max}. If the reception angle falls between the two of them, we assume the message comes from another street and then the vehicle is in an intersection. As it cannot determine the distance to the intersection center, it waits before forwarding a random amount of time, t'_j, from the distribution in 3.

$$t'_j \sim U(0, T_j).$$ (3)

Again, the first vehicle to forward inhibits the rest in the same intersection to do the same. If a vehicle that considers itself inside a junction receives a duplicate with a lower TTL, it needs to determine if it comes from the same intersection. This is done by applying a generic threshold distance, d_j. If the other vehicle is closer than this distance, it will assume that it is located in the same intersection.

2.2 State of the Art

Two similar works from the literature on urban dissemination are UV-CAST and TAF. Both are totally distributed, use a distance-based contention and do not need infrastructure support.

UV-CAST (Urban Vehicular Broadcast) [13] is composed by two operation modes: disconnected and well-connected. Every vehicle finds out in which mode it is according to the beacons from one-hop neighbors. If they are at the edge of a connected group, they are in the disconnected mode and wait to find new neighbors before forwarding. Otherwise, they are well-connected and apply a broadcast suppression scheme. If, according to a digital map, a vehicle is located in an intersection, it has a higher priority for forwarding.

TAF (Two Angles Forwarding) and other two similar algorithms are presented in [9]. A vehicle checks the reception angles of all the duplicates of the same message during the contention wait. Specifically in TAF, a receiver calculates the angles in the triangle formed by itself and the last two relays from which it heard the same message. If the cosines of the angles in which the vertex is not itself are both lower than a threshold, it will retransmit the packet at the end of its computed wait even though it may have not won the contention, but not otherwise.

3   Exploration Description

Now we list the parameters of the schemes explained above that needed further tuning. We also describe the metrics that we use to determine the values that offer the best performance.

3.1   Parameters Subject to Study

According to the descriptions in Sect. 2, there are three key parameters: T_{max}, T_j and $\Delta\alpha$.

T_{max} is the maximum per-hop delay for a vehicle that is not located in a junction. This parameter is important because it helps to prevent situations in which several vehicles try to forward almost simultaneously. In addition, it has to be small enough to consider the scenario almost static during the contention. The same value should work properly in very different traffic situations. Also, it directly affects the latency of the scheme.

T_j is the maximum wait for vehicles in junctions. It must be less or equal to T_{max} and it affects the performance in a similar way.

$\Delta\alpha$ is the difference between α_{max} and α_{min}. It defines what is considered a junction, given that a vehicle determines its position in one by comparing the reception angle with these two thresholds. As explained above, the reception angle is calculated by using the relay's reported location and the receiver knowledge of its own trajectory.

From the descriptions above, the reader can note that the base roadway scheme only depends on T_{max}, the map-based scheme depends on T_{max} and T_j, and the angle-based scheme depends on the three parameters. Hence, to isolate their effects, the first step will be to tune T_{max} with simulations of the roadway scheme. Then, we will fix the resulting value for the map-based scheme to find out T_j. And last, we will configure the angle-based scheme with those values and make a sweep of $\Delta\alpha$.

3.2   Metrics

We can group the metrics we use in this study into three categories: success, overhead and latency.

Success – The final goal of a multi-hop broadcast is to reach as many nodes as possible in a given area. We define the success with two different metrics. The *long-reach success* is the proportion of cases where the dissemination goes further than the second hop – i.e. the message leaves the source area. It is normalized to that of a simple flooding in the same situation. The other metric is the *coverage*, or number of vehicles that received the message in the long-reach cases.

Overhead – A high overhead is undesirable, as it occupies the limited shared bandwidth with useless data. It can be measured with the *redundancy ratio*, that we define as the ratio of vehicles that act as relays from the total number of receivers. Another metric that echoes the overhead is the *number of lost packets*, as congestion leads to this effect.

Latency – The third performance indicator is the latency of the scheme. We may use the per-hop delay or the end-to-end delay. The *per-hop delay* accounts for distance-based and MAC contention and for propagation time. The *end-to-end delay* is averaged over all the receivers, may they be at one or several hops away from the source.

4   Simulations Configuration

As in our preliminary study, we have used Veins [12] as our simulation framework because it offers the possibility of importing real maps through OpenStreetMap [2], realistic movements thanks to SUMO [8], an implementation of 802.11p for OMNeT++ [1] and the Simple Obstacle Shadowing [11] propagation model for building shadowing. We have also used VACaMobil [3] in order to maintain a constant traffic density throughout every run of the simulations. More information about the network configuration is listed in [5]'s Table 2.

The scenario for our simulations is a $2 \, km \times 2 \, km$ area around the Castellana Street in Madrid, shown in Fig. 1b. It is sufficient for our study because in our previous article we noticed that, though the absolute values differ, the curves shapes remain the same for different scenarios.

The traffic densities go in the range from 25 to 100 vehicles per square kilometer The origin of the message is a fixed unit in the center of the scenario. The preset radius of interest (the ROI) is $1 \, km$.

Lastly, in the angle-based method, a vehicle determines if another vehicle is forwarding from the same intersection by using a threshold distance, d_j. It made no sense to try to adjust d_j by simulations because it is highly dependent on the given city and we would only overfit it to our scenario. Instead, we have studied the widest diagonal in junctions from a set of four different city maps: New York (USA), Madrid (Spain), Rome (Italy) and Cologne (Germany), available via OpenStreetMap. The median – the most usual value – was, respectively, $9.89 \, m$, $9.24 \, m$, $9.64 \, m$ and $9.61 \, m$. Accordingly, we have set $d_j = 10 \, m$.

5   Results

We prepare to discuss the simulation results. Due to space constraints, we omit the graphs of metrics that were not affected by the studied parameter.

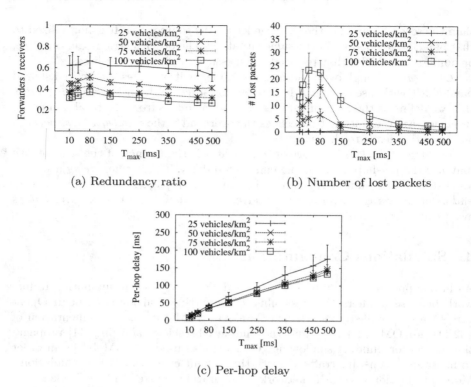

(a) Redundancy ratio   (b) Number of lost packets

(c) Per-hop delay

Fig. 2. Simulation results of the roadway scheme with different T_{max} values.

5.1 Tuning of T_{max}

We use the roadway scheme to explore the influence of this parameter. When varying it from 10 ms to 500 ms, the long-reach success and the coverage remained constant for every traffic density. The rest of the results are shown in Fig. 2. There, we can see that the forwarding ratio (Fig. 2a) descends slightly when the maximum wait is longer. When the time range is short, several vehicles that are close to each other may pass the message to the MAC layer before receiving the other relays' duplicates. This leads to the high number of lost packets for short waits shown in Fig. 2b. As we could expect, the average per-hop delay is proportional to T_{max} as seen in Fig. 2c. Given that this parameter does not affect the success, we search a good trade-off between overhead and latency. The former is improved when the value is greater or equal to 350 ms, while the latency worsens as the value gets higher. So we choose $T_{max} = 350$ ms.

5.2 Tuning of T_j

We fix $T_{max} = 350$ ms in the map-based scheme to study the effect of T_j alone. In order to better understand the simulated points, the x-axis of the graphs in

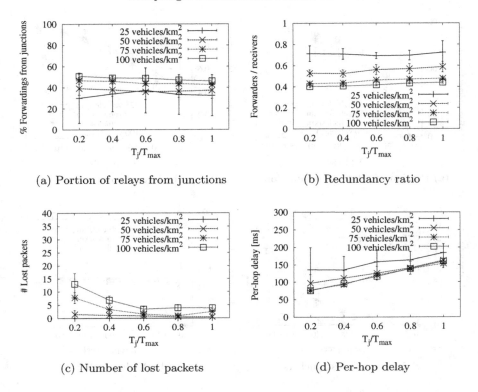

(a) Portion of relays from junctions

(b) Redundancy ratio

(c) Number of lost packets

(d) Per-hop delay

Fig. 3. Results of the map-based scheme with fixed T_{max} and different T_j values.

Fig. 3 represent the relation between T_j and T_{max} instead of the absolute values. Again, the success is not related to a wait time. We also find a very limited effect in the redundancy ratio of Fig. 3b. The slight rise is caused by vehicles in a junction that are also the furthest from the previous relay. They wait so much that another vehicle forwards first, though it does not inhibit them. It is almost balanced out by the slightly higher number of vehicles that forward from junctions (Fig. 3a) when their wait is shorter. Again, a very short maximum delay has the same problems of redundancy and losses (Fig. 3c) as T_{max}. The average per-hop delay, shown in Fig. 3d, is clearly influenced by the vehicles that have to wait less because they are in intersections. Following a similar reasoning to that for T_{max}, we find that $T_j/T_{max} = 0.6$ is the best compromise between losses and delay. This corresponds to $T_j = 210$ ms.

5.3 Tuning of $\Delta\alpha$

By using the T_{max} and T_j values found above, the only parameter left to config-ure the angle-based scheme is $\Delta\alpha$. It defines what is assumed to be an intersection and what not, because α_{min} and α_{max} are the thresholds for the reception angle. This can be observed in Fig. 4a. When $\Delta\alpha$ is a flat angle to either side, every

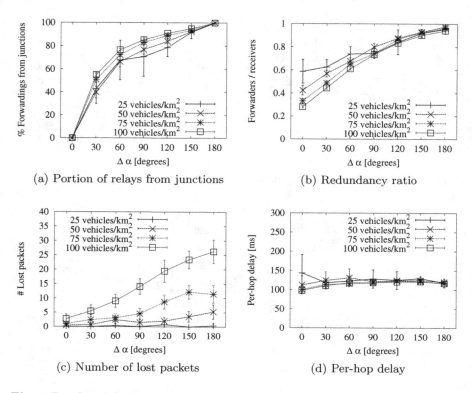

(a) Portion of relays from junctions

(b) Redundancy ratio

(c) Number of lost packets

(d) Per-hop delay

Fig. 4. Results of the angle-based scheme with fixed T_{max} and T_j, and varying $\Delta\alpha$.

reception angle indicates that the vehicle is in an intersection. Hence, all the forwardings are done from intersections, because every vehicle believes it is in one. And when $\Delta\alpha$ is $0°$, no one considers itself inside a junction, so none of the forwardings is done from one. $\Delta\alpha$ does not affect the success of the scheme, but it does have a strong impact on the forwarding ratio (Fig. 4b). When it is a wide angle, many vehicles consider themselves inside a junction. Hence, the number of retransmissions grows significantly. This leads to many lost packets, as seen in Fig. 4c. It also creates a curve of per-hop delay that is quite flat (Fig. 4d). The reduction in latency that we could expect when most vehicles have a shorter wait time is compensated with the long MAC contentions. Given the high packet loss and latency with wide angles, we limit this parameter to $\Delta\alpha = 60°$.

5.4   Comparative of the Schemes with the Final Values

Now, we can compare the three schemes in their best configuration. For reference, we have included the simulation results of a simple flooding scheme with a random jitter before forwarding. When a vehicle receives a new message, it selects a random delay from an uniform distribution between 0 and 190 ms. This value was selected so as to approximately match the average per-hop delay of the other schemes. This way, the dissemination through the whole ROI takes a similar time for all of them. As time passes, vehicles will be entering the ROI (becoming new targets) or leaving it (becoming unreachable). By keeping the end-to-end delays comparable, the number of reachable targets is consistent, too.

The simulation results can be seen in Fig. 5. First, we can see the long-reach success normalized to that achieved by simple flooding in Fig. 5a. The three studied schemes are close to the flooding, being the two urban adaptations the ones with highest ratios. We see the same results for the coverage (Fig. 5b).

In return for the higher coverage, the urban schemes require more overhead. This can be noted in the forwarding ratio in Fig. 5d, as well as in the number of lost packets in Fig. 5d. We can see that the angle-based scheme is the worst in this sense, with a redundancy ratio greater than 0.6 even in high densities. We can see in Fig. 5c that this is due to the greater number of vehicles forwarding from junctions. An important factor for this is the definition of intersection in each urban scheme. In the angle-based scheme, a vehicle may be physically close to a junction rather than in it, but it will consider itself inside it, whilst the map-based scheme will not allow this. In addition, a map does not account for sidewalks and other open spaces that let the signal travel. Another factor is the distance threshold used in the angle-based scheme to decide if a neighboring relay is in the same intersection as a waiting vehicle. In wide junctions like a big roundabout, it may be too short, letting two or more vehicles in the same intersection forward the message.

Lastly, Fig. 5f and g show the latency. Due to the shorter wait for vehicles in intersections, the two urban schemes have a slightly shorter average per-hop delay, though this effect is softened in the average end-to-end delay.

6   Conclusions

In this article, we have studied several parameters of the three schemes that we considered for information dissemination in urban VANETs in [5]. We have reached a set of specific values for them that will ensure a good performance for each of the schemes. In a comparison of the three variations using the final configuration, the adaptations for urban environments improve the success in the dissemination with regard to the roadway scheme, though the latter offers reasonably good results, too. We had already reached a similar conclusion in our previous study. Between the two urban schemes, the angle-based variation achieves a bit higher coverage than the map-based one at the cost of a relevant overhead. Hence, we think that the map-based option offers a better compromise between gains and losses, and should be the one to use in an urban scenario.

A new option would be to marry the best of both in a mixed scheme, that would allow a vehicle to detect a junction in more than one way and that would also help in better identifying relays from the same intersection. Another possibility is to help the dissemination go further with one-time floodings in difficult situations, like the beginning of the dissemination. We intend to explore these options as future work.

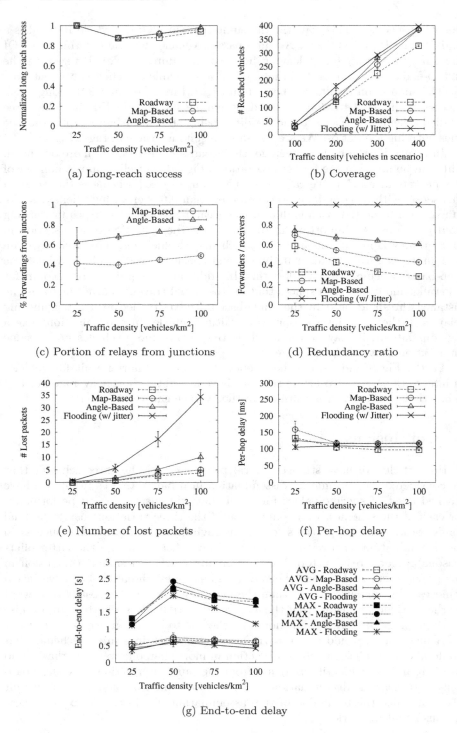

(a) Long-reach success

(b) Coverage

(c) Portion of relays from junctions

(d) Redundancy ratio

(e) Number of lost packets

(f) Per-hop delay

(g) End-to-end delay

Fig. 5. Comparative of the different schemes with the final values.

Other line of future work that we find important is to validate our conclusions with a different city map. Due to space constraints it was impossible to include it in this article. A comparison with other map-based scheme from the literature, like UV-CAST, would be interesting as well.

Acknowledgments. This work was partially founded by the Spanish Ministry of Science and Innovation within the framework of projects TEC2010-20572-C02-01 "CONSEQUENCE" and TEC2014-54335-C4-2-R "INRISCO".

References

1. OMNeT. http://www.omnetpp.org. Accessed Jun 2015
2. OpenStreetMap. http://www.openstreetmap.org. Accessed Jun 2015
3. Baguena, M., Tornell, S., Torres, A., Calafate, C., Cano, J.C., Manzoni, P.: VACaMobil: VANET Car Mobility manager for OMNeT++. In: IEEE International Conference on Communications Workshops (ICC), pp. 1057–1061, June 2013
4. ETSI: European Standard EN 302 636-4-1 V1.2.1: Intelligent Transport Systems (ITS); Vehicular communications; GeoNetworking; Part 4: Geographical addressing and forwarding for point-to-point and point-to-multipoint communications; Subpart 1: Media-Independent Functionality, July 2014
5. Garcia-Lozano, E., Campo, C., Garcia-Rubio, C., Cortes-Martin, A.: Bandwidth-efficient techniques for information dissemination in urban vehicular networks. In: 11th ACM Symposium on Performance Evaluation of Wireless Ad Hoc, Sensor and Ubiquitous Networks (PE-WASUN 2014), pp. 61–68, September 2014
6. Garcia-Lozano, E., Campo, C., Garcia-Rubio, C., Cortes-Martin, A., Rodriguez-Carrion, A., Noriega-Vivas, P.: A bandwidth-efficient service for local information dissemination in sparse to dense roadways. Sensors **13**(7), 8612–8639 (2013)
7. Korkmaz, G., Ekici, E., Ozguner, F.: Black-burst-based multihop broadcast protocols for vehicular networks. IEEE Trans. Veh. Technol. **56**(5), 3159–3167 (2007)
8. Krajzewicz, D., Erdmann, J., Behrisch, M., Bieker, L.: Recent development and applications of SUMO - Simulation of Urban MObility. Int. J. Adv. Syst. Meas. **5**(3—-4), 128–138 (2012)
9. Salvo, P., De Felice, M., Cuomo, F., Baiocchi, A.: Infotainment traffic flow dissemination in an urban VANET. In: IEEE Global Communications Conference (GLOBECOM 2012), pp. 67–72, December 2012
10. Sanguesa, J.A., Fogue, M., Garrido, P., Martinez, F.J., Cano, J.C., Calafate, C.T., Manzoni, P.: RTAD: a real-time adaptive dissemination system for VANETs. Comput. Commun. **60**, 53–70 (2015)
11. Sommer, C., Eckhoff, D., German, R., Dressler, F.: A computationally inexpensive empirical model of IEEE 802.11p radio shadowing in urban environments. In: 8th IEEE/IFIP Conference on Wireless On demand Network Systems and Services (WONS 2011), Bardonecchia, Italy, pp. 84–90, January 2011
12. Sommer, C., German, R., Dressler, F.: Bidirectionally coupled network and road traffic simulation for improved IVC analysis. IEEE Trans. Mob. Comput. **10**(1), 3–15 (2011)
13. Viriyasitavat, W., Tonguz, O., Bai, F.: UV-CAST: an urban vehicular broadcast protocol. IEEE Commun. Mag. **49**(11), 116–124 (2011)

Cooperative Decision-Making ITS Architecture Based on Distributed RSUs

Asier Moreno[1]([⊠]), Enrique Onieva[1], Asier Perallos[1],
Giovanni Iovino[2], and Pablo Fernández[1]

[1] Deusto Institute of Technology (DeustoTech),
University of Deusto, Bilbao, Spain
{asier.moreno,enrique.onieva,perallos,
pablo.fernandez}@deusto.es
[2] INTECS SpA, Via Umberto Forti 5, Pisa, Italy
giovanni.iovino@intecs.it

Abstract. This paper describes a new cooperative Intelligent Transportation System (ITS) architecture which aim is to enable collaborative sensing services targeting to improve transportation efficiency and performance. This objective will be carried out by applying a combination of cooperative applications and methods for data sensing, acquisition, processing and communication amongst road users, vehicles, infrastructures and related stakeholders.

The advantages afforded by the proposed system due to the use of a distributed architecture, moving the system intelligence from the control centre to the peripheral devices are exposed. The global architecture of the system as well as the interaction between its components and the development of a set of services, gathering the sensed-data and providing relevant information to the users/drivers is also presented.

Keywords: Intelligent Transportation Systems · Wireless Sensor Networks · Distributed intelligence · Wireless communications · Ubiquitous computing

1 Introduction

Nowadays, a centralized architecture is commonly used for traffic management systems. All the information from motorways authorities, weather stations and measurement points on the road is gathered by a Traffic Management Centre (TMC). Then the information is analysed and decisions are taken in the TMC and sending back to the on-road infrastructure. The architecture of classical ITS [1] is thus purely hierarchical, with sensed data flowing from the leaves (i.e., road-side sensors) to the root [2].

This kind of approach presents some disadvantages [3], not scaling adequately and showing a lack of flexibility. Usually such a vertical architecture is not suitable to accept and integrate changes and exhibits latency and security issues related to the centralization of the communications which produces a bottleneck in the system.

For these reasons research activities in ITS and especially in C-ITS (Cooperative ITS) have changed the vision behind the definition of new ITS architectures, switching from the hierarchical and vertical approach to a new vision, which is more horizontal and distributed [4].

© Springer International Publishing Switzerland 2015
J.M. García-Chamizo et al. (Eds.): UCAmI 2015, LNCS 9454, pp. 84–90, 2015.
DOI: 10.1007/978-3-319-26401-1_8

The aim of this work is to define an innovative and fully distributed architecture to enable cooperative sensing in Intelligent Transportation Systems (ITS) environments. The main idea behind the project relies on a local distributed intelligence, operating on a limited geographical scale, where data is timely distributed and processed without the need to contact a central subsystem. To this aim, the concept of "gateway" is introduced: a logical entity that offers capabilities similar to those provided by centralized approaches (e.g., data storage or event processing) but operating on a local scope with the possibility to exchange messages with other gateways.

2 Cooperative Decision-Making ITS

A new cooperative architecture is proposed, where the intelligence of the system is distributed over some of the elements in the infrastructure which host a software platform for running ITS applications. Communication with the remote centre happens only for the transmission of aggregated data for long-term operations while real-time data will be processed and stored locally, nearby the source of the events.

2.1 Global System Architecture

The architecture relies on a local distributed storage and intelligence, which operates on a limited geographical scale where data are distributed and processed in real-time without the need to contact the control centre. Moreover sensed data will be processed in a cooperative manner performing content aggregation and integration since the earliest stages, while only statistical data for long-term evaluation are sent to the control centre. In order to achieve distributed intelligence and cooperative sensing two key concepts are defined: the gateways (GW) and the local/global areas. A logical view of the architecture is reported in Fig. 1.

Gateway (GW). A gateway refers to a physical entity that implements the reference architecture, the Data Distribution Platform (DDP) and the Collaborative Learning Unit (CLU). A GW is able to join Local/Global Areas and is connected to different subsystems (VS: Vehicular Subsystems, PS: Personal Subsystems, etc.)

Local/Global Area. An area is composed by: a set of gateways (at least one), communications among these gateways, and criteria to define the area perimeter (e.g. based on the density of population, traffic, ICT elements, etc.).

2.2 Software Architecture of Platform on GWs

Based on the generated distributed system, the GWs, autonomously, will analyse the information gathered and determine the best traffic strategies for dealing with roadway incidents. To do so, each of the GWs hosts a software platform designed for running ITS applications. This software architecture is composed of various modules:

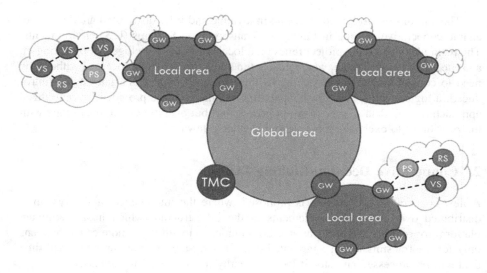

Fig. 1. Global system architecture

- **Connectors**, used to extend the gateway interoperability via integration interfaces with external subsystems and technologies such as Wireless Sensor Networks, Vehicular Networks, Road-side Subsystems, etc.
- **DDP/Logical Layer**, providing the basic capabilities needed by the ITS services. The key component of the logical layer, the Data Distribution Platform (DDP), includes the mechanism to communicate between applications and services by managing an events-based architecture.
- **ITS Services and Applications**, higher level services or end-user applications implementing traffic and travel models to respond to roadway incidents. An example of the services that can be provided will be shown in Sect. 4.
- **External Components**, software components running in the same OS and which are required by other components in order to work properly.

The proposed software architecture will be executed on a GNU/Linux operating system. This choice is made due to the success stories of this OS being flexible enough to run on a wide set of hardware. All the services, connectors and applications will be provided as OSGi [5] bundles exposing their functionalities to other bundles through the service layer. Thus an OSGi reference framework and a JAVA Runtime Environment are required in order to be able to run the GWs software platform.

3 Architecture's Main Components

3.1 DDP: Data Distribution Platform

The role of the DDP is to enable a scalable and highly adaptable system able to receive data from the architecture subsystems and to provide a set of capabilities (basic services) used by ITS applications and services. The DDP is therefore responsible for providing the mechanisms for the communication between the different layers using a publisher/subscriber (P/S) events-based architecture.

Other software components would only have to be concerned to inform the DDP about the events in which they are interested. It will be the DDP who has to redirect messages to these components interested, inside the Local Area or in other Local Areas. Instead of implementing a high number of point-to-point links between sensors/actuators, actors and gateways at all layers, the DDP in the Logical layer will implement a kind of data space, using an appropriate middleware [6] directly supporting many-to-many communications using the P/S pattern.

3.2   CLU: Collaborative Learning Unit

To achieve the architecture's goal of autonomous operation, the CLUs will include a set of components that will respond to events received via the DDP (Fig. 2). The distributed traffic management will be achieved through the collaboration of the CLUs in the Area enabling cooperative intelligence. The output will feed up also the cooperative networks, resulting in notifications that influence the reality of interest.

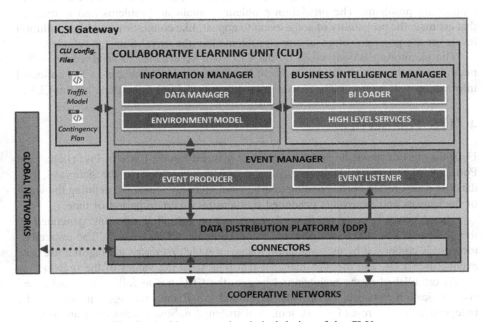

Fig. 2. Architecture and technical design of the CLU

- **Events manager:** this module controls the flow of the events at the CLU side; communicating with the DDP to obtain relevant events for the CLU considering its geographical position, the GW's attached WSN, the position of other GWs, etc.

- **Information manager:** this module provides updated information about the GW environment (related sensors, road conditions, etc.) to the CLU services. It also processes the Traffic Models and the Contingency Plans configuration files.
- **Business intelligence manager:** it has a set of high-level services responsible for responding to incidents that arise on the road: accidents, delays, CO_2 levels, etc. As the situations are varied, services implemented by the CLU will have different dynamically adjusted behaviours provided by the integrated AI in the CLUs.

The CLUs will be always updated with new traffic models and contingency plans reported by the TMC. These configuration files consist of two sets of data, which may be updated dynamically and thus allow the change in the behaviour of the CLUs. On the one hand, topological information of the elements is established. On the other hand, a table with the rules that specify what information is relevant to that particular CLU is also stored, so it can properly subscribe to events provided from the DDP.

Regarding the intelligence integrated in the CLUs, one of the main challenges is to develop stable and distributed algorithms not requiring very high computational resources. The CLU has to solve routing problems as a necessary task for the implementation of several use cases. This is due the fact that almost in every incident detected; it has to provide a warning signal and an alternative route to avoid it.

Other types of problems that have to be faced by the CLU are the prediction and monitoring problems. The prediction problems contain all problems and techniques that estimate the probability of some event to appear, like congestion and high pollution levels; or the possible values of some problems like the travel time for vehicles.

The monitoring actions taken by the CLU will be oriented to send/receive information about the state of the environment (accidents, blocked lanes, etc.) The collected information will be necessary for a proper decision making to be done by the CLU.

4　ITS Test Services

Until the start of the deployment tests, being planned to take place in Pisa (Italia) and Portugal; to test the CLU implementation and the operation of the gateways, two datasets were created corresponding to urban and highway scenarios, defining the value of the sensors and the events generated by them for a certain period of time.

The objective is to see the flow of events, not only the flow of events generated by the use cases, but rather the communications between CLUs as well. The tests environment is composed by the simulation manager, which recreates the ingoing use case events, the CLUs, and the web manager that represents the values of the sensors.

As established in the architectural design, the CLU has to follow an event-based communication between the Logical layer and the Events manager in order to be independent of the rest of the system. A distributed publisher/subscriber architecture has been deployed for achieving this goal of autonomous operation. The CLUs have to subscribe to relevant events (changes in sensor values for example) which, in this prototype, will be published periodically by the Simulation manager attending to the provided datasets. The use of this distributed architecture along with the provided datasets allows for the future integration of the CLUs in the real scenario without further changes needed.

A web application for the real time monitoring of the sensors and actuators has been incorporated to the testing solution. With this web application, the administrator can test the functionality and the correct operation of the system in a simulated environment prior to the physical deploy of the RSUs on the road. Figure 3 shows a screenshot of the developed C# map-based Rich Internet Application [7].

Fig. 3. Web Manager application

5   Conclusion and Future Work

This work, based on the ICSI European project, exposes a new paradigm in the ITS domain, moving the system intelligence from the control centre to the peripheral devices. The presented architecture uses a set of gateways, installed in the road infrastructure to process and gather all the sensors data independently and in a distributed way, without the need to contact a central subsystem.

The presented architecture, with the participation of the sensors networks on the road, the data distribution platform, the collaborative learning units and finally the ITS applications, encompasses the entire process of capture and management of available road data, enabling the generation of services to promote transportation efficiency and performance, among others.

Acknowledgement. This work has been partially funded by the European Commission under the Seventh Framework Programme. Intelligent Cooperative Sensing for Improved Traffic efficiency (ICSI) project. Grant agreement no.: 317671.

References

1. Weiland, R.J., Purser, L.B.: Intelligent Transportation Systems, Transportation in the New Millennium. Transportation Research Board, Washington (2000)
2. Weiß, C.: V2X communication in Europe-From research projects towards standardization and field testing of vehicle communication technology. Comput. Netw. **55**, 3103–3119 (2011)
3. Papadimitratos, P., La Fortelle, A., Evenssen, K., Brignolo, R., Cosenza, S.: Vehicular communication systems: enabling technologies, applications, and future outlook on intelligent transportation. IEEE Commun. Mag. **47**, 84–95 (2009)

4. Paul, A., Haley, D., Grant, A.: Cooperative intelligent transport systems: 5.9-GHz field trials. Proc. IEEE **99**, 1213–1235 (2011)
5. Rellermeyer, J.S., Alonso, G., Roscoe, T.: R-OSGi: Distributed Applications Through Software Modularization. In: Cerqueira, R., Campbell, R.H. (eds.) Middleware 2007. LNCS, vol. 4834, pp. 1–20. Springer, Heidelberg (2007)
6. Eugster, P., et al.: The many faces of publish/subscribe. ACM Comput. Surv. (CSUR) **35**, 114–131 (2003)
7. Fraternali, P., Rossi, G., Sánchez-Figueroa, F.: Rich internet applications. IEEE Internet Comput. **14**, 9–12 (2010)

A Data Analytics Schema for Activity Recognition in Smart Home Environments

Giancarlo Fortino[1], Andrea Giordano[2], Antonio Guerrieri[1]([envelope]),
Giandomenico Spezzano[2], and Andrea Vinci[2]

[1] Dipartimento di Ingegneria Informatica, Modellistica, Elettronica e Sistemistica,
Università della Calabria, 87036 Rende, CS, Italy
g.fortino@unical.it, aguerrieri@deis.unical.it
[2] Institute for High Performance Computing and Networking (ICAR),
CNR – National Research Council of Italy,
Via P. Bucci 41C, 87036 Rende, CS, Italy
{giordano,spezzano,vinci}@icar.cnr.it

Abstract. Recent advancements in the fields of embedded systems, communication technologies and computer science open up to new application scenarios in the home environment. Anyway, many issues raised from the inherent complexity of this new application domain need to be properly tackled. This paper proposes the *Cloud-assisted Agent-based Smart home Environment (CASE)* architecture for activity recognition with sensors capturing the data related to activities being performed by humans and objects in the environment. Moreover, the potential of analytics methods for discovering activity recognition in such environment has been investigated. CASE easily allows to implement Smart Home applications exploiting a distributed multi-agent system and the cloud technology. The work is mainly focused on activity recognition albeit CASE architecture permits an easy integration of other kinds of smart home applications such as home automation and energy optimization. The CASE effectiveness is shown through the design of a case study consisting of a daily activity recognition of an elder person in its home environment.

Keywords: Smart homes · Internet of Things · Activity recognition · Cloud computing · Multi agent system · Analytics · Wireless sensor and actuator networks

1 Introduction

In the context of the Internet of Things (IoT) [1] many devices have been enhanced with respect to their ordinary role to be proactive and collaborative with other devices [2]. In this background, the Smart Homes [3] are advancing as a disruptive trend in the literature. Regarding Smart Homes, many progresses have been done in the past few years on several fields: *Home Automation and Domotics* [4], *Energy Optimization* [5], *Distributed Sensing and Actuation* [6],

© Springer International Publishing Switzerland 2015
J.M. García-Chamizo et al. (Eds.): UCAmI 2015, LNCS 9454, pp. 91–102, 2015.
DOI: 10.1007/978-3-319-26401-1_9

Activity Recognition [7], *Ambient Assisted Living* [8,9], *Indoor Positioning Systems* [10], and *Home Security* [11].

A very important and interesting application scenario for the Smart Homes is emerging in the last few years. Given the growing in population age, more and more elder people living alone require assistance 24/7. *Activity Recognition* [7] using data mining techniques can be successfully adopted for this purpose. Indeed, applying these techniques on data coming from the home environment permits to recognize and analyze human activities in real time and, eventually, to send alarms to relatives or doctors of the monitored person.

This paper proposes a novel platform, called *Cloud-assisted Agent-based Smart home Environment (CASE)*, that easily allows the distributed sensing and actuation in Smart Home environments. CASE is a layered architecture which permits the physical entities (i.e. sensors and actuators) to be transparently integrated with a distributed multi-agent system and a cloud infrastructure. CASE architecture enables agents, which implement specific applications and analytics services, to be dynamically uploaded either on the cloud system, exploiting its heavy computational resources, or close to the physical entities fostering real-time computation.

Together with the platform, a general activity recognition schema will be shown and its matching with the CASE platform will be portrayed. CASE activity recognition considers both environmental sensors spread on the home environment and mobile wearable sensors worn by the home inhabitants. A case study has been drawn out which aims to underline the CASE features and benefits.

The reminder of the paper is organized as follows: Sect. 2 introduces the related work, Sect. 3 presents the proposed architecture and shows how it can be used in the activity recognition field, and Sect. 4 provides a case study. Finally, some conclusions and future work are drawn.

2   Related Work

Nowadays, Smart Homes represent an important research field both in academia and in industry [3]. One of the major challenges in the realization of these applications is interoperability among various devices and deployments. Thus, the need for a new architecture - comprising of smart control and actuation - has been identified by many researchers. In this context, the increase of ageing population is growing the need to implement Activity Recognition [12] in the Smart Homes. Several works have been done in this direction.

Authors of [13] introduce an activity recognition system for single person smart homes using Active Learning. They apply data mining techniques to cluster in-home sensor samplings so that each cluster represents a human activity. The users have to label each cluster with the corresponding activity so to allow the system learning how to recognize future activities. The system has been designed to detect not only single but also overlapping activities.

In [7,14] authors present an automatic approach to activity discovery and monitoring for assisted living in a real world setting. It does not use supervised methods for activity recognition, but it automatically discovers activity patterns. Moreover, the system is designed to discover variations in such patterns and is also able to handle real life data by dealing with different sensor problems.

The work in [15] shows a prototype used to forecast the behaviour and wellness of the elderly by monitoring the daily usages of appliances in a smart home. Elderly people perform activities at regular intervals of time. When daily activities are performed regularly, it means that the elderly man/woman is in a state of wellness. In this work, Predictive Ambient Intelligence techniques are used involving the extraction of patterns related to sensor activations.

In [16] authors introduce an ontology-based hybrid approach to activity modeling that combines domain knowledge based model specification and data-driven model learning. Central to the approach is an iterative process that begins with seed activity models created by ontological engineering. The "seed" models are deployed, and subsequently evolved through incremental activity discovery and model update. The rationale of this work is to provide (on single-user single-activity scenarios) generic activity models suitable for all users and then create individual activity models through incremental learning.

Aim of this paper is to propose a novel platform that, with respect to the state of the art in the Smart Home Activity Recognition field, allows:

- the cloud-assisted integration between environmental sensory data with data coming from wearable sensors which permits to better detect human activities;
- the possibility to dynamically evolve the classification model by adding or updating classifiers as soon as new activities are discovered;
- an easy integration of different kinds of smart home applications with the activity recognition one.

3   Cloud-Assisted Agent-Based Smart Home Environment

In this section we introduce the basic concepts of the *Cloud-assisted Agent-based Smart home Environment (CASE)* architecture which allows to easily design and develop optimized complex smart home applications. CASE architecture is particularly suitable in those scenarios where complex human activities (e.g. cooking, sleeping etc.) need to be figured out from raw sensors data. In our approach, we distinguish two kinds of sensors: environmental sensors and mobile sensors. Environmental sensors are typically placed in fixed positions in the home environment while mobile sensors are, for example, worn directly by humans, and their positions dynamically change when people move around the home area. Combining both environmental and human-related data with analytics methods allows discovering and analysing complex activities which usually can not be derived solely from environmental data neither from the human-related ones.

In the next section, the CASE architecture is described in order to better clarify the rationale and the basic concepts underlying the proposed approach.

3.1 CASE Architecture

The CASE architecture can be seen as composed by three coarse-grained layers (see Fig. 1):

Fig. 1. Physical architecture.

IoT Layer. It consists of the collection of all sensors, actuators or more complex devices which are spread across the home environment or worn by humans.

Virtualization Layer. It is the layer focused on abstracting the physical part so to simplify the upper layers work by supplying a uniform interface to heterogeneous IoT devices. This layer also addresses all the low level issues such as connectivity, reliability and resilience.

Analytics Layer. The first two layers allow to develop simple monitoring on the sensed data as well as simple actuation strategies. Anyway, passing from the raw sensory data to a complex model of reality, which is able to recognize high level human activities, requires the adoption of complex algorithms which may fall into several research fields such as data-mining, swarm intelligence and so on. Since their complexity, such algorithms frequently need the high availability of computational resources that the cloud provides. All these kinds of algorithms/techniques are called hereafter *Analytics Services*.

By using the CASE architecture it is possible to build applications related to the smart home context. In particular, the CASE effectiveness in the case of monitoring of human activities for recognizing critical or dangerous situations will be shown in Sect. 4.

The main issues addressed by the CASE architecture concern: the heterogeneity of physical elements (i.e. sensors, actuators and other devices), the real-time distributed nature of the smart home and the inherent complexity of the analytics. CASE hides heterogeneity by means of the *IoT Devices Abstraction Layer* which *wraps* the physical entities that are managed through a well-defined *Object Interface* as detailed in Sect. 3.1. The real-time distributed nature of these kinds of application and the inherent complexity of the analytics involved are addressed adopting a distributed multi-agent system (MAS) and the cloud technology. The distributed MAS aims to keep the computation close to the sources of information (i.e., the physical devices), thus decreasing the need for remote communications so to foster fast actuations based on real-time changes in the environment. Furthermore, it could ensure dynamic adaptivity by enabling the use of Swarm Intelligence algorithms. The Cloud technology may be suitably exploited to carry out heavy computational tasks which could be required for running complex analytics.

CASE architecture is composed by a set of computing nodes of two kinds: *fixed* and *mobile*. The fixed computing nodes are single-board computers like Raspberry PIs or BeagleBoards. They manage the fixed environmental sensors and actuators to which are connected. The single-board computers can be effectively placed across the home area because of their low costs, low energy consumptions and small dimensions. The mobile computing nodes are achieved using smartphones. This is a valuable solution because nowadays smartphones are very cheap and commonly used. Indeed there should not be any problem for a person who wears sensors to also bring along a smartphone.

Each computational node contains both the IoT devices abstraction layer and the agent server. IoT devices abstraction layer and Agent Server are located in the same computing nodes in order to guarantee that agents exploit the local physical part. Instead of transferring data to a central processing unit, processes are transferred (by injecting fine-grained agents onto the nodes) toward the data sources. As a consequence, a minimum amount of data needs to be transferred over a long distance (i.e. toward remote hosts) so local access and computation is fostered in order to achieve good performance and scalability.

IoT Devices Abstraction Layer. The Iot Devices abstraction layer aims to hide heterogeneity by supplying a well-established *Object Interface* (OI) permitting the physical parts to be suitably integrated with the rest of the system. All the physical stuff/devices must be arranged in a set of *Virtual Objects* (VOs) implementing OI [17].

A VO could be defined as a collection of physical entities like sensors and actuators, together with their computational abilities. It can be composed of just a simple sensor or it can be a more complex object that includes many sensors, many actuators, computational resources like CPU or memory and so on.

In general, VO outputs can be represented by *punctual values* (e.g. the temperature at a given point of a room) or *aggregated values* (e.g. the average of moisture during the last 8 h). Also, the values returned by VOs could be just the measurement of sensors or could be the result of complex computations (e.g. the temperature at a given point of space computed by means of interpolation of the values given by sensors spread across the environment).

Furthermore, a VO could supply actuation functionality by changing the environment on the basis of external triggers or internal calculus.

These different kinds of behaviour that VO can expose must be taken into account. VO is therefore conceived as a complex object that can read and write upon many simple physical resources. More in detail, we consider that each VO exposes different *functionalities*. Each functionality can be either sensing or actuation and can be refined by further parameters that dynamically configure it.

The previous assumption leads to the definition of *resource* as the following *triplet*:

$$[VOId, FunctionId, Params]$$

where VOId uniquely identifies the VO, FunctionId identifies the specific functionality and Params is an ordered set of parameter values that configure the functionality.

Besides read and write operations (i.e. sensing and actuation), it is provided for VOs to be able to manage events that occur in the physical part. Agents can define events by supplying *logical rules* in which one or more VOs could be involved [17]. The IoT Devices Abstraction Layer is in charge of notifying the agents of the events' occurrences.

CASE Multi-agent System. The Multi Agent component of the CASE architecture is made up of the following entities: *Agents*, *Messages* and the *Agent Server*. Figure 2 shows these entities and how they interact among themselves and with the *IoT Devices Abstraction Layer*.

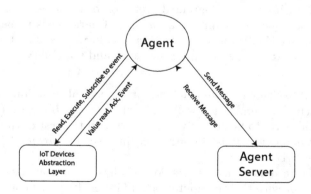

Fig. 2. CASE multi-agent entities.

An *Agent* is an autonomous entity which executes its own behaviour interacting with other agents via Agent Server. In addition, each agent can interact with the physical part exploiting functionalities exposed by the IoT Devices Abstraction Layer (i.e. using the Object Interface) which, in turn, is in charge of notifying the events that occur in the physical part to the agent.

A *Message* is the atomic element of communication between agents. It carries an application specific content together with information about the sender agent and the receiver one.

The *Agent Server* is the container for the execution of agents. It offers functionalities concerning the life cycle of the agents as well as functionalities for agents' communication. Agent servers are arranged in a peer-to-peer fashion where each agent server hosts a certain number of agents and permits them to execute and interact among themselves transparently. In other words, when an agent requests the execution of a functionality, its host agent server is in charge of redirecting transparently the request to the suitable agent server.

CASE Cloud. In the CASE cloud part a set of CASE nodes are deployed and run on a cloud infrastructure. Such nodes lack of the Iot Devices Abstraction Layer since, obviously, there are no physical entities connected. For this reason each node consists of the only agent server. The communication between the nodes connected with the physical part and the nodes in the cloud occurs by means of message exchange (see Sect. 3.1).

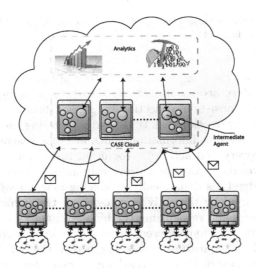

Fig. 3. CASE cloud.

Agents located on the cloud nodes act as intermediary between the CASE MAS and cloud analytics services. The feature of adding new agents at runtime can be used to link new services in the cloud during the execution of the system (no reboot is needed).

The CASE cloud part is PaaS, namely it provides a software stack and a set of libraries for the application execution. Anyway, it also can be seen as SaaS because the CASE user, i.e. the application developer, can inject his application by remotely add the needed agents.

3.2 CASE Activity Recognition

Even though the CASE architecture can be effectively used in many smart home application domains, this work is mainly focused on the activity recognition task because it can be suitably exploited to analyse human behaviour so to realize and prevent dangerous situations which may occur in home environments. In this section the activity recognition module of the CASE architecture is presented.

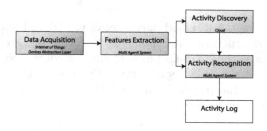

Fig. 4. Activity recognition tasks flow. Each task is executed in a different layer of the CASE architecture, as labeled.

In Fig. 4 are shown the four main tasks for the in home activity recognition: *data acquisition, feature extraction, activity discovery, activity recognition*. The data acquisition task consists in collecting the sensor data from the home environment. The feature extraction task is focused on filtering the acquired data in order to extract the relevant information which are then rearranged and passed to the activity discovery and activity recognition tasks. The activity discovery task uses the features to discover new previously unknown activities in order to enlarge the knowledge thus dynamically producing new *classifiers*. Such classifiers are eventually used by the activity recognition task which is in charge of processing the features and recognizing the high level activities in real time.

Each task is carried out in a different layer of the CASE architecture (Fig. 4). In particular, the data acquisition task is assigned to the IoT Devices Abstraction Layer, the feature extraction is carried out by *extractor agents*. The activity discovery task is assigned to the CASE cloud part. Indeed, it typically involves complex data mining algorithms so it can suitably exploit the large computational resources of the cloud technologies. The activity discovery task produces as output new *classifier agents* which are dynamically deployed on the agent servers. These agents run in the computational nodes physically placed in the home environment so they can classify the activities fast enough to fulfil the real time requirements.

4   Case Study

In order to highlight the effectiveness of the proposed platform, a case study has been designed inspired by the CASAS project [14]. Such case study concerns a single apartment, which is instrumented with various proximity sensors. Each sensor provides boolean information (on/off) on the presence of someone in its sensed area. The apartment comprises of five rooms: a kitchen, a dining room, a living room, a bedroom and a bathroom. In addition, the person who lives in the apartment always wears wearable sensors consisting of three axis accelerometers. Each room hosts a fixed CASE node where the environmental sensors are connected to. A mobile CASE node, e.g., a smartphone always carried by the person, can receive all the data of the wearable sensors.

Figure 5 shows the main logical flow involved in this case study. At the bottom, two activity recognition processes are designed to be continuously executed: the first uses the environmental sensors' data (i.e. the proximity sensors) to recognize daily activities, while the second uses the wearable sensors to recognize the body postures of the apartment inhabitant. These two tasks will feed a single log, composed by triplets ⟨DATE, TIMESTAMP, ACTIVITY⟩, as shown in Fig. 5. In this log, an activity could be both a daily live activity, such as cooking or watching tv, or a body posture, such as standing still or sitting.

A third component has been designed to use this log in order to detect anomalies so to produce alerts through the exploitation of a set of high level inference rules.

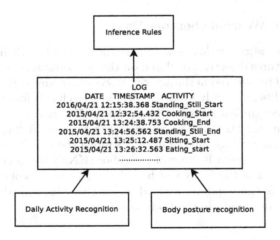

Fig. 5. Case study main flow

4.1   Mining on Environmental Sensors Data

The use of the algorithms presented in [13] is proposed to recognize daily activities in the presented setting. A general schema of activity recognition has been given in Sect. 3.2. The data generated from ambient sensors produce events represented by a quadruple:

$$\{DATE, TIMESTAMP, SENSORID, STATUS\}$$

that represents a status change (*on/off*) of the sensor identified by *SENSORID*, at the time *DATE, TIMESTAMP*.

The raw data are then processed by collecting consecutive sensor firings segmented per room. The result of this operation is a list of occupancy episodes, in the form of (*roomID, startTime, duration, usedSensors*), where *roomID* uniquely identifies a room, *startTime* is the beginning time of the occupancy episode, *duration* is how long the episode lasts, *usedSensors* is the set of the sensors that was used during a particular occupancy episode.

These episodes are the features that feed the activity discovery and recognition tasks.

The activity discovery task uses the frequent itemset mining Apriori algorithm for identifying the relevant occupancy episodes which are then clustered [13]. The output of this task is a set of clusters, that can be updated over time. Each cluster is represented by a tuple (*UsedSensors, MeanStartTime, MeanDuration*) which needs to be manually labelled.

The set of labelled clusters constitutes the model for the activity recognition task, where each new occupancy episode is assigned to the most similar cluster, and will be used to feed the afore introduced activity log (see Fig. 5).

4.2   Mining on Wearable Sensors Data

CASE wearable sensors are designed to periodically send to their Mobile CASE Node a set of features directly calculated on the accelerometer sensor nodes [18]. Such features will be selected in the activity discovery/training phase through the SFFS [19] algorithm as already proposed in [18]. The chosen features act as input to the activity recognition system, designed in a CASE Agent, which will run a classifier recognizing the body postures and movements defined (i.e. *standing still, sitting, laying, walking, falling down*). Among the classification algorithms available in the literature, a K-Nearest Neighbor (KNN)-based classifier [20] will be used. The output of the KNN will be calculated every second to have in the CASE Agent a real-time update. Instead, the activity log introduced above will be fed everytime an update in the body posture is ready.

4.3   Inference Rules

The activity log, fed by both the environmental and the wearable sensors activity recognition tasks, represents the knowledge base of an expert system (composed of a set of collaborating Cloud Agents) which is able to produce alerts on the basis of a set of high level inference rules.

In the following some simple inference rule examples are listed:

Condition One	Condition Two	Alert
Cooking	Lying	Faint
Shower	Lying	Faint
Night	Too long standing still	Illness
Toileting	Too long sitting	Illness
Any activity	Falling down	Accidental fall or faint

Whenever a Cloud Agent will detect that one of these rules is satisfied, it will generate an alarm to notify an anomaly event. This feature of the system is particularly important in a Smart Home environment where elder assistance is performed. A wider set of alarms can be defined at cloud level based on specific habits of people living in a smart home.

5 Conclusion

The paper has proposed Cloud-assisted Agent-based Smart home Environment (CASE). CASE is a novel platform for the distributed sensing and actuation in Smart Home environments which allows a simple integration between physical entities (such as sensors and actuators), a distributed multi-agent system, and a cloud infrastructure. In the CASE architecture, agents are disseminated both on local nodes and on the cloud to manage sensors/actuators or to execute complex algorithms.

The designed case study shows how to use the CASE platform to perform activity recognition in smart home combining both environmental and wearable sensors data. Moreover, the case study portrays how the data coming from the activity recognition can be exploited to feed a knowledge base that will be used by Cloud Agents to evaluate inference rules.

Future work will be devoted both to an improvement of the platform and to the realization of a wider use case that comprehends not only the activity recognition task but also home automation and energy optimization.

Acknowledgment. This work has been partially supported by "Smart platform for monitoring and management of in-home security and safety of people and structures" project that is part of the DOMUS District, funded by the Italian Government (PON03PE_00050_1).

References

1. Miorandi, D., Sicari, S., De Pellegrini, F., Chlamtac, I.: Internet of things. Ad Hoc Netw. **10**(7), 1497–1516 (2012)
2. Fortino, G., Guerrieri, A., Russo, W.: Agent-oriented smart objects development. In: 2012 IEEE 16th International Conference on Computer Supported Cooperative Work in Design (CSCWD), pp. 907–912, May 2012

3. Bierhoff, I., van Berlo, A., Abascal, J., Allen, B., Civit, A., Fellbaum, K., Kemppainen, E., Bitterman, N., Freitas, D., Kristiansson, K.: Smart home environment, COST, Brussels (2007)
4. Alkar, A.Z., Buhur, U.: An internet based wireless home automation system for multifunctional devices. IEEE Trans. Consum. Electron. **51**(4), 1169–1174 (2005)
5. Serra, J., Pubill, D., Antonopoulos, A., Verikoukis, C.: Smart HVAC control in IoT: energy consumption minimization with user comfort constraints. Sci. World J. **2014**, 1–11 (2014)
6. Fortino, G., Guerrieri, A., O'Hare, G., Ruzzelli, A.: A flexible building management framework based on wireless sensor and actuator networks. J. Netw. Comput. Appl. **35**, 1934–1952 (2012)
7. Rashidi, P., Cook, D.J.: Com: a method for mining and monitoring human activity patterns in home-based health monitoring systems. ACM Trans. Intell. Syst. Technol. **4**(4), 64:1–64:20 (2013)
8. Pavón-Pulido, N., López-Riquelme, J.A., Ferruz-Melero, J., Vega-Rodríguez, M.A., Barrios-León, A.J.: A service robot for monitoring elderly people in the context of ambient assisted living. J. Ambient Intell. Smart Environ. **6**(6), 595–621 (2014)
9. Dohr, A., Modre-Opsrian, R., Drobics, M., Hayn, D., Schreier, G.: The internet of things for ambient assisted living. In: 2010 Seventh International Conference on Information Technology: New Generations (ITNG), pp. 804–809, April 2010
10. Richter, P., Toledano-Ayala, M., Soto-Zarazúa, G.M., Rivas-Araiza, E.A.: A survey of hybridisation methods of GNSS and wireless LAN based positioning system. J. Ambient Intell. Smart Environ. **6**(6), 723–738 (2014)
11. Sang-Hyun, L., Lee, J.G., Kyung-Il, M.: Smart home security system using multiple ANFIS. Int. J. Smart Home **7**(3), 121–132 (2013)
12. Rashidi, P., Mihailidis, A.: A survey on ambient-assisted living tools for older adults. IEEE J. Biomed. Health Inform. **17**(3), 579–590 (2013)
13. Hoque, E., Stankovic, J.A.: AALO: activity recognition in smart homes using active learning in the presence of overlapped activities. In: 6th International Conference on Pervasive Computing Technologies for Healthcare, PervasiveHealth 2012, pp. 139–146 (2012)
14. Cook, D.J., Krishnan, N.C., Rashidi, P.: Activity discovery and activity recognition: a new partnership. IEEE Trans. Syst. Man Cybern. **43**(3), 820–828 (2013)
15. Suryadevara, N., Mukhopadhyay, S., Wang, R., Rayudu, R.: Forecasting the behavior of an elderly using wireless sensors data in a smart home. Eng. Appl. Artif. Intell. **26**(10), 2641–2652 (2013)
16. Chen, L., Nugent, C., Okeyo, G.: An ontology-based hybrid approach to activity modeling for smart homes. IEEE Trans. Hum.-Mach. Syst. **44**(1), 92–105 (2014)
17. Giordano, A., Spezzano, G., Vinci, A.: Rainbow: an intelligent platform for large-scale networked cyber-physical systems. In: Proceedings of the 5th International Workshop on Networks of Cooperating Objects for Smart Cities (UBICITEC), pp. 70–85 (2014)
18. Fortino, G., Giannantonio, R., Gravina, R., Kuryloski, P., Jafari, R.: Enabling effective programming and flexible management of efficient body sensor network applications. IEEE Trans. Hum.-Mach. Syst. **43**(1), 115–133 (2013)
19. Pudil, P., Novovičová, J., Kittler, J.: Floating search methods in feature selection. Pattern Recogn. Lett. **15**(11), 1119–1125 (1994)
20. Cover, T., Hart, P.: Nearest neighbor pattern classification. IEEE Trans. Inf. Theor. **13**(1), 21–27 (1967)

Teaching a Virtual Robot to Perform Tasks by Learning from Observation

Cristina Tîrnăucă[1]([✉]), José L. Montaña[1], Carlos Ortiz–Sobremazas[1],
Santiago Ontañón[2], and Avelino J. González[3]

[1] Universidad de Cantabria, Santander, Spain
{cristina.tirnauca,joseluis.montana,carlos.ortizsobremazas}@unican.es
[2] Drexel University, Philadelphia, USA
santi@cs.drexel.edu
[3] University of Central Florida, Orlando, USA
gonzalez@ucf.edu

Abstract. We propose a methodology based on Learning from Observation in order to teach a virtual robot to perform its tasks. Our technique only assumes that behaviors to be cloned can be observed and represented using a finite alphabet of symbols. A virtual agent is used to generate training material, according to a range of strategies of gradually increasing complexity. We use Machine Learning techniques to learn new strategies by observing and thereafter imitating the actions performed by the agent. We perform several experiments to test our proposal. The analysis of those experiments suggests that probabilistic finite state machines could be a suitable tool for the problem of behavioral cloning. We believe that the given methodology is easy to integrate in the learning module of any Ubiquitous Robot Architecture.

1 Introduction

"People living comfortably in digital environments in which the electronics are sensitive to their needs, personalized to their requirements, anticipatory to their behavior and responsive to their presence": a possible future with Ambient Intelligence as stated by Philips Research Technologies[1]. Ambient Intelligence (AmI) is a buzzword. Many AmI systems incorporate only low-level type intelligence. Very often, they are built in the absence of Artificial Intelligence (AI), while the emphasis is concentrated on their hardware component: with sensors, communication protocols, and, in general, ubiquitous computing. As an example, many smart cities projects consist primarily in the distribution of thousands of sensors over the urban space. This limited amount of intelligence represents an inconvenience, at least in early stages of an AmI system, but it is rapidly being solved with emerging software Machine Learning (ML) applications that will result in a balanced combination of ubiquitous technologies and AI methodologies. ML has received attention inside the AI community from the beginning.

---

[1] http://www.research.philips.com/technologies/projects/ami/.

© Springer International Publishing Switzerland 2015
J.M. García-Chamizo et al. (Eds.): UCAmI 2015, LNCS 9454, pp. 103–115, 2015.
DOI: 10.1007/978-3-319-26401-1_10

Neural Networks, Inductive Learning from Examples, Case-Based Reasoning, Decision Trees (DTs), Bayesian Networks (BNs), Support Vector Machines and other Data Mining techniques like k-clustering contribute decisively in the whole process of knowledge discovery and representation. Nowadays, ML is widely used, so AmI will likely also need to handle this technology. Moreover, one main requirement for AmI is to learn by observing users. For example, several systems understand user commands, but they are not intelligent enough to avoid doing things that the user does not want to do. Basic ML methods will enable AmI systems to learn by observing users, thus making these systems more adapted to them.

This paper is devoted to the study of basic ML methods that will enable AmI systems to learn by observing users. In our formulation, the problem of behavioral learning consists of cloning the way in which a task is performed by some agent just by observing it in action. We think that this point of view is general enough to deal with relevant specific applications in AmI such as the generation of the software needed by intelligent autonomous agents like robots in order to fulfill their duties.

As a formal framework to study the behavioral cloning problem we propose to use the theoretical corpus of a learning paradigm named Learning from Observation (LfO). One of the pioneers of this field is M. Bauer [1], who shows how to make use of knowledge about variables, inputs, instructions and procedures in order to learn programs, which basically amounts to learning strategies to perform abstract computations by demonstration, a topic that was especially popular in robotics [7]. Another early mention of LfO comes from Michalski et al. [8], who define it merely as unsupervised learning. Gonzalez et al. [5] discussed LfO at length, but provided no formalization nor suggested an approach to realize it algorithmically. More recent work on the more general LfO subject came nearly simultaneously but independently from Sammut et al. [14] and Sidani [16]. Fernlund et al. [3] used LfO to build agents capable of driving a simulated automobile in a city environment. Pomerleau [12] developed the ALVINN system that trained neural networks from observation of a road-following automobile in the real world. Moriarty and Gonzalez [9] used neural networks to carry out LfO for computer games. Könik and Laird [6] introduced LfO in complex domains with the SOAR system, by using inductive logic programming techniques. Other significant work done under the label of learning from demonstration has emerged recently in the Case-Based Reasoning community. Floyd et al. [4] present an approach to learn how to play RoboSoccer by observing the play of other teams. Ontañón et al. [11] use learning from demonstration for real-time strategy games in the context of Case-Based Planning. Finally, another related area is that of Inverse Reinforcement Learning [10], where the focus is on reconstructing the reward function given optimal behavior (i.e., given a policy, or a set of trajectories). One of the main problems here is that different reward functions may correspond to the observed behavior, and heuristics need to be devised to only consider families of reward functions that are interesting.

2 Behavioral Models Based on Discrete-Time Finite-State Deterministic and Stochastic Processes

Imagine some agent A performing a task in a certain environment. In the LfO formulation, the behavior of the agent can be captured by at least three different types of variables: its perception X of the environment taking values in some space $\mathcal{X}$, its unobservable internal state $C \in \mathcal{C}$, and the perceptible actions it executes, $Y \in \mathcal{Y}$. We interpret the agent behavior as a discrete-time process $Z = \{Z_1, ..., Z_k, ...\}$ (which can be either deterministic or stochastic), with state space $\mathcal{I} = \mathcal{X} \times \mathcal{C} \times \mathcal{Y}$; $Z_t = (X_t, C_t, Y_t)$ is a variable that captures the state of the agent at time t.

The observed behavior of an agent in a particular execution defines a *trace*: $T = [(x_1, y_1), ..., (x_n, y_n)]$ where x_t and y_t represent the specific perception of the environment and action of the agent at time t. The pair of variables X_t and Y_t represents the *observation* of the agent A, i.e., $O_t = (X_t, Y_t)$. Thus, for simplicity, we can write a trace as $T = [o_1, ..., o_n]$. We assume that the random variables X_t and Y_t are multidimensional discrete variables. Under this statistical model, we distinguish three types of behaviors: type 1 (that includes strict imitation behavior) corresponding to a process that eventually depends on time (independent of previous states and actions); type 2 (reactive behavior) where Y_t eventually depends on time t, present state X_t and non-observable internal state C_t; type 3 (planned behavior) when the action Y_t eventually depends on time t, previous states $X_1, \ldots, X_t$ and actions $Y_1, \ldots, Y_{t-1}$, and non-observable internal state C_t. Note that we use *eventually* to include the case in which there is in fact no dependency.

When a behavior B does not explicitly depend on time, we say that it is a *stationary* behavior. Also, we distinguish between *deterministic* and *stochastic* behavior.

In this paper we model only stationary behaviors that do not explicitly depend on the internal state. We focus on behaviors of type 2 and 3, and we limit the "window" of knowledge in the case of planned behavior to one previous observation (the experiments can be easily extended to allow a more generous "memory", with the obvious drawback of an increased number of features). This gives rise to three possibilities for the current action Y_t:

- Y_t depends only on current state X_t (Model 1)
- Y_t depends on previous and current state: X_t, X_{t-1} (Model 2)
- Y_t depends on previous and current state: X_t, X_{t-1}, and on previous action Y_{t-1} (Model 3)

Note that the actual strategies of the agent may be of more complex types (see Sect. 4), but the cloned strategy is restricted to one of the three models presented above.

An example of the kind of information available for each of the three models in the training phase is presented in Fig. 1 (we assume the learning trace is $T = [(x_1, y_1), \ldots, (x_n, y_n)]$).

Model 1		Model 2			Model 3			

1st feat.	Class
x_1	y_1
x_2	y_2
...	...
x_n	y_n

1st feat.	2nd feat.	Class
—	x_1	y_1
x_1	x_2	y_2
...	...	...
x_{n-1}	x_n	y_n

1st feat.	2nd feat.	3rd feat.	Class
—	—	x_1	y_1
x_1	y_1	x_2	y_2
...	...	...	...
x_{n-1}	y_{n-1}	x_n	y_n

Fig. 1. Training examples for behavior cloning

3 Behavioral Cloning Algorithms for Reactive and Planned Behaviors

We describe in this section the kind of learning machines that we propose for modeling reactive and planned behaviors. Note that the only information we have is a trace with pairs (state, action): we do not know if the trace was produced by a deterministic or a stochastic agent, or whether it uses an internal state. But we would like to have a mechanism that predicts, in each state, the action to perform.

If the learned strategy is a deterministic one, this can be done via a classifier, using more or less features depending on the model (see Fig. 1). We experimented with a decision tree algorithm [15], a probabilistic neural network (PNN) [2], the k Nearest Neighbor (kNN) algorithm, the RProp algorithm for multilayer feedforward networks [13] and the Naïve Bayes (NB) algorithm.

On the other hand, if we want to train a stochastic model, the agent should be able to perform more than one action in a given state, and in order to achieve this we propose the use of probabilistic finite automata, which we describe below.

3.1 Probabilistic Finite Automata

A probabilistic finite automaton (PFA) has a finite alphabet of *symbols* Σ and a finite set of *states* Q. There is a transition probability function $\phi(q, a, q')$ with values in $[0, 1]$ defined on $Q \times \Sigma \times Q$, whose meaning is the probability of emission of symbol a while transitioning from state q to q'. This function must be a true probability for every $q \in Q$. We also need an initial probability value $\iota(q)$ for each state q, satisfying $\sum_{q \in Q} \iota(q) = 1$.

Then, the conditional probability of a symbol a given the state q, is

$$\mathbb{P}(a \mid q) = \sum_{q' \in Q} \phi(q, a, q')$$

We propose to train a PFA $\mathcal{A}$ to model an unknown behavior by observing its trace T. To this end, we define the alphabet Σ of automaton $\mathcal{A}$ to be the set of all actions $\mathcal{Y}$ that the agent can perform. The state space Q depends on the model: it is either $\mathcal{X}$ (Model 1), or $\mathcal{X} \times \mathcal{X}$ (Model 2) or $\mathcal{X} \times \mathcal{Y} \times \mathcal{X}$ (Model 3).

Training the automaton $\mathcal{A}$ from a trace $T = [(x_1, y_1), (x_2, y_2), \ldots, (x_n, y_n)]$ consists of determining the initial probability values $\{\iota(q) \mid q \in Q\}$ and the transition probability function values $\{\phi(q, a, q') \mid q, q' \in Q, a \in \Sigma\}$. For any state $q \in Q$, let $\sharp q$ be the number of occurrences of symbol q in trace T. Note that in the case of Model 1, $\sharp q = |\{i \in \overline{1, n} \mid x_i = q\}|$, for Model 2, if $q = (x, x')$, then $\sharp q = |\{i \in \overline{2, n} \mid x_{i-1} = x, x_i = x'\}|$, and for Model 3, if $q = (x, y, x')$, then $\sharp q = |\{i \in \overline{2, n} \mid x_{i-1} = x, y_{i-1} = y, x_i = x'\}|$. Similarly, we define $\sharp(q, a)$ and $\sharp(q, a, q')$ for $a \in \Sigma$ and $q, q' \in Q$ as follows.

Model 1: $q = x, a = y, q' = x'$
$\sharp(q, a) = |\{i \in \overline{1, n} \mid x_i = x, y_i = y\}|$
$\sharp(q, a, q') = |\{i \in \overline{1, n-1} \mid x_i = x, y_i = y, x_{i+1} = x'\}|$
Model 2: $q = (x'', x), a = y, q' = (x, x')$
$\sharp(q, a) = |\{i \in \overline{2, n} \mid x_{i-1} = x'', x_i = x, y_i = y\}|$
$\sharp(q, a, q') = |\{i \in \overline{2, n-1} \mid x_{i-1} = x'', x_i = x, x_{i+1} = x', y_i = y\}|$
Model 3: $q = (x'', y'', x), a = y, q' = (x, y, x')$
$\sharp(q, a) = |\{i \in \overline{2, n} \mid x_{i-1} = x'', x_i = x, y_{i-1} = y'', y_i = y\}|$
$\sharp(q, a, q') = |\{i \in \overline{2, n-1} \mid x_{i-1} = x'', x_i = x, x_{i+1} = x', y_{i-1} = y'', y_i = y\}|$

Note that in the case of Models 2 and 3, $\sharp(q, a, q')$ is zero by definition if the last element of state q is different than the first element of state q'. Next, we estimate the values of ι and ϕ with the following formulas.

$$\iota(q) := \frac{\sharp q + 1}{n + |Q|} \qquad \phi(q, a, q') := \frac{\sharp(q, a, q') + 1}{\sharp q + |Q| \times |\Sigma|}$$

We use Laplace smoothing to avoid zero values in the testing phase for elements that never appeared in training. It is easy to see that $\mathbb{P}(a \mid q)$ becomes $(\sharp(q, a) + |Q|)/(\sharp q + |Q| \times |\Sigma|)$, and this is precisely the probability of performing the action a when in state q.

3.2 Evaluation Metrics

We propose two methods for evaluating the performance of the cloning algorithms.

Predictive Accuracy. This is a standard measure for classification tasks. Let M be the model trained by one of the learning algorithms using the trace obtained by observing an agent A (that follows a certain strategy) on a fixed set of maps. This model can be either deterministic (in which case, there is only one possible action at any point in time) or stochastic (the action is chosen randomly according to some probability distribution).

Now, let $T = [(x_1, y_1), \ldots, (x_n, y_n)]$ be the trace of the agent A on a different previously unseen map. We denote by $M([x_{t-1}, y_{t-1},]x_t)$ the action predicted by the model M for the state x_t, possibly knowing previous state x_{t-1} and action y_{t-1}. If M is a stochastic model, $M([x_{t-1}, y_{t-1},]x_t)$ is a random variable over

$\mathcal{Y}$ with the probability distribution $\{\mathbb{P}(a|q)\}_{a \in \mathcal{Y}}$, where $q = x_t$ for Model 1, $q = (x_{t-1}, x_t)$ for Model 2 and $q = (x_{t-1}, y_{t-1}, x_t)$ for Model 3.

The predictive accuracy $Acc_M(T)$ is measured as follows:

$$Acc_M(T) = \frac{1}{n} \sum_{t \in \overline{1,n}} \sharp(M, T, t),$$

where $\sharp(M, T, t) = 1$ if $M([x_{t-1}, y_{t-1},]x_t) = y_t$ and 0 otherwise.

Monte Carlo Distance. To assess the quality with which a model M reproduces the behavior of an agent A we propose a Monte Carlo-like measure based on estimating the cross entropy between the probability distributions associated with both the model M and the agent A. We propose to estimate cross entropy from traces, for this reason it is a Monte Carlo estimation. More concretely, let $T = [o_1, \ldots, o_n]$ be a trace generated[2] according to model M on a fixed map (different than the one used in training), and let $S = [o'_1, \ldots, o'_m]$ be the trace generated by the agent on the same map. We define the Monte Carlo distance between model M and agent A as follows (estimated through traces T and S):

$$H(T, S) = -\frac{1}{n} \sum_{i=1}^{n} log \left[\frac{1}{m} \sum_{j=1}^{m} \mathbb{I}_{\{o'_j\}}(o_i) \right] \tag{1}$$

Here $\mathbb{I}_{\{o'_j\}}$ means the indicator function of set $\{o'_j\}$. Obviously the previous measure in Eq. (1) is empirical. It is assumed that for large enough traces it is closed to the true cross entropy between the behavior corresponding to model M and the behavior exhibited by agent A.

Using Laplace smoothing, the previous formula becomes:

$$H(T, S) = -\frac{1}{n} \sum_{i=1}^{n} log \left[\frac{\sum_{j=1}^{m} \mathbb{I}_{\{o'_j\}}(o_i) + 1}{m + |\mathcal{X} \times \mathcal{Y}|} \right] \tag{2}$$

4 Experiments

We have run our experiments with a simulator of a simplified version of a Roomba, which is a series of autonomous vacuum cleaners sold by iRobot[3]. The original Roomba vacuum cleaner uses a set of basic sensors that helps it perform tasks. For instance, it is able to change direction whenever it encounters an obstacle. It uses two independently operating wheels that allow 360 turns in

---

[2] The model predicts the next action, but the next state is given by the actual configuration of the map; in the case that it is impossible to perform a certain action because of an obstacle, the agent does not change its location.

[3] According to wikipedia, "iRobot Corporation is an American advanced technology company founded in 1990 and incorporated in Delaware in 2000. Roomba was introduced in 2002. As of Feb 2014, over 10 million units have been sold worldwide".

place. Additionally, it can adapt to perform other more creative tasks using an embedded computer in conjunction with the Roomba Open Interface.

In our implementation, the robot can only move Up, Down, Left and Right while there is no obstacle in front of it. Although it is possible for the agent to start anywhere, the traces we generate are always with the agent starting in the top-left corner of the map.

4.1 Training Maps

The environment in which the agent moves is a 40×60 rectangle surrounded by walls, which may contain all sorts of obstacles. For testing, we have randomly generated obstacles on an empty map. In the sequel, we briefly explain the six maps used in the training phase. Each of them is meant to represent a real-life situation, as indicated by their title (the list is by no means exhaustive) (Fig. 2).

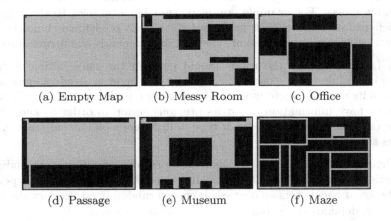

(a) Empty Map   (b) Messy Room   (c) Office

(d) Passage   (e) Museum   (f) Maze

Fig. 2. Training maps

Empty Map. The empty map consists of a big empty room with no obstacles.

Messy Room. The messy room simulates an untidy teenager bedroom, with all sorts of obstacles on the floor, and with a narrow entry corridor that makes the access to the room even more challenging for any "hostile intruder".

The Office. The office map simulates a space in which several rooms are connected to each other by small passages. In this case, obstacles are representing big furniture such as office desks or storage cabinets.

The Passage. The highlight of this map is an intricate pathway that leads to a small room. The main room is huge and does not have any obstacle in it.

The Museum. This map is intended to simulate a room from a museum, with the main sculpture in the center, and with several other sculptures on the four sides of the room, separated by small spaces.

The Maze. The most part of this map consists of narrow pathways with the same width as the agent. There is also a little room which is difficult to find.

4.2   Agent Strategies

We have designed a series of strategies with different complexities. When describing a strategy, we must define the behavior of the agent in a certain situation (which defines its state X_t) that depends on the configuration of obstacles in its vicinity (prefix **Rnd** is used for stochastic strategies).

Walk. The agent always performs the same movement in a given state. As an example, a possible strategy could be to go `Right` whenever there are no obstacles, and `Up` whenever there is only one obstacle to the right (stationary deterministic of type 2, it only depends on current state X_t).

Rnd_Walk. In this strategy, the next move is picked up randomly from the set of available moves. For example, an agent that has obstacles to the right and to the left can only move `Up` or `Down`, but there is no predefined choice between those two (stationary stochastic of type 2, it only depends on current state X_t).

Crash. In this strategy the robot should perform the same action as in the previous cell while there exists this possibility. Whenever it encounters a new obstacle in its way, the agent must choose a certain predefined action. Therefore, it needs to have information about its previous action in order to know where to move (stationary deterministic of type 3, it depends on current state X_t and previous action Y_t).

Rnd_Crash. This strategy is similar to the previous one: the agent maintains its direction while possible. The main difference is that the action to perform when the agent encounters an obstacle is chosen randomly (stationary stochastic of type 3, it depends on current state X_t and previous action Y_{t-1}).

ZigZag. It consists of different vertical movements in two possible directions, avoiding the obstacles. It has an internal state which tells the robot if it should advance towards the left or the right side with this vertical movements: it initially goes towards the right side, and once it reaches one of the right corners, the internal state changes so that the robot will start moving toward the left side (stationary deterministic of type 3, it depends on current state X_t, previous action Y_{t-1} and internal state C_t).

Rnd_ZigZag. This strategy is similar to the previous one, with the only difference that once it reaches a corner the internal state could either change its value or not, and this is randomly assigned (stationary stochastic of type 3, it depends on current state X_t, previous action Y_{t-1} and internal state C_t).

4.3   Evaluation

In our evaluation the simulation time is discrete, and at each time step, the vacuum cleaner can take one of these 5 actions: up, down, left, right and stand still, with their intuitive effect (if it tries to move into an obstacle, the effect is equivalent to the stand still action). So the control variable Y can take 5 different values: Up, Down, Left, Right, Stand. The vacuum cleaner perceives the world through the input variable X having 4 different binary components: up, down, left, right, each of them identifying whether the vacuum cleaner can see an obstacle in that direction.

Predictive Accuracy. For each pair map/strategy we have generated a trace of 1500 observations. In the training phase, we used, for each strategy, a single file obtained by concatenating the traces from the above mentioned six maps. Therefore, each machine was trained using 9000 observations coming from different types of maps. In the testing phase, for each of the three randomly generated maps and each of the six strategies, we generated traces of 1500 observations. The numbers in the following three tables represent average values of the predictive accuracy computed for each of those randomly generated maps. Note that the only stochastic model is the PFA.

Model 1	PFA	DT	PNN	KNN	RProp	NB
Walk	0.999	1.000	1.000	1.000	0.558	0.506
Rnd_Walk	0.282	0.318	0.318	0.316	0.298	0.291
Crash	0.530	0.532	0.532	0.532	0.514	0.295
Rnd_Crash	0.424	0.441	0.441	0.441	0.428	0.367
ZigZag	0.472	0.350	0.350	0.350	0.348	0.474
Rnd_ZigZag	0.483	0.494	0.494	0.494	0.470	0.477
Avg.	0.532	0.523	0.522	0.522	0.436	0.402

Model 2	PFA	DT	PNN	KNN	RProp	NB
Walk	0.363	0.502	0.005	0.006	0.502	0.005
Rnd_Walk	0.277	0.294	0.290	0.287	0.277	0.277
Crash	0.488	0.502	0.437	0.488	0.406	0.278
Rnd_Crash	0.431	0.395	0.389	0.395	0.361	0.372
ZigZag	0.558	0.492	0.489	0.484	0.482	0.481
Rnd_ZigZag	0.458	0.589	0.574	0.584	0.550	0.477
Avg.	0.439	0.462	0.364	0.374	0.430	0.315

Model 3	PFA	DT	PNN	KNN	RProp	NB
Walk	0.358	0.338	0.338	0.336	0.501	0.337
Rnd_Walk	0.282	0.304	0.293	0.287	0.293	0.289
Crash	0.716	0.701	0.635	0.645	0.626	0.480
Rnd_Crash	0.952	0.958	0.914	0.934	0.914	0.929
ZigZag	0.919	0.961	0.892	0.944	0.896	0.857
Rnd_ZigZag	0.909	0.956	0.890	0.944	0.894	0.855
Avg.	0.689	0.703	0.660	0.682	0.687	0.625

Analyzing the results, we can see that our hierarchy of models behaves as expected: type 3 behavior is very well captured by Model 3 (the one that uses information about both previous state and previous action), while type 2 behavior is better explained by Model 1 (in which we only take into account the current state). Note that even though intuitively, the more info we have, the best we can predict, in the case of type 2 behavior, using this extra information can do more harm than good. Another anticipated result that was experimentally confirmed is that Model 1 would be very good in predicting the **Walk** strategy, because the agent always performs the same action in a given state, and that **Rnd_Walk** would be the most unpredictable strategy of all (a notable exception is in the case of Model 2, for which, surprisingly, PNNs and KNNs have even worse accuracy for the **Walk** strategy).

It is noteworthy the high accuracy rates of Model 3 for **Rnd_Crash**, **ZigZag** and **Rnd_ZigZag**, all type 3 strategies. Also, this model gives somewhat lower, but still good enough, prediction rates for the **Crash** strategy.

If we were to chose a classifier, we would opt for DTs, which gives, with only one exception (Model 3, **Walk**), best results among deterministic models.

Using a PFA is, most of the times, either the best option, or very close to the best one, especially when predicting the behavior of more complex strategies. Note that PFAs are notably better for describing type 3 behaviors. Also, although intuitively a stochastic model should be better than a deterministic model in describing the behavior of a random process, in our experiments, this is not the case (PFAs outperform DTs mostly when learning deterministic strategies).

Monte Carlo Distance. In this case the models were trained with the same trace obtained by putting together the observations of the agent's behavior on the set of six maps described in Sect. 4.1 (therefore, each of them had 9000 observations). In order to compare the distance between the agents's behavior and the behavior of a given learned strategy, we used the same three randomly generated maps as before. For each of the classifiers (DT, PNN, KNN, RProp, NB) and for each of the six predefined strategies (**Walk**, **Rnd_Walk**, **Crash**, **Rnd_Crash**, **ZigZag**, **Rnd_ZigZag**), we generated the trace T produced by an agent whose next action is dictated by the classifier on each of the three randomly generated maps. On the other hand, we generated the trace S of each of the six predefined strategies on those three maps. In Fig. 3 we present the average of $H(T, S)$ for each pair classifier/strategy (see Eq. (2)). For stochastic models, the next action, instead of being predefined, is obtained by sampling according to the probability distribution given by the trained model.

Analyzing the results, we can see that PFAs are the best in cloning the agent's behavior for all six strategies, and that the deterministic approach only equals its performance for the **Walk** strategy. Also note that random behaviors are harder to reproduce than their deterministic counterparts.

	PFA	DT	PNN	KNN	RProp	NB
Walk	0.752	0.752	0.752	0.752	7.348	7.348
Rnd_Walk	4.562	7.027	7.027	7.027	7.315	7.315
Crash	1.441	3.877	3.877	3.877	7.348	7.348
Rnd_Crash	5.349	6.734	6.734	6.734	7.352	7.352
ZigZag	1.774	4.863	4.863	4.863	7.322	7.322
Rnd_ZigZag	1.796	6.926	6.926	6.926	7.325	7.325
Avg.	2.612	5.030	5.030	5.030	7.335	7.335

Fig. 3. Monte Carlo distance between original and cloned behavior

5   Conclusions and Future Work

We have proposed several models for behavioral cloning and two evaluation metrics. First, we used ML classifiers to predict the action of the agent in a given state (a deterministic model). Then, we trained a PFA to estimate the probabilities of the agent's actions in a given state (a stochastic model). In both cases, we measured the predictive accuracy on new unseen data: deterministic approaches turned out to give slightly better results, but the difference was negligible. Nevertheless, when comparing the trace of the learned strategy with the trace of the original agent on a randomly generated map, we could experimentally check that PFAs do a better job than any of the classifiers under study.

As future work, we plan to extend this methodology to a more realistic type of robot, which can perform rotations of different angles and whose position is represented by real values on the map. Also, the set of agent's strategies should be extended to include non-stationary type behaviors and other more sophisticated behaviors, such as the outward-moving spiral of the Roomba robot.

Finally, another future work direction is getting our models to deal with a greater fixed amount of memory, with the obvious computational limitation induced by our fully observable state space, which is directly proportional with the amount of memory required by the trained automaton. A possible solution is to deal with non-observable internal states using a few amount of them. Another possible approach is the use of some notion of context learning in order to reduce the number of possible states.

Acknowledgments. The authors gratefully acknowledge the financial support of project BASMATI (TIN2011-27479-C04-04) of Programa Nacional de Investigación and project PAC::LFO (MTM2014-55262-P) of Programa Estatal de Fomento de la Investigación Científica y Técnica de Excelencia, Ministerio de Ciencia e Innovación (MICINN), Spain.

References

1. Bauer, M.A.: Programming by examples. Artif. Intell. **12**(1), 1–21 (1979). http://dx.doi.org/10.1016/0004-3702(79)90002-X
2. Berthold, M.R., Diamond, J.: Constructive training of probabilistic neural networks. Neurocomputing **19**(1–3), 167–183 (1998). http://dx.doi.org/10.1016/S0925-2312(97)00063-5
3. Fernlund, H.K.G., Gonzalez, A.J., Georgiopoulos, M., DeMara, R.F.: Learning tactical human behavior through observation of human performance. IEEE Trans. Syst. Man Cybern. B **36**(1), 128–140 (2006). http://doi.ieeecomputer society.org/10.1109/TSMCB.2005.855568
4. Floyd, M.W., Esfandiari, B., Lam, K.: A case-based reasoning approach to imitating robocup players. In: Wilson, D., Lane, H.C. (eds.) Proceedings of the 21st International Florida Artificial Intelligence Research Society Conference, Coconut Grove, Florida, USA, pp. 251–256. AAAI Press, 15–17 May 2008. http://www.aaai.org/Library/FLAIRS/2008/flairs08-064.php
5. Gonzalez, A.J., Georgiopoulos, M., DeMara, R.F., Henninger, A., Gerber, W.: Automating the CGF model development and refinement process by observing expert behavior in a simulation. In: Proceedings of the 7th Conference on Computer Generated Forces and Behavioral Representation, May 12–14, 1998, Orlando, Florida, USA (1998)
6. Könik, T., Laird, J.E.: Learning goal hierarchies from structured observations and expert annotations. Mach. Learn. **64**(1–3), 263–287 (2006). http://dx.doi.org/10.1007/s10994-006-7734-8
7. Lozano-Pérez, T.: Robot programming. Proc. IEEE **71**(7), 821–841 (1983)
8. Michalski, R., Stepp, R.: Learning from observation: conceptual clustering. In: Michalski, R., Carbonell, J., Mitchell, T. (eds.) Machine Learning Symbolic Computation, pp. 331–363. Springer, Heidelberg (1983). http://dx.doi.org/10.1007/978-3-662-12405-5_11
9. Moriarty, C.L., Gonzalez, A.J.: Learning human behavior from observation for gaming applications. In: Lane, H.C., Guesgen, H.W. (eds.) Proceedings of the 22nd International Florida Artificial Intelligence Research Society Conference, Sanibel Island, Florida, USA. AAAI Press, 19–21 May 2009. http://aaai.org/ocs/index.php/FLAIRS/2009/paper/view/100
10. Ng, A.Y., Russell, S.J.: Algorithms for inverse reinforcement learning. In: Langley, P. (ed.) Proceedings of the 17th International Conference on Machine Learning, Stanford University, Stanford, CA, USA, pp. 663–670. Morgan Kaufmann, June 29–July 2, 2000
11. Ontañón, S., Mishra, K., Sugandh, N., Ram, A.: On-line case-based planning. Comput. Intell. **26**(1), 84–119 (2010). http://dx.doi.org/10.1111/j.1467-8640.2009.00344.x
12. Pomerleau, D.: ALVINN: an autonomous land vehicle in a neural network. In: Touretzky, D.S. (ed.) Advances in Neural Information Processing Systems 1 (NIPS 1998), pp. 305–313. Morgan Kaufmann (1988). http://papers.nips.cc/paper/95-alvinn-an-autonomous-land-vehicle-in-a-neural-network
13. Riedmiller, M., Braun, H.: A direct adaptive method for faster backpropagation learning: the RPROP algorithm. In: IEEE International Conference on Neural Networks, vol. 1, pp. 586–591, IEEE (1993). http://dx.doi.org/10.1109/icnn.1993.298623

14. Sammut, C., Hurst, S., Kedzier, D., Michie, D.: Learning to fly. In: Sleeman, D.H., Edwards, P. (eds.) Proceedings of the 9th International Workshop on Machine Learning, Aberdeen, Scotland, UK, pp. 385–393, Morgan Kaufmann, 1–3 July 1992
15. Shafer, J.C., Agrawal, R., Mehta, M.: SPRINT: a scalable parallel classifier for data mining. In: Vijayaraman, T.M., Buchmann, A.P., Mohan, C., Sarda, N.L. (eds.) Proceedings of 22th International Conference on Very Large Data Bases, Mumbai (Bombay), India, pp. 544–555, Morgan Kaufmann, 3–6 Sep 1996. http://www.vldb.org/conf/1996/P544.PDF
16. Sidani, T.: Automated machine learning from observation of simulation. Ph.D. thesis, University of Central Florida (1994)

Facing up Social Activity Recognition Using Smartphone Sensors

Pablo Curiel[✉], Ivan Pretel, and Ana B. Lago

Deusto Institute of Technology - DeustoTech,
MORElab – Envisioning Future Internet, University of Deusto,
Avda. Universidades 24, 48007 Bilbao, Spain
{pcuriel,ivan.pretel,anabelen.lago}@deusto.es

Abstract. In the last years context awareness has become a reality in real-world applications. However, building comprehensive context recognition systems which are able to recognize both low and high-level context information remains a challenge. In this paper, we discuss environment recognition as a means to address the issue of recognizing a high-level user context, social activity. In many countries, bars, pubs and similar establishments are one of the main places where social engagement takes place, and thus we propose recognizing these types of environments using data collected from mobile device sensors as a proxy for inferring social activity. For this purpose, we discuss the common defining characteristics of these establishments and the sensors we will use to recognize them. After that, we introduce the design of our system. Finally, we present the preliminary evaluation carried out to assess the validity of our proposal.

Keywords: Mobile sensing · Multimodal sensors · Environment recognition · Activity recognition · Context awareness

1 Introduction

The area of context recognition has greatly benefited from latest advances in mobile technologies. Early works which addressed the problem of recognizing user context relied in ad-hoc architectures for either equipping spaces with a sensing infrastructure or attaching sensors to human body [1,2]. However, current smartphones are equipped with a wide variety of sensors, like accelerometer, gyroscope, geomagnetic and luminosity sensors, microphone or GPS among others, thus becoming an ideal replacement for those early ad-hoc sensing stations.

In addition, smartphones are ubiquitous by nature, as they have become part of our daily lives and we carry them with ourselves everywhere and everytime. For this reason, context information is especially important in the mobile computing area, where user context, and thus their needs, change rapidly [10].

In fact, in the last years context awareness has become a reality in real-world applications [9]. In particular, usage of simple context information like location

© Springer International Publishing Switzerland 2015
J.M. García-Chamizo et al. (Eds.): UCAmI 2015, LNCS 9454, pp. 116–127, 2015.
DOI: 10.1007/978-3-319-26401-1_11

is moderately widespread in commercial applications like Foursquare, to suggest interesting venues nearby, or Twitter, to tell which topics are trending in each user's location. Google also makes extensive usage of user location for services like its search engine or in newer applications like Google Keep, which offers location-based reminders. More recently, more complex context recognition is gaining presence in everyday products. For instance, several physical activity tracking application and devices, which are popular nowadays, can distinguish a number of activities like walking, running, cycling or climbing stairs.

However, building comprehensive context recognition systems remains a challenge, as many complex or high-level activities do not always follow a clearly recognizable pattern that can be interpreted using low-level sensor data [6]. This is the case of many high-level user activities (e.g., cooking or reading) or user environment or surroundings (e.g., home, workplace, bar or public transport).

In this paper we address the issue of environment recognition as a means to tackle a high-level user activity: socialization. Detecting when users are engaged in social contexts would enable services like "social reminders". Products like coupon or discount applications targeted at groups or marketing campaigns aimed at attracting current clients' friends as new customers could also benefit from this knowledge, as they would be able to present promotions in the most appropriate moment. It could even enable healthcare related applications, like detection of potentially troublesome decreases in social interactions of a user. However, directly inferring a social interaction using smartphone sensors is not feasible. For this reason, in the present work we address this issue by means of environment recognition: detecting when a user is in a bar, pub, restaurant or a similar establishment. In many countries these kinds of establishments are one of the main places of social engagement and people of all ages gather there frequently, on weekly or even daily basis. Therefore, we consider recognizing these kinds of venues a useful proxy for social engagement recognition.

The remaining of this paper is structured as follows. The next section discusses related work in context and environment recognition. In Sect. 3 we present the data collection, processing and the feature extraction processes. Section 4 describes the evaluation carried out and the results obtained. Finally, in Sect. 5, conclusions and future work are exposed.

2   Related Work

One studied approach for recognizing the environment is using only audio information, what is known as computational auditory scene recognition.

For instance, Peltonen et al. [12] recorded audio samples in 26 different everyday scenes and studied the classification performance with several experimental configurations. They extracted 10 different features from those audio sequences and classified them using both k-Nearest Neighbours (k-NN) and Gaussian Mixture Models (GMM). Among the tested features, Band-energy and Mel-frequency cepstral coefficients (MFCC) proved to be the best for k-NN and GMM respectively. With the latter setup and audio sequences of 30 seconds they achieved an average recognition rate of 63.4 %. However, they also explored longer audio sequences, confirming that recognition rate increased accordingly. Besides, using kNN with Band-energy features they also tested more general environment classifications which showed better results (94.7 % recognition rate for Vehicle vs. Other contexts and 86.3 % for Indoor vs. Outdoors environments).

In [10], the authors also studied context inference based only on environmental noise. They recorded 3-second samples for 11 everyday contexts and classified them using a Hidden Markov Models (HMM). Similarly to Peltonen et al. they use MFCC as main features for recognition. They achieved a 92 % accuracy, with individual scenes ranging from 75 % to 100 %.

The SoundSense [8] framework proposes a mixture of supervised and unsupervised audio classification for real-time analysis of user context. It separates recognition in two steps: a general audio categorization into voice, music or ambient sound and a finer intra-category classification. For the general classification, a supervised learning approach is used, with a combination of a Decision Tree and a HMM, achieving over a 90 % of accuracy. For the intra-category classification, the authors propose an unsupervised and adaptive Bayesian classifier which is capable of identifying and learning previously undiscovered sounds. The preliminary evaluation of this algorithm showed disparate results, with perfect classification for some contexts, like Driving, and poor for others which have less representative sound signatures, like Bus riding.

Other approach for environment recognition is fusing data from different sensors.

Räsänen [14] et al. studied the combination of audio and acceleration features for classifying both user activities and environments. For this purpose, they captured around 22 h of 5 activities and 9 environments using mobile phones. They later trained two classifiers with both audio and acceleration data separately. Finally, they obtained combined outcomes from both using weighted linear models, repeating this process with varying weights (from a pure acceleration to a pure audio classifier). They concluded that, for activities, the combined classifier outperformed the separate ones, whereas for environments the former was not better than the pure audio classifier.

Following this research line, in [3] Han et al. also studied user context recognition building separate classifiers for audio and acceleration data collected from mobile phone sensors. However, instead of combining outcomes from both they suggest a hierarchical approach in which the audio classifier provides a more specific context classification depending on the output from the acceleration classifier. In the present work, in particular, the audio classifier is used for classifying the transportation mode when the acceleration classifier infers that the user is moving but is neither walking nor running. In addition, GPS and Wi-Fi signals are also used for refining the outcomes from the previous classifiers.

Finally, Parviainen et al. [11] present an algorithm for both activity and environment recognition using mobile sensor data fusion and with support for per-user adaptation. Apart from the most extended acceleration and audio features, they rely on data provided by GPS, WiFi, GSM Bluetooth interfaces. Their work focuses on exploring the benefits of adaptation for environment classification performance. For this purpose, they implemented an adaptation algorithm for a Bayesian maximum a posteriori classifier. Their results confirm this theory, as the precision of the classifier using the test set improves from a 50 % to a 68 % when adapting the trained classifier using the new data.

3   System Design

3.1   Sensors Used

For the task of deciding which data sources to use for recognizing bar-like establishments, we considered the main characteristics all of them share. In general, we can describe them as:

- Noisy places with continuous murmur, music playing or TV on, among other noises.
- People either sitting or standing, depending on the kind of establishment, but in either case in stationary positions.
- Low-light locations, specially low in the case of pubs, for instance, and less dark in others like restaurants. But in general they can be described as dimly and artificially lighted places.

Consequently, we will use audio, acceleration and luminosity as data sources for the recognition task.

3.2   Context Data Capturing

In order to train and test classification algorithms, we first need an annotated data set which contains a diverse list of both bar-like establishments and other non-bar environments. For this purpose, we developed an Android application which gathers the following data.

Audio Root Mean Square (RMS) Power and Decibels (dBs). From the microphone. In contrast to several existing works, which rely on more advanced features like MFCC, we considered audio power features more suitable for our work. One of our main objectives is achieving a generalizable model, which is able to correctly classify previously unseen environments. However, the strength of MFCC is identifying specific sounds, as it models the psychoacoustic properties of the human ear [10], and therefore it is best suited to recognize previously discovered sounds. As a matter of fact, previous works which have addressed environment recognition using MFCC and similar features, have reported that bar-like establishments where one of the most problematic cases [12].

3-axial Acceleration. From acceleration, gyroscope and geomagnetic sensors. In Android, the acceleration sensor provides values which combine both user and gravitiy acceleration. In addition, this acceleration values follow a device-coordinate system, which means that for the same real-world acceleration, values returned vary depending on the orientation of the phone. To solve these issues, we use the gyroscope to compute and subtract the gravitational component from the acceleration and the geomagnetic sensor to obtain the device orientation, with which this acceleration is transformed to the earth coordinate system.

Ambient Luminosity. From the luminosity sensor.

Screen Status. Provided by the Android framework. It will be later used for transforming the luminosity data, as described in Sect. 3.3.

The capture application was designed to record data as realistic as possible, minimizing the bias introduced due to the capture process itself. Hence, it needs minimal user interaction: starting the capture when desired, updating the current environment when it changes and stopping the capture. In addition, the data capture runs in a background service, and thus it does not interfere in the normal device operation.

To carry out a preliminary evaluation of our proposal, we captured 100 h of data using an LG Nexus 4 device and 20 h using an HTC Desire 816. Pursuing the aim of a generalizable model, these capture sessions consist of mostly non-repeated locations, with two exceptions to this rule. On the one hand, some contexts, like commuting, were captured more than once due to their shorter duration. On the other hand, capture sessions were repeated in some environments, like home, but in each of them the user activity varied. In any case, regarding bar-like establishments, all captured sessions correspond to different venues.

3.3   Data Processing

Once we capture the raw data using the Android application we must process it before it can be fed into the classification algorithms. First we carry out a data fusion process, in which data coming from the different sensors is combined at a constant and uniform sampling rate. Second, we make some transformations to improve the properties of the data for the classification task. Finally, we extract the final features that will be used in the classifiers. These tasks are performed using R language version 3.1.

Data Fusion. Not all sensors are capable of providing samples at the same rate, neither sampling times are synchronized for all of them. Besides, as the devices used for data capturing were used normally while this data gathering was running, some sensors suffered from occasional increases, delays or halts in their sampling rates. For this reason, this data fusion step is needed.

Following the 50 Hz sample rate used by default, we fuse data at this constant rate. Both when there are interruptions in sampling of any sensor or for the special case of the luminosity sensor, which works at a slower rate, linear interpolation is used to compute the missing values.

In addition, we also generated down-sampled versions of the fused data. Both sampling and processing sensor data at higher rates has a negative impact in battery life, so finding the best compromise between energy consumption and prediction accuracy is an important aspect. The selected additional sample rates were 20, 10, 5, 2 and 1 Hz.

Data Transformation. In this step we apply transformations to the raw data variables in order to both adapt them for the classification task characteristics and to generate new ones which may be better suited for the task.

As discussed in the previous section, acceleration is processed to generate both linear (with no gravity component) and earth-coordinate versions of it. In addition, these features are augmented with the acceleration vector norm.

Regarding audio variables, they are too noisy in their raw form, at least for higher sample rates. Thus, we also generated filtered versions of both RMS and DBs variables using a low pass filter.

Concerning luminosity, it exposes a remarkable issue. Due to normal operation of the mobile phone while data were captured, it was placed inside pockets for long periods, resulting in repeated zero values which do not correspond to the true luminosity of the environment. To tackle this problem, we process luminosity data and fill those zero values when the screen is turned off (we assume that if both conditions are satisfied then there are great chances that the device is inside the pocket) with the closest sample observed when the screen was turned on. Additionally, luminosity data follow a heavily skewed, long-tail distribution which can be tricky for some classifiers. Thus we also generated a log-transformed version of this variable which presents a more normalized shape.

Feature Extraction. The final step before feeding the data into a classifier is feature extraction. As it is common in the literature, we split data into window frames to compute these features.

In our case, as data capture sessions may involve more than one environment, we split the data into these groups first. When doing so, we discard data recorded both at the end of an environment and at the beginning of the next one using the confidence interval provided by the user. This way, we ensure that all data are correctly labelled.

Once data are grouped into environments, we perform the window splitting. For each window frame, we compute the mean, median, standard deviation, minimum and maximum values of all the variables. These aggregated measures make up our features for the classification task.

Regarding window frame sizes, intuitively we can tell that they must be big enough for capturing the characteristics of the environment instead of being confused by short duration events. Hence, we generated different window-sized versions of the data in order to search for the best size. Selected window sizes where 10, 30, 60, 90, 120, 180, 240 and 360 seconds.

4   Evaluation

The first step before building any classifier is splitting the collected data into training and test sets. We split the 100 h captured with the Nexus 4 into 70 h for training and 30 for testing. The 20 h of data captured with the Desire were dedicated to the test set, in order to evaluate how well the classifiers are able to generalize to different users and devices. Regarding classifier training, we used 10×5-fold cross validation.

As we have discussed in the previous section, there are several configuration parameters to study: the best features to use, the most suitable window sizes and the classifier performance decay with decreasing sensor sampling rates. Additionally, we trained four different classifiers for a more thorough comparison: a random forest, a support vector machine (SVM) using a Gaussian radial basis function kernel, k-Nearest Neighbours (k-NN) and a Naive Bayes classifier. For the remaining of this section, where not explicitly denoted different measures, when talking about comparisons between parameters or models, recall, specificity, area under the ROC curve (AUC) and accuracy are being considered.

For all these evaluation tasks we used R in its 3.1 version. For training and testing classifiers we used the caret [5] package (version 6.0-41), and more specifically, the randomForest [7] package (version 4.6-7) for using random forests, kernlab [4] (version 0.9-20) for the SVM, the R built-in class package for k-NN and klaR [15] package (version 0.6-12) for the Naive Bayes classifier. And to test the statistical significance of the different comparisons, we used the Friedman Rank Sum Test from the R built-in stats package and the Nemenyi post-hoc test from the PMCMR [13] package (version 1.1).

4.1   Feature Comparison

The aim of this comparison is finding out which features contribute most to the recognition task, that is, which have the most discriminating power, as well as evaluating whether the proposed data transformations help in improving classifiers' accuracy. These comparisons where made for all models and window sizes.

Acceleration Features Comparison. With acceleration features we compared two aspects: if adding the vector norm was useful and if either linear or earth-acceleration lead to better results than base acceleration.

In general, vector norm can be a useful feature to add to the 3-axis acceleration. For random forest, SVM and k-NN, it leads to better classification results for the three types of acceleration. However, improvement is in general subtle (around 1 % on average for all window sizes) and not always statistically significant. For Naive Bayes, vector norm also contributes to better results for base acceleration. However, for linear and earth-acceleration it shows no improvement.

Regarding the comparison of the three types of acceleration, there are more disparate results. For all classifiers and window sizes, there is no significant difference between linear and earth acceleration. Comparing base acceleration to the transformed ones, both random forest and SVM show statistically significant better results (up to a 4 % better) with the latter. Naive Bayes also improves (up to a 4 % too) with earth acceleration, though differences are only partially significant (for some window sizes). Finally, k-NN does show a slight improvement for both transformed acceleration types, but only significant for the recall measure.

Audio Features Comparison. With audio features we also compared two aspects: whether either of the feature types (RMS and dBs) outperformed the other and if the noise reduction filter is better than the unfiltered version.

Comparing the two feature types, dBs are significantly better than RMS except for the random forest, which shows no difference between both. This improvement ranges from a 4 to a 9 % in the case of the SVM, from 6 to 15 % for k-NN and from 2 to 8 % for Naive Bayes.

In the case of the filtering, differences are less noticeable. Except for k-NN, in which RMS works better with the unfiltered version, the filtered feature leads to better results that its unfiltered counterpart. However, this difference is, in general, only partially significant.

Luminosity Features Comparison. With luminosity features we studied whether the two transformations applied are useful.

First, the log transformation of the luminosity variable does not lead to significant improvement in the classifier performance. Both the random forest and k-NN show no difference, while for SVM and Naive Bayes there is a subtle improvement (up to a 2 %), yet only partially significant.

Comparing the fixed to the raw version leads to similar conclusions. Neither the forest nor k-NN show differences between them, while SVM and Naive Bayes experiment a small and partially significant improvement of up to a 2 %.

However, combining both transformations we get a slightly bigger improvement. While for k-NN, once again, there is no gain, random forest shows a small improvement (up to a 1 %, yet no statistically significant) and SVM improves up to a significant 3 %. Finally Naive Bayes shows up to a 3 % decline in recall, which is compensated with a noticeable increase of up to an 11 % in specificity.

Contribution of Each Sensor. The last step in feature comparison is studying the contribution of the features extracted from each sensor to the classifier performance. This was done training the classifiers with the best performing feature of each sensor as concluded in the previous comparisons. Then, extra classifiers where trained excluding in each of them one of the feature types. The results are the following.

Audio features are the ones which contribute most to the classifiers. The decline in performance without it for the four classifiers ranges from a significant 15 % to a 20 %. Acceleration features are less important, but nevertheless their contribution ranges from a significant 1 % to a 10 %. In contrast, luminosity features are only useful for SVM and Naive Bayes, with partially significant improvements up to 3 % and 8 % respectively.

4.2   Window Size Comparison

Once the best performing features for each model had been selected, we used them to make window comparisons.

Regarding window sizes, even though the best performing one varies for each classifier, a common pattern can be seen. First, as it was expected, smaller window sizes show worse results than larger ones, as they have greater risk of capturing short duration events rather than general characteristics of each environment. However, this performance decline is only statistically significant for windows of 10 and 30 seconds.

Considering each classifier independently, random forest shows the best performance for 240-second windows. However, average performance loss for smaller windows like 120 or 90-second ones is around a 2%. In the case of the SVM, the best performing window is of 120 seconds. However, even 60-second windows are competitive with this classifier, with less than a 2% performance decline on average. The k-NN classifier works best with 180-second windows, yet the mean loss with 60-second ones is less than a 2%. In fact, this is the only classifier of the four tested which shows competitive results with windows of 10 seconds, with an average decline of 3%. Finally, Naive Bayes stands out with 240-second windows, but suffers from a mean loss of less than a 2% for 120-second windows.

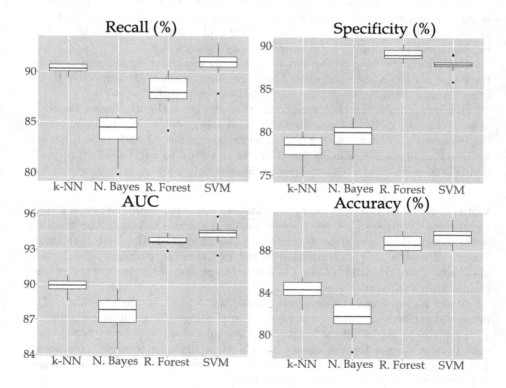

Fig. 1. Comparison of the four different classifiers

4.3 Classifier Comparison

Having selected both the best performing features and the best window sizes, we can compare how well each classifier performs the recognition task. In Fig. 1, performance measures obtained from the cross validation repetitions for the four discussed models are presented. As it can be observed, the best performing classifier is SVM, which outperforms the others in recall, AUC and accuracy. However, differences in performance with random forest, which even beats SVM in specificity, are small and not statistically significant. The other two classifiers offer an acceptable yet significantly worse performance, except for recall, where k-NN has a solid performance.

4.4 Sample Rate Comparison

Lastly, we studied how decreasing the sampling rate of the sensors impacts classifier performance. As expected, smaller window sizes suffer more than bigger ones when this parameter is decreased. However, even for the smallest windows, dropping the sample rate to 10 Hz results in a non-significant performance drop of around a 1 %. Smaller sampling rates begin to show statistically significant declines, but for moderate-sized windows like 90 seconds even a 1 Hz sampling rate shows a performance loss of less than a 4 %.

4.5 Test Set Results

After studying the best performing configuration, we selected the SVM with linear acceleration, filtered dBs and log-transformed fixed luminosity as the best

Table 1. Nexus 4 Test Results Confusion Matrix (in percentages)

	Bar	Pub	Café	Sports bar	Disco	Restaurant		
Bar	97	37	99	91	91	93		
Other	3	63	1	9	9	7		
Bar	1	5	0	73	48	26	15	9
Other	99	95	100	27	52	74	85	91
	Walk	Home	Work	Wait	Train	Road	Shop	Museum

Table 2. HTC Desire 816 Test Results Confusion Matrix (in percentages)

	Bar	Café	Sports bar	Disco	Restaurant		
Bar	93	6	4	52	15		
Other	7	94	96	48	85		
Bar	1	0	0	2	1	27	2
Other	99	100	100	98	99	73	98
	Walk	Home	Work	Wait	Train	Road	Shop

classifier, which achieves average results in cross-validation of 91 % recall, 87.9 % specificity, an AUC of 0.94 and 89.4 % accuracy. Next, the results obtained fitting this classifier to the test data split in 120-second windows are detailed.

With the test data captured with the Nexus 4 (whose confusion matrix can be observed in Table 1) we obtained a 93.8 % recall, a 90.6 % specificity, an AUC of 0.98 and a 92.2 % accuracy, which are remarkable results. However, with the second test set results are much less satisfactory, as while achieving an specificity of 98 %, recall and accuracy drop to a 21.8 % and 60 % respectively. The reason for these results is that, as it can be observed in Table 2, the classifier is failing to detect most bar-like environments, while it successfully classifies almost all other environments. In fact, only "Bar" establishments are successfully classified.

Given the disappointing results with this second test set, we tried training the classifier with this second test dataset to evaluate its performance using cross-validation. In this case, results were much more satisfactory, even better than the ones achieved with the training data of the Nexus 4, with a 87 % recall, a 96.8 % specificity, an AUC of 0.97 and a 92 % accuracy.

All these results suggest that the proposed system, once trained with enough data, is at least capable of generalizing to new environments captured by the same user and device. However, results with the second dataset raise the question of whether it would be capable of generalizing also to new users and devices. Thus, carrying out a more comprehensive data collection campaign, involving more users and devices must be the next step to follow.

5   Conclusion

In the present article we have introduced an environment recognition system using smartphone sensors. In particular, as a means to address the recognition of a high-level context like the user being involved in social activities, we have proposed a classifier for bars, pubs and similar establishments, which are a common place for social engagement in many countries.

With the aim of building a classifier which generalizes well enough to correctly recognize previously unvisited venues, we have discussed the sensors used for data gathering and the features extracted from them as well as the data collection process. The preliminary results obtained seem promising regarding the recognition of new locations for the same user. However, generalization to new users seems to be more troublesome.

Thus, future work will involve a new data collection campaign which involves more users in order to better study these aspects. Another path to explore in search for better recognition results is classification with separate classes for each type of bar-like establishment of interest, as this could potentially enable to better capture the particular characteristics each of these environments has.

References

1. Bao, L., Intille, S.S.: Activity recognition from user-annotated acceleration data. In: Ferscha, A., Mattern, F. (eds.) PERVASIVE 2004. LNCS, vol. 3001, pp. 1–17. Springer, Heidelberg (2004)
2. Choudhury, T., Consolvo, S., Harrison, B., Hightower, J., Lamarca, A., Legrand, L., Rahimi, A., Rea, A., Bordello, G., Hemingway, B., Klasnja, P., Koscher, K., Landay, J., Lester, J., Wyatt, D., Haehnel, D.: The mobile sensing platform: an embedded activity recognition system. IEEE Pervasive Comput. **7**(2), 32–41 (2008)
3. Han, M., Vinh, L.T., Lee, Y.K., Lee, S.: Comprehensive context recognizer based on multimodal sensors in a smartphone. Sensors 12(9), 12588 (2012). http://www.mdpi.com/1424-8220/12/9/12588
4. Karatzoglou, A., Smola, A., Hornik, K., Zeileis, A.: kernlab - an S4 package for kernel methods in R. J. Stat. Softw. 11(9), 1–20 (2004). http://www.jstatsoft.org/v11/i09/
5. Kuhn, M., Wing, J., Weston, S., Williams, A., Keefer, C., Engelhardt, A., Cooper, T., Mayer, Z., Kenkel, B., The R Core Team, Benesty, M., Lescarbeau, R., Ziem, A., Scrucca., L.: caret: Classification and regression training (2015). http://CRAN.R-project.org/package=caret, R package version 6.0-41
6. Lane, N., Miluzzo, E., Lu, H., Peebles, D., Choudhury, T., Campbell, A.: A survey of mobile phone sensing. IEEE Commun. Mag. **48**(9), 140–150 (2010)
7. Liaw, A., Wiener, M.: Classification and regression by randomforest. R News 2(3), 18–22 (2002). http://CRAN.R-project.org/doc/Rnews/
8. Lu, H., Pan, W., Lane, N.D., Choudhury, T., Campbell, A.T.: Soundsense: Scalable sound sensing for people-centric applications on mobile phones. In: Proceedings of the 7th International Conference on Mobile Systems, Applications, and Services, MobiSys 2009, pp. 165–178. ACM, New York (2009). http://doi.acm.org/10.1145/1555816.1555834
9. Lukowicz, P., Pentland, A.S., Ferscha, A.: From context awareness to socially aware computing. IEEE Pervasive Comput. **11**(1), 32–41 (2012)
10. Ma, L., Smith, D., Milner, B.: Environmental noise classification for context-aware applications. In: Mařík, V., Štěpánková, O., Retschitzegger, W. (eds.) DEXA 2003. LNCS, vol. 2736, pp. 360–370. Springer, Heidelberg (2003)
11. Parviainen, J., Bojja, J., Collin, J., Leppnen, J., Eronen, A.: Adaptive activity and environment recognition for mobile phones. Sensors 14(11), 20753 (2014). http://www.mdpi.com/1424-8220/14/11/20753
12. Peltonen, V., Tuomi, J., Klapuri, A., Huopaniemi, J., Sorsa, T.: Computational auditory scene recognition. In: IEEE International Conference on Acoustics, Speech, and Signal Processing (ICASSP) 2002, vol. 2, pp. 1941–1944. IEEE (2002)
13. Pohlert, T.: PMCMR: Calculate Pairwise Multiple Comparisons of Mean Rank Sums (2015). http://CRAN.R-project.org/package=PMCMR, R package version 1.1
14. Räsänen, O., Leppänen, J., Laine, U.K., Saarinen, J.P.: Comparison of classifiers in audio and acceleration based context classification in mobile phones. In: 19th European Signal Processing Conference, EUSIPCO 2011, Barcelona, Spain, pp. 946–950, August 2011. http://www.eurasip.org/Proceedings/Eusipco/Eusipco2011/papers/1569422049.pdf
15. Weihs, C., Ligges, U., Luebke, K., Raabe, N.: klaR analyzing german business cycles. In: Baier, D., Decker, R., Schmidt-Thieme, L. (eds.) Data Analysis and Decision Support, pp. 335–343. Springer-Verlag, Heidelberg (2005)

RBox: An Experimentation Tool
for Creating Event-Driven
Recommender Algorithms for Web 2.0

Edmundo P. Leiva-Lobos[(⊠)] and Michael Palomino[(⊠)]

Departamento de Ingeniería Informática,
Universidad de Santiago de Chile, Santiago, Chile
{edmundo.leiva,michael.palomino}@usach.cl

Abstract. This article introduces a software environment called RBox, built to experiment with recommender systems (RS), regardless of the application domain. In spite of the ubiquity of RS on the Web 2.0 this research field still lacks a unique way of representing collective intelligence. To solve this problem, this article adopts a generic event-driven approach providing a unique RBox data schema. Thus, it is possible to achieve the abstraction of collaborative events that occur on Web 2.0 such as *ranking, tagging* and *voting*. A comparison with other tools illustrates the contribution of RBox to the RS field. For instance, this tool enables reusing algorithms and executing experiments that were originally intended for a specific application domain, for other ones. Finally, considering RS tools' limitations, the next versions of RBox will integrate ubiquitous computing and context-aware recommender systems .

Keywords: Recommender systems · Event-driven approach · Experimentality · Ubiquity

1 Introduction

The aim of ubiquitous computing is to build personalized applications based on the context surrounding users in order to support everyday activities. However, an obstacle to achieving this goal is Web's information overload. This causes high cognitive load for the users; especially when they look for topics of their interest [11]. Recommender systems (RS) rose in order for responding to this challenge. This research field still lacks a unique way to represent collective intelligence and standardization for experimenting with its algorithms [4, 13]. In fact, there is no tool available for researchers in this RS field to define and test algorithms independently from the recommendation domain. In recent years, however, there has been progress in achieving the integration of this collective intelligence, represented by progress in developing tools and frameworks. In this scenario, this paper proposes RBox as a higher alternative.

2 Related Works

Over the last few years, there have been few tools or frameworks aimed at creating or researching recommendation algorithms, and likewise, others that have contributed, such as IDEs that can generate code or components like RBox does. In short, RBox is

© Springer International Publishing Switzerland 2015
J.M. García-Chamizo et al. (Eds.): UCAmI 2015, LNCS 9454, pp. 128–133, 2015.
DOI: 10.1007/978-3-319-26401-1_12

software for creating recommender algorithms for web 2.0 based on an event-driven approach.

We have compared twelve tools: (1) C/Matlab Toolkit [9]; (2) Weka[1] that contains a popular algorithm collection of automatic learning machines; Apache Mahout project[2] provides an open source platform for systems with collaborative filtering recommendation; (3) RACOFI [10]; platform for multidimensional recommendation scores based on collaborative filtering; (4) SDVFeature[3] recommendation systems with collaborative filtering based on matrix factorization; (5) Crab[4], as a Python framework to build recommendation engines based on collaborative filtering to be integrated with scientists Python packages; (6) SUGGEST[5] builds recommendation systems in production environments but without experimentation characteristics; (7) EasyRec[6], which provides only a service to be used in Web applications; (8) RecommenderLab, [8] which is a framework for developing and testing algorithms aimed toward ecommerce, highly dependent on context; (9) MyMediaLite [6], which is a library of APIs to experiment and use algorithms based on common scenarios recommendation; (10) LensKit [5] is a platform to investigate recommender systems based on collaborative filtering; (11) AIBench [7] is a IDE and framework that speeds up coding, implementation, testing and optimization techniques of Artificial Intelligence.

Special mention is given to the twelfth tool: Synergy [14]. It proposes a scheme of data to work with generic collaborative filtering RS. Its key is to change the matricial or tensorial representation of the data used by most algorithms currently in use, replacing them with events such as tagging content, expressing opinions, and voting, among others. In general, none of these 12 tools is able to generate components that can be reused in other systems in a plug-in format as does RBox.

3 RBox Basics

The field of recommender systems has experienced dramatic growth [1, 4], mainly due to the worldwide increase of social networks and electronic commerce which are the basis of this kind of system. This has led to research, development and implementation of specific algorithms to rescue collective intelligence [3] from specific domains to provide recommendations in those contexts.

As a result, two direct consequences have been detected. The first is that, due to the diversity of domains, datasets belonging to each of them have specific representations. Transitively, the second consequence is that, given this diversity of data representation schemes, there is no tool available to researchers in this area to define and test algorithms independently from their recommendation domain of origin. In recent years,

---

[1] http://www.cs.waikato.ac.nz/ml/weka/.

[2] http://mahout.apache.org/.

[3] http://mloss.org/software/view/333/.

[4] http://muricoca.github.com/crab/.

[5] http://glaros.dtc.umn.edu/gkhome/suggest/overview/.

[6] http://easyrec.org/.

however, there has been progress with regard to achieving the integration of this collective intelligence, which in practice has meant progress in developing tools and frameworks.

3.1 Design Issues

RBox it is a desktop application for researcher users, which allows them to test and compare the results of different algorithms for collaborative filtering recommendation in an investigative process, enabling: population of the dataset for experimentation, defining algorithms, algorithm parameterization, running tests, releases of plug-ins with algorithms and associated settings. Moreover, RBox is designed under the concept of plug-in [12] using the java.util.ServiceLoader class included in Java 6.0. Under this model, RBox defines the software parts that allow users to define both the algorithms and precision metrics used at runtime as interchangeable components used in the experiments. Using this scheme, RBox can define three key issues in RS research. First, it can define similarity algorithms, to compare the proximity of elements (e.g. users or items) and then generate a list to recommend. Second, it can define recommendation algorithms themselves. Finally, it can design evaluation metrics which allow users to evaluate recommendation algorithms by means of error metrics and metric classification. For the first group, algorithms are required to works with a type of event that has an associated numerical value (rating). The second group is more generic. Experimenters must implement the metric type that they need according to the algorithm that will be evaluated.

To allow the operation of the algorithms regardless of data domains, a Generic data model is used, which is event-driven [14] and allows data mapping from the original data sets.

3.2 Generic Data Model

Even-driven approach in RBox means that interactions are associated with a value depending on the type of event concerned, as does Synergy [14]. In the case of collaborative tagging, it is the tag itself. In the case of valuation, it is an integer that indicates the degree of acceptance of the item reviewed by the user. This arises after having seen that interaction among users and content can be varied, and after realizing that there is not one way to generically evaluate different recommendation algorithms for a specific context. Thus, treating all interactions similarly removes dependencies from any specific interaction dimension. In this model (Fig. 1), it is represented as the set of users U; C is the set of items; I is the set of possible interactions (types of interaction); E is the set of events; and V is the vector of values associated with an interaction. Using elementary set theory:

$$U = \{u_1, u_2, \ldots u_n\} \quad E = \{(s, p, o, t) \mid s \text{ in } U, p \text{ in } I, o \text{ in } C, t \text{ is time}\}$$
$$C = \{c_1, c_2, \ldots c_m\} \quad I = \{i_1, i_2, \ldots i_n\} \quad V = \{(e, a) \mid e \in E, a \text{ is some value}\}$$

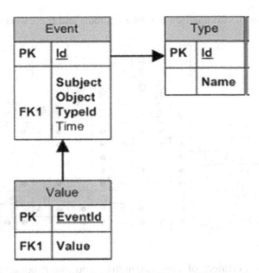

Fig. 1. ERD of data model (Source: [14], p. 4)

Each event is generated by a user or Subject. Item or object (Objects) recommendations are provided for the Subject. Each event is of some type, and the type of event identifies the type of interaction between the subject and the object. Besides, the interaction generates some value, so the event is associated with one or more values. For example, by giving a value to a film (rating) the event would have a numerical value within a range of values (e.g., 0–1, 1–3, 1–5).

4 Comparing RBox

Eight criteria have been established for benchmarking different tools reviewed with RBox. They characterize solutions to the problems of domain diversity and lack of research environments for the experimentation in RS. Table 1 summarizes this.

The criteria are: (1) Domain mappability is the ability of the tool to transform recommendation algorithms that are located in a specific domain and map them into a different one (e.g. from book to movies), (2) Experimentability is the feature that allows the tool to be used to evaluate and experiment with different algorithms by means of running tests. Through the results of these tests, it is possible to evaluate and compare them, (3) Maintainability refers to how easily the software is corrected if there are flaws or is extended to include it new features. Generally, this criterion should be supported by well-known design patterns, by the use of frameworks and well- documented standard programming languages; (4) Flexibility (or extensibility) allows the use of various algorithms of recommendation, even if new attributes or characteristics of the user interaction with the items are included; (5) Configurability means adapting the operation of the software through its parameters, thus, different algorithms can be configured according to its particular need, given the criteria of the researcher; (6) Recommender as outcome is able of generating components plug-ins, so, it can be

Table 1. Comparison between RS tools and frameworks.

	Rbox	Synergy	Apache Mahout	LensKit	MyMedia Lite	RecommenderLab	C/Matlab Toolkit	Crab	EasyRec	RACOFI	SUGGEST	SDVfeature	Weka	AIBench
Mappability between domains	●	●	●	●	●		●	●	●		●	●	●	
Experimentability	●	●		●	●		●	●					●	●
Maintainability	●			●	●								●	●
Flexibility/Extensionabilty	●		●	●	●								●	●
Configurability	●			●	●			●		●		●		
Recommender as outcome	●													
OpenSource	●		●	●	●	●	●	●				●	●	●
Recommendation-oriented	●	●	●	●	●	●			●	●	●			

re-used both in an environment of experimentation and in a production environment in real time; (7) Open Source means that the software code is available under open source agreements; (8) Recommendation-oriented the tools are restricted to the construction of recommender algorithms, instead of being a tool for general purpose.

The reader may note that mappability between domains applies for most of the tools. However, except for RBox, in these cases, "mappability" is reached via programming effort through API or frameworks without guidance. On the other hand, in the case of RBox, there is a standardized way of mapping via a mapper. This component gathers data from a social network through a crawling process which is translated to the unique event schema used by RBox. With this scheme, the user interactions are managed as a generic event, enabling evaluating algorithms independent of domain.

5   Conclusions and Future Work

RBox puts forward an approach that makes a significant leap towards the aggregation of RS domains that are usually scattered. This way, users are able to reuse recommendation algorithms from different domains, experiment with new algorithms and generate a plug and play version of these algorithms to be built-in real domains. Thus, RBox users can focus their time and effort mainly on research, being relieved of creating specific algorithms for particular domains. However, the new generation of recommender systems, so-called Context Aware Recommenders [2] require further awareness or contextual information that is not provided by the current version of RBox. In fact, ubiquitousness requires more adaptive and personalized recommendations. Nowadays, recent researchers are combining ubiquitous computing and recommender systems in the so-called ubiquitous recommendation systems [11], which will be the aim of the new version of RBox.

Acknowledgements. This work was supported by the National Science and Technology Commission of Chile FONDEF project called "Observatorios Escalables de la Web en Tiempo Real" [D09I1185], between 2011–2013.

References

1. Adomavicius, G., Tuzhilin, A.: Toward the next generation of recommender systems: a survey of the state-of-the-art and possible extensions. IEEE Trans. Knowl. Data Eng. **17**, 734–749 (2005)
2. Adomavicius, G., Tuzhilin, A.: Context-aware recommender systems. In: Ricci, F., Rokach, L., Shapira, B., Kantor, P.B. (eds.) Recommender Systems Handbook, pp. 217–253. Springer, New York (2011)
3. Alag, S.: Collective Intelligence in Action. Manning Publications Co., Greenwich (2008)
4. Candillier, L., Jack, K., Fessant, F., Meyer, F.: State-of-the-art recommender systems. In: Collaborative and Social Information Retrieval and Access: Techniques for Improved User Modeling, pp. 1–23. IGI Global (2009)
5. Ekstrand, M.D., Ludwig, M., Konstan, J.A., Riedl, J.T.: Rethinking the recommender research ecosystem: reproducibility, openness, and LensKit. In: Proceedings of the Fifth ACM Conference on Recommender Systems, pp. 133–140. ACM, Chicago (2011)
6. Gantner, Z., Rendle, S., Freudenthaler, C., Schmidt-Thieme, L.: MyMediaLite: a free recommender system library. In: Proceedings of the Fifth ACM Conference on Recommender Systems, pp. 305–308. ACM, Chicago (2011)
7. Glez-Peña, D., Reboiro-Jato, M., Maia, P., Rocha, M., Díaz, F., Fdez-Riverola, F.: AIBench: a rapid application development framework for translational research in biomedicine. Comput. Methods Prog. Biomed. **98**, 191–203 (2010)
8. Hahsler, M.: Recommenderlab: A Framework for Developing and Testing Recommendation Algorithms (2011)
9. Lebanon, G.: C/Matlab Toolkit for Collaborative Filtering. http://www.cs.cmu.edu/~lebanon/IR-lab.htm
10. Marcel, M.A., Ball, M., Boley, H., Greene, S., Howse, N., Lemire, D., McGrath, S.: RACOFI: A Rule-Applying Collaborative Filtering System (2003)
11. Mettouris, C., Papadopoulos, G.: Ubiquitous recommender systems. Computing **96**, 223–257 (2014)
12. O'Conner, J.: Creating Extensible Applications With the Java Platform. http://www.oracle.com/technetwork/articles/javase/index-140417.html
13. Ricci, F., Rokach, L., Shapira, B.: Introduction to recommender systems handbook. In: Ricci, F., Rokach, L., Shapira, B., Kantor, P.B. (eds.) Recommender Systems Handbook, pp. 1–35. Springer, New York (2011)
14. Tareen, B., Lee, J., Lee, S.: Synergy: a workbench for collaborative filtering algorithms on user interaction data. In: International Workshop on User Data Interoperability in the Social Web (2010)

Supporting Smart Community Decision Making for Self-governance with Multiple Views

Gustavo Zurita[1], José A. Pino[2], and Nelson Baloian[2(✉)]

[1] Management Control and Information Systems Department,
Universidad de Chile, Santiago, Chile
gzurita@fen.uchile.cl
[2] Computer Science Department, Universidad de Chile, Santiago, Chile
{jpino,nbaloian}@dcc.uchile.cl

Abstract. Size and evolution of current cities present a great challenge to their inhabitants to make them develop in a harmonious and sustainable way. People living in large cities find many obstacles to participate in the urban development decisions affecting them directly. A tool which supports citizens in gathering, combining and visualizing the information, as well as proposing, discussing and selecting the best ideas for urban improvement would certainly help them to accomplish this task, thus contributing to the development of a more participatory society and a smarter city with better reaction capabilities to changes in the environment. In this work we present a smart city application, intended for citizens living in an urban community enabling them to present and share their opinions, comments and interests. The application also should support citizens to make decisions. Those decisions should influence local authorities concerning community improvements. The application may be used with any subject relevant to an urban community and thus, it could be useful in many scenarios of citizens' participation and decision making. It includes multiple views: time-based, spatial and relational.

Keywords: Smart city · Smart community · Multiple views

1 Introduction

According to the United Nations [1], over the last year the balance between those living in urban areas and those living in rural areas tipped irrevocably over to the urban side. Size and evolution of current cities present a great challenge to their inhabitants to make them develop in a harmonious and sustainable way. An instance in Chile is presented in [35]: a 2012 law establishes several constraints to the installation of new telecommunication antennas by mobile phones service providers. Some of these constraints concern the minimum distance allowed from the new antenna to previous antennas, hospitals and schools. Moreover, the law forces the company which is installing the antenna to propose and finance some works to improve the urban environment of the area where the antenna is to be located, which is defined by a circle with a 500 m. diameter and centered at the place where the antenna is going to be located.

© Springer International Publishing Switzerland 2015
J.M. García-Chamizo et al. (Eds.): UCAmI 2015, LNCS 9454, pp. 134–143, 2015.
DOI: 10.1007/978-3-319-26401-1_13

These urban improvement works should be approved by the people living in the area, who have the possibility of analyzing the project and raising concerns during certain time frame after the project is proposed, typically 30 days. In order to be able to properly react in such a short time, it is highly recommendable that people use Information Technology (IT) allowing them to analyze the necessary information in an effective and efficient way [2–4].

In this work we present a smart city application, intended for citizens living in an urban community enabling them to present and share their opinions, comments and interests. The application also should support citizens to make decisions. Those decisions should influence local authorities concerning community improvements. The application may be used with any subject relevant to an urban community and thus, it could be useful in many scenarios of citizens' participation and decision making.

Users of this application may share information about proposals on geo-referenced subjects on a map. Examples of such proposals are described in [5, 6]. The application can be run from any type of computer device, such as desktop PCs, Tablet PCs, or smartphones. Mobility and pervasiveness may favor the choice of Tablet PCs or smartphones [5, 7–9, 36].

2 Smart City Definitions

The term Smart Cities may have its origins in the Smart Growth proposed by Bollier in 1998 [10], which advocated new policies for urban planning. The term has been adopted since 2005 by a number of technology companies such as Cisco [11], Siemens [12], and IBM [13] for the application of complex information systems to integrate the operation of urban infrastructure and services such as buildings, transportation, electrical and water distribution, or public safety. It has since evolved to mean almost any form of technology-based innovation in the planning, development, and operation of cities. Smart city mainly focuses on applying the next-generation IT to all contexts of human life, regularly embedding sensors and equipment to hospitals, power grids, railways, bridges, tunnels, roads, buildings, water systems, dams, oil and gas pipelines and other objects in every corner of the world [14]. The concept of Smart City has become popular across the world and is currently the center of attention for industry and governments globally [15]. In spite of this, its exact definition is still not well-established [16, 17]. Several working definitions of Smart City have been put forward and adopted in both practical and academic use; we selected nine definitions which belongs to the most relevant papers found in the literature: (1) Partridge [18], "A city where the ICT strengthen the freedom of speech and the availability of public information and services". (2) Bowerman [19], "A city that monitors and integrates conditions of all of its critical infrastructures, including roads, bridges tunnels, rails, subways, airports, seaports communications, water, power, even major buildings can better optimize its resources, plan its preventive maintenance activities, and monitor security aspects while maximizing services to its citizens". (3) Caragliu et al. [20], "A city that invests in human and social capital and traditional and modern (ICT) communication infrastructure in order to sustain the economic growth and a high quality of life, with a wise management of natural resources, through participatory governance". (4) Kehoe et al. [21], "It makes optimal use of all the interconnected information available today to better understand and control its operations and optimize the use of limited resources". (5) Rios [4], "A city that gives inspiration, shares culture, knowledge, and life, a city that motivates its inhabitants to create and flourish in their own lives". (6) Harrison [3], "A city connecting the physical infrastructure, the ICT infrastructure, the social infrastructure, and the business infrastructure to leverage the collective intelligence of the city". (7) Anttiroiko et al. [22], "A city that reflects a particular idea of local community, one where city governments, enterprises and residents use ICTs to reinvent and reinforce the community's role in the new service economy, create jobs locally and improve the quality of community life". (8) Giffinger [23], "A city well performing in a forward-looking way in economy, people, governance, mobility, environment, and living, built on the smart combination of endowments and activities of self-decisive, independent and aware citizens". (9) Washburn [24], "The use of Smart Computing technologies to make the critical infrastructure components and services of a city–which include city administration, education, healthcare, public safety, real estate, transportation, and utilities—more intelligent, interconnected, and efficient".

There are two aspects in the above definitions which are most relevant for our proposal: one is which topics of a city are covered by the definitions and the other one is the common part of all definitions.

2.1 Topics Covered by a Smart City

It is common sense that a metropolitan area can be classified as smart when safety, enhanced public services, healthcare monitoring, green sustainability, high social interaction, and efficient transportation systems become available to any citizen in any location [14, 25]. This condition then requires to design, develop, deploy, and maintain public and private infrastructures, based on advanced and integrated materials, sensors, electronics, computer systems, and databases. Analyzing the definitions presented in the previous section, and the review of the literature [3, 24–28], we can identify eight key topics covered by a Smart City. The aspects covered by Smart City are: **smart energy, smart building, smart mobility, smart infrastructure, smart technology, smart healthcare, smart governance, and smart people.**

2.2 Common Aspects to Smart City Definitions

According to our analysis and to [29], the common aspects to the Smart City definitions are: people (smart people), technology (smart infrastructure, smart technology, smart mobility) and governance (smart governance). These can be regarded as the drivers to achieve a Smart City. **Smart People** are individuals or organizations that are engaged in the success of the smart city [4]. They use their creativity in leveraging the city infrastructure in order to create social, economic and environmental values. Smart people must be committed to lifelong learning, and sharing of knowledge [19, 29]. These characteristics enable them to create a sustainable smart economy, smart environment and smart education system. **Smart Technology** is the platform that allows the interaction among smart people. This platform is referred to as the technology of the city. Technology in a smart city includes all the infrastructure, ICT, applications (smart technologies), digital networks (smart infrastructure) and mobile devices (smart mobility) [19, 29]. These technologies are used as a communication channel where smart people share knowledge, skills and services. The technology is leveraged in order to maximize the value to smart people [20]. **Smart Governance** includes policies, regulations and directives that encourage collaboration, partnership and participation within the smart city. Governance ensures that the actors within the Smart City act in a predictable and monitored manner. Governance oversees the standardization of how various stakeholders interact within the smart city [19].

2.3   Smart Community

The notion of using Internet technology to work together towards a common goal is the foundation of smart communities [15, 30]. A **smart community** is a group of citizens that work together to leverage information technologies in the creation of economic, cultural and social value or for supporting decision-making of actions which are to be implemented by the government or local authorities. Smart people of a Smart community can include citizens, government or even business organizations [15, 30]. In other words, a smart community is a system where citizens and organizations (public and private) use smart technology to enhance the way they conduct their everyday business and decisions. This enhancement can lead to advantages, such as new revenue streams, attaining new knowledge that can be used to improve the efficiency of business functions or government decisions, better life conditions, higher level of participation in community life, better community decision making, etc. Smart Communities are a kind of Smart City enabling and empowering citizens, supporting their individual and common quests for well-being [6].

3   Smart People as Sensors

There are initiatives that investigate the power of collective, although imprecise intelligence of citizens in a Smart Cities scenario. The main visionary goal is to automate the organization of spontaneous and impromptu collaborations of large groups of people participating in collective actions (Smart Communities according to our understanding), such as in the notable case of urban crowdsensing [5]. In a crowdsensing environment, people or their mobile devices act as both sensors that collect urban data and actuators that take actions in the city, possibly upon request. According to [5], managing the crowdsensing process is a challenging task spanning several socio-technical issues: from the characterization of the regions under control to the quantification of the sensing density needed to obtain a certain accuracy; from the evaluation of a good balance between sensing accuracy and resource usage (number of people involved, network bandwidth, battery usage, etc.) to the selection of good incentives for people to participate (monetary, social, etc.). To tackle these problems, the researchers in [5] propose a crowdsensing platform with three main original technical aspects: (1) an innovative geo-localized social model to profile users along several variables, such as time, location, social interaction, service usage, and human activities; (2) a matching algorithm to autonomously choose people to involve in participations and (3) to quantify the performance of their sensing.

According to [8], as a special form of crowdsourcing [2], mobile crowdsensing aims to provide a mechanism to involve participants from the general public to efficiently and effectively contribute and utilize context-related sensing data from their mobile devices in solving specific problems in collaborations. Mobile crowdsensing leverages human intelligence to collect, process, and aggregate sensing data using individuals' mobile devices to realize a higher-quality and more efficient sensing solution. A specific scenario of use of this mobile crowdsensing concept is presented in [7], and [31].

4 Multiple Views

Multiple Coordinated Views is a specific exploratory visualization technique that enables users to explore their data, that is displayed in two or more different forms [32]. In fact, the overall premise for the technique is that users understand their data better if they interact with the presented information and view it through various representations. These multiple representations describe the situation where there may be multiple interpretations of the data, and hence different viewpoints from those interpretations. This is obviously useful in education, since the learner may understand the information better through a certain presentation rather than through another one. Through multiple views and multiform representations the user can easily compare the data from two or more representations. Specifically, systems that solely use two side- by-side views are named dual view systems [33].

5 A Smart Community Application

As we said in the introductory section, we want to design an application for a Smart community which supports its members to discuss issues relevant to the community which may also include a decision making process. The design principles of this application consider the idea of supporting smart people forming a smart community for improving self-governance and participation including the ideas of Multiple Views and smart people as sensors. In order to allow people to use it wherever they are, the application has been implemented as a web application which can be accessed and run with smartphones, tablets or desktop PCs. However, due to the design of the interface a tablet would be the most convenient device in order to be mobile and have a good overview of the application at the same time. Functions are provided for users in order to share messages, comment on posts, add categories to messages, and check the various messages associated with certain categories. Messages can be private or public; and it can be geo-referenced on the map.

The application allows users to log in into a session creating a new user to the system or using her/his credentials of Facebook or Twitter. The idea is that a new session is created for a new discussion and/or decision topic. Users contribute in various forms: Create a new entry, which are called as "feeds" in the application, comment a feed (own or from another user), like a follow-up in a conversation, and "vote" for or against a feed, very much similar to whatever is possible to do in social sites like Twitter or Facebook. Users can also associate two more important elements to a feed: one is a geographical location, and the other is one or more tags. The geographical location may be added automatically if the user clicks a pushdown button on the interface and if the device she/he is using does have a GPS. The other way is to click over a map which is displayed along with the feeds when the feed is being created. The point associated with the feed will be highlighted with a mark, which will display the feed's title if clicked. Tags can be assigned by selecting them from a pre-stored list, which can be entered at the creation of the session, or by typing a new tag. Feeds can be private or public. The idea is that the user can take some time in order to "prepare" the feed and refine it several times before publishing it when he/she is satisfied with its current form and content.

The most interesting features of the application are those related to browsing the already entered information. There are three browsing modes: one is a list of all feeds ordered by date and time of issue. They are shown at the left hand side of the screen as a green box with the title, content, the author's name, the timestamp, a button to show-hide the tags originally assigned by the author or assigned later by other users, and another button to show-hide the comments the feed has received from other users. At the beginning of feeds list there is a button labeled with a "+" for creating new feeds.

The Second view is a map showing the markers to which the feeds have been associated. This map is downloaded directly from GoogleMaps and therefore they have all the features provided by them, such as zooming in and out, navigating through the whole world, etc. The third view is a conceptual map in which nodes are shown as a cyan colored circle and labelled with the name of all tags that have been associated to a feed. The nodes are connected by a line to a green rectangle labelled with the title of the feed. Thus, when one feed has more than one tag the visual effect is a subgraph in which two or more nodes labelled with the tag names are connected to a central rectangle containing the title of the feed.

As we previously mentioned, the innovative aspect proposed by this work is the implementation of an interface with small-multiple views of the same information (geo-localized, tagged feed of an online forum) which are synchronized: when one feed is selected by the user from the feeds list then its corresponding mark on the map view and the green box in the concept map representing it are also highlighted. When a mark in the map view is selected (by clicking on it), its corresponding feed in the feeds list and the corresponding box in the concept map are also highlighted. When one node of the concept map is selected (by clicking on it) then all the feeds associated with it are also highlighted in the map view and the feeds list. If the selected node in the concept map is a tag, more than one feed might be highlighted in the other views. Consequently, when more than one feed are found by the search engine, all of them are highlighted in the three views. The idea behind providing multiple views is that they allow users to explore data from various points of view and this will help them to understand them better, browse them in various ways and see relations on one view which are not clear in another. The application has been implemented so that it can be used in the web. It means it can be accessed and run on any computer device having a

HTML5 compatible web browser like Google Chrome, Firefox, Opera, etc. It also means the application can be used on smartphones, tablets or desktop PCs. Tablets are the best devices because of their screen size and mobility, which adds ubiquity and therefore the possibility of crowdsensing, since the users can act as human sensors of what is going on in the neighborhood [5, 7–9].

6 Usability Test of the Application

The application was tested with real users. The community is a condominium called Santa Carolina, near Santiago, Chile. The community includes inhabitants of 32 homes covering a property of about 50 acres. The community faced the need to select projects to be developed during 2015. Several projects had been proposed beforehand, such as public lighting improvement, roads repair, installation of a security hut, and generation of a manual of use of public spaces. The application was used to support the project selection process by the community members. At the end of the testing period, users were asked to fill out a usability questionnaire to evaluate the application structure, its ease of use, its ease to understand, its appearance, and the user experience. The questionnaire was adapted from [34].

The period of use was defined between Nov. 24 and Nov. 30, 2014. Ages of participants ranged 18–47 years old. All administrators' projects were loaded to the application with their corresponding categories. Then, during a week the community members could post their comments on the projects, cast votes and visualize information according to time line, geographic map and conceptual map. Besides, they could create new projects and categories, and associate categories to the projects already in the system. Seventy-five percent of the community members participated in the experiment. A total of 23 projects were presented, 15 of them were geo-referenced, and 19 were associated to categories. The number of comments was 55 and 48 votes were received (31 positive, 17 negative). The number of participants was 24, with 20 of them accessing through their Facebook or Twitter accounts.

The next assertions can be stated based on the results of the usability questionnaire: (1) Application structure: The structure of the application together with its coherence were well evaluated, mainly with the choices "I agree" and "I strongly agree". (2) Ease of use: Most aspects were well evaluated, mostly with the "I agree" choice. However, interactivity was badly evaluated, mostly with the "I disagree" option. (3) Ease of understanding: help and feedback had a mixed evaluation, mostly with the "I agree" and "I disagree" options. Search for information was very well evaluated, with the "I strongly agree" option. (4) Appearance: it was well evaluated, with the "I agree" choice. (5) User experience: most people chose "I agree" with the statement of having a nice experience using the application.

7 Conclusions and Future Work

The smart city application described in this paper is an attempt to achieve the development of communities of citizens living under the concept of smart people, smart technology and smart governance. The application's user interface introduces multiple views and it can benefit users in the sense of better understanding of the competing projects and therefore it may increase community members' participation. It is possible to raise issues concerning the real-world applicability of the tool mentioning the advantages for the community of having a face-to-face meeting. In our experiment, e.g., it is clearly positive the condominium inhabitants meet together to talk about the possible projects to develop by their community. However, the application was not developed as a replacement of a face-to-face meeting; rather, the application can complement one or more face-to-face meetings. Thus, people who cannot be present at a face-to-face meeting can still participate in the decision making process. Also, people using the application have more time to ponder the advantages and disadvantages of each project, talk to other people or within the family about them before casting votes, and perhaps change their minds at any time. Therefore, the time frame for an asynchronous discussion is much more convenient than the duration of just one face-to-face meeting.

It is easy to draw a parallel between the scenario for this experiment and the scenario which was mentioned in the introduction, where a community of neighbors has to analyze the proposal of urban improvements proposed by a company which is going to install a communication antenna in their neighborhood [35]. This application will help them counter-propose, discuss and select the projects they would like to be implemented.

References

1. UN world's population increasingly urban with more than half living in urban areas. News (2014)
2. Batty, M., et al.: Smart cities of the future. Eur. Phys. J. Spec. Top. **214**(1), 481–518 (2012)
3. Harrison, C., et al.: Foundations for smarter cities. IBM J. Res. Dev. **54**(4), 1–16 (2010)
4. Rios, P.: Creating "The smart city" (2012)
5. Cardone, G., et al.: Fostering participation in smart cities: a geo-social crowdsensing platform. IEEE Commun. Mag. **51**(6), 112–119 (2013)
6. Daniel, S., Doran, M.-A.: geoSmartCity: geomatics contribution to the smart city. In: Proceedings of the 14th Annual International Conference on Digital Government Research, ACM (2013)
7. Aihara, K., et al.: Crowdsourced mobile sensing for smarter city life. In: 2014 IEEE 7th International Conference on Service-Oriented Computing and Applications (SOCA), IEEE (2014)
8. Hu, X., et al.: Multidimensional context-aware social network architecture for mobile crowdsensing. IEEE Commun. Mag. **52**(6), 78–87 (2014)
9. Yan, T., et al.: mCrowd: a platform for mobile crowdsourcing. In: Proceedings of the 7th ACM Conference on Embedded Networked Sensor Systems, ACM (2009)

10. Bollier, D.: How Smart Growth Can Stop Sprawl: A Fledgling Citizen Movement Expands. Essential Books, Washington, DC (1998)
11. Cisco Dubai: The smart city (2005)
12. Siemens: Stadt der Zukunft (2004)
13. IBM: Smarter cities: New York 2009 (2009)
14. Komninos, N., Schaffers, H., Pallot, M.: Developing a policy roadmap for smart cities and the future internet. In: eChallenges e-2011 Conference Proceedings, IIMC International Information Management Corporation, IMC Information Management Corporation (2011)
15. Phahlamohlaka, J., et al.: Towards a smart community centre: SEIDET digital village. In: Kimppa, K., Whitehouse, D., Kuusela, T., Phahlamohlaka, J. (eds.) ICT and Society. IFIP Advances in Information and Communication Technology, vol. 431, pp. 107–121. Springer, Heidelberg (2014)
16. Boulton, A., Brunn, S.D., Devriendt, L.: Cyberinfrastructures and 'smart' world cities: physical, human and soft infrastructures. In: Derudder, B., Hoyler, M., Taylor, P.J., Witlox, F. (eds.) International Handbook of Globalization and World Cities, p. 198. Edward Elgar, Northampton (2011)
17. Chourabi, H., et al.: Understanding smart cities: an integrative framework. In: 2012 45th Hawaii International Conference on System Science (HICSS), IEEE (2012)
18. Partridge, H.L.: Developing a human perspective to the digital divide in the 'smart city' (2004)
19. Bowerman, B., et al.: The vision of a smart city. In: 2nd International Life Extension Technology Workshop, Paris (2000)
20. Caragliu, A., Del Bo, C., Nijkamp, P.: Smart cities in Europe. J. Urban Technol. **18**(2), 65–82 (2011)
21. Kehoe, M., et al.: Smarter cities series: a foundation for understanding IBM smarter cities. Redguides for Business Leaders, IBM (2011)
22. Anttiroiko, A.-V., Valkama, P., Bailey, S.J.: Smart cities in the new service economy: building platforms for smart services. AI Soc. **29**(3), 323–334 (2014)
23. Giffinger, R., et al.: Smart cities-ranking of European medium-sized cities. Vienna University of Technology (2007)
24. Washburn, D., et al.: Helping CIOs understand "smart city" initiatives: defining the smart city, its drivers, and the role of the CIO, Forrester Research, Inc., Cambridge, MA (2010)
25. Su, K., Li, J., Fu, H.: Smart city and the applications. In: 2011 International Conference on Electronics, Communications and Control (ICECC), IEEE (2011)
26. Piro, G., et al.: Information centric services in smart cities. J. Syst. Softw. **88**, 169–188 (2014)
27. Naphade, M.: Smarter cities and their innovation challenges. Computer **44**(6), 32–39 (2011)
28. Singh, S.: Smart cities: a $1.5 trillion market opportunity. Forbes, Editor, Forbes blog (2014)
29. Al-Hader, M., et al.: Smart city components architecture. In: International Conference on Computational Intelligence, Modelling and Simulation 2009, CSSim 2009, IEEE (2009)
30. Baskin, C., Barker, M., Woods, P.: Towards a smart community: rethinking the strategic use of ICTs in teaching and learning. Australas. J. Edu. Technol. **19**(2), 192–210 (2003)
31. Roitman, H., et al.: Harnessing the crowds for smart city sensing. In: Proceedings of the 1st International Workshop on Multimodal Crowd Sensing, ACM (2012)
32. Roberts, J.C.: State of the art: coordinated & multiple views in exploratory visualization. In: Fifth International Conference on Coordinated and Multiple Views in Exploratory Visualization 2007, CMV 2007, IEEE (2007)
33. Convertino, G., et al.: Exploring context switching and cognition in dual-view coordinated visualizations. In: International Conference on Coordinated and Multiple Views in Exploratory Visualization 2003, Proceedings, IEEE (2003)

34. de Barros Pereira, H.B.: Análisis experimental de los criterios de evaluación de usabilidad de aplicaciones multimedia en entornos de educación y formación a distancia. Universitat Politècnica de Catalunya (2002)
35. Baloian, N., Frez, J., Zurita, G.: Smart cities: supporting citizen participation in city planning. In: Proceedings of the CSIT, Yerevan Armenia (2013)
36. Guerrero, L., Ochoa, S., Pino, J.A., Collazos, C.: Selecting computing devices to support mobile collaboration. Group Decis. Negot. 15(3), 243–271 (2006)

Building Smart Adaptable Cyber-Physical Systems: Definitions, Classification and Elements

Borja Bordel[✉], Ramón Alcarria, Marina Pérez-Jiménez,
Tomás Robles, Diego Martín, and Diego Sánchez de Rivera

Technical University of Madrid, Madrid, Spain
bbordel@dit.upm.es, {ramon.alcarria,
tomas.robles,diego.martin.de.andres}@upm.es,
marina.perez@isom.upm.es,
diego.sanchezderiveracordoba@gmail.com

Abstract. The provision of systems that join the information technologies with the physical world has been one of the most popular issues in research in the last fifteen years. Nevertheless, the complexity associated with these systems prevented many authors from providing a theoretical formalization. Even it is difficult to find a consensus name or a definition for this new type of systems. Therefore, in this work we propose a theoretical and technical formalization for these solutions, which includes a name at the forefront of research: smart adaptable cyber-physical systems (SACPS). We also present a complete definition for the SACPS, and explain the elements and subsystem interaction.

Keywords: Smart Adaptable Cyber-Physical Systems · SACPS · RFID · Wearable technologies · Wireless HAN · Cybernetic devices

1 Introduction

Making a research in the smart environment field is complicated. The causes are, overall, the term's ambiguity and the lack of a bibliographic base (extended and coherent) which fixes the limits, elements, technologies, etc. in this kind of systems.

Therefore, the main objective of this work is presenting a new concept, with technical character and without ambiguity, which delimits the application area of the (until now) so-called "smart environment". We are talking about Smart Adaptable Cyber-Physical Systems (SACPS).

The rest of the paper is organized as follows: In section two we review the previous efforts of some authors for defining this type of systems and try to extend them with the now-a-days knowledge. Section three presents a classification for SACPS. Finally, section four is dedicated to the elements which make up a SACPS and to their functions.

J.M. García-Chamizo et al. (Eds.): UCAmI 2015, LNCS 9454, pp. 144–149, 2015.
DOI: 10.1007/978-3-319-26401-1_14

2 History, Definition and Related Work

The first efforts for integrating information technologies in the physical world were based on electronics. Thus, from 2000, several terms have appeared in the literature and, overall, have been proposed in conferences, to refer to smart distributed electronic systems (more or less embedded in the physical world): Smart Home [1, 2], Smart Office [3], Intelligent Home [4], Smart Environments [5], Adaptive Versatile Environments [6], Interactive Spaces [7], Problem-Solving Environments [8], etc.

In a parallel way, for these terms some definitions appeared. Thereby, in 2000, [9] said that "A smart space is a region of the real world that is extensively equipped with sensors, actuators and computing components". The problem of this definition, viewed today, lies in the fact that it is incomplete, because the "intelligent factor" disappears, as the definition only considers hardware components. Due to that, in 2002, other authors decide to propose their own definition. [1] defines a Smart Environment as "a system that is able to autonomously acquire and apply knowledge about the environment and adapt to its inhabitants' preferences and requirements in order to improve their experience". This second option, however, is unspecific. Although it explains the expected operation way (from a high level point of view), including the human factor and not including any reference to hardware or software elements, makes difficult to determine when a system agrees with the definition and when not.

So much so that, in 2005, the same authors in [5] proposed a new definition: "A smart environment is a physical world that is interconnected through a continuous network abundantly and invisibly with sensors, actuators and computational units, embedded seamlessly in the everyday objects of our lives". This last definition, much more complex, was endorsed by other authors, such as the famous KITECH (Korea Institute of Industrial Technology), nevertheless, as in the first case; this definition does not include any reference to the "intelligent part" of the system.

From 2010, more or less, the interest on these systems decrease, and researches abandon attempts to formalize the theoretical framework. At this moment, a new concept captures all interest: the Cyber-Physical Systems (CPS). The most popular definition, presented in [10], defines the CPS as "integrations of computation and physical processes. Embedded computers and networks monitor and control the physical processes, usually with feedback loops where physical processes affect computations and vice versa."

In 2010, hardware infrastructure for ubiquitous systems has started maturing, what allows defining CPS from a more behavioral and specific point of view. However, although any future attempt must apply CPS's principles, this name also groups systems that are "not enough smart" (for example, as we said, in 2002 it became clear that smart systems have to "adapt to its inhabitants' preferences and requirements").

In order to join the CPS's principles with all previous knowledge, we define the Smart Adaptable Cyber-Physical Systems (SACPS).

A Smart Adaptable Cyber-Physical Systems (SACPS) is a physical world that is interconnected through a continuous network abundantly and invisibly with sensors, actuators and computational units, embedded seamlessly in the everyday objects and/or clothes. The resulting system must be monitored from a control process management entity, and must define feedback loops where information and collected data from sensors affect physical processes. The system must be adaptable to different domains and be oriented to prosumer user, for which must implement self-configuration and dynamic self-adaptation capabilities.

In this definition, as we can see, all aspects previously seen are present:

The first definition's part refers the communications physical infrastructure and its relation with the external world. As can be seen, it is really similar to the definition proposed in [5] for the "Smart Environments", to which a reference to the modern wearable technologies has been added.

The second part, in relation with process control and feedback loops, is directly related with the work philosophy in CPS (orient to process, Big Data, etc.).

The third and last part (relative to system self-configuration and its adaptation to prosumer user) gathers the necessity (showed in [1]) to make the system autonomous and adaptable to the users' preferences and requirements.

3   Elements in a SACPS Layered Model

All SACPS are parts of the physical world, which connects with the rest of the reality through a permeable interface that allows the transference of materials, objects, energy, user, etc. (see Fig. 1(a)).

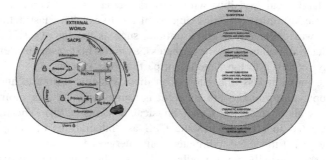

Fig. 1. (a) Relation between the external world and a SACPS. (b) Layered model of a generic SACPS

However, despite they can be considered as a unit, inside each SACPS various subsystems can be distinguished. Each subsystem will encapsulate some elements and functions from the complete systems. Namely:

Physical subsystem: It includes all the elements from the ordinary world that are part of the SACPS, but which they have not been modified to include any electronic instrument, communication device or process element. This subsystem also includes the power supply, the physical space occupied by the system and all the information stored in several variables, own the physical world (temperature, blood pressure...). Here are also integrated all users that take advantage of the SACPS's services, but which are not experts neither in the system's technology base nor in its specific application field. In what follows, we will name as "habitants" to this kind of users.

Cybernetic subsystem: It includes all the elements from the ordinary world that have been modified in some way, in order to integrate (seamless) electronic instrumental, communication devices and/or process elements. Smart furniture, wearables or any other similar device (we will call "cybernetic devices" to them) belong to this subsystem. This subsystem is, besides, in charge of monitoring the physical subsystem and acting over it. Cybernetic devices, at the same time, can be made of up to three different modules: sensorisation module, process and execution module, and communications module. Sensorisation module includes all electronic instrumentation and the device's actuators, such as displays, LED, etc. Process and execution module includes, if there was one, the device's microcontroller unit and all its peripherals. This part is in charge of executing the task ordered from the smart subsystem, controlling sensors and actuators, executing micro-services, etc. Finally, communications module includes all the infrastructure and software, necessary to allow the communication among the cybernetic devices, and between the device and the smart. Depending on how many modules implements a cybernetic device; we can distinct three classes of devices:

- Tagged cybernetic device: We use this name with devices that only implement the communications module. Furthermore, that module can only communicate with other cybernetic devices with which link connection will be available (never with the smart subsystem). The amount of information which can communicate is, besides, limited. The employed terminology comes from RFID technology, where this kind of modules is called "tag RFID".
- Peripheral cybernetic device: These devices implement the sensorisation module and a reduce functions communications module. Because these devices do not have a complete communications module, they only can communicate with other cybernetic devices with which link connection exits. This time, however, there are not limitations in the amount of transmittable data.
- Full cybernetic device: Finally, devices of this group implement the three possible modules (with full functions). These devices, typically, will receive information from their sensors and from close peripheral devices and tagged objects. With this information it will execute the delegated task, and will inform to the smart subsystem if it were necessary.

Smart subsystem: It includes all the infrastructure, applications, software, and management systems which controls and monitorizes the other subsystems, processes received data and feedbacks future process with the information extracted from these data. It can be divided in other two subsystems: communications subsystem (that makes possible the information flow with the cybernetic subsystem) and data analysis, process control and decision making subsystem. Here, besides, it will be implemented the politics that will allow the self-configuration and dynamic self-adaptation of the SACPS. This subsystem, moreover, includes those users which are not experts in the SACPS's base technology, but they are experts in the system's application field (prosumer users). These users, as can act directly over the smart subsystem, so that they can adjust the global behavior of the SACPS to their requirements.

It is usual in this kind of technologies (see [10]) representing the system as a set of concentric layers, where as you progress inward, you get way from the physical world. Then, the layered model for a generic SACPS can be expressed as in Fig. 1(b).

4   Classification of SACPS

Within the set of SACPS several classifications can be made: depending on the application field, depending on the number of elements, etc. The nature of the main data source considered differentiates all SACPS in these three categories:

Actor-focused systems: These systems are totally oriented to obtain data from SACPS's habitants. The interest is focused on how the users behave and what they feel. Due to the nature of these systems, it is indispensable that data sampling, processing, and decision making to be at real-time and execute in high-speed (with the purpose of supplying feedback as soon as possible). Of course, this does not impede, in addition, other systems for data analysis to be included. From an electronic point of view, these systems are extensively equipped with biometrical sensors and wearable devices (see Fig. 2); all of them powered in an independent and continuous way, in order to guarantee a permanent access to users' data. Systems thought for helping in some types of rehabilitation, or labor stress detection, are some of the applications of the SACPS of this category.

Object-focused systems: In these systems the interest is focused on the interactions among the devices which make up the SACPS. In these systems, moreover, habitants

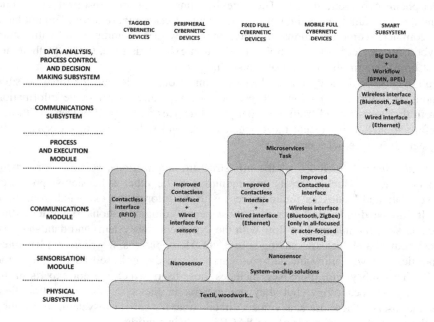

Fig. 2. Base technologies employed in SACPSs

become elements with the same importance, and at the same level, than furniture, objects. Applications deployed in this type of systems do not demand, in general, a continuous data supply, so data sampling can be based on collection-stored-delivery schemes. Furthermore, at hardware level, a more relaxed scheme of data sampling allows the extensive use of communication systems where one of the extremes is passive (see Fig. 2). Traceability systems, control process and stock management, are typical application examples that belong to this group of SACPS.

All-focused systems: These systems are really complex, as they integrate both visions from the previous groups. On the one hand, they implement applications typical to the object-focused systems, where habitants and object are treated in the same way. On the other hand, the information provided by the actor-focused systems is also necessary here, so user monitoring infrastructure must be included. At electronic level, they are systems really similar to actor-focused ones, although, at application level, they implement (besides) functionalities typical from object-focused systems. It is a really useful point of view in systems destined to critical or dangerous resources management such as explosives or toxic gases. In these situations, knowing infrastructure information (stock, etc.) is as important as knowing actor information (i.e. the biological state of worker that manipulate the material).

References

1. Das, S.K., Cook, D.J.: The role of prediction algorithms in the MavHome smart home architecture. IEEE Wirel. Commun. **9**(6), 77–84 (2002)
2. Das, S.K., Cook, D.J.: Agent based health monitoring in smart homes. In: Proceedings of the International. Conference on Smart Homes and Health Telematics (ICOST), Singapore, Sept 2004. Keynote Talk
3. Le Gal, C., Martin, J., Lux, A., Crowley, J.L.: Smart office: design of an intelligent environment. IEEE Intell. Syst. **16**(4), 60–66 (2001)
4. Lesser, E.: The intelligent home testbed. In: Proceedings Of Autonomy Control Software Workshop, Jan 1999
5. Das, S.K., Cook, D.J.: Smart Environments: Technology, Protocols, and Applications. Wiley, Chichester (2005)
6. Youngblood M., Cook D.J., Holder L.B.: Managing adaptive versatile environments. In: Proceedings of IEEE International Conference on Pervasive Computing and Communications, pp. 351–360 (2005)
7. Fox, A., Johanson, B., Hanrahan, P., Winograd, T.: Integrating information appliances into an interactive space. IEEE Comput. Graphics Appl. **20**(3), 54–65 (2000)
8. Srivastava M.B.: Smart Kindergarten: sensor-based wireless networks for smart problem-solving environments. In: Proceedings ACM Conference on Mobile Computing and Networking (2001)
9. Nixon, P., Dobson, S., Lacey, G.: Managing smart environments. In: Proceedings of the Workshop on Software Engineering for Wearable and Pervasive Computing, June 2000
10. Lee, E.: Cyber physical systems: design challenges. In: Proceedings on 11th IEEE International Symposium on Object Oriented Real-Time Distributed Computing (ISORC), pp. 363–369 (2008)

Comparative Analysis of Artificial Hydrocarbon Networks and Data-Driven Approaches for Human Activity Recognition

Hiram Ponce[✉], María de Lourdes Martínez-Villaseñor,
and Luis Miralles-Pechúan

Universidad Panamericana Campus México,
Augusto Rodin 498, Col. Insurgentes-Mixcoac, Mexico, D.F., Mexico
{hponce, lmartine, lmiralles}@up.edu.mx

Abstract. In recent years computing and sensing technologies advances contribute to develop effective human activity recognition systems. In context-aware and ambient assistive living applications, classification of body postures and movements, aids in the development of health systems that improve the quality of life of the disabled and the elderly. In this paper we describe a comparative analysis of data-driven activity recognition techniques against a novel supervised learning technique called artificial hydrocarbon networks (AHN). We prove that artificial hydrocarbon networks are suitable for efficient body postures and movements classification, providing a comparison between its performance and other well-known supervised learning methods.

Keywords: Human activity recognition · Artificial organic networks · Artificial hydrocarbon networks · Wearable sensors · Supervised learning · Classification

1 Introduction

Human activity recognition (HAR) deals with the integration of sensing and reasoning in order to better understand people actions. Research related to human activity recognition has become relevant in pervasive and mobile computing, surveillance-based security, context-aware computing, and ambient assistive living [1]. Recognizing body postures and movements is especially important to improve the quality of life of the disabled and the elderly. Health systems and assistive technologies can deliver personalized support based on activity recognition.

Two main approaches are used to perform the task of activity recognition: vision-based and sensor-based activity recognition [1, 2]. The vision-based approach requires image processing of video sequences or digital visual data provided by cameras. No wearable or smartphone sensors are required, but it depends on the image quality. Quality of cameras, lighting, and environments, among others, are factors that determine image quality. Visually monitoring the actor behavior entails privacy issues. The sensor-based approach is focused on activity monitoring using wearable [2] or smartphone sensors and technologies [3]. The drawback of this approach is that the

© Springer International Publishing Switzerland 2015
J.M. García-Chamizo et al. (Eds.): UCAmI 2015, LNCS 9454, pp. 150–161, 2015.
DOI: 10.1007/978-3-319-26401-1_15

actor must wear sensors or smartphones for extended periods of time. Calibration of sensors and battery charges issues are also frequent [2].

By building an activity model, systems are able to interpret sensor data and infer body postures and movements. Activity models can be built mainly using data-driven or knowledge-driven methods [1]. Data-driven or bottom-up approaches learn activity models using data mining and machine learning techniques. HAR systems frequently use supervised learning approaches. Decision trees, Bayesian networks, Markov models, Support Vector Machines, and classifier ensembles are reported in [17] as classifier algorithms used by state-of-art HAR systems. The learning algorithm chosen for a HAR system differs depending on its purpose. It also has benefits and drawbacks. Recognized activities, types of devices and sensors, level of energy, and classification flexibility level are factors that have to be taken into account when designing an online or offline HAR system. Human activity recognition systems have many different requirements, so in order to determine if a certain learning technique is well suited for activity recognition, a comparative analysis must be performed [17].

In this paper we describe a comparative analysis of data-driven activity recognition techniques against a novel supervised learning technique called artificial hydrocarbon networks (AHN). In particular, the latter method has proved to be very effective for regression and classification problems. For instance, artificial hydrocarbon networks algorithm has been used in uncertain and imprecise domains, offering excellent response in modeling and control approaches [4–6] and preserving stability [4, 7]. Since sensor-based activity recognition is quite imprecise and noise introduces uncertainty on it, then artificial hydrocarbon networks can be used as an alternative to tackle these problems. Thus, we aim to determine that artificial hydrocarbon networks are suitable for efficient body postures and movements classification, providing a comparison between its performance and ten other well-known supervised learning methods.

The rest of the paper is organized as follows: in Sect. 2 we discuss the data-driven approaches for classification of body postures and movements. We present our artificial hydrocarbon networks approach for human activity recognition in Sect. 3. We describe our experiments in Sect. 4, and discuss the results in Sect. 5. Finally, we conclude and outline our future work in Sect. 6.

2 Data-Driven Approaches for Classification of Body Postures and Movements

Sensor-based activity recognition has evolved from using sensors for adaptive systems in the context of home automation [8] to extensive use of different type of sensors in a great diversity of research areas and scenarios of ubiquitous and mobile computing [1]. Wearable and dense sensors are used for activity monitoring. Wearable sensors refer to sensors embedded in personal clothes or accessories. The most frequently used sensors are accelerometers and GPS sensors. Bao et al. [9] and Pantelopoulos et al. [10] present surveys of wearable systems. Wearable sensors can be obtrusive, and uncomfortable to wear for long periods of time. They are not suitable for monitoring complex activities. Dense sensors are usually attached to commonly used objects avoiding the trouble of wearing them at all times. This approach is more suitable for ambient assisted living. The scope of this paper focuses on activity recognition from wearable sensors.

Activity models based in wearable sensors use generative and discriminative methods. Surveys [1, 11] report Naïve-Bayes, Hidden Markov Model, k-nearest neighbor, decision trees classifiers, C4.5, and Support Vector Machine (SVM) as frequently used methods for activity recognition.

3   Artificial Hydrocarbon Networks Approach for Human Activity Recognition

In this section, artificial hydrocarbon networks algorithm is explained to get an overview of this supervised learning method. Then, it is described how this algorithm can be used as an approach for human activity recognition.

3.1   Artificial Hydrocarbon Networks

Artificial organic networks (AON) technique [4, 7] is a class of learning algorithms inspired on chemical organic compounds that can package information (e.g. data patterns) in modules so-called molecules. Artificial organic networks technique defines mechanisms similar to chemical organic compounds (i.e. through heuristics) that generate organized and optimized structures in terms of chemical energy. It can be proved that these artificial organic networks preserve some chemical characteristics like [4]: modularity, inheritance, organization and structural stability.

From the above, artificial hydrocarbon networks (AHN) is a supervised learning method based on artificial organic networks [4, 7]. This technique is inspired on chemical hydrocarbon compounds; and, similarly to chemical hydrocarbons, artificial hydrocarbon networks only use two atomic units: hydrogen and carbon atoms that can be linked with at most one and four other atoms, respectively. Then, these molecules can form other types of structures so-called compounds, which include nonlinear relationships among all molecules [4]. In fact, these types of networks are really adequate for modeling issues, as well as being used in real applications like system prediction, or searching for patterns in unknown or uncertain data. Examples of their applications can be found in literature [4–7].

A graph-model representation of artificial hydrocarbon networks is shown in Fig. 1. This graph-model can be explained as (1). Currently, these networks receive a set of inputs X that is evaluated through n_i molecules that form the i th compound C_i using a set of coefficients H_i regard X ng to the hydrogen atoms of each compound in the whole structure. At last, artificial hydrocarbon networks compute a set of response outputs $\hat{Y}$ using a linear combination of all compounds weighted by the parameters α_i known as stoichiometric coefficients. To this end, artificial hydrocarbon networks can be trained using the so-called simple AHN-algorithm, or simple-AHN (see [4] for more details). That algorithm is a supervised training method that finds the set of all hydrogen values H_i and stoichiometric coefficients α_i, given a training dataset of the form as X, Y representing multi-categorical inputs X and target outputs Y. Moreover, the simple-AHN algorithm minimizes a loss function such that $\hat{Y}$ approximates Y, using a learning rate coefficient $0 < \eta < 1$ [4, 7].

$$\hat{Y} = \sum_i \alpha_i C_i(X, H_i, n_i) \tag{1}$$

To this end, this work adopts the linear and saturated compound topology [4, 5], such that, $i = 1$ and the only compound is formed by n molecules. In that sense, the training process of an AHN-model will consider the learning rate η and the number of molecules n in that compound.

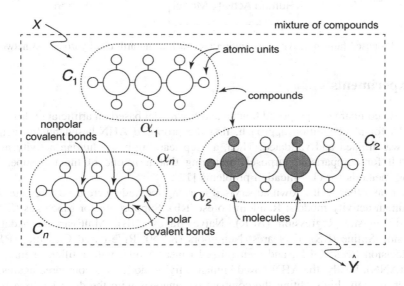

Fig. 1. Example of an artificial hydrocarbon network.

3.2 Human Activity Recognition Based on Artificial Hydrocarbon Networks

We propose using artificial hydrocarbon networks technique as a supervised learning method for building a data-driven human activity model that allows recognition retrieval. An artificial saturated linear compound that receives multiple inputs and generates an output response was used. Figure 2 shows our proposed human activity recognition approach based on AHN. As noted in Fig. 2, first the human activity model is trained using a database with previous attribute-target information. The training process is computed using the simple-AHN algorithm [4]. Then, a query based on the same type of attributes described in the database can be asked to the human activity model based on AHN. Lastly, that AHN-model calculates a proper output target approximation.

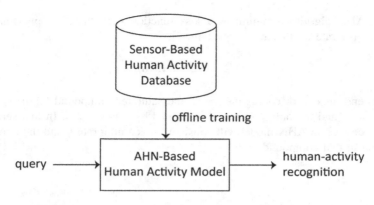

Fig. 2. Proposed human activity recognition approach using artificial hydrocarbon networks.

4 Experiments

In order to compare our proposed human activity model based on artificial hydrocarbon networks for a recognition approach, first the proposed AHN-based human activity model was trained and validated. Then, a deep learning-based human activity model was built for comparison purposes, assuming that it is one of the top supervised learning methods for classification problems [12].

Later on, other well-known supervised learning methods were used to create other nine human activity models: Random Forest (RF), Support Vector Machines (SVM), Boosted Logistic Regression (BLR), Naïve Bayes (NB), Multivariable Adaptive Regression Spline (RS), K-Nearest Neighbors (KNN), Rule-based Classifier (RBC), C4.5 decision trees (C4.5), and Generalized Linear Model with artificial neural networks (ANN). Lastly, the AHN-based human activity model was compared against the other ten models, highlighting the comparative analysis with the deep learning-based model. Following, a description of the dataset is presented, then the methodologies for building both AHN-based and deep learning-based models are explained, and a comparative analysis is discussed lastly.

4.1 Dataset Description

Classifiers were trained and tested using a public domain dataset collected with the use of four accelerometers positioned in the waist, thigh, ankle and arm (Fig. 3) [2] downloaded from UCI Repository [13]. The authors collected data from four people in different static postures and dynamic movements. The dataset contains 165,633 samples and five classes (sitting-down, standing-up, standing, walking, and sitting) collected on eight hours of activities of four healthy subjects. The person's position is the model output. There are five possible positions (sitting-down, standing-up, standing, walking, and sitting). Model inputs represent user data such as name, gender, age, height, weight, body mass, and sensor axis values. We have four sensors and for each

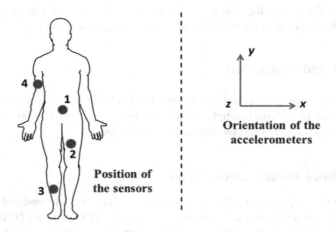

Fig. 3. Wearable device built for data collection [2].

of them we collect the values of the x, y and z axes. Name and gender are text values, height and body mass are real values and the rest are integer.

4.2 Feature Selection

We applied the RFE (Recursive Feature Selection) method [14] with 30,000 samples to select the most important attributes. The RFE method is variable elimination wrapper, so models are constructed from a combination of attributes. First, the algorithm constructed a model with each of the attributes independently, and evaluated the results. The algorithm classified the model inputs from highest to lowest according to the accuracy of the generated models. Later it built models gathering attributes from the best one to the worst. The output was the precision of the models created with each combination of attributes. The algorithm chose the combination of attributes that generated the best model. In this case the best model was proved to be that with all features. To this end, feature selection [16] was done for eliminating those characteristics that do not provide any relevant information to the process, which they are typically features with very little variation or are highly dependent to others. At last, feature selection allows realizing more precise, simpler models, and in less time [16].

4.3 Methodology

For our comparative analysis, we chose ten classifiers, nine traditional methods reported as frequently used for human activity recognition in [1, 11], and H20 Deep Learning package for R Studio. For each of the methods, we applied five times cross-validation with ten partitions. Then we calculate the accuracy of the different configurations of each model as the mean of the fifty models generated. With the best configuration of each model, a new model was created using all the samples of the training set. Subsequently, we used the model to predict test samples.

5   Results and Discussion

For training and testing purposes, we randomly divide the dataset in two subsets: a training data set of 100,000 samples and a testing data set of 50,000 samples, the remaining samples of the original dataset were excluded.

5.1   AHN-Based Human Activity Model

The structure of the proposed AHN-based human activity model consisted in an artificial saturated linear compound [4] with ten molecules as shown in (2); where, CH_k means a molecule of order k, and straight lines represent simple bonds (or relationships). Also, it was trained using the simple-AHN algorithm reported in [4] with a learning rate coefficient of 0.1 (this selection was based on empirical results for classification problems presented in literature [4]) to find suitable values of H. It is remarkable to say that the simple-AHN algorithm has better performance when input attributes have small values, thus all features in both training and testing sets were standardized using the mathematical expression (3); where, x_{iq} represents the q sample value of the i th attribute, μ_x is the mean of the i th attribute, σ_x is the standard deviation of the i th attribute, and z_{iq} is the q standardized value of x_{iq}.

$$CH_3 - CH_2 - \cdots - CH_2 - CH_3 \tag{2}$$

$$z_{iq} = \frac{x_{iq} - \mu_x}{\sigma_x} \tag{3}$$

Once the training model was obtained, the AHN-based human activity model was validated with the testing data set obtaining a 98.14 % of accuracy (see Table 1). Lastly, this model was employed to predict a human activity based on the sensor attributes as shown in Fig. 2. It is remarkable to say that simple-AHN algorithm does not require random initialization, as other methods [4].

5.2   Deep Learning-Based Human Activity Model

Deep learning (DL) algorithms implement a methodology based on abstract models created from the inputs. These algorithms use a variety of learning techniques designed to extract features of the data hierarchically. That is, the upper level features are formed from the characteristics of the lower levels. This technique allows constructing more accurate and better predictive models for a wide range of problems [15]. These learning techniques apply to non-linear transformations for data representations.

They use a set of concatenated output layers where one layer is the input to the next layer. The larger and higher is the number of layers the more increases the capacity for

Table 1. Confusion matrix of the proposed AHN-based human activity model.

		Predicted values					
		sitting	*sittingdown*	*standing*	*standingup*	*walking*	Error
	sitting	14290	48	64	63	31	0.01421
	sittingdown	36	3353	16	14	25	0.02642
Real values	*standing*	126	60	14098	65	119	0.02557
	standingup	17	14	18	3748	43	0.02396
	walking	20	59	40	52	13581	0.01243
	Total	14489	3534	14236	3942	13799	0.01860

abstraction. Some deep learning algorithms are based on neuroscience and simulate the behavior of neurons in the brain and nervous system. The algorithm tries to establish a relationship between a stimulus and responses. Unlike traditional algorithms that are based on developing very specific methods to solve specific problems. Deep learning methods apply useful techniques aimed for generic problems. The applications of these algorithms can range from detecting fraud in credit card stock prediction results.

For deep learning model, we used the following settings: "Tanh" (Hyperbolic tangent activation function) as the activation function. The "Tanh" is very used in neural networks; this function produces numbers between -1 and 1. Thirty epochs were set for iteration. The rate of learning parameter was set in 0.01. When the rate lowers, the convergence is slower and the model is more stable. Finally, we used three hidden layers with 500, 250, and 500 nodes.

5.3 Comparative Analysis of Data-Driven Human Activity Models

We compare the accuracy of our proposed human activity model based on artificial hydrocarbon networks against other ten models, as shown in Fig. 4. The deep learning-based model (DL) was the top resultant model with 99.59 % of accuracy, while the proposed AHN-based model reached 98.14 % of accuracy. It is evident from Fig. 4 that the proposed model is one of the top three methods, i.e. it is in the first quartile (>95.07 %) of the experimental results. Random forest (RF) also competes with 99.48 % against DL and AHN models. In addition, Fig. 4 shows the mean accuracy (93.06 %) of the human activity models reported for example in [2], giving a qualitative meaningful to our proposed AHN-based model.

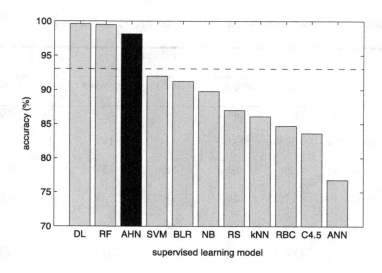

Fig. 4. Comparative analysis of accuracy (%) in different data-driven human activity models based on supervised learning methods. Black bar represents the proposed AHN-based model with 98.14 % of accuracy, which it is greater than the mean accuracy (93.06 %) of the human activity models reported for example in [2].

Tables 1 and 2 show the confusion matrix of the AHN-based and the DL-based models, respectively; where, the diagonal represents the true positive values. Notice that deep learning-based model has some zero false positive values in contrast with the AHN-based model. Moreover, Table 3 shows the accuracy of the models for activities. It can be seen from Table 3 that the proposed AHN-based model is stable when classifying activities (0.67 % of standard deviation) as well as deep learning-based model (0.65 % of standard deviation). In fact, the latter model is less accurate for detecting the *standing-up* activity, while in AHN is less accurate for detecting the *sitting-down* activity.

Table 2. Confusion matrix of the deep learning-based human activity model.

		Predicted values					
		sitting	*sittingdown*	*standing*	*standingup*	*walking*	Error
	sitting	15116	1	0	1	0	0.00013
	sittingdown	1	3557	4	23	6	0.00947
Real values	*standing*	0	6	14215	18	29	0.00371
	standingup	8	22	22	3666	11	0.01689
	walking	0	3	31	18	13242	0.00391
	Total	15125	3589	14272	3726	13288	0.00408

Table 3. Summary of accuracy values (%) of AHN-based and DL-based models for each activity.

Activity	Accuracy	
	AHN-based model	DL-based model
Sitting	98.58	99.99
Sitting-down	97.36	99.05
Standing	97.44	99.63
Standing-up	97.60	98.31
Walking	98.76	99.61

6 Conclusions and Future Work

In this paper we presented a classifier based on a novel supervised learning technique called artificial hydrocarbon networks (AHN). We described a comparative analysis between ten well-known data-driven activity recognition techniques against our AHN-based activity model. We focus our comparison on the performance of deep learning technique, which resulted with the best performance.

From the results of the comparative analysis we conclude that the activity model created with our classifier based on artificial hydrocarbon networks (AHN), had a performance that was left inside the three best models of our experiments. In addition, these results positioned the accuracy of AHN model above the mean accuracy of other results reported in the literature [2].

We consider that artificial hydrocarbon networks (AHN) are suitable for efficient body postures and movements classification, given a database with five activity classes gathered from four subjects wearing accelerometers. This comparative analysis executed in the domain of Human Activity Recognition (HAR), supports that the novel artificial hydrocarbon networks supervised learning technique is very effective for classification problems. In fact, this comparative analysis suggests that AHN should be used instead of deep learning when low time and low memory consuming are demanding, and accuracy is not crucial for solving the HAR problem (e.g., DL is 1.45 % more accurate than AHN in this HAR problem).

For future work, we are planning to do more experiments using different inertial sensors, e.g. accelerometers, in order to prove the classifier flexibility level of AHN. Also, we try to build a new database collected from users with different characteristics to determine if the activity model supports new users for more complex activities.

References

1. Chen, L., Hoey, J., Nugent, C.D., Cook, D.J., Yu, Z.: Sensor-based activity recognition. IEEE Trans. Syst. Man Cybern. Part C Appl. Rev. **42**(6), 790–808 (2012). doi:10.1109/TSMCC.2012.2198883
2. Ugulino, W., Cardador, D., Vega, K., Velloso, E., Milidiú, R., Fuks, H.: Wearable computing: accelerometers' data classification of body postures and movements. In: Barros, L.N., Finger, M., Pozo, A.T., Gimenénez-Lugo, G.A., Castilho, M. (eds.) SBIA 2012. LNCS, vol. 7589, pp. 52–61. Springer, Heidelberg (2012)
3. Reyes, J.L.: Smartphone-Based Human Activity Recognition. Springer Theses. Springer, Cham (2015). ISBN 978-3-319-14273-9 (Print) 978-3-319-14274-6 (Online)
4. Ponce, H., Ponce, P., Molina, A.: Artificial Organic Networks: Artificial Intelligence Based on Carbon Networks. Studies in Computational Intelligence, vol. 521. Springer, Cham (2014)
5. Ponce, H., Ponce, P., Molina, A.: Adaptive noise filtering based on artificial hydrocarbon networks: an application to audio signals. Expert Syst. Appl. **41**(14), 6512–6523 (2014)
6. Molina, A., Ponce, H., Ponce, P., Tello, G., Ramirez, M.: Artificial hydrocarbon networks fuzzy inference systems for CNC machines position controller. Int. J. Adv. Manuf. Technol. **72**(9–12), 1465–1479 (2014)
7. Ponce, H., Ponce, P.: Artificial organic networks. In: Proceedings of IEEE Conference on Electronics, Robotics, and Automotive Mechanics, pp. 29–34 (2011)
8. Mozer, M.C.: The neural network house: an environment that adapts to its inhabitants. In: Proceedings of the AAAI Spring Symposium on Intelligent Environments, pp. 110–114 (1998)
9. Bao, L., Intille, S.S.: Activity recognition from user-annotated acceleration data. In: Ferscha, A., Mattern, F. (eds.) PERVASIVE 2004. LNCS, vol. 3001, pp. 1–17. Springer, Heidelberg (2004)
10. Pantelopoulos, A., Boubakis, N.: A survey on wearable systems for monitoring and early diagnosis for the elderly. IEEE Trans. Syst. Man Cybern. Part C **40**(1), 1–12 (2010)
11. Acampora, G., Cook, D.J., Rashidi, P., Vasilakos, A.V.: A survey on ambient intelligence in healthcare. Proc. IEEE **101**(12), 2470–2494 (2013). doi:10.1109/JPROC.2013.2262913
12. Hinton, G.E., Osindero, S., Teh, Y.W.: A fast learning algorithm for deep belief nets. Neural Comput. **18**(7), 1527–1554 (2006)
13. Lichman, M.: UCI Machine Learning Repository. School of Information and Computer Science, University of California, Irvine, CA (2013). http://archive.ics.uci.edu/ml

14. Granitto, P.M., Furlanello, C., Biasioli, F., Gasperi, F.: Recursive feature elimination with random forest for PTR-MS analysis of agroindustrial products. Chemometr. Intell. Lab. Syst. **83**(2), 83–90 (2006)
15. Bengio, Y.: Learning deep architectures for AI. Found. Trends Mach. Learn. **2**(1), 1–127 (2009)
16. Liu, H., Motoda, H.: Feature Selection for Knowledge Discovery and Data Mining, vol. 454. Springer, New York (2012)
17. Lara, O.D., Labrador, M.A.: A survey on human activity recognition using wearable sensors. IEEE Trans. Commun. Surv. Tutorials **15**(3), 1192–1209 (2013)

Activity Recognition in Intelligent Assistive Environments Through Video Analysis with Body-Angles Algorithm

A First Step for Future Behaviour Recognition

Carlos Gutiérrez López de la Franca$^{(\boxtimes)}$, Ramón Hervás,
and José Bravo

Laboratorio MamI, Escuela Superior de Informática de Ciudad Real,
Universidad de Castilla-La Mancha, Paseo de la Universidad 4,
13071 Ciudad Real, Spain
Carlos.Gutierrez5@alu.uclm.es,
{Ramon.Hlucas,Jose.Bravo}@uclm.es

Abstract. *Activity Recognition* in a scientific setting is a field that is extremely popular, in which numerous and diverse proposals exist that tackle the creation of systems capable of recognising activities through different types of sensors. Given the relative maturity of *Activity Recognition* in comparison to *Behaviour Recognition*, most of the existing proposals in this last field are based in *Activity Recognition* but with the difference of analysing the activities throughout time. Therefore, the objective of this article is to describe the first phases of development of a larger scale research (doctoral thesis) with which we will intend to analyse the *Behaviour* of people with focus not only based on *Activity Recognition* but also with a strong component centered around *smart environments with context awareness* and supported by the foundations of *The Psychology of behaviour*.

Keywords: Behaviour Recognition · Activity Recognition · Kinect · Body-Angles Algorithm · Psychology · Serious games · Cognitive rehabilitation · Multisensing environments · Natural interaction · Context awareness

1 Introduction

Human behaviour is complex and it is influenced by many factors. Because of this, when analysing we have to be aware of the increasing amount of influence of these factors. In the same way that we may erroneously think that *Activity Recognition* is only done by *video analysis*, it would be a mistake to consider that **Behaviour Recognition** can only be done through *Activity Recognition* throughout time, though most of the previous projects would suggest by supporting themselves only in *Activity Recognition* to analyse **human behaviour**. Determining the *activity* that the subject of study is doing is very important, but it is not the only factor taken into account to deduct their behaviour, *context* (psychological profiles of the person, their environment, and their goals) are also fundamental.

© Springer International Publishing Switzerland 2015
J.M. García-Chamizo et al. (Eds.): UCAmI 2015, LNCS 9454, pp. 162–173, 2015.
DOI: 10.1007/978-3-319-26401-1_16

At the time of the reading of the present article, it is very important to keep in mind that it fulfils a double objective. On the one hand, *introducing the line of work and research* that we are attempting to develop during the following years, and on the other hand, *explain to a greater degree of detail* the phase in which it is currently being developed within that line of work. Because of this, the article is divided in 3 parts.

We will start with point 2, describing the long term objective of the project from the highest level of abstraction to the lowest, representing this last one the part of the project in which we are currently working. The second part of the article will describe in detail the current phase of development of the project during points 3, 4 and 5. The third point will introduce the subproject in development, the 4th will cover state of the art and the 5th point will describe the most important part of the subproject in more detail. The 6th point corresponds with the third part of the article and will explain in detail the tests that have been done to the system that is implemented, as well as its results, with the goal of starting to evaluate the usefulness and accuracy percentage of said system. Lastly, the 7th point will group the ideas that will be implemented in more advanced phases of development.

2   Proposed Research Line

The final goal of this research project is the creation of a system capable of analysing and recognising the **behaviour** of the monitored people. This system will support itself in different *modules* or *layers* that represent both the different *subsystems* that compose it, as well as *the different levels of abstraction* within the system. At the highest level of abstraction the system provides the **detected behaviours**, while at the lowest level of abstraction will provide the **actions or detected activities**. An *activity* is formed by a *sequence of actions*. The greater the number of actions that compose an *activity*, the greater the complexity. It is considered that a *basic activity is that which is composed of one action*, therefore the concepts of *action* and *basic activity* are equal.

Therefore, with the most basic information obtained from the *layers* of the lowest level of abstraction of the system, and combining this information obtained from each of the *modules* or *subsystems*, we will try to get as a final result the behaviour exhibited from each study subject.

There are two main *motivations* from this project. In first place a great deal of the existing proposals base themselves only on detecting changes in the pattern of activity performance throughout time. With this project we try to enrich that vision. In second place, the *computerized analysis of human behaviour* is still in its beginning steps. There are existing proposals that can recognise activities, proposals that analyse the emotions that people express, but there are not a lot of existing proposals that go a step further. Knowing the **behaviour** of the person would enable several applications, not only based on **behaviour detection**, like *detection of erratic behaviour (wandering) on people with dementia* [10], but also based on the **modification and adaptation** of it, as well as **applications capable of adapting to the behaviour of the user**. This way we can obtain improvements in the quality of life in people *without any kind of cognitive issue* (through *adaptive applications* minimizing the situation that can generate *stress* or *negative reactions* in users) as well as in people that present some *cognitive pathology* (*learning therapy and behaviour modification*).

There are several factors that influence **human behaviour**. These factors can be divided mainly in two: *factors inherent to the subject* and those *fruit of the present moment* that the subject is living through. The *inherent* factors to the subject are those that come from their past like *genetic factors, vital experiences, social situation* in which they have grown, how their brain process information or the *culture* that they have inherited and knows (memes or cultural genes). On the other hand, the present moment that the subject lives through also *exerts a very powerful influence* over the knowledge that the subjects adopts, such as the *emotion* that they feel at that moments, the *activity* that the subject is doing, the *physical state* that they find themselves in or the *environment/context* in which they are localized.

All of these factors that influence the behaviour that a human being adopts can be grouped in three great aspects: **Activity Recognition**, **Context Information** and **Psychological Fundaments**. All three forms what we call *Behaviour-Aware Computing*, and this concept is the one that settles the presented research field.

3 First Subproject in Development

The first phase in development corresponds to the subproject dedicated to the creation of the *Activity Recognition* module, as other of the system's components depend on it.

To extract the information from the monitored spatial environment uses two tools: **Kinect** (version 1) allows us to analyse posture and movements that people in the environment are doing, and the **Estimote** sensors, embedded in objects of daily use, give the module information about the context in which the actions are occurring, making the *Activity Recognition* module *sensitive to context* [6] (see Fig. 1).

This project is divided in two phases. The first phase applies to the development of the **core** of the project, the *Activity Recognition* subsystem. The second phase consists in the development of a practical application that takes advantage of the created *core*. This way it is possible to test in depth and take advantage of the *Activity Recognition* before developing the rest of the system's modules that interact with it. The final application is a *game* focused on helping *children with cognitive problems*.

4 State of the Art

The *monitoring* or *recognition* of *movements/actions/gestures/activities* is a topic of study that generates a lot of interest, because their specific applications and the fields in which they can be applied are innumerable. Because of this, *for some time*, there have been related projects [4, 16] but the majority are very recent, mainly because during their compilation, there has been special interest in the proposals that make use of novelty sensor devices, particularly *Kinect*.

The collected proposals go from a system to guide people with *dementia* in the perform *activities of daily living* [4], to a system that allows the evaluation the *performance* of a *dancer* [1], going through a *physical rehabilitation* [12], activity recognition

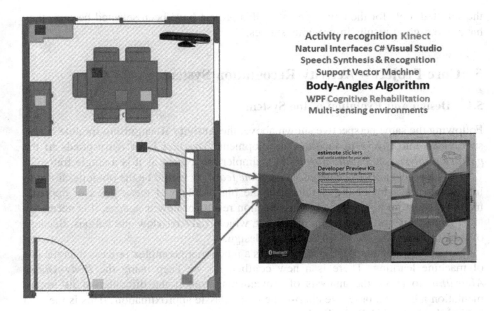

Fig. 1. Extraction of information of the monitored environment

for the *physical rehabilitation through mobile devices with accelerometer* [14], detection of *elderly frailty with accelerometry* [7], detection of *stereotypical behaviour in autistic children* [9], an *analysis of the current outlook* of research in the field of Activity Recognition [5] and monitor the activities that occur in *an isolation room of a psychiatric hospital* with the objective of giving detailed information on their mental state to the personnel, as well as influence on the technological elements of the environment to try and help the isolated patient [17].

Another kind of proposals centre around the use of **alternative recognition strategies**, like the recognition of activities in which the *observer in 1st person* takes part [15], a study of activity recognition when information from *skeleton tracking is not available* [18] or *gesture* recognition [3] and *hand* gesture [13].

Lastly, there are also proposals that support themselves on **objects from the environment** (taking context into account) to do the *activity analysis*. Some of those examples are the detection of activities done in a *house* with *simple ubiquitous sensors* [16], a system of activity recognition of daily living that takes *context* into account, this is, *the objects* the user *interacts with* [8], a system of the same idea as the previous one but centered around activities and *culinary* objects [2] and lastly, monitoring the activities and state of a *dog* through sensors embedded in their *collar* [11].

The study of the previous works cited sheds as first indicator that *Kinect* has demonstrated, with its limitations, to being a useful tool in the environment of *Activity Recognition*. In second instance we observe that the most used methods/algorithms are the *Hidden Markov Models, Dynamic Time Warping* and *Support Vector Machine*, the last one being the predominant in the group of mentioned articles. Because of this, the selected tools for the development of this project have been selected because they have given good results in previous studies.

5   Core Project – Activity Recognition System

5.1   Design and Evolution of the System

Following the same perspective shown above, the **Activity Recognition** module is also subdivided into *layers* to facilitate development. The first layer corresponds to the *posture analysis*, as a *static posture* is a simpler movement as it is a single frame.

It is clear that a focus centered on *machine learning* would be the obvious choice to implement a system of these traits. But the big problem of these types of approximations is that, to obtain precise classification results of new instances, it is necessary to generate a big and varied training dataset, which is always slow and tedious. Because of this, the **Body-Angles Algorithm** was design.

But the development of the algorithm is a much more complex process than the use of machine learning. There is a new conflict, do we keep using the **Body-Angles Algorithm** to allow the analysis of movements, even if the difficulty of its implementation increases, or do we choose the more classic approximation? This is the idea behind the **Extended Body-Angles Algorithm**.

At this point a *new question* arises. We have to *validate the created* analysis *model*, comparing its results to the ones that could be obtained from an approximation based on a more traditional focus, but can the traditional focus based on machine learning be taken advantage of for more than just comparing and validating the algorithm? This is where the **Triple Activity Recognition System** is born (Fig. 2).

With the **Triple Activity Recognition** System we subdivide the **Activity Recognition** system in 3 different *modules*. Each one of the 3 *modules* will be provided with the information that has been collected from the environment through *Kinect* and *Estimote*. With this information each module elaborates their answer, meaning, the activity that has been done according to it. The final result of the triple system is obtained combining and comparing the 3 *answers* given by the modules. If there are discrepancies these would be solved attending to the opinion of the module that has been given greater decision making power (that with a higher accuracy rate). Having *3 opinions* we get a more robust system. The modules are:

- **Extended Body-Angles Algorithm Module**
- **Machine Learning Module** $\longrightarrow$ It will be trained with both the raw data from the sensors as well as the angles calculated from the algorithm, to check if this last one can be used to enrich the typical approach.
- **Reactive/Conditional Module** $\longrightarrow$ Some activities can be recognised if a series of conditions are met, like for example the subject holding an object or two joints of the individual form a certain angle. With this module we will contrast if the performed activity meets the sequence of defined conditions for some of the defined activities that it supports.

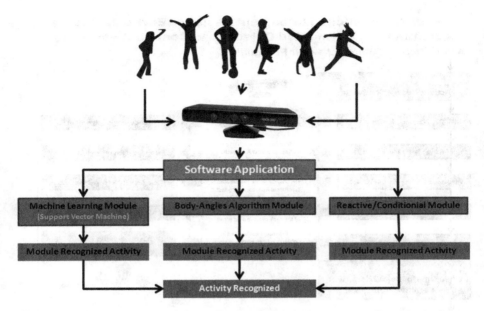

Fig. 2. *Triple Activity Recognition System*

The evolution followed during this project, as well as the order of the project, the defined sub-targets and what results come up from those sub-targets, it becomes obvious in Fig. 3.

5.2 Body-Angles Algorithm

It allows comparing the *similarity* between the *postures* of two human bodies, without the need of using a dataset with multiple instances of each of the supported postures. With the **Body-Angles Algorithm** one only need to have an instance of the reference with which to make the comparison. To make this possible we need to extract information from the human bodies so it won't depend on any individual factor as height of the individual, the exact position that it occupies within the environment or the actual environment. This means that the unit of information to use should be able to be extrapolated to any context, and if it fulfils that the unit of information has the same value in both bodies, we can assure that the posture of both is exactly the same, which makes it unnecessary to have more than one instance to compare it to. This unit of information is the *angle that two joints form in the human body*.

Whichever the human skeleton that is being analysed from *Kinect*, whichever position it occupies in the environment, and whichever the environment, if the angle that joint **J1** and **J2** form is the same on both skeletons, means that both have that **bone** that is between both joints is in the exact same posture. To check the full skeleton, the *angled formed between all pairs of adjacent joints* is checked. The algorithm takes into account the 20 joints that *Kinect* can provide.

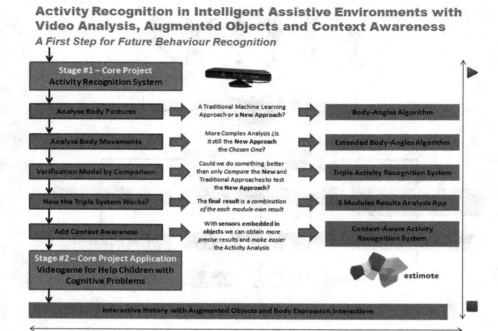

Fig. 3. Evolution of the development of the **Activity Recognition** module

To obtain the angle that a pair forms, it assigns one of the two joints as centre of the coordinate system. It is possible to find out the angle that it forms with another joint in terms of that centre applying *trigonometry*, and poses the problem as the assigned joint as the centre of the coordinate system, and is also the centre of a *goniometric circumference*. To do the math, as additional data it is necessary to obtain which one of the *4 quadrants* of that goniometric circumference, the joint that is not centre of coordinates. The trigonometric calculus is done in two dimensions projecting the skeleton on the XY plane and the ZY plane (reducing the complexity of the calculus without ignoring the depth). Also, to reduce the impact of errors in precision that *Kinect* commits, it is considered an acceptable error margin, that for now it is fixed in ±5 degrees (we will later validate that decision).

The ***Extended Body-Angles Algorithm*** compares the existing similarity between *movements* done by human bodies. Instead of comparing just one posture, it compares the *sequences of postures* that form the movements (Fig. 4).

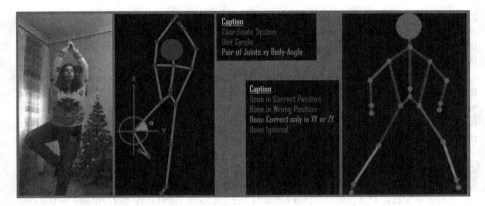

Fig. 4. Graphic example of the *Body-Angles Algorithm* working

6 Body-Angles Algorithm Test

As it has been indicated in the previous part, we're currently developing, among other things, the *Extended Body-Angles Algorithm* from the *first version* of the *Body-Angles Algorithm*, as this last one is already implemented. Because of this we have done a study with the goal of testing the accuracy rate that it can give.

This study has consisted in reproducing yoga postures and variations of those, in front of *Kinect*, with the objective of having the *Body-Angles Algorithm* analyse it and

Body-Angles Algorithm Test Results UCAmI 2015				
Results of Each Study Subject				
Subject	Total Tests	Successful Tests	Unsuccessful Tests	Success Rate
Subject #1	400	358	42	89.5 %
Subject #2	150	137	13	91.33 %
Subject #3	160	151	9	94.375 %
Subject #4	400	360	40	90 %
Subject #5	325	262	63	80.615 %
Total Results of Study Subjects				
Yoga Pose	Total Tests	Successful Tests	Unsuccessful Tests	Success Rate
The Tree	150	129	21	86 %
Tree v2	170	124	46	72.94 %
Tree v3	150	145	5	96.67 %
Warrior B	220	192	28	87.27 %
Warrior B v2	220	219	1	99.55 %
Chair	145	112	33	77.24 %
Chair v2	140	107	33	76.43 %
Mountain	240	240	0	100 %
Total	1435	1268	167	88.36 %

Fig. 5. *Body-Angles Algorithm* test results

give as a result which posture the volunteer was doing in each case. In first instance the reference models for the postures were recorded onto the system's database, meaning, the only instance that the algorithm needs to use as a model to compare the posture that is being done to.

We have used postures and variations of those postures to make a more demanding test of the algorithm. In fact some of the variations are not official yoga poses, but variations created for this experiment in order to have postures that are mostly alike, but have a small difference. This way we test the *precision* of the algorithm better than using a group of postures that are different among them.

Figure 5 collects the results of the performed tests and Fig. 6 shows a capture of the developed application to perform the tests. In it we can see how the algorithm calculates the percentage of similarity of the performed posture with each of the saved reference models. The posture that obtains the greatest similarity percentage is the one that the algorithm gives as a result. The application makes an automatic accounting of the number of tests in which the algorithm has gotten it right with the posture that was being done.

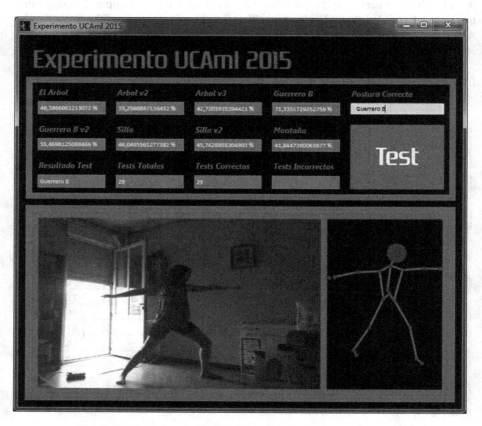

Fig. 6. Look of the application to test the *Body-Angles Algorithm*

As it can be seen, there aren't significant differences between the results with different test subjects. The groups of selected Yoga postures are beginner level so the level of knowledge of Yoga of the subject did not influence the results.

7 Conclusions and Future Work

Other than the applications and objectives that we hope to reach and develop in the future, and the ones that have been mentioned throughout the document, future work will focus mainly on the *improvement* of the *Triple Activity Recognition Subsystem*, with particular emphasis on the *improvement* on the *Body-Angles Algorithm*, as it is the most novel contribution. On top of it being the *most novel contribution*, it has been demonstrated that it is capable of obtaining good results recognising activities (in the performed tests it has obtained an *accuracy rate* of **88.36 %**) with the great advantage of *not needing to train the algorithm*, and in consequence, *not needing to generate a big dataset* with multiple instances per activity. Also, even though the creation and implementation of the *Body-Angles Algorithm* is a more complex process than using a *machine learning tool*, the internal processing of the created algorithm, once implemented, is simpler as it is based on values comparison, and *not on complex mathematical artifacts*.

The main improvement tries to implant in the algorithm has to do with the *ubiquity* of the system. The current implementation corresponds with a first simplified version of the algorithm in which the user has to be aware of the use of *Kinect*, and has to do the postures or movements in front of it. In later versions of the algorithm instead of projecting the skeleton on the XY and ZY planes in regards to *Kinect*, it will do the same operation but it will *translate the centre of reference to the person*, in which the obtained angles on both planes will be the same independently of the position that the user has in regards to *Kinect*. This way *Kinect* will go **unseen in the environment**.

As we have previously mentioned, on point 3, this first subproject corresponding to the *Activity Recognition Subsystem* is divided in 2 phases. At the moment of writing these lines, we are working on the development of the *Extended Body-Angles Algorithm*, the creation of the *Triple Activity Recognition System* and the implementation of the *3 Modules Results Analysis App* tool (see Fig. 3). Therefore, on top of the *improvement* of the *Body-Angles Algorithm*, in the future *phase 2* will be developed.

The second phase is the development of a *game* focused on **helping children with cognitive problems**. The game will be a type of *interactive story-teller*. The child will be presented a story, and to advance in it, they will be proposed a series of tasks to do. These tasks can be: activities or movements that the *Activity Recognition* module can recognise, achieve or use some of the objects that have an *Estimote* sensor integrated or any other interaction or prize that increases the cognitive benefits of using the application. The proposed tasks are related to what the story tells, and to be able to reach the end it will be necessary that the child correctly does those tasks.

With the game we try to stimulate aspects like **memory, attention, senses** and being able to do **analysis therapies and behaviour modification**. Once the game is developed, with the use of the neuroheadset *Emotiv Epoc*, we will try and check if it generates the benefits previously mentioned in the health of the children that use it.

In third place, and in relation to the *results of the tests* of the **Body-Angles Algorithm**, indicating that, if on this occasion we have chosen a first evaluation based on the accuracy percentage of the algorithm, in future publications there will be a more complex statistical evaluation and more detail on the obtained results.

Lastly, the fourth line of future work, as we have indicated, consists in development the rest of the modules of the *Behaviour Recognition System*.

Acknowledgments. This work was conducted in the context of UBIHEALTH project under International Research Staff Exchange Schema (MC-IRSES 316337) and the coordinated project grant TIN2013-47152-C3-1-R (FRASE), funded by the Spanish Ministerio de Ciencia e Innovación.

References

1. Alexiadis, D.S., Kelly, P., Daras, P., O'Connor, N.E., Boubekeur, T., Moussa, M.B.: Evaluating a dancer's performance using kinect-based skeleton tracking. In: Proceedings of the 19th ACM International Conference on Multimedia, pp. 659–662. ACM, Scottsdale (2011)
2. Bansal, S., Khandelwal, S., Gupta, S., Goyal, D.: Kitchen activity recognition based on scene context. In: International Conference on Image Processing (ICIP), pp. 3461–3465. IEEE, Melbourne (2013)
3. Biswas, K.K., Basu, S.K.: Gesture recognition using Microsoft Kinect®. In: Automation, Robotics and Applications (ICARA) 5th International Conference, pp. 100–103. IEEE, Wellington (2011)
4. Boger, J., Hoey, J., Poupart, P., Boutilier, C., Fernie, G., Mihailidis, A.: A planning system based on Markov decision processes to guide people with dementia through activities of daily living. IEEE Trans. Inf. Technol. Biomed. **10**(2), 323–333 (2006)
5. Brush, A., Krumm, J., Scott, J.: Activity recognition research: the good, the bad, and the future. In: Pervasive Workshop How to do Good Research in Activity Recognition, Helsinki, Finland (2010)
6. Dey, A.K.: Understanding and using context. Pers. Ubiquit. Comput. **5**(1), 4–7 (2001)
7. Fontecha, J., Navarro, F.J., Hervás, R., Bravo, J.: Elderly frailty detection by using accelerometer-enabled smartphones and clinical information records. Pers. Ubiquit. Comput. **17**(6), 1073–1083 (2013)
8. Fu, J., Liu, C., Hsu, Y.P., Fu, L.C.: Recognizing context-aware activities of daily living using RGBD sensor. In: IEEE/RSJ International Conference on Intelligent Robots and Systems (IROS), pp. 2222–2227. IEEE, Tokyo (2013)
9. Goncalves, N., Costa, S., Rodrigues, J., Soares, F.: Detection of stereotyped hand flapping movements in Autistic children using the Kinect sensor: a case study. In: Autonomous Robot Systems and Competitions (ICARSC), pp. 212–216. IEEE, Espinho (2014)
10. Hervas, R., Bravo, J., Fontecha, J.: An assistive navigation system based on augmented reality and context awareness for people with mild cognitive impairments. IEEE J. Biomed. Health Inform. **18**(1), 368–374 (2014)
11. Ladha, C., Hammerla, N., Hughes, E., Olivier, P., Plötz, T.: Dog's life: wearable activity recognition for dogs. In: Proceedings of the ACM International Joint Conference on Pervasive and Ubiquitous Computing, pp. 415–418. ACM, Zurich (2013)

12. Leightley, D., Darby, J., Li, B., McPhee, J.S., Yap, M.H.: Human activity recognition for physical rehabilitation. In: IEEE International Conference on Systems, Man, and Cybernetics (SMC), pp. 261–266. IEEE, Manchester (2013)
13. Ramirez-Giraldo, D., Molina-Giraldo, S., Alvarez-Meza, A.M., Daza-Santacoloma, G., Castellanos-Dominguez, G.: Kernel based hand gesture recognition using kinect sensor. In: XVII Symposium on Image, Signal Processing, and Artificial Vision (STSIVA), pp. 158–161. IEEE, Antioquia (2012)
14. Raso, I., Hervás, R., Bravo, J.: m-Physio: personalized accelerometer-based physical rehabilitation platform. In: Proceedings of the Fourth International Conference on Mobile Ubiquitous Computing, Systems, Services and Technologies, pp 416–421, Florence, Italy (2010)
15. Ryoo, M.S., Matthies, L.: First-person activity recognition: what are they doing to me? In: Computer Vision and Pattern Recognition (CVPR), pp. 2730–2737. IEEE, Portland, (2013)
16. Tapia, E.M., Intille, S.S., Larson, K.: Activity recognition in the home using simple and ubiquitous sensors. In: Ferscha, A., Mattern, F. (eds.) Pervasive Computing. LNCS, vol. 3001, pp. 158–175. Springer, Berlin Heidelberg (2004)
17. Veltmaat, M.J.T., van Otterlo, M., Vogt, J.: Recognizing activities with the Kinect. Technical report, Radboud University Nijmagen (2013)
18. Yang, Z., Zicheng, L., Hong, C.: RGB-depth feature for 3D human activity recognition. Commun. Chin. 10(7), 93–103 (2013)

Autonomous Evaluation of Interaction Resource Adequateness for Ambient Intelligence Scenarios

Gervasio Varela[✉], Alejandro Paz-Lopez, José A. Becerra,
and Richard J. Duro

Integrated Group for Engineering Research,
University of A Coruña, Ferrol, Spain
{gervasio.varela,alpaz,ronin,richard}@udc.es

Abstract. One of the main problems of Ambient Intelligence systems is that developers have to design and implement different user interfaces for each combination of user and environmental characteristics. This paper deals with alleviating this problem through the implementation of a UI development framework, called Dandelion, which postpones until run-time the implementation of the UI for a specific scenario. In particular, we address the autonomous evaluation of the adequateness of interaction devices for the scenario in order to facilitate the final automatic generation of an adapted UI.

Keywords: Human-computer interaction · Ambient-intelligence · Fuzzy-logic · User interfaces

1 Introduction

Ambient Intelligence (AmI) systems are expected to offer a ubiquitous user experience where the functionalities of the system are accessible in any place, at anytime, while keeping the interaction with the user transparent and natural [1, 2, 4].

In order to achieve this kind of user interaction experience, AmI user interfaces (UIs) are usually built by relying on different combinations of physical devices distributed throughout the environment [3–5]. These devices represent heterogeneous interaction resources that come from different manufacturers, employ different technologies, and use a variety of modalities to interact with the users. Obviously, to be ubiquitous, the user interfaces must operate in a diversity of physical environments with different types of users, while providing a natural and transparent user experience. Thus, depending on the user abilities and environment conditions, different sets of devices and interaction modalities will provide a better and more natural user experience [1–3].

Ambient Intelligence developers are required to bear in mind this heterogeneity of usage scenarios (combinations of user characteristics and environment conditions) when designing and implementing their systems. Thus, they must predict which kind of users are going to be supported by the system, and under what environmental conditions the system is going to operate. Then, for each specific usage scenario identified,

© Springer International Publishing Switzerland 2015
J.M. García-Chamizo et al. (Eds.): UCAmI 2015, LNCS 9454, pp. 174–186, 2015.
DOI: 10.1007/978-3-319-26401-1_17

they must decide, in advance, which particular set of devices is going to provide the most adequate user experience.

As can be easily imagined, it is very difficult and costly to predict the different usage scenarios where the system is going to be operated, and even if the developers are able to predict some of them, they are required to design a new user experience, with different devices, for each one. Furthermore, at some point, an unpredicted usage scenario (an unknown physical place, a change in user abilities or preferences, etc.) is going to arise, and ideally, the user interface should be able to continue operating and offering a natural user experience.

In order to achieve a truly ubiquitous and natural user experience in Ambient Intelligence UIs, the particular selection of which interaction modalities and devices are going to be used for each case should be postponed until run-time [1, 2]. This way, it will be possible to know the devices available, as well as the characteristics and conditions of the current usage scenario, and exploit them to drive the design of the user experience for that usage scenario.

Some projects have advanced in the development of context-adaptive UIs for Ambient Intelligence and Ubiquitous Computing systems, like the Multi-Access Service Platform [2] or the Egoki framework [1], nevertheless they have been focused on graphical user interfaces adapted to the end user devices in the case of MASP, and to the user abilities in the case of Egoki. From the field of physical user interfaces there are some solutions like the Personal Universal Controller [5], which automatically generates UIs for remote appliances. Nevertheless, they are also focused on graphical user interfaces that provide access to remote physical devices, and not on directly using those devices to build a multimodal UI.

In this paper we introduce an UI adaptation system that has been implemented as a part of the Dandelion UI development framework [6]. We will pay special attention to the mechanism used to evaluate the adequateness of an interaction device for a concrete usage scenario. This evaluation mechanism exploits information about the scenario to autonomously obtain, at run-time and in real-time, a measure of how adequate each device available in an environment is to provide a natural user experience in a particular scenario. This evaluation mechanism can be used for two different purposes, on the one hand, as a recommendation system for prototyping purposes. On the other hand, to dynamically select, at run-time, a new set of interaction devices for a new usage scenario.

This paper is organized as follows. Section 2 provides an overview of the UI adaptation system of Dandelion. Section 3 presents a detailed description of the autonomous, and real-time, device adequateness evaluation mechanism. Section 4 describes an example use case of the evaluation mechanism, and finally, in Sect. 5 some conclusions and future work are presented.

2 Context-Adaptive Ambient Intelligence User Interfaces

As indicated in the introduction, the autonomous interaction resource evaluation mechanism presented in this paper has been built integrated into a UI development framework for Ambient Intelligence systems called Dandelion [6]. This framework supports the development of portable AmI UIs capable of adapting, in real-time, to the characteristics of different usage scenarios. The Dandelion framework is designed and built around the idea of decoupling the developers, as much as possible, from the particular set of interaction devices used for each scenario. As can be seen in Fig. 1, the framework is designed using a multi-layered approach, where different layers of abstraction increase the level of decoupling between developers and devices.

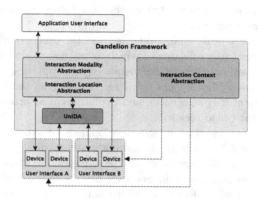

Fig. 1. Overview diagram of the Dandelion framework architecture.

On the one hand, the three layers shown on the left side of Fig. 1, the Interaction Modality Abstraction layer (IMA), the Interaction Location Abstraction Layer (ILA) and the Uniform Device Access layer (UniDA), create a UI development framework for Ambient Intelligence that allows developers to design and build their UIs at a very high-level of abstraction. The combination of these three abstraction layers enable developers to design and implement a single user interface logic, and then deploy it with a different set of interaction devices on each usage scenario.

In short, The Uniform Device Access layer [7] is a device technology abstraction framework that transforms a network of heterogeneous devices, from different technologies and manufacturers, into a homogeneous network where all the devices can be accessed in the same way, using a small set of generic APIs, and without requiring specific knowledge about each technology. The Interaction Modality Abstraction layer, combined with UniDA, enables developers to use any kind of device, independently of their modality and functionalities, to interact with the user. It allows developers to design and implement the UI logic using high-level interaction concepts, completely isolated from the devices modalities and technologies. And finally, The Interaction Location Abstraction layer isolates developers from the physical distribution of the devices, allowing developers to deploy the abstract UI using any distributed device available.

On the other hand, the Interaction Context Abstraction layer, on the right side of Fig. 1, is in charge of automating the adaptation of the UI to each usage scenario.

Thus, due to the abstraction capabilities provided by these three layers, the process of adapting an AmI UI to a new context, i.e. a new usage scenario, is reduced to performing a selection of a new set of interaction devices, among those available, appropriate for providing an adequate and natural user experience in the new scenario, and then deploy the abstract UI using this new set of devices.

In Dandelion, in order to achieve dynamic UI adaptation to new scenarios, this selection process is performed autonomously, at run-time and in real-time, by the Interaction Context Abstraction layer (ICA). As displayed in Fig. 2, and as will be seen with more detail in Sect. 3, the ICA receives a set of context models and the interaction requirements of the application as input, and it uses a series of Computational Intelligence algorithms to process them and provide a new selection of interaction devices as output.

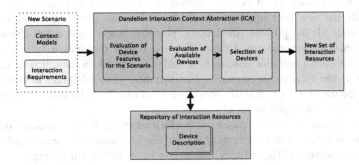

Fig. 2. Overview of the UI adaptation to context mechanism of the Dandelion framework

3 Autonomous Evaluation of Interaction Resource Adequateness for an Ambient Intelligence Usage Scenario

In this section we are going to describe the operation of the Dandelion Interaction Context Abstraction layer, with particular focus on how the ICA decides, automatically, which devices are the most adequate to provide a user adapted and natural interaction experience in a particular scenario. As shown in Fig. 2, the selection process is divided into three separate steps:

First, when the device selection process is started, the Dandelion ICA uses the information provided in the context models (modeled using fuzzy variables) to automatically evaluate all the possible device characteristics, and provide a fuzzy evaluation of what values of those characteristics are considered the most desirable for the particular usage scenario.

Second, the previously generated evaluation of device characteristics is used to query a repository of interaction resources (IRs) and evaluate, for each device available, how adequate it is for the new usage scenario. This degree of adequateness is calculated by a metric that compares the fuzzy description of the devices, to the fuzzy evaluation of characteristics generated in the previous step.

The result of this device evaluation process is a list of devices scored according to their adequateness to provide a user experience adapted to the abilities and characteristics of one specific usage scenario. This list is then used by the ICA to dynamically update a mapping between the abstract UI and the end devices, thus modifying, at run-time and in real-time, the UI.

In the next subsections we are going to show a more detailed description of how the adequateness degree of the devices is evaluated.

3.1   Evaluation of Interaction Resource Features for the Scenario

While all the three phases of the interaction resource (IR) selection procedure have an important role in the process, the first phase is the one that will have the greatest impact on the list of devices selected for the new scenario.

In this first phase, the ICA must decide what kind of modalities and physical characteristic the new user interface should have. For that purpose, the ICA automatically evaluates all the possible modalities, physical shapes, and other characteristics that an interaction resource could have. This evaluation provides a fuzzy measure of how adequate each particular feature is in order to provide a natural user interaction experience in the new usage scenario. For instance, how adequate is being able to provide voice messages or an alarm sound, or what physical characteristics, like shape or size, are the most appropriate.

This evaluation of device features is performed using fuzzy variables that model which value of a particular feature or characteristic is considered the most adequate for the new usage scenario. These fuzzy values can have different meanings and domains depending on the kind of information we are modeling, and we have identified four different categories of features or characteristics:

- *Interaction Modalities.* A device can use one or many interaction modalities (keyboard, touch, voice, etc.). The evaluation of adequateness of a modality consist in a fuzzy value that we call the *granularity*, it ranges from 0.0 to 10.0, and it is an indication of the level of complexity of the modality supported by the scenario. A finer granularity (larger number) indicates support for a greater complexity, for example a keyboard with a large number of small keys, or a device with complex voice commands. While a coarser granularity (smaller number) indicates support for lower complexity, like a keyboard with a small number of big keys.
- *Physical Shape.* Devices can have different physical shapes (toy, table, display, etc.). The evaluation of shapes for a scenario is also modeled using a *granularity* value where a finer granularity represents a great similarity to the specified shape.
- *Physical Characteristics.* A fuzzy specification of different physical properties of the devices, like the size, the weight or whether the device is mobile or static.
- *Usage Characteristics.* A fuzzy specification of device usage requirements, like the recommended user age or the required experience with technological device.

This fuzzy evaluation of the most adequate device features for the scenario is automatically generated by three different fuzzy-rule inference systems (FIS) as shown in Fig. 3. Each one of them is in charge of generating one of the three different aspects of the device evaluation.

The modality evaluation builder is composed of a series of small Fuzzy Inference Systems (FIS); each one of them specialized in a particular modality. As shown in the

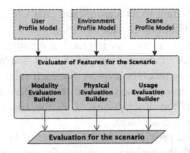

Fig. 3. Detailed view of the Ideal IR generator, which automatically evaluates the properties of devices of a particular usage scenario represented by the three context models.

example of Fig. 4, they receive different properties of the user, environment and scene as input, and produce a granularity value for one particular modality as output. This way, it is easy to add new modalities just by including a new small FIS.

```
RULE 1:
    IF user_visual_acuity IS normal AND user_cognitive_abstract_signs IS normal
    THEN modality_symbol IS high_granularity;
RULE 2:
    IF user_visual_acuity IS somewhat_impaired AND user_cognitive_abstract_signs IS normal
    THEN modality_symbol IS low_granularity;
RULE 3:
    IF user_cognitive_abstract_signs IS somewhat_impaired OR user_cognitive_abstract_signs IS
    impaired OR user_cognitive_abstract_signs IS severely_impaired
    THEN modality_symbol IS not_supported;
. . .
```

Fig. 4. Example of FIS dedicated to evaluating the granularity of an interaction modality, abstract signs, for a particular usage scenario.

The evaluation of physical properties of the devices is generated by two different FIS; one specialized in evaluating the physical characteristics of the device (size, portability, etc.), and the other one in evaluating the granularity of different physical shapes (toy, table, keyboard, embedded, etc.).

Finally, the evaluation of usage properties is generated by one FIS that relies on the information provided by the user model in order to evaluate the usage characteristics of the IRs, like the ICT abilities required by the user or the user's recommended age.

All the different FIS have been implemented using the JFuzzyLogic library [8], a Java library that facilitates the implementation of fuzzy inference systems. Their rules, generated manually using expert knowledge, have been programmed using the standard Fuzzy Control Language (FCL), which allows developers to easily customize the adaptation process by modifying the rules or adding new ones.

3.2 Calculating Adequateness of the Interaction Resources for the Scenario

As indicated in Fig. 2, once we have evaluated the adequateness of each device feature for a particular usage scenario, the next step consists in evaluating how adequate is each particular device, according to its features and characteristics, to provide a natural user experience in that particular scenario.

For that purpose, the ICA queries an interaction resource repository, as shown in Fig. 2, that keeps a database of descriptions of the IRs available in different physical environments. The repository receives a query for each interaction operation required by the UI, and it uses an *adequateness metric* to compare the evaluation of device features for the scenario to the descriptions of all the IRs deployed in the physical location of the particular usage scenario.

This adequateness metric provides a fuzzy measure of how similar are the features of the IR to the features with the highest evaluation for the scenario. Therefore, as these evaluations indicate the most adequate features for a particular usage scenario, this metric can be considered to provide a measure of how adequate an IR is for a concrete usage scenario.

As displayed in Fig. 5, the adequateness metric is a fuzzy measure between *0.0* and *10.0* obtained from the combination of multiple specific metrics of each one of the aspects of an Interaction Resource:

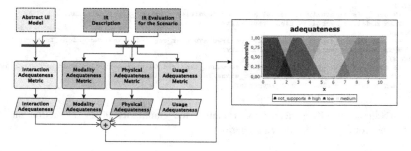

Fig. 5. The IR adequateness metric is calculated by an aggregation of four independent adequateness measures (Interaction, Modality, Physical and Usage adequateness).

- *Modality adequateness.* Provides a measure of how adequate an IR is for a specific usage scenario regarding its modalities.
- *Physical adequateness.* Provides a measure of how adequate is the physical description of the IR for a particular usage scenario, including the adequateness of its physical shape.
- *Usage adequateness.* Provides a measure of how adequate the usage characteristics of the IR are for one usage scenario.
- *Interaction adequateness.* Provides a measure of how adequate the interaction capabilities of the IR are to implement one particular interaction operation required by the UI.

For each query, the repository calculates the adequateness factor of each IR deployed in the physical location specified, and then, it answers with a list of IR descriptions sorted by their adequateness value. For that purpose, the repository keeps a database of IR descriptions. These descriptions are fuzzy objects that specify the characteristics and features of an IR in the same terms of the evaluation introduced in the previous section. What modalities are supported and with what granularity, which are the physical and usage characteristics of the IR and, additionally, it also includes information about the interaction operations supported by the IR (input, output, selection, etc.).

As both the evaluation of IR features and the IR description are objects made up of fuzzy attributes, in order to compare then and implement the adequateness metric, we need a mechanism to compare fuzzy objects, i.e. a similarity metric capable of dealing with uncertain and imprecise information. We are using the Fuzzy Geometric Model (FGM) proposed by Bashon [9], which is a generalization of the Euclidean distance adapted to fuzzy objects.

The Fuzzy Geometric Model performs the calculation of similarity between fuzzy objects in two steps:

1. Calculate the similarity among each corresponding pair for attributes.
2. Aggregate the similarities of all the pairs of attributes in order to give a final judgment of how similar the objects are.

For the first step, the calculation of the similarity between each pair of attributes, the FGM uses the following three equations.

The distance between two fuzzy sets $A_{ij}, B_{ij} \in F(U_j)$ is defined by the mapping $dis : F(Uj) \times F(Uj) \rightarrow [0, 1]$ shown in Eq. 1, where Uj stands for the domain of the j th attribute, and $i = 1,2,...,$ m_j stands for the number of linguistic terms defined by the membership functions $\mu_{A_{ij}}$ and $\mu_{B_{ij}}$ (in our case: $\mu_{A_{ij}}(x) = \mu_{B_{ij}}(x)$ for all $x \in U_j$). Equation 1 calculates the distance between the values of each pair of attributes $(x_1, x_2 \in U_j)$ taking into account only one of the specific linguistic terms of the fuzzy set for any.

$$dis(A_{ij}, B_{ij}) = |\mu_{A_{ij}}(x_1) - \mu_{B_{ij}}(x_2)| \tag{1}$$

Equation 2 shows a normalized generalization of the Euclidean distance, $d_F : at_{F_1} \times at_{F_2} \rightarrow [0, 1]$, that calculates the distance between two pairs of fuzzy attributes by taking into account the shape of the membership function that characterizes their membership to the fuzzy set. This is done by comparing the attribute distances regarding all the different linguistic terms (m_j).

$$d_F(a_j, b_j) = \frac{\sqrt{\sum_{i=1}^{m_j} dis(A_{ij}, B_{ij})^2}}{\sqrt{m_j}} \tag{2}$$

Finally, the similarity, $S_F : at_{F_1} \times at_{F_2}$, between each corresponding pair of fuzzy attributes a_j and b_j is defined by Eq. 3, where k_j (≥ 0) is a weight used to customize the contribution of each attribute to the final calculation of the object similarity.

$$S_F(a_j, b_j) = \frac{1 - d_F(a_j, b_j)}{1 + k_j d_F(a_j, b_j)} \tag{3}$$

Once we have calculated the similarity between each of the corresponding attributes, step two consists in aggregating all of them to produce an overall measure of how similar the two objects are. This can be achieved in multiple ways, but we have decided to use the weighted average of attribute similarities, because it allows us to customize the importance of each attribute in the final similarity metric. The overall fuzzy object similarity metric is provided by Eq. 4, where $\alpha_j \in [0, 1]$:

$$FuzSim(F_s, F_t) = \frac{\sum_{j=1}^{r} \alpha_j S_F(a_j, b_j)}{\sum_{j=1}^{r} \alpha_j} \tag{4}$$

As previously introduced, the FGM, i.e. the *FuzSim* function, in combination with some simple heuristics, is used to implement the Modality, Physical, and Usage similarities:

- *Modality adequateness.* It is calculated using a combination of heuristics and FGM similarity. It compares the granularity of each modality supported by the IR to their respective evaluation for the scenario. If the granularity of the IR is less than or equal to the evaluation of the maximum for the scenario, the adequateness is 1.0, because the scenario supports a more complex modality than the one specified by the IR. Otherwise, it compares the two values according to Eq. 5, where g_s and g_f are the granularity values of modalities M_s and M_f respectively. Finally, the modality adequateness value is adjusted using a simple heuristic (see Eq. 5) that penalizes the complexity of modalities.

$$ModAdq(M_s, M_f) = FuzSim(g_s, g_f) - 0.01 * g_f \tag{5}$$

- *Physical adequateness.* It is calculated as the weighted aggregation of the application of the *FuzSim* function to two different objects: the shape of the IR and its physical characteristics (size, etc.). Its definition can be seen in Eqs. 7 and 8, where *sp* stands for the shape granularity, *Ch* for the physical characteristics object, *sz* for the size attribute, *st* for the status attribute, and *d* for the usage distance attribute of the physical characteristics.

$$PhAdq(Ps, Pf) = 0.35 FuzSim(sp_s, sp_f) + 0.65 PhCSim(Ch_s, Ch_f) \tag{6}$$

$$PhCSim(Ch_s, Ch_f) = 0.5 SF(sz_s, sz_f) + 0.35 SF(st_s, st_f) + 0.15 SF(d_s, d_f) \tag{7}$$

- The usage similarity is calculated using the *FuzSim* function with the weights shown in Eq. 9, where Ug stands for the usage characteristics object, age for the recommended age attribute, and ict for the ICT literacy attribute.

$$UsgAdq(Ug_s, Ug_f) = 0.2SF(age_s, age_f) + 0.8SF(ict_s, ict_f) \qquad (8)$$

Finally, the overall FIO adequateness is calculated using the following equation if the interaction similarity is greater than or equal to 0.25. When the interaction similarity is less than 0.25, *Adequateness = 0.0*.

$$\begin{aligned} Adequateness = &0.10IntrAdq(I_s, I_f) + 0.65ModAdq(M_s, M_f) \\ &+ 0.15PhAdq(P_s, P_f) + 0.10UsgAdq(Ug_s, Ug_f) \end{aligned} \qquad (9)$$

As can be seen, we have considered the modality adequateness as the more relevant factor for the calculation of the overall adequateness because we think that modality is the factor that has more impact on the natural interaction perception of the UI. Regarding interaction adequateness, we have set a limit for its lower value. If the interaction similarity is too low (less than 0.25), the adequateness is 0.0, because if an IR does not match the interaction requirements of the UI, it will be useless.

4 Use Case Example

In this section we are going to present the results obtained for the autonomous, real-time, IR evaluation mechanism in a real Ambient Intelligence UI.

During the last years our group has been participating in the development of an intelligent evacuation management system for passenger ships such as cruises or ferries. The objective of the system is dual. On the one hand, it has to monitor the status of the ship in order to detect emergency situations (fire, flooding, etc.) and notify this situation to the ship crew. On the other hand, in case of evacuation of the ship, the system must provide guidance to passengers, in real-time, to leave the ship safely.

For this last goal, the system needs a UI that is able to adapt, dynamically, to the changing conditions of the ship, that can vary dramatically during the evolution of an emergency (limited visibility, noise, flooded corridors, etc.), and diverse characteristics and possible disabilities of the passengers. Therefore, the UI must be implemented as a combination of multiple distributed signaling devices embedded in the ship (screens, sound systems, light signals, etc.) that must be used complementarily and redundantly to show evacuation directions to the passengers. Furthermore, the devices must be changed at run-time and in real-time, as the users move from one location to another, and the environment conditions change.

For illustration purposes, and in order to keep this description simple and within the space of the paper, we have manually generated the models of six different usage scenarios by combining two physical places and three users. In the real system, the environment and situation models would be generated automatically by monitoring the environment, while the user model would be created by the crew during the passenger registration process (elder person, child, blind person, etc.).

Once the system detects a context change (a user moving from one place to another, o a new environment condition), it will ask the Dandelion ICA for a new selection of devices, thus starting the Dandelion UI adaptation process, that will autonomously execute the IR evaluation mechanism presented in this paper.

The first step consists in automatically generating an evaluation of device features for the usage scenario. Figure 6 shows the evaluations automatically generated for six different usage scenarios. As can be seen, the granularity values for the modalities change considerably according to user characteristics and environment conditions. For example, the deaf user has very low values for sound and speech based modalities, while the blind user has very low values for modalities requiring vision abilities.

| | | MODALITIES | | | | | | | | | USAGE | |
		sound	speech rec	speech prod	touch	wimp	gesture	keyboard	symbol	video	age	ict
CABIN	Deaf User	0,970	0,970	0,970	7,457	5,890	9,025	9,025	9,025	9,025	50	7
	Blind User	9,025	9,025	9,025	7,457	3,593	9,025	6,912	0,970	0,970	50	7
	Standard User	8,377	9,025	8,377	8,377	6,681	9,025	9,025	7,827	7,187	40	5
DECK	Deaf User	0,970	0,970	0,970	6,044	3,593	6,963	6,763	7,913	4,677	50	7
	Blind User	5,328	5,328	5,328	6,044	3,593	6,963	6,728	3,078	2,080	50	7
	Estándar User	5,143	5,328	5,143	6,666	4,409	6,963	6,763	7,229	4,409	40	5

| | | PHYSICAL | | | PHYSICAL SHAPE | | | | | | |
		size	status	distance	display	button	remote	toy	embedded	keyboard	surface
CABIN	Deaf User	7,913	6,250	208,239	8,905	3,909	7,898	3,750	9,025	6,896	6,861
	Blind User	7,913	6,250	208,239	4,964	6,086	7,520	3,750	9,025	6,226	6,861
	Standard User	7,913	6,250	208,239	8,396	3,750	7,898	3,750	9,025	6,912	6,913
DECK	Deaf User	6,912	3,750	201,394	5,623	7,588	7,588	3,750	9,025	7,360	5,000
	Blind User	6,912	3,750	201,394	4,107	7,617	7,617	3,750	7,913	7,317	5,000
	Estándar User	6,912	3,750	201,394	6,337	6,778	7,588	3,750	9,025	6,497	5,883

Fig. 6. Evaluation of IR features for the six proposed usage scenarios. Two different physical locations in a ferry ship (the cabins and the main deck), and three different users (a deaf user, a blind user, and a standard user without any severe disability).

The next step consists in evaluating the adequateness of the different interaction devices available. Figure 7 shows the adequateness values generated for the six usage scenarios and five different interaction devices. A smartphone using a graphical UI, a sound alarm system, a speech synthesis system, a display showing direction information, and a lighting signal for low visibility environments. As can be seen, different devices have different adequateness values according to their modalities and features. For example, the devices using sound modalities have very low adequateness values for the deaf user, even if they have good physical and user adequateness values. The contrary happens with the blind user, that has good adequateness values in sound-based devices. In the case of the standard user, while the user abilities does not impose any limitation, the environment conditions affect the selection, with sound-based modalities having lower adequateness values in the deck environment due to high ambient noise.

As can be seen, the IR evaluation mechanism is able to automatically provide an evaluation, in the form of fuzzy value called adequateness, of how adequate a device is for an usage scenario.

		Cabin					Deck				
		Smartph.	Sound P.	Speech S.	Display	Signal	Smartph.	Sound P.	Speech S.	Display	Signal
Deaf U.	Adequateness	0,870	0,299	0,299	0,900	0,876	0,543	0,293	0,293	0,868	0,886
	Interaction	1,000	1,000	1,000	1,000	1,000	1	1	1	1	1
	Modality	0,930	0,000	0,000	0,960	0,930	0,442	0	0	0,96	0,93
	Physical	0,506	0,741	0,741	0,583	0,549	0,446	0,698	0,698	0,489	0,495
	Usage	0,892	0,882	0,882	0,882	0,892	0,892	0,882	0,882	0,882	0,892
Blind U.	Adequateness	0,244	0,917	0,910	0,255	0,272	0,248	0,905	0,81	0,531	0,396
	Interaction	1,000	1,000	1,000	1,000	1,000	1	1	1	1	1
	Modality	0,000	0,950	0,940	0,000	0,000	0	0,95	0,905	0,427	0,213
	Physical	0,368	0,741	0,741	0,445	0,549	0,393	0,559	0,559	0,436	0,456
	Usage	0,892	0,882	0,882	0,882	0,892	0,892	0,882	0,882	0,882	0,892
Standard	Adequateness	0,816	0,918	0,911	0,898	0,879	0,463	0,785	0,871	0,89	0,912
	Interaction	1,000	1,000	1,000	1,000	1,000	1	1	1	1	1
	Modality	0,930	0,950	0,940	0,960	0,930	0,391	0,756	0,93	0,96	0,95
	Physical	0,488	0,741	0,741	0,565	0,549	0,471	0,698	0,495	0,514	0,698
	Usage	0,383	0,893	0,893	0,893	0,922	0,383	0,893	0,922	0,893	0,893

Fig. 7. Adequateness values automatically generated for five different interaction devices under the six proposed usage scenarios.

5 Conclusions

In this paper we have presented a mechanism to autonomously evaluate the degree of adequateness of interaction devices to implement an Ambient Intelligence UI for a concrete usage scenario.

The method proposed uses a set of context models and a series of fuzzy inference systems to evaluate which device features are the best for a scenario. Then, a novel device adequateness metric is introduced. It compares the fuzzy description of the interaction devices with the fuzzy evaluation of device features obtained from the previous step.

The interaction resource evaluation mechanism has been demonstrated in a real world example for a ship evacuation system. The results obtained are quite encouraging and we are now implementing a fuller version within the Dandelion framework.

Acknowledgments. This work has been partially funded by the Xunta de Galicia and European Regional Development Funds under grants GRC 2013-050 and redTEIC network (R2014/037).

References

1. Aizpurua, A., Cearreta, I., Gamecho, B.: Extending in-home user and context models to provide ubiquitous adaptive support outside the home. In: Martín, E., Haya, P.A., Carro, R.M. (eds.) User Modeling and Adaptation for Daily Routines. LNCS (HCI), pp. 25–59. Springer, London (2013)
2. Blumendorf, M., Albayrak, S.: Towards a framework for the development of adaptive multimodal user interfaces for ambient assisted living environments. In: Stephanidis, C. (ed.) Universal Access in Human-Computer Interaction. Intelligent and Ubiquitous Interaction Environments. LNCS, vol. 5615, pp. 150–159. Springer, Heidelberg (2009)
3. Dadlani, P., Peregrin Emparanza, J., Markopoulos, P.: Distributed user interfaces in ambient intelligent environments: a tale of three studies. In: Proceedings of the 1st DUI, pp. 101–104. University of Castilla-La Mancha (2011)
4. Zuckerman, O., Gal-Oz, A.: To TUI or not to TUI: evaluating performance and preference in tangible vs. graphical user interfaces. Int. J. Hum. Comput. Stud. **71**(7–8), 803–820 (2013)

5. Nichols, J., Myers, B.A., Rothrock, B., Nichols, J.: UNIFORM: automatically generating consistent remote control user interfaces. In: CHI 2006 (2006)
6. Varela, G.: Autonomous adaptation of user interfaces to support mobility in ambient intelligence systems. In: EICS 2013 - Proceedings of the ACM SIGCHI Symposium on Engineering Interactive Computing Systems, pp. 179–182 (2013)
7. Varela, G., Paz-Lopez, A., Becerra, J.A., Vazquez-Rodriguez, S., Duro, R.J.: UniDA: uniform device access framework for human interaction environments. Sensors 11(10), 9361–9392 (2011)
8. Cingolani, P., Alcala-Fdez, J.: jFuzzyLogic: a java library to design Fuzzy logic controllers according to the standard for Fuzzy control programming. Int. J. Comput. Intell. Syst. 6(sup1), 61–75 (2013)
9. Bashon, Y.M.: Contributions to Fuzzy object comparison and applications. Ph.D. thesis, University of Bradford (2013)

Detection of the Student Creative Behavior Based on Diversity of Queries

Cristian Olivares-Rodríguez[1,2] and Mariluz Guenaga[2(✉)]

[1] Universidad Andres Bello, Santiago, Chile
colivares@unab.cl
[2] DeustoTech - University of Deusto, Bilbao, Spain
mlguenaga@deusto.es

Abstract. Creativity is a skill of the twenty-first century, because in today's society both solving problems and changing environmental conditions are part of everyday life. However, evaluation of this skill is done through explicit methods which take a long time to implementation, they are not part of any student daily tasks, or have a high level of subjectivity. Therefore, we propose an implicit model for detecting student creative behavior based on the diversity of queries issued by students during a task search information to solve a problem. The diversity of the queries is calculated through the opportunities for such queries linked to each point of view. The method has shown very promising results on a small group of students. This shows that the diversity of queries is a good indicator of student creative behavior, so it is feasible to establish an implicit model for the detection of this ability, which is in daily use by students and, therefore, not need additional time to complete.

1 Introduction

Creativity has been defined as an ability of the twenty-first century [1] and it should be incorporated in schools, because it has been shown that students with good performance in math, language or science does not necessarily achieve good performance in search solutions for solving problems in unfamiliar contexts [2].

We focus on search because in this process, creativity could emerge if there is chance to make unlikely associations. Indeed, diversity provides an opportunity to be serendipitous in search tasks [3]. But, specificity provides positive rewards, because students take less risks. Therefore, students are in front of a tradeoff between exploration and exploitation, which is depicted in issued queries by them.

In this work we propose a method to classify the creative search behavior based on issued queries by students, since these encode the students association skills. Diversity of a query is modeled by its similarity against a set of emerged points of view from a query analysis. Therefore, the student could reach a creative solution when its queries have a high diversity, so new opportunities emerge to develop new concepts. Our experimental setup has involved 71 students of primary school, which have solved a general challenge through our platform.

© Springer International Publishing Switzerland 2015
J.M. García-Chamizo et al. (Eds.): UCAmI 2015, LNCS 9454, pp. 187–192, 2015.
DOI: 10.1007/978-3-319-26401-1_18

Each student provides a set of queries issued and a solution to the challenge, which are used to compute our proposed model based on diversity. Therefore, a diversity model of queries was used to classify student creative behavior with acceptable results (76 % of accuracy).

In this article, we describe a brief background regarding to creativity and search, regarding to educational context (Sect. 2). After that, we provide a formal definition of the proposed model (*Divers-Q*), which is developed on a real learning context (Sect. 3). Then, we define the methodology (Sect. 4) and we depict the main results (Sect. 5). Finally, we summarize our contributions and some future works (Sect. 7).

2   Background

This work focuses on the analysis of the student creative behavior, we propose that creative behavior can be inferred from the diversity of queries issued by the students during a problem-solving session.

Creativity does not have a unique definition, but Mednick [4] defined that a creative person is able to reach novel solutions to complex problems by making as many concept associations as possible (fluency), as diverse as possible (flexibility) and as unexpected as possible (originality). Koestler proposes the bissociation process [5] as a way to reach creative solutions by means of novel concepts associations in our mind. And also, a creative process was defined by Amabile [6] such as follows: a *conceptualization* phase, where the purpose is to establish several problem definitions from several points of view; a *search* phase, that aims to reach new concepts, relate them in order to make new associations and establish new solutions; and a *development* phase, where the purpose is to implement the solution and to update the domain knowledge. Amabile defined that the whole process is influenced by creative-relevant skills: associative and executive. The first one is related with the ability to make associations of concepts, in a short period of time [4]. And, the second one is related to the ability to control the search of alternatives.

There are some procedures to measure the creativity, but they are based on huge questionnaires [7] or they are highly subjective. Nevertheless, an empirical evaluation of divergent thinking (DT) by providing *unusual uses* is commonly used as a measure of the creativity. The evaluation of DT is a weighting function of every response based on fluency, flexibility and originality. This evaluation is made by experts, such as it is defined by Benedek [8].

While several studies have focused on to analyze patterns of search, we are working on to relate such patterns with the creative behavior. Weber and Jaimes developed a query log analysis over 2.3 million of anonymous users of Yahoo! seach engine just in U.S. [9]. The scope of such work was to determine who, how and what Web search is used for. They described three general kind of users in terms of topics, queries and demographic data: (1) informational or diverse, (2) navigational or bookmark, and (3) transactional. Usta et al. developed an analysis of search behavior of K-12 students over a commercial educational search engine log [10]. The more relevant findings of this work are that (1) a more likelihood of query repetitiveness in contrast to a general search engine and (2) the student's queries were shorter (2.16 terms on the average) than general web queries (2.5 terms on the average) submitted by users between 10 and 18 years old.

3   Creative Search Behavior ($Diversity\text{-}Q$)

An association task provides insight about the creative variables [4] and the information search can be seen as an association task, where each user is asked to provide a set of queries regarding to a target need (Eq. 1).

$$Q^{u_j}(n^s) = [(q_1, t_1), (q_2, t_2), \dots, (q_n, t_n)] \tag{1}$$

where q_i are the queries issued by a user u_j in a given time t_i and n^s is a target need provided by the system to drive the association task. More precisely, such target need is an information requirement defined by a goal, a description and a set of statements which put the target in context. The user strategy to relate a given query to an information need is hidden in the user mind, but it has been shown that the creative potential is highly related to association skills [8]. Therefore, we propose that a query model can be learnt in order to automatically recognize the creative search behavior.

Given a target need n^s and a set of users U, a pool of queries association task P is defined (Eq. 2).

$$P(n^s) = \begin{bmatrix} Q^{u_1}(n^s) \\ \vdots \\ Q^{u_U}(n^s) \end{bmatrix} \tag{2}$$

This pool encodes several points of view provided by every users to n^s. Also, the queries of a particular user u provide insights about the user's path to reach relevant or interesting knowledge, and each query is related to one or many points of views (v) such is defined in the Eq. 3.

$$Q^{u_i}(n^s) = \begin{bmatrix} s(q_1^{u_i}, v_1) \; s(q_1^{u_i}, v_2) \cdots s(q_1^{u_i}, v_j) \\ \vdots \\ s(q_n^{u_i}, v_1) \; s(q_n^{u_i}, v_2) \cdots s(q_n^{u_i}, v_j) \end{bmatrix} \tag{3}$$

where $s(q, v)$ is a similarity measure between a query q and a point of view v, but points of views are unknown a priori. Thus, we figure out a subset of unknown point of views, $V_k \subset V$, by following a unsupervised learning model and by using a subset of queries P_p of p selected users from $P(n^s)$. Where each point of view v is a centroid of a cluster and every query q is represented in a binary model of bag of words.

Similarity $s(q, v)$ is the chance that a user moves towards a point of view v by means of a query q when the search results arise. Diversity of query will be higher if the chances to move towards points of view are quite similar to each other. Therefore, a user session is completely defined by its queries issued (Eq. 3) and the points of view V_k.

4   Experimental Setup

We have developed a search task on 71 students of fifth and sixth grade from Spain, but we have considered just 53 students in order to evaluate the proposal because they have provided at least one query in the whole process.

We have designed a general challenge, which defines the target need n^s (Eq. 1). Once students have been accepted the challenge, they have 35 minutes to reach a creative solution. During the search, they could search information on Wikipedia[1] through our platform by using a Python module[2].

We have applied the unusual uses test for a *Chair* (*Silla*) (in one minute) and we have manually evaluated the user creativity taking into account their flexibility, fluency and originality. This evaluation have been done in a blind process by six diverse professionals, which evaluated by a 5-Likert scale at each dimension. The solutions have been evaluated based on a rubric of creativity used at the University of Deusto. Thus, a student is considered creative if their DT evaluation or the solution evaluation is higher than a *th* threshold.

We have learnt the subset of points of view by using the k-Means algorithm, considering several values of k. We have evaluated the quality of *Diversity-Q* model by a classification problem: creative and non creative students. The learning algorithms considered were Naïve Bayes (*NB*), Decision Tree (*dTree*) and three versions of the SVM algorithms. In order to evaluate the accuracy of the learning algorithms we have performed a cross-validation method.

5   Results

The *Diversity-Q* model provides a good description of creative search behavior, because the classifiers reach acceptable accuracy even for small values of k. Meanwhile, the classification performance is independent of the k value at three learning models: *SVM-Linear*, *SVM-Sigmoid* and *NB*.

We see at Fig. 1 that Decision Tree Algorithm has the worst performance to classify student creative behavior. This performance keeps similar for almost every value of *th*. The SVM algorithms show similar results to each other, thus the kernel used is not so relevant. Nevertheless, a polynomial kernel provides better results over small values of k and *th* (Fig. 1(a) and (b)), which is crucial for reduce the time performance by keeping high accuracy. Surprisingly, Naïve Bayes algorithm provides a similar accuracy to SVM algorithms, even for small values of k.

---

[1] https://es.wikipedia.org.
[2] https://github.com/goldsmith/Wikipedia.

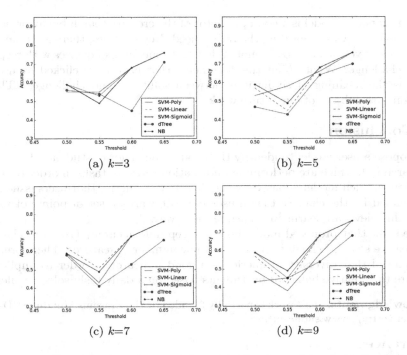

Fig. 1. Classification accuracy against several values of threshold th and k.

The parameter th becomes crucial for the classification task. While higher is th the accuracy is better, which is strongly related with the blind evaluation of the students by a diverse group of professionals. When a low th has been used, there is a high number of students considered creative, but they are really not.

6   Discussion and Limitations

Weber and Jaimes work provided a detailed analysis about the user behavior on a commercial search engine and the Usta et al. work shown the students behavior over an educational platform. While, the search goals are unknown in these works, we have designed a framework where the challenge is known in advance but user intents are still unknown. Our proposal provides implicit relations between the student behavior and the target need.

We applied an experimental setup over set of 71 students, but it is required to develop a more exhaustive experimentation regarding to size and diversity of sample.

We have used a commonly applied test for divergent thinking developed by Benedek et al. [8]. Also, we've used a formal rubric to measure for creative level of solutions. Both measures have been helpful to properly identify the most creative students. Nevertheless, a more detailed analysis is required because both measures depend on expert criteria.

The proposed model is a good predictor of the creative search behavior based on the points of view regarding the target need. Nevertheless, there are relations which are not yet taken into account: What is the meaning of queries with respect to the challenge? What about the documents that have been clicked by users? What is the meaning of similarities between solutions and challenges? These questions are subject of our future work.

7   Conclusion

We propose a user model to identify the creative behavior of students (how they are searching), which are performing information retrieval tasks in order to solve a challenge. Such model is based on the diversity of queries that users issue and it is defined by the chances that a user moves towards a set of points of view, where this views are learnt in a unsupervised way.

We show that proposed model has an acceptable accuracy (76 %) to classify the creative search behavior, even with a few number of features. Therefore, we have proved that diversity of queries is a good indicator in order to implicitly measure the creative behavior of students based on a daily task: solve problems.

Acknowledgments. This work is partially founded by the Erasmus Mundus SUD-UE program (http://www.sudue.eu).

References

1. Kyllonen, P.C.: Measurement of 21st century skills within the common core state standards. In: Invitational Research Symposium on Technology Enhanced Assessments, pp. 7–8, May 2012
2. OCDE: Pisa: programme for international student assessment. http://www.oecd.org/pisa/ (2014). Accessed 1 May 2015
3. André, P., Schraefel, M.C., Teevan, J., Dumais, S.T.: Discovery is never by chance: designing for (un) serendipity. C and C 2009, pp. 305–314 (2009)
4. Mednick, S.: The associative basis of the creative process. Psychol. Rev. **69**, 220–232 (1962)
5. Koestler, A.: The Act of Creation. Dell Publishing Co, New York (1964)
6. Amabile, T.: The social psychology of creativity: a componential conceptualization. J. Pers. Soc. Psychol. **45**, 357–376 (1983)
7. Torrance, E.P.: The nature of creativity as manifest in its testing. In: Sternberg, R.J. (ed.) The Nature of Creativity: Contemporary Psychological Perspectives. Cambridge University Press, New York (1988)
8. Benedek, M., Neubauer, A.C.: Revisiting mednick's model on creativity-related differences in associative hierarchies. Evidence for a common path to uncommon thought. J. Creat. Behav. **47**(4), 273–289 (2013)
9. Weber, I., Jaimes, A.: Who uses web search for what: and how. In: Proceedings of the fourth ACM international conference on Web search and data mining, pp. 15–24, ACM (2011)
10. Usta, A., Altingovde, I.S., Vidinli, I.B., Ozcan, R., Ulusoy, O.: How k-12 students search for learning?: analysis of an educational search engine log. In: Proceedings of the 37th International ACM SIGIR Conference on Research & #38; Development in Information Retrieval. SIGIR 2014, pp. 1151–1154. ACM, New York, NY, USA (2014)

Collaboration-Centred Cities Through Urban Apps Based on Open and User-Generated Data

Diego López-de-Ipiña[1]([⊠]), Unai Aguilera[1], and Jorge Pérez[2]

[1] Deusto Institute of Technology, DeustoTech,
University of Deusto, 48007 Bilbao, Spain
{dipina,unai.aguilera}@deusto.es
[2] eServices, TECNALIA, Bilbao, Spain
jorge.perez@tecnalia.com

Abstract. This paper describes the IES Cities platform conceived to streamline the development of urban apps which combine heterogeneous datasets provided by diverse entities, namely, Government, citizens, sensor infrastructure and so on. Particularly, it focuses on the Query Mapper, a key component of this platform devised to democratize the development of Open Data based mobile urban apps. The advantages from the developers' perspective brought forward by IES Cities are evaluated by describing an exemplary urban app created on top of it. This work pursues the challenge of achieving effective citizen collaboration by empowering them to prosume urban data across time.

Keywords: Smart city · Linked data · Apps · Crowdsourcing · HTML5

1 Introduction

The increasing urbanisation is making city authorities, governments, companies and even citizens to start thinking on alternative ways to manage the resources within a city not only pursuing more efficiency, i.e. to do more with less, but also seeking to find ways to achieve a higher level of satisfaction among citizens and economic agents within a city. Indeed, the success of a city to retain and attract people and companies highly relies on its appeal, economic dynamicity and awareness of the real needs of the diverse societal sectors that populate it. Only when these three premises are met we can truly start talking about truly Smart Cities, i.e. those cities that meet citizens' needs.

Since the first public administrations started sharing their data as Open Data, the idea of Open Government has spread around the world. Open Data implies [1]: (a) more efficient and effective government, (b) innovation and economic growth, (c) transparency and accountability and (d) inclusion and empowerment. These arguments favour the "open by default" paradigm, but the openness of government data is only one of the ingredients needed to address Open Government. Involving local entrepreneurs and citizens is a must. Indeed, most cities, territories and countries, which have started adopting Open Government policies, have serious lacks on exploiting the potential of Open Data. They have focused their attention only on implementing their open data portals, placing low effort on bringing open data closer to entrepreneurs and citizens through suitable APIs, easily consumable by application developers.

© Springer International Publishing Switzerland 2015
J.M. García-Chamizo et al. (Eds.): UCAmI 2015, LNCS 9454, pp. 193–204, 2015.
DOI: 10.1007/978-3-319-26401-1_19

The IES Cities platform is a CIP European project aiming to promote user-centric mobile micro-services that exploit both open data and user-supplied data. It contributes with an urban apps-enabling technological solution. It focuses on enabling citizens to create, improve, extend and enrich the open data associated to a city in which micro-services, i.e. urban apps, are based. The main stakeholders of the resulting urban apps ecosystem are the citizens, SMEs and public administration within a city. This platform is grounded on the progress achieved lately in two key technological areas: (a) *open government and urban sensor generated datasets* and (b) *smartphones equipped with different sensors*, e.g. GPS, which can execute urban apps, i.e. offering services for citizens in different domains (e.g. transport, security and so on). Furthermore, it aims to demonstrate through a range of two-phase pilots in four European cities (Bristol, Majadahonda, Rovereto and Zaragoza) how the resulting apps can actually satisfy the needs and demands of their citizens by fostering citizen-council collaboration.

This paper has the following structure. Section 2 reviews related work. Section 3 describes the IES Cities platform. Section 4 describes a core component of the platform, namely Query Mapper, whose purpose is to streamline the consumption and production of urban data. Section 5 validates the platform by describing an urban app created for Zaragoza. Finally, Sect. 6 draws some conclusions and outlines future work.

2   Related Work

This work proposes assembling Smarter Cities around Linked Data [2], Crowdsourced Data [3] and Open APIs approaches.

Since the introduction of the term crowdsourcing and crowd-sourced data by Howe in its seminal paper [4], data generated by citizens has been used for collecting encyclopaedia data, cartography data and environmental data among other sets of data. These huge datasets are used for education, urban planning, disaster relief and so on. In the Smart City context, some initiatives have emerged to give citizens the chance to participate providing data about the city, e.g. FixMyStreet[1]. Citizens can act as mobile sensors that monitor the variables of the city, and the data provided by them as crowd-sourced data. Data commonly provided by citizens are: (a) *atmospheric data* (temperature, pressure, air humidity, soil humidity and so on); (b) *environmental data* (gas emissions, pollutants, noise level and so forth), which is measured by the physical sensors of their smartphones or accompanying Bluetooth connected sensing devices; and (c) *data directly sensed and edited by their citizens* such as damaged street furniture, bumps in the road, vandalism and so forth. These data can be used by authorities, decision-makers, and urban planners to perform thought through interventions.

TheDataTank (TDT) [5] is a tool to transform online data of different formats into a user-friendly RESTful API. The data owner provides the URI base of her data and the meta-data needed to interpret the data set: Once this is done, data is provided using pagination to improve the response to the client. The query mapper described in Sect. 4 follows a similar data transformation approach but enhances exploitability by enabling

---

[1] http://www.fixmystreet.com/

querying heterogeneous datasets through SQL and returning results in JSON format, the *lingua franca* of web developers.

There are several initiatives trying to promote Open APIs for Smart Cities and territories. CitySDK[2] is a free and open-source project providing ways for citizens to release data. The SDK provides also libraries that third parties can use to reuse data released by citizens. Open311[3] offers a platform for citizens to communicate issues about public spaces and services. It also offers a public API for third parties to develop new applications using the data provided by citizens. Ushahidi [6] represents a set of tools to democratize information, increase transparency and lower barriers for individuals to share their stories. This platform enables easy crowdsourcing of information through multiple channels, including SMS, email, Twitter and the web. It includes Crowdmap, a tool that enables sharing a story on a map with the addition of photos and videos.

This work seeks citizen participation and contribution to a city's datasets or knowledge base by enabling them to contribute with data through their smartphones' urban apps Some important concerns around user-generated data are its provenance, trustworthiness and privacy control. To deal with provenance, the W3C has developed the PROV Data Model [7]. Trustworthiness is tackled in this work by delegating data validation to the consuming app business logic. The flexible and fine-grained mechanism to control access to published data in IES Cities is described in Sect. 4.

3 The IES Cities Platform

IES Cities promotes urban mobile services that exploit both Open Data and user-generated data in order to develop innovative services. It encourages the reuse of already deployed sensor networks in cities and the existing Open Government related datasets. It envisages smartphones as both a sensors-full device and a browser, i.e. hybrid app player, which is carried by almost every citizen.

IES Cities' main contribution is to devise a technological platform to foster the development of Open Data apps, which are then consumed from citizens' smartphones. This platform is being deployed in four different European cities providing their citizens the opportunity to get the most out of their cities' data. Our assumption is that urban apps will be assembled from structured and non-structured data in the form of RDF, CSV, XML or even HTML pages which can be scrapped. However, information in such models should be mapped into JSON, a *de facto lingua franca*, for web and mobile developers to truly promote the consumption of urban datasets.

IES Cities accelerates the development and deployment of new urban services that exploit city knowledge in the form of several heterogeneous datasets such as Open Government repositories, user-generated data through smartphone apps or even social data. The platform manages the whole lifecycle of city-related data and provides facilities to exploit that knowledge in a uniform, web developer-friendly, manner, i.e. through the SQL query language and the JSON format to exchange data between urban

---

[2] http://www.citysdk.eu

[3] http://open311.org/

apps and the platform's back-end. Furthermore, the platform annotates user-generated data with provenance and fine-grained access control metadata for datasets so that quality assurance, reliability and security can be enforced. The goal is to ensure that user-generated data truly enrich and complement existing council-provided data. Besides, the platform provides support to host app specific datasets so that the whole presentation and business logic can rely on the client-side and all the data manipulation responsibility is delegated to the platform. Finally, IES Cities also incorporates a Logging module through which statistics can be gathered and analytics applied regarding apps and datasets usage. The platform and each app manager can thus monitor the operation and usage of their IES Cities-compliant assets.

3.1   IES Cities Architecture

The IES Cities platform's client/server architecture is depicted in Fig. 1, comprising the following layers: (a) client layer, (b) business layer and the (c) data layer.

The *IES Cities Client Layer* is composed of the IES Cities Player and the Web Interface. The *IES Cities player* is a mobile application that serves as the main entry point to browse through, review and select those urban services run in a user's smartphone. The *Web Interface*[4] allows different actions depending on the type of user (citizens, city councils and service developers), e.g. to browse, search, review and access to applications, datasets and usage stats being generated by the platform.

The *IES Cities Business Layer* is responsible for the management of the main entities handled by the solution, namely councils, apps, datasets, users and usage stats. IES Cities is devised to host the urban apps and datasets ecosystem of a city. It promotes the usage and consumption of such apps and datasets by citizens, enterprises and the council itself. All the functionality of the IES Cities platform is offered through a RESTful API[5] which groups operations in the following categories: (a) *Account interface* which offers CRUD operations to deal with the main entities tackled by the project; (b) *Logging module* which enables server-side components to register diverse events associated to apps life cycle (e.g. `AppStart`, `AppProsumer` and so on), player interactions (e.g. `PlayerAppSearch`), or dataset-related (e.g. `DatasetRegistered`); and the (c) *Query Mapper* which offers methods to enable the query and insertion of data through SQL. Figure 2 shows the Swagger-generated web interface on top of the IES Cities RESTful API.

The *IES Cities Data Layer* allows accessing different heterogeneous datasets, e.g. ideally those modelled as 5* Linked Data but also other open data available in less rich formats such as CSV or XML files, in an homogeneous manner. In order to make this possible, when a data provider registers a new dataset: it has to describe the contents by providing a description of its data model and its access details. Through the data *wrapper abstraction*, IES Cities enables to access any type of data source, even non-structured data sources, e.g. tweets accessed through Twitter public API, and to map it into a format, which can be exploited directly by the Query Mapper component.

---

[4] http://iescities.com/

[5] http://iescities.com/IESCities/swagger/

Different database management systems can actually host the data. Currently, a document-oriented NoSQL database engine (i.e. Scalaris), a relational database management system (i.e. PostgreSQL) and the Virtuoso RDF store are hosted within the back-end. In addition, external CKAN and Socrata remote repositories can also be consumed.

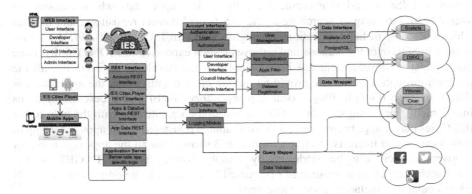

Fig. 1. IES Cities platform architecture.

Fig. 2. IES Cities' RESTful API with details for data (Query Mapper associated) category.

3.2 IES Cities Operation

The *modus operandi* of the platform is as follows. Firstly, the municipality registers with the IES Cities server its datasets descriptions, by means of a web form. It indicates where the dataset can be located and accessed (URI), what is the original format of the data (CSV, RDF, XML and so on), a description of the dataset expressed in JSON-Schema and, optionally, a mapping script between the original data source format and JSON, and *vice versa*. Secondly, a developer finds which datasets are available by browsing or searching in the IES Cities' dataset repository, and decides which ones best fit her application. Through a RESTful JSON-based API, she issues queries in SQL over the datasets and retrieves results expressed in JSON. Thirdly, once the application development has been completed, the developer registers it with the platform through a web form, providing among other details where the application is (URI), its type (Google Play, Local app repository, Web) and a description of its functionality, including snapshots. Finally, end-users, i.e. citizens, with the help of the IES Cities player app, browse or search for available registered urban apps according to their location and interests. As illustration, Fig. 3 shows how all the apps registered for a given council can be retrieved by simply issuing an HTTP GET to the `context/entities/council/{councilid}/apps`, getting back a JSON result containing metadata about those apps.

4 The Query Mapper

The Query Mapper component's underlying philosophy is to create a relational view for all mapped data sources, allowing the execution of queries to retrieve the data. An assortment of Data Wrappers assists the Query Mapper with datasets that cannot be mapped into a relational model. Through such wrappers, SQL queries are translated into API calls or execution of business logic to extract the results. A good example is the Social Data Wrapper, which enables to issue SQL queries about social data posts. The functionality of this module is exposed under the category `data` (see Fig. 2) in IES Cities API:

- *Querying using SQL.* The query mapper provides methods to query a dataset using the SQL query language. The registered dataset must be compatible with these types of queries, which requires that the dataset is fully relational or that it is backed by a data source that can be transformed by the Query Mapper to a relational view.
- *Querying using SPARQL.* The query mapper also provides support for querying datasets using SPARQL. In this case, only datasets mapped to SPARQL data sources can be queried using this language. This functionality can be used by more experienced developers to access modelled as RDF graphs.
- *Update using SQL.* This module also contains functionality to insert or remove data through SQL from the registered datasets. Indeed, through the Query Mapper, CRUD operations over datasets are fully supported.

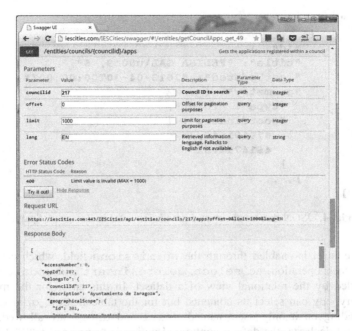

Fig. 3. RESTful API invocation through Swagger interface.

4.1 Mapping Data Sources

Datasets registered in the IES Cities platform require a mapping description in order to be connected with the data sources. Mappings are described in JSON and can have different attributes depending on the type of the dataset being connected. However, all JSON descriptions must contain the `mapping` attribute, which defines the type of the connected data source. Currently, the supported data sources are: `database`, `sparql`, `json` and `csv`. There is also the possibility to create developer-generated, application-driven datasets, by specifying the schema of the required storage in JSON.

For example, let us consider the JSON file contents' extract in Fig. 4 from the publicly available JSON file provided by Zaragoza council at https://www.zaragoza.es/api/recurso/turismo/alojamiento.json, which provides details about accommodation options in such city.

Figure 5 shows the required mapping to register such dataset within IES Cities. The `mapping` field declares that the input data source is JSON; the `uri` field points to the source URL; the `root` field defines the JSON key field where the mapping starts from; the `key` field selects the attribute from the set of mapped objects to be used as the primary key for the main relational table generated from this JSON; and the `refresh` field defines the interval to retrieve the new data and update the internal structures, since JSON files can change periodically. Observe that the optional `table` field indicates the name of the main relational table generated which would otherwise be named as the `root` field. In order to give place to a third normal form-based relational database, the mapper produces two additional tables from the given JSON contents, namely, `hotel_geometry` and `hotel_geometry_coordinates`.

```
"result": [
    {
      "id": 1,
      "title": "FELISA GAL\u00c9, 6",
      "lastUpdated": "2013-04-30T00:00:00Z",
      "geometry": {
        "type": "Point",
        "coordinates": [
          678191.46,
          4614794.52
        ]
      }, ...
    }
]
```

Fig. 4. JSON dataset about accommodation offer in Zaragoza, Spain.

Access control is enabled through the `permissions` field, which can be configured for each operation, i.e. `select`, `delete`, `insert` and `update`, of every table provided by the relational view of a dataset. In this case, for the main table `hotel` everybody can select its contents, but for the table `hotel_geometry` and those depending on it only users named `user1` and `user2` are allowed. For the operations not declared, the default-configured option is "access": "NONE", which implies that nobody can delete, update or insert contents into these tables using the RESTful API. This makes sense for this dataset since the council regulates it. However, for app-specific datasets, the app should be assigned to a user id with rights to modify the contents of the generated dataset.

Finally, Fig. 6 shows the result of querying the hotels JSON dataset earlier mapped through a JOIN-rich SQL query and the results of such query returned in JSON format.

5   IES Cities-Aided Urban Apps

A total of 16 apps has been developed within the project and published in Google Play[6], ranging from apps that allow people to decide where trees are planted (Bristol's Democratree) to collaborative maps where citizens add new points of interest and routes (Majadahonda's In-Route).

5.1   Apps Evaluation Methodology

In the trialling of IES Cities apps, an adaptation of the Compass Acceptance Model [11] has been taken as reference for the evaluation process. This model captures the end user feedback and performs assessment of the apps. The original CAM contains *ease of use*, *usefulness*, *cost* and *mobility* evaluation factors. Ease of use and usefulness are

---

[6] https://play.google.com/store/search?q=iescities&c=apps

```
{
    "mapping": "json",
    "uri":
"https://www.zaragoza.es/api/recurso/turismo/alojamiento.
json",
    "root": "result",
    "key": "id",
    "refresh": 86400,
    "table": "hotel"
    "permissions": {
        "select": [
            {
                "table": "hotel",
                "access": "ALL"
            },
            {
                "table": "hotel_geometry",
                "access": "USER",
                "users": ["user1", "user2"]
            }
        ]
    }
}
```

Fig. 5. JSON mapping to register accommodation JSON dataset in IES Cities.

simple to grasp as relates to the platform and apps. Cost includes factors such as effort to adopt the platform as well as actual monetary cost of the platform and apps. To replace mobility we have added "interaction with the city". This factor measures the extent to which apps bring the citizen closer to the city and its function. The degree of acceptance of the proposed urban apps by the different stakeholders is being assessed by applying the following three-step methodology:

1. *Definition of a range of Key Performance Indicators (KPIs).* These have been defined regarding the types of users and for the different apps uses. Some common KPIs defined across apps are number of downloads, number of active users, etc.;
2. *Set-up of a range of data sources to feed the KPIs.* The following data sources are being used: (i) *user questionnaires* to ask users directly about their opinion and experience with the application; (ii) *logging data* from logs of events generated by the apps in use; (iii) *Google Play*, i.e. the marketplace where our apps are uploaded, to obtain usage statistics and; (iv) *in-app questionnaires* which are periodically launched within the apps to gather usage feedback;
3. A *mapping of data sources to KPIs has been performed.* From the available data sources values for the KPI variables are collected and assigned.

The preliminary evaluation results obtained by applying this methodology are demonstrating that apps have a high degree of average acceptance, over 80 %.

5.2   Zaragoza's Complaints and Suggestions App

This app (see Fig. 7), uses Open Data to get an overview of reports and faults in public infrastructure. It demonstrates how a developer with the help of the IES Cities platform can create an urban app relying on semantic data, without technical knowledge of the query and data modelling language in this case, SPARQL and RDF, respectively. Thanks to IES Cities, a web developer only needs to create a query in the standard SQL language and send it to the Query Mapper. In fact, both a data entry point and a service entry point have been defined for this service. The first one enables SPARQL queries to be submitted to an SPARQL endpoint. Since the Zaragoza council wants to comply with standards, such as the Open311, but it also wants to commit towards Open Data of the highest standards, i.e. 5* Linked Data, Open311's GeoReport[7] records have been mapped into RDF triples representing the same info in a semantic form. This was achieved through a Data Wrapper element as depicted in Fig. 1. Those RDF triples constitute the Open311 RDF repository made available through a simple XSLT transformation, which can now be queried through SPARQL. On the other hand, a programmatic REST API, usable by any web developer, without knowledge of semantic technologies, has also been enabled at http://www.zaragoza.es/ciudad/risp/open311.htm.

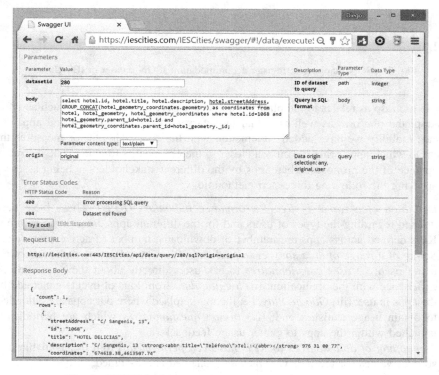

Fig. 6. RESTful API invocation to `data/query/280/sql`.

---

[7] http://wiki.open311.org/GeoReport_v2/

Fig. 7. Zaragoza complains & suggestions screenshots.

The IES Cities platform capabilities to accelerate urban app development are demonstrated by the fact that developers have only to submit SQL queries through a REST API to the IES Cities Query Mapper (data/query/{datasetid}/sql). This component talks to the Zaragoza SPARQL endpoint and maps the results into JSON so that they are easily processed by the Complaints & Suggestions app, an HTML5 app.

During initialization, and after the user login, the app queries for available complaints and suggestions, and displays the result on a map (see 3rd snapshot in Fig. 7). The requested information is minimal in order to reduce network usage. New complaints and suggestions are submitted by simply filling a form to which location information is automatically attached by means of the device's geo-location capabilities (see 1st snapshot in Fig. 7). The most recent complains are viewed by selecting the corresponding menu option (see 2nd snapshot in Fig. 7). By clicking on the marker of a report, a description of the report is shown and access to full details given.

From the data owner's point of view, i.e. Zaragoza's council, the enrichment of its datasets by third parties presented some issues, e.g. the fact that data not previously approved could be published and that there is no mechanism to control the quality and quantity of data a citizen can add. In order to address this, IntelliSense techniques and other consolidation techniques were considered so that the user is suggested related earlier submitted reports before submitting her own. A mechanism to also enable end-users to vote up or down reports was also considered to progressively reduce the relevance of spurious complains and reports taking into account the crowd opinion about them. However, in the actual real deployment of the app, end-user suggestions and complaints are manually validated before they are viewed and voted for by final users. Hence, a sanity check of reports is performed by a public administration moderator. There are plans to integrate a trustworthiness evaluator, to partially automatize and speed up the current manual evaluation that a human operator has to accomplish, with the consequent associated delay, in order to validate every single report submitted.

6 Conclusion and Further Work

The IES Cities platform allows councils to manage their datasets and urban apps ecosystem, aimed to increase the quality of life of their citizens and to foster economy promotion by allowing both administration provided and end-user generated data exploitation. The IES Cities' Query Mapper component streamlines developers work when implementing apps that consume open data and generate data, by means of an SQL-based interface, which returns as result the *lingua franca* of web developers, i.e. JSON. An exemplary real app currently deployed in the Spanish city of Zaragoza has been described, highlighting the properties of IES Cities to enable an easier consumption and generation of Open Data.

In future work, the data collected on the trials of the 16 apps currently available will be analysed. For that, engagement campaigns are currently in place in order to ensure the highest possible adoption of the proposed apps, selected taking into account the actual needs expressed by different councils and their citizens. The end outcome will be an open source available platform and a range of exemplary apps, which will prove the potential of fostering a stronger collaboration among citizens and councils to progress towards Smarter Cities.

References

1. Open Data Institute.: Open Data Barometer - 2013 Global Report, (2013). http://www. opendataresearch.org/dl/odb2013/Open-Data-Barometer-2013-Global-Report.pdf
2. Heath, T., Bizer, C.: Linked data: evolving the web into a global data space. In: Synthesis Lectures on the Semantic Web, 1st edn. Morgan & Claypool Publishers, San Rafael (2011)
3. Kittur, A., Pendleton, B.A., Suh, B., Mytkowicz, T.: Power of the few vs. wisdom of the crowd: wikipedia and the rise of the bourgeoisie. In: Proceedings of the 25th Annual ACM Conference on Human Factors in Computing Systems (CHI 2007), ACM (2007)
4. Howe, J.: The rise of crowdsourcing. Wired Mag. **14**(6), 1–4 (2006)
5. The Data Tank - an open data management systems maintained by OKFN Belgium, (2015). http://thedatatank.com/
6. Ushahidi open source software for information collection, visualization and interactive mapping, (2015). http://ushahidi.com/
7. W3C.: PROV model primer. working group, (2013). http://www.w3.org/TR/2013/NOTE-prov-primer-20130430/, Note 30 April 2013
8. European Union Open Data Portal, (2015). https://open-data.europa.eu/en/data/
9. Groth, P., Gil, Y.: Editorial - using provenance in the semantic web. In: Web Semantics: Science, Services and Agents on the World Wide Web, vol. 9(2), pp. 83–244. Elsevier (2011)
10. Fix My City application, (2014). http://www.fixmycity.de/
11. Amberg, M., Hirschmeier, M., Wehrmann, J.: The Compass Acceptance Model for the analysis and evaluation of mobile services. Int. J. Mob. Commun. **2–3**, 248–259 (2004)

Ambient Intelligence for Transport

Surveillance System for Isolated Public Road Transport Infrastructures

Carmelo R. García$^{(\boxtimes)}$, Alexis Quesada-Arencibia, Teresa Cristóbal,
Gabino Padrón, and Francisco Alayón

Institute for Cybernetic Science and Technology, University of Las Palmas de Gran
Canaria, Campus Universitario de Tafira, 35017 Las Palmas, Spain
{rgarcia,aquesada,gpadron,falayon}@dis.ulpgc.es
teresa.cristobalb@gmail.com

Abstract. In the context of public passenger transport by road, the
surveillance of the transport network is a responsibility of transport
authorities and companies. In the context of intercity transport, there
are isolated places where this task is difficult to carry out due to lack
access to basic resources such as electricity and communications. In this
paper we present an intelligent surveillance system proposal for such
places, that is able to monitor selectively and autonomously, making use
of the on-board equipment: tracking system, image sensors and communications system. This paper describes how these elements have been
combined to implement a surveillance system with the ability to recognize the different physical contexts in the transport network.

Keywords: Intelligent transport systems · Public transport
management

1 Introduction

The use of surveillance systems in public infrastructure is increasingly due to
economic, security, safety and efficiency reasons. These systems are improving
their performance incorporating the technological advances, being increasingly
frequent cases of surveillance systems for massive transit and large transport
infrastructures.

In this paper a surveillance system for network of public transport of passengers by road is presented. It uses video images of the public transport network
acquired by mobile cameras that are controlled in an intelligent way, using elements currently available on the public transport infrastructure (vehicle location
and mobile communications systems). The proposed system is specially designed
for monitoring bus stops located in non-urban areas. It has been designed to operate in non-urban transport contexts, e.g., isolate rural areas, where the deployment of traditional surveillance systems is difficult, because the availability of
basic infrastructure, such as electricity and communications infrastructures, is
not always guaranteed.

© Springer International Publishing Switzerland 2015
J.M. García-Chamizo et al. (Eds.): UCAmI 2015, LNCS 9454, pp. 207–215, 2015.
DOI: 10.1007/978-3-319-26401-1_20

This document is structured as follows: next we will describe the objectives in detail, related works and others proposals, the proposed system in the fourth section and finally, conclusions and future work.

2   Goals and Challenges

The aim of the proposed system is the surveillance, by image recording, of those parts of the transport network that are isolated, lacking electricity and communications resources, allowing in special circumstances real-time surveillance. In the context of public transport of passengers by road, these places are the bus stops located in isolated non-urban areas. The images provided by the system must permit its users to analyse the state of the different elements of the bus stops (furniture, billboards, pavement, etc.) and detect situations that hinder the accessibility of vehicles and bus stops. To achieve this goal, image sensors installed in fleet vehicles in conjunction with some other elements already installed in the infrastructure must be used, allowing an intelligent surveillance in these places. For this purpose, the infrastructure elements that have a relevant role are the location system and the mobile communications system.

To achieve the objective described in the preceding paragraph, the system must be easily integrated into the infrastructure already available on the transport network and must operate autonomously without interfering the tasks usually done in the transportation network. Also, the system must have a high degree of interoperability so that it can be adapted to different types of companies, being easily scalable in order to increase the number of image sensors and locations to be monitored. To fulfill these requirements, specifications and recommendations of authorities and international organizations about transport systems must be used.

3   Related Works

Surveillance systems provide the capability of collecting proper information in order to enhance the safety in both, private and public places. Raty [1] reviews the use of different technologies, such as multimedia surveillance [2], wireless sensor networks [3], distributed multi agent systems [4], communications middleware [5], context awareness [6] and mobile robots [7]. Because of the importance of public transport infrastructures in the life of citizens, it is increasingly frequent the use of this type of systems in this kind of infrastructures. Velastin [8] describes an architecture of a surveillance system for public transport infrastructures that takes into account the distributed nature of the detection processes and the need to allow different types of devices and actuators, being this architecture the initial step to provide intelligent ambient in public transport network. Bigdeli [9] describes a real-life trial system that uses various video analytic systems to detect relevant events and objects in a mass transport environment. Ahmad [10] proposes the use of WiMAX technology in the surveillance of vehicles of public transport and a scheme that estimates the utility of different cameras and puts some low utility cameras offline. As a result, a high utility of the video surveillance system is obtained when the throughput at high vehicular speeds become insufficient. Protto et al. [11] describes the ISTIME project that explores distributed and local sensors, for non-destructive electromagnetic monitoring of critical transport infrastructures.

The proposed system, by an intelligent processing of the different contexts of the transmission system, allows video surveillance functions in isolated parts of the public transport where traditional surveillance systems are difficult to deploy. This intelligent behaviour, based on the use of technologies of positioning and communications technologies, is a distinguishing feature of surveillance systems used in public road transport.

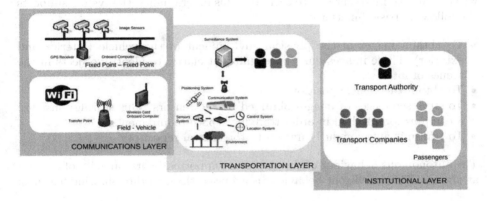

Fig. 1. Surveillance system architecture.

4   System Description

The maintenance of the places of the transport network is an important activity because their status is an important factor that affects transport accessibility and the perception of citizens about this public service. A transport network can have thousands of stops located in a widely dispersed geographic area which may include isolated areas that lack basic infrastructure such as electricity supply and communications. This section describes a proposal of an intelligent system for the surveillance of bus stops in a transport network. This system uses a network of mobile imaging sensors installed on buses that selectively acquire images showing the state of the stops when the vehicles arrive to them. The selective acquisition is performed using the vehicle positioning system; when the vehicle approaches to the bus stop the image sensors are autonomously activated and the image acquisition is stopped when the vehicle moves away from the bus stop. The acquired images are referenced in space and time, stored in the on-board computer and, finally, transferred to an image repository in an autonomous way. To achieve this functionality the system uses the location system to detect when the vehicle arrives to an upload points located in the transport network, and use the Wifi network to transfer the image files. To build the system the architectural specification for intelligent transport systems (ITS) ITERIS has been used [12].This consists of three sections: the functions required by the ITS, the entities that participate and finally the data flow between these entities. The proposed system architecture is illustrated in Fig. 1.

4.1 Features

As already mentioned, the purpose of the system is the surveillance, by images autonomously acquired, of relevant places of a network of public transport by road. Autonomy in this context means the ability to selectively acquire images without human intervention. To carry out this functionality, the system supports the following basic functions:

- To obtain images of the physical environment of the vehicle (interior and exterior). These images must have sufficient clarity to identify objects in the scenes of interest.
- To obtain the vehicle position.
- To store sequences of images obtained by the sensors. This storing must use a compression method in order to reduce space requirements.
- To transmit autonomously images to the central repository.

The autonomous behaviour of the system is supported by its capacity of context awareness. This intelligent behaviour is achieved through the following features:

- To be able to locate the vehicle in the transport network.
- Intelligent images acquisition. To do this, it is necessary to identify the different places of the vehicles routes and decide when the images acquisition should start and when it should stop. To support this functionality, the data required are the geographical coordinates of the vehicle, its speed and its location on the transport network.
- Intelligent transmission of images. Specifically the system must detect when the vehicle arrives to an upload image point and know when the transfer can be made. The information required to support this functionality are: the geographical coordinates of the vehicle, its speed, its location in the transport network, the geographical coordinates of the images upload points and the scheduled time during which the vehicle will be stopped in these points.

4.2 Entities (Elements of the Infrastructure)

The hardware and software elements necessary to support the described functionalities are illustrated in Fig. 2. The hardware entities are:

- Vehicle sensors system. Currently in the public transport by road, a wide variety of sensors are used to acquire various relevant aspects of the physical environment. Image sensors are increasingly used in stations, bus stops and

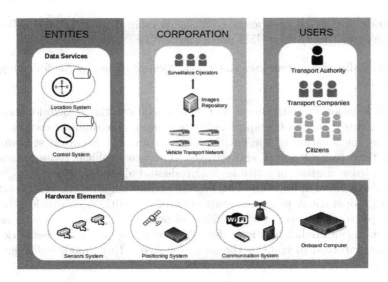

Fig. 2. Hardware and software entities.

vehicles for security purposes of the people and the infrastructure on the transport network. The camera used is certified to IP66. This means that it is protected against dust and strong jets of water from all directions. It has night vision capability supported by infrared lighting (23 LEDs) with a range up to 20 meters. Fixed optics is 3.6 mm. It controls the gain, brightness, sharpness, the change in operating modes (day/night) and the white balance automatically.

- Vehicle positioning system. The proposed system uses the positioning technology most widely used in the world of transport, the Global Positioning System (GPS). This system, in its standard version, provides a maximum positioning error of 100 meters. This error depends on aspects such as atmosphere conditions, earth curvature and even a random error introduced by the system itself. To improve positioning accuracy of a GPS standard configuration, it can use Differential Global Positioning System (DGPS). This configuration is based on the use of periodic transmissions of positioning corrections in order to correct the position of the vehicles.

- Vehicle data communication system. One of the technological advances that have promoted the development of the transport systems is the mobile communications. The proposed system uses Wifi technology to transfer files containing sequences of images acquired by the vehicles. This technology provides an adequate quality of service when the vehicle is moving at speed not exceeding 10 Km/h.

- On-board computer. It controls the images acquisition and storing process, the image files transmissions and it also executes all the processes that support the context awareness. This is a computer with reduced size and weight (11.5 × 10.1 × 2.7 cm and 330 grams). The main resources of the current configuration are: 2 GHz low-power CPU, 2 GB main memory, 64 GB solid-state storage drive (SSD), four USB ports and a Wi-Fi interface.

Additionally, the system uses the information provided by the following data services:

- Vehicle location system. Based on the bus position, the vehicle location system situates it on the transport network using a geographical database that contains the location of the entities of the transport network: stations, bus stops, time control points and garages. The geographical representation of these entities consists of latitude, longitude and altitude.
- Control system of operations. This system verifies whether the vehicle activity fulfills its operations planning: start time of expeditions, transition times of bus stops, transition times of time control points, etc. Using this information, the system can predict how long the vehicle will stop at a given network point and then, proceed to transfer the images stored if this time is sufficient.

4.3   Data Flow

How the system is able to process context to operate autonomously is explained in this section. Specifically, how it is able to carry out the selective acquisition of image sequences at bus stops and how to perform image files transmission to the repository.

The selective acquisition process of images at bus stops is performed autonomously, without human intervention, when the vehicle is in an area near to the stop, about 200 meters, called acquisition area. This is done using the positioning data of the vehicle, supplied regularly (every second) by the GPS receiver on the vehicle. These data are: latitude, longitude, altitude, speed and quality of the measurement. When the quality of the measure indicates that this is a reliable position (this means that the error is less than 100 meters) then checks if the vehicle is located about 200 meters from the position of the next bus stop. The position of the next bus stop is provided by the vehicle location system and the distance is obtained by calculating the Euclidean distance between two points. If the distance obtained is less than 200 meters, the system infers that it is in the acquisition area and proceeds to activate the images sensors and the images sequence is stored in the on-board computer. While the vehicle is in the acquisition area, the image sensors is acquiring continuously. When the distance between the vehicle position and the bus stop exceeds 200 meters, the system stops the images acquisition.

The transmission of image sequences files is also done autonomously, without human intervention. This process starts when the vehicle is at a point of automatic data transfer. These points are places with Wifi coverage, and to carry out the transmission the following condition must be met:

- The vehicle is closer than 100 meters from the transfer point.
- The vehicle is stopped (zero GPS velocity) during a sufficient period of time.

To check these conditions, the system uses the positioning data of the vehicle provided by the GPS receiver (latitude, longitude, altitude, speed and quality of the measurement). When the quality of the measure indicates that this is a reliable position, the system checks if the distance between the vehicle and a transfer point is less than 100 meters. The position of the transfer points is provided by the vehicle location system and the distance is obtained by calculating the Euclidean distance between those two points. If the distance obtained is less than 100 meters, then the system infers that the vehicle is in a coverage area for wireless data transfer. When the vehicle is located in a transfer point, before establishing communication for image files transmission, the system wait until the vehicle is stopped (zero GPS velocity). Obtaining the time interval the vehicle must be stopped in the transfer point (data provided by the control system of the operations of the vehicle), the system decides if the image files transmission can be carried out.

5 Test Carried Out

To determine whether the proposed system can be deployed in a real context of a public transport company, we have made a series of studies and tests in real conditions. The aim of these studies was to know if the data required by the system are usually available in vehicles of a public transport company by road. As explained in the previous section, the data required by the system are the vehicle's position, its speed, vehicle location on the network, geographical positions of the bus stops and geographical positions of the transfer points of data. All these data are handled in fleets of public transport vehicles equipped with operations control systems. Currently, this kind of system is very common in the public transport of passengers because this is a main element to guarantee the quality of service.

The aim of the field tests carried out was to establish the hardware system requirements. Specifically, the tests were performed to determine the minimum required resolution of the images, the compression technique necessary to reduce storage requirements and, once these parameters has been established, to calculate the required storage space and the required transfer time to transmit the image files using the wireless infrastructure. The results are:

- Image resolution and compression technique. Within the range of sensors commonly used in mobile environments, we can find resolutions from 176×120 to 720×480. A resolution between 320×280 to 640×480 is sufficient for the purposes of the system, requiring less network bandwidth and less storage space than higher resolution. About compression, the three compression standards most commonly used are: H.264, MPEG-4 and Motion JPEG. The H.264 was selected, because this is the latest standard, offering significant savings in bandwidth and storage.
- Storage space and bandwidth required. Using the H.264 compression, with 4CIF resolution of 704×576, with a bit rate of 600 kbps approximated, trans-

mitting 30 images per second, involves a total of 540 MB/h. Assuming approximately two hours of images acquisition at bus stops per day, the space requirement is about 1 GB/day.

- Failure infrastructure. The critical elements of the infrastructure are the Wi-Fi access points installed in the automatic data transfer points of the transportation network. Considering that the per day of storage space required is about 2 GB and the available image storage space in the on-board computer is about 60 GB, then a vehicle can perform the images recording during 30 days without performing an image transfer to the central repository. To mitigate the effects of this fault condition, the automatic data transfer points can be installed in transport network places of frequent passage of vehicles (stations, main stations and garages).

6 Conclusion

This paper has presented a proposal for a monitoring system using video images of relevant places of a public transport network by road. In order to be able to monitor any bus stop of the transport network, the system uses image sensors installed in vehicles. For this reason the system has a distributed architecture of mobile sensors. The system operates autonomously, with ability to operate without human intervention. This capability is achieved by processing the context using commonly available data on the vehicles of a fleet of public transport. The system is suitable for monitoring isolated points, as in the case of bus stops located in isolated rural areas.

References

1. Raty, T.D.: Survey on contemporary remote surveillance systems for public safety. IEEE Trans. Syst. Man Cybern. C Appl. Rev. **40**(5), 493–515 (2010)
2. Cucchiara, R.: Multimedia surveillance systems. In: Proceedings of 3rd International Workshop Video Surveillance & Sensor Networks (VSSN), p. 310 (2005)
3. Chandramohan, V., Christensen, K.: A first look at wired sensor networks for video surveillance systems. In: Proceedings of 27th Annual IEEE Conference on Local Computer Network (LCN), pp. 728–729 (2002)
4. Valencia-Jimenez, J.J., Fernandez-Caballero, A.: Holonic multiagent systems to integrate multi-sensor platforms in complex surveillance. In: Proceedings IEEE International Conference Video Signal Based Surveillance (AVSS), p. 49 (2006). doi:10.1109/AVSS.2006.58
5. Detmold, H., Dick, A., Falkner, K., Munro, D.S., Van Den Hengel, A., Morrison, P.: Middleware for video surveillance networks. In: Proceedings 1st International Workshop Middleware Sensor Network (MidSens), pp. 31–36 (2006)
6. Bandini, S., Sartori, F.: Improving the effectiveness of monitoring and control systems exploiting knowledge-based approaches. Pers. Ubiquit. Comput. **9**(5), 301311 (2005). doi:10.1007/s00779-004-0334-3
7. Tseng, Y., Wang, Y., Cheng, K., Hsieh, Y.: iMouse: an integrated mobile surveillance and wireless sensor system. Computer **40**(6), 60–66 (2007). doi:10.1109/MC.2007.211

8. Velastin, S.A., Boghossian, B.A., Lo, B.P.L., Sun, J., Vicencio-Silva, M.A.: PRIS-MATICA: toward ambient intelligence in public transport environments. IEEE Trans. Syst. Man Cybern. A Syst. Hum. **35**(1), 164–182 (2005)
9. Bigdeli, A., Lovell, B.C., Sanderson, C., Shan, T., Chen, S.: Vision processing in intelligent CCTV for mass transport security. In: Workshop on Signal Processing Applications for Public Security and Forensics, SAFE 2007, pp. 1–4, IEEE (2007)
10. Ahmad, I., Habibi, D.: High utility video surveillance system on public transport using wimax technology. In: 2010 IEEE Wireless Communications and Networking Conference (WCNC), pp. 1–5 (2010)
11. Potto, M., et al.: Transport infrastructure surveillance and monitoring by electro-magnetic sensing: the ISTIMES project. Sensors **2010**(10), 10620–10639 (2010). doi:10.3390/s101210620
12. ITERIS. National ITS Architecture 7.1. United States Department of Transportation. http://www.iteris.com/itsarch/index.htm (2015). Acceded 16 May 2015

ITS Architecture for Provision of Advanced Information Services for Public Transport by Road

Carmelo R. García[✉], Alexis Quesada-Arencibia, Teresa Cristóbal,
Gabino Padrón, and Francisco Alayón

Institute for Cybernetic Science and Technology, University of Las Palmas de Gran
Canaria, Campus Universitario de Tafira, 35017 Las Palmas, Spain
{rgarcia,aquesada,gpadron,falayon}@dis.ulpgc.es
teresa.cristobalb@gmail.com

Abstract. In this work a system architecture model for the provision of advanced information services in the context of public transport of passengers by road is presented. The main aim of this model is to provide a frame for systematic development of ubiquitous services integrated in transport infrastructures. The proposed architecture is based on standard specification about ITS architectures and ubiquitous paradigm. To illustrate the utility of the proposed model, a case of use is presented, specifically an intelligent surveillance system for on route public transport vehicles that has been developed using the proposed model.

Keywords: Intelligent transport systems · Public transport management

1 Introduction

Like many productive sectors, the information technologies advances have facilitated the development of people and goods transport. Since seventies of the last century to the present, this sector has benefited from technological advances and the leading exponent of this symbiosis is a scientific field called Intelligent Transport Systems (ITS) whose purpose is to design, implement and deploy technology solutions that benefit the transport sector and its users.

In this work a system architecture model for the provision of advanced information services in the context of public transport of passengers by road is presented. The main aim of this model is to provide a frame for systematic development of ubiquitous services integrated in transport infrastructures, having the developed services a high level of interoperability and scalability. These advanced services, deployed in different places of the transport network, process autonomously the context in order to improve and facilitate the public transport. The proposed architecture is based on standard specification about ITS architectures and ubiquitous paradigm.

The topics described in this paper are the following: first, the goals and challenges are presented, the second section is dedicated to related works, the

© Springer International Publishing Switzerland 2015
J.M. García-Chamizo et al. (Eds.): UCAmI 2015, LNCS 9454, pp. 216–224, 2015.
DOI: 10.1007/978-3-319-26401-1_21

system architecture model is explained in the fourth section, a case of use is described in the next section, and finally, the conclusions.

2   Goals and Challenges

The ITS aim is to develop systems that improve the transport user safety and the efficiency, to increase the citizens mobility, and to decrease the environmental impact of the transport activity. To achieve this goal, a wide range of systems based on different technologies has been developed, specially technologies related to communications, sensors and computing, The main purpose of the system architecture model presented in this work is to provide a frame for systematic development of intelligent ambient in the context of the public passenger transport by road networks. Systematic development means that the intelligent ambient are made using common specifications and using ITS standard specifications, with the aim to achieve a high level of:

- Integration. The services must be easily deployed in the transport infrastructures and using the resources of these infrastructures.
- Interoperability. The intelligent ambient services must be executed using different technologies and in different kind of transport companies, for example: urban, intercity transport and long distance transport, as well as small, medium or big companies.
- Scalability. The intelligent ambient must be easily expansible in order to increase the number of places and the amount of users that can be benefited from the proposed architecture model.

Additionally, to facilitate the usability, the deployed services in the different intelligent ambient must be autonomous. This is the reason why the system architecture model uses the ubiquitous computing paradigm. Specifically, using this paradigm the following challenges can be faced [1]:

- Effective use of the smart spaces. A smart space is an open or closed area in the public transport network where sensors, controllers, actuators and ubiquitous software are able to adapt to the environment for providing smart objects.
- Scalable location. As intelligent spaces grow in sophistication, the interaction between user computing and environment increases. This affect to bandwidth and the required power. This challenge has special relevant in places of massive transit.

3   Related Works

Since the last century, the transport authorities have paid much attention to the ITS field, because this field has provided systems that have produce great economic and social benefits. For example, in the European context, we can find the COOPERS [2] and OASIS [3] initiatives for the development of intelligent and cooperative systems to improve the safety and mobility of citizens.

The result is a wide range of ITS cases that using information and communications technologies solve different transport problems. As a consequence of this wide range of ITS systems and technologies, the transport authorities and organizations have promoted the development of normalization specifications and architecture models for integration and compatibility of ITS. For example; the E-FRAME initiative [4] for development of a European architecture specification of ITS, or in the USA case, the ITERIS architecture specification [5], or the Japan specification [6].

In Table 1 the functional areas and functions are presented, following the European ITS Framework Architecture. The areas covered by the proposed architectural model are highlighted in bold.

The development of the information and communications technologies has been one of the driving forced that have allowed the ITS development [7], being the travellers services one of the topics that has aroused great interest in researches, especially the services related to localization and navigation [8]. To develop interoperable ITS services, researches are using models based on e-Business, specifically the Service Oriented Architecture (SOA), that permits to develop distributed systems where the components have a loose coupling [9]. The work of Aloisio [10], where a web architecture for developing of ITS services is proposed, is an example of this line of research.

Considering the goals of the proposed architecture, the works where ubiquitous computing and ambient intelligent paradigms are used to make proposes of ITS must be cited. For example, Velastin [11] presents a surveillance system for transport infrastructures, based on distributed architecture of sensors and actuators, as a first step to incorporate ambient intelligence in these infrastructures. Arikava [12] explain a traveller assistant for massive transit points based on ubiquitous paradigm. García [13] presents a proposal of framework to develop ubiquitous information services for public transport by road. Finally, Zhou [14] proposes a system based on ambient intelligence that improves the public transport buses accessibility for people with special needs.

4   Architecture Description

As described above, three are the bases of the proposed architecture model: standard specifications about ITS architectures, the paradigms of ubiquitous computing and SOA model. Standard specifications about ITS architectures are used to guarantee a high level of compatibility, integration, interoperability and scalability of the intelligent information services to develop. Ubiquitous computing paradigm to achieve context awareness in the different ambient of public transport network, so the provided information services are able to predict and adapt to the needs of transport users. The SOA paradigm is assumed by the proposed architecture model in order to use non-standard transport infrastructure elements, isolating theirs specific characteristics.

Table 1. Functional areas and functions - European ITS framework architecture.

Functional areas	Functions
1. General	1.1 Architectural properties
	1.2 Data exchange
	1.3 Adaptability
	1.4 Constraints
	1.5 Continuity
	1.6 Cost/Benefit
	1.7 Expandability
	1.8 Maintainability
	1.9 Quality of data content
	1.10 Robustness
	1.11 Safety
	1.12 Security
	1.13 User friendliness
	1.14 Special needs
2. Infrastructure planning and maintenance	2.1 Transport planning support
	2.2 Infrastructure maintenance management
3. Law enforcement	3.1 Policing/Enforcing traffic regulations
4. Financial transactions	4.1 Electronic financial transactions
5. Emergency services	5.1 Emergency notification and personal security
	5.2 Emergency vehicle management
	5.3 Hazardous materials and incident notification
6. Travel information and guidance	6.1 Pre-trip information
	6.2 On-trip driver information
	6.3 Personal information services
	6.4 Route guidance and navigation
7. Traffic, incidents and demand management	7.1 Traffic control
	7.2 Incident management
	7.3 Demand management
	7.4 Safety enhancements for vulnerable road users
	7.5 Intelligent junctions and links
8. Intelligent vehicle systems	8.1 Vision enhancement
	8.2 Automated vehicle operation
	8.3 Longitudinal collision avoidance
	8.4 Lateral collision avoidance
	8.5 Safety readiness
	8.6 Pre-crash restraint deployment
9. Freight and fleet management	9.1 Commercial vehicle pre-clearance
	9.2 Commercial vehicle administrative processes
	9.3 Automated roadside safety inspection
	9.4 Commercial vehicle on-board safety monitoring
	9.5 Commercial fleet management
10. Public transport management	10.1 Public transport management
	10.2 Demand responsive public transport
	10.3 Shared transport management
	10.4 On-Trip public transport information
	10.5 Public travel security

The main modules of this proposal are the following:

- Transport Infrastructure Module (TIM). This component is formed by all the hardware elements and communications integrated in the transport infrastructure. This module is composed by two subsystems: the communication module and the sensing module that integrates all the sensors and actuators deployed in the transport network.

  - Communications system. This module integrates all the communications networks, both privates and public, used by other components of the architecture. This system provides all the communications technologies used in the transport activity: communication between vehicles (V2V), between vehicle and infrastructure (V2I, I2V) and between infrastructures (I2I) by technologies and protocols, such as;
    - Local communications: RS-232, RS-485, IR, IEEE 802.15.1 (Bluetooth), IEEE 802.15.4 (ZigBee), IEEE 802.11 (Wifi), etc.
    - Long distance communications: GSM, GPRS, 3G, etc.
    - Broadband Mobile Communications: IEEE 802.16 (WiMax), iBurst.
  - Sensing system. This module is configured by all the sensors and actuators technologies deployed in the transport network (stations, bus stops, garages, intermodal transit points, etc.) and vehicles. The sensors and actuators are grouped in two types:
    - Infrastructure sensors: images sensor, wireless sensor network (WSN).
    - Vehicle sensors: Vehicular sensors ad-hoc network.
- Corporative Services Module (CSM). All the processes and services related to transport activity are integrated in this module. Therefore, this is provided by transport operators and authorities. CSM is structured in two parts:

  - Monitoring system that provides all the data produced by infrastructure surveillance systems and by vehicles alarm systems.
  - System services that covers all processes that provide data related to different transport tasks:
    - Control operations.
    - Payment.
    - Planning operations.
    - Travellers information.

  New features such as high availability in anywhere and anytime of the information services using new computing paradigm, for example cloud computing, are responsibility of this module.
- User Service Module (USM). All the ubiquitous services provided in the different intelligent ambient of the transport network belong to this module. All the data produced by the CSM and communications resources provided by the TIM are used by the ubiquitous services, such as: on-route assistants, payment systems, emergence warning systems, etc. To access to these ubiquitous services by transport users, the user smart devices play a main role.

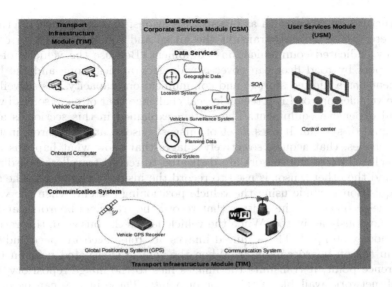

Fig. 1. General vision of the vehicle surveillance system.

The SOA model is used in the proposed architecture model to make the interface between CSM and USM modules, and the web technology to implement this interface. The main element of this interface is the registering and discovering system. By this scheme the sensors data are collected by the monitoring system, then these data are accessed by the CSM services for publishing purposes and finally, these services are discovered by the user intelligent services, following this common scheme:

- Step 1: Data initiation. Before doing anything, the variables necessary for running the service have to be initiated.
- Step 2: Service publication. Any information service declares to user applications that it is starting to operate.
- Step 3: Running the service logic. The developer will encapsulate his code here and this will be run.

5   Case of Use

To illustrate the utility of the proposed model, a case of use is presented in this section. Specifically, an on route public transport vehicles surveillance system has been tested.

In passenger public transport, especially in massive transit transport networks, the safety against vandalism and criminal behaviour is a requirement assumed by transport authorities and companies. For this reason, the use of surveillance systems based on image and sound sensors is very frequent in transport infrastructures in places such as bus stops, stations, massive transit intermodal points, etc. These systems transmit the image and sound signals to a control centre by dedicated communications equipment. Because the vehicles of public transport by road fleet can cover a wide geographical zone and the board equipment has a limited storage and communications capacity, the surveillance of these vehicles on road is a technological challenge that often is solves by specific and expensive equipment. The system explained in this section is a case of this kind of system. It uses a set of images sensors, at least three, installed in the vehicles, that acquire selectively images that show what happens inside the vehicles. Two of the sensors are dedicated to record travellers boarding on buses, and the other sensor is used to record the inside of the buses. The selective acquisition is made using the vehicle positioning system; when the vehicle approaches a bus stop, the sensors that record the travellers boarding and exit are autonomously activated. When the vehicle leaves the bus stop, this record is autonomously stopped. The acquired images are referenced in space and time, stored in the on-board computer. When the vehicle is situated near an image transference point, it transmits the images files to the image repository, using the Wifi network available in this type of points. These images can be used in case of incidents happened during the vehicle service, and can even be used to identify passengers. Figure 1 shows the system.

As already mentioned, the purpose of the system is the autonomous surveillance by images of public transport vehicles. In this context, autonomously means to be able to acquire, store and transmit images selectively without human intervention. To achieve this capacity, the following functionalities are required:

- To acquire images inside of vehicles.
- To know the vehicle position.
- To store the frames acquired by the sensors.
- To transmit images to central repository.
- In case of emergency, real time images transmission to monitoring centre.

The autonomous system behaviour is reached by its context awareness capacity. This intelligent behaviour is achieved using the following functionalities of the Transport Infrastructure Module:

- Sensors system. The vehicle image sensors must work in adverse environmental conditions (water, dust, temperature), to acquire images with low light, to control brightness and sharpness automatically.
- Vehicle positioning system. The proposed system uses GPS to get the vehicle geographic coordinates (latitude, longitude, and altitude), velocity and measurement quality.
- V2I communication infrastructure. The Wifi technology is used to transmit the images frame, stored in the on-board computer, to the corporative images repository. On the vehicle side, the on-board computer provides this communication resource, and on the side of the infrastructure, this resource is provided by the access points installed in the images transference points. For emergency situations, 3G communications is used to transmit real-time images

to the monitoring centre. The on-board computer provides this communication resource too.

- On-board computer. This element is used to store the frames, to execute all the processes to support the context awareness and to make the transmissions of frames automatically.

Additionally, the surveillance system requires data provided by services belonging to the Corporative System Module:

- Vehicle localization System. Using the vehicle positioning data, this system placed the vehicle in points of the transport network (bus stops, station, control points, images transference points etc.). For this purpose, a geographical data base representing all the transport network points is used.
- Vehicle operations control system. Using the data provided by this system, the surveillance system knows how long the vehicle is stopped at an image transference point.

6 Conclusion

In this work an architecture model for developing and deploying of ubiquitous services in the context of public road transport has been presented. In the context of this work, the ubiquitous services are deployed in different places of the public transport network that support context awareness work autonomously in order to improve or facilitate the public transport activity. To achieve a high level of integration in the transport infrastructures, the proposed model is based on standard specifications about ITS architectures. The ubiquitous computing paradigm permits the services to have the context awareness capacity. To illustrate the utility of the proposed architecture model, an intelligent images surveillance system for public transport vehicles on road based on the proposed model has been described. Using elements and services available in vehicles and certain parts of the transport network, this system performs selectively and autonomously the imaging inside the bus and the transmission of the frames.

References

1. Satyanarayanan, M.: Pervasive computing: vision and challenges. IEEE Pers. Commun. 8, 10–17 (2001). C.M. University, Ed
2. COOPERS. Cooperative networks for intelligent road safety. European Commission, http://cordis.europa.eu/project/rcn/79301_en.html (2010). Acceded 10 May 2015
3. OASIS - Operación de Autopistas Seguras, Inteligentes y Sostenibles. INDRA, http://www.indracompany.com/sostenibilidad-e-innovacion/proyectos-innovacion/oasis-operacion-de-autopistas-seguras-inteligentes- (2011). Acceded 15 May 2015
4. E-FRAME: Extend framework architecture for cooperative systems. European Commission's Directorate General for Mobility and Transport, http://www.transport-research.info/web/projects/project_details.cfm?id=44407 (2008). Acceded 16 May 2015

5. ITERIS. National ITS Architecture 7.1. United States Department of Transportation, http://www.iteris.com/itsarch/index.htm (2015). Acceded 16 May 2015
6. Yokota, T., Weiland, R.: ITS ITS Technical note 5. Technical note for developing countries, World Bank, pp. 10–11 (2014)
7. Dado, M., Spalek, J., Janota, A.: Present and future challenges of ICT for intelligent transportation technologies and services. In: Proceeding of the 2009 1st Conference on Wireless Communications, Vehicular Technology, Information Theory and Aerospace and Electronic Systems Technology, Wireless VITAE 2009, Denmark (2009)
8. European Global Navigation Satellite Systems Agency. Personal LBS Positioning and Navigation, GNSS Market report, Issue 4 (2015)
9. Papazoglou, M., Traverso, P., Dustdar, S., Leymann, F.: Service-oriented computing: state of the art and research challenges. Computer 40(11), 38–45 (2007)
10. Aloisio, G., Carteni, G., Sponziello, A., Laudadio, T.: Design strategies for web based ITS applications - a proposed architecture in design of intelligent transport systems application. In: Proceedings of the International Conference on e-Business, ICE-B is Part of ICETE - The International Joint Conference on e-Business and Telecommunications, Barcelona, Spain (2007)
11. Velastin, S.A., Boghossian, B.A., Lo, B.P.L., Sun, J., Vicencio-Silva, M.A.: PRISMATICA: toward ambient intelligence in public transport environments. IEEE Trans. Syst. Man Cybern. A Syst. Hum. 35(1), 164–182 (2005)
12. Arikawa, M., et al.: NAVITAME: supporting pedestrian navigation in the real world. IEEE Pervasive Comput. Mob. Ubiquit. Syst. 6(3), 21–29 (2007)
13. García, C.R., Pérez, R., Lorenzo, A., Quesada, A., Alayón, F., Padrón, G.: OnRoute: a case of ubiquitous computing framework for providing public transportation information services. In: Proceeding of UCAm I: 5th International Symposium on Ubiquitous Computing and Ambient Intelligence, p. 2011, Mexico, Rivera Maya (2011)
14. Zhou, H., Hou, K.-M., Zuo, D., Li, J.: Intelligent urban public transportation for accessibility dedicated to people with disabilities. Sensors 2012(12), 10679–10692 (2012)

Low-Cost Service to Predict and Manage Indoor Parking Spaces

Cándido Caballero-Gil$^{(\boxtimes)}$, Jezabel Molina-Gil, and Pino Caballero-Gil

Department of Computer Engineering and Systems,
University of La Laguna, Tenerife, Spain
{ccabgil,jmmolina,pcaballe}@ull.es

Abstract. Since the number of vehicles on the road has been growing rapidly during the last few years, the lack of parking spaces has become a usual problem for many people. Taking advantage of the emerging concept of connected car, the popularity of smartphones and the rise of Internet of Things, this work proposes a solution to predict where the best available parking spots are. The proposal includes both a centralized system to predict empty indoor parking spaces based on cellular automata, and a low-cost mobile application based on different technologies to help the driver to find empty parking spaces. On the one hand, cellular automata are used to model the behavior of drivers in parking facilities. Specifically, the system applies the idea behind the game of life to capture some features of parking occupancy based on common user behaviors, in order to reduce the time to find empty parking spots. On the other hand, the proposal involves a smartphone application that uses accurate technologies for indoor positioning. The client software is a lightweight Android application that provides different indoor positioning solutions, such as precise positioning systems based on Quick Response codes or Near Field Communication tags, or semi-precise positioning systems based on Bluetooth Low Energy beacons. The proposed service takes into account that it will be gradually adopted by users. The results obtained from a preliminary implementation show how the proposal improves the parking experience and increases efficiency of parking facilities in terms of time and energy costs.

Keywords: Location-Based service · Indoor parking · Intelligent transport system · Smartphone application · Sensors · Cellular automata

1 Introduction

Every day, more parking availability is required due to the increasing number of vehicles. The lack of parking involves many disadvantages such as discomfort and time consumption, which cause stress to drivers. This stress increases the risk of road accidents when drivers are looking for empty parking spots. Besides, this issue is an important cause of extra carbon dioxide emissions, which deteriorate the environment of the ecosystem, especially when many people are simultaneously searching empty parking spaces at peak rush hours.

© Springer International Publishing Switzerland 2015
J.M. García-Chamizo et al. (Eds.): UCAmI 2015, LNCS 9454, pp. 225–236, 2015.
DOI: 10.1007/978-3-319-26401-1_22

Smartphones and sensor technologies are common in our daily life, so taking advantage of them could help to provide ubiquitous solutions for parking problems. In the design of a solution based on those devices, an additional difficulty appears when vehicles enter places, such as indoor parking facilities, where the use of GPS (Global Positioning System) or triangulation from mobile cells is not possible or precise enough to provide useful data. Thus, generally in indoor parking facilities it is necessary to drive around the garage to look for empty parking spots. Many indoor parking facilities use a basic system that automatically detects the arrival and departure of vehicles through various sensors, in order to conclude whether there is still some empty parking space or not, and to display updated parking space occupancy information. However, due to the unavailability of GPS in indoor facilities, where most urban parking spaces are located, current parking systems cannot provide indoor navigation.

In this paper, a novel approach for parking solution based on advanced but cheap technologies is introduced. The proposal is designed to create a user-friendly experience in order to maximize its adoption. The new service has been simulated and the obtained conclusion is that the service is low-cost and energy-efficient for end-users and an effective solution for service providers and operators of parking facilities.

This work is structured as follows. Section 2 briefly describes some related works. Then, Sect. 3 provides details of the proposed parking system, including the approach based on cellular automata. Section 4 presents the main features of the development of the parking locator service based on smartphones and a server. Some results of a functional demonstration of the service are shown in Sect. 5. Finally, the work is closed with some conclusions and open problems.

2   Related Works

This paper proposes a novel parking service that combines a system to predict availability in parking spaces and a smartphone application to indicate parking occupation through different kinds of sensors. Thus, the following subsections briefly revise some works related to each one of those two topics.

2.1   Parking Prediction

Figure 1 shows, with an example, a typical behavior of drivers in a parking space according to which all users park their vehicles in the spots closest to the exit.

In general, the behavior of vehicles in parking spaces may be modeled like the population growth in urban environments, which has been studied in several works [1,2]. The prediction of parking availability in real time has also been studied through intelligent approaches [3].

The system to predict parking availability described here is completely different because it is based on the Game of Life, which is a Cellular Automaton introduced by John Conway in 1970 [4]. According to this model, cells are self-replicating machines [5] that reproduce themselves autonomously. By studying

Fig. 1. Example of actual parking occupancy

the behaviour of vehicles growing in parkings we have use some kinds of CA. In order to model the parking occupancy we need the map and the exits that will be the seed for the model of vehicles occupancy.

To the best of our knowledge, only the recent works [6,7] present a system for parking recommendation based on CA (Cellular Automata). However, such a system has a focus not directed towards indoor facilities, uses different technologies and is not completed with a practical application for the drivers.

2.2 Parking Availability with Low-Cost Sensors

Smartphone-based indoor positioning occupancy solutions have been widely studied in recent years, but such applications are yet to be substantiated. An intelligent parking system relies on the acquisition of parking space occupancy status information in real time. This kind of information can be obtained by various detection sensors, which can be divided into two categories: intrusive and non-intrusive sensors [8]. On the one hand, intrusive sensors have to be installed in every parking space, thus involving a high cost because this type of sensors includes active infrared sensors, inductive loops, magnetometers, magneto-resistive sensors, pneumatic road tubes, piezoelectric cables or weigh-in-motion sensors. On the other hand, non-intrusive sensors can be microwave radar, passive acoustic array sensors, passive infrared sensors, ultrasound or video image processing. Their main advantage is that they can be installed easily by mounting the device on the ground or the ceiling of any parking space. However, some of them could present many problems in some parking topologies. These sensors and related infrastructure can be used in the development of a parking service in existing facilities without requiring any major additional hardware or installation cost. Although the installation and maintenance of these kind of non-intrusive sensors do not result in invasive procedures or traffic disruptions, and cost less than intrusive sensors, the cost is higher than the one of our proposal, which is based on QR codes, NFC tags or BLE beacons.

QR (Quick Response) code is the trademark for a type of matrix or two-dimensional barcode first designed for the automotive industry in Japan and now used for many different applications. Its cost of production is priceless because it can be easily printed on any piece of paper. Several works have addressed the parking problem by using QR codes [9,10].

NFC (Near Field Communication) is a set of ideas and technology that enables smartphones and other devices to establish radio communication with each other by touching the devices together or bringing them into proximity to a distance of typically 10 cm (3.9 in) or less. Its associated cost is low, and some authors have used NFC solutions to solve the parking problem [11, 12].

BLE (Bluetooth Low Energy) beacons are transmitters that use Bluetooth 4.0 to broadcast signals that can be heard by compatible devices. They can be powered by batteries or fixed power sources such as USB adapters. When a smart device is in a beacon's proximity, the beacon recognizes it and is able to interact with it. In particular, the proposal presented here has been implemented with BLE devices within the Physical Web [13], a new project from Google's Chrome team that provides a lightweight discovery and interaction layer to the Internet of Things. This system is cheap and does not require a beacon per parking space. Instead, just one beacon is necessary per section including from 8 to 16 rows of cars, depending on the walls and other obstacles.

Existing intelligent parking services can be improved to provide more efficient use with a predictable parking cost based on a new generation of technologies and infrastructures for intelligent parking systems [14]. On the one hand, Wireless Local Area Networks (WLANs) and 2G/3G or Long Term Evolution (LTE) networks enable ubiquitous Internet access with a smartphone. On the other hand, the concept of the connected car is being substantiated by major vehicle and tech manufacturers, which are developing related products and services such as Android Auto by Google or Apple CarPlay [15–19].

Indoor mapping is another critical tool necessary to develop a new generation of intelligent parking systems [20]. Several companies, such as Aisle411, Google, Micello, Navteq, Nokia or PointInside, have developed various indoor map products for a range of points of interest, such as shopping centers and airports, throughout North America, Europe and Japan. In addition to indoor maps, an accurate indoor positioning solution would play an enabling role in next generation intelligent parking systems, along with GPS positioning for universal navigation and intelligent information services.

3   CA-Based System to Predict Parking Occupancy

This paper proposes a low-cost solution for indoor parking facilities that does not require any fixed physical component to control parking availability. The idea, as shown in Fig. 2, is composed of a server that manages information about parking spaces occupation and applies a predictive method, and a smartphone application that helps users both to find where there are empty parking spaces with a high probability, and where their vehicles are parked. Such an application is based on QR codes, NFC tags or Physical Web Beacons.

3.1   Prediction of Parking Occupancy

In order to model the occupancy and release behavior of parking spaces, different use cases have been studied. For instance, the parking shown in Fig. 1 has just one Point Of Exit (POE) and in that case it is clear that users try to park their

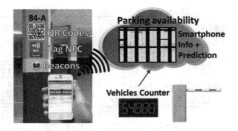

Fig. 2. Low-cost indoor parking system

vehicles in places near to the POE. Indeed, there are some studies that state a relationship between the choice of parking space and the distance to ticket machines, entrances, exits, final destinations, etc. [21].

Besides, distinct behaviors can be distinguished inside the parking facility depending on the hour of the day, the day of the week, etc. Thus, occupancy of parking spaces seems not to be a random decision but to follow clear rules.

3.2 CA to Model Parking Occupancy

This work uses the concept of cellular automata to predict parking occupancy. A cellular automaton is a discrete model that comprises a regular grid of cells, where each cell is in one of a finite number of states. The best known CA have one or two dimensions. Here, only two-state and two-dimensional CA are used.

Taking into account users' behavior, basically three stages can be distinguished during parking occupancy: Stage 1 (Filling), Stage 2 (Swapping) and Stage 3 (Emptying). The first and last stages correspond, respectively, to the opening and closing of the parking facilities. Vehicle behavior with respect to a parking space is defined in each stage depending on the space state (Empty or Occupied). In this work, a modified Conway's Game of Life is used for the parking model [4], where alive cells correspond to occupied parking spots while dead cells are empty parking spots.

The used model defines a matrix where different positions can be parking spaces or lanes. Roads can be horizontal or vertical and can have one or two lanes, and every parking space must be accessible from a road. The model includes a loop whose iterations define the state of each parking space.

Figure 3 shows an example of the rules applied in the proposed system, defined following the actual behavior pattern seen in parking spaces in order to simulate it. Thus, the system calculates the next value of each cell $x(i, j)$ having into account the values of all its neighbors $x(i, j - 1), x(i, j + 1), x(i - 1, j), x(i + 1, j), x(i - 1, j - 1), x(i + 1, j - 1), x(i - 1, j + 1)$ and $x(i + 1, j + 1)$.

This model follows from a study of indoor facilities with parking fees, where the conclusion is that driver behavior can be modeled using a modified version of the Game of Life. During the Filling Stage, vehicles tend to occupy parking spaces in a predefined way. During the Emptying Stage, vehicles tend to release

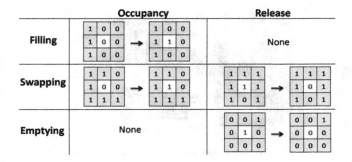

Fig. 3. Example of rules defining occupancy and release for each stage

parking spaces in a random way. Finally, during the Swapping Stage, empty parking spaces mainly surrounded by occupied ones are quickly occupied, empty parking spaces mainly surrounded by empty ones remain empty, occupied parking spaces mainly surrounded by empty ones are quickly released, and occupied parking spaces mainly surrounded by occupied ones are quickly released.

The adjustment of the Game of Life to the proposed model is shown below:

– Filling Stage
  • Empty cells with three or more neighbors become occupied.
  • Empty cells with two or fewer neighbors remain empty.
  • Occupied cells remain occupied.
– Swapping Stage
  • Empty cells with six or more neighbors become occupied.
  • Empty cells with five or fewer neighbors remain empty.
  • Occupied cells with six or more neighbors are released.
  • Occupied cells with three to five neighbors remain occupied.
  • Occupied cells with two or fewer neighbors are released.
– Emptying Stage
  • Empty cells remain empty.
  • Occupied cells with seven or more neighbors are released.
  • Occupied cells with three to six neighbors become occupied.
  • Occupied cells with two or fewer neighbors are released.

3.3   System Simulation Using Matlab

The actual situation seen in Fig. 1 has been recreated using MATLAB, as shown in Fig. 4, where each cell corresponds to a parking space. With this simulation of the proposed CA-based model, empty parking spaces can be predicted specially during the Filling stage.

Thus, Fig. 4 shows a simulation of driver behavior in the scenario of a parking facility with one POE, once chosen an adequate CA initial state that takes into account where the POE is. As can be seen, the simulation grows in a similar way to the real scenario shown in Fig. 1.

Fig. 4. Simulation of cellular automata to predict parking occupancy using matlab

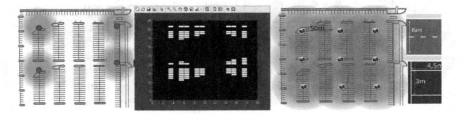

Fig. 5. Example of parking facility with 4 POEs and configuration with BLE Beacons

The proposed tool allows modeling different parking spaces with different topologies ranging from parking spaces with more or fewer rows or columns, POEs, number of lanes, sections, etc. For instance, the map on the left in Fig. 5 shows a parking facility with four POEs, and, as can be seen, once chosen an adequate CA initial state taking into account where the POEs are, the model reflects that users tend to park near the four access points. In this paper we have performed more than 100 simulations in several scenarios ranging from 60 to 2000 parking spaces and from 1 to 8 POEs.

4 Smartphone-Based Service to Locate Parking Spaces

The parking solution proposed in this work is composed of two components. First, as described in the previous Section, a CA-based model has been described to help to predict parking occupancy. Second, a smartphone-based service is described in this Section to help the user to locate both empty parking spaces and the parked vehicle thanks to a combination of different technologies. In order to facilitate the adoption of this technology, the user app will be designed to be light and automatic. As shown in Fig. 6, the proposed platform has been implemented through a distributed architecture that uses the smartphone to detect a variety of sensors and send a signal to a server. That server centralizes all the information regarding empty, occupied and possibly occupied parking spots. However, in addition to that and having into account that not every driver will have the application running on its smartphone, the described predictive tool helps to estimate which parking spaces are available in the parking facility.

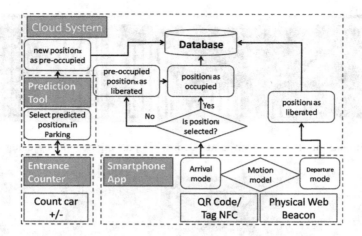

Fig. 6. High-level architecture of the indoor parking system

The high-level architecture of the proposal fuses three kinds of indoor sensors for location, and is based on a server that receives information from a vehicles counter, user smartphone applications and the tool for parking prediction.

Service providers establish the interfaces to bridge parking facilities and users over the Internet, and develop tools to create and maintain the parking facilities database. Operators of parking facilities use information from user applications and the predictive tool to monitor the occupancy of each parking space and to publish online the parking space occupancy prediction information in real time. Thus, the Internet is used in the proposed scheme to connect the different parties, including parking facilities, customers and service providers.

The information of each parking space includes its geographical coordinates, occupancy status, etc. A lightweight client program is running on users' smartphones to access the service through the Internet, to collect the data of the parking facilities of its interest and to keep an send the information about the parking space occupancy.

4.1   Server and Database

The server and database have been developed by using several frameworks that allow us to create an efficient and scalable solution. The involved technologies are the following:

- Node.js is an open source, cross-platform runtime environment for server-side and networking applications. Applications are written in JavaScript, and can be run within the Node.js runtime on multiple platforms. Commonly used for real-time web applications.
- MongoDB is a cross-platform document-oriented database. Classified as a NoSQL database, MongoDB eschews the traditional table-based relational database structure in favor of JSON-like documents with dynamic schemas.

- Express.js is a Node.js web application framework, designed for building single-page, multi-page, and hybrid web applications.
- Mongoose is a framework that allows to model data from a MongoDB database, allowing CRUD operations (Create, Read, Update and Delete).
- Embedded JavaScript (EJS) cleans the HTML out of your JavaScript with client side templates.
- Angular.js is an open-source web application framework that provides a framework for client-side Model-View-Controller (MVC) architecture.
- Bootstrap is a front end that works as an interface for the user, unlike the server-side code that resides on the "back end" or server.

4.2   Smartphone-Based Indoor Positioning Solution

The parking service exploits an accurate positioning solution based on QR codes, NFC tags or BLE Physical Web Beacons. In its development, the user operations are conducted on the parking client software. The application has been developed for the Android operating system and has been tested with a Samsung smartphone that runs Android 4.4. The software development has been done with Android Studio. The main Application Programming Interfaces (APIs) and resources used for the smartphone application are:

- An image-based floor map has been used as indoor map.
- Physical Web API has been used to acquire the measurements of the physical web beacons for indoor positioning.
- Zxyng API has been used to capture QR codes [22].

Indoor Positioning Using QR Codes or NFC Tags. QR codes and NFC tags are cheap technologies that can be used to solve the indoor location problem. These technologies are really convenient for the proposal because they can be easily used to remind where a vehicle is parked or to indicate which parking space is being used. These technologies are easy to use but have the inconvenience that they are not automatic, so, in order to occupy a parking space, the user has to take a picture of the QR code or put its smartphone close to the NFC tag. Thus, it is possible that many users do not use the technology because they forget to perform this simple step. The release of a parking space is automatic because the smartphone can detect the connection with the car handsfree and/or movement.

Indoor Positioning Using BLE Beacons. BLE beacons have also been widely used for indoor positioning as this kind of positioning solution is cost-efficient and can be operated in conjunction with communication services. Besides, the interaction between BLE beacons and the smartphone can be automated so that the user does not have to do anything neither in the arrival nor in the departure. The inconvenience is that location is not as precise as with QR or NFC solutions.

Unlike traditional solutions, which are usually based on specific hardware tags for positioning, the proposed solution uses the built-in hardware of a smartphone to collect the signals of the beacons and performs positioning estimation information from the cloud. Thus, for instance in the parking on the right in Fig. 5, nine beacons are enough to cover all parking spaces with enough precision.

5   Functional Demonstration of Parking Locator

This section describes a simple demonstration of the proposed parking service by showing some experimental results. The conclusion is that the parking service based on both prediction and availability of information from users' smartphones improves the user experience of customers through the parking recommendation and the reminder of the location of their parked vehicles. In addition to this, it is also demonstrated that the system is energy saving because the trip of a vehicle to the parking space is shorter. Figure 7 shows the difference between the distances that a user has to traverse to find an empty parking space depending on the information he/she knows. As can be seen, users with additional information go directly, while users without such information go wandering inside the parking facility until finding the parking space. It demonstrates the improvement of the proposal even in a very simple parking scenario. Figure 7 also shows an efficient and an inefficient route from the entrance in position $(1,2)$ of our matrix to a parking space in position (i,j). The measures to define the efficiency of such routes to a parking space in position (i,j) are given by the following expressions:

$$D(A \rightarrow B) = (1,2) \rightarrow (i,j) \tag{1}$$

- i: Number of rows. In the example there are 8 rows.
- j: Number of columns. In the example there are 12 columns.
- S_i: Size of a row item. In the example it is 3 meters.
- S_j: Size of a column item. In the example it is 4,5 meters.
- $Tsec$: Size of sections. In the example there are 4 items in each section.

Thus, on the one hand, the equation of an efficient route is:

$$D(A \rightarrow B)^{ef} = \begin{cases} (j-1) * S_j \ \forall (j \% 3) \neq 1 \\ (j+1) * S_j \ \forall (j \% 3) = 1 \end{cases} + (i-2) * S_i \quad if \quad (i \geq 3) \tag{2}$$

On the other hand, the equation for the inefficient route of Fig. 7 is:

$$D(A \rightarrow B)^{inef} = (Tsec + 2) * S_i + (2 * S_j)) * \lfloor (j-1)/3 \rfloor + \lambda_i$$
$$\lambda_i = \begin{cases} (i-2) * S_i & if \quad (\lfloor (j-1)/3 \rfloor \% 2 = 0) \\ (Tsec + 4 - i) * S_i & if \quad (\lfloor (j-1)/3 \rfloor \% 2 = 1) \end{cases} \tag{3}$$

In general, users try to park as close as they can to a POE, if they do not know where is the best empty parking space, they search through all the parking. On the contrary, if users have such information, they go directly to the best space, saving time and fuel and increasing their comfort. After the user has parked the vehicle, the smartphone disconnects from the vehicle's Bluetooth and the

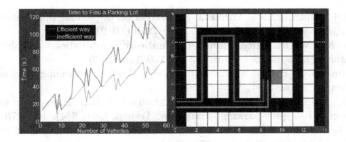

Fig. 7. Comparison between traversed distances to find an empty parking spot

Parking Locator App is launched so that the user can take a picture of the QR code or put the smartphone near the NFC tag. If there are BLE beacons, this information is automatically stored. Finally, when the user wants to come back to the vehicle and needs to find the route to it, he/she uses the function "Find my car", which leads him/her from the current location to the parked vehicle. In order to find the best walking route, the pathfinding framework [23] is used.

6 Conclusions

The main objective of this work is the development of a low-cost solution for indoor parking facilities that combines a system to predict availability in parking spaces and a smartphone application to indicate parking occupation through different kinds of sensors. The proposal is a complete service that also help the driver by offering an orientation service to take him/her to an available parking space or to the parked vehicle. The proposed predictive tool is based on a modified cellular automata to predict the behavior of vehicles inside the parking. The designed tool is based on a web application and a mobile application that uses QR codes, NFC tags and/or BLE beacons. On the one hand, the web application provides the availability estimation based on estimated and actual occupation of parking spaces. On the other hand, the mobile application has been developed focusing on the simplicity and the usefulness for the final user. For this reason, it synchronizes with the car's Bluetooth to automate the whole process. Both the web and the Android application have been tested and the results obtained from their use are promising.

Acknowledgments. Research supported by the projects TIN2011-25452, IPT-2012-0585-370000, RTC-2014-1648-8 and TEC2014-54110-R.

References

1. Clarke, K., Hoppen, S., Gaydos, L.: A self-modifying cellular automaton model of historical. Environ. Plan. B **24**, 247–261 (1997)
2. Herold, M., Goldstein, N.C., Clarke, K.C.: The spatiotemporal form of urban growth: measurement, analysis and modeling. Remote sens. Environ. **86**(3), 286–302 (2003)

3. Caicedo, F., Blazquez, C., Miranda, P.: Prediction of parking space availability in real time. Expert Syst. Appl. **39**(8), 7281–7290 (2012)
4. Gardner, M.: Mathematical games: the fantastic combinations of John Conways new solitaire game life. Sci. Am. **223**(4), 120–123 (1970)
5. Von Neumann, J., Burks, A.W., et al.: Theory of self-reproducing automata. IEEE Trans. Neural Netw. **5**(1), 3–14 (1966)
6. Horni, A., Montini, L., Waraich, R.A., Axhausen, K.W.: An agent-based cellular automaton cruising-for-parking simulation. Transp. Lett. **5**(4), 167–175 (2013)
7. Horng, G.-J.: Using cellular automata for parking recommendations in smart environments. PLoS ONE **9**(8), e105973 (2014)
8. Mimbela, L.E.Y., Klein, L.A.: Summary of vehicle detection and surveillance technologies used in intelligent transportation systems. Southwest Technology Development Institute, New Mexico State University, Vehicle Detector Clearinghouse (2003)
9. Hammadi, O.A., Hebsi, A.A., Zemerly, M.J., Ng, J.W.: Indoor localization and guidance using portable smartphones. In: IEEE/WIC/ACM International Joint Conferences on Web Intelligence and Intelligent Agent Technology, pp. 337–341 (2012)
10. Costa-Montenegro, E., Gonzalez-Castano, F.J., Conde-Lagoa, D., Barragans-Martinez, A.B., Rodriguez-Hernandez, P.S., Gil-Castineira, F.: QR-maps: An efficient tool for indoor user location based on QR-codes and google maps. In: IEEE Consumer Communications and Networking Conference, pp. 928–932 (2011)
11. Kim, M.S., Lee, D.H., Kim, K.N.J.: A study on the nfc-based mobile parking management system. In: IEEE International Conference on Information Science and Applications, pp. 1–5 (2013)
12. Sorden, G., Hinsley, M.: Location-based services, US Patent App. 13/688,011, 28 November 2012
13. Physical Web, (2014). https://google.github.io/physical-web
14. Levine, U., Shinar, A., Shabtai, E.: System and method for parking time estimations, US Patent 7,936,284, 3 May 2011. www.google.com/patents/US7936284
15. Google, Android auto (2015). www.android.com/auto
16. Apple, Car play (2015). www.apple.com/ios/carplay
17. BMW, ConnectedDrive (2015). www.bmw.es/connecteddrive
18. Ford, Ford sync (2015). www.ford.com/technology/sync
19. Generals Motors, On star (2015). https://www.onstar.com
20. Khoshelham, K., Elberink, S.O.: Accuracy and resolution of kinect depth data for indoor mapping applications. Sensors **12**(2), 1437–1454 (2012)
21. van der Waerden, P., Borgers, A., Timmermans, H.: Travelers micro-behavior at parking lots: a model of parking choice behavior. In: Processing of the 82nd Annual Meeting of the Transportation Research Board 1212 (2003)
22. Official zxing ("zebra crossing") project (2015). https://github.com/zxing/zxing
23. PathFinding project (2015). http://qiao.github.io/PathFinding.js/visual/

Detection and Report of Traffic Lights Violation Using Sensors and Smartphones

Francisco Martín-Fernández[✉], Pino Caballero-Gil, and Cándido Caballero-Gil

Departament of Computer Engineering, University of La Laguna, 38202 La Laguna, Spain
{fmartinf,pcaballe,ccabgil}@ull.edu.es

Abstract. Since technology is advancing at a rapid pace, new smart electronic devices are continually emerging to solve everyday problems. One of the most important problems of the world is related to road safety, so the mitigation of traffic accidents has become one of the biggest challenges for researchers. As a result, many proposals have emerged within the Intelligent Transport System (ITS) initiative. This paper proposes a new ITS-based system to automatically detect and warn about the breach of traffic lights. In the proposal, the vehicle that violates traffic lights self-reports of it, so the system can warn nearby vehicles to make they drive with greater caution. This self-reporting is done in a completely anonymously way so that users do not stop using the application. Besides, the method uses cryptographic algorithms to guarantee trust, integrity and authenticity of the information. The proposed system has been designed and implemented using sensors, smartphones and a server in the cloud, and the obtained results are promising.

Keywords: Road safety · Intelligent Transport System · Traffic light violation · Smartphone application

1 Introduction

Diverse problems related to road traffic have increased worldwide as a result of the population growth, ranging from big urbanized zones to dense populated areas. These traffic adverse circumstances can reduce the efficiency of transport infrastructure and increase travel time, fuel consumption and pollution. One of the consequences of the widespread of Information and Communication Technologies (ICT) is the existence of countless applications that help to drive.

Currently, decisions of drivers depend on what they see and/or hear. However, a system that includes interactive and cooperative driving and an effective traffic control would provide a third channel to receive additional data that cannot be directly seen or heard by drivers, but that might be very helpful for their decision-making.

The so-called Intelligent Transport System (ITS) is a set of technological solutions designed to optimize different modes of transport. One of its main

© Springer International Publishing Switzerland 2015
J.M. García-Chamizo et al. (Eds.): UCAmI 2015, LNCS 9454, pp. 237–248, 2015.
DOI: 10.1007/978-3-319-26401-1_23

purposes is to prevent adverse traffic circumstances, and to reach it, ITS is based on varied technologies.

Vehicular Ad-hoc NETworks (VANETs) are a key part of the ITS where information is exchanged among vehicles and/or with a communication infrastructure. Thus, every vehicle is assumed to have an information transmitter commonly known as On Board Unit (OBU). Regarding the communication infrastructure, it can be implemented in various ways. For instance, the infrastructure can be arranged along the road in the form of points of communication commonly referred as Road Side Units (RSUs).

A difficult problem in road safety is the discovery of users that fail to stop at red traffic lights. There may be several causes of traffic light violations. One of them is the duration of the traffic lights. Traffic lights with a very short duration cause that users ignore the red light, what produces a ripple effect that can cause many accidents. In order to try to overcome this problem, different solutions exist such as new traffic signal mechanisms, red-light speed cameras to detect offenders, etc., which reduce traffic jams in urban centers around the world. These solutions are effective but very expensive to be widespread.

According to the Traffic Safety Facts Report of the National Highway Traffic Safety Administration (NHTSA) [15], there were more than 2.3 million reported intersection-related crashes, resulting in more than 7,770 fatalities and approximately 733,000 injury crashes in the USA. In particular, the Fatality Analysis Reporting System (FARS) of the NHTSA reports that red-light running crashes alone caused 762 annual deaths, and that 165,000 people are injured annually by red-light runners. Besides, the Insurance Institute for Highway Safety (IIHS) reports that half of the people killed in red-light running crashes are not the signal violators, but drivers and pedestrians hit by red-light runners.

This paper is organized as follows. Section 2 briefly introduces some background of related work. Section 3 explains the theoretical solution proposed to protect the security of the scheme. Section 4 describes in detail the proposed scheme of the sensor platform. In Sect. 5, the user application of the system is presented. Section 6 provides a short explanation about the implementation of the proposal and its time performance. Finally, some conclusions and open problems close the paper in Sect. 7.

2   Related Works

The need of improving road traffic management is evident worldwide. Governments are worried about the growing number of vehicles on roads and of traffic-related deaths. For this reason, they are trying to improve traffic safety by exploring the potential of the ITS through numerous research projects funded by public entities and/or the automotive industry [1]. The current ITS state-of-the-art is based primarily on a series of initiatives from both academia and industry, addressed mainly to try to enable the future development of VANETs.

Several proposals exist to punish those users that violate traffic lights [4,5]. One of such proposals, called red light camera, has been operating for several

years in regions such as China, Hong Kong, United Kingdom and North America
[2]. A red light camera is a type of traffic enforcement camera that captures an
image of any vehicle that enters an intersection after jumping a red traffic light. It
takes automatically a picture to the vehicle that run the red light and the photo
can be used as evidence that assists authorities in their enforcement of traffic
laws. Generally, the camera is triggered when a vehicle enters the intersection
(passes the stop-bar) after the traffic signal has turned red.

In [8], authors present an adaptive traffic light system based on wireless
communication between vehicles and fixed controller nodes deployed in intersections. Such traffic light system is based on short-range wireless communication
between vehicles, which uses a controller wireless node placed in the intersection
that determines optimum values for the traffic lights phases.

The work from Google [7] presents several methods for automatically mapping the three-dimensional positions of traffic lights and robustly detecting traffic
light state on board equipment in cars with cameras. They used these methods
to map more than four thousand traffic lights, and to perform on board traffic
light detection for thousands of drivers through intersections.

The work [11] proposes the use of RFID for dynamic traffic light sequences.
It avoids problems that usually arise with systems that use image processing
and beam interruption techniques. RFID technology with appropriate algorithm
and database were applied to a multi-vehicle, multi-lane and multi-road junction
area to provide an efficient time management scheme. A dynamic time schedule
was worked out for the passage of each column. The simulation showed that the
dynamic sequence algorithm could adjust itself even with the presence of some
extreme cases. The conclusion is that the system could emulate the judgment
of a traffic police officer on duty, by considering the number of vehicles in each
column and the routing properties.

A modern traffic light for six roads and four junctions has been implemented
by programming in the PIC16F877A microcontroller [12]. The system works
efficiently over the present traffic controlling system with respect to less waiting
time, efficient operation during emergency mode and suggestions of alternate
route.

To the best of our knowledge, there is no proposal to notify the vehicles in an
area where there is a nearby vehicle that has jumped a traffic light. Nor is there
a solution allowing a vehicle to report that it has broken the law at a traffic light,
anonymously. Anonymity can encourage using this system. The authorities can
benefit by analyzing data generated by the system. In this way, it can detect if
a traffic light is more likely to be violated than another one. Besides, this can
serve to study and adjust the timing of traffic lights.

3   Security Scheme

The proposed system should maintain user anonymity, and integrity and authenticity of information, in order to promote the application to be used. The aim is
not to find the users who skip the traffic lights, but to warn above that a user has

jumped a traffic light, without being able to trace his/her identity. Therefore, a reliable and secure anonymity scheme is needed to inspire confidence to all users. The proposal uses a cloud server, a sensor platform and smartphones to achieve this aim. The smartphones are used to identify the vehicles. The sensor platform is located in traffic lights and communicates with the smartphones. The cloud server is responsible to notify to the other nearby vehicles.

In order to maintain this level of security, OpenSSL was used in the implementation. OpenSSL is an open-source implementation of the SSL and TLS protocols. OpenSSL supports a number of different cryptographic algorithms. In particular, this work uses the last version 1.0.2 released in January.

For the establishment of a secure communication channel, a Certificate Authority (CA) has been implemented in the cloud server. A certificate authority is an entity that issues digital certificates to certify the ownership of a public key. This allows others to rely upon signatures or on assertions made by the private key that corresponds to the certified public key. In this model of trust relationships, a CA is a trusted third party, trusted both by the subject (owner) of the certificate and by the party relying upon the certificate.

The integrity of the message and the authenticity of the sender are protected through the use of a digital signature scheme. Thus, the vehicle uses its private key during the process of digital signature of the message sent to the server, and the server uses the user's public key to verify the digital signature of the message. Specifically, the scheme is based on the Elliptic Curve Digital Signature Algorithm (ECDSA) [10] that offers a variant of the Digital Signature Algorithm (DSA), which uses elliptic curve cryptography.

The implementation is based on a digital signature scheme with the following parameters, where $\times$ denotes elliptic curve point multiplication by a scalar:

- $Curve$: Equation defining an elliptic curve field.
- G: Elliptic curve base point, generator of the $Curve$ with prime order n.
- n: Integer order of G, so that $n \times G = O$.
- d_A: Private key integer randomly selected in the interval $[1, n-1]$.
- Q_A: Public key curve point denoted by $Q_A = d_A \times G$.
- m: Message to sign.

On the one hand, n order to sign a message m, Algorithm 1 is used.

Algorithm 1. Signature Algorithm

---

1 Calculate $e = h(m)$, where $h(\cdots)$ is the SHA-3 cryptographic hash function;
2 Let z be the L_n leftmost bits of e, where L_n is the bit length of n;
3 Select a cryptographically secure random integer k from $[1, n-1]$;
4 Calculate the curve point $(x_1, y_1) = k \times G$;
5 Calculate $r = x_1 \bmod n$. If $r = 0$, go back to step 3;
6 Calculate $s = k^{-1}(z + rd_A) \bmod n$. If $s = 0$, go back to step 3;
7 The signature is the pair (r, s);

Algorithm 2. Verification Algorithm

---

1 Check that Q_A is not equal to the identity element O;
2 Check that Q_A lies on the curve;
3 Check that $n \times Q_A = O$;
4 Verify that r and s are integers in $[1, n-1]$. Otherwise, the signature is invalid;
5 Calculate $e = h(m)$, where $h(\cdots)$ is the same function used in the signature generation, SHA-3;
6 Let z be the L_n leftmost bits of e;
7 Calculate $w = s^{-1} \bmod n$;
8 Calculate $u_1 = zw \bmod n$ and $u_2 = rw \bmod n$;
9 Calculate the curve point $(x_1, y_1) = u_1 \times G + u_2 \times Q_A$;
10 The signature is valid if $r \equiv x_1 \pmod{n}$. Otherwise it is invalid;

On the other hand, each signature is verified by the server with Algorithm 2.

In order to protect user anonymity, k-anonymity is used for the digital signature. The concept of k-anonymity was first formulated in [14] as an attempt to solve the problem that given person-specific field-structured data, produce a data release with scientific guarantees that the individuals who are the subjects of the data cannot be re-identified while the data remain practically useful.

In particular, a release of data is said to have the k-anonymity property if the information for each person contained in the release cannot be distinguished from at least $k - 1$ individuals whose information also appear in the release. In particular, the implemented schema guarantees k-anonymity through the application of the ideas in [3], according to vehicle every user is randomly associated to a group that share cryptographic material such as a par of privates pubic keys and a group certificate so that this data are used to sign. In this way, users do not reveal their particular identities but only their group identifier.

4   Sensor Platform

Sensing systems for ITS are based on networked system vehicles and infrastructures, i.e. on smart vehicle technologies. Infrastructure sensors are in general tough devices that are installed in the road. These sensors may be disseminated during road construction or by sensor injection machinery for rapid deployment. There are many types of sensors: vehicle counters, weather stations, cameras to detect traffic jams, radars to detect high speeds, etc. These sensors can be ranged from very simple (such as sensors to detect the number of vehicles on a road section) to highly advanced (such as cameras to detect vehicles with a special software). Usually, the more complex sensors are the most expensive. A camera with visual detection of vehicles is a very expensive system, and it is used to avoid the violations of traffic lights.

In order to add intelligence to traffic lights, the proposed system uses a light sensor that provides information in real time about the traffic light color. This, together with a Bluetooth Low Energy (BLE) module, allows transmitting the state of the traffic light to nearby vehicles, as a beacon notification.

Bluetooth road sensors are able to detect Bluetooth MAC addresses from Bluetooth devices in passing vehicles. If these sensors are interconnected, they are able to provide interesting data. Compared to other traffic measurement technologies, Bluetooth measurement has some differences:

- High Accuracy and the devices are quick to set up easily.
- Limited to a number of Bluetooth devices that can be broadcasting in a vehicle so counting and other applications are limited.
- Non-intrusive measurements what can lead to lower-cost installations for both permanent and temporary sites.

The sensor platform that is used consists of several electronic modules for composing a small, fully integrated system in any type of traffic light.

In this work, RFDuino [13], which is an Arduino shrunk to the size of a fingertip and made it wireless, is used as the board, exactly the 2216 model, with a Dual AAA Battery Shield. The shield has a step-up switching regulator that allows the batteries to be drained down to low voltages while still providing a stable 3.3 V to the RFduino.

The Bluetooth Low Energy module used for the RFDuino is the RFD22102 RFduino DIP. This module has the technical specifications shown in Table 1.

The format of a BLE message include a 1 byte preamble, 4 byte access codes correlated with the RF channel number used, a Packet Data Unit (PDU) that can be between 2 to 39 bytes and 3 bytes of CRC. Thus, the shortest packet would have 10 bytes and the longest packet would have 47 bytes. The transmission times of these packages range from 8 microseconds to the smallest package up to 300 milliseconds for the largest. The PDU for the advertising channel consists of the 16-bit PDU header, and depending on the type of advertising, the device address and up to 31 bytes of information. Also, the active scanner may request up to 31 bytes of additional information from the advertiser if the advertising mode allows such an operation. It means that a sizeable portion of data can be received from the advertising device even without establishing a connection. Advertising intervals can be set in a range of 20 ms to 10 s. It specifies the interval between consecutive advertising packets.

The sensor, which is connected to the traffic light, captures its color and state emitted by a beacon, and constantly sends this information to all vehicles near the traffic lights. To ensure the integrity of each beacon, a digital signature scheme is used.

ISO/IEC 9796-2 [9] scheme 1 based on SHA-1 hash and RSA is applied for the digital signature, because its length is only 22 bytes, so it fulfills the storage requirements of BLE beacons. ISO/IEC 9796-2 is a standard signature scheme widely used in the smart card industry for public key certificates and message authentication because it quite simple to implement.

All traffic lights have a generic certificate to sign beacons, given by the CA of the Directorate General of Traffic.

The beacon is formatted as shown in Fig. 1, where:

- idTrafficLight: Unique identifier for the traffic light.

Table 1. RFD22102 BLE Technical Specs

Specification	Value
Part number	RFD22102
Category	Bluetooth LE RF module
Type	Transceiver/Controller
Band	2.4 GHz
CPU	16 MHz ARM Cortex-M0
Flash	128 kb
Ram	8 kb
Multi frequency	Yes
Package-case	DIP RFduino footprint
Packaging	Bulk clamshell
RoHS compliant	Yes
Low supply voltage	1.9 V
Typical supply voltage	3 V
High supply voltage	3.6 V
Transmit current	18 mA, 4 uA ULP
Receive current	18 mA, 4 uA ULP
FCC approved	Yes
IC approved	Yes
ETSI CE tested	Yes
Transmit power	4 dbm

- bearing: Compass direction used to describe the direction of the traffic light (represented in degrees (0–360)).
- state: State of the traffic light (green, red, etc.)
- signature: Digital signature of the message.

This beacon is received by the smartphone, which is responsible for processing information and report anonymously if it did not respect the traffic signal.

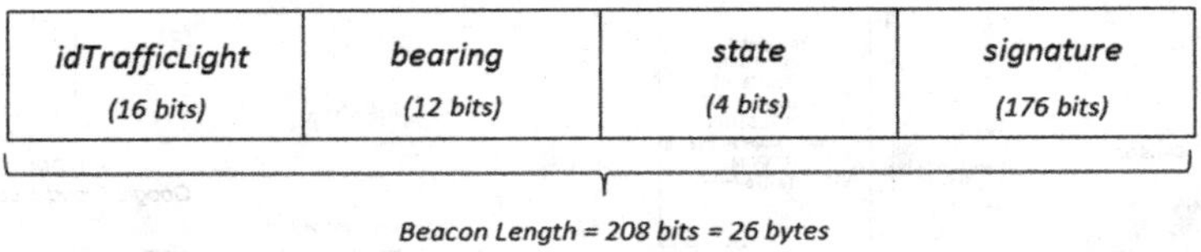

idTrafficLight	bearing	state	signature
(16 bits)	(12 bits)	(4 bits)	(176 bits)

Beacon Length = 208 bits = 26 bytes

Fig. 1. Format of the beacon transmitted by the traffic light

5   User Application

A mobile application has been implemented to read the BLE beacon that the traffic light emits, and processes (See Fig. 2).

In order to monitor all system users and establish communications, including the use of a server, that is responsible for the control and monitoring, is proposed. The different system technologies are shown in Fig. 3.

Depending on the information contained in the beacon, and the speed that the vehicle has at that time, the application detects in background if the vehicle did not respect the traffic lights. If the vehicle driver violated the traffic light, the smartphone sends a message to a server that controls and manages such events. The server is responsible for searching its database to find nearby vehicles at

Fig. 2. User interface of the mobile application

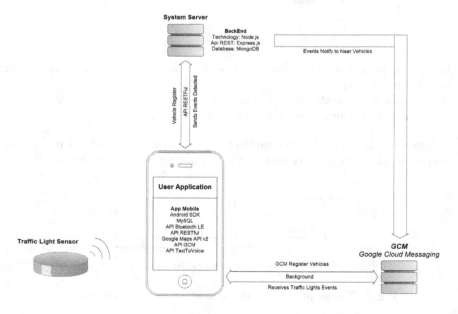

Fig. 3. Use flow and technologies used in the system

that time. This is possible because the server knows the position of each vehicle using the system, since all vehicles send every 5 seconds their current positions. Once it has located all vehicles near the traffic lights, a push notification that reaches all smartphones of nearby vehicles is generated. The application informs the driver via voice that there is another driver who has skipped a traffic light in its area, so it recommends driving with special caution. The application also displays on a map, the position of the traffic light.

The server is a full-stack Javascript implementation. As cross-platform runtime environment for server-side and networking applications Node.js is used. In order to connect the mobile application with the server through REST Web Services, the work uses Express.js. To store the vast amount of data on the server, a NoSQL database called MongoDB is used.

6   Implementation Analysis

The implemented system uses sensors, smartphones and cloud servers to automatically detect and anonymously report that a driver has failed to respect a traffic light. Figure 4 shows an overview of the system operation.

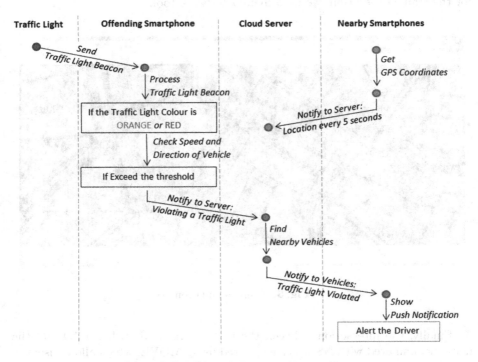

Fig. 4. Overview of the system operation

Table 2. Size of sent packets

Packet	Size (in bits)
Beacon from traffic light to smartphone (via BLE)	208
Data event from smartphone to server (via WiFi/GPRS/3G/LTE)	248
Push notification from cloud server to smartphones	272

The system can also be used by road authorities to detect traffic lights that are less respected. Thus, an action plan can be established to investigate the causes for searching solutions (longer duration of light color, etc.).

The system has several processes that send various data packets. In Table 2, the size of the different data packets used in the proposed system is shown.

Different batteries of tests were used to check the time separately for each scheme component and the total time. The simulations were done using multiple software packages to add credibility and develop a realistic simulation. Thus, the scenario that has been used for simulations comprises a real traffic situation in the city of Madrid (Spain) in 2014 [6] (See Fig. 5). In order to simulate the architecture and communications of a VANET, a tool called NS-2 was used, and for the traffic generation, we used SUMO software tool.

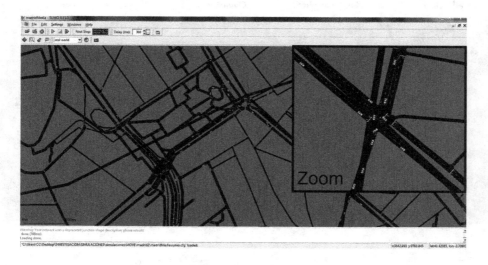

Fig. 5. Traffic simulation

Finally, the interaction between the traffic generated with SUMO and the network simulated with NS-2 was generated using MOVE, which allows users to rapidly generate realistic mobility models for VANET simulations.

As a result, the times represented by the averages of all tests, shown in Table 3, prove that efficiency has been achieved.

Table 3. Average time required to send different data

Component	Time (in Milliseconds)
Sending the beacon from the traffic light to the smartphone	0.17
Smartphone data processing	51
Sending event from smartphone to cloud server	116
Cloud Server data processing	104
Notification push from cloud server to smartphones	142
Total	**413.17**

7   Conclusions

Novel methods to try to avoid traffic accidents are becoming a major technological research. Among the main causes of traffic accidents, one of the most
dangerous is the violation of traffic lights. There are several proposals to detect
violators of traffic lights, but all are based on complex systems using video cameras to denounce such violators. This paper proposes a new system based on
self-reports of offending vehicles in order to warn nearby vehicles. For this, the
system makes use of sensors, placed at traffic lights, which emit their current
status as beacon data. Each vehicle is paired with a smartphone that is responsible for reading and processing these beacons to discern whether the vehicle is
violating traffic lights or not. If so, the smartphone notifies anonymously to a system in the cloud that the nearby traffic light has been violated. Then the cloud
system notifies all nearby vehicles that there is a vehicle with outlaw behavior.
The proposed system uses different cryptographic protocols to provide security
to all communications and in particular to achieve anonymity, authenticity and
integrity messages. This work is part of a work in progress but the first beta
implementation shows promising results.

Acknowledgments. Research supported by TIN2011-25452, BES-2012-051817, IPT-
2012-0585-370000, RTC-2014-1648-8 and TEC2014-54110-R.

References

1. Bin, T., Morris, B.T., Ming, T., Yuqiang, L., Chao, G., Dayong, S., Shaohu, T.:
   Hierarchical and networked vehicle surveillance in ITS: a survey. IEEE Trans.
   Intell. Transp. Syst. **16**(2), 557–580 (2015)
2. Bochner, B., Walden, T.: Effectiveness of red light cameras. Transp. Eng. J. **80**(5),
   18 (2010)
3. Caballero-Gil C., Molina-Gil J., Hernandez-Serrano J., Leon O., Soriano M., On
   the revocation of malicious users in anonymous and non-traceable VANETs. In:
   XIII Reunion Española sobre Criptologia y Seguridad de la Informacion, pp. 87–91
   (2014)

4. Charette, R., Nashashibi, F.: Traffic light recognition using image processing compared to learning processes. In: ICEE/RSI International Conference on Intelligent Robots and Systems, pp. 333–338 (2009)
5. Choi, C., Park, Y.: Enhanced traffic light detection method using geometry information. Int. J. Comput. Control, Quant. Inf. Eng. **8**(8), 1264–1268 (2014)
6. de Trafico, D.G.: Portal Estadistico Parque de Vehiculos. http://www.dgt.es/. Accessed 2015
7. Fairfield, N., Urmson, C.: Traffic light mapping and detection. In: IEEC International Conference on Robotics and Automation (ICRA), pp. 5421–5426 (2011)
8. Gradinescu, V., Gorgorin, C., Diaconescu, R., Cristea, V., Iftode, L.: Adaptive traffic lights using car-to-car communication. In: IEEE Vehicular Technology Conference, VTC2007-Spring, pp. 21–25 (2007)
9. ISO/IEC 9796–2:2010: Information technology, Security techniques, Digital signature schemes giving message recovery, Part 2: Integer factorization based mechanisms. ISO (2010)
10. Johnson, D., Menezes, A., Vanstone, A.: The elliptic curve digital signature algorithm (ECDSA). Int. J. Inf. Secur. **1**(1), 36–61 (2001)
11. Al-Khateeb, K.A., Johari, J.A., Al-Khateeb, W.F.: Dynamic traffic light sequence algorithm using RFID. J. Comput. Sci. **4**, 517–524 (2008)
12. Kham, N.H., Nwe, C.M.: Implementation of modern traffic light control system. Int. J. Sci. Res. Publ. **4**(6), 82–89 (2014)
13. RFDuino: http://www.rfduino.com/. Accessed May 2015
14. Sweeney, L.: k-anonymity: a model for protecting privacy. Int. J. Uncertainty Fuzziness Knowl. Based Syst. **10**(5), 557–570 (2002)
15. U.S. Department of Transportation, Traffic Safety Facts 2008 Report. National Statistics (2008)

Detecting Aggressive Driving Behavior
with Participatory Sensing

Miguel Angel Ylizaliturri-Salcedo[✉], Monica Tentori,
and J. Antonio Garcia-Macias

CICESE Research Center, Ensenada, Baja California, Mexico
mylizali@cicese.edu.mx, {mtentori,jagm}@cicese.mx

Abstract. Aggressive driving increases the risk of accidents, and it is
normally a consequence of the impatience, frustration, or anger of drivers.
In this paper, we present a case study showing the feasibility of using
participatory sensing to enable drivers to report and gain awareness on
aggressive driving behavior. We describe the design and development of
the Driving Habits System prototype, a mobile application that enables
drivers deploying sensing campaigns to collect data about their driving
habits. We also discuss the results from a 5-weeks deployment study,
where 23 drivers used the system in their everyday lives in the city of
Ensenada, Mexico. Our results indicate that our prototype was useful
and easy to learn. Its design allows drivers to raise awareness on their
driving behaviors and motivates them to engage on a participatory sensing campaign to identify issues on the factors that affect driving. We
close discussing design issues for ubiquitous applications to be used while
driving and the potential impact of such tools in promoting self-reflection
and behavior change.

1 Introduction

Aggressive driving increases the risk of collisions, and is common on drivers,
motivated by impatience, annoyance or hostility. According to [12], aggressive
driving can be recognized by: running red lights, traffic weaving, tailgating and
forced merging. Some research projects have proposed using smartphones for
identifying different maneuvers that relate with aggressive driving [5]. In this
work we propose making drivers to reflect into their own data as they are driving,
allowing to raise awareness on aggressive driving behaviors, and promoting safer
driving styles.

Although, works like MIROAD [2,5] show that the use of sensors in smartphones, combined with classifiers, are appropriate to infer driving behaviors,
little has been said about how this data could be used to provide drivers with
awareness of their driving behaviors and eventually promote positive behavior change. Nowadays, apps like Automatic (automatic.com), Zubie (zubie.co),
Dash & Drive Smart (dash.by) and TalkyCar (http://goo.gl/LvQtw7) use a
smartphone and OBD-II interface devices to assessing the quality of driving in

© Springer International Publishing Switzerland 2015
J.M. García-Chamizo et al. (Eds.): UCAmI 2015, LNCS 9454, pp. 249–261, 2015.
DOI: 10.1007/978-3-319-26401-1_24

terms of the number of aggressive behaviors a driver may exhibit like braking, accelerating, and speeding.

However, some of these apps are only available for the market in USA; and when they are used in developing countries with challenging road conditions, the issues that affect road quality can provide a biased evaluation of the aggressive driving behaviors, producing drivers' frustration and discouraging their usage and jeopardizing adoption. Also, there is limited evidence of how these commercial applications could be used to deploy participatory sensing campaigns for gathering collective knowledge. These related efforts open new research questions around the design of mobile technologies making use of specialized sensors and taking advantage of the notions of participatory sensing that are appropriate and easy to use while driving.

In this work, we describe the design of the Driving Habits System prototype for conducting participatory sensing campaigns on aggressive driving behaviors and present a case study in the concrete scenario of the city of Ensenada, Mexico. We finish this work with some design issues for ubiquitous applications intended to be used while driving and its potential impact in promoting self-reflection and behavior change.

2   The Driving Habits System

The Driving Habits System is a mobile application designed to enable drivers deploy participatory sensing campaigns and gather data about aggressive driving behaviors and the quality of roads. We followed a user centered design methodology to iteratively design our prototype. First, we conducted 11 interviews with pedestrians (n=4), drivers (n=6) and transit officers (n=1), and 10 hours of non-participatory observation. Then, we conducted three participatory design sessions (one hour long in average) with a multidisciplinary team with expertise interaction design (n=1), and in human computer interaction and ubiquitous computing (n=3). We evaluated the design of our prototype during a focus group with drivers with at least one-year experience (n=5) and experts in human computer interaction (n=1). In what follows, we describe the resulting prototype.

The main component of the Driving Habits System is a mobile sensing application running in Android devices (Fig. 1) for monitoring aggressive driving behaviors. We define an aggressive behavior as any of the four aggressive maneuvers that the Driving Habits System is capable of recognizing: swerving, braking, accelerating and speeding. The Driving Habits System automatically registers an aggressive behavior event when it recognizes and geo-localizes one single maneuver that exceeds a normal driving threshold.

The application's interface is similar to a traditional GPS navigation system, as this interface is familiar to drivers and we wanted to reduce the cognitive effort associated with the use and interpretation of the information being displayed.

There are two visualizations notifying drivers when incurring in aggressive driving behaviors. First, the driver's trajectory is drawn in colors depending on the vehicle's speed on top of a traditional navigation map (Table 2). Second, next

Fig. 1. The driving habits system. Upper left, the application main screen, Bottom left, the ELM327 device plugged into the vehicle OBD-II port, center, the android device running the application mounted over the dashboard, Upper right, the emotion status survey, Bottom right, the aggressive behavior event survey.

to the map, the user can review a tile with four icons indicating how aggressive the driver is related to each one of the aggressive behaviors. Both the color of the icons and user trajectory changes in response to the driver's performance, from green to yellow and red, based on the aggressiveness level of their driving: green, less aggressive; yellow, somewhat aggressive; and red very aggressive (Table 3).

The Driving Habits System also provides audio feedback when detecting an aggressive behavior event by reproducing a short beep and a verbal prompt using the Android voice synthesizer. Following a conversational interaction model, the system asks the driver to fill an icon-based survey to specify the reason of incurring in an aggressive behavior event (*e.g.*, "Carlos, why did you swerve?").

Drivers use the survey interface for detailing the contextual reasons that might be the cause of that specific aggressive behavior event (*e.g.*, "I swerved to avoid a street bump", Fig. 1, bottom right), or to discard the event automatically detected by the system. This way the survey enables drivers to report a pothole, a street bump, an obstacle, a traffic jam, or even the aggressive behavior of another driver. If the driver is unable or chooses not to answer the survey, it will be dismissed automatically after 15 seconds of waiting for a response. The same notification and survey mechanism is used for requesting drivers to report their current emotional state when beginning a trip (Fig. 1, upper right). This survey presents positive and negative emotions, like, being angry, sad, or happy, defined by the circumflex emotion model [9].

2.1   Using the System

To show how the Driving Habits System could be used in practice, here we present an example scenario of use:

As Carlos begins driving, he touches the play button, indicating he is willing to share his driving data. The voice assistant component uses the Android voice

Table 1. Aggressive driving behavior representation and its thresholds.

Behavior	Icon	Event threshold
Swerving		The accelerometer senses a lateral acceleration change of ±4 m/s² [2].
Braking		The accelerometer and the ELM327 device infer a longitudinal deceleration of 2.4 m/s² [2].
Accelerating		The accelerometer and the ELM327 device senses a longitudinal acceleration of 2.8 m/s² [2].
Speeding		The ELM327 device senses speeds over 80 km/h. The trajectory color on map follows the next rules: Blue<=0, green 0<speed<=35, yellow 35<speed<=60, orange 60<speed<=80, red 80<speed [4].

synthesizer loudly to say: "The services are active". At this moment the Driving Habits System begins to record data. The system asks, loudly, "Hi Carlos, how do you feel today?", and presents the icon-based emotion self-report survey with eight icons showing emoticons related with the emotional status (Figure 1, upper right). As this time Carlos is happy, he chooses a yellow icon representing a happy face. At this moment, the four icons representing his aggressive behaviors are green. When Carlos begins to drive, his trajectory is depicted over the map, in green colors because he is driving below 35 km/h. In a moment of distraction, he did not react with enough time to brake softly, because the next intersection traffic light is about to change to red. When braking suddenly, the system reproduces a beep, and says: "Carlos, you made a sudden brake, why is that?", and presents an icon-based aggressive event survey (Figure 1, bottom right). The color of the braking icon changes from green to yellow indicating to Carlos, his behavior is somewhat aggressive. Carlos touches the screen and waits to be able to continue driving. When arriving to his destination, Carlos touches the pause button and the Driving Habits System says loud "The services are paused", indicating that he finished collecting the data.

2.2   Architecture

To provide the above mentioned functionality the system uses an Android device running the Driving Habits System Application (i.e. a tablet with 7 in. size display and at least 4 GB of free internal memory) (Fig. 1, bottom left) connected via Bluetooth to an ELM327 interface device plugged into the OBD-II vehicle's port available on all vehicles since 1996. The Android device keeps the collected data in a local repository, and when Wi-Fi access point is available, usually when the device's battery is being charged, sends the data to an application server that stores a representation of the driver's data.

Inferring aggressive driving events. As the works reported in the literature [2,5], the algorithms based in accelerometer data require calibration for recognizing the orientation of the device related to the vehicle's moving direction in order to identify properly when the vehicle is going forward or backwards; in other words, braking or accelerating. The normal operation of the vehicle produces vibration, affecting the accelerometer readings. Also falling into a pothole or slamming a door can be easily confused with braking or swerving. One alternative is trusting exclusively in the engine operation data collected from the OBD-II port, insensible to the quality of the road, but this would not provide information about the lateral vehicle's movement, essential for recognizing the swerving maneuvers, nor the perceived sensation of movement. For addressing this issue, as in [5] we use both data sources (Table 1), and in this work we propose human intervention for event recognition using participatory sensing to identify the events related with the quality of the road.

The Driving Habits System extracts and processes raw data from the Android device's accelerometer, following the schema proposed in [2] for detecting erratic driving behaviors. Following their method, the Driving Habits System application recognizes the vehicle's direction during the initial movement and later computes two acceleration vectors: longitudinal and lateral, quantifying the forces that affect the vehicle's movement. Then analyzes these vectors in three seconds long overlapping windows, using the thresholds in (Table 1) (Fig. 2).

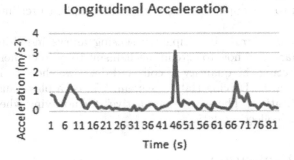

Fig. 2. Aggressive braking event example. In the time 46 s, a change of -3 m/s^2 happens.

The use of the ELM327 interface device in the vehicle's OBD-II port allows us to gather additional operation data (*i.e.* vehicle starting, the engine revolutions per minute, and the odometer reported speed). The Driving Habits System analyzes a three-element tuple {speed, revolutions per minute, timestamp} using three seconds overlapping windows. This information is used for drawing the trace with the vehicle's speed over the map, using the colors according to Table 2. The threshold for aggressive speeding is based in [4]. Also, for minimizing the noise effect from the accelerometer, this information is processed for detecting the braking and accelerating aggressive behavior events using the same thresholds for the accelerometer (Table 1).

Geo-referencing the vehicles position and the aggressive driving events. The Driving Habits System application samples the Android device's GPS sensor data at a rate of one time per second. This allows estimating the current vehicle location, represented by a four-element tuple {longitude, latitude, GPS speed, timestamp}. This information is used to form a trip descriptor, composed by a set of location tuples that describe the traveled trajectory and the set of aggressive driving events detected when using the Driving Habits System application.

Promoting user participation. Participatory sensing campaigns cause user burden, as the participant incurs in energy and monetary expenses, due to the effort required for sensing, processing, and communicating data [3]. We based our incentive model in system utility [10], providing feedback related with the aggressive driving events. This information promotes both awareness and self-reflection about the driving behavior.

Sharing the gathered data. As a permanent data connection demands additional expenses from the user [3], and this data connection is not available when the vehicle is located in zones without mobile network coverage, we chose to store the gathered data in the Android device. There is a Wi-Fi listening service in the application, and when it detects one convenient connection, it synchronizes the information to our application server without explicit user intervention.

Providing privacy control. Participatory sensing allows individuals to decide what data to share, and how to extend mechanisms to protect their privacy [11]. Despite this affecting the quantity of collected data, we chose to let the drivers decide when using the Driving Habits System. We use a play-pause button and an audible notification "The services are active" for notifying when the Driving Habits System is collecting data.

3   System Evaluation

We evaluated the system for 5-weeks in the city of Ensenada Mexico to understand the potential adoption, and perceived utility of the Driving Habits System in real-life situations.

3.1   Methods

23 participants were recruited, all graduate students, 10 are female, 7 of the participants are in the 18–25 age range, and 16 into the 26–36 years old. We used the Spanish-version of the Driving Habits Questionnaire for screening purposes on their driving [7]. None of them identifies themselves as an aggressive driver.

We used the Car Technology Acceptance Model (CTAM) survey [8] for assessing the Driving Habits System acceptance. The CTAM survey comprises 9 categories provided as a five level Likert scale questionnaire [6]. We calculated the mean, standard deviation and Cronbach's alpha [1] for each category. The Cronbach's alpha ($0 \leq \alpha \leq 1$) shows the degree of internal consistency between the questions in the category, where the closer values to 1 implies a stronger relationship between questions.

Finally, participants filled a survey with a set of five questions extracted from the Spanish-version of the Driving Habits Questionnaire. We performed a t-Student test for comparing their driving behavior awareness before and after participating in the study. We supplemented these surveys along with a semi-structured interview where we asked questions on technology adoption, self-awareness and potential behavior-change on driving habits. Interviews lasted 25 min on average (sd 8:43 min), for a total of 10 hours of recording.

3.2   Results

Use and Adoption. We collected 508 valid trips, equivalent to 2,751.49 km of mobility traces (with an average trip distance of 6.43 km, sd 5.41 km). This data represents 101.61 hours of total use of the Driving Habits System, (average trip duration 12 min and sd 9.10 min). 85.04 % of those trips where correlated with an initial emotional state manually reported by drivers when starting a trip (Table 2). From this data 68.69 % were positive emotions.

When driving, the participants performed some aggressive driving behaviors events. The Driving Habits System gathered 3,970 events (Table 3). After the Driving Habits System presented the aggressive behavior survey, the participants explained 1,739 events, providing further contextual information.

System Acceptance. According to the CTAM questionnaire results (Table 4), the most remarkable aspects of our design correspond with the effort expectancy

Table 2. Participants answers to the "How do you feel today?" question

Category responses	Response	Answers	
		Quantity	Percentage
No answer	Dismissed	76	14.96 %
Negative emotion	Stressed	15	2.95 %
	Irritated	8	1.57 %
	Tired	19	3.74 %
	Sad	41	8.07 %
Positive emotion	Energetic	43	8.46 %
	Relaxed	116	22.83 %
	Happy/Quiet	190	37.40 %

Table 3. Aggressive driving behaviors events detected by the system

Behavior	Collected events	Events by participant				Events survey answered	
		Mean	SD	Min	Max	Quantity	Percentage
Speeding	506	22	22.92	0	74	287	56.71 %
Swerving	1128	49	82.20	0	395	349	30.93 %
Braking	1963	85	90.46	0	322	935	47.63 %
Accelerating	373	16	18.04	0	71	168	45.04 %

and self-efficacy. However, these categories obtained some of the lowest Cronbach's α values in the questionnaire, along with the facilitating conditions. This could be consequence of the existence of a trade-off between the goals that integrate these questionnaire categories. In general, all the categories have mean values pointing to a positive acceptance of the Driving Habits System, being the perceived safety the lower score, indicating that drivers have some concerns pointing to the demanded attention when answering the aggressive events surveys and the distraction potential as we explain further.

Table 4. Statistics of the car technology acceptance model questionnaire

Survey outcomes	Mean	SD	Cronbach's α
Performance expectancy	3.25	1.04	0.6887
Effort expectancy	4.66	0.65	0.3133
Attitude towards using technology	3.72	0.91	0.7502
Social influence	3.65	1.04	0.8290
Facilitating conditions	3.47	1.43	0.4641
Self-efficacy	4.26	1.10	0.5915
Anxiety	3.72	0.92	0.7410
Behavioral intention to use the system	3.67	0.87	0.7526
Perceived safety	2.98	1.17	0.7242

In what follows, we relate the CTAM questionnaire results and show the interpretation from the qualitative analysis of the interviews performed at the withdrawal stage of the study.

Performance expectancy. 13 of the 23 participants indicated that the Driving Habits System helped them to improve their performance as drivers and provided awareness on their own driving habits. "I am more aware of over speeding events. The car inertia [when going down hill] heavily increases speed and I wasn't aware of [how fast the car is when going downhill]." [Participant 22] Also, 8 of the 23 participants emphasized installation with the system is somewhat problematic, as it requires too much of their attention that sometimes users are not in a position to give away. "My concern was to install and turn on [the system], it wasn't automatic, if I'm going late, and [the system] is asking me "How do you feel today?" [Participant 13]

Effort expectancy. All the 23 participants indicated that learning how to use the Driving Habits System was easy, and 20 of them highlighted the system is easy to use. "The way to indicate when an incident happen was easy, it shows you the options, it was intuitive [to use] the icons" [Participant 22]

Attitude towards using technology. 14 all the participants indicated that using the Driving Habits System makes more interesting and fun to drive: "It was fun to put the tablet over the car dashboard, I found the buttons accessible" [Participant 21]

Social influence. 18 of the 23 participants indicated their desire to show the Driving Habits System to their family and friends. In other hand, only 9 of the 23 participants indicated that their passengers were worried about the use of the Driving Habits System, because it could be associated to driving risks related with distractions. "When driving with a passenger, he demanded me to put attention in driving instead of attending the system, sometimes he felt that I'm being more focused in the system" [Participant 1]

Facilitating conditions. As 19 of the 23 participants owns an Android compatible device, and all 23 participant's vehicles are provided with an OBD-II interface, they didn't find any technical issue regarding the use of the Driving Habits System. As participants in the study we also provide them with the Android tablet.

Self-efficacy. 21 of the 23 participants answered that the Driving Habits System allows them to realize their usual activities and solving its problems without needing any help. They declared that even in some cases, passengers without any previous instruction got proficient operating the system, and taking the responsibility of answering the context surveys on some detected events: "[I didn't label some events], because [the passengers] heard the voice and they already knew that I'd braked or accelerated, and they provided an answer, the system doesn't interrupt us, they really liked" [Participant 23]

Anxiety. Only 9 out of the 23 participants responded having a concern about using the system, and 14 of them indicated being concern about having an accident. "I have three concerns: one: distraction, two: causing an accident, three: getting a ticket because I'm driving distracted" [Participant 6]. Despite those feelings, only 2 participants indicated being uncomfortable about using the Driving Habits System.

Behavioral intention to use the system. 16 of the 23 participants said that if they have access to the Driving Habits System, they would use it, and 13 of the 23 participants indicated that if the Driving Habits System were public available, they would use it because their characteristics. "I would use it when driving alone, because you don't feel so lonely, [the Driving Habits System] it becomes your companion" [Participant 20]. The intention of use would be influenced also by the possible positive contribution to their community and the society well-being product of using the Driving Habits System.

Perceived safety. 9 of the 23 participants expressed that the Driving Habits System could be insecure. They explained that the system demands for attention in case of committing many driving events. That's why some drivers opted for not labeling more events. "The times when I provided feedback was when someone was with me [a passenger], then it could be better to use voice commands" [Participant 7]

Driving Behavior Awareness

Individual driving behavior awareness. Table 5 details the five questions from the Spanish-adaptation of the Driving Behavior Questionnaire and the quantitative results of this survey. As mentioned in the study design section, participants identified themselves as good and safe drivers, and this perception had not significant changed after the study intervention. When using a t-Student test, we did not find a significant difference in this set of questions, but this is reasonable due to the short period of time that the participants used the system. Despite this, some participants expressed the system did increase their awareness about their own driving profile and how their emotions could impact their driving in specific situations. "You answer that you're happy, and then, you start to drive, and it notifies you about several events, it makes me think that my emotional status in fact affects my driving, sometimes when I'm in a hurry, it's better to breathe and relax and avoid committing an imprudence for being rushed" [Participant 13]

Table 5. Change of perception

Question	Pre-intervention		Post-intervention	
	Mean	SD	Mean	SD
Im a good driver	4.174	1.072	4.091	0.868
Im safe as a driver	4.087	1.276	4.455	0.8
I commit mistakes as a driver	2.957	1.397	3.227	1.307
I avoid to break the law as a driver	4.087	1.125	4.045	1.133
My emotions affect my driving	3	1.128	3.227	1.066

4   Conclusions and Future Work

Our results indicate that the Driving Habits System was useful, and easy to use and learn. Drivers explained the reason of 42 % of the aggressive behavior events, and 34 % of them were related to external factors, showing how the problems on the urban infrastructure could induce a bias in the aggressive driving assessment when used in our cities. Some participants expressed concerns around safety. Participants commented they were slightly distracted by the notifications being displayed by the system, and in numerous occasions they did not answer system's requests, as they preferred to direct their full attention to aspects related to driving instead of focusing on interacting with the system. Nowadays, most vehicles allow to deactivate some input features available in the vehicle's dashboard to avoid traffic accidents; doing the opposite, like in our case, perturbed some participants. This opens up questions around the proposal of appropriate "vehicle micro interactions" to investigate how long a participant is willing to interact with the system while driving, and when and how these micro interactions are safe.

Our results also show that the interaction modality we chose for our prototype was not the best one. Although, participants appreciated the use of a voice synthesizer to gain awareness of their driving behavior, they regretted the absence of a similar input modality. Not having a way to input feedback through voice entry commands also reduced the number of events participants labeled – only 42 % of all the aggressive behavior events were explained. The use of a full and bidirectional voice interface, with anthropomorphic characteristics, that is, to use natural language and speech, will heavily improve and simplify user interaction. Our findings also indicate that passengers played an active role as copilots, and helped drivers by interacting with the Driving Habits System. This shows that systems designed for vehicles use must take into consideration collective experiences. This requires systems to adapt their behavior to avoid interfering in the social experience that may happen when having a group of people in the vehicle, as our design somewhat interrupted conversations. Context detection mechanisms to inform when and how to provide notifications will make a more enjoyable experience for the group of people in the vehicle. Alternatively, passenger-only options could facilitate the capturing of data and user interaction.

Our study is limited by the reduced number of participants, and the limited variation in age and driving profiles of our recruited participants. In consequence, our findings cannot be generalized. However, it is important to note that our aim was to exemplify the potential impact of having such a tool in a specific context – like the city of Ensenada. Also, as our study was short and although we had some insights that participants changed some of their driving habits, we could not answer questions around behavior change and demonstrate how permanent this change could be.

As future work we aim to explore the characteristics of the appropriate in-vehicle micro-interactions for finding the right balance that allows raising continuous awareness on aggressive driving without increasing the risk perception as our current design did. Also, exploring new useful incentives. Incorporating features into our system to allow participants take advantage from the collected data from other drivers on road conditions and other drivers' status. For example, provide contextual hints to support the decision process of drivers by taking into consideration road issues (*e.g.*, "if you continue driving by this street, you'll find potholes"), and getting feedback from transit or government authorities on the infrastructure problems reported for incentivizing the use and engage participants on data capturing. Also, it is necessary to conduct a longer study aiming to measure the potential change of behavior, in order to find if the use of these systems promotes the adoption of better driving practices and its effects on drivers' awareness.

References

1. Cronbach, L.J.: Coefficient alpha and the internal structure of tests. Psychometrika **16**(3), 297–334 (1951). http://link.springer.com/10.1007/BF02310555
2. Dai, J., Teng, J., Bai, X., Shen, Z., Xuan, D.: Mobile phone based drunk driving detection. In: Proceedings of the 4th International ICST Conference on Pervasive Computing Technologies for Healthcare. IEEE (2010). http://eudl.eu/doi/10.4108/ICST.PERVASIVEHEALTH2010.8901
3. Ganti, R., Ye, F., Lei, H.: Mobile crowdsensing: current state and future challenges. IEEE Commun. Mag. **49**(11), 32–39 (2011). http://ieeexplore.ieee.org/xpls/abs_all.jsp?arnumber=6069707
4. Traffic Regulations for the Municipality of Ensenada, Baja California (2000). https://www.ebajacalifornia.gob.mx/pdfs/reg_transitoens.pdf
5. Johnson, D.A., Trivedi, M.M.: Driving style recognition using a smartphone as a sensor platform. In: 2011 14th International IEEE Conference on Intelligent Transportation Systems (ITSC), pp. 1609–1615, Oct 2011. http://ieeexplore.ieee.org/lpdocs/epic03/wrapper.htm?arnumber=6083078
6. Likert, R.N.Y.U.: A technique for the measurement of attitudes. Arch. Psychol. **22**(140), 5–55 (1932)
7. de Cózar, E.L., Ibáñez, J.G.M., Perales, M.C., Barbany, J.M.A., Arce, J.S.: Spanish adaptation of the driver behaviour questionnaire and comparison with other european adaptations. In: 5th Conference of the International Test Commission: Psychological and Educational Test Adaptation Across Languages and Cultures Building Bridges Among People, Brusells (2006). http://www.uv.es/metras/docs/2006_ITC_lopez_de_cozar.pdf
8. Osswald, S., Wurhofer, D., Trösterer, S., Beck, E., Tscheligi, M.: Predicting information technology usage in the car : towards a car technology acceptance model. In: Proceedings of the 4th International Conference on Automotive User Interfaces and Interactive Vehicular Applications (AutomotiveUI 2012), pp. 51–58. ACM (2012). http://dl.acm.org/citation.cfm?doid=2390256.2390264
9. Posner, J., Russell, J.A., Peterson, B.S.: The circumplex model of affect: an integrative approach to affective neuroscience, cognitive development, and psychopathology. Dev. Psychopathol. 17(3), 715–34 (2005). http://www.pubmedcentral.nih.gov/articlerender.fcgi?artid=2367156
10. Riahi, M., Papaioannou, T.G., Trummer, I., Aberer, K.: Utility-driven data acquisition in participatory sensing. In: Proceedings of the 16th International Conference

on Extending Database Technology - EDBT 2013, p. 251 (2013). http://dl.acm.org/citation.cfm?doid=2452376.2452407

11. Shilton, K., Burke, J., Estrin, D., Hansen, M., Srivastava, M.: Participatory privacy in urban sensing (2008). http://escholarship.org/uc/item/90j149pp.pdf

12. Tasca, L.: A review of the literature on aggressive driving research (2000). http://www.aggressive.drivers.com/papers/tasca/tasca.pdf

Human Interaction and Ambient Intelligence

Building Personalized Activity Recognition Models with Scarce Labeled Data Based on Class Similarities

Enrique Garcia-Ceja$^{(\boxtimes)}$ and Ramon Brena

Tecnológico de Monterrey, Campus Monterrey, Av. Eugenio Garza Sada 2501 Sur,
Monterrey, Nuevo León, Mexico
e.g.mx@ieee.org, ramon.brena@itesm.mx

Abstract. With the recent advent of new devices with embedded sensors, Human Activity Recognition (HAR) has become a trending topic in the last years because of its potential applications in pervasive health care, assisted living, exercise monitoring, etc. Most of the works on HAR either require from the user to label the activities as they are performed so the system can learn them, or rely on a trained device that expects a "typical" ideal user. The first approach is impractical, as the training process easily become time consuming, expensive, etc., while the second one drops the HAR precision for many non-typical users. In this work we propose a "crowdsourcing" method for building personalized models for HAR by combining the advantages of both *user-dependent* and *general* models by finding class similarities between the target user and the community users. We evaluated our approach on 4 different public datasets and showed that the personalized models outperformed the user-dependent and general models when labeled data is scarce.

Keywords: Activity recognition · Wearable sensors · Accelerometer · Model personalization

1 Introduction

In the last years Human Activity Recognition (HAR) [1] has gained a lot of attention because of its wide range of applications in several areas such as health and elder care, sports, etc. [2–4]. Inferring the current activity being performed by an individual or group of people can provide valuable information in the process of understanding the context and situation in a given environment and as a consequence, personalized services can be delivered. Recently, the use of wearable sensors has become the most common approach to recognize physical activities because of its unobtrusiveness and ubiquity –specifically the use of accelerometers [4–6] because they are already embedded in several devices and they raise less privacy concerns than other types of sensors.

One of the problems in HAR systems is that the labeling process for the training data tends to be tedious, time consuming, difficult and prone to errors.

© Springer International Publishing Switzerland 2015
J.M. García-Chamizo et al. (Eds.): UCAmI 2015, LNCS 9454, pp. 265–276, 2015.
DOI: 10.1007/978-3-319-26401-1_25

This problem has really hindered the practical application of HAR systems, limiting them to the most basic activities, for which a general model is enough, as is the case for the pedometer function or alerting the user who spends too much time quiet sitting down; both functions now available in some fitting devices and smartwatches.

On the other hand, when trying to offer personalized HARs, there is the problem that at the initial state of a system there is little or no information at all (in our case, sensor data and labels). In the field of *recommender systems* (e.g., movie, music, book recommenders) this is known as the *cold-start problem* [7] and it includes the situation when there is a new user but nothing or little is known about him/her, in which case it becomes difficult to recommend an item, service, etc. It also encompasses the situation when a new item is added to the system but since no one has yet rated, purchased or used that item, then it is difficult to recommend it to the users.

In this work, we will focus in the situation when there is a new user in the system and we want to infer his/her physical activities from sensor data with high accuracy even when there is little information about that particular user, assuming that the system already has data from many other users and also that their associated data is already labeled. We are thus attempting to use a "crowdsourcing" approach which consists in using collective data to fit personal data. The key insight in our approach is that instead of building a model with all the data from all other users, we will use the scarce labeled data from the target user to select a subset of the other users' data based on class similarities to build a personalized model. The rational behind this idea is that the way people move varies between individuals so we want to exclude instances from the training set that are very different from those of the target user in order to remove noise.

This paper is organized as follows: Sect. 2 presents some related work. Section 3 details the process of building a Personalized Model. The experiments are described in Sect. 4. Finally in Sect. 5 we draw our conclusions.

2   Related Work

From the reviewed literature, broadly three different types of models in HAR can be identified–namely: *General*, *User-Dependent*, and *Mixed* models.

General Models (GM): Sometimes also called *User-Independent Models*, *Impersonal Models*, etc. and from now on we will refer to them as GMs. For each specific user i a model is constructed using the data from all other users j, $j \neq i$; the accuracy is calculated testing the model with the data from user i.

User-Dependent Models (UDM): They are also called *User-Specific Models*, here we will refer to them as UDMs. In this case, individual models are trained and evaluated for a user using just her/his own data.

Mixed Models (MM): In [8] they call them Hybrid models. This type of model tries to combine GMs and UDMs in the hope of adding their respective strengths, and usually is trained using all the aggregated data without distinguishing between users.

There are some works in HAR that have used the UDM and/or GM approach [9–11]. The disadvantages of GMs are mostly related to their lack of precision, because the data from many dissimilar users is just aggregated. This limits the GM HAR systems to very simple applications such as pedometers and detection of long periods of sitting down. The disadvantages of UDM HAR systems are related to the difficulties of labeling the specific users' data, as the training process easily become time consuming and expensive, so in practice users avoid it.

For UDMs, several techniques have been used to help users label the data, as it is the weakest link in the process. For example, in [12] a mobile application was built in which the user can select several activities from a predefined list. In [13], they first video-recorded the data collection session and then manually labeled the data. Some other works have used a Bluetooth headset combined with speech recognition software to perform the annotations [14] whereas in [15] the annotations were made manually by taking notes. Anyway, labeling personal activities remains being very time-consuming and undesirable indeed.

From the previous comments, apparently MMs look like a very promising approach, because they could cope with the disadvantages of both GM and UDM, but in practice combining the stregths of both has been an elusive goal; as noted by Lockhart &Weiss [8], no such system has made it to actual deployment.

There have been several works that have studied the problem of scarce labeled data in HAR systems [16,17] and used Semi-supervised learning methods to deal with the problem, however they follow a *Mixed* model approach, i.e., they do not distinguish between users.

Model *personalization/adaptation* refers to training and adapting classifiers for a specific user according to his/her own needs. Building a model with data from many users and using it to classify activities for a target user will introduce noise due to the diversity between users. Lane et al. [18] showed that there is a significant difference for the *walking* activity between two different groups of people (20–40 and > 65 years old). Parviainen et al. [19] also argued that a single general model for activity classification will not perform well due to individual differences and proposed an algorithm to adapt the classification for each individual by only requesting binary feedback from the user. In [20] they used a model adaptation algorithm (Maximum A Posteriori) for stress detection using audio data. Zheng et al. [21] used a collaborative filtering approach to provide targeted recommendations about places and activities of interest based on GPS traces and annotations. They manually extracted the activities from text annotations whereas in this work the aim is to detect *physical* activities from accelerometer data. Abdallah et al. [22] proposed an incremental and active learning approach for activity recognition to adapt a classification model as new sensory data arrives. In [23] they proposed a personalization algorithm that uses clustering and a Support Vector Machine that first, trains a model using data from user A and then personalizes it for another person B, however they did not specify how should user A be chosen. This can be seen as a 1 → n relationship in the sense that the base model is built using data from a specific user A and the personalization of all other users is based solely on A. The drawback of this approach is that user A may be very different from all other users which could lead to poor final models. Our work differs from this one in that we follow a n → 1 approach which is more desirable in real world scenarios, i.e., use data already labeled by the community users to personalize a model for a specific user. In work [18] they personalize models for each user by first building Community Similarity Networks (CSN) for different dimensions such as: physical similarity, lifestyle similarity and sensor-data similarity. Our study differs from this one in two key aspects: First, instead of looking for inter-user similarities we find similarities between classes of activities. This is because two users may be similar overall but still, there may be activities that are performed very differently between them. Second, we just use accelerometer data to find similarities since other types of data (age, locations, height, etc.) are usually not available or impose privacy concerns. Furthermore, we evaluated the proposed method on 4 different public datasets collected by independent researchers.

In this work we will use an approach that is between GMs and UDMs, so it could be seen as a variation of Mixed Models, but here we use a small amount of the user's available data to select a subset of the other users' activities instances to complement the data from the considered user, instead of just blindly aggregating all other users' data. This selection is made based on class similarities and the details will be presented in Sect. 3.

3   Personalized Models

In this section we describe how a Personalized Model (PM) is trained for a given target user u_t. A General Model (GM) includes all instances from users U_{other}, where U_{other} is the set of all users excluding the target user u_t. In this case there may be differences between users on how they perform each activity (e.g., some people tend to walk faster than others) so this approach will introduce noisy instances to the train set and thus, the resulting model will not be very accurate when recognizing activities for u_t.

The idea of building a PM is to use the scarce labeled data of u_t to select instances from a set of users $U_{similar}$, where $U_{similar}$ is the set of users similar to u_t according to some similarity criteria. Building PMs for activity recognition was already studied by Lane et al. [18], with the limitations we already explained in the preceding section. In our approach, we look for similarities per class instead of a per user basis, i.e., the final model will be built using only the instances that are similar to those of u_t for each class. Procedure 1 presents the proposed algorithm to build a PM based on class similarities.

The procedure starts by iterating through each possible class c. Within each iteration, instances of class c from the u_t train set τ_t and all the instances of class c that belong to all other users are stored in $data_{all}$. The function $subset(set, c)$ returns all the instances in set of class c which are then saved in $data_t$. Function $instances(U)$ returns all the instances that belong to the set of users U. Next, all instances in $data_{all}$ are clustered using k-means algorithm for

---

Procedure 1. Build PM

1: T ← {}   ▷ Start with an empty train set
2: **for** c in C **do**   ▷ For each class
3:    $data_t$ ← $subset(\tau_t, c)$ ▷ τ_t is the target user's train set
4:    $data_{other}$ ← $subset(instances(U_{other}), c)$
5:    $data_{all}$ ← $data_t \cup data_{other}$
6:    Cluster $data_{all}$ using k-means for $k = 2..UpperBound$ and select the optimal k according to some clustering quality index.
7:    S ← $\arg\max_{g \in G} |data_t \cap g|$ ▷ G is the set of the resulting k groups
8:    T ← T $\cup$ S $\cup$ $data_t$
9: **end for**
10: $weight$(T)   ▷ Assign a weight to each instance such that the importance of τ_t increases as more training data of the target user is available.
11: Build model using training set T.

$k = 2...UpperBound$. For each k, the *Silhouette* clustering quality index [24] of the resulting groups is computed and the k that produces the optimal quality index is chosen. A clustering quality index [25] is a measure of the *quality* of the resulting clustering based on compactness and separation. The *Silhouette* index was chosen because it has been shown to produce good results with different datasets [25]. Next, instances from the cluster in which the majority of instances from $data_t$ ended up are added to the final training set T. Also all instances from $data_t$ that ended up in other clusters are added to T to make sure all the data from u_t are used. After the *for* loop, all instances in T are assigned an *importance* weight as a function of the size of τ_t such that instances from the u_t train set have more impact as more training data is available for that specific user. The exponential decay function $y = (1-r)^x$ was used to assign the weights where r is a decay rate parameter and $x = |\tau_t|$. The weight of all instances in T that are not in τ_t is set to y and the weight of all instances in τ_t is set to $1 - y$. Finally, the model is built using T with the new instances' weights. Note that the classification model needs to have support for instance weighting. In this case we used a decision tree implementation called rpart [26], which supports instance weighting.

4   Experiments and Results

We conducted our experiments with 4 publicly available datasets. *D1: Chest Sensor Dataset* [27,28]; *D2: Wrist Sensor Dataset* [29,30]; *D3: WISDM Dataset* [31,32]; *D4: Smartphone Dataset* [13,33]. For datasets D1 and D2, 16 common statistical features on fixed length windows were extracted. The features were: mean for each axis, standard deviation for each axis, maximum value of each axis, correlation between each pair of axes, mean of the magnitude, standard deviation of the magnitude, mean difference of the magnitude, and area under the curve of the magnitude. D3 already included 46 features and D4 already included 561 extracted features from the accelerometer and gyroscope sensors.

Several works in HAR perform the experiments by first collecting data from one or several users and then evaluating their methods using *k-fold cross valida-tion* (being 10 the most typical value for k) on the aggregated data. For a $k = 10$ this means that all the data is randomly divided into 10 subsets of approximately equal size. Then, 10 iterations are performed. In each iteration a subset is chosen as the test set and the remaining $k - 1$ subsets are used as the train set. This means that 90 % of the data is completely labeled and the remaining 10 % is unknown, however, in real life situations it is more likely that just a fraction of the data will be labeled. In our experiments we want to consider the situation when the target user has just a small amount of labeled data. Our models' evalu-ation procedure consists of sampling a small percent p of instances from u_t to be used as the train set τ_t and use the remaining data to test the performance of the General Model, User-Dependent Model and our proposed Personalized Model. To reduce sampling variability of the train set we used proportionate allocation stratified sampling. We chose p to range between 1 % to 30 % with increments of 1. For each p percent we performed 5 random sampling iterations for each user.

Figures 1, 2, 3 and 4 show the results of averaging the accuracy of all users for each p percent of data used as train set. For D1 (Fig. 1) the PM clearly outperforms the other two models when the labeled data is between 1 % and 10 % (the curve for PM-2 will be explained soon). The GM shows a stable accuracy since it is independent of the user. For the rest of the datasets the PM shows an overall higher accuracy except for D2 (later we will analyze why this happened).

Table 1 shows the average number of labeled instances per class for each p percent of training data. For example for D3 we can see how just using 3 labeled instances per class the PM achieves a good classification accuracy (≈ 0.8).

Table 2 shows the difference of average overall accuracy and recall (from 1 % to 30 % of labeled data) between the PM and the other two models. Here we can

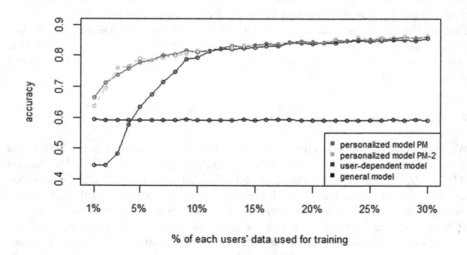

Fig. 1. D1: Chest sensor dataset

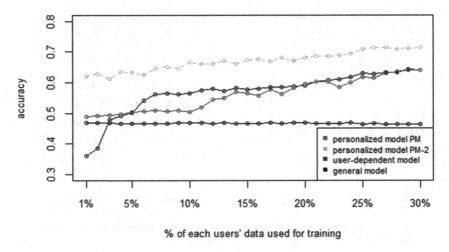

Fig. 2. D2: Wrist sensor dataset

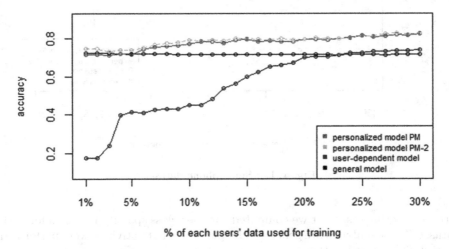

Fig. 3. D3: WISDM dataset

see how the PM significantly outperforms the other two models in all datasets except for the accuracy in D2 when comparing PM - UDM in which case the difference is negligible. This may be due to the user-class sparsity of the dataset, i.e., some users just performed a small subset of the activities. This situation will introduce noise to the PM. In the extreme case when a user has just 1 type of activity it would be sufficient to always predict that activity. However, the PM is trained with the entire set of possible labels from all other users in which case the model will predict labels that are not part of that user. To confirm this, we visualized and quantified the user-class sparsity of the datasets and performed

Table 1. Average number of labeled instances per class.

	1 %	5 %	10 %	15 %	20 %
D1	1	7	14	21	28
D2	1	1	2	3	3
D3	1	2	3	4	5
D4	1	3	6	9	12

Table 2. Difference of average overall accuracy/recall (from 1 % to 30 % of labeled data) between the PM and the other two models.

	PM - GM	PM - UDM
D1	22.5 %/18.4 %	5 %/8 %
D2	9.3 %/9.4 %	−0.80 %/17 %
D3	6 %/7 %	22.15 %/34 %
D4	4 %/4 %	25.5 %/28 %

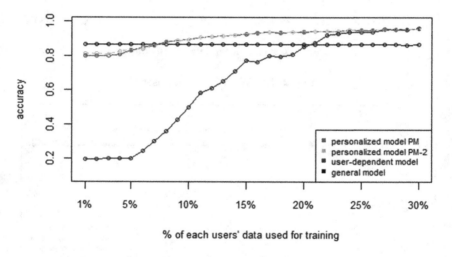

Fig. 4. D4: Smartphone dataset

further experiments. First we computed the user-class sparsity matrices for each dataset. These matrices are generated by plotting what activities were performed by each user. A cell in the matrix is set to 1 if a user performed an activity and 0 otherwise. The sparsity index is computed as 1 minus the proportion of 1's in the matrix. In datasets D1 and D4 all users performed all activities giving a sparsity index of 0. Figures 5 and 6 show the user-class sparsity matrices of datasets D2 and D3 respectively. D2 has an sparsity index of 0.54 whereas for D3 it is 0.18. For D2 this index is very high (almost half of the entries in the matrix are 0) furthermore the number of classes for this dataset is also high (12). From the matrix we can see that several users performed just a small number of activities (in some cases just 1 or 2 activities). One way to deal with this situation is to train the model excluding activities from other users that were not performed by the target user. Figures 1, 2, 3 and 4 (gray dotted line PM-2) show the results of excluding types of activities that are not in u_t. As expected, for datasets with low or no sparsity the results are almost the same (with small

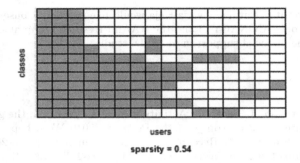

users

sparsity = 0.54

Fig. 5. D2: wrist sensor dataset user-class sparsity matrix

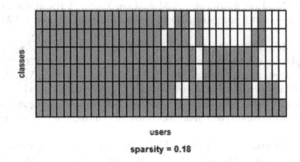

users

sparsity = 0.18

Fig. 6. D3: WISDM dataset user-class sparsity matrix

variations due to random initial k-means centroids). For D2 which has a high sparsity the accuracy significantly increased. This shows evidence that the user-class distribution of the dataset has an impact on the PM and that this can be alleviated by excluding the classes that are not relevant for a particular user.

5 Conclusions

In this work we proposed a method based on class similarities between a collection of previous users and a specific user to build Personalized Models when labeled data for this one is scarce, getting thus the benefits from a "crowdsourcing" approach, where the community data is fit to the individual case. We used the small amount of labeled data from the specific user to select meaningful instances from all other users in order to reduce noise due to inter-user diversity. We evaluated the proposed method on 4 independent human activity datasets. The results showed a significant increase in accuracy over the General and User-Dependent Models for datasets with small sparsity. In the case of datasets with high sparsity, the performance problems were alleviated in a great extent by excluding types of activities from other users that were not performed by the target user.

Acknowledgements. Enrique Garcia-Ceja would like to thank Consejo Nacional de Ciencia y Tecnología (CONACYT) and the AAAmI research group at Tecnológico de Monterrey for the financial support in his PhD. studies.

References

1. Brush, A., Krumm, J., Scott, J.: Activity recognition research: the good, the bad, and the future. In: Proceedings of the Pervasive 2010 Workshop on How to Do Good Research in Activity Recognition, Helsinki, Finland, pp. 17–20 (2010)
2. Martínez-Pérez, F.E., González-Fraga, J.Á., Cuevas-Tello, J.C., Rodríguez, M.D.: Activity inference for ambient intelligence through handling artifacts in a healthcare environment. Sensors **12**(1), 1072–1099 (2012)
3. Han, Y., Han, M., Lee, S., Sarkar, A.M.J., Lee, Y.-K.: A framework for supervising lifestyle diseases using long-term activity monitoring. Sensors **12**(5), 5363–5379 (2012)
4. Mitchell, E., Monaghan, D., O'Connor, N.E.: Classification of sporting activities using smartphone accelerometers. Sensors **13**(4), 5317–5337 (2013)
5. Banos, O., Galvez, J.-M., Damas, M., Pomares, H., Rojas, I.: Window size impact in human activity recognition. Sensors **14**(4), 6474–6499 (2014)
6. Andrea Mannini and Angelo Maria Sabatini: Machine learning methods for classifying human physical activity from on-body accelerometers. Sensors **10**(2), 1154–1175 (2010)
7. Schein, A.I., Popescul, A., Ungar, L.H., Pennock, D.M.: Methods and metrics for cold-start recommendations. In: Proceedings of the 25th Annual International ACM SIGIR Conference on Research and Development in Information Retrieval, pp. 253–260. ACM (2002)
8. Lockhart, J.W., Weiss, G.M.: Limitations with activity recognition methodology & data sets. In: Proceedings of the 2014 ACM International Joint Conference on Pervasive and Ubiquitous Computing: Adjunct Publication, UbiComp 2014 Adjunct, pp. 747–756. ACM, New York (2014)
9. Varkey, J.P., Pompili, D., Walls, T.A.: Human motion recognition using a wireless sensor-based wearable system. Pers. Ubiquit. Comput. **16**(7), 897–910 (2012)
10. Khan, A.M., Lee, Y.-K., Lee, S.Y., Kim, T.-S.: A triaxial accelerometer-based physical-activity recognition via augmented-signal features and a hierarchical recognizer. IEEE Trans. Inf. Technol. Biomed. **14**(5), 1166–1172 (2010)
11. Zhang, M., Sawchuk, A.A.: A feature selection-based framework for human activity recognition using wearable multimodal sensors. In: Proceedings of the 6th International Conference on Body Area Networks, ICST (Institute for Computer Sciences, Social-Informatics and Telecommunications Engineering), pp. 92–98 (2011)
12. Lara, Ó.D., Pérez, A.J., Labrador, M.A., Posada, J.D.: Centinela: a human activity recognition system based on acceleration and vital sign data. Pervasive Mob. Comput. **8**(5), 717–729 (2012)
13. Anguita, D., Ghio, A., Oneto, L., Parra, X., Reyes-Ortiz, J.L.: Human activity recognition on smartphones using a multiclass hardware-friendly support vector machine. In: Bravo, J., Hervás, R., Rodríguez, M. (eds.) IWAAL 2012. LNCS, vol. 7657, pp. 216–223. Springer, Heidelberg (2012)
14. Khan, A.M., Lee, Y.-K., Lee, S., Kim, T.-S.: Accelerometers position independent physical activity recognition system for long-term activity monitoring in the elderly. Med. Biol. Eng. Comput. **48**(12), 1271–1279 (2010)

15. Garcia-Ceja, E., Brena, R.F., Carrasco-Jimenez, J.C., Garrido, L.: Long-term activity recognition from wristwatch accelerometer data. Sensors **14**(12), 22500–22524 (2014)
16. Guan, D., Yuan, W., Lee, Y.-K., Gavrilov, A., Lee, S.: Activity recognition based on semi-supervised learning. In: 13th IEEE International Conference on Embedded and Real-Time Computing Systems and Applications, 2007, RTCSA 2007, pp. 469–475 (2007)
17. Stikic, M., Van Laerhoven, K., Schiele, B.: Exploring semi-supervised and active learning for activity recognition. In: 12th IEEE International Symposium on Wearable Computers, 2008, ISWC 2008, pp. 81–88. IEEE (2008)
18. Lane, N.D., Xu, Y., Lu, H., Hu, S., Choudhury, T., Campbell, A.T., Zhao, F.: Enabling large-scale human activity inference on smartphones using community similarity networks (Csn). In: Proceedings of the 13th International Conference on Ubiquitous Computing, UbiComp 2011, pp. 355–364. ACM, New York (2011)
19. Parviainen, J., Bojja, J., Collin, J., Leppänen, J., Eronen, A.: Adaptive activity and environment recognition for mobile phones. Sensors **14**(11), 20753–20778 (2014)
20. Lu, H., Frauendorfer, D., Rabbi, M., Mast, M.S., Chittaranjan, G.T., Campbell, A.T., Gatica-Perez, D., Choudhury, T.: StressSense: detecting stress in unconstrained acoustic environments using smartphones. In: Proceedings of the 2012 ACM Conference on Ubiquitous Computing, UbiComp 2012, pp. 351–360. ACM, New York (2012)
21. Zheng, V.W., Cao, B., Zheng, Y., Xie, X., Yang, Q.: Collaborative filtering meets mobile recommendation: a user-centered approach. In: AAAI, vol. 10, pp. 236–241 (2010)
22. Abdallah, Z.S., Gaber, M.M., Srinivasan, B., Krishnaswamy, S.: StreamAR: incremental and active learning with evolving sensory data for activity recognition. In: 2012 IEEE 24th International Conference on Tools with Artificial Intelligence (ICTAI), vol. 1, pp. 1163–1170 (2012)
23. Vo, Q.V., Hoang, M.T., Choi, D.: Personalization in mobile activity recognition system using K-medoids clustering algorithm. Int. J. Distrib. Sens. Netw. **2013**(315841), 12 (2013). doi:10.1155/2013/315841
24. Rousseeuw, P.J.: Silhouettes: a graphical aid to the interpretation and validation of cluster analysis. J. Comput. Appl. Math. **20**, 53–65 (1987)
25. Arbelaitz, O., Gurrutxaga, I., Muguerza, J., Pérez, J.M., Perona, I.: An extensive comparative study of cluster validity indices. Pattern Recogn. **46**(1), 243–256 (2013)
26. Therneau, T.M., Atkinson, E.J.: An introduction to recursive partitioning using the rpart routines. Technical report 61 (1997)
27. Casale, P., Pujol, O., Radeva, P.: Personalization and user verification in wearable systems using biometric walking patterns. Pers. Ubiquit. Comput. **16**(5), 563–580 (2012)
28. Activity recognition from single chest-mounted accelerometer data set (2012). https://archive.ics.uci.edu/ml/datasets/Activity+Recognition+from+Single+Chest-Mounted+Accelerometer. Accessed 2015
29. Bruno, B., Mastrogiovanni, F., Sgorbissa, A.: A public domain dataset for adl recognition using wrist-placed accelerometers. In: 2014 RO-MAN: The 23rd IEEE International Symposium on Robot and Human Interactive Communication, pp. 738–743 (2014)
30. Dataset for adl recognition with wrist-worn accelerometer data set (2014). https://archive.ics.uci.edu/ml/datasets/Dataset+for+ADL+Recognition+with+Wrist-worn+Accelerometer. Accessed 2015

31. Kwapisz, J.R., Weiss, G.M., Moore, S.A.: Activity recognition using cell phone accelerometers. SIGKDD Explor. Newsl. **12**(2), 74–82 (2011)
32. Activity prediction dataset (2012) . http://www.cis.fordham.edu/wisdm/dataset. php. Accessed 2015
33. Human activity recognition using smartphones data set (2012). http://archive. ics.uci.edu/ml/datasets/Human+Activity+Recognition+Using+Smartphones. Accessed 2015

Sign Language Recognition Using Leap Motion

A Support Vector Machine Approach

Luis Quesada[1(✉)], Gustavo López[2], and Luis A. Guerrero[1,2]

[1] Escuela de Ciencias de La Computación E Informática,
Universidad de Costa Rica, San Pedro, Costa Rica
{luis.quesada,luis.guerreroblanco}@ucr.ac.cr
[2] Centro de Investigaciones En Tecnologías de La Información Y Comunicación,
Universidad de Costa Rica, San Pedro, Costa Rica
gustavo.lopez_h@ucr.ac.cr

Abstract. Several million people around the world use signs as their main mean of communication. The advances in technologies to recognize such signs will make possible the computer supported interpretation of sign languages. There are more than 137 different sign language around the world; therefore, a system that interprets those languages could be beneficial to all, including the Deaf Community. This paper presents a system based on a hand tracking device called Leap Motion, used for signs recognition. The system uses a Support Vector Machine for sign classification. We performed three different evaluations of our system with over 24 people.

Keywords: American Sign Language · Leap Motion · Support Vector Machine · Automatic sign language recognition

1 Introduction

Sign language is a kind of visual language that consists of a sequence of grammatically structured human gestures. It is the most common way to communicate among people with hearing or speech disabilities.

Contrary to popular belief, there are no standards in sign language, for example, each country has a different sign language, and some countries have more than one. Moreover, there is no relation between sign languages and spoken languages.

The 2013 edition of Ethnologue of Languages listed 137 different sign languages [1]. American Sign Language (ASL), the sign language of the Deaf Community in the United States, is used by most of 28 million people who have some degree of hearing loss in the United States [2].

ASL has inspired Human-Computer Interaction researchers to try and merge natural user interfaces (NUI) and automatic sign language recognition. Most research has focused on identifying optimal features and classification methods to correctly recognize a given sign from a set of possible ones.

In 2013 a device called Leap Motion was released. This device facilitated computer supported hand recognition. Moreover, the data gathered by the device are relatively accurate and can be used in several classification methods.

J.M. García-Chamizo et al. (Eds.): UCAmI 2015, LNCS 9454, pp. 277–288, 2015.
DOI: 10.1007/978-3-319-26401-1_26

This paper proposes a sign recognition system, that combines a the Leap Motion for hand tracking and a Support Vector Machines (SVM) as classification method. This approach has already been described by other authors. However, our main contribution is that we got better results using fewer data points. Other authors use 45 float numbers to characterize one sign, and we use only 30. Moreover, we found that it is possible to modify our approach for using even fewer float numbers to characterize a sign.

We performed three different evaluations to test our sign recognition system. First, we assessed the Leap Motion's hand tracking capabilities. Afterwards, we tested SVM implementation accuracy when classifying data gathered using the Leap Motion. Finally, we performed an experiment with 24 users (external to this research) and tested the system as a whole.

The rest of the paper is structured as follows: Sect. 2 describes the Leap Motion, the SVMs, and some related work. Section 3 details our system implementation. Section 4 describes the evaluation performed to test our system and its results. Finally, in Sect. 5 concludes the results.

2 Background and Related Work

This section introduces the Leap Motion Controller and its characteristics. Then SVMs are briefly described. Finally, several sign language recognition systems are described and compared with our solution.

2.1 Leap Motion

The Leap Motion is a hand tracker released in 2013. Placed face up on a surface, the controller senses the area above it in a range of approximately 24 inches on the vertical axis.

Leap Motion's precision is about 0.00039 inches, it operates in a close proximity at a rate of 200 frames per second (depending on processing capabilities), and it tracks up to 27 joints per arm, including hands, wrist and elbow joints [3].

Each recognized point is represented by an ordered triple (x, y, z) that specifies a point in 3-dimensional space. Figure 1 shows the recognized joints and the coordinate system used.

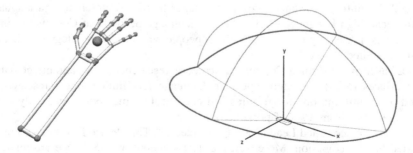

Fig. 1. Graphical representation of recognized hand and Leap Motion coordinates

Leap Motion employs a right-handed Cartesian coordinate system; all axes intersect in the center of the device. The X-axis lies horizontally parallel to the long edge of the device, with a range of 24 inches at a maximum 150° angle. The Z-axis also lies horizontally parallel to the short edge of the device, reducing away from the user's body, i.e., closer to the person the higher the values, with a range of 24 inches at a maximum of 120° angle. The Y-axis is vertical, increasing upwards [4].

Leap Motion uses two high precision infrared cameras and three LEDs. Leap Motion was released with an API that allows access to hand's identifiers and approximate dimensions. It also allows access to joint's normalized direction vectors. These data can be gathered up to 100 times per second. Leap motion's API can be accessed using different programming languages, including: C ++, Objective C, Java and Python [3].

2.2 Support Vector Machines

SVMs are supervised learning models that use training observations to recognize patterns and perform classification or regression analysis. Each observation is represented in a 2-dimensional plane [5].

During training, each observation is positioned. After training, vectors are traced to divide observations of different classes. To classify the signs, each new observation is positioned, and a prediction is provided using the established vector.

Several kernels are available for being used in SVMs. Kernel defines how classifications are performed. Although SVMs were originally defined to perform binary classification, multiclass problems can be solved using multiple binary classifiers [5].

2.3 Computer Supported Sign Language Recognition

Automatic sign language recognition is still an open research topic [2]. Given that sign languages are not standardized around the world -and even inside a country-, more than one sign language can be used and tested. The task of automatic recognition of those languages is not trivial [6].

During last years, the efforts for automatic sign language recognition include the application of custom gloves and generic recognition devices like the Microsoft Kinect.

Zafrulla, et al. discuss the use of the Kinect versus the use of their own gloves-based system named CopyCat to recognize a set of 1000 ASL phrases and words. They show how the Kinect has a good recognition rate. However, they face some limitations which include that the person must be standing. The recognition rates are not better than previous implementations using gloves [7].

Sun, Zhang and Xu used Kinect to recognize signs supported by image processing. The method had an accuracy mean of 84.1 % using selected signs and gestures [8].

The Leap Motion release provided another option for researchers to develop new strategies for sign language recognition. Several researches have been conducted testing the Leap Motion to recognize sign language. The main weakness of the Leap Motion is its lack of accuracy when something obstructs the device and the hand [9].

SVM and the neural nets algorithms have been applied to accomplish sign language recognition. Chuan, Regina, and Guardino [10] reported results of an experiment using both approaches and compared them. They used data of the palm (5 reference float numbers) and from each finger (2 vectors and 2 float numbers) to recognize signs [10]. The results were similar to the Kinect approach discussed in [8], around 80 % and 85 % accuracy.

Our solution uses a SVM as well, but considering only one vector and one coordinate in recognition area for each finger. These reduce drastically the amount of fit data needed by the SVM. Next section presents an overview of the implemented system, including the SVM and a detail of the measures taken from the Leap Motion.

3 Implementation

Our sign language recognition system was developed using Leap Motion for hand tracking and data gathering, and a SVM as a classification mechanism. Leap Motion API was accessed using Python 2.7. Our SVM was constructed with a Gaussian kernel, parameters:

- γ (Gamma) = 0.0001
- degree = 3
- random_state = None
- C = 100
- kernel = 'rbf'
- shrinking = True
- cache_size = 200
- max_iter = −1
- tol = 0.001
- class_weight = None
- probability = False
- verbose = False
- coef0 = 0.0

Our SVM uses one-against-one classification approach for multiclass classification. This approach was firstly described by Knerr, Personnaz and Dreyfus in 1990 and it was applied to neural networks [11].

In one-against-one multiclass classification for SVMs, all possible two-class classifiers are evaluated, giving a total of n(n−1)/2 classifiers. Our implementation uses Scikit-learn library to implement the SVM [12].

Even though Leap Motion allows tracking of up to 27 joints, we only use five of them as input for the SVM. We decided to use the corresponding coordinate of the tip of the distal phalanx and direction vector of the distal phalanx (i.e., the normalized direction of the bone from base to tip). Each direction vector and finger's tip coordinates represents a unique combination that characterize a sign.

We selected these values based on empirical pre-experimentation. We ran several datasets and concluded that these values show equal or better results than recent works [10].

Table 1 shows an example of one observation for the number one sign. As it can be seen, six float (data type) numbers are used to characterize each finger. Therefore, each training observation used 30 float numbers.

Table 1. Number one sign representation.

Finger	Coordinates (x, y, z)	Direction vector (distal phalanx)
Thumb	(56.56, 176.98, 45.14)	(−0.56, 0.10, 0.81)
Index	(61.30, 245.06, −0.61)	(−0.03, −0.19, 0.98)
Middle	(76.30, 163.49, 57.51)	(0.10, −0.01, −0.99)
Ring	(89.88, 166.17, 70.06)	(0.19, −0.07, −0.97)
Pinky	(105.65, 173.56, 70.35)	(0.17, 0.03, −0.98)

SVM training was performed with data gathered from the Leap Motion. Training was performed with 250 observations, all with the right hand of a right handed person.

Training observations were gathered in sequence and the hand moved randomly inside the Leap Motion recognition area.

After training, the recognition method was characterized. Since the moment the leap motion recognizes a hand placed over it, data is classified. Developers empirically decided that to allow better tracking, hand should be placed in a five sign before classifying.

Another design feature is that we read every 10 frames. Therefore, the same sign must be placed for ≈ ¼ second. After a five sign is recognized, the system is ready for any other sign. In order to notify the user of a classification, five consecutive frames must be classified as the same.

4 Evaluation and Results

We performed three types of evaluations. Leap Motion recognition potential and SVM classification potential were executed by the researchers. A user evaluation was performed with people external to this research.

4.1 Leap Motion's Recognition Potential

The first evaluation executed was to measure the Leap Motion's recognition potential. Several research papers address this for other sign languages such as: Arabic [13], Australian [9], and even American [10]. We will discuss this last research finding and compare them to our results in Sect. 4.3.

We considered 26 letters in the ASL alphabet, using the graphical representation of gathered data we determined if the Leap Motion was able to recognize all fingers. Each sign was performed in two positions:

1. User-sensor: In this setting the sign was performed as if the sensor was the other person.

2. User-user (Sensor between): In this setting signs were performed as if other person was seeing them and the leap motion was placed between the 2 persons.

Figure 2 shows the graphical representation of the positions used during the tests.

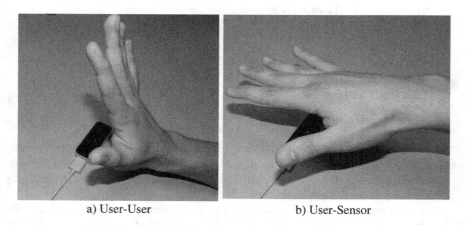

a) User-User   b) User-Sensor

Fig. 2. Leap Motion's recognition evaluation settings.

Table 2 shows the evaluation results. Only 6 sings could not be identified by the Leap Motion. A sign is not identifiable if the visualization does not match the sign. Considering both positions (front and under) only six signs were not recognized: K, M, N, P, Q and T.

Table 2. ASL alphabet recognition using the Leap Motion.

Letter	User-Sensor	User-User	Letter	User-Sensor	User-User	Letter	User-Sensor	User-User
A	Yes	No	J	Yes	No	S	Yes	No
B	Yes	No	K	No	No	T	No	No
C	Yes	No	L	Yes	Yes	U	Yes	Yes
D	Yes	Yes	M	No	No	V	Yes	Yes
E	Yes	No	N	No	No	W	Yes	Yes
F	Yes	Yes	O	Yes	Yes	X	Yes	No
G	No	Yes	P	No	No	Y	Yes	Yes
H	No	Yes	Q	No	No	Z	Yes	Yes
I	Yes	No	R	Yes	Yes			

M, N and T signs are occasionally recognized, but only 100 % recognition was considered successful. The main reason for K, P, and Q, not to be recognized is that thumb, index and middle fingers are placed in a way that prevents a straight line to be traced between the Leap Motion and the fingers.

4.2   Support Vector Machine Classification Potential

Understanding that only 20 of the 26 ASL letters are identifiable using Leap Motion, we proceed to evaluate SVMs performance to classify these 20 letters. Training and evaluation of all letters was performed in the User-Sensor position (see Fig. 2), except G and H that were only identifiable in the User-User position.

Three tests were performed:

1. Separate letters in three categories of correct classification: always, sometimes and never. Each evaluator (2 researchers) performed each sign in random order and the response was compared with the sign. This was performed three times. If the six results were correct, the sign was labeled as correct, if one or more were incorrect, the sign was labeled as sometimes, if there were no correct classifications, the sign was labeled with never.
2. Letters labeled as sometimes or never were evaluated again. This time evaluators tried to achieve correct classification, attempt count was the response (max 10).
3. Check the signs that were labeled as never even with the new test cases. Tested these sing to determine if there were patterns in the classification.

In the first test, the category "always" include the signs B, C, I, U, V, and Y letters. The second category (sometimes) includes signs wrongly classified. The L sign was misclassified as the U sign one time. The same error occurs with sign R (confused by U), X (confused by D), D (confused by U) and G (confused by L). All these confused signs are similar, for example, X and D signs differ only by the flexion of the distal phalanx of the index finger.

Another signs were wrongly classified twice: E, F, H, O, and W. The signs A, E, S and W were wrongly classified between 3 and 6 times in this test.

The second test gave to the "sometimes" category a new chance. This result in a new set of well classified signs: D, F, H, G, R and X. The signs A, E, O, S and W were again misclassified most of the times. See Appendix (Table 3) for more details.

Thus, we concluded the signs B, C, D, F, G, H, I, L, R, U, V and Y can be recognized by the Leap Motion and classified by the SVM. Signs for letters J and Z are recognized by the Leap Motion. However, they are not considered in the rest of evaluations because the correct representation of those letters is a gesture (i.e., requires movement).

In the third and last test we tried to find an explanation for each one of the letters that were not correctly classified. The A and S signs were confused too many times by the SVM. Moreover, the Leap Motion tracks these signs wrongly, maybe because these differ only by the thumb finger position.

The O and W signs were a particular case. One of the researchers failed almost all the O sign classifications. The second researcher failed all the W sign classifications. Repeating the test with other people, using only the O and W signs, we concluded the researcher hand's shape was the cause.

The E sign was classified correctly in a few occasions. It was confused with various signs without patterns; this was independent of the person who performed the sign. An inconsistent training set for the SVM is probably the main cause of this behavior.

Based on these results, we selected a set of 11 signs (including one control sign) and we ask 24 persons to perform a user evaluation. The next section describes the experiment.

4.3 User Evaluation

We selected 11 signs with different shapes; one sign was used as the control sign between them. The control sign selected was the number 5 sign (ASL) because is too easy to track by the Leap Motion and always correctly classified (100 % accuracy in pre-experiments). The shape of each sign is show in Fig. 3.

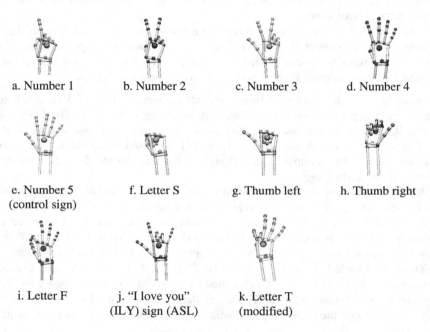

a. Number 1	b. Number 2	c. Number 3	d. Number 4
e. Number 5 (control sign)	f. Letter S	g. Thumb left	h. Thumb right
i. Letter F	j. "I love you" (ILY) sign (ASL)	k. Letter T (modified)	

Fig. 3. Selected signs.

The signs show different difficulties. The numbers (Fig. 3.a, b, c, and f), letter S and thumb left (Fig. 3.f and g) only vary in one finger position.

We defined 3 scripts with 20 sign each, randomly ordered. Each script contained 2 items of each sign. The first script order was: d, a, f, c, g, b, h, k, k, i, a, i, j, j, c, g, b, f, h, d. The second script was: c, k, f, d, a, j, k, j, f, h, b, i, b, g, i, c, h, d, a, g. The third script was: a, b, d, f, k, c, i, j, h, h, a, k, f, i, g, d, b, j, c, g.

We ask 24 persons to perform each sign following the order defined by the script. Between each sign, the person must perform the control sign. For example, the instructions were:

1. Perform "number 5" sign (system ready)
2. Perform "number 4" sign
3. Perform "number 5" sign (system ready)
4. Perform "number 1" sign
5. etc....

The selected persons to perform the signs were right-handed men and women between 20 and 35 years old. All of them have no sign language experience. They were instructed how to perform each sign during the experiment.

After obtaining the data from the 24 persons, we got the following results. The SVM had 100 % accuracy of the number 2 sign. Three signs were classified with a very good accuracy (> 90 %): letter A, thumb left and "I love you" sign. Figure 4 shows the accuracy percentage for each sign.

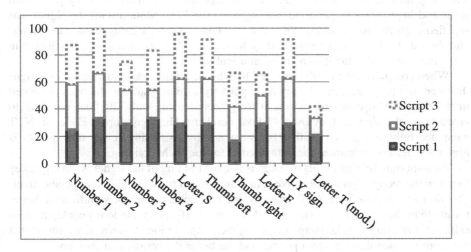

Fig. 4. Accuracy percentage by sign.

The worst results were obtain by letter F, letter T modified and thumb right. The F and T modified signs are very similar. The 70 % of the classification intents to recognize the T modified, the SVM failed classifying as the letter F. For more details, see Appendix (Table 4).

The thumb right sign correct classification depends by the sequence each person followed to perform the sign. If the person brings the fingers to the palm (almost like a fist) first, and then flip the hand, the SVM classify correctly the sign. However, the person flips the hand first and then brings the fingers to the palm, the Leap Motion lost the tracking and the SVM failed.

We performed a statistical analysis of the gathered data. The first test was to determine if the script used during the evaluation had a significant impact in the results obtained. An ANOVA analysis did not found statistical significance across scripts ($F_0 = 0.48$; $p = 0.624$).

After assuring that the script did not have significant effect on the results, we performed an ANOVA analysis to compare the mean of the results for each sign evaluated (Fig. 3). The ANOVA analysis found statistical significance across signs ($F_0 = 16.13$; $p = 0.000$). This result is evident when number two sign and modified letter T sign (Fig. 4) are compared, they have 100 % recognition accuracy and 40 % respectively.

5 Discussion

This section presents an in-depth discussion on our results. Moreover, we compare them with a similar research.

Even thought Chuan, Regina, and Guardino [10] reported results of using SVMs and Leap Motion for hand recognition, our approach was different. They performed signs and kept trying to get good reading from the Leap Motion until the signer was satisfied with the recognition. We tested the Leap Motion's recognition capabilities, and did not force signs. Therefore, they have got 100 % accuracy on recognition in signs that are very difficult to achieve in a real scenario.

When comparing the results reported by Chuan, Regina, and Guardino of the signs that were not fully recognized, they have got very similar results to the ones presented in this paper. However, our results were gathered using only 30 float numbers to characterize the sign, as they used 45 float numbers. The signs for A, E, K, M, N, T were not fully recognized neither by them nor by us. Using fewer float points is important because minimize the data needed for the SVM training.

An important finding of this research is that the training of the signer is directly a key factor in the recognition process. We tested our system from two different perspectives. The first set of tests were performed by the researchers that got significantly better results than the second test. The second test was perform by random people, without skills neither using sign language nor using the Leap Motion. Moreover, we found that the more practice these random people had the better the results that they got.

During the user evaluation patterns emerged and allowed us to found that the order in which the sign movements were performed affected the SVM's accuracy. This result was not statistically verified. For instance, when performing the thumb right sign if the user first turn the hand and then move his/her fingers to the palm of the hand, the sign was not always correctly recognized. However, if the user first move his/her fingers to the palm and then turn the hand the results were much better. Similar results were found in other signs.

Acknowledgments. This work was partially supported by the Escuela de Ciencias de la Computación e Informática at Universidad de Costa Rica (ECCI-UCR) grand No. 320-B5-291, by Centro de Investigaciones en Tecnologías de la Información y Comunicación de la Universidad de Costa Rica (CITIC-UCR), and by Ministerio de Ciencia, Tecnología y Telecomunicaciones (MICITT) and Consejo Nacional para Investigaciones Científicas y Tecnológicas (CONICIT) of the Government of Costa Rica.

Appendix

This appendix shows the SVM classification potential by researcher ("sometimes" category) and the user evaluation results (each sign was performed 48 times). The selected signs for the user evaluation were detailed in Fig. 3.

Table 3. Number of attemps until the sign was correctly recognized (maximum 10 attemps).

Letter	Researcher 1	Researcher 2	Letter	Researcher 1	Researcher 2
A	5	4	O	1	>10
D	1	3	R	1	2
E	7	3	S	1	>10
F	1	4	W	>10	1
H	1	1	X	1	3

Table 4. User evaluation results.

Sign	SVM classification		Misclassified signs (number of appearances)
	Correct	Incorrect	
Number 1	41	7	Number 2 (4), ILY sign (3)
Number 2	48	0	–
Number 3	36	12	Number 2 (8), ILY sign (4)
Number 4	37	11	Letter F (9), Number 1 (2)
Letter S	44	4	Thumb left (4)
Thumb left	45	3	Letter S (2), ILY sign (1)
Thumb right	33	15	Letter S (10), Letter T (3), Number 1 (2)
Letter F	38	10	Letter T (8), Number 4 (2)
ILY sign	44	4	Number 3 (4)
Letter T	14	34	Letter F (31), Number 4 (3)

References

1. Lewis, P., Simons, G., Fennig, C.: Ethnologue: Languages of the World. SIL International, Dallas (2009)
2. Hanson, V.: Computing technologies for deaf and hard of hearing users. In: Sears, A., Jacko, J. (eds.) Human Computer Interaction Handbook: Fundamentals, Evolving Technologies, and Emerging Applications, pp. 886–893. CRC Press, Boca Raton (2012)
3. Leap motion. http://www.leapmotion.com
4. Guna, J., Jakus, G., Pogačnik, M., Tomažič, S., Sodnik, J.: An analysis of the precision and reliability of the leap motion sensor and its suitability for static and dynamic tracking. Sensors **14**(2), 3702–3720 (2014)
5. Cortes, C., Vapnik, V.: Support-vector networks. Mach. Learn. **20**(3), 273–297 (1995)
6. Caridakis, G., Asteriadis, S., Karpouzis, K.: Non-manual cues in automatic sign language recognition. Pers. Ubiquit. Comput. **18**(1), 37–46 (2014)

7. Zafrulla, Z., Brashear, H., Starner, T., Hamilton, H., Presti, P.: American Sign Language recognition with the kinect. In: Proceedings of the 13th International Conference on Multimodal Interfaces, pp. 279–286. ACM, New York (2011)
8. Sun, C., Zhang, T., Xu, C.: Latent support vector machine modeling for sign language recognition with kinect. ACM Trans. Intell. Syst. Technol. **6**(2), 1–20 (2015)
9. Potter, L., Araullo, J., Carter, L.: The leap motion controller: a view on sign language. In: Proceedings of the 25th Australian Computer-Human Interaction Conference: Augmentation, Application, Innovation, Collaboration, pp. 175–178. ACM. New York (2013)
10. Chuan, C., Regina, E., Guardino, C.: American Sign Language recognition using leap motion sensor. In: International Conference on Machine Learning and Applications, pp. 541–544. IEEE Press, New York (2014)
11. Knerr, S., Personnaz, L., Dreyfus, G.: Single-layer learning revisited: a stepwise procedure for building and training a neural network. Neurocomputing **68**, 41–50 (1990)
12. Scikit-learn: machine learning in python. http://scikit-learn.org/
13. Mohandes, M., Aliyu, S., Deriche, M.: Arabic sign language recognition using the leap motion controller. In: IEEE International Symposium on Industrial Electronics, pp. 960–965. IEEE Press, New York (2014)

Sketching Stereoscopic GUIs
with HTML5 Canvas

Diego González-Zúñiga[1], Toni Granollers[2], and Jordi Carrabina[1(✉)]

[1] CEPHIS, Universitat Autònoma de Barcelona, 08193 Barcelona, Spain
diekus@acm.org, jordi.carrabina@uab.cat
[2] GRIHO, Universitat de Lleida, 25003 Lleida, Spain
antoni.granollers@udl.cat

Abstract. Creating the layout of an application graphical user interface is an important part of any system development process. Mock-ups, usability studies, focus groups and sketching are techniques that help define this layout and ship the best UI for the required task. But with the addition of 3D depth into the GUI assortment, a gap is exposed when trying to draft the GUI due to the fact that depth cannot be easily represented using traditional 2D methods like paper or existing software. With this article we present a tool that allows designers and developers to draft graphical user interfaces that comply with stereoscopic side-by-side formats. The tool is created using the HTML5 canvas element, in conjunction with the browser's console to live edit any sketch, and created layouts can be saved and shared in devices capable of showing compatible stereoscopic images.

1 Introduction

Graphical User Interface (GUI) development is an area that has gained much attention in the last decade. The availability of multimedia technology, the World Wide Web and advances in GPU power, coupled with the awareness that user-centered design and usability are key elements of a system, have encouraged advances in this area. Frameworks and platforms like Adobe Flash, Adobe Flex, Oracle's JavaFX, Microsoft Silverlight and Microsoft's Windows Presentation Foundation provided a way to make animation and multimedia elements first class citizens of a GUI toolbox. With this plethora of new options available for user interfaces, the process of designing them became more relevant. UI prototyping, usability studies and sketching become a best practice among the development process that keeps the teams headed in the right direction. Additionally, specialized software like SketchFlow, ForeUI and Balsamiq are used for creating wireframes, mock-ups and prototypes of user interfaces, in order to detect problems and iterate sooner.

These tools are important because they are a mean of exploring ideas before investing in them. Whether it is for a proof of concept, design exploration, technical exploration, or a combination of all three, failing to do so can incur in expensive iterations of previous done work.

With the study of stereoscopic 3D for user interfaces, and the possibilities it brings to UI layout and interaction, there is still a gap to fill related to prototyping for these

© Springer International Publishing Switzerland 2015
J.M. García-Chamizo et al. (Eds.): UCAmI 2015, LNCS 9454, pp. 289–296, 2015.
DOI: 10.1007/978-3-319-26401-1_27

new kind of applications. This article presents a tool that permits the creation of stereoscopic mock-ups and prototypes, allowing reviewing and sharing of 3D GUIs in stereoscopic displays.

2   State of the Technology

2.1   Stereo 3D in Applications

The stereoscopic effect is commonly used in movies and videogames to enhance the sense of immersion of the exposing media. The stereo format is now common and 3D is a standard feature in many TV sets sold nowadays. Movies with 3D versions account for the first 7 places in the all-time box office revenue [1]. Stereo technology has reached a maturity that has allowed a commoditization that exposes challenges for a new generation of content, both media and user generated.

One area that has not progressed at the same pace as entertainment, 3D-wise, is software. Software applications have been shyer to introduce depth. Nonetheless, research has shown that 3D is good for aesthetic and functional reasons: when the S3D UI is designed from the beginning for a holistic user experience, that is, one that grants depth a utilitarian function. Mobile application examples, like the phonebook contact app designed by Häkkilä et al. [2], or the in-car infotainment systems presented by Broy et al. [3] show that 3D representations have a potential to improve the user experience and attractiveness of a user interface without a negative impact on the their workload. Highlighting and selecting items [4], changing a user's gaze pattern in familiar UIs like search engine result pages [5] and other experiments that measure the desirability factor of the stereo effect in certain UIs prove the benefits of adding depth to graphical interfaces. However, so far there is no way of sketching a stereoscopic UI that can be viewed in a compatible device.

2.2   Sketching

According to Buxton [6] and Fällman [7], design is a complex word to define, so an insight towards its definition can be found towards the archetypal activity of design. Independent of the area where design is done, the common action of designers of all kinds is sketching. The importance of sketching can be linked to different areas of software development. For rapid concept development, basic composition layout, client communication, visual exploration, or refining visual solutions, there is no quicker method to explore several solutions than sketching. Sketching allows to define, in a hasty way, a concept that is made as a preliminary study. The outputs that this process delivers can be converted into mock-ups, which would give a clear idea of the full size scale model of the UI that is been considered. Sketching is generally done using pen and paper. More and more sketches and mock-ups blend in software that is designed to wireframe websites and mobile apps.

2.3 Canvas

HTML5 brings new functionality that adds multimedia elements into the core mark-up language. Tags like video, audio and canvas rule out the need for proprietary plug-ins that allow for rich interactive applications. Of these new features, canvas represents a resolution-dependent bitmap that can be used to render graphs, game graphics or other visual images on the fly. An analogy could be made that a canvas is a blank sheet of paper on the web. It exposes a JavaScript drawing context that is able to paint lines, paths and other figures on itself. Additionally, it can work with specific browser features like RequestAnimationFrame to efficiently render animations or poll information from external peripherals that have JavaScript APIs, making it a versatile element for graphing and *sketching*.

3 Challenge and Alternatives

Having mentioned all the relevant areas that relate to our work, we now note the challenge and available alternatives when trying to define a stereoscopic graphical user interface. Our main objective always was to be able to represent a sketch of GUI on a stereo capable device and easily assess its depth factor and to have the ability to change and sketch more elements on the fly: the concept of prototyping, fast drafting for 3D UIS. Our challenge is to "sketch" a tool that sketches 3D GUIS. Related work has been made by Broy et al. [8] where transparent acrylic glass "frameboxes" are built using laser cutters to reference automobile dashboards and mobile screens. Another way of prototyping stereo GUIs, proposed by the same authors is denominated "MirrorBox", which uses a number of aligned semi-transparent mirrors that generate three virtual layers on which to position UI elements. While these methods allow the prototyping of S3D UIs, we wanted a method that could be extrapolated to bigger screens and that allowed the saving and sharing of concepts for later consumption in stereo screens or projectors. The main challenge was to create an app that could easily create sketches that would support the application design process, independent of screen size, desired allocated depth and proprietary technology.

4 Stereo 3D Sketching for GUIs (Sketcheo3D)

Our sketching tool, dubbed "Sketcheo3D" is a browser application that allows to easily create a mock-up of the graphical user interface of a stereoscopic application. It creates these mock-ups by drawing in several layers of pairs of canvases. Drawing elements in the z-axis is achieved by using the SXS3DCNV JavaScript library [9], which allows to draw geometric shapes, paths and images using HTML5 canvas. This framework exposes JavaScript functions that allow to directly manipulate the bitmap on the canvas by calling them on the browser console. The tool includes pre-built UI elements (see Fig. 1) that can be inserted to create the sketch. It can also be 'hacked' to use external created images to replicate a design, which gives the tool a lot of versatility since it can represent a final "look", layout and depth effect of a user interface before building it.

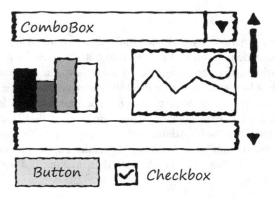

Fig. 1. Some of the sketch UI elements available.

This tool is proposed as an open and extendable way to create 3D UI sketches. It achieves this by providing several operation modes that give full control of the bitmap to the developer or designer. The most common way of utilizing the tool is by directly placing elements on the canvas using a mouse and visualizing the sketch live in a stereoscopic device. The application toolbar allows to change the offset between elements that will be positioned on screen, thus, creating the depth effect. This offers a way to sketch full GUIs very rapidly, which is one of the main characteristics of sketches. Figure 2 shows a sketch of a login screen in the designer. The menu toolbar sits at the bottom and exposes the available UI controls (from Fig. 1).

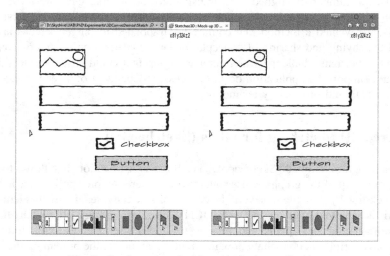

Fig. 2. Login screen sketch made in the application.

Another operation mode involves using the browser's console to on the fly add elements and perform more complex instructions, like drawing paths, and altering the drawing context's style, which allows changing colors, translating elements, cloning parts of the current bitmap, etc. This is done with a combination of functions defined by the application itself, functions from the SXS3DCNV drawing toolkit and even direct access to variables from any underlying script. Using the console allows rapid creation of refined prototypes. Figure 3 shows a more distinguished version of the log-in screen sketched in Fig. 2, by directly adding a custom background using a function of the 3D JavaScript kit.

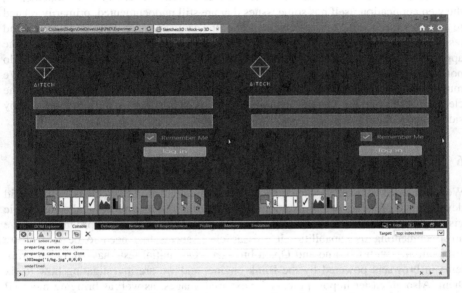

Fig. 3. Skinned login screen mock-up from Fig. 2.

Another form of further customizing the end results and adapting the application outcome to a brand's look and feel is to create a theme. Themes consist in images that correspond to each basic UI control and that replace the default provided sketch-like imagery. Figure 3 also shows a custom theme made to match a more specific look, while maintaining the depth and functionality of other sketches. With this we want to state that Sketcheo3D is built as a sketching solution, but at the same time is itself a sketch, a draft of how can we use technology to build modular and expandable solutions that help with managing new features presented by new media.

Finally, the created sketch can be saved as an image, to be distributed, shared or visualized in any stereoscopic display capable of showing side by side stimulus. We see this beneficial as it allows the generated ideas easily make their way into meetings in an array of different formats, from printed to projected. They can be stored, disposed of, and most importantly, iterated upon.

5 Limitations

As stated before, this tool is a sketch. As such, it is rapidly evolving and helping us not only test the layout of different 3D graphical user interfaces, but is also built in a way that allows it to adapt to different scenarios, from basic sketching to being able to feature custom in-house design. It is built using only open technologies, and based in the latest standards while adapting the stereoscopic principles to create innovative software UIs. The core technologies are HTML, Canvas and JavaScript. Nonetheless, the web application itself has some issues that are still undocumented, primarily related to each browser's different implementation of the canvas feature. For our examples and testing purposes, we have used Internet Explorer 11. We have also verified that the application works in Firefox 35 and Safari 8, nonetheless Chrome 40 and Opera 27 do not paint all elements of the toolbar UI, making the tool unusable in these browsers. We must adapt our application to the way the Blink engine (which they share) renders the clearing of the canvas. Another limitation in our sketch is that we only support side by side stereoscopic format.

6 Future Work

We consider Sketcheo3D a sketch because it is an application that comes from a rapid development of ideas. A few iterations have led to a tool that allows real stereoscopic visualization of UI elements in different depth planes. It is a work in progress, and we are documenting its capabilities in this article. Aspects that need to be refined are compatibility with Chrome and Opera browsers. Our initial tests have drawing problems in browsers powered by the Blink engine, and we are investigating how to fix them. Also an easier import process for external images, as well as bringing more UI element templates is under development.

Fig. 4. Sketcheo3D running on a PC, iPhone and Nokia phone.

We note the need for proper documentation, and a JavaScript wrapper of certain functions of the underlying SXS3DCNV library to Sketcheo3D counterpart, as well as code optimizations and general bug fixes. With this said, our tool sketch has proven to be easy to use, fast to create, and useful to explore different layouts that involve depth for stimuli we create for other experiments.

7 Conclusions

We have sketched a tool that allows the creation of sketches of graphical user interfaces. It uses current web technologies to draft layouts that use depth. The benefits and differentiator of this tool is based primarily on the fact that it can show actual stereoscopic images, with the positions defined by parameters defined by developers or designers. The tool is flexible and can adapt to different window (screen) sizes, and is able to run on different platforms (Windows, Mac) and different devices (Fig. 4 shows the app running in a Windows PC, on an iPhone and in a Nokia phone).

Finally, we have an ongoing iteration process that will continue to develop the app, and we have uploaded the current version to the web address http://diekus.net/r/Sketcheo3D/.

Acknowledgments. Supported by the Spanish Ministry of Finance and Competitiveness (proj. no. IPT-2012-0630-020000) and funded by the Catalan Government scholarship 2012FI_B677.

References

1. International 3D & Advanced Imaging Society: 3D Update at CES 2015, Las Vegas (2015)
2. Häkkilä, J., Posti, M., Koskenranta, O., Ventä-Olkkonen, L.: Design and evaluation of mobile phonebook application with stereoscopic 3D user interface. In: CHI 2013 Extended Abstracts on Human Factors in Computing Systems on - CHI EA 2013, p. 1389. ACM Press, New York (2013). doi:10.1145/2468356.2468604
3. Broy, N., André, E., Schmidt, A.: Is stereoscopic 3D a better choice for information representation in the car? In: Proceedings of the 4th International Conference on Automotive User Interfaces and Interactive Vehicular Applications - AutomotiveUI 2012, p. 93. ACM Press, New York (2012). doi:10.1145/2390256.2390270
4. Huhtala, J., Karukka, M., Salmimaa, M., Häkkilä, J.: Evaluating depth illusion as method of adding emphasis in autostereoscopic mobile displays. In: Proceedings of the 13th International Conference on Human Computer Interaction with Mobile Devices and Services - MobileHCI 2011, p. 357. ACM Press, New York (2011). doi:10.1145/2037373.2037427
5. Gonzalez-Zuniga, D., Chistyakov, A., Orero, P., Carrabina, J.: Breaking the pattern study on stereoscopic web perception. In: Urzaiz, G., Ochoa, S.F., Bravo, J., Liming, L.C., Oliveira, J. (eds.) Ubiquitous Computing and Ambient Intelligence, Context-Awareness and Context-Driven Interaction, pp. 26–33. Springer, Heidelberg (2013). http://link.springer.com/chapter/10.1007/978-3-319-03176-7_4
6. Buxton, B.: Sketching User Experiences, pp. 97–115 (2007). doi:10.1016/B978-012374037-3/50064-X

7. Fallman, D.: Design-oriented human-computer interaction. In: SIGCHI Conference on Human Factors in Computing Systems (CHI 2003), pp. 225–232 (2003). doi:10.1145/642611.642652

8. Broy, N., Schneegass, S., Alt, F., Schmidt, A.: FrameBox and MirrorBox. In: Proceedings of the 32nd Annual ACM Conference on Human Factors in Computing Systems - CHI 2014, pp. 2037–2046. ACM Press, New York (2014). doi:10.1145/2556288.2557183

9. González-Zúñiga, D., Carrabina, J.: Hacking HTML5 canvas to create a stereo 3D renderer. In: Proceedings of the IEEE 10th Symposium on 3D User Interfaces (2015)

An Alternative to W3C Task Model for Post-WIMP

Miguel A. Teruel, Arturo C. Rodríguez, Francisco Montero,
Elena Navarro$^{(\boxtimes)}$, Víctor López-Jaquero, and Pascual González

LoUISE Research Group, Computer Systems Department,
University of Castilla – La Mancha, Albacete, Spain
{miguel,arturorodriguez,fmontero,victor,
pgonzalez}@dsi.uclm.es, elena.navarro@uclm.es

Abstract. The way people interact with computers has greatly evolved over the last years. Nowadays, WIMP (Windows, Icons, Menus, Pointer) systems are being replaced and Post-WIMP systems are becoming more and more popular as new interaction techniques, based on virtual reality, gesture recognition, wearable computers and so on, are becoming more usual for end users. The languages used to specify Post-WIMP systems have to change in order to cope with the increasing complexity of these systems. Therefore, this paper presents a Post-WIMP task meta-model, based on CSRML, as an alternative to the current W3C one. This proposal offers two main advantages regarding the specification of Post-WIMP systems. First, since the current W3C task meta-model does not have the required mechanisms to specify collaboration, a cornerstone of current Post-WIMP applications, several elements and relationships have been included in this new meta-model to specify it. Second, this new meta-model features the required expressiveness to represent the awareness information that Post-WIMP users should be provided with during the interaction with the system. A case study related to a Post-WIMP first person shooter game, based on a virtual reality interface, is used to show how this new task meta-model works.

Keywords: Post-WIMP · CSRML · W3C task model · Collaboration · Awareness

1 Introduction

Over the past two decades, HCI researchers have developed a broad range of new interfaces that diverge from the traditional "Window, Icon, Menu, Pointing device" (WIMP). However, WIMP interfaces seem to be not optimal for carrying out complex tasks such as computer-aided design, simultaneous manipulation of large amounts of data, or highly interactive games. They also show deficiencies when applications are required to monitor input signals continuously, show 3D models, or simply, portray an interaction for which there is no standard widget. Post-WIMP is a term coined to describe work about user interfaces that go beyond the paradigm of windows, icons, menus and a pointing device, i.e. WIMP interfaces [2]. This new generation of interfaces has been fueled by both the advances in technology and an improved understanding of human psychology. Defined by van Dam [2] as interfaces "containing at

© Springer International Publishing Switzerland 2015
J.M. García-Chamizo et al. (Eds.): UCAmI 2015, LNCS 9454, pp. 297–308, 2015.
DOI: 10.1007/978-3-319-26401-1_28

least one interaction technique not dependent on classical 2D widgets such as menus and icons", some examples of these Post-WIMP interaction styles are: (i) virtual and augmented reality, (ii) tangible interaction, (iii) ubiquitous and pervasive computing, (iv) context aware computing, (v) handheld or mobile interaction, (vi) perceptual and affective computing, and (vii) lightweight, tacit or passive interaction. Although some people may classify previous interaction styles as disparate innovations coming from unrelated worlds, they share noticeable and important commonalities, such as a considerable awareness demand to help us to understand, connect, and analyze the work at hand.

In this work we propose an alternative to the current task meta-model from W3C [11] by considering two of the main cornerstones of such systems, namely *awareness* and *collaboration* and focus on its application in the development of a system that involves ubiquitous computing and virtual reality. This type of systems usually include agents that implicitly interact between them and the system in order to perform tasks without the user necessarily being aware of it. However, the system must be able to gather information concerning to the user and the environment, interpret it and adapt itself accordingly. Moreover, agents, human or not, can perform autonomous tasks or collaborative tasks. For this reason, Collaborative Systems Requirements Modelling Language (CSRML) [10] has been chosen as the basis of our proposal since it features capabilities for specifying collaboration and awareness demands. However, the CSRML task model had to be modified in order to make it compliant with the W3C's, as well as enriched with Post-WIMP awareness elements.

This paper is organized as follows. Section 2 introduces the background related to the current W3C task model. Section 3 proposes our task meta-model for Post-WIMP interfaces, defined as an extension of that proposed by W3C. Section 4 presents a case study based on a Post-WIMP game that will be modeled by using both task models. Finally, conclusions are gathered in Sect. 5.

2   Current W3C Task Model

Traditionally, task models (AMBOSS, CTT, LOTOS, TaskMODL, etc.) provide a description of WIMP interactive systems. They represent the static information of users and application tasks and their relationships at both structural (task decompositions) and temporal levels (temporal relationships). However, this description obviates the details about how processes and interactions are accomplished. Each task specified in the task model is an activity or process whose achievement is necessary to fulfill the user's goals. Analysts can represent tasks at various abstraction levels. They could consider an activity as an atomic task or decompose it into subtasks in order to provide a more detailed specification and then, establish temporal relationships between them.

The W3C task model is based on the widely adopted ConcurTaskTrees (CTT) notation [7] and aims to unify the task modeling. The meta-model for the W3C task model notation features a hierarchical structure among tasks and offers several operators (LOTOS operators [1]), also used in CTT, to define the temporal relationships between tasks. Moreover, this model provides a taxonomy of types of task. The Task meta-model elements (Fig. 1) are the following:

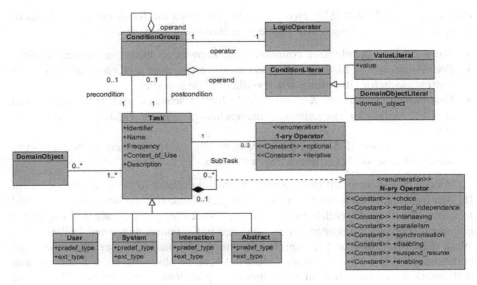

Fig. 1. Current W3C Task meta-model (extracted from [11])

- *Task*: action to be performed from the user perspective. From the structural point of view there are two kinds of tasks: *atomic tasks* (indivisible actions) and *composed tasks* (decomposable into subtasks). Moreover, four different types of tasks can be defined: (i) *User:* internal cognitive activity not directly performed through the user interface; (ii) *System:* action performed by the application itself; (iii) *Interaction:* actions performed by users that may result in an instantaneous system feedback; and (iv) *Abstract:* tasks that have subtasks belonging to different categories.
- *Domain Object*: an object of the domain model related to a task.
- *Condition Group*: a logical operation to specify pre- and postconditions of a task.
- *Logic Operator*: operator that connects the operands of the Condition Group and specifies the type of logical operation.
- *Condition Literal*: literal value or object of the domain model used as operand in a logical operation.
- *N-ary Operator*: operator that establishes a temporal restriction between subtasks.
- *1-ary Operator*: operator that establishes whether a task is optional or/and iterative.

The task meta-model shown in Fig. 1 enables analysts to describe tasks models of WIMP interaction effectively. It uses the composition relationships to specify hierarchical structure of tasks along with temporal operators. Although these operators are expressive enough to describe the temporal relationships between tasks, it would be reasonable also to include a new meta-class to establish the temporal relationships in an individual way and associate one operator with each temporal relationship.

However, modern applications clearly tend to be collaborative (e.g. games, text editors, social networks, developments IDEs, etc.), with a considerable number of users interacting concurrently. Moreover, user interfaces of these applications have greatly evolved towards Post-WIMP. Jacob et al. [6] identified the following four aspects of the real world that a Post-WIMP application should support:

- *Naïve Physics*: people have common sense knowledge about the physical world.
- *Body Awareness & Skills*: people have awareness of their own physical bodies and possess skills for controlling and coordinating their bodies.
- *Environment Awareness & Skills*: people have a sense of their surroundings and possess skills for negotiating, manipulating, and navigating within their environment.
- *Social Awareness & Skills*: people are generally aware of others in their environment and have skills for interacting with them.

As can be observed, all these aspects are mainly related to the *awareness* concept [8]. For instance, when several users are editing a document at the same time, they need to know who they are collaborating with and what changes they are making to the document. This need has been widely analyzed in Computer Supported Collaborative Work (CSCW). Ellis et al. [3] identified the strong relationship between awareness and collaboration in the 3C collaboration model. As can be observed, since awareness and collaboration are everywhere in contemporary applications, especially in Collaborative Virtual Environments (CVE) [4], a task meta-model should enable us to specify such features. Therefore, since the current W3C specification was originally designed to specify WIMP environments, in this paper we introduce an enriched task meta-model for Post-WIMP based on CSRML in order to deal with these avant-garde systems.

3   A Task Modeling Language for Post-WIMP

Having highlighted the shortcomings of the current W3C Task Model to deal with Post-WIMP applications, this section presents the CSRML [10] task model adapted to Post-WIMP task specification. This language has been selected because it supports the requirements specification of collaborative systems, one of the main cornerstones of Post-WIMP. The elements used for the task modeling are described in the following and illustrated in Figs. 2, 3 and 4. Moreover, the graphical representation of such elements can be seen in Fig. 5.

- *Task*: The concept of task of W3C has been extended to include its importance by using a color code (green, yellow, orange, red), being the green color the least important and the red the most important one. In addition, the 4 types of tasks of W3C have been included, but its definition has been refined: (i) *Abstract task*: it is an abstraction of a set of concrete tasks; (ii) *System task*: it is a refinement of an abstract task that is carried out by the system or a non-human agent in an autonomous way (e.g. collect data of the environment or make a database backup); (iii) *User task*: it is a refinement of an abstract task that is carried out by the system or a human agent in an autonomous way (e.g. a cognitive task for making decision); and (iv) *Interaction task*: every task that involves a communication between agents and the system and a reaction of the system. This kind of task can be performed by one or several participants. There are 4 types of interaction tasks: *Individual task* is

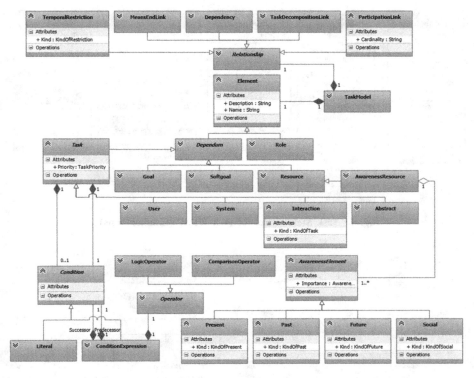

Fig. 2. Task Meta-model for Post-WIMP (Hierarchy and compositions)

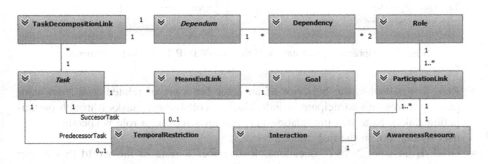

Fig. 3. Task Meta-model for Post-WIMP (Associations)

a task that a role can perform without any kind of interaction with other roles. *Collaboration/Communication/Coordination* tasks require 2 or more roles to be involved in order to perform any kind of collaboration/communication/coordination between them.

- *Legacy Elements*: In order to make this task model compliant with W3C's, several elements had to be added to its meta-model (bottom left-hand corner of Fig. 2).

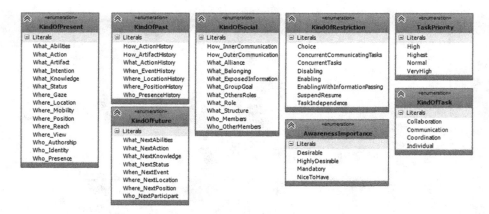

Fig. 4. Task Meta-model for Post-WIMP (Enumerations)

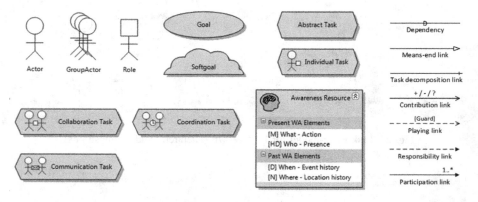

Fig. 5. Graphical representation of the Post-WIMP Task Model elements

- *Role*: It establishes the behavior of an actor for a set of related tasks. An actor playing a role can participate in individual or collaborative tasks (through participation links). Note that the relation between an actor and a role is specified in the user model, not in the task model.
- *Goal*: It answers "why?" questions. It describes a state of the world that a user would like to achieve. However, a goal does not prescribe how it should be achieved.
- *Softgoal*: It is a condition in the world that the user wants to achieve, but unlike the concept of (hard) goal, this condition it is not sharply defined. A softgoal is typically a quality attribute that constrains other element, such as a goal, a task or a resource.
- *Resource*: It is an entity that the user needs to achieve a goal or perform a task. The main concern about a resource is whether it is available and from whom.

- *Awareness Resource*: This element represents a perception of a required awareness that a user needs to accomplish a task. This element is represented as a set of Awareness Elements attached to a participation link between a role and a task.
- *Awareness Element*: An Awareness Resource shows all the Awareness Elements that can be set (if they are needed) with their importance according to the contribution they have to the accomplishment of a task. These awareness elements are an extension of those identified by Gutwin and Greenberg [5] for Post-WIMP environments, in order to be compliant with the different awareness elements identified by Jacob et al. [6]. For instance, the element *Presence– Where – Reach* is related with Jacob's body awareness; the element *Future – Where – Next Position* has to do with environment awareness; and *Social & group dynamics – What – Group goal* is an example of Social Awareness. Furthermore, these awareness elements are categorized into four categories, related to the present, past, future and social aspects (see Fig. 4). Finally, their importance can be established as nice to have (N), desirable (D), highly desirable (HD) or mandatory (M).
- *Participation Link*: It denotes who is involved in a task. It has an attribute to specify its cardinality, i.e., the number of users that can be involved in a task. It can optionally have an awareness resource attached to it to represent that the role has a special perception need to participate in the task, without which, the accomplishment of the task could be negatively affected or even the role could not participate in the task.
- *Task Decomposition Link*: It describes the essential elements of a task. A task decomposition link relates a task to sub-tasks to perform, sub-goals to achieve, resources that are needed, and softgoals that typically define quality goals for the task.
- *Means-end Link*: A means-end link documents which softgoal, task, or resource contributes to achieve a goal.
- *Dependency*: It is a relationship between a *depender* and a *dependee* for a *dependum*. The *depender* and the *dependee* are actors and the *dependum* can be a goal, a task, a resource, or a softgoal. The *depender* depends on the *dependee* for achieving a goal, performing a task, or using a resource. If the *dependee* fails to provide the *depender* with the required *dependum*, it becomes difficult or impossible for the *depender* to achieve the goal, perform the task, or use the resource.

4 Case Study

In order to demonstrate how the Task Model proposed for Post-WIMP works (hereinafter abbreviated as PWTM), a case study is presented in the following which consists in a virtual reality (VR) multi-device distributed first person shooter (FPS) game. In this manner, players will play geographically distributed but they will feel like they are playing together in the same virtual battlefield. The different devices that the user will use to play the game are the following ones:

- *Virtual reality display*: it will be used to provide the user with immersive 3D graphics as well as for capturing the user' head movements to control the character gaze.
- *Hands tracker*: a tracking device will capture the position of the user's dominant hand that is used to simulate a gun. Hence, the direction and trigger of the character gun will be controlled by using this device.
- *Virtual reality moving interface*: treadmill-like device enabling the game to capture the users' movement and translating them to the virtual, but not allowing them to shift physically in the real world.
- *Bluetooth haptic actuators*: these actuators will be located over the user's body to make them feel when and in which part of his body the character is damaged. Hence, 7 actuators will be used which are located on the user's head, limbs, chest and back.
- *Surround sound headset with microphone*: this device provides users with positional sound, making them able to guess the direction of the shots and other characters steps. This device also includes a microphone to communicate with other users.
- *Biometric watch*: an e-watch will motorize the players' heart rate and the system could stop the game provided a player is extremely tired.

Once the hardware environment has been defined, the following tasks will be performed by a user when playing the game: *Defeat Enemy* (main task), *Move, Communicate, Revive Player* (two players can bring to life to other player of the same team when the three of them are virtually together and the alive players crouch), *Shoot, Aim, Pull The Trigger, Get Power-ups, Deploy Power-Up* (system task), *Show End* (system task) and *Monitor player's hearth rate* (system task that will prevent the player from get extremely tired). Moreover, since the game to implement is both collaborative and Post-WIMP, users must be provided with awareness information about the game environment (i.e. player's status, other players' location and actions, the game terrain, etc.). Concretely, the awareness information to be provided by the system is the following:

- *Own status*: information about the player's health and active power-ups.
- *Connected players*: a list will show both the connected players and their teams.
- *Allies location*: the location of the user's team members is shown on a mini-map.
- *Power-ups position*: new power-ups deployed are shown on the mini-map.
- *Received damage*: when the user's character is hit by a bullet, the user will feel a vibration on his own body, thus getting awareness information of the shooting direction (e.g. if the character is hit from behind, the user will feel a vibration on his back).
- *Caused damage*: when a character is hit, positional aural information is provided.
- *Steps and shooting sound*: the weapons and characters steps will produce certain sounds that can make the user aware of the enemies' location.

Once the game tasks and awareness needs have been explained, they will be modelled by using both the current W3C task model (W3CTM from here on out) and the proposed one for Post-WIMP.

4.1   Using W3C Task Model to Specify the Game Tasks

Figure 6 shows an instance of the W3CTM for our case study. As can be seen, the task *PlayGame* is the root of the task tree, decomposed into other tasks: *MonitorUserHR*, *DefeatEnemy* and *ShowEnd*. *DefeatEnemy* is an abstract task. *Move, LookAt, Revive-Player, Communicate, Listen* and *DeployPowerUp* can be performed concurrently. *DeployPowerUp* enables *GetPowerUp* since this task cannot be performed if there is no power-up available in the scenario. *GetPowerUp* enables *Shoot*. The task *Move* can be performed in two different ways, so it is decomposed into *Walk* and *Run*, and the N-Ary operator between them will be the Choice operator. Moreover, the system shows the movement on the map concurrently. In order to get a power-up, the user must move across the virtual scenario. Once the user passes through the virtual item representing the power-up, the system informs the user with the task *ShowPowerUp*. *Shoot* task is further decomposed into two sub-tasks: *Aim* and *PullTheTrigger*. Both tasks can be performed concurrently. When a team wins the game, the system informs the user of the end of the game.

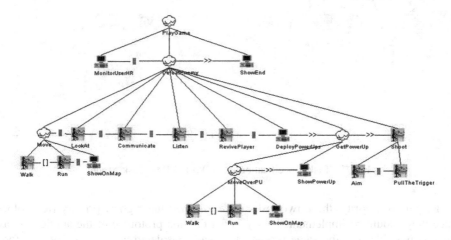

Fig. 6. Tasks specification using W3C Task Model

4.2   Post-WIMP Task Model to Specify the Game Tasks

As can be seen in Fig. 7, the specification of the case study by using our proposal, Post-WIMP Task Model (PWTM), enriches the one created by using the W3C proposal (Fig. 6), adding new elements and relationships for modeling collaboration and awareness features. Since this new model is based on a Goal-Oriented RE language [9], the goal *Achieve the defeat of the enemies* has been added to the task model, because this is the main aim of users who perform the task *Play game*. Moreover, three resources, namely *Speed, Reach* and *Power*, corresponding to the three different Power-Ups, have also been included in the task model. Another difference is that the interaction tasks have been more detailed by defining their kind and priority. As an example, the task *Communicate* is considered as a communication task, since it enables team members to communicate with each other. Besides, tasks *Listen* and *Pull trigger* are considered coordination tasks. These coordination tasks are a special kind of collaborative tasks in which certain pieces of information (noise and health in our example) get coordinated among several players. In addition, the task *Revive player* is a collaborative task since two different characters have to approach a dead one to revive it. Finally, other tasks such as *Look at game scenario* or *Walk* are individual tasks since only one user is required to perform them.

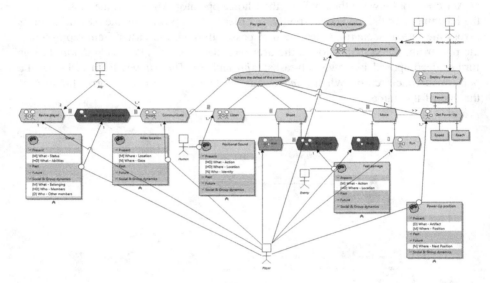

Fig. 7. Tasks specification using Post-WIMP Task Model

Regarding priority, these two tasks were assigned the highest priority (red color) since they should be implemented early to get the first prototype of the application as soon as possible. For the same reason, *Aim* was considered a high priority task too, while *Listen* and *Deploy Power-Up* are considered as normal priority tasks, because in our first prototype, it is not absolutely necessary to have the sound and power-up systems fully implemented.

As shown in Fig. 7, PWTM does not have systems tasks. Hence, when a task is performed by the system, it will be denoted by the participation of the role "System" in such task (e.g. the *Deploy Power-Up* task is performed by the system). Moreover, four other roles take part into this specification, namely the *Player*, his *Allies* and *Enemies*, or any *Human* player, i.e., each one (a super-role) of the three previous ones. However, it is worth noting that the association of the user with the roles he can play is made in the user model rather than in the task model. Moreover, participation links are used to specify which users are involved in which interaction tasks. For instance, two different participation links are related to the task *Communicate*, because when performing this task, one player (1) speaks with one or more (1..*) of his allies.

Five different awareness resources are attached to the participation links to represent the awareness information required to perform the tasks. First, the player must ([M]) have the awareness resource *Allies location* to provide him with the location of his allies to perform the task *Communicate*, as such communication can only be performed if the team members are close enough. Additionally, it would be nice to have ([N]) information about the other players' gaze in order to coordinate joint attacks. Moreover, when performing the task *Look at game scenario*, players need awareness information about their own *status*, and it is also highly desirable ([HD]) to be aware of their own abilities (active Power-Ups). Finally, they need to know which group they belong to, as well as who the members of the team are. Lastly, it is desirable ([D]) to be aware of who are the members of teams. Besides, the other goal present in this diagram is *Avoid players tiredness*. It is achieved by means of the task *Monitor players' heart rate which,* in turn would disable ([>) the task Move, not allowing the players to move until their physical status gets recovered. Hence, it has been shown how the task meta-model enables to specify collaboration and awareness in a proper manner, being these two aspects paramount in the development of contemporary Post-WIMP systems.

5 Conclusions and Future Work

During the last years, not only the visual appearance of user interfaces has changed, but also the way people interact with computers. As a matter of fact, the classical WIMP interfaces are giving way to the avant-garde Post-WIMP systems, which go beyond Windows, Icons, Mouse and Pointers (WIMP). Such Post-WIMP interaction is based on gesture recognition, virtual reality, and wearable computers and so on. Therefore, since interactive systems have evolved, the mechanisms required to specify them have to evolve as well. This fact constitutes the main motivation of this work, which is the development of an alternative to the task model currently in revision by the W3C to make it suitable for the specification of the requirements of a Post-WIMP system. Since collaboration is one of the cornerstones of such systems, our proposal is based on the task model of CSRML [10], which implements the widely known 3C collaboration model [3]. Furthermore, in order to provide this model with the awareness needs of a Post-WIMP system identified by Jacob [6], the awareness model of CSRML, namely Gutwin's Workspace Awareness [5], has been enriched to make the model able to deal with Post-WIMP special features (e.g. context awareness, social awareness, etc.). Moreover, a case study based on a Post-WIMP game has been used to show how the same system is modelled by using both the current W3C task model and our proposal, PWTM. It has allowed us to illustrate that the Post-WIMP characteristics related to awareness and collaboration are more properly specified by using PWTM because W3CTM has not enough expressiveness to describe awareness information neither collaboration as each type of user has to be specified in a different diagram.

Despite this model has shown to be suitable for Post-WIMP systems, further work needs to be done. In order to improve the specification of Post-WIMP system requirements, our next work will focus on a context model to complement this task model. By using such model, it will be possible to specify how Post-WIMP applications will self-adapt to their execution context (i.e. to the available hardware, user's disabilities or environmental characteristics such as lighting or noise, etc.). Besides, the implementation of the case study presented in this work has already begun. A playable prototype based on the task specification created by using the PWTM has been implemented.

Acknowledgments. This work is funded by the Spanish Ministry of Economy and Competitiveness and by the FEDER funds of the EU under the project Grant insPIre (TIN2012-34003). It has also been funded by Spanish Ministry of Education, Culture and Sport thanks to the FPU scholarship (AP2010-0259).

References

1. Bolognesi, T., Brinksma, E.: Introduction to the ISO specification language LOTOS. Comput. Netw. ISDN Syst. **14**(1), 25–59 (1987)
2. Van Dam, A.: Post-WIMP user interfaces. Commun. ACM **40**(2), 63–67 (1997)
3. Ellis, C.A., Gibbs, S.J., Rein, G.: Groupware: some issues and experiences. Commun. ACM **34**(1), 39–58 (1991)
4. García, A.S., Molina, J.P., Martínez, D., González, P.: Enhancing collaborative manipulation through the use of feedback and awareness in CVEs. In: 7th ACM SIGGRAPH International Conference on Virtual-Reality Continuum and Its Applications in Industry (VRCAI 2008), p. 1. ACM Press, Singapore, Thailand (2008)
5. Gutwin, C., Greenberg, S.: A descriptive framework of workspace awareness for real-time groupware. Comput. Support. Coop. Work **11**(3), 411–446 (2002)
6. Jacob, R.J.K., Girouard, A., Hirshfield, L.M., Horn, M.S., Shaer, O., Solovey, E.T., Zigelbaum, J.: Reality-based interaction: a framework for post-WIMP interfaces. In: SIGCHI Conference on Human Factors in Computing Systems (CHI 2008), pp. 201–210 (2008)
7. Paternò, F.: Model-Based Design and Evaluation of Interactive Applications. Springer, London (2000)
8. Steinmacher, I., Chaves, A.P., Gerosa, M.A.: Awareness support in global software development: a systematic review based on the 3C collaboration model. In: Kolfschoten, G., Herrmann, T., Lukosch, S. (eds.) CRIWG 2010. LNCS, vol. 6257, pp. 185–201. Springer, Heidelberg (2010)
9. Teruel, M.A., Navarro, E., López-Jaquero, V., Montero, F., González, P.: Comparing goal-oriented approaches to model requirements for CSCW. In: Maciaszek, L.A., Zhang, K. (eds.) Evaluation of Novel Approaches to Software Engineering. vol. 275, pp. 169–184. Springer-Verlag, Heidelberg (2012)
10. Teruel, M.A., Navarro, E., López-Jaquero, V., Montero, F., González, P.: CSRML: a goal-oriented approach to model requirements for collaborative systems. In: Jeusfeld, M., Delcambre, L., Ling, T.-W. (eds.) ER 2011. LNCS, vol. 6998, pp. 33–46. Springer, Heidelberg (2011)
11. W3C: MBUI - Task Models, http://www.w3.org/TR/task-models/

Virtual Touch FlyStick and PrimBox:
Two Case Studies of Mixed Reality
for Teaching Geometry

Andrés Ayala[1], Graciela Guerrero[1], Juan Mateu[1], Laura Casades[2],
and Xavier Alamán[1(⊠)]

[1] Universidad Autónoma de Madrid (UAM), Madrid, Spain
{cesar.ayala,rosa.guerrero,
juan.mateu}@estudiante.uam.es, xavier.alaman@uam.es
[2] Florida Secundaria, Catarroja, Valencia, Spain
laura.casades@gmail.com

Abstract. This article presents a case study of the use of two new tangible interfaces for teaching geometry in a secondary school. The first tangible device allows the user to control a virtual object in 6 degrees of freedom by sensing isotonic and isometric muscle contractions. The second tangible device is used to modify virtual objects, changing attributes such as position, size, rotation and color. An experiment on using these devices was carried out at the "Florida Secundaria" high school: students learned geometric concepts by interacting with a virtual world using the tangible interfaces.

Keywords: Virtual worlds · Mixed reality · Tangible user interfaces · E-learning

1 Introduction and Related Work

In the literature [1, 2], virtual worlds are defined as computer generated environments that use two or three dimensional computer generated images to represent elements of the physical world or imaginary scenarios. In these worlds, users are able to perform a wide range of interactions with the synthetic elements of the virtual world and with other users [3].

The development of virtual world technologies has opened new opportunities in the educational field. According to the USA National Science Foundation, virtual worlds have the potential to play a significant role in education [4].

Mixed reality combines physical world elements with the virtual world [5]. According to Milgram's taxonomy [6] there are two possible scenarios for mixed reality: real experiences with virtual overlays, which is called augmented reality (AR), o virtual experiences that are complemented with real world components, which is called augmented virtuality (AV). The project described in this paper is an AV environment, thus the physical interactive component is central: we will call it the tangible interface [7]. Two prototypes of tangible interfaces have been developed to evaluate the experience of using mixed reality for education, based in the middleware developed by Mateu [8].

© Springer International Publishing Switzerland 2015
J.M. García-Chamizo et al. (Eds.): UCAmI 2015, LNCS 9454, pp. 309–320, 2015.
DOI: 10.1007/978-3-319-26401-1_29

There are some projects in the literature related to this one. Starcic et al. [9] describe a system for teaching geometry using tangible interfaces, aimed to inclusive education. This study concludes that tangible user interfaces (TUI) are appropriate for learning geometry in the particular case of students with motor skill problems.

Other project using mixed reality for education is the environment proposed by Nikolakis et al. [10]. In this project, the student learns geometry using a haptic glove that allows creating scenes involving geometric objects. This project was assessed with high school students, with the conclusion that the mixed reality environment provides a more efficient problem solving approach to learning geometry.

However, to our knowledge, all the existing projects in this area use ad-hoc 3D applications for the virtual reality part of the system. In our Virtual Touch architecture, mixed-reality is implemented using a full fledged virtual world, thus enabling the teachers extending the educational applications, or even creating new ones by themselves,

2   Description and Implementation of the System

Two interface devices have been developed to enable the creation of mixed reality educational applications. The first tangible device is FlyStick, which allows the user to control a virtual object in 6 degrees of freedom by sensing isotonic and isometric muscle contractions. The second tangible device is PrimBox, which can be used to modify virtual objects, changing attributes such as position, size, rotation and color.

Both devices use a set of sensors that communicate with the virtual world through a middleware. The Phidgets technology was chosen for the sensor implementation, because it provides a low cost and reliable hardware, as well as interface libraries for a handful of programming languages, including C#, which fits with the middleware's source code.

The architecture for this mixed reality environment is based on the middleware developed by Mateu et al. [8], which allows integrating different types of tangibles and different types of base technologies.

2.1   Virtual Touch FlyStick

This device allows users manipulating a virtual object with six degrees of freedom (three translations and three rotations). In order to provide precision and ease of use, it was designed taking into account the way in which humans transmit information to a device through their limbs. A human limb can send and receive information through two types of muscle contractions: using force or displacement. Devices capable of interpreting force interactions are called "isometric", while those that interpret movements are called "isotonic".

Isometric devices are also referred as pressure devices because they use sensors that capture the force produced by muscle contraction against a resistance. These devices exert a force of equal magnitude in the opposite direction to the applied force.

Isotonic devices are also called displacement devices, because these sensors capture the movement of the human limb without exerting any significant resistance on it. These devices offer freedom of movement because they do not exert a significant drag on the limb.

Research done by Zhai et al. [11] recommends the use of isotonic sensors when speed and short distances are a primary concern, and the use of isometric sensors when trajectory quality and coordination are more important.

Virtual Touch FlyStick captures both types interactions through various embedded sensors, as shown in Fig. 1. By combining the data obtained from a digital gyroscope, an accelerometer and magnetometer placed inside the tangible device, isotonic movements are captured. Meanwhile an analog pressure sensor captures the data to determine the amount of force applied to the device (isometric interaction) while the user performs a movement with the tangible device.

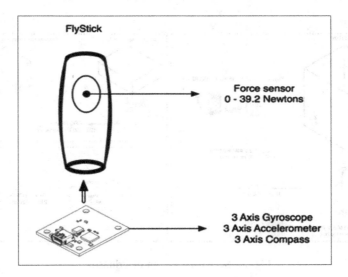

Fig. 1. Schematic design of FlyStick

A 3D printer was used for the construction of the components that make up the structure of the tangible device.

2.2 Virtual Touch PrimBox

According to Girvan and Savage [12] the best approach for teaching through virtual worlds is the methodology of constructivism. Dickey [13] also shows that constructivist learning is the best suited methodology in virtual worlds. Virtual Touch PrimBox is based on the constructivist approach where the user can create and build objects in the virtual world using tangible objects (in the real world) as interface, without the need of using built in menus, textboxes, and other traditional interfaces commonly employed.

PrimBox is a 13.4 × 12 × 11.3 cm cube that contains four Phidgets sensors, which are connected to a USB port of the computer that is running the middleware:

- One RFID reader, which senses the RFID tags that are embedded in the physical objects that represent the different geometrical figures.
- Three linear potentiometers (sliders), located in the three axis of the cube, which sense the change of displacement done by the user. These changes represent changes of magnitude of attributes such as size, rotation, position and color, related to a virtual object.

The selection of an attribute for edition is done by placing a card with an embedded RFID tag over a RFID reader inside a closed box, as shown in Fig. 2. Each card represents a different attribute: dimension, color, rotation and position.

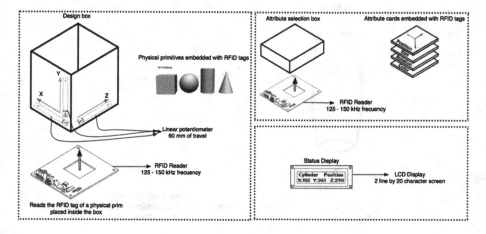

Fig. 2. Schematic design of PrimBox

In addition to the two clusters of sensors, a Phidget LCD is placed as an output device; it provides information regarding the type of attribute selected and the magnitude for each axis.

To use PrimBox, the user first places a physical object inside the main container. Then a virtual object (with the same appearance as the physical object) is created in the virtual world. In this moment, the attributes of the virtual object can be modified by changing the position of the three sliders which represent the 3-dimensional axis (x,y,z) or the primary colors (r,g,b), depending on the attribute card placed in the selection box. The LCD display shows the type of object placed (cube, sphere, etc.), the attribute being affected (position, color, etc.) and the magnitude of each axis. The changes made by the user are displayed in real time in both worlds. Users can select already created objects in the virtual world for further editing, just by clicking on them.

3   Case Studies: Applying the System at a High-School

The two tangible interfaces have been evaluated in "Florida Secundaria" high school (Valencia, Spain). The experience was organized in 4 sessions of three hours. The first session was devoted to an introduction to virtual worlds. In this first session, students explored the virtual world, learned how to create, move and rotate objects, how interact with other avatars and how to customize the look of their avatar.

In the other three sessions, the students performed several educational activities within the virtual world, where they used the tangible user interfaces PrimBox and FlyStick (see Figs. 3 and 4).

Fig. 3. A student working on activity 1 using the PrimBox tangible.

Fig. 4. A student working on activity 3 using the FlyStick tangible.

The activities were aimed at teaching geometry, with the main objective of developing spatial vision, taking advantage of the three-dimensional virtual world.

In this experience we settled a group that made the experience using the mixed reality applications, and a control group that worked the same materials with a traditional methodology (using a blackboard). In total 60 students participated in the experience (30 students using mixed reality and 30 students using a traditional methodology).

For each group, the students were chosen randomly. After choosing the students we found that in the group using virtual worlds, **23.0** % of the pupils had special educational needs, compared with **16** % of pupils in the group using traditional methodologies. The special educational needs were mainly dyslexia, attention deficit disorder and hyperactivity (ADHD) and learning difficulties with some curricular adaptations.

The sessions were conducted on students of second and third year of secondary education (ESO). We prepared three activities (see Table 1):

Table 1. Educational activities performed

	Tangible	Activity description	Main goal
Activity 1	VT PrimBox	One student is interacting with the virtual world constructing a geometrical figure following the oral instructions provided by a second student that is seeing a real world model	Using geometry language
Activity 2	none	Building a three-dimensional geometric figure from the different views (front, top, bottom and side views).	Developing the perception of space
Activity 3	VT FlyStick	The students, interacting with the tangible interface, generate various conic curves in the virtual world (circle, parabola, ellipse and hyperbola)	Understanding conic sections

4 Analysis of the Results

In order to evaluate the experience we have used:

- An introductory questionnaire about virtual worlds.
- A usability test about PrimBox and FlyStick.
- A semi-structured interview with the Math teacher.
- Exercises and tests on the subject, to check the learning effectiveness.

In the introductory questionnaire of virtual worlds, we found that most of the students were aware of virtual worlds and even had played with them previously (see Table 2). That means that virtual worlds are attractive to students and motivation is high: virtual worlds capture their attention and interest. Regarding ease of use, we found that virtual worlds were perceived as simple to use and to interact with, so the learning curve was very low.

With respect to the usability questionnaire (see Table 3), students found simple and easy the interaction with the tangible interfaces provided (PrimBox and FlyStick),

Table 2. Result of the survey about introduction of virtual worlds (26 students)

Kind of question	Questions about virtual worlds (Session 1: Introduction to virtual worlds)	Yes	No
Previous Knowledge	Did you know virtual worlds previously?	17 (65.4 %)	9(34.6 %)
	Have you ever played with virtual worlds before?	15(57.7 %)	11(42.3 %)
Easy to use and interactivity	Did you find it easy to interact in a virtual world?	25 (96.2 %)	1(3.8 %)
	Do you think that it's difficult changing the properties of objects in a virtual world?	10 (38.5 %)	16 (61.5 %)
	Have you found difficult to do collaborative activities in a virtual world?	4(15.4 %)	22(84.6 %)
Useful to learn Maths and Geometry	Do you think that the virtual worlds helps you to understand X, Y, Z coordinates?	19(73.1 %)	7(26.9 %)
	Do you think that virtual worlds can help you to learn Maths?	22(84.6 %)	4(15.4 %)
Motivation	Did you like the session about virtual worlds?	25(96.2 %)	1(3.8 %)
	Would you like to perform activities using virtual worlds in class?	25(96.2 %)	1(3.8 %)
	Would you like to perform activities using virtual worlds from home?	18(69.2 %)	8(30.8 %)

as well as the activities in virtual world. The only problem was the Internet connection that sometimes was slow.

In activities 1 and 2 we have not appreaciated significative differencies between the results obtained by students in second course of ESO (13–14 years-old) vs. students in third course of ESO (14–15 years-old). In activity 3, however, we have seen worse results in the second course of ESO (70 % average of correct answers) compared with the results in the third course of ESO (79 % average of correct answers). It seems that students in the second-year of ESO do not have the same spatial vision as students in the third-year of ESO.

The contents discussed in the sessions were not directly related to the student's age, but with the methodology used. In general, students using the Virtual Touch system were able to assimilate more difficult and abstract contents.

In activity 3, two competence tests were used to assess learning (see Figs. 5 and 6). The first test took place just after the activity was performed (one group using FlyStick and the control group in a normal class). The second test took place two weeks later. Although the results of the first test were better for the students using the traditional methodology, the students that had used FlyStick got better results in the second test: Virtual Touch methodology allowed better retainment of the knowledge. This suggests

Table 3. Usability and user experience survey using Virtual Touch system (23 students)

Questions about usability and user experience (Session 2: Usability survey)	Yes	No
Has been it easy using the tangible elements?	8 (61.5 %)	5(38.5 %)
Is virtual Touch easy to use?	9(69.2 %)	4(30.8 %)
Is it quick to learn how to use the system?	11(84.6 %)	2(15.4 %)
Have you felt comfortable using Virtual Touch?	10(76.9 %)	3(23.1 %)
Virtual Touch facilitates group work?	11(84.6 %)	2(15.4 %)
Have you needed the help or assistance of the teacher?	2(15.4 %)	11(84.6 %)
Have the simulation of the activities in the virtual world been too complex?	5(38.5 %)	8(61.5 %)
Has the effort to solve the activities been very high?	1(7.7 %)	12(92.4 %)

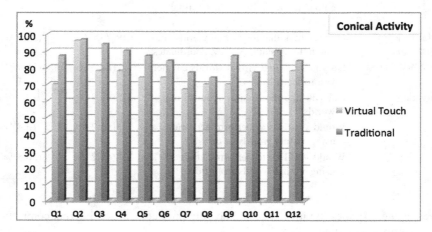

Fig. 5. Comparative results: Virtual Touch and Traditional methodology (1st test)

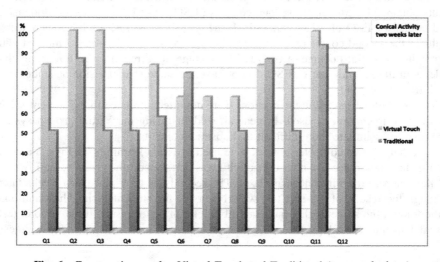

Fig. 6. Comparative results: Virtual Touch and Traditional (two weeks later)

Table 4. Semi-structured interview with the teacher

Semi-structured interview made to the teacher	Answers
Have you ever played with virtual worlds before?	No
Have you found interesting the Virtual Touch system?	Yes
Have you needed technical support for using Virtual Touch?	Yes
Do you think that virtual worlds could improve the teaching of Mathematics?	Yes • Virtual worlds can help to visualize scenarios on which subsequently apply mathematical processes • Virtual worlds can allow developing spatial vision of students • Virtual worlds are a creative and motivation environment • In a virtual world, students can share and collaborate on certain tasks in real time without worrying about the physical place where they are
Did you find difficult to use the tangible?	No
Did you require a lot of effort to create training activities in the virtual world?	Yes
In your opinion, the major advantages of the Virtual Touch system are…	The tangible interface allowed recreating movements, which did not require great accuracy in the virtual world, in a more comfortable and closer to the student way
In your opinion, the major disadvantages of the Virtual Touch system are…	• Teachers need some training about the Virtual Touch system • It would be convenient to have a resource bank • The need for a complex infrastructure (server, ports, viewers…) • The difficulty of designing activities that fit within the curriculum of the course
Do you think the student may be distracted in the virtual world?	Yes
Rate the sessions	• The students had a great willingness to perform activities • In some activities students with special educational needs did as well as the other students. • There should be a mechanism to assess the work of each avatar, like controlling the behavior of avatars.
Assessment of tangible:	

(*Continued*)

Table 4. (*Continued*)

Semi-structured interview made to the teacher	Answers
"Virtual Touch FlyStick"	• Advantages: Ergonomic, lightweight, easy to install and use. • Disadvantages: Improve the button to tilt the cutting plane (the button is too hard).
Assessment of tangible: "Virtual Touch PrimBox"	• Advantages: easy to handle, easy to install and use. • Disadvantages: The size of tangible. Couldn't it be reduced?

that using VirtualTouch learning is more meaningful, probably because motivation makes students remember better the concepts in a long term.

These activities took into account that students with special educational needs are more problematic when understanding an activity. However, students with special educational needs improved their results in the experience with respect to their previous qualification in Mathematics in a 86 %. Doing activities with virtual worlds and tangible interfaces enabled them to improve mathematical competence, acquiring better performance.

After the experiences, we also made a semi-structured interview with the teacher of Math. In Table 4 a summary of the interview is presented.

Table 5. Strong and weak points identified

Strong points	Weak points
Meaningful learning	Distraction in some students
Active learning	Need to have good equipment (high band width, computer with good graphic cards, configuration ports to connect with server
Reduce impulsivity	Evaluate the novelty factor in a long period
Improve the motivation	Need to create and adapt all activities and teaching materials
Effective with pupils with special educational needs	Need to perform training for teachers
Promotes collaborative activities	Difficulty controlling the behavior of avatars
Improve spatial vision in a three dimensional environment	
Tangible provided are appropriate for inclusive education (for example: low fine motor skills)	

5 Conclusions and Future Work

We can conclude that students are more motivated using the Virtual Touch system. However, the novelty factor probably is having an impact. As a future work, we need to evaluate Virtual Touch in a longer time span.

Virtual Touch allows active learning because students are doing the activities by themselves; the teacher only gives some initial instructions. Although students dedicated more time to do the exercises in the sessions using Virtual Touch, this system reduces the impulsivity of students to answer the questions and the students are more patient and relaxed while they are doing the activities. We observed that the students stayed one and half hour doing the activities in a good level of concentration, while it is quite difficult to maintain the interest and concentration so long using a traditional methodology. As future work, this has to be confirmed by repeating the experiment some more times.

The tangible interfaces provided were appropriate for students with special needs, such as students with physical disabilities, who have difficulty performing movement, translation or rotation of geometric figures using the mouse.

In Table 5 we present a summary of the strong and weak points identified.

Acknowledgments. We want to thank the Florida Secundaria for all their support during the experience. The work reported in this paper was partially funded by the Spanish Research Plan (project TIN2013-44586-R) and by the Madrid Research Plan (project S2013/ICE-2715).

References

1. Herbert, A., Thompson, F., Garnier, F.: Immaterial art stock: preserve, document and disseminate the pioneering works of art created inside online immersive platforms. In: 2nd European Immersive Education Summit (EiED 2012), Paris, France, pp. 101–113 (2012)
2. Frutos-Perez, M.: Practice, context, dialogue: using automated conversational agents to extend the reach and depth of learning activities in immersive worlds. In: World Conference on Educational Multimedia, Hypermedia and Telecommunications, Reino Unido, pp. 70–77 (2011)
3. Dickey, M.D.: Brave new (interactive) worlds: a review of the design affordances and constraints of two 3D virtual worlds as interactive learning environments. Interact. Learn. Environ. **13**(1–2), 121–137 (2005). Trece ed.
4. Borgman, C.L.: Fostering Learning in the Networked World: The Cyberlearning Opportunity and Challenge, 2nd edn. University of California, Los Angeles (2011)
5. Bull, G., Bredder, E., Malcolm, P.: Mixed reality. Learn. Lead. Technol. **40**(5), 10–11 (2013)
6. Milgram, P., Takemura, H., Utsumi, A., Kishino, F. Augmented reality: a class of displays on the reality-virtuality continuum. In: SPIE, pp. 282–292. The International Society for Optical Engineering (1995)
7. Hiroshi., I. Tangible bits: beyond pixels. In: 2nd International Conference on Tangible and Embedded Interaction, New York, NY, USA, 2008, pp. 15–25 (2008)

8. Mateu, J., Lasala, M.J., Alamán, X.: VirtualTouch: a tool for developing mixed reality educational applications and an example of use for inclusive education. Int. J. Hum. Comput. Interact. **30**(10), 815–828 (2014)
9. Starcic, I., Cotic, A., Zajc, M.: Design-based research on the use of a tangible user interface for geometry teaching in an inclusive classroom. Br. J. Educ. Technol. **44**(5), 729–744 (2013)
10. Nikolakis, G., Fergadis, G., Tzovaras, D., Strintzis, M.G.: A mixed reality learning environment for geometry education. In: Vouros, G.A., Panayiotopoulos, T. (eds.) SETN 2004. LNCS (LNAI), vol. 3025, pp. 93–102. Springer, Heidelberg (2004)
11. Zhai, S., Milgram, P., Drascic, D.: An evaluation of four degree-of-freedom input techniques. In: INTERACT 1993 and CHI 1993 Conference Companion on Human Factors in Computing Systems, New York, NY, USA, pp. 123–125 (1993)
12. Girvan, C., Savage, T.: Identifying an appropriate pedagogy for virtual worlds: a communal constructivism case study. Comput. Educ. **55**(1), 342–349 (2010)
13. Dickey, M.D.: Teaching in 3D: pedagogical affordances and constraints of 3D virtual worlds for synchronous distance learning. Distance Educ. **24**(1), 105–121 (2003)

User Interfaces for Self-reporting Emotions: A Systematic Literature Review

Carolina Fuentes[1]([✉]), Carmen Gerea[1], Valeria Herskovic[1], Maíra Marques[2], Iyubanit Rodríguez[1], and Pedro O. Rossel[3]

[1] Departamento de Ciencia de la Computación,
Pontificia Universidad Católica de Chile, Santiago, Chile
{cjfuentes,cgerea,iyubanit}@uc.cl, vherskov@ing.puc.cl
[2] Departamento de Ciencias de la Computación,
Universidad de Chile, Santiago, Chile
mmarques@dcc.uchile.cl
[3] Departamento de Ingeniería Informática,
Universidad Católica de la Santísima Concepción, Concepción, Chile
prossel@ucsc.cl

Abstract. Affective computing has focused on emotion acquisition using techniques of objective (sensors, facial recognition, physiological signals) and subjective measurement (self-report). Each technique has advantages and drawbacks, and a combination of the information generated from each could provide systems more balanced and accurate information about user emotions. However, there are several benefits to self-reporting emotions, over objective techniques: the collected information may be more precise and it is less intrusive to determine. This systematic literature review focuses on analyzing which technologies have been proposed to conduct subjective measurements of emotions through self-report. We aim to understand the state of the art regarding the features of interfaces for emotional self-report, identify the context for which they were designed, and describe several other aspects of the technologies. A SLR was conducted, resulting in 18 selected papers, 13 of which satisfied the inclusion criteria. We identified most existing systems use graphical user interfaces, and there are very few proposals that use tangible user interfaces to self-report emotional information, which may be an opportunity to design novel interfaces, especially for populations with low digital skills, e.g. older adults.

1 Introduction

Emotions are central to many human processes (e.g. perception, understanding), and may enhance the effectiveness of some systems [22]. Emotions are composed of behavioral, expressive, physiological, and subjective reactions (feelings) [4]. An instrument may measure only one of these components [4].Therefore, many technological instruments have been proposed, e.g. some that seek to recognize emotions through computer vision or physiological sensors, and others that require users to input their feelings.

© Springer International Publishing Switzerland 2015
J.M. García-Chamizo et al. (Eds.): UCAmI 2015, LNCS 9454, pp. 321–333, 2015.
DOI: 10.1007/978-3-319-26401-1_30

Ubiquitous computing is technology that "disappears", with the goal of designing computers that fit the human environment [26]. An example of this type of technology are Tangible User Interfaces (TUIs). TUIs allow users to manipulate digital information and physically interact with it [11]. TUIs take advantage of users' knowledge of how the physical world works [13], which may make them especially suitable for users without much knowledge of the digital world.

There are several scenarios in which systems benefit from acquiring information about users' emotions, but in which users have low digital skills and therefore may have difficulty expressing these emotions. For example, a training center to introduce older and underprivileged adults to computing has trouble gathering their opinions and feelings about the course. TUIs may be less intimidating, taking advantage of their knowledge of the physical world and blending into the environment.

The goal of this work is to study which types of interfaces currently exist or have been proposed that deal with user emotions. This will allow us to understand whether populations such as the one mentioned above are well served by these interfaces. We aim to understand the characteristics of interfaces dealing with emotions, to provide as a contribution an overview of the important elements and considerations when designing an interface for users to report their feelings. To achieve this goal, we conducted a systematic literature review (SLR). SLR is a means of identifying, evaluating and interpreting all available research relevant to a particular research question, or topic area, or phenomenon of interest [15]. This technique is useful for reviewing existing evidence about a technology and identifying gaps in current research.

This paper is organized as follows. In Sect. 2, we define relevant terms for our literature review. Section 3 describes our methodology, describing the research questions, search strategy, selection criteria and how we extracted the data. Section 4 summarizes the results, and finally, in Sect. 5 we present the discussion, conclusions, and directions for future research.

2   User Interfaces: A Brief Introduction

This section presents a brief overview of the concepts of *Interaction Style* and *Types of user Interfaces*.

The concept of interaction may be understood as a metaphor of translation between two languages, while an interaction style is defined as a dialogue between computer and user [5]. Interaction style may also be defined as the way that a user can communicate or interact with a computer system [3]. Many different interaction styles have been proposed [3,5], e.g. natural language (speech or typed human language recognition), form-fills and spreadsheets, WIMP (windows, icons, menus, pointers), point-and-click, three dimensional interfaces (virtual reality).

A user interface is the representation of a system with which a user can interact [12]. To the best of our knowledge, there is not one agreed upon taxonomy to define every possible type of user interface. Command-line interfaces

(CLI) are interfaces in which the user types in commands [14]. Graphical user interface (GUI) represent information through an image-based representation in a display [12,14]. Natural user interfaces (NUI) allow users to interact by using e.g. body language, gestures, or facial expressions [14,27].Organic user interface (OUI) define an interface that may change its form, shape or being [8,16]. Tangible user interface (TUI) is a user interface in which a person uses a physical object in order to interact with digital information [10].

3   Literature Review Methodology

In general, a SLR can be divided in three phases. Even though - due to space concerns - we do not show each of the phases completely, our work was developed following them. The phases are the following ones: [15,19]:

1. Planning the review: Define a protocol that specifies the plan that the SLR will follow to identify, assess, and collate evidence.
2. Conducting the review: Execute the planned protocol.
3. Reporting the review: Write up the results of the review and disseminate the results to potentially interested parties.

3.1   Need for a Systematic Literature Review

Recently, there have been several proposals of user interfaces and interaction styles to report, register and share human emotions. This SLR aims to identify which technologies are being used, who the target users are, and how the technology has been evaluated. We aim to identify trends in this area, under-served populations of users, and avenues of future research.

3.2   Research Questions

The goal of this review is to find how software technologies support self-report of emotional information. However, this question is too generic, so it was subdivided into several questions, that focus on specific aspects of the evaluation.

To define our research questions we followed the Population, Intervention, Comparison, Outcome and Context (PICOC) structure [15] (Table 1). This structure helps capture the attributes that should be considered when defining research questions in a SLR. This review does not aim to compare interventions, so the attribute comparison is not applicable.

A set of research questions was defined, related to understanding the types of interfaces, interactions, evaluation methodologies, of novel interfaces and technologies to self-report emotions. Hence, our SLR aims to answer the following research questions:

Table 1. Research questions as structured by the PICOC criteria

Criteria	Description
Population	Describe the specific type of population for which the tool was designed, e.g. students, elderly, children, users with disabilities, patients
Intervention	Describe approaches, i.e. methods, strategies, techniques that support types of interaction to register and share emotions
Comparison	N/A
Outcome	Describe the effectiveness of emotional self-report technologies, the improvements that technology provides, how emotional expression is eased through technology
Context	Describe the domain of use of the user interface

(RQ1) What type or style of interaction does the technology for emotion self-reporting provide?

(RQ2) What type of user interface is used to self-report emotions?

(RQ2.1) Who is the target user of the technology?

(RQ3) How are the self-reported emotions validated?

(RQ4) Does the proposed technology allow sharing emotions?

(RQ4.1) With who?

(RQ5) Was the proposed technology evaluated?

(RQ5.1) Who participated in the evaluation process?

(RQ5.2) What was the performed task in the evaluation process?

(RQ5.3) How long was the evaluation process?

(RQ5.4) How many users participated in the evaluation process?

(RQ6) Which are the benefits of using technology to register emotions?

3.3 Search Strategy

Based on these questions, we identified the keywords to be used to search for the primary studies. The initial set of keywords was: *emotion/s, mood/s, affect/s, share, interaction, self-report.* With these keywords, the search string was built using boolean AND and OR operators, resulting in the following search string:

(emotion **OR** emotions **OR** mood **OR** moods **OR** affect **OR** affects) **AND** (share **OR** interaction **OR** "self-report")

The search for primary studies was done on the following digital libraries: ACM Digital Library[1], IEEE Xplore Digital Library[2], ScienceDirect[3] and

---

[1] http://dl.acm.org.

[2] http://ieee.org/ieeexplore.

[3] http://www.sciencedirect.com.

Table 2. Number of the papers selected by each digital library

Digital Library	Number of papers
ACM	43
IEEE Xplore	115
ScienceDirect	22
Springer Link	147
Total	**327**

Springer Link[4]. These libraries were chosen because they are among the most relevant sources of scientific articles in several computer science areas [19]. Table 2 presents the number of papers that the search on each of the digital libraries produced.

We removed duplicates automatically (and then re-checked manually), finding 56 duplicated papers that were excluded. After this step, there were 271 papers in our corpus.

3.4 Selection Criteria

Once the potentially relevant primary studies had been selected, we evaluated them to decide whether they should be included in the review. For this, the following inclusion and exclusion criteria were defined:

1. Inclusion Criteria:
   (a) The paper is in English.
   (b) The paper is a peer-reviewed article and it was obtained from a journal, conference or workshop.
   (c) The paper was published on or before May 2015.
   (d) The paper is focused on technologies for reporting/registering/communicating human emotions.
   (e) The paper reasonably presents the technology and its validation.
   (f) The paper present as measuring subjective emotions as its main purpose.
2. Exclusion Criteria:
   (a) The paper is not available online.
   (b) The paper is a survey or SLR.
   (c) The paper does not include validation of the technology.
   (d) The paper includes human-robot/agent interaction.
   (e) The paper does not include an objective measurement of emotions.

Four researchers individually read the titles and abstracts of the 271 selected papers, and applied the criteria to accept or reject papers from the study. The papers all researchers agreed should be accepted or rejected (as well as papers with only 1 acceptance) were automatically included or removed. A fifth researcher was asked to decide for papers with 2 or 3 acceptances (25 papers in total). After this step, out of our corpus of 271 papers, 18 papers remained.

---

[4] http://link.springer.com.

3.5 Data Extraction

For this step, three researchers read the 18 selected papers, with the focus on answering the research questions introduced in Sect. 3.2. The obtained information was compiled into an ad-hoc Excel template. Moreover, during this detailed reading and analysis, the application of exclusion criteria was refined in some cases. Thus, 5 papers were excluded and only 13 papers remained for the data analysis step. These papers are presented in Table 3.

Table 3. Primary studies selected

Year	Conference (ID/Ref.)		Journal (ID/Ref.)	
2005	C15	Sánchez et al. [24]		
2007			J13	Isbister et al. [9]
2009	C06	Lin et al. [18]		
2009	C12	Laurans et al. [17]		
2009	C17	Bardzell et al. [1]		
2010			J01	Yu et al. [28]
2013			J02	Oliveira et al. [21]
2013			J14	Schubert et al. [25]
2013	C16	Caon et al. [2]		
2013	C18	Read and Belpaeme [23]		
2014			J05	Niforatos and Karapanos [20]
2014			J09	Doryab et al. [6]
2015	C11	Gallacher et al. [7]		

4 Results

This section presents the results produced by our SLR. Table 4 shows the per-year distribution of selected studies, separated by publication type. 85 % of the reviewed papers were published between 2009 and 2015. The following sections present the results, structured as answers to the research questions.

Table 4. Summary of studies by publication type and by publication year

Venue	2004	2005	2006	2007	2008	2009	2010	2011	2012	2013	2014	2015
Conference	-	1	-	-	-	3	-	-	-	2	-	1
Journal	-	-	-	1	-	-	1	-	-	2	2	-
Total	0	1	0	1	0	3	1	0	0	4	2	1

4.1   Results of Interaction Styles and Type of Interfaces

Out of the analyzed papers, 70 % presented a GUI interface, with WIMP, point-and-click, Menu and Q&A interaction styles (see Table 5). Only 30 % were TUI interfaces. The target user from the reviewed studies is in 70 % of cases generic (there is no specific target population), and only 15 % include users with specific characteristics such as patients, caregivers, workers.

Table 5. Classification of research question Q1 and Q2

Paper	Style of interaction	Type of interface				Target user
		GUI	TUI	WEB	NUI	
[C06]	Point and click, other		x			All users
[C11]	Other		x			Office workers
[C12]	Other		x			All users
[C15]	WIMP, point and click	x				People using chat
[C16]	WIMP, point and click	x				All users
[C17]	WIMP, point and click, menus, Q &A	x				All users
[C18]	WIMP, point and click	x				Robot
[J01]	WIMP, point and click, menus, Q &A	x			x	Patient, caregiver
[J02]	WIMP, point and click, menus	x		x		All users
[J05]	WIMP, other	x			x	All users of mobile phones
[J09]	Menus, Q & A	x				Patients bipolar disorder
[J13]	Other		x			All users
[J14]	WIMP, point and click					All users

4.2   Validation of Registered Emotions

Out of the analyzed studies, 80 % used additional mechanisms to validate the self-reported emotions (Table 6). The validations were e.g. measurement of physiological signals (facial expressions, gestures, heart rate).

4.3   Sharing Emotions

Sharing emotions is allowed in 65 % of the reviewed proposals. They allow sharing emotions with several types of users (Table 7). The interfaces that allow emotion sharing are in 60 % of cases GUIs, and in 40 % of cases TUIs.

Table 6. Classification of research question Q3

Paper	Type of interface	Validated
[C06]	TUI	Heart rate
[C11]	TUI	N/A
[C12]	TUI	Comparative study with IAPS, self-validate
[C15]	GUI	According to the tone of the conversation
[C16]	GUI	Multimodal input exploiting touch gestures and facial expression recognition
[C17]	GUI	Physiological measures and semi structured prose review
[C18]	GUI	N/A
[J01]	GUI, NUI	N/A
[J02]	GUI, WEB	Captured physiological signals, biometric
[J05]	GUI, NUI	Pictures of ones face
[J09]	GUI	Sensors and a factor inference engine
[J13]	TUI	Feedback
[J14]	GUI	Post-performance rating

Table 7. Classification of research question Q4

Paper	Type of interface	Share emotion	With who
[C06]	TUI	Yes	Friends
[C11]	TUI	Yes	Business partner
[C15]	GUI	Yes	Other
[C16]	GUI	Yes	Other
[C17]	GUI	Yes	Other
[J01]	GUI, NUI	Yes	Other
[J02]	GUI, WEB	Yes	Other
[J13]	TUI	Yes	Other
[C12]	TUI	No	N/A
[C18]	GUI	No	N/A
[J05]	GUI, NUI	No	N/A
[J09]	GUI	No	N/A
[J14]	GUI	No	N/A

4.4   Methodologies of Evaluation

This SLR studied evaluation methods to understand which are commonly used in this type of interface (Table 8). 85 % include an evaluation of the proposed technology, and most used mixed-methods approaches. The chosen participants were students, or users with particular characteristics, or in some cases, any

Table 8. Classification of research question Q5

Paper	Evaluated	Participants	Task	Time	N participants
[C12]	Yes (quanti-tative)	Students	Testing prototype using IAPS and move the handle of the emotion slider away or towards them	N/A	51
[C18]	Yes (quanti-tative)	Children, adults	Locate labels on the AffectButton	N/A	58
[J09]	Yes (quanti-tative)	Bipolar patients	Using MONARCA prototype, correlation, significance test, scale for depression	11 months	10
[J14]	Yes (quanti-tative)	Students	Using interface , Listen to the music and track emotion	N/A	30
[J02]	Yes (quali-tative)	Computer literate	Observations and semi-structured Interviews	N/A	10
[C11]	Yes (both)	Office workers	Testing prototype by users, questionnaires, pre and post interviews, in the field observation, survey	4 weeks	25(interviews) + 34(survey)
[C15]	Yes (both)	Group of hci researchers	Questionnaires, observation	N/A	10
[C17]	Yes (both)	Participants were familiar with Internet video	Four-tier approach(physiological, behavioral, subjective, and self-reporting data sources), scale and observation, video recorded	90 min per participant	21
[J01]	Yes (both)	Depressed students, pairs of individuals, caregivers	Fill out questionnaires, set and emoticon, capturing pictures	More than 3 weeks	28
[J05]	Yes (both)	Office workers	Use the mobile application,scale of psychological well-being, exit-interviews, picture capture	3 weeks	27
[J13]	Yes (both)	General participants	Use of objects	1 h per participant	24
[C06]	No	N/A	N/A	N/A	N/A
[C16]	No	N/A	N/A	N/A	N/A

available user. Only two studies conducted evaluation with users in a real context, e.g. a mental illness such as depression. Regarding the length of study, out of the studies with evaluation, 55 % specified how long it took them to make the evaluation. The average number of participants was 30 ($min = 10$, $max = 59$).

4.5   Benefits of Register Emotions

We identified the benefits of using technology to register emotions (Table 9). 50 % suggest an *improvement* on the goals of the study, which were either supporting self-reflection, encouraging people to reflect on their emotions, or improving emotion identification by participants. 45 % show evidence that technologies to report emotions *facilitate* tasks such as user experience studies and cultural research. This research suggests there is no particular evidence of differences in this aspect between articles published in conferences and journals.

Table 9. Classification of research question Q6

Paper	Type of Interface	Benefits of technology to register emotions
[C06]	TUI	Facilitate
[C11]	TUI	Improve
[C12]	TUI	Facilitate
[C15]	GUI	Improve
[C16]	GUI	Improve
[C17]	GUI	Other
[C18]	GUI	Improve
[J01]	GUI, NUI	Improve
[J02]	GUI, WEB	Facilitate
[J05]	GUI, NUI	Improve
[J09]	GUI	Improve
[J13]	TUI	Facilitate
[J14]	GUI	Facilitate

4.6   Discussion

The most common interaction style was WIMP, with a GUI interface. We did not find a well-defined interaction style for TUI interfaces, which may have several explanations: TUIs are newer and not as well established as GUIs, and there are fewer research projects that study TUIs in multiple real contexts. This may open an interesting field of research, that tries to uncover the interaction styles that are relevant for new interfaces, considering their particular characteristics.

It is interesting to note that 80 % of the analyzed interfaces implemented a second method to validate the emotions users reported. It is important and noteworthy that researchers recognize that due to the drawbacks, all instruments inherently have, emotions should ideally be validated both through objective and subjective methods.

Over 60 % of the reviewed studies allowed emotion sharing. This opens up another interesting aspect that needs further research, privacy: how do users feel about sharing something that is deeply personal, such as an emotion?

Registering emotions was considered to have several benefits, e.g. allowing users to self-reflect on emotional states. Delivering appropriate instances of self-reflection may benefit users, especially in contexts such as systems related to mental health, or for users at a higher risk for depression.

One challenge that is still open is to conduct evaluations of these systems with real users in real contexts of use. Naturally, this is a difficult task, as in any research with real users - however, evaluations should begin to incorporate real users to be able to truly understand the impact of self-reporting emotions.

5   Conclusions and Future Work

This work presented a SLR regarding interfaces for emotional self-report. We analyzed several dimensions of the interfaces, e.g. used technology, target user, evaluation process and benefits. The main contribution of this research is to present a rigorous and formal SLR that characterizes research in the area of user interfaces for self-reporting emotions.

In general, researchers have identified that it is important to share emotions with other users. However, our results show that most self-report interfaces for emotions are GUIs. This may mean that some categories of users (older adults, children who do not yet know how to read) may be left out of these technologies, which suggests the importance of studying these users to propose technologies with new interaction styles specific to them.

We found a small number of relevant papers, which is a motivation to continue expanding our literature review. For example, we can consider other digital libraries (e.g. Scopus[5], Wiley Online[6]) to widen the scope of our literature review and take into account a greater number of primary studies. It would be especially interesting to explore clinical-focused journals to expand the scope of our review. The small number of papers is also a signal that this area of research requires more studies (especially involving users in real contexts) and interfaces (with new interaction styles).

Acknowledgements. This project was partially funded by CONICYT Chile PhD scholarship, CONICIT and MICIT Costa Rica PhD scholarship and Universidad de Costa Rica, and Fondecyt (Chile) Project No. 1150365.

References

1. Bardzell, S., Bardzell, J., Pace, T.: Understanding affective interaction: Emotion, engagement, and internet videos. In: Proceedings of the 3rd International Conference on Affective Computing and Intelligent Interaction and Workshops (ACII 2009), pp. 1–8. IEEE, September 2009
2. Caon, M., Khaled, O.A., Mugellini, E., Lalanne, D., Angelini, L.: Ubiquitous interaction for computer mediated communication of emotions. In: Proceedings of the Humaine Association Conference on Affective Computing and Intelligent Interaction (ACII 2013), pp. 717–718. IEEE Computer Society, September 2013
3. Design, I.: Interaction Style (2014). http://www.interaction-design.org. Accessed May 2015
4. Desmet, P.: Measuring emotion: development and application of an instrument to measure emotional responses to products. In: Blythe, M., Overbeeke, K., Monk, A., Wright, P. (eds.) Funology: From Usability to Enjoyment. Funology, Human-Computer Interaction Series, vol. 3, pp. 111–123. Springer, Dordrecht (2005)
5. Dix, A., Finlay, J., Abowd, G.D., Beale, R.: Human-Computer Interaction, 3rd edn. Pearson Education Limited, Harlow (2004)

---

[5] http://www.scopus.com.
[6] http://onlinelibrary.wiley.com.

6. Doryab, A., Frost, M., Faurholt-Jepsen, M., Kessing, L.V., Bardram, J.E.: Impact factor analysis: combining prediction with parameter ranking to reveal the impact of behavior on health outcome. Pers. Ubiquit. Comput. **19**(2), 355–365 (2015)
7. Gallacher, S., O'Connor, J., Bird, J., Rogers, Y., Capra, L., Harrison, D., Marshall, P.: Mood squeezer: Lightening up the workplace through playful and lightweight interactions. In: Proceedings of the 18th ACM Conference on Computer Supported Cooperative Work & Social Computing (CSCW 2015), pp. 891–902. ACM, March 2015
8. Holman, D., Vertegaal, R.: Organic user interfaces: designing computers in any way, shape, or form. Commun. ACM **51**(6), 48–55 (2008)
9. Isbister, K., Höök, K., Laaksolahti, J., Sharp, M.: The sensual evaluation instrument: developing a trans-cultural self-report measure of affect. Int. J. Hum. Comput. Stud. **65**(4), 315–328 (2007)
10. Ishii, H.: Tangible bits: beyond pixels. In: Proceedings of the 2nd International Conference on Tangible and Embedded Interaction, pp. xv-xxv. ACM, February 2008
11. Ishii, H.: The tangible user interface and its evolution. Commun. ACM **51**(6), 32–36 (2008)
12. Jacko, J.A.: Human Computer Interaction Handbook: Fundamentals, Evolving Technologies, and Emerging Applications. CRC Press, Boca Raton (2012)
13. Jacob, R.J., Girouard, A., Hirshfield, L.M., Horn, M.S., Shaer, O., Solovey, E.T., Zigelbaum, J.: Reality-based interaction: a framework for post-wimp interfaces. In: Proceedings of the SIGCHI Conference on Human Factors in Computing Systems (CHI 2008), pp. 201–210. ACM, April 2008
14. Jain, J., Lund, A., Wixon, D.: The future of natural user interfaces. In: Extended Abstracts on Human Factors in Computing Systems (CHI EA 2011), pp. 211–214. ACM, May 2011
15. Kitchenham, B., Charters, S.: Guidelines for performing Systematic Literature Reviews in Software Engineering. Technical report EBSE 2007–01, Keele University and Durham University, July 2007
16. Lahey, B., Girouard, A., Burleson, W., Vertegaal, R.: Paperphone: understanding the use of bend gestures in mobile devices with flexible electronic paper displays. In: Proceedings of the SIGCHI Conference on Human Factors in Computing Systems (CHI 2011), pp. 1303–1312. ACM, May 2011
17. Laurans, G., Desmet, P., Hekkert, P.: The emotion slider: A self-report device for the continuous measurement of emotion. In: Proceedings of the 3rd International Conference on Affective Computing and Intelligent Interaction and Workshops (ACII 2009), pp. 1–6, September 2009
18. Lin, C.L., Gau, P.S., Lai, K.J., Chu, Y.K., Chen, C.H.: Emotion Caster: Tangible emotion sharing device and multimedia display platform for intuitive interactions. In: Proceedings of the 13th International Symposium on Consumer Electronics (ISCE 2009), pp. 988–989. IEEE, May 2009
19. Lisboa, L.B., Garcia, V.C., Lucrédio, D., de Almeida, E.S., de Lemos Meira, S.R., de Mattos Fortes, R.P.: A systematic review of domain analysis tools. Inf. Softw. Technol. **52**(1), 1–13 (2010)
20. Niforatos, E., Karapanos, E.: EmoSnaps: a mobile application for emotion recall from facial expressions. Pers. Ubiquit. Comput. **19**(2), 425–444 (2015)
21. Oliveira, E., Martins, P., Chambel, T.: Accessing movies based on emotional impact. Multimedia Syst. **19**(6), 559–576 (2013)
22. Picard, R.W.: Affective computing: challenges. Int. J. Hum. Comput. Stud. **59**(1–2), 55–64 (2003)

23. Read, R., Belpaeme, T.: Using the AffectButton to measure affect in child and adult-robot interaction. In: Proceedings of the 8th ACM/IEEE International Conference on Human-Robot Interaction (HRI 2013), pp. 211–212. IEEE Press, March 2013
24. Sánchez, J.A., Kirschning, I., Palacio, J.C., Ostróvskaya, Y.: Towards mood-oriented interfaces for synchronous interaction. In: Proceedings of the 2005 Latin American Conference on Human-Computer Interaction (CLIHC 2005), pp. 1–7. ACM, October 2005
25. Schubert, E., Ferguson, S., Farrar, N., Taylor, D., McPherson, G.E.: The six emotion-face clock as a tool for continuously rating discrete emotional responses to music. In: Aramaki, M., Barthet, M., Kronland-Martinet, R., Ystad, S. (eds.) CMMR 2012. LNCS, vol. 7900, pp. 1–18. Springer, Heidelberg (2013)
26. Weiser, M.: The computer for the 21st century. In: Baecker, R.M., Grudin, J., Buxton, W.A.S., Greenberg, S. (eds.) Human-Computer Interaction, pp. 933–940. Morgan Kaufmann Publishers Inc., San Francisco (1995)
27. Wigdor, D., Wixon, D.: Brave NUI World: Designing Natural User Interfaces for Touch and Gesture. Elsevier, Amsterdam (2011)
28. Yu, S.H., Wang, L.S., Chu, H.H., Chen, S.H., Chen, C.C.H., You, C.W., Huang, P.: A mobile mediation tool for improving interaction between depressed individuals and caregivers. Pers. Ubiquit. Comput. 15(7), 695–706 (2011)

LaGeR Workbench:
A Language and Framework for the Representation and Implementation of Device-Agnostic Gestural Interactions in 2D and 3D

Erick Mata-Montero and Andrés Odio-Vivi[✉]

Escuela de Ingeniería en Computación,
Instituto Tecnológico de Costa Rica, Cartago, Costa Rica
emata@itcr.co.cr, andresodio@gmail.com

Abstract. The recent rise of virtual and augmented reality applications, ambient intelligence, as well as video games have encouraged the proliferation of gestural input devices such as the Razer Hydra, Leap Motion Controller, and Kinect 3D. Because these devices do not relay data in a standard format, application developers are forced to use a different Application Programming Interface (API) for each device.

The main objective of this research was to define and implement LaGeR (Language for Gesture Representation), a language for the representation and interpretation of two and three dimensional device-agnostic gestures. Through LaGeR, developers can define gestures that will then be processed regardless of the device and the APIs involved. To ease the use of LaGeR, a LaGeR Workbench was developed as a set of tools and software libraries to convert gestures into LaGeR strings, recognize those strings as gestures, visualize the originating gestures in 3D, and communicate those detections to subscribing programs. In addition, LaGeR's effectiveness was validated through experiments in which LaGeR Workbench was used to give users control of representative functionality of the Google Chrome web browser by using two-hand gestures with a Razer Hydra device. LaGeR was found to be simple yet expressive enough to represent gestures and develop gesture-based device-agnostic applications.

Keywords: Pointing devices · Virtual reality · Gestural input · Regular languages · Publish-subscribe/event-based architectures

1 Introduction

In recent years, traditional interaction devices such as the mouse, keyboard, and classic video game controllers have been extended with various gesture-based alternatives. Although gestural input methods already existed in academia and in the industry (e.g., Immersion CyberGlove and VPL DataGlove), they were costly and thus limited in availability and impact.

© Springer International Publishing Switzerland 2015
J.M. García-Chamizo et al. (Eds.): UCAmI 2015, LNCS 9454, pp. 334–345, 2015.
DOI: 10.1007/978-3-319-26401-1_31

The mass adoption of gesture-based interaction devices became firmly established after milestones such as the release of the Nintendo Wii with its motion controls (2006), the iPhone with its touch screen (2007), and the Kinect with its three-dimensional camera and movement tracking (2010), among others. More recently, devices such as the Razer Hydra (2011) and Leap Motion 3D Controller (2013) have facilitated high-precision gesture-based interaction at a low cost.

Unfortunately, the proliferation of devices for gesture-based interaction has not been accompanied by the definition of standards, which forces software developers to adapt their programs to each device's API.

This document is organized as follows: Sect. 2 defines our general and specific research goals. Section 3 summarizes related work. Section 4 describes the tools, architecture and experiments used to build and test LaGeR and LaGeR Workbench. Section 5 describes LaGeR. It starts with a discussion of the conceptual spatial model, which is an extension of the traditional Rose of the Winds; then it presents LaGeR's syntax and semantics; and concludes with a discussion of some pragmatic aspects such as scale invariance and gesture imprecision tolerance. Section 6 analyzes our main results and Sect. 7 presents conclusions and future work.

2   Research Goals

The main goal of this research is to define, implement, and test a language for the representation and interpretation of concurrent, two- and three-dimensional, device-agnostic, symbolic unistroke gestures. LaGeR strings will be interpreted and used at the operating system level as well as at the application level. The specific goals are:

1. Propose a generic way of representing the movement of two points (e.g., index fingers of a user's hand) according to the data provided by movement sensors (e.g., touchpad, Razer Hydra, and Xbox controller analog sticks).
2. Define a regular language that uses such a representation to specify gestures.
3. Identify mechanisms to tolerate inexact data (e.g., a user tries to move the input device in a straight line, but is not perfectly steady).
4. Demonstrate the expressiveness and effectiveness of the language by means of a proof of concept. This will require the creation of a workbench, that is, a collection of tools and software libraries to convert sensor movements into LaGeR strings, recognize them as gestures, visualize them in 3D, communicate their detection to subscribing programs, and allow injecting standard input events (e.g., keystrokes) into the system.

3   Related Work

Our first two specific goals were to propose a generic way of representing the movement of two points, together with a language that would leverage it to specify gestures. [9] presents a very complete survey of gesture recognition techniques and implementations, including the analysis of consecutive frames from video inputs (e.g., [6]). This led us to consider discretizing the sensor data, defining a vector space in $\mathbb{R}^3$ where the sensor would describe the position of points with constant periodicity. Our final representation was based on this general approach but addresses those issues in a novel way (see Sect. 5).

Our third specific goal involves recognizing gestures in a way that is tolerant of inexact data. We considered several different methods [1,4,5] until we came up with the idea of directly comparing input and candidate gestures represented as LaGeR strings by means of the Damerau-Levenshtein distance [2]. This measure of distance counts the minimum number of operations required to transform one string into another and has been successfully used for spell checking, measuring DNA variations, and other applications [2,8].

Our final specific goal has been to develop a proof of concept. To do so, we were inspired by the all-in-one nature of Gesture Script [7], which prompted the creation of a LaGeR workbench. Our input handling leveraged the VRPN middleware [11] and the 1€ Filter [3] in order to support multiple devices and reduce jitter, respectively.

A more comprehensive analysis of related work can be found in the Master's thesis from which this paper is derived [10].

4 Tools, Architecture and Experiments

4.1 Hardware and Software

The following hardware and software resources were used in this research:

1. Razer Hydra: Low-cost, gesture-based input device that uses magnetic fields to accurately track the orientation and position of two wands to within 1 mm and 1°, respectively.
2. VRPN (version 07.33): Open-source middleware that abstracts hundreds of input devices and allowed us to obtain the X, Y, and Z coordinates of each Razer Hydra wand in real-time. VRPN includes an implementation of the 1€ Filter [3] which smoothes the jitter.
3. Boost (version 1.55): C++ libraries for threading, inter-process communication and mathematical operations.
4. OpenGL (version 3.x): Open-source graphic libraries used to visualize LaGeR-coded gestures in 3D.
5. libXtst (version 1.2.2): Open-source libraries for used for injecting keystrokes into a graphical Linux desktop environment via the X Window System.

4.2 LaGeR Workbench Architecture

To implement LaGeR Workbench, the following C++ libraries were programmed and thoroughly tested:

1. liblager_connect: Allows the exchange of messages between programs that use LaGeR Workbench by providing a message queue and the necessary mechanisms for gesture subscription and notification.
2. liblager_recognize: Takes a LaGeR string, compares it to a set of stored gesture strings, and returns the closest match. See Algorithm 3 for more details.
3. liblager_convert: Takes data produced by the movements of an input device and converts it into the corresponding LaGeR string. Data is obtained from VRPN and converted with Algorithms 1 and 2.

We then leveraged them to write the following programs:

1. lager_viewer: Allows the user to visualize LaGeR gesture strings. Different colors are used for each sensor, and a gradient represents the direction of movement (from dark to light).
2. lager_recognizer: Receives subscriptions to gestures described as LaGeR strings and then notifies subscribers when a sufficiently similar gesture has been produced by an input device.
3. lager_gesture_manager: Provides an interactive, command line interface menu that allows the user to manage a file of LaGeR gesture strings. Actions include adding, visualizing, editing, and deleting gesture strings. Gestures can either be added directly via a gesture-based input device or by entering their LaGeR strings manually.
4. lager_injector: Provides an example implementation that loads a file with LaGeR gesture strings, registers them with lager_recognizer, and injects commands into the X Window System to control applications according to the gestures performed by the user.

In addition to these software modules, a polyhedron navigator called Great Stella [12] was used to create and visualize the rhombicuboctahedron that models 3D movements (see Sect. 5).

Algorithm 1. Conversion of LaGeR movements

Require: Sensor position sample
1: **if** Euclidean distance between the samples > MIN_SAMPLE_DIST **then**
2:    Calculate the θ and ϕ angles which correspond to the movement from the previous to the most recent position
3:    Round the angles to the nearest $45°$ interval
4:    Use the angles to perform a look-up in a conversion table and obtain the corresponding LaGeR literal (see Table 1)
5:    **return** LaGeR literal
6: **else**
7:    Ignore the sample
8: **end if**

4.3   Experiments

The objective of the first experiment — "Test 1" — was to check the basic functioning of the system under controlled conditions. To do so, we used lager_gesture_manager and lager_viewer to define and catalog nine primitive gestures. Then, a user was asked to reproduce each of them with the input device, ten times in a row, in the following order: horizontal line, vertical line, triangle, square, circle, line forward, line backward, simultaneously separating two sensors horizontally, and simultaneously joining two sensors horizontally. For each input gesture, the best-match cataloged gesture was calculated (see Algorithm 3).

Algorithm 2. Grouping of LaGeR literals

Require: Sensor position sample
 1: Obtain the LaGeR literal for the sample (see Algorithm 1)
 2: Store the sample's timestamp and literal
 3: **if** The other sensor has moved since the last time its movements were grouped **and** time elapsed since that movement < MOVEMENT_GROUPING_TIME **then**
 4:     Store the timestamps of the last grouped movements for both sensors
 5:     Replace the last group of literals in the input string by the movement literal for sensor 0, followed by the movement literal for sensor 1 and the separator '.'
 6: **else**
 7:     Append the literal for the current sensor and a '_' in the position for the other sensor's literal to the input string.
 8: **end if**

Algorithm 3. Recognizing LaGeR gestures

Require: LaGeR string for input gesture
 1: **for all** Candidate gesture strings **do**
 2:     Expand the input string and candidate gesture string to LCM (see Subsect. 5.4: Scale Invariance)
 3:     Calculate Damerau-Levenshtein distance between input string and candidate gesture's string
 4:     Convert distance to percentage of strings' length
 5: **end for**
 6: **if** Least distance < MIN_DISTANCE_PCT **then**
 7:     **return** Corresponding candidate gesture
 8: **else**
 9:     **return false**
10: **end if**

The second experiment — "Test 2" — focused on reproducing more realistic conditions for a given application. In this case, we used lager_gesture_manager and lager_viewer to define a set of more complex gestures which corresponded to common actions for browsing the Web with Google Chrome. In addition to using lager_recognizer, we linked it to Google Chrome via lager_injector so that the user could truly control the browser and see the concrete result of her actions on screen. The test consisted of ten repetitions of the following sequence of actions: Open Google Chrome (draw capital G), Open new tab (draw capital T), Load CNN website (draw CNN in caps), Zoom in (separate sensors horizontally), Zoom out (join sensors horizontally), Refresh page (draw clockwise circle), Close tab (draw capital X), Open new tab (draw capital T), Load Google website (draw capital G), Close tab (draw capital X)

Both experiments were carried out with a novice user, in order to avoid biases caused by training and adaptation effects.

5   LaGeR: A Language for Gesture Representation

5.1   Spatial Model

We approximate a unistroke 3D gesture by a finite sequence of chronologically ordered points in 3D space. Points are assumed to be captured and relayed by an interaction device at regular time intervals. Two consecutive points (x, y, z) and $(x', y'z')$ in the sequence define a vector or *atomic* (straight line) move from point (x, y, z) to point (x', y', z').

In a two-dimensional space, each atomic move from point (x, y) to point (x', y') can be approximated by a relative move in one of eight cardinal directions as suggested by the Rose of the Winds model. This of course introduces errors that can be diminished by, for example, adjusting the sampling rate of the interaction device or using more than eight cardinal directions.

In this research, we generalize the Rose of the Winds model to a 3D natural counterpart, namely, a rhombicuboctahedron (see Fig. 1). As a result, by using angle differences of 45 degrees, we get 26 cardinal directions or atomic moves that we can see as vectors emanating from the center of the rhombicuboctahedron toward the center of each facet.

Each of the 26 atomic moves can be described using spherical coordinates (r, θ, ϕ) where r is the radius, θ the polar angle, a ϕ the azimuthal angle (see Fig. 2). However, given that sampled points will be normalized as far as speed,

Fig. 1. A rhombicuboctahedron [13].

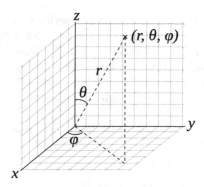

Fig. 2. Spherical coordinates [14].

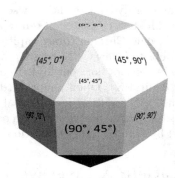

Fig. 3. Spherical coordinates on faces of rhombicuboctahedron.

magnitude and duration, we omit the radius component, which results in a rhombicuboctahedron as the one partially depicted in Fig. 3. Coincidentally, the English language alphabet consists of 26 letters, which naturally leads to using each of them to represent a unique atomic move. Table 1 presents the mapping of letters onto their corresponding normalized spherical coordinates.

LaGeR should also be able to capture two important aspects of gestural interactions, namely, concurrency of gestures and immobility (pauses in one or more of the concurrent gestures). This has been achieved by simple syntactic and semantic rules as explained in the following subsections.

5.2   Syntax

The following context-free grammar defines the syntax of LaGeR. Even though this could be captured by a regular grammar, we used a CFG because it is more concise and leads to a cleaner syntax-directed specification of LaGeR's semantics.

$G_{LaGeR} = (N_{LaGeR}, T_{LaGeR}, P_{LaGeR}, <gesture>)$

where

$N_{LaGeR} = \{<atomic\_move>, <concurrent\_moves>, <gesture>\}$

$T_{LaGeR} = \{a, b, c, d, e, f, g, h, i, j, k, l, m, n, o, p, q, r, s, t, u, v, w, x, y, z, ., -, \#\}$

and the rules of P_{LaGeR} are:

$<gesture> \rightarrow$
   $<concurrent\_moves> \# \mid <concurrent\_moves> . <gesture>$
$<concurrent\_moves> \rightarrow$
   $<atomic\_move> \mid <atomic\_move><concurrent\_moves>$
$<atomic\_move> \rightarrow$
   $a \mid b \mid c \mid d \mid e \mid f \mid g \mid h \mid i \mid j \mid k \mid l \mid m \mid n \mid o \mid p \mid q \mid r \mid s \mid t \mid u \mid v \mid w \mid x \mid y \mid z \mid \_$

5.3 Semantics

The following is a summarized syntax-driven description of LaGeR's semantics.

<$atomic\_move$> is either a letter from the English language alphabet or
"_". In the former case, the letter is interpreted as a move from the previously
recorded (x, y, z) position of an interaction device to its new (x', y', z') position.
Point (x, y, z) is interpreted as the center of a rhombicuboctahedron and point
(x', y', z') is approximated by the center of the corresponding facet as defined
in Table 1. In the latter case, the terminal symbol "_" denotes a "no move",
which is detected when an interaction device does not show a perceivable change
of position in a time interval of predefined duration. Each <$atomic\_move$> is
generated by an input device in (potential) motion.

<$concurrent\_moves$> is a string l that describes one or more atomic moves
that happen at the same time[1]. In general, if we have k interaction devices /
inputs, the length of string l is exactly k. In addition, for all $1 \leq j \leq k$ the j-th
symbol of string l always corresponds the j-th input. In this research, $k = 2$.

Table 1. Mapping of spherical coordinates onto LaGeR literals

θ	ϕ	LaGeR symbol	θ	ϕ	LaGeR symbol
0	0, 45, 90, 135, 180, 225, 270, 315	a	90	180	n
45	0	b	90	225	o
45	45	c	90	270	p
45	90	d	90	315	q
45	135	e	135	0	r
45	180	f	135	45	s
45	225	g	135	90	t
45	270	h	135	135	u
45	315	i	135	180	v
90	0	j	135	225	w
90	45	k	135	270	x
90	90	l	135	315	y
90	135	m	180	0, 45, 90, 135, 180, 225 270, 315	z

For example, consider a user who moves a Razer Hydra's left sensor one unit
to the right and two units towards the front, while the right sensor remains
immobile. In LaGeR, a move to the right corresponds to direction $(90°, 90°)$
and is represented by an 'l', and the move forward corresponds to direction
$(90°, 180°)$ and is represented by an 'n'. As the right sensor remains motionless,
the corresponding LaGeR string for this 3D symbolic unistroke concurrent two
sensor gesture is L_n_.n_.

---

[1] How atomic moves from different input devices are defined as happening at the same
time is determined by Algorithm 2.

$<gesture>$ corresponds to a sequence of $<concurrent\_moves>$ that have occurred in ascending chronological order and have gestural unity, i.e., that correspond to a gesture that LaGeR's interpreter understands. In this research, the end of gesture indicator is either temporal (enough time has passed without movements performed by the user) or tactile (the users has pressed a button in the interaction device). In both cases, an end-of-gesture "#" marker is inserted to facilitate parsing of LaGeR strings.

5.4   Pragmatics

Transforming sequences of points in 3D space into LaGeR strings is a change of domain that presents several challenges and opportunities. On the potentially negative side, precision is lost by approximating vectors in a discrete 3D space with only 26 cardinal points for each atomic move. Our experiments are aimed at proving that in spite of the loss of precision, this is not significant. On the positive side, strings can be manipulated very efficiently to identify gestures and deal with scale invariance and tolerance to imprecision.

Scale Invariance. Let w be the LaGeR string generated by lager_convert as the translation of an input user gesture. Let w' be the string that has been previously generated with lager_gesture_manager and cataloged as the string to match in order to recognize w as a gesture of type w'. We assume that applications expect gestures to be scale invariant. Thus, gestures such as "small square" and "large square" would be considered the same.

A straightforward approach to normalize the scale of the input gesture is to compare the length of w and w'. If they are the same, the Damerau-Levenshtein distance is used to determine if they are close enough. Otherwise, the least common multiple $LCM(|w|, |w'|)$ is calculated, each string is expanded by the corresponding factor and then the Damerau-Levenshtein distance is used to determine if they are close enough (see Algorithm 3). For example, if the cataloged string w' is "a_.b_.b_.c_.c_.c_.", and the input string w is "a_.b_.c_.c_.", we have $|w'| = 18$, $|w| = 12$, and $LCM(18, 12) = 36$. Therefore, we expand w' and w by a factor of 2 and 3, respectively. This means that each $<concurrent\_moves>$ of w' is concatenated with itself once and each $<concurrent\_moves>$ of w is concatenated with itself twice. Thus, we obtain the following two new strings:

$$w' = a\_.b\_.b\_.c\_.c\_.c\_. \rightarrow a\_.a\_.b\_.b\_.b\_.b\_.c\_.c\_.c\_.c\_.c\_.c\_.$$

$$w = a\_.b\_.c\_.c\_. \rightarrow a\_.a\_.a\_.b\_.b\_.b\_.c\_.c\_.c\_.c\_.c\_.c\_.$$

Gesture Imprecision Tolerance. By changing the domain of 3D coordinates to strings, we reduced the problem of matching gestures to using the Damerau-Levenshtein distance between two LaGeR strings. Thus, imprecise user movements are tolerated.

6 Analysis of Results

Figure 4 shows the results of Test 1 as a series of charts plotting the Damerau-Levenshtein distance (as a percentage of the string's length) between the input string with respect to the best-match gesture string in the catalog for each run, compared to the detection threshold (30 %). Points plotted below the 30 % line correspond to a positive identification, with an X representing a false positive. All basic gestures were detected successfully except for one mismatch (run 8 of the Circle trial detected a Square) and one correctly identified gesture which was beyond the threshold (run 4 of the Line Backward trial).

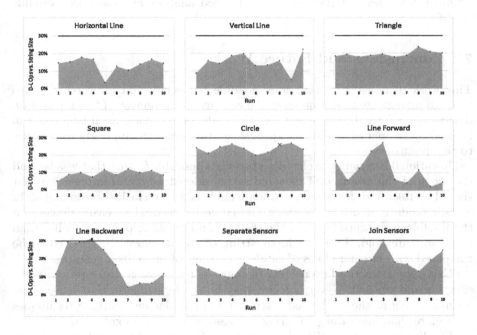

Fig. 4. Test 1 results.

Figure 5 shows the results of Test 2 in the form of two plots depicting the time it took the user to carry out each run, as well as the number of errors made. Task duration declined throughout the test, most likely due to training effects. The error rate declined as well, though not as markedly. It is possible that as the user gained confidence, she started to prioritize task completion speed, negating some of the training benefits.

Furthermore, qualitatively speaking the user reported that the system felt responsive and that she was able to complete the runs quickly. Both tests were conducted on a laptop computer, with response times for short gestures below 200 ms, intermediate gestures around 500 ms, and the longest gesture

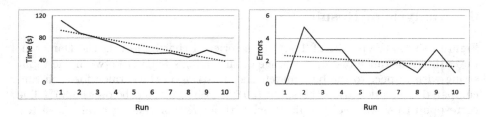

Fig. 5. Test 2 results.

("OpenCNN") around 1000 ms. More detailed analysis and data are available in [10].

7   Conclusions and Future Work

This work demonstrated that it is possible to specify and interpret gestures through a language that represents the concurrent movement of two interaction devices by using a rhombicuboctahedron model of 3D space. Such language can be used by an operating system to provide gesture events to applications agnostic to the input device.

Rotational invariance of closed gestures is a desirable feature that was beyond the scope of this research. This could be considered a type of imprecision that should be tolerated, for example, when a circle is drawn clockwise starting at 12 o'clock versus starting at 3 o'clock. Closed gestures could be easily detected if the Euclidean distance between the starting and finishing point is smaller than a certain threshold. Then, an input string of atomic moves (letters) could be compared with circular shifts of cataloged strings of predefined gestures.

Using the Damerau-Levenshtein distance to recognize gestures proved to be effective and efficient. Nevertheless it may be too inflexible in that it uses just a single string as the predefined gesture to match. Machine learning techniques with more than one cataloged string per gesture are worth exploring.

Finally, even though VRPN makes it straightforward to conduct our tests with other interaction devices, they should be carried out to fully assess the device-independence character of LaGeR. Furthermore, the spatial precision of the devices may require extra fine-tuning of LaGeR Workbench parameters, which combined with the aforementioned improvements would greatly improve usability for ambient computing scenarios such as freestanding, unsupported hand movements.

References

1. Bai, X., Yang, X., Yu, D., Latecki, L.J.: Skeleton-based shape classification using path similarity. Int. J. Pattern Recogn. Artif. Intell. **22**(04), 733–746 (2008). Accessed http://knight.cis.temple.edu/~latecki/Papers/IJPRAI08.pdf

2. Bard, G.V.: Spelling-error tolerant, order-independent pass-phrases via the damerau-levenshtein string-edit distance metric. In: Proceedings of the Fifth Australasian Symposium on ACSW Frontiers (2007). Accessed http://crpit.com/confpapers/CRPITV68Bard.pdf

3. Casiez, G., Roussel, N., Vogel, D.: 1€ filter: a simple speed-based low-pass filter for noisy input in interactive systems. In: Proceedings of the SIGCHI Conference on Human Factors in Computing Systems. (2012). doi:10.1145/2207676.2208639

4. Chen, Q., Georganas, N.D., Petriu, E.M.: Hand gesture recognition using haar-like features and a stochastic context-free grammar. IEEE Trans. Instrum. Measur. **57**(8), 1562–1571 (2008). Accessed http://www.discover.uottawa.ca/~qchen/my_papers/I%5C&M_published.pdf

5. Han, C.Y., Everding, B., Wee, W.G.: Graph matching for object recognition and recovery. Pattern Recogn. **37**(7), 1557–1560 (2004). Accessed http://www.cipprs.org/papers/VI/VI2003/papers/S8/S8_he_132.pdf

6. Lee, J., Cakmak, M., DePalma, N.: Gesture recognition with temporally local to global representations. Atlantic 1–6 (2008). Accessed http://www.mendeley.com/download/public/2829371/3769593392/fde19992241d33f9d577e01abba7b1eb96b7c213/dl.pdf

7. Lu, H., Fogarty, J., Li, Y.: Gesture script: recognizing gestures and their structure using rendering scripts and interactively trained parts. In: CHI 2014, Toronto, Ontario, Canada (2014). Accessed http://yangl.org/pdf/gscript.pdf

8. Majorek, K.A., Steczkiewicz, K., Muszewska, A., et al.: The RNase h-like superfamily: new members, comparative structural analysis and evolutionary classification. Nucleic Acids Research **42**(7), 4160–4179 (2014). Accessed http://nar.oxfordjournals.org/content/42/7/4160.long

9. Mitra, S., Acharya, T.: Gesture recognition: a survey. IEEE Trans. Syst. Man Cybern. Part C Appl. Rev. **37**(3), 311–324 (2007). Accessed http://www.cs.nccu.edu.tw/ whliao/hcie2007/gesture_recognition.pdf

10. Odio, A.: LaGeR: Lenguaje para descripción de gestos bidimensionales y tridimensionales. Master's thesis, Instituto Tecnológico de Costa Rica, Cartago, Costa Rica (2015)

11. Taylor II, R.M., Yang, R., Weber, H., Hudson, T.: Virtual reality peripheral network (2014). Accessed http://www.cs.unc.edu/Research/vrpn/

12. Webb, R.: Stella: polyhedron navigator (2015). Accessed http://www.software3d.com/Stella.php

13. Wikipedia (s.f.): Rhombicuboctahedron. In Wikipedia (2015). Accessed https://en.wikipedia.org/wiki/Rhombicuboctahedron

14. Wikipedia (s.f.): Spherical coordinate system. In Wikipedia (2015). Accessed http://en.wikipedia.org/wiki/Spherical_coordinate_system

ICT Instrumentation and Middleware Support for Smart Environments and Objects

An Evaluation of Two Distributed Deployment Algorithms for Mobile Wireless Sensor Networks

Francisco Aguilera, Cristina Urdiales$^{(\boxtimes)}$, and Francisco Sandoval

ISIS Group, ETSI Telecommunications, University of Malaga, 29071 Malaga, Spain
{cristina,sandoval}@dte.uma.es

Abstract. Deployment is important in large wireless sensor networks (WSN), specially because nodes may fall due to failure or battery issues. Mobile WSN cope with deployment and reconfiguration at the same time: nodes may move autonomously: (i) to achieve a good area coverage; and (ii) to distribute as homogeneously as possible. Optimal distribution is computationally expensive and implies high traffic load, so local, distributed approaches may be preferable. This paper presents an experimental evaluation of role-based and behavior based ones. Results show that the later are better, specially for a large number of nodes in areas with obstacles.

Keywords: Mesh mobile sensor networks · WSN · Deployment · SPF · BDM

1 Introduction

Wireless sensor networks (WSN) are conformed by a set of spatially distributed sensors that connect to each other. Sensor nodes have some degree of autonomy and they include a processing unit, along with the sensor(s) and the communication chip. In many applications, networks have to be deployed over a large area in hard to predict configurations. Furthermore, a node battery life mostly depends on the amount of traffic that it is generating/routing. If a node falls, part of the network might get isolated. Furthermore, in WSN deployment has a strong impact not only in terms of coverage but also in connectivity and throughput [1]. WSN usually rely on a mesh topology, which is more redundant, but also more robust and easier to expand and modify. Unfortunately, it is also harder to set up and maintain.

Mobile WSN (MWSN) are a potential solution to this problem [2]. MWSN can modify their positions to reorganize the network on a need basis. This solution is particularly adequate for deployment in hazardous or remote areas, or in large areas involving a large number of nodes. MWSN may be deployed by multiple robots systems (MRS), so that each node can decide when and where to move itself.

This work focuses on creating and testing a robot swarm to deploy a mobile WSN as efficiently as possible in terms of coverage and energetic efficiency.

© Springer International Publishing Switzerland 2015
J.M. García-Chamizo et al. (Eds.): UCAmI 2015, LNCS 9454, pp. 349–356, 2015.
DOI: 10.1007/978-3-319-26401-1_32

The key idea under this concept is to use as little nodes as possible to cover a given area and to make it last as long as possible before batteries need to be replaced. Robot nodes have been used to repair MWSN by replacing fallen nodes [3], but deployment typically requires robot coordination and localization. A common approach to localization is Received Signal Strength (RSS) based triangulation, since GPS sensors are battery consuming, heavy and expensive for this kind of application. In most approaches, a static beacon infrastructure is fixed for mobile nodes to locally position themselves [4,5].

There are two main distributed deployment strategies. In centralized deployment algorithms, a master node gathers information about the whole network and makes all decisions. This process is computationally expensive and usually involves techniques like Genetic Algorithms [6] or, to distribute calculation, Particle Swarm Optimization [7]. However, these approaches usually required more complex hardware and involve a higher traffic load. Alternatively, distributed algorithms require less complex calculation and less intense communication, since no node needs to be particularly aware of the state of the rest. These algorithms consider that local dispersion leads naturally to global dispersion, so each node makes decisions according to local factors, e.g. RSS.

We are going to evaluate two different distributed approaches. These approaches are representative of rule based deployment and behavior based deployment, respectively. The first one is the Backbone Dispersion Algorithm (BDA) [8]. In BDA, nodes move randomly until they fulfill some termination conditions. Each node only needs to evaluate how many nodes it can connect to. Once a robot stops, it won't move again. This algorithm is simple and requires little communication among node. However, its constraints do not fit well with the requirements of e.g. hierarchical networks. In these cases, a behavior based deployment algorithm may be required. We are going to use a Social Potential Fields (SPF) algorithm to represent this second group. This algorithm was originally proposed for swarm robots [9] and can be easily extended to mobile WSN by using RSS as an additional source of data. These algorithms basically model a set of forces of attraction and repulsion depending on the local environment of the node to determine its emergent motion.

From this point on, we will refer to nodes as robots, where each robot includes the communication module, required sensors and a processing unit, plus onboard distance sensors to avoid collisions.

2 Deployment Algorithms

BDA [8] depends on a set of deployment rules:

- At least two robots and one of them belongs to the backbone: the robot keeps moving and avoiding obstacles to spread the network as much as possible
- A single robot that belongs to the backbone: to prevent loss of connectivity to the network the robot stops until another robot gets nearby
- At least a robot, but no robot belonging to the backbone: the robot joins the backbone, stops and notifies its change of status to the rest of the network
- No robot: the robot moves backwards until it finds some robot to connect to

To implement the SPF [9], each robot is affected by two different forces:

- A repulsion force f_{r1} that forces the robot away from other nearby robots or obstacles to prevent collisions.
- A second repulsive force f_{r2} that aims at expanding the network.
- An attraction force (clustering force) f_c that grows along with the distance between robots to prevent loss of communication.

Robots stop when these forces reach an equilibrium. To avoid the well known oscillation problem, an equilibrium threshold f_u is used.

In BDA, no distance estimation is required [10]: robots are either connected or not. In SPF, however, we need to estimate distances to obstacles, including other robots within communication range. Each robot estimates these distances using the Friis equation [11] and RSS from nearby robots. Although this estimation is rough, it works correctly for reactive algorithms like BDA where no optimization is required. Distances allowed between robots mostly depend on our communication range and safety concerns, i.e. how close to obstacles we let the robot be. In our case we are going to operate with IEEE 802.14.4 standard and small robots. Hence, we use the following (heuristically estimated) parameters.

$$f_r 1(r) = -\frac{0.01}{r^8} \tag{1}$$

Using this adjustment, the repulsion equilibrium point between robots is equal to 1 m. However, since our f_u is equal to 0.5, this force only operates when robots are closer than 60 cm from each other. On the other side, the attractive force starts to be noticed when robots are at least 1.5 m away:

$$f_c(r) = -\frac{20}{r^6} + \frac{2}{r^{0.2}} \tag{2}$$

Finally, the second repulsion force tries to keep a distance of approximately 2 m between each two robots:

$$f_r 1(r) = -\frac{60}{r^7} \tag{3}$$

3 Evaluation Parameters

In order to evaluate the results of deployment algorithms, we need to define a set of parameters of interest, first.

Coverage is used as a quality measure in networks. Specifically, we are going to evaluate blanket coverage: any point of the region is sensed by at least one sensor. If node i covers a round area A_i, given N sensors in a full area A, coverage C can be calculated as:

$$C = \frac{\cup_{i=1...N} A_i}{A} \tag{4}$$

Equation 4 can be modeled using a probabilistic grid of M cells [12], where each cell i yields the overall probability of detecting an event on that location P_i.

$$C = \sum_{i=1}^{M} \frac{P_i}{M} \tag{5}$$

Since events at cell i can be detected independently by several nodes, P_i needs to be calculated as follows:

$$P_i = 1 - \bar{P}_i = 1 - \prod_N (1 - P_{ij}) \tag{6}$$

N being the number of nodes and P_{ij} being the probability of node j detecting an event at cell i.

Regarding energetic efficiency, we need to take into account two different energy costs: (i) deployment and (ii) maintenance. Deployment costs mostly depend on two parameters [13]: distance d that each node covers to reach its final location; and time t to reach the final location. After the deployment is complete, energy cost is usually related to how regularly nodes are distributed. Uniformity U for N nodes can be defined as:

$$U = \frac{1}{N} \sum_{i=1} U_i \tag{7}$$

$$U_i = \left(\frac{1}{K_i} \sum_{j=1}^{K_i} (D_{i,j} - M_i)^2 \right)^{1/2} \tag{8}$$

K_i, j being the number of nodes close to node i, $D_{i,j}$ being the distance between nodes i and j and M_i being the average distance between node i and its closest ones. The better U is, the lower the network energy consumption.

There are many other factors that affect energy consumption after deployment, mostly related to routing strategies. In order to evaluate them indirectly, efficiency can be roughly estimated in terms of the average power that nodes require to send a message to the rest of the network P_m:

$$P_m = \frac{1}{N} \sum_{i=1}^{N} P_{mi} \tag{9}$$

$$P_{mi} = \frac{1}{N} \sum_{i=1}^{N-1} P_{ij} \tag{10}$$

P_{mi} being the power required at node i to send a message to the rest of the network and P_{ij} being the power required to send a message from node i to node j. In networks where messages need to be retransmitted through k nodes,

$$P_{ij} = P_{i1} + ... + P_{ik} \tag{11}$$

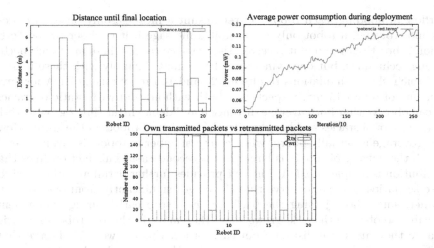

Fig. 1. BDA deployment for 20 robots in an environment without obstacles (Color figure online)

4   Experiments and Results

Although the following tests have been performed with a small number of physical robots (TI CC4305137) in real environments, in order to evaluate the impact of our different deployment strategies, we need a large number of robots. Hence, the following experiments have been performed using the freeware Player/Stage environment. Player allows us to control both a real and a simulated robot in an almost transparent way [14].

Table 1. Deployment of a mesh network using BDA and SPF

N	Dply	Obst	t	d	C	U	P_m	Msg_{Tx}
20	BDA	N	2 m 3 s	2.140	79.33 %	0.578	0.052	34.8 %
20	BDA	Y	3 m 8 s	3.218	76.78 %	0.574	0.051	32.5 %
100	BDA	N	6 m 48 s	30.077	58.13 %	0.533	0.119	34.7 %
100	BDA	Y	7 m 31 s	40.145	52.302 %	0.524	0.113	33.36 %
20	SPF	N	1 m 6 s	1.698	95.11 %	0.706	0.071	32.7 %
20	SPF	Y	1 m 46 s	2.360	99.33 %	0.806	0.078	35.3 %
100	SPF	N	2 m 38 s	18.499	93.67 %	0.727	0.176	42.8 %
100	SPF	Y	2 m 59 s	20.513	88.44 %	0.706	0.166	42.7 %

In our mesh network simulations, nodes transmit at -10 dBm, corresponding to our measures using the real robots. We are going to focus uniquely on two simple routing mechanisms: flooding and closest neighbor. In order to avoid overflow in flooding, each robot can retransmit a message only once. In closest neighbor routing, a robot only retransmit a message if it is closer to the destination robot than the one it received the message from. There are much better routing techniques, but deployment can be evaluated simply with these two.

Table 1 shows simulations results for 20 and 100 robots using BDA for environments of 6 and 15 m^2, respectively, both without and with static obstacles. We can observe that both average distance d and deployment time t grow slightly in presence of obstacles and largely with the number of robots in the group. However, coverage is actually poorer when a large number of robots is involved, even though the density of robots is larger in the second case. This fact outlines that distribution is subpar in BDA. Figure 1 provides further detail at robot level for these scenarios. We can observe that d changes significantly from one robot to another, since those joining the backbone first stop early during deployment. We can also observe that P_m grows when they move in the 100 robots scenario, because they are more distant from each other. Finally, we can observe that, after deployment, the ratio of retransmitted packets for each robot with respect to own transmitted packets changes significantly from one robot to the next and, in most cases, is quite large. As a general rule, robots on the network boundaries retransmit less packages than the rest, although robots in very crowded areas also have a lower retransmission rate because nearby robots take part of the job.

Figure 2 shows BDA deployment at two stages of a simulation with 100 robots in an environment without obstacles. We can observe in Fig. 2a one of the main issues of this approach: during deployment, many robots get trapped in the center of the network. Although the problem eventually fixes itself, deployment time gets considerably increased when this happens (particularly when the number of robots is large). In order to keep deployment time limited, we stop the simulation as soon as at least 80 % of the swarm is deployed. Figure 2b shows the final location of the robots in this simulation. We can easily observe that there are uncovered areas and distribution is not homogeneous. An additional drawback of this approach is that robots tend to conform lines. These formations are particularly weak with respect to node failures, that might lead to disconnections of a mild number of nodes.

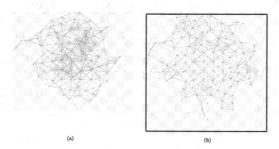

(a)   (b)

Fig. 2. BDA deployment: (a) trapped robots; (b) final configuration

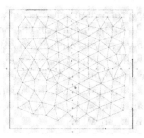

Fig. 3. SPF deployment for 100 robots in an environment without obstacles

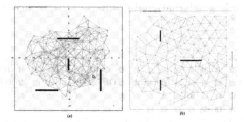

Fig. 4. Deployment for 100 robots in an environment with obstacles using: (a) BDA; (b) SPF

The presented results improve largely if we switch to SPF deployment. Table 1 shows results for 20 and 100 robots using SPF for environments of 6 and $15\,m^2$, respectively, both without and with static obstacles. We can easily observe that deployment is faster, robots move less, and both coverage and uniformity improve. It can also be observed that P_m and $M\bar{s}g_{Tx}$ grow with the number of robots more than in BDA coverage. This happens because robots are better distributed and not so many of them are far from the rest or in very crowded areas. Figure 3 shows the result of a 100 nodes network deployment in an environment without obstacles. All simulation in these environments return similar results. We can observe that nodes spread quite uniformly over the whole area.

All commented results are more evident in environments with obstacles. Figure 4 shows a sample environment with three obstacles. BDA is very affected by the location and shape of these obstacles, whereas SPF deployment basically adapts to the obstacles to obtain a configuration as similar as possible to Fig. 3.

5   Conclusions

We have presented an experimental evaluation of two representative distributed deployment algorithms for mobile WSN: rule based (BDA) and behavior based (SPF) ones. Nodes deploy faster and more homogeneously using SPF, plus they cover less distance in general. These effects are more acute the larger the network is. Average power and message retransmission is actually larger in SPF, because nodes are better distributed. In BDA, nodes on the boundaries and those in high density node areas do not have to retransmit so often. However, most loaded nodes fall quite early and, hence, full areas of the network get disconnected. In SPF, traffic load is better distributed, so the network lasts longer. SPF also adapts much better to areas with obstacles. In brief, SPF seems more suitable for deployment in large, dynamic, unstructured areas. Future work will focus on extending this study to hierarchical WSN.

Acknowledgements. This work has been partially supported by the Spanish Ministerio de Educacion y Ciencia (MEC), Project n. TEC2011-06734, by Junta de Andalucia, Project n. TIC 7839 and by International Campus of Excellence Andalucia Tech.

References

1. Robinson, J., Ng, E., Robinson, J.: A performance study of deployment factors in wireless mesh networks. IEEE Infocom **2007**, 2054–2062 (2007)
2. Yick, J., Mukherjee, B., Ghosal, D.: Wireless sensor network survey. Comput. Netw. **52**(12), 2292–2330 (2008)
3. Mei, Y., Xian, C., Das, S., Hu, Y.C., Lu, Y.H.: Repairing sensor networks using mobile robots. In: Proceedings of the ICDCS International Workshop on Wireless Ad Hoc and Sensor Networks (IEEE WWASN 2006) (2006)
4. Batalin, M.A., Sukhatme, G.S.: Coverage, exploration and deployment by a mobile robot and communication network. Telecommun. Syst. J. Spec. Issue Wirel. Sens. Netw. **26**(2–4), 181–196 (2004)
5. Hattori, K., Owada, N.T.T.K.Y., Hamaguchi, K.: Autonomous deployment algorithm for resilient mobile mesh networks. In: Proceedings of Asia-Pacific Microwave Conference, pp. 662–664 (2014)
6. Ferentinos, K.P., Tsiligiridis, T.A.: Adaptive design optimization of wireless sensor networks using genetic algorithms. Comput. Netw. **51**(4), 1031–1051 (2007)
7. Kukunuru, N., Thella, B.R., Davuluri, R.L.: Sensor deployment using particle swarm optimization. Int. J. Eng. Sci. Technol. **2**(1), 5395–5401 (2010)
8. Damer, S., Ludwig, L., LaPoint, M.A., Gini, M., Papanikolopoulos, N., Budenske, J.: Dispersion and exploration algorithms for robots in unknown environments. In: Unmanned Systems Technology VIII. SPIE Digital Library (2006)
9. Reif, J.H., Wang, H.: Social potential fields: a distributed behavioral control for autonomous robots. Robot. Auton. Syst. **27**(3), 171–194 (1999)
10. Ludwig, L., Gini, M.: Robotic swarm dispersion using wireless intensity signals. Distrib. Auton. Robot. Syst. **7**, 135–144 (2006)
11. Han, C., Yim, J., Lee, G.: A review of friis equation based indoor positioning. Adv. Sci. Technol. Lett. **30**, 101–105 (2013)
12. Ghosh, A., Das, S.K.: Review: coverage and connectivity issues in wireless sensor networks: a survey. Pervasive Mob. Comput. **4**(3), 303–334 (2008)
13. Heo, N., Varshney, P.K.: A distributed self spreading algorithm for mobile wireless sensor networks. In: IEEE Wireless Communication and Networking, pp. 1597–1602 (2003)
14. Gerkey, B.P., Vaughan, R.T., Howard, A.: The player/stage project: tools for multi-robot and distributed sensor systems. In: Proceedings of the 11th International Conference on Advanced Robotics, pp. 317–323 (2003)

SELICA: Advanced Sensor Identification System for Secure and Sustainable Food Chain Management

A Real Experience of Using Smart Environments to Address Industrial Needs

Unai Hernandez-Jayo[✉], Janire Larrañaga, Nekane Sainz, and Juan José Echevarria

Deusto Institute of Technology (DeustoTech), University of Deusto, 48007 Bilbao, Spain
{unai.hernandez, janire.larranaga, nekane.sainz, juanjose.echevarria}@deusto.es

Abstract. In this paper the systems developed in the framework of the SELICA project are described. The project aims to monitor the fresh-food cold chain and control its temperature and humidity levels. After a preliminary analysis of the cold chain, two blackspots were detected: load and unload areas and the means of transport. For this purpose a set of temperature and humidity sensors integrated into passive RFID tags are used. The reading of these tags is done by embedded systems which are also in charge of sending these data to the central management system. SELICA project is a work in progress with real industrial experience that has produced the prototypes described in this paper.

1 Introduction

The quality of fresh-food products depends on the control of the supply chain, including the transport, storage and distribution stages. Fresh-food as fruits, vegetables, meat or fish can suffer damage and loss their quality throughout the logistic process. Among the different factors affecting the life of the product, the temperature and humidity are certainly two of the most important ones, which can be affected directly if the cold chain is broken during complex transport and storage stages: the use of different means of transport, multi storage locations with different ambient conditions, etc. These issues aggravate due to the large distance from the origin to the destination because of the growing demands for off-seasons products and the off-shoring of the producers and consumers.

It is in this scenario where Information and Communications Technologies can play an important role offering to the end-consumers and wholesalers innovative solutions that help them to provide control and monitoring systems that can report them more information about the life cycle of a product during the supply chain. From the end-consumer point of view, these implementations can give him extra information about the degree of conservation and freshness of the product, information that

© Springer International Publishing Switzerland 2015
J.M. García-Chamizo et al. (Eds.): UCAmI 2015, LNCS 9454, pp. 357–368, 2015.
DOI: 10.1007/978-3-319-26401-1_33

nowadays only can be taken out from the packing and expiration dates printed on the product. From the perspective of the wholesaler, these systems offer mechanisms to meet failure and quality loss in real time during the whole supply chain, preventing that damaged goods reach the market.

Perishable products such as vegetables, fruits, meat, fish or dairy products require refrigerated transport. These elements are at risk of losing market value due to changes in the cold chain during transport, storage and/or final distribution stages.

Poorly operated supply chains, as shipments that are not cleared in time, in which boxes are left outside of the cold area, may deter the quality and product life, the inherent risk to the public health.

This paper is structured as follows: in Sect. 2 the scenario for a real fresh-food supply chain is explained, the problems with the shelf-life products, the requirements for the transportation as well as the references for possible solutions are included. In following sections the description of the load – unload area (Sect. 3) and the transportation solution (Sect. 4) are presented. Finally the paper ends with its main conclusions at Sect. 5.

2   Background

This paper gives an ICT (Information and Communication Technology) solution for the cold chain supervision for a farmers' co-op. This company is dedicated to manufacturing prepared salads. Thus they first harvest vegetables from their green farm suppliers, mainly tomatoes, lettuce and carrots, and then they take them back to the factory and prepare the salads. These salads are sent to the warehouse and logistic distribution center.

From the logistic distribution center, the salads are distributed to the retail stores. For the farmers' co-op it is crucial to know and to check that the temperature and humidity is kept within a range during all the transportation process. Nowadays there is only supervision inside farmers' co-op facilities but there is no report about what happens during the transportation from the cooperative to the end-client and during the load/unload process.

The aim of this paper is to introduce a solution for temperature and humidity supervision of the supply chain. In order to obtain the best solution we need to combine ICT and logistics knowledge to:

- select how to transport the product,
- choose the best "relation price/output" ICT solution,
- integrate the ICT solution in the fresh-food supply chain,
- and integrate this information into farmers' co-op Management Center.

According to last references, RFID is the technology for logistics [1, 2]. Passive RFID tags are cheap and were designed for easy attachment to any product: however, there are some reports on some drawbacks [3]. These include short range detection, reliability, and limited range for many products at the same time. Despite of these drawbacks, there is always a workaround to combine transportation and RFID technology in order to facilitate the real time supervision and control of the supply chain.

The last initiatives in the use of RFID technology in developing countries [4] where agriculture is the main activity, show that whenever RFID is applied to the fresh-food chain, it improves the shelf-life of the products in a 30 % and this means more earnings [5].

The solution presented in this paper adds temperature and humidity information to the tracking transportation process, and reports these values to Co-op Management Center.

In the first phase of the project, and after a thorough study of the requirements, the project has fulfilled the following goals:

(1) Traceability of the products from farmers' co-op to the end-consumer.
(2) Monitoring temperature and humidity in real time.
(3) Integration of this information in the management systems of farmers' co-op.

Therefore, the scope of SELICA project tries to satisfy companies' needs related to improved monitoring, tracking and traceability control in order to guarantee the quality of the products, and this work sets the stage for it [6]. The technical developments described in the following sections, contribute to develop future work packages during the project, specially the ones which are currently under development. In this work, the sustainability and life cycle of fresh-product is under analysis. The goal of this work is to determinate the environmental impact of the whole process, from the product's harvest, its manufacturing and the delivery to the final consumer.

2.1 Scope of SELICA Project

Based on the defined objectives and with the knowledge acquired during the analysis of previous approaches, the scope of the project was defined according to the scenario represented in Fig. 1.

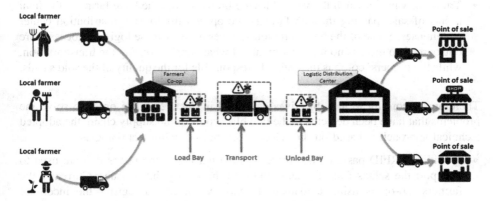

Fig. 1. Scenario of SELICA project

The scope of the system focuses on monitoring the parameters of temperature and humidity of the places through which vegetables and salads pass. Therefore, two main blackspots are detected during the requirements analysis stage (Fig. 2):

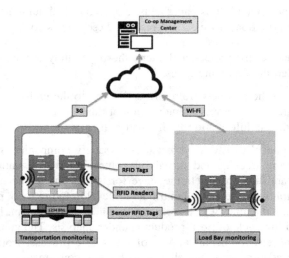

Fig. 2. The detected blackspots at the food chain

- Load area: places where the fresh products are loaded into the transport. Two of these locations have been detected in SELICA scenario: the exit at farmers' co-op where the salads wait for checking in the transport and the entrance to the logistic distribution center where the products also must be received (all the products must be inspected and identified). As both locations are similar, during the designed pilot only one of the loading areas has been monitored.
- Trucks or vans in which the vegetables are brought from the local farms to the final points of sale, passing through farmers' co-op and the logistic distribution center warehouses. Some of the transportation services used on these logistic processes are outsourced so there is no information about what happens during the transportation, while the farmers' co-op is the untimely responsible for the quality of the sold salads.

Therefore, according to the objectives described in Sect. 2 and in order to solve the problems that have been detected at the two blackspots of the supply chain, the adopted technical approach is based on the selection of the following technologies:

- Traditional RFID passive tags: these tags are placed on the boxes that are used to transport the salads from farmers' co-op to the final point of sales. Currently the farmers' co-op is using a manual traceability system to register the incoming vegetables and the output salads, so this system will also help them improve their actual management system and keep their product database updated with information that will automatically be reported by the infrastructures deployed on the load/unload areas (described in Sect. 3) and on transportation (Sect. 4).

- Battery free temperature sensor RFID tags: these novel sensors tags will be placed on the pallets used to transport the boxes with the salads. In this way, farmers' co-op central management system is reported about the ambient temperature of the boxes contained in a specific pallet.
- Low cost embedded systems able to be easily deployed at both blackspots and with wireless communication capabilities. These embedded systems are in charge of reading the information provided by both RFID tags and send it to the Co-op Management Center. Then, this central system will register all the events at the food supply chain, and hence the actual lack of information will be solved.
- RFID readers: the readers will be deployed inside the truck and at the load/unload areas. Their operation is basically to read tags and immediately send the data to the embedded systems for further processing.

This approach has been selected for the following reasons:

1. As the boxes on the pallet are staked, there are no significant differences of temperature among them, thus it is not necessary to place a tag with a sensor on each box.
2. The substrate of traditional RFID tags is paper, so they can be easily attached on the boxes. However, the substrate of sensor RFID tags is a printed circuit board, so it is more complicated to place on the boxes, what leads us to place them on the pallets.
3. At load/unload areas, pallets are accumulated while they are being processed in the transport or the warehouse, so they can be either in the shade or exposed to the sun. Once the temperature sensor tags are placed on the pallets, the temperature variation that depends on the location of the pallet can be reported to the management system.
4. Due to the price of these sensor tags, we assume the placement of one of them on each box impractical. On the other hand, the price of traditional tags is currently close to cents of Euro, so from an economic perspective, this is the best solution for the project.

3   Load/Unload Area System Description

The loading and unloading area is considered a place where the cold chain is susceptible to breakage since it is when the products spend more time outdoors. In order to control the temperature at which foods are subjected at this point of the chain, a RFID identification solution with temperature and humidity control has been developed which consists of the following elements: (1) UHF RFID reader, (2) UHF RFID antennas (3) RFID tags with integrated temperature and humidity sensor, (4) conventional RFID tags, (5) embedded system based on Raspberry Pi Model B (6) LED indication system (7) trigger button for the reading process of the boxes and a (8) Wi-Fi module that provides Internet access to embedded system.

3.1   Software of the Embedded System

In the present section of the paper, the operation of the program, developed in Python and runs in the Raspberry Pi Model B embedded platform is described. Note that this program is the responsible person for interacting with the RFID reader program, which will be explained more in detail in the next section.

At the beginning of the program, the system remains waiting with the LED lit up in blue for the goods to be placed at the point of loading and unloading and the actuator button to be pressed by the operator. When the operator presses the button, the system communicates with the RFID reader and starts reading the boxes.

If no identifier is detected in the reading process, the LED will turn red and the system will return to the starting point. But if in the reading process, the reader detects the RFID tags placed on the pallet, both the temperature sensor integrated tag and the conventional tags placed on the boxes, the system will link these tags to their virtual counterparts in order to feed the cold chain monitoring system.

The batch information (boxes + pallet) is encoded and a call to a web service is executed, using the Wi-Fi module included in the embedded system. Then, the information is processed in the Co-op Management Center, where the identifiers of the boxes are linked to the pallet and its temperature. This allows monitoring the dynamic conditions through all the stages of the cold chain, including processing, storage, or transportation days of the product, providing a useful tool to find any breakage on it (Fig. 3). When the web service responses with an acknowledge to the request, the LED will turn green and will blink for some seconds, and will return to the starting point. However, if an error occurs while sending the data, the red LED will turn red and will flash for a few seconds in order to notify the operator about the error.

In order to verify that the information is sent and stored correctly, the batches and their temperatures stored at the Management Center can be accessed via web.

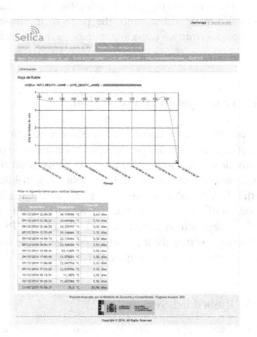

Fig. 3. Control web site at co-op management center

3.2 RFID Reader Software Description

In order to perform the reading of the RFID tags, a program in C language running inside the RFID reader has been implemented. Note that the RFID reader is interfaced through a Telnet session. On a reading request from the embedded system, the reader will start with the reading process.

In the first place, the reader will try to find the tag with the temperature and humidity sensor in order to obtain the temperature value. To do so, the reader will look for the identifiers within a known range that correspond with the temperature sensor tags, and once detected that tag, the reader writes the activation command on the temperature sensor in the corresponding user memory location. If the write command is executed correctly, the reader will attempt to read the temperature returned by the built-in temperature sensor. Therefore, the program tries to read the position where the sensor puts the measured temperature value.

Finally, this value is converted to Celsius before being returned to the embedded system so that it can encode it in the web request to Co-op Management Center.

3.3 Solution Testing

The solution designed for the unloading areas has been tested at a logistic distribution center facility. The tests were done in a large dock with multiple unload zones. The space available in each of these unload areas is delimited by two side pillars, with a distance of 5 m between them. The antennas are placed anchored to the aforementioned pillars with the same configuration as in the truck; thus, one of the antennas was set at 1.60 m and the other antenna at 40 cm height (Fig. 4).

It is in each of these areas where carriers place their trucks to proceed to the unload of the pallet with boxes. The operator responsible for the unload will place the goods in the reading area, approximately at the center of the unload zone and at a distance of one meter. Once the goods are placed, the identification process starts. Note that during trials, the boxes were placed without a specific order. This is because in an actual use

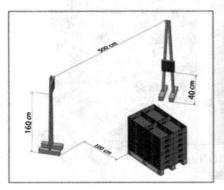

Fig. 4. Monitoring at load/unload area in the logistic distribution center

case, the operator responsible for carrying the reading process will not care about placing the boxes with the tag in a concrete orientation.

Both antennas read the information of all tags available in its radiation field. To prevent duplicate readings, a filtering process is done before reporting the embedded system.

As explained before, to obtain the temperature data of the batch, it is necessary to execute a writing operation in the tag's user memory. In field tests, it has been observed that when the RFID tag is in the back of the pallet (in both configurations), the minimum signal conditions to execute the write operation are not met, and therefore the temperature cannot be recovered. Generally, write operations on the tags require more power than reading. Hence, when the tag is in the back of the pallet, both the pallet and the boxes on it largely attenuate the signal.

So that the operator does not have to be aware of how to place the boxes in the unloading zone (and thus changing its working procedures), we have developed a support system for reading tags with a portable UHF RFID reader.

The used reader is the Intermec IP30 that runs a.NET application that basically retrieves the temperature from the sensor tag and executes the web service calls to send the information to the control center.

4   Transportation Solution Description

When a transport unit arrives at the load/unload area, the embedded system deployed on-board connects with the Co-op Management Center in order to receive information about the pallet and boxes that will be delivered to the logistic distribution center. In this area, as it has been described in Sect. 3, boxes are matched up with the pallet using the RFID tags located at the boxes and pallets (Fig. 5). Then, thanks to the RFID readers deployed inside the truck, the on-board system is able to recognise if all the

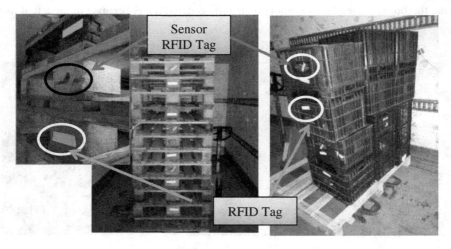

Fig. 5. RFID tags location: boxes and pallets.

batches (pallet + boxes) are loaded into the transport and if it is ready to start the delivery. At the same time, the driver is reported with this information on a nomad device (it can be a tablet, PDA or smartphone) that is connected with Bluetooth to the embedded system. In case there is any missing box, the on-board embedded system sends, via Bluetooth, the identifier of those boxes to the driver's device so that he can claim them to Co-op Management Center. Thus, discrepancies between orders/supplies and shortages are avoided.

Once the truck starts the route, the on-board system is able to store the GPS coordinates and send this information along with the temperature and humidity values recorded by the temperature sensor RFID tags placed on the pallets. In this way, Co-op Management Center's control application (Fig. 3) is updated in real time with data of the state of the products during the whole logistic process. Finally, when the truck arrives at the logistic distribution center, the on-board system detects and reports the pallets and boxes that are unloaded as well as the temperature and humidity values of the sensors in that moment. All this information is really important to detect possible spots where the cold chain is broken.

4.1 Embedded on-Board System Description

The embedded on-board system is an easily configurable set of electronic devices that can be deployed in different transport units (trucks, vans, etc.). The main task of the on-board system is to detect passive RFID tags and temperature sensor RFID tags, and to communicate with the Co-op Management Center and with the driver's mobile unit by means of its embedded Bluetooth and WIFI modules. Moreover, as it has been described previously, this on-board system also integrates geopositioning capacities, so the device can also provide information to the driver in order to optimize the route and so improve the quality of the service.

The core of the on-board system is the embedded platform that centralises all the information and communications capabilities. Its function is to acquire all the information from the RFID readers distributed in the vehicle and to send it to the central server for the evaluation of the temperature and humidity of the products.

For the development of this component a Beaglebone Black board by Texas Instrument has been chosen. This embedded platform developed by Texas Instruments provides all the performance, capacity and connectivity required by the on-board system.

In order to adapt the voltage coming from the battery and to establish the RS232 connection, a printed circuit board has been developed. Finally, to protect the embedded platform from possible bumps and splashes, it has been placed inside an IP67 sealed box.

4.2 RFID Reading System Description

As it has been described above, two types of identification tags have been used in the project: conventional C1G2 UHF RFID tags, provided by Confidex and temperature and humidity sensor RFID tags provided by Farsens. Farsens has a portfolio of different passive RFID sensor tags, but for the SELICA project we have selected the HYGRO-FENIX battery-less relative humidity and temperature sensor tag. It is an EPC Class-1 Generation-2 (C1G2) RFID tag built in a compact PCB format. This tag includes a relative humidity and temperature sensor from ST Microelectronics with a relative humidity range from 0 % to 100 % rH and a temperature range from −40 °C to +120 °C. With a 2 W ERP setup, the battery-less temperature sensor can communicate up to a distance of 1.5 m.

The core of the HYGRO-FENIX hardware is the ANDY100 integrated circuit and the HTS221 relative humidity and temperature sensor. ANDY100 IC has been designed specifically for wireless communications, including a RF front-end for UHF RFID power harvesting. The hardware of the tag sensor also includes a voltage regulator module, an EPC C1G2/ISO18000-6C digital processor, a non-volatile memory and a SPI master module that can be controlled via EPC C1G2 standard memory access commands.

The selected temperature sensor RFID tags force the use of a compliant RFID reader that allows reading and writing the control registers of the tag. Moreover, as the embedded system will be deployed on the boxcar of the truck, it must be considered that the system cannot hamper the normal performance of the loading and unloading of goods. Complying with the requirements referred, the reader that has finally been selected is the ThingMagic Vega reader. This reader meets the ThingMagic M5 command stack, which ensures integration with the embedded platform. For this purpose, a specific class has been developed that allows access to the functions necessary for the project: identification of the tags and temperature and humidity

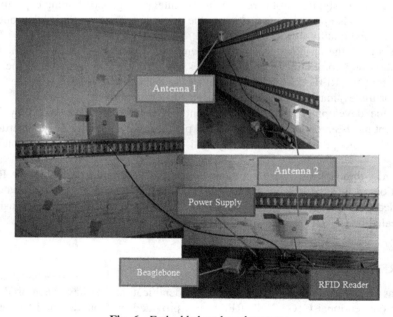

Fig. 6. Embedded on-board system

recording. The MAX232 communications interface included in the embedded platform allows the connection of the reader (RS232 level) with the Beaglebone Black (embedded system) card (3V3 TTL level).

RFID tags are read thanks to two high gain antennas located at the door and in the back of the boxcar. For this deployment, two Patch-A0006 antennas from Poynting Europe have been selected. These antennas cover the 900 MHz band and they have been designed with a low VSWR over RFID bands, they are weatherproof and easy to install. The whole embedded on-board system is shown in Fig. 6.

5   Conclusions and Future Work

In this paper the environmental sensing applications based on RFID and embedded systems developed in the framework of SELICA project are presented. These solutions try to address the temperature and humidity monitoring issues in the supply chain of fresh products.

RFID technology is the core of the proposed solutions, but in spite of its reliability, there are some factors that affect its performance in the proposed scenarios. Unload areas in the logistic distribution center have a metal lifting platform that facilitate the unloading of pallets from the trucks. Furthermore all the unload zones are very close to each other, which could cause pallets from adjacent unload areas to be read. Similar problems appear in the boxcar due to its metallic and isolated nature.

Depending on the location of the metallic surface, it may completely isolate the field generated by the reader, making the communication with the tags impossible. Inside boxcar, the problem with multiple reflections affects the readers so that they have to discriminate replicated information.

Therefore, it is a factor to consider, since it can be very damaging to the system. It is also possible that the placement of metallic material benefits the system, as the electromagnetic waves would bounce on it.

The results show that each use case is unique and difficult to replicate, which is why the design of a traceability system using RFID technology should consider the needs of each specific case beforehand.

As future work, and in order to improve the number of successful readings, it is quite important to determine the best relative position of tags and readers, taking into account the nature, actions and tools needed during the load and unloading process, such as: the skills of the worker, the materials of the pallets and boxes, the interferences created by the pallet-trucks and so on.

On other hand, SELICA project is still running. The current work package is devoted to measure the sustainability and life cycle of the fresh-products, from the farm to the retail storages. To carry out these processes the information provided by the systems described in this paper is very important.

Acknowledgments. This work has been funded by the Ministry of Economy and Competitiveness of Spain under INNPACTO funding program (SELICA project, IPT-2012-0381-060000). Special thanks to Inkoa Sistemas S.L, Garaia Co-op, Farsens S.L and planet Media Studios S.L. for their support.

References

1. Fu, H.P., Chang, T.H., Lin, A., Du, Z.-J., Hsu, K.-Y.: Key factors for the adoption of RFID in the logistics industry in Taiwan. Int. J. Logistics Manage. **26**, 61–81 (2015)
2. Ringsberg, H.A., Mirzabeiki, V.: Effects on logistic operations from RFID- and EPCIS-enabled traceability. Br. Food J. **116**, 104–124 (2013)
3. Boeck, H., Wamba, S.F.: RFID and buyer-seller relationships in the retail supply chain. Int. J. Retail Distrib. Manage. **36**, 433–460 (2008)
4. Sharma, S., Patil, S.V.: Development of holistic framework incorporating collaboration, supply-demand synchronization, traceability and vertical integration in agri-food supply chain. Int. J. Inf. Syst. Supply Chain Manage. **4**(4), 18–45 (2011)
5. Jedermann, R., Nicometo, M., Uysal, I., Lang, W.: Reducing food losses by intelligent food logistics. Philos. Trans. R. Soc. A: Math. Phys. Eng. Sci. **372**(2017), 2013302 (2014)
6. Van der Vorst, J.G.A.J., Tromp, S.-O., van der Zee, D.-J.: Simulation modelling for food supply chain redesign; integrated decision making on product quality, sustainability and logistics. Int. J. Prod. Res. **47**, 6611–6631 (2009)

Mobile Phone Sensing:
Current Trends and Challenges

Iván R. Félix, Luis A. Castro[⊠], Luis-Felipe Rodríguez,
and Érica C. Ruiz

Sonora Institute of Technology (ITSON), Ciudad Obregon, Mexico
rogelio.felix@gmail.com, luis.castro@acm.org,
{luis.rodriguez,erica.ruiz}@itson.edu.mx

Abstract. The efforts to improve user experience and expand the services offered through mobile phones over the past few years have led to new ways of recollecting data and inferring knowledge about people and their surroundings. This emerging area is known as mobile phone sensing and has been supported by a plethora of devices and sensors. Mobile phone sensing has enabled researchers to migrate from presumably bias-prone surveys and large observational teams to accurate, timely, and in-situ data collection about subjects of research. In doing so, this area has been experiencing different waves of technological development. In this paper, we analyze and discuss three waves of development and present a review of related literature in the area.

Keywords: Mobile phone sensing · Opportunistic sensing · Participatory sensing

1 Introduction

In social and behavioral sciences, and related fields, several research methods rely on direct observation of the subjects or on their memories. In this regard, mobile phone sensing is an emerging area that has been helping researchers obtain data from large groups of persons with lower costs and more advantages at the time of analyzing data for it can be collected when it happens, where it happens, and stored in remote repositories for detailed scrutiny.

In this work, we present the results of a literature review in the area and discuss different trends that have been pervading mobile phone sensing. In the following sections, we discuss how technology has provided a large range of types of sensors and how researchers have started to use them. We first discuss how these have been implemented in custom-built devices. Then we discuss how researchers have taken advantage of mobile phone that incorporate sensors (Sect. 2). In Sect. 3, we present the methodology used for literature review. After that, we present results about the usage of the different types of sensors. In Sect. 5, we describe some trends and challenges that are to be addressed in this emerging field. Finally, in Sect. 6, we present some concluding remarks.

© Springer International Publishing Switzerland 2015
J.M. García-Chamizo et al. (Eds.): UCAmI 2015, LNCS 9454, pp. 369–374, 2015.
DOI: 10.1007/978-3-319-26401-1_34

2 Mobile Phone Sensing: Three Waves of Development

Mobile phone sensing is a relatively new research area that has been developing during the last few years, which can be split into three different waves that have been gaining attention as the area unfolds: (1) the creation of custom-built sensing devices, (2) the use of on-device built-in sensors, and (3) the use of commercial sensors.

2.1 The Creation of Custom-Built Sensing Devices

The first wave of mobile sensing used several devices that were built to meet a particular research need. These sensing devices were mainly crafted when technology was mature enough to combine sensors that would fit in a box that subjects could carry with them in an unobtrusive way. In some studies, they used sensing devices with self-storage methods and analyzed the information as soon as they downloaded it from these devices, like in [1].

As soon as the capabilities of feature phones increased, they became the companion to their custom-built sensing devices. Advanced feature phones could store a considerable amount of information, could communicate with external sensors and remote servers, and had an acceptable processing power. While the custom-built device sensed the environment (or the subject), feature phones usually communicated with this device via Bluetooth to collect and save the data in their storage or send it through the network to remote servers for further analysis. Also, feature phones enabled researchers to inform subjects of their status (with a glance to the phone's screen background [2]) as well as correct sensor bad readings.

2.2 The Use of Built-in Sensors

The second major wave in mobile phone sensing started with the emergence of smartphones. By 2007, mobile phones began embedding sensors for a better user experience (e.g., accelerometer and gyroscope) and for novel types of services that involved knowing user location and orientation (e.g., GPS and compass).

Recent papers have shown that researchers are able to infer several aspects of persons, like the quality of their sleep [3], their level of stress [4], their wellbeing [3], their surroundings [5], and even personality traits [6]. Beyond that, the usefulness of mobile phones with built-in sensors does not end at a personal level, but they have contributions at the social level where researchers look for ways to infer social behavior and interactions patterns [7], or at community level where they help map and identify urban situations, like noise pollution in a city [8], or predicting bus arrival [9].

2.3 The Use of Commercial Sensors

In the literature, two main uses for commercial sensors along mobile phones were found: (1) as a tool to get the ground truth (i.e., they are used to compare with the results of a study with an alternate method), and (2) as a companion to the mobile phone.

To illustrate the first usage, in [10] they developed an algorithm that uses built-in mobile phone sensors to infer when a person is sleeping and the amount of time they slept. Then, they compared the results with proven-to-work commercial applications that can get that information: (a) Jawbone Up that uses a wrist band, and (b) the Zeo Sleep Manager Pro that uses a head band. For the second goal, in [11], they used the Emotiv Epoc Electroencephalography (EEG) headset to control the address book dialing app of the smartphone with the mind of the subject.

3   Research Procedure

In this section, we describe the research procedure used for searching the papers presented in this work. The search is by no means exhaustive.

1. *Google Scholar.* First we used the search phrase mobile sensing and selected papers from the first five result pages whose title and abstract were relevant for our purposes. Secondly, we used the search phrase mobile phone sensing and again selected from the first five result pages of the search engine papers whose title and abstract were relevant for our purposes. Thirdly, we used again the search phrase mobile phone sensing but this time we applied a filter, to obtain papers that were published between 2013 and 2015, and, as previously stated, selected from the first five result pages whose titles were relevant for our purposes.
2. *References on downloaded papers.* We analyzed the references from the papers, and selected the ones that included the following keywords: mobile, phone, smartphone and sensing in their title, or a composite phrase using two or more of those words. The selected items from the references were looked up on Google Scholar and filter out the ones that were not relevant for our goals.

4   Results

We next describe the aggregated papers grouped and classified, by the types of sensors used by year of publication. Using the previous procedure, we found 43 papers that we considered relevant to the purpose of this work. It is important to mention that some papers include more than one type of sensor, therefore they were counted more than once. Due to space constraints, not all papers were discussed in the text.

4.1   Types of Sensors Used Per Year

From the papers found, different types of sensor were used, mainly form three sources: (a) from the smartphone itself (built-in), (b) from custom-built external devices, and (c) from commercial external devices. Generally, the sensors that fit in these three sources are called hard sensors. However, there is another type of sensor based on software, i.e., logs of the use of the mobile phone (e.g., call logs, SMS logs, internet usage logs, calendar logs, social networks logs) [6, 12]. Usually, these sensors have been used to infer social, or personality traits of the user.

In our results, most of the sensors used are hard sensors, where the accelerometer, GPS, Bluetooth and microphone are the most commonly used (see Fig. 1). The built-in sensors are the most accessible and less obtrusive as no additional devices are needed. Whereas in soft sensors the application logs, SMS logs and call logs seem to be the most useful (see Fig. 1).

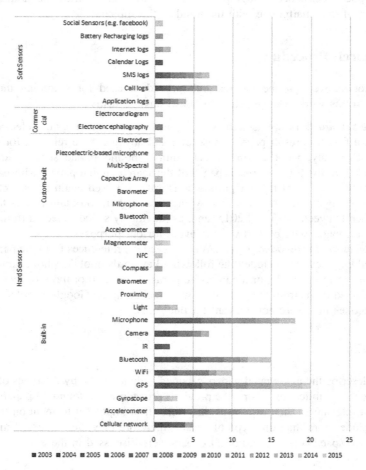

Fig. 1. The numbers of papers using each type of sensor per year

5 Current Trends and Challenges in Mobile Phone Sensing

Up until now, smartphones have played mainly two roles in mobile sensing. First, mobile phones are an augmented sensing device, capable of collecting raw data from its environment, processing them to give them some meaning or inferring situations about users, their surroundings, or people they interact with. Still, there are some data analyses that require too much processing time and therefore a lot of power, thus smartphones may not be the most suitable devices to process the data. Secondly, mobile phones are devices used as a means to link to external sensing devices, with the capacity of storing and processing data, and communicating with remote repositories, thus becoming a platform for deploying specialized sensors in extensive campaigns.

Despite the fact that smartphones from different vendors share many features, they usually differ in their development platform. In general, this difference can result in an increase of costs for creating a sensing tool. Several projects have attempted to decrease the technical burden by creating tools that do not require programming experts [12, 13].

One of the most daunting challenges in mobile phone sensing is making sense of the data collected. In this task, the use of machine learning or pattern recognition algorithms is paramount. However, as of today, due to the data quality (i.e., bad sensor readings, noisy readings, and unlabeled data) and the restrictions of machine learning algorithms, this task is very challenging. Finally, another challenge is energy. Modern mobile phones, although with better batteries, consume even more power than their predecessors.

6 Conclusions

Mobile phone sensing is an area that is taking advantages of the mobile phones properties (e.g., ubiquitous) and has been used to help researchers gather data. Mobile phones have become generally more powerful, as they embed larger capacities (e.g., more memory, more processing power, improved data transmission, more sensors). In the transition from feature phones to smartphones, different techniques to exploit the potential of mobile phones have been applied. We found mainly three different waves of development, (1) when phones did not include sensors and researchers primarily created their own, (2) when phones did include sensors and researchers started using them, and (3) when commercial sensors appeared and researchers exploited them, since they are specialized, cheap, and accurate. We also found that during all the time during the development of mobile sensing, built-in hard sensors are the most used, where the accelerometer, Bluetooth, GPS, and microphones are the ones that have been used in almost all the years we looked upon.

There is still room for some improvements as different development platforms exist and technical knowledge is required in order to take advantage of the capabilities of modern mobile phones, but there is some work that might help to overcome these challenges. We hope that the results and discussion in this paper can be used to motivate technological developments or research in this emerging area.

Acknowledgements. This work was partially funded by National Council for Science and Technology in Mexico (CONACYT) through a scholarship provided to the first author, and the Sonora Institute of Technology (ITSON).

References

1. Choudhury, T., Pentland, A.: Sensing and modeling human networks using the sociometer. In: 2012 16th International Symposium on Wearable Computers, pp. 216–216. IEEE Computer Society (2003)
2. Consolvo, S., McDonald, D.W., Toscos, T., Chen, M.Y., Froehlich, J., Harrison, B., Klasnja, P., LaMarca, A., LeGrand, L., Libby, R.: Activity sensing in the wild: a field trial of ubifit garden. In: Proceedings of the SIGCHI Conference on Human Factors in Computing Systems, pp. 1797–1806. ACM (2008)
3. Lane, N.D., Lin, M., Mohammod, M., Yang, X., Lu, H., Cardone, G., Ali, S., Doryab, A., Berke, E., Campbell, A.T.: Bewell: sensing sleep, physical activities and social interactions to promote wellbeing. Mob. Netw. Appl. **19**(3), 345–359 (2014)
4. Lu, H., Frauendorfer, D., Rabbi, M., Mast, M.S., Chittaranjan, G.T., Campbell, A.T., Gatica-Perez, D., Choudhury, T.: Stresssense: detecting stress in unconstrained acoustic environments using smartphones. In: Proceedings of the 2012 ACM Conference on Ubiquitous Computing, pp. 351–360. ACM (2012)
5. White, J., Thompson, C., Turner, H., Dougherty, B., Schmidt, D.C.: Wreckwatch: automatic traffic accident detection and notification with smartphones. Mob. Netw. Appl. **16**(3), 285–303 (2011)
6. Chittaranjan, G., Blom, J., Gatica-Perez, D.: Who's who with big-five: analyzing and classifying personality traits with smartphones. In: 2011 15th Annual International Symposium on Wearable Computers (ISWC), pp. 29–36. IEEE (2011)
7. Rachuri, K.K., Musolesi, M., Mascolo, C., Rentfrow, P.J., Longworth, C., Aucinas, A.: EmotionSense: a mobile phones based adaptive platform for experimental social psychology research. In: Proceedings of the 12th ACM International Conference on Ubiquitous Computing, pp. 281–290. ACM (2010)
8. Rana, R.K., Chou, C.T., Kanhere, S.S., Bulusu, N., Hu, W.: Ear-phone: an end-to-end participatory urban noise mapping system. In: Proceedings of the 9th ACM/IEEE International Conference on Information Processing in Sensor Networks, pp. 105–116. ACM (2010)
9. Zhou, P., Zheng, Y., Li, M.: How long to wait?: predicting bus arrival time with mobile phone based participatory sensing. In: Proceedings of the 10th International Conference on Mobile Systems, Applications, and Services, pp. 379–392. ACM (2012)
10. Chen, Z., Lin, M., Chen, F., Lane, N.D., Cardone, G., Wang, R., Li, T., Chen, Y., Choudhury, T., Campbell, A.T.: Unobtrusive sleep monitoring using smartphones. In: 2013 7th International Conference on Pervasive Computing Technologies for Healthcare (PervasiveHealth), pp. 145–152. IEEE (2013)
11. Campbell, A., Choudhury, T., Hu, S., Lu, H., Mukerjee, M.K., Rabbi, M., Raizada, R.D.: NeuroPhone: brain-mobile phone interface using a wireless EEG headset. In: Proceedings of the Second ACM SIGCOMM Workshop on Networking, Systems, and Applications on Mobile Handhelds, pp. 3–8. ACM (2010)
12. Froehlich, J., Chen, M.Y., Consolvo, S., Harrison, B., Landay, J.A.: MyExperience: a system for in situ tracing and capturing of user feedback on mobile phones. In: Proceedings of the 5th International Conference on Mobile Systems, Applications and Services, pp. 57–70. ACM (2007)
13. Perez, M., Castro, L., Favela, J.: Incense: a research kit to facilitate behavioral data gathering from populations of mobile phone users. In: Proceedings of UCAmI, Cancun, Mexico, pp. 25–34 (2011)

A Lightweight Distributed Architecture to Integrate Fuzzy Relevant Objects in Real-Time Environments

Javier Medina[✉], Francisco Javier Quesada, and Macarena Espinilla

Department of Computer Science, University of Jaen, Jaen, Spain
{jmquero,fqreal,mestevez}@ujaen.es

Abstract. The development of intelligent environments from scratch means an arduous and complex process. In these environments, the integration of sensors and the design of processing information in real time are key aspects in order to generate feasible solutions. To shed light on this context, in this contribution, we present an architecture for information processing based on object distribution services. The capture and processing of data are developed ubiquitously within mobile devices and ambient computers by means of peer to peer based on fuzzy temporal subscriptions. The main advantage of the use of fuzzy temporal subscriptions is that the information is received by a subscriber when it reaches a desired level of relevance for this subscriber, implying a decrease in the communication burden in the architecture. In order to illustrate the usefulness and effectiveness of our proposal, a scene of an user performing an activity in an intelligent environment is described by means of his interactions with the environmental objects and the identification of users by marker-based tracking.

Keywords: Intelligent environments · Ambient middleware · Object distribution services · Real-time processing · Marker-based tracking

1 Introduction

Internet of Things (IoT) [23] is emerging as a new paradigm where Ambient Intelligence [30] and Ubiquitous Computing [29] converge [21]. These paradigms locate the information processing in the everyday objects properly, but there are new challenges which arise in order to develop collective intelligence in these frameworks.

In this context, there are two key issues that should be addressed. On the one hand, the integration of the heterogeneous data and, on the other hand, the information processing.

The first issue is the integration of data from heterogeneous sources, which is critical to provide an affluent ambient layer. There is a wide range of sensors that can be deployed in an intelligent environment that collect multiple data,

© Springer International Publishing Switzerland 2015
J.M. García-Chamizo et al. (Eds.): UCAmI 2015, LNCS 9454, pp. 375–386, 2015.
DOI: 10.1007/978-3-319-26401-1_35

such as, mobile, wearables, ambient devices. The mobile devices integrate movement, location and connectivity by means of sensors and wide-range protocols (accelerometer, GPS, NFC, Wi-Fi, etc.). Meanwhile, ambient devices are collecting information from our environment using low-power protocols (Z-Wave or ZigBee) in light sensors, or WLAN protocols in vision or audio sensors.

In summary, each sensor can send and receive the data from the sensor network in the lowest level of the communication layer providing physical interaction with the hardware. To do so, there are different languages or platforms in the sensor network such as C++, Android, Objective-C, Java or Ruby. Because of this, the mosaic of devices, languages and protocols needs for be accessible homogeneously to develop real scenes with heterogeneous sensors.

The second issue is the information processing that requires structural data and procedures to generate new information from low-layer information [10]. In the literature, several approaches have been proposed to manage these issues, in which the efforts have been focused on providing general and ad hoc models. With respect to the standard structural models, it is noteworthy SensorML [2], developed by Open Geospatial Consortium which includes geolocation or discovering in a XML schema. Concerning the semantic annotating for sensors, it is relevant the W3C Semantic Sensor Networks (SSN) specifications [4,8]. Regarding ad hoc models, there are approaches which provide own models which fit better within ad hoc reasoning processes or streaming requirements [3,7,24,25].

Furthermore, a key aspect in the second issue is the middleware infrastructure in which input/output data are connected by remote services in distributed environments. The adequate distribution of services in ambient environments is vital to provide sensitivity to real time [1] for distributing the information processing in several central processing units [17,27]. There are several relevant open middlewares that provide sturdy solutions in ubiquitous and ambient contexts. Among them, it is noteworthy ZeroC Ice [11,28] that is an object-oriented distributed computing tool with support for several languages and platforms as well as Global Sensor Network (GSN) that applies sliding window management [26] in changing data stream [14]. Finally, OpenIot increases the characteristics of GSN adding top-k subscriptions over sliding windows (top-k/w subscriptions) [20] and semantic open-linked data techniques. The subscription process has been demonstrated to be adequate for IoT, highlighting the implementation of Data Distribution Service for Real-Time Systems (DDS) by Object Management Group (OMG)[1].

The aim of this contribution is to provide a straightforward architecture to process heterogeneous information from real-time in intelligent environments. This architecture is based on a peer-to-peer communication in which fuzzy relevant objects are distributed in subscriptions in a sliding window in time.

To do so, the contribution is structured as follows: the use of appropriate techniques in our proposal is discussed in Sect. 2 and the proposed architecture is described in Sect. 3. In Sect. 4, a scene developed under the proposed architecture

---

[1] http://www.omg.org/spec/DDS/1.2/.

using video processing as well as ambient and mobile sensors is described. Finally, in Sect. 5, conclusions and future works are pointed out.

2   Requirements and Cost-Value Approach

This contribution is focused on the development of an straightforward architecture in which heterogeneous information provided by a sensor network is spread in real time.

To do so, it is necessary to process the information provided by mobile, ambient and vision sensors. Some previous solutions deal with data using heavy computing techniques in desktop computers, delegating light devices to wrappers of raw data. For example, GSN needs for MySQL to manage and store the data streams or OpenIot provides subscription services just in server side. Moreover, there are some problems to integrate GSN in light devices within other platforms or languages [9].

In this contribution, a minimum scalable architecture is proposed in which each sensor (mobiles, ambient and vision) sends stream of processed data to subscribers in a dynamic way. Furthermore, each sensor transmits its streams in real time to top-k/w subscriptions [20] under a fuzzy [31] approach based on the relevant information for each subscription. The main advantage of this fact is that the centralization is not necessary, providing a peer-to-peer communication where the most relevant fuzzy objects are distributed in a sliding window in time.

Furthermore, due to the fact that each sensor depends on each manufacturer platform, a metalanguage middleware is required in order to deploy the subscription services. In this contribution, ZeroC Ice is chosen as middleware because it supports transparent communication for several languages (C++, .NET, Java, Python, Objective-C, Ruby, PHP, and JavaScript) and protocols (TCP, UPD and SSL).

Finally, regarding data representation, a fuzzy Entity-Attribute-Value (EAV) model [22] is proposed in order to describe objects from the ambient environment. This basic similar description for semantic representation is used in OpenIot by means of Resource Description Framework and the Linked Sensor Middleware [15]. As is detailed in next sections, the entity-attribute-value model is suitable to decompose the objects in distributed nodes and to integrate them in real time.

3   Architecture for Distributed Fuzzy EAVs in $alpha$/w Subscriptions

In this section, the proposed architecture for streaming fuzzy objects under the subscription paradigm with relevant information is described. Figure 1 illustrates the processing and flow of information from devices to subscribers under our approach that are described in detail in the following subsections. To do so, first, the meta model based on a fuzzy representation of EAVs is presented for

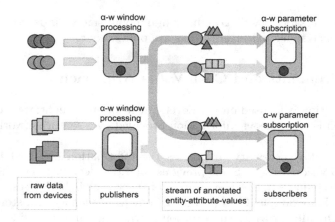

Fig. 1. Flow of information from devices to subscribers

defining the relevance of each data source. Then, the relevant information to be transmitted is defined by Top-α/w distributed publishers/subscriber. Finally, the dynamic nature of the architecture is addressed.

3.1   Metadata Model: Fuzzy Temporal EAV

In this section, the fuzzy version of EAV to handle imprecise environmental object representations in our proposal is described.

Fuzzy entities, attributes and values has been used satisfactorily in many real-world applications due to information is often vague or ambiguous [18], providing the following advantages: (i) *flexibility* to represent concepts, physical or virtual objects, (ii) *data processing independence* and (iii) *interoperability* to be analyzed and processed by computers or humans.

The proposed environmental model is defined as a set of fuzzy temporal entities within a set of attributes wit a set of fuzzy temporal values. This representation comes from a generalization of an ad hoc structure [3].

The temporal dimension of the data from mobile, ambient and vision source has been defined by a time-stamp that inserts the reading or changing data in milliseconds in the Unix time format. This stamp is used from sliding window to stream the most recent data at an interval in time.

The relevance of data has been defined by a fuzzy value between [0,1] [31] that is estimated by the publisher. Therefore, each node that generates and streams the data must define how relevant are the data, based on the context of the measure. For example, it can represent the probability, uncertainty or importance, enabling subscribers to apply an alpha-cut [31] to receive only relevant data.

So, each fuzzy temporal EAV in our proposal is defined by the following elements:

- *Id.* An universal identifier of the object.
- *Type.* A type description of the entity (e.g. Person, Mobile, Ambient Device).
- *Relevance.* A fuzzy relevance value between [0,1].
- *Stamp.* A time stamp from the last modification in milliseconds.
- *Attributes.* A set of attributes that characterized the object in which each attribute is defined by
  - *Id.* An universal identifier of the attribute.
  - *Type.* A type description of the attribute (e.g. Location, Movement, Open).
  - *Values.* A set of values where each value is defined by
    - *Type.* The nature of the value (e.g. Integer, Double, String, Float, Location2D, Location3D).
    - *Relevance.* A fuzzy relevance value between [0,1].
    - *Stamp.* A time stamp from the last modification in milliseconds.

3.2 Top-α/w Distributed Publishers/subscribers

Our approach in based on a peer to peer communication based on fuzzy temporal subscriptions to transmit preprocessed information, which is relevant to the subscriber, offering a distributed ubiquitous (mobile, ambient or desktop) sensor network.

This approach provides several advantages:

- The information processing is distributed in several central processing units.
- The subscribers can define (as far as possible) the time and relevant data for notification.
- The subscribers obtain processed instead of raw data facilitating the handle of their own information management.

In order to define the relevant data, each subscriber can define temporal constrains and a fuzzy threshold of relevance:

- TNotification. The minimal time that the publish must wait to notify to the subscriber.
- TWindow. The temporal window of relevant data to be summarized. This is, the set of values where $t - stamp < TWindow$, where t is current time.
- Alpha-Cut. The minimal alpha value of relevance that entities and values must overcome. The publisher apply this alpha-cut filtering the objects where $relevance > \alpha$.
- Aggregation operator $\cup$. Based on the nature of data, subscribers can specify optionally an operator to summarize the data, for example: min, max or average. If there not exists any operator, all samples where $relevance > \alpha$ in the temporal window are sent.

In the publisher side, the devices receive the data from their sensors, storing them in a temporal window. When the notification time interval of each subscriber expires, they send the relevant data applying the fuzzy temporal filtering, see Fig. 1. In this approach, the crisp definition of the temporal component is required to avoid the possible duplication of data in consecutive intervals due to vague or imprecise temporal windows.

4   Description of a Real Scene Based on Fuzzy EAVs in *alpha*/w Subscription

In this section, a description of a real scene in an intelligent environment is presented, which is modeled and processed under our proposed architecture. The presented scene show an a user makes a tea in an intelligent environment, specifically in a kitchen. First of all, the user goes into the kitchen and takes a cup from the cupboard. Then, he fills the cup of water and heats it in the microwave. Finally, he drinks the tea and goes out of the room.

In the following subsection, the sensor network of the intelligent environment is described in which the scene has been carried out and, then, the real-time publishers/subscribers are indicated.

4.1   Sensor Network of the Intelligent Environment

The sensor network in the kitchen integrates several sensors that provided heterogeneous data:

- Mobile devices that provide information of the scene in terms of accelerometer and touching tags (NFC).
- Ambient sensors based on switch that are located at the doors that separates the areas of the smart environment, the doors of some home appliances (microwave, fridge, etc.) as well as at the doors of kitchen furniture.
- Vision sensor and vision marks. The vision sensor corresponds with an IP camera that records the images from the scene and provide the location and identification using vision marks located in a T-shirt with four vision markers, see Fig. 2.

It is noteworthy that in this scene a T-shirt has been worn by the user that includes four id markers (two larger in frontal and back side and two smaller

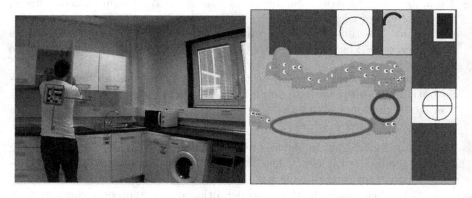

Fig. 2. (A) A frame and mark detection from scene (B) Projection of 3D positions from tracker publisher in room map.

in sleeves) in order to identify the user and his location by using an open source project: Minimal library for Augmented Reality applications (Aruco) [6] to detect markers.

So, candidate markers are detected, obtaining the identifiers and calculates the rotation and translation transformation matrix (R,S). Moreover, providing the real size of markers, the model view projection matrix (H) is obtained to estimate a 3D position from marker view to 3D position from the camera view. Finally, a naive modification has been integrated to provide the dynamic size of marker based on its identifier.

4.2 Real-Time Publishers/Subscribers

One of the main advantages of our proposal is that data processing is distributed. In the proposed scene, the following nodes have been deployed:

– *A mobile publisher.* This node is a multi-sensor source that streams motion from an accelerometer and reading events from NFC tags using a top-α/w processing. On the accelerometer signal, a single raw value of motion has been calculated as the square root of the sum of the squares of the components X, Y and Z $motion = \sqrt{x^2 + y^2 + z^2}$. Besides, it is included a fuzzification process to estimate the *relevance* of the fuzzy object based on the motion value using a membership function of a fuzzy set which represents the concept of *being in movement*. The membership degree is calculated by a linear increasing membership function $I[a, b]$, where lower or equal values to a are 0, greater or equal to b are 1, and a linear function that changes smoothly from 0 to 1 in a straight line in values between a and b. In this case, the domain values from the mobile accelerometer are in range $[0, 2]\,\mathrm{m/s}^2$ and we have defined a linear increasing function $I[0, 0.5]$ that calculates the relevance of motion values from mobile sensor in range $[0, 1]$.
  The semantic of the tags in the scene simulates the automatic opening door of the kitchen using a NFC tag. In Fig. 3, we show the events received (in red dots) when the user enters and leaves the room. Any fuzzification has been associated to NFC events where relevance has been evaluated as 1 (crisp value).
  In addition, using the Google Account Id from the mobile, we can identify the user and generate an ad hoc fuzzy EAV for each mobile. An example of stream data from mobile publisher is: $\{id : \text{``}PerryMason\text{''}, stamp :$ $1432207248128\}, attributes : [\text{``}Movement\text{''} : \{value : 7.3, relevance :$ $0.9, stamp : 1432207248118\}, \text{``}Tag\text{''} : \{value : \text{``}touchoven\text{''}, relevance :$ $1.0, stamp : 1432207248081\}]$.
– *An ambient publisher.* This node streams open/closed events from ambient sensor based on switch using a top-α/w processing.
  The open/close sensor returns asynchronously two trigger: a change of state and low-battery state. We include a fuzzification process to estimate the *relevance* of the fuzzy objects from the change of state based on the low-battery messages. When a low-battery state is included in the measure, we set

relevance = 0.5. Otherwise, *relevance* = 1.0. In addition, using the *id* from each ambient sensor, we can generate an ad hoc fuzzy EAV for each measure. An example of stream data from ambient publisher is:$\{id$: *"Oven"*, *stamp* : 1432207248128$\}$, *attributes* : [*"Open"* : $\{value$: *true*, *relevance* : 0.5, *stamp* : 1432207248118$\}$].

In Fig. 3 are shown the events received in the scene from a subscriber. These are, three events (in green dots) when the user opens the cupboard and when he opens the microwave.

– *An tracker publisher*. This node streams location and identification events from users using a top-α/w processing.

The 3D location and the user identification has been integrated in a stream publisher within Aruco detection. A temporal fuzzification has been associated to 3D positions where relevance has been evaluated using linear increasing membership function $I[TWindow, 0]$ that prioritizes the most recent data in the interval $[t_0 - TWindow, t_0]$ using the difference between the current time t_0 and the time of the mark detection *stamp*. This semantic represents An example of stream data is: $\{id$: *"PerryMason"*, *stamp* : 1432207248128$\}$, *attributes* : [*"Location3D"* : $\{value$: $XYZ(4.25, 2.70, 1.23)$, *relevance* : 0.8, *stamp* : 1432207248118$\}$].

In Fig. 2 the 3D transformations from the real scene into a sketch map are depicted. Table 1 shows the performance of vision markers to identify and track the user. The detection percentage in the scene is significant (closer to 40 %), providing a smooth tracking. The average of distance to consecutive marker detection is 2,67, this is, the number of frames between a marker detection and the next. However, there is a lack of information in non frontal poses, as the value of maximal distance to consecutive marker detection determines. It is shown in Fig. 2: with red ellipse, the lack of markers when the T-shirt is distorted by drinking cup movements; with blue ellipse, the undetected cornered frames when user leaves the room. At the end of this movements, the sleeve markers,

Table 1. Statistical data from marker detection

Number of frames	583
Number of marker detections (ms)	219
Percentage of marker detection	37,57 %
Average time of marker detection	55,47 ms
Number of frontal and back marker detections	212
Number of sleeve marker detections	7
Average of distance to consecutive marker detection	2,67
Standard deviation of distance to consecutive marker detection	10,86
Max of distance to consecutive marker detection	131

Table 2. Data stream reduction from accelerometer in mobile device

Number of samples from accelerometer (ns) in mobile device	873
Samples from accelerometer per second	19,41
Number of aggregated samples from accelerometer in $TNotification = 1000\,\text{ms}$	43
Number of accelerometer events from subscriptions (αs) $TNotification = 1000\,\text{ms}$, $TWindow = 1000\,\text{ms}$, $\alpha = 0.15$ and $\cup = MAX$	32
Ratio of reduction (ns/αs)	27,28

Table 3. Data stream reduction from vision sensor

Number of marker detections (ms)	219
Number of events from vision sensor from subscriptions (αs) with $TNotification = 1000\,\text{ms}$, $TWindow = 1000\,\text{ms}$, $\alpha = 0.15$ and $\cup = MAX$	17
Ratio of reduction (ms/αs)	12,89

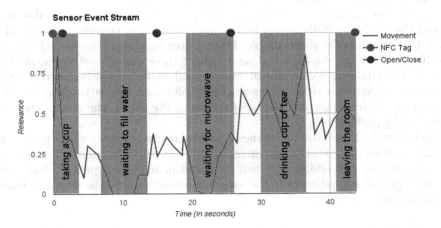

Fig. 3. Stream events from mobile and ambient publishers. $\alpha = 0.15$, $TWindow = 1000\,\text{ms}$, $TNotification = 1000\,\text{ms}$. Accelerometer aggregator $\cup = MAX$. None ambient and NFC aggregator (Color figure online).

however they are not numerous, provide a vital information to track the user when goes out of the room.

On the other hand, the data stream reduction from accelerometer and vision sensor, which generate both high-frequency data, with $TNotification = 1000\,\text{ms}$ and $\alpha = 0.15$ subscriptions are shown in Tables 2 and 3. We highlight the significant ratio reduction from number of raw data to events from subscription.

The collected data from the scene are accessible in the URL[2].

---

[2] http://ceatic.ujaen.es/smartlab/ucami_smartlab_scene.zip.

5 Conclusions and Future Works

In this contribution a lightweight distributed architecture for intelligence environments in real time has been presented. We have evaluated previous open approaches focusing on the information processing in centralized computers, such as GNS or OpenIot.

For this reason, interesting topics included in GSN or OpenIot has been translated to our solution using an open multi platform middleware (ZeroC Ice). We have proposed an architecture based on top-k/w subscription, which restricts information processing to a certain window of relevant elements recently observed on the stream, which we call as α/w subscription. So, we have proposed a fuzzy processing of objects conducted in light devices where each subscriber can defined a alpha-cut of relevance. Other parameters to enrich the information processing to the context of the user, such as parametrizing membership function [16], are going to be considered in future works.

Concerning the data representation model, we have defined a distributed fuzzy entity-attribute-value scheme integrated in the middleware. Related works use similar models, such as Tuple Space, in mobile middlewares due to their simplicity, flexibility, performance and scalability [5, 19].

In the design of the architecture, we have defined a publisher/subscriber model that is dynamically linked by machine-to-machine communications. This paradigm increases the composition of interactive capabilities in the IoT [13]. In results, we have developed a real scene where three distributed nodes publish data from mobile devices, ambient sensors and video processing in real time. The scene integrates a video processing based on vision marker tracking in order to capture the identification and the location of the users. The results show an encouraging performance.

In future works, we aim to use these id vision marks in vision sensor with camera auto-calibration, where static marks located in walls determine the absolute location of users. In addition, it will be useful in multi-occupancy, identifying the activities of several users in the same space and associating activities based on multi sensors events.

Acknowledgements. This contribution has been supported by research projects: CEATIC-2013-001, UJA2014/06/14 and TIN-2012-31263.

References

1. Balan, R.K., Satyanarayanan, M., Park, S.Y., Okoshi, T.: Tactics-based remote execution for mobile computing. In: Proceedings of the 1st International Conference on Mobile Systems, Applications and Services, pp. 273–286. ACM, May 2003
2. Botts, M., Robin, A.: OpenGIS sensor model language (SensorML) implementation specification. OpenGIS Implementation Specification OGC, 07–000 (2007)
3. Castro, J.L., Delgado, M., Medina, J., Ruiz-Lozano, M.D.: Intelligent surveillance system with integration of heterogeneous information for intrusion detection. Expert Syst. Appl. **38**(9), 11182–11192 (2011)

4. Compton, M., Barnaghi, P., Bermudez, L., Garcia-Castro, R., Corcho, O., Cox, S., Taylor, K.: The SSN ontology of the W3C semantic sensor network incubator group. Web Semant. Sci. Serv. Agents. World Wide Web **17**, 25–32 (2012)
5. De, S., Nandi, S., Goswami, D.: Tuple space enhancements for mobile middleware. Int. J. Commun. Netw. Distrib. Syst. **12**(3), 299–326 (2014)
6. Garrido-Jurado, S., Muñoz-Salinas, R., Madrid-Cuevas, F.J., Marín-Jiménez, M.J.: Automatic generation and detection of highly reliable fiducial markers under occlusion. Pattern Recogn. **47**(6), 2280–2292 (2014)
7. Gomez-Romero, J., Patricio, M.A., García, J., Molina, J.M.: Ontology-based context representation and reasoning for object tracking and scene interpretation in video. Expert Syst. Appl. **38**(6), 7494–7510 (2011)
8. Neuhaus, H., Compton, M.: The semantic sensor network ontology. In: AGILE Workshop on Challenges in Geospatial Data Harmonisation, Hannover, Germany, pp. 1–33 (2009)
9. Perera, C., Zaslavsky, A., Christen, P., Salehi, A., Georgakopoulos, D.: Connecting mobile things to global sensor network middleware using system-generated wrappers. In: Proceedings of the Eleventh ACM International Workshop on Data Engineering for Wireless and Mobile Access, pp. 23–30. ACM, May 2012
10. Haefner, K.: Evolution of Information Processing Systems: An Interdisciplinary Approach for a New Understanding of Nature and Society. Springer, Heidelberg (2011)
11. Henning, M.: A new approach to object-oriented middleware. IEEE Internet Comput. **8**(1), 66–75 (2004)
12. Henning, M., Spruiell, M.: Choosing middleware: why performance and scalability do (and do not) matter, 1 September 2009. http://www.zeroc.com/articles/IcePerformanceWhitePaper.pdf
13. Kortuem, G., Kawsar, F., Fitton, D., Sundramoorthy, V.: Smart objects as building blocks for the internet of things. IEEE Internet Comput. **14**(1), 44–51 (2010)
14. Kifer, D., Ben-David, S., Gehrke, J.: Detecting change in data streams. In: Proceedings of the Thirtieth international conference on Very Large Data Bases (VLDB Endowment), vol. 30, pp. 180–191, August 2004
15. Le-Phuoc, D., Nguyen-Mau, H.Q., Parreira, J.X., Hauswirth, M.: A middleware framework for scalable management of linked streams. Web Semant. Sci. Serv. Agents. World Wide Web **16**, 42–51 (2012)
16. Liu, H., Jacobsen, H.A.: A-ToPSS: a publish/subscribe system supporting imperfect information processing. Proceedings of the Thirtieth International Conference on Very large Data Bases (VLDB Endowment), vol. 30, pp. 1281–1284, August 2004
17. Liu, G.: Distributing network services and resources in a mobile communications network. US Patent No. 5,825,759. US Patent and Trademark Office, Washington, DC (1998)
18. Ma, Z.: Fuzzy Database Modeling of Imprecise and Uncertain Engineering Information. Springer, Heidelberg (2006)
19. Picco, G.P., Balzarotti, D., Costa, P.: Lights: a lightweight, customizable tuple space supporting context-aware applications. In Proceedings of the 2005 ACM Symposium on Applied Computing, pp. 413–419. ACM, March 2005
20. Pripužić, K., Žarko, I.P., Aberer, K.: Top-k/w publish/subscribe: a publish/subscribe model for continuous top-k processing over data streams. Inf. Syst. **39**, 256–276 (2014)

21. Marie, Pierrick, Desprats, Thierry, Chabridon, Sophie, Sibilla, Michelle: Extending Ambient Intelligence to the Internet of Things: New Challenges for QoC Management. In: Hervás, Ramón, Lee, Sungyoung, Nugent, Chris, Bravo, José (eds.) UCAmI 2014. LNCS, vol. 8867, pp. 224–231. Springer, Heidelberg (2014)
22. Nadkarni, P.: The EAV/CR model of data representation. Technical report, Center for Medical Informatics, Yale University School of Medicine (2000)
23. Kopetz, H.: Internet of things. In: Kopetz, H. (ed.) Real-Time Systems, pp. 307–323. Springer, New York (2011)
24. Rodríguez, N.D., Cuéllar, M.P., Lilius, J., Calvo-Flores, M.D.: A fuzzy ontology for semantic modelling and recognition of human behaviour. Knowl.-Based Syst. **66**, 46–60 (2014)
25. Roggen, D., Lukowicz, P., Ferscha, A., Millán, J.D.R., Tröster, G., Chavarriaga, R.: Opportunistic human activity and context recognition. Computer 46, 36–45 (2013). IEEE Computer Society (EPFL-ARTICLE-182084)
26. Salehi, A.: Design and implementation of an efficient data stream processing system. Doctoral dissertation, École Polytechnique Féd'erale de Lausanne (2010)
27. Verissimo, P., Rodrigues, L.: Distributed Systems for System Architects, vol. 1. Springer Science & Business Media, New York (2012)
28. Villanueva, F.J., Villa, D., Moya, F., Barba, J., Rincón, F., Lopez, J.C.: Lightweight middleware for seamless HW-SW interoperability, with application to wireless sensor networks. In: Design, Automation & Test in Europe Conference & Exhibition (DATE 2007), pp. 1–6. IEEE, April 2007
29. Weiser, M.: The computer for the 21st century. Sci. Am. **265**(3), 94–104 (1991)
30. Zelkha, E., Epstein, B., Birrell, S., Dodsworth, C.: From devices to ambient intelligence. In: Digital Living Room Conference, vol. 6, June 1998
31. Zadeh, L.A.: Fuzzy sets. Inf. control **8**(3), 338–353 (1965)

Smart Sensor Design for Power Signal Processing

Francisco-Javier Ferrández-Pastor$^{(\boxtimes)}$, Higinio Mora-Mora,
Jose-Luis Sanchez-Romero, and Mario Nieto-Hidalgo

Department of Computing Technology, University of Alicante,
P.O. Box 90, 03080 Alicante, Spain
fjferran@dtic.ua.es

Abstract. Ubiquitous systems used to improve quality of life include integration of multiple data and knowledge representing behaviour of people. These systems produce several sources of raw data (environmental, wearable sensors) to produce new processed data (behaviour patterns, people actions). In the domestic environment, daily and frequent people activities use all kinds of electric devices (appliances). Connection and disconnection of these devices provide useful data to know patterns of use, usual or unusual events and people behaviour. Currently, specialised systems for power load and monitoring are costly to install. This work proposes the design and development of low cost and embedded hardware tools (smart sensors) to obtain power consumption information used on ambient assisted living services. Non-intrusive load monitoring (NILM) design based in Wavelet transform (WT) processing, and Field-Programmable Gate Arrays (FPGAs) hardware implementation, provide the necessary support to develop this kind of embedded devices.

Keywords: Smart sensor · FPGA · Wavelet transform · Power management · Human activity recognition

1 Introduction

Advances on consumption signal processing improve the development of energy management systems and smart grids (used at home, buildings, etc.). Power signals are captured, monitored, stored in databases, and processed in numerous and specific solutions. The aim is to assure the signal quality, measure power consumption, classify loads and provide support services in energy management systems. These services require to capture power consumption signal and to implement specific mathematical methods. Capturing power signals is carried out by specialised hardware systems whereas software algorithms process the signals to obtain information. [9]. There are mathematical paradigms frequently used in power signal processing (e.g. Wavelet [10] and Fourier transform [15]). Considering this, a method to embed signal processing algorithms on hardware implementations using non intrusive methods would provide useful devices specialised in energy management systems.

© Springer International Publishing Switzerland 2015
J.M. García-Chamizo et al. (Eds.): UCAmI 2015, LNCS 9454, pp. 387–393, 2015.
DOI: 10.1007/978-3-319-26401-1_36

The first problem to be faced is the integration of mathematical processing on low-cost hardware architecture with the capacity to implement rule based algorithms. Reconfigurable architectures (to facilitate new configurations) and mathematical transform that enable detection and identification of device connections have to be integrated. FPGAs are a good choice if it is necessary to perform a fast processing and reconfiguration [3]. Mathematical processing should be easy to implement and provide capabilities for classification and signal identification. Wavelet transform (WT) have a wide range of facilities which depend on the type of wavelet and its application [2].

2   Related Work

In power management systems, the electric signal is processed to analyse events produced by the consumption devices or to detect faults in the distribution system. These events are characterized by means of different feature extraction methods. There is a wide variety of systems to process the power signals, mainly classified in two groups: high frequency [13] and low frequency systems [7]. An event detection module detects the on/off transition of appliances by analysing the changes in the power levels. The events can be defined in terms of steady-state or transient changes. Transient analysis captures electrical events, such as high frequency noise in electrical current or voltage, generated when an appliance is turned on/off [5,12]. There are difficulties with this method for detecting appliances whose consumption varies continuously or that have multiple states once connected. In order to address some of these issues, [16] measured both real and reactive power. The mathematical transform selected is Wavelet Transform (WT). Wavelet analysis has been widely applied in signal analysis, image processing, numerical analysis, and so on [6].The main applications of wavelet transform in electrical systems are analysis of electrical power systems [10], power quality information [4], fault detection and location [11] and signal processing [8]. FPGA technology (Field Programmable Gate Array) is used by hardware designers to prototype computer architectures in a variety of applications [14].

3   Electrical Signal Analysis: Smart Sensor Design

There are different services and applications in power systems in which high performance is required: electric disaggregation to detect appliances, management of energy consumption, detection of power quality, harmonics or fault detection are some examples. The electrical signal in power systems is processed by using two approaches: steady-state and transient signals. In Steady-state (low data rate) signal is in a dynamic equilibrium; in transient state (high data rate) signal has sudden changes in response to a change from equilibrium. Transient signals are caused by connection/disconnection of devices or by faults in the systems. Between two different steady states there are several transient events.

Power management systems need to know which devices are involved on power consumption and when the connection/disconnection occurs. Appliances

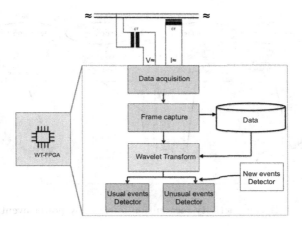

Fig. 1. Smart Sensor Design: functional modules.

identification methods provides valuable information in these scenarios. Power meters provide data (power curve shown) which are processed by specialized algorithms to detect events (identification, classification, etc.).

This work embeds power signal processing (using WT) and event detection modules on an hardware reconfigurable architecture (FPGA). The design proposed is shown in Fig. 1 with the following modules:

- *Data acquisition:* In this module power sensors (power meters, current transformer, voltage divider,..) obtain electric data (current and/or voltage).
- *Frame capture:* In this module data streams are captured to create working windows. The size of this window is configurable and a memory datalog is included for buffering data. Frequency levels between 1 Hz–20 KHz work from 1 sample each second to 400 samples each 20 ms.
- *Root Mean Square (RMS) and Wavelet Transform (WT):* This module performs RMS and WT on data obtained in the frame capture module.
- *Detection/Identification:* This module integrates the knowledge by means of rules defined by experts.

4   Experimental Prototype: Smart Sensor Test

The smart sensor design has four modules: data acquisition, frame capture, wavelet transform and detector modules. The methodology employed to develop an smart sensor for power signals processing, following this design, is:

1. Testing and validating each module using hardware and software support.
2. Processing all modules together. Testing and validating.
3. Finally, the design is implemented on hardware using FPGA modules integrated into low cost embedded systems.

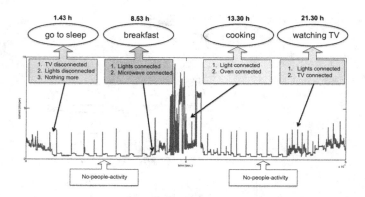

Fig. 2. Human activity recognition inferred by power events.

The experimental prototype has the following modules:

- Hardware module: National Instrument myRIO with a dual-core ARM®
  Cortex™-A9 real-time processing and Xilinx FPGA customizable I/O.
- Software module: Logical numerical computing environment provides by Lab-
  view FPGA.

4.1 Event Detection Using Root Mean Square (RMS) Data and Wavelet Transform (WT) Coefficients

Wavelet Transform allows to make a multi resolution analysis (MRA) to detect
and classify device connections [1]. Multi-resolution analysis obtains low-pass
approximations $S_{m0,n}$ and high-pass details $T_{m,n}$ from the signal $S(t)$ (Fig. 3).
An approximation contains the general trend whereas details embody the
high-frequency contents. In multiresolution analysis, approximations and detail
coefficients are obtained through a succession of convolution processes. These
coefficients are then used to detect signatures of appliance patterns.

When certain criteria are met (windows size and type of wavelet) it is possible
to obtain the wavelet coefficients that may be used to identify the consumption
of individual devices and appliances. Coefficients $S_{m0,n}$ and $T_{m,n}$ correspond to
approximation and detail information in different frequency bands. Each device

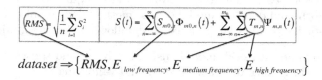

Fig. 3. Feature generation using RMS data and WT coefficients

Table 1. Confusion Matrix obtained

Appliance Connec./disconnec.	Human activity	Not human activity
Human activity	65	30
Not human activity	2	750
Predicted	67	785
Precision	97,0 %	96,1 %

aggregates different Energy E_{Ψ_i} obtained with this coefficients. RMS of signals and frequency information provided by WT are used to detect and classify devices connection. Feature generation is build with RMS and WT coefficients (Fig. 3). The method used for classification is k-Nearest Neighbors algorithm.

4.2 FPGA Implementation: Experiments

Data acquisition and frame capture have been carried out in a real environment: current sensors in main electrical panel of domestic scenario has been tested. Different appliances were connected: fridge, microwave, electric oven, washing machine, TV, lights and electronic devices have provided the frame data. Figure 2 shows the power signal captured during a day in the home analized. Sequence of specific events, captured in time periods, create logical behaviour patterns implemented by rules to detect usual or unusual events. Different detection modules require different WT processing. The bottleneck is therefore the development of this modules because several processing data are required. Implementing mathematical operations on hardware architectures improve processing capacity (time response) and enhance the possibility for successful developing of embedded systems. In this work a mathematical analysis (WT) is used by different detection hardware modules (based in FPGA implementation). Wavelet Transform offers time-frequency information used by each module working in parallel (Table 1).

5 Conclusions

Currently, there are power management systems composed by hardware sensors for acquiring power data and software to process them. Development of approaches that integrate basic sensors and data processing devices embedded reduce their cost and generalise their use. The method proposed in this work use an appropriate hardware architecture (FPGA) and an efficient mathematical paradigm (WT). The aim is to develop devices with high capacities and low cost. FPGA are completely reconfigurable and Wavelet transform is implemented with simple algorithms offering at once time-frequency information. Integration of mathematical processing on embedded systems increases system capabilities to develop intelligent sensors. When this integration includes advanced processing and rules to detect and to identify specific events the sensor become "smart". In this paper, an approach to the design of smart sensor in power systems is proposed. The design has been carried out by including a hardware architecture based on FPGA and processing based in WT and RMS data. Through theoretical analysis and empirical experimentation, promising results were obtained. The main modules described in the design have been tested using power data captured in real environment.

References

1. Akansu, A.N., Haddad, P.R.: Multiresolution Signal Decomposition: Transforms, Subbands, and Wavelets. Academic Press, San Diego (2000)
2. Albanesi, M.G., Lombardi, L.: Wavelets for multiresolution shape recognition. In: Del Bimbo, A. (ed.) ICIAP 1997. LNCS, vol. 1311. Springer, Heidelberg (1997)
3. Arrais, E., Roda, V., Neto, C., Ribeiro, R., Costa, F.: FPGA versus DSP for wavelet transform based voltage sags detection. In: Proceedings of the 2014 IEEE International Conference on Instrumentation and Measurement Technology (I2MTC 2014), pp. 643–647, May 2014
4. Brito, N., Souza, B., Pires, F.: Daubechies wavelets in quality of electrical power. In: Proceedings of the 8th International Conference on Harmonics and Quality of Power, vol. 1, pp. 511–515, October 1998
5. Chang, H.H., Lin, C.L., Lee, J.K.: Load identification in nonintrusive load monitoring using steady-state and turn-on transient energy algorithms. In: 14th International Conference on Computer Supported Cooperative Work in Design (CSCWD 2010), pp. 27–32 (2010)
6. Hariharan, G., Kannan, K.: Review of wavelet methods for the solution of reaction diffusion problems in science and engineering. Appl. Math. Model. **38**(3), 799–813 (2014)
7. Hart, G.: Non-intrusive appliance load monitoring. Proc. IEEE **80**(12), 1870–1891 (1992)
8. He, H., Cheng, S., Zhang, Y., Nguimbis, J.: Home network power-line communication signal processing based on wavelet packet analysis. IEEE Trans. Power Deliv. **20**(3), 1879–1885 (2005)
9. Jiang, L., Luo, S., Li, J.: An approach of household power appliance monitoring based on machine learning. In: Fifth International Conference on Intelligent Computation Technology and Automation (ICICTA 2012), pp. 577–580 (2012)
10. Kim, C.H., Aggarwal, R.: Wavelet transforms in power systems. I. General introduction to the wavelet transforms. Power Eng. J. **14**(2), 81–87 (2000)
11. Liang, J., Elangovan, S., Devotta, J.: A wavelet multiresolution analysis approach to fault detection and classification in transmission lines. Int. J. Electr. Power Energ. Syst. **20**(5), 327–332 (1998). http://www.sciencedirect.com/science/article/pii/S0142061597000768
12. Marceau, M., Zmeureanu, R.: Noninstrusive load disaggregation computer program to estimate the energy consumption of major end uses in residential buildings. Energ. Convers. Manag. **41**(13), 1389–1403 (2000). http://www.sciencedirect.com/science/article/pii/S0196890499001739
13. Ruzzelli, A., Nicolas, C., Schoofs, A., OHare, G.: Real-time recognition and profiling of appliances through a single electricity sensor. In: 7th Annual IEEE Communications Society Conference on Sensor Mesh and Ad Hoc Communications and Networks (SECON 2010), pp. 1–9 (2010)

14. Sanchez, J.L., Mora, H., Mora, J., Jimeno, A.: Architecture implementation of an improved decimal cordic method. In: IEEE International Conference on Computer Design (ICCD 2008), pp. 95–100 (Oct 2008)
15. Santoso, S., Grady, W., Powers, E., Lamoree, J., Bhatt, S.: Characterization of distribution power quality events with fourier and wavelet transforms. IEEE Trans. Power Deliv. **15**(1), 247–254 (2000)
16. Streubel, R., Yang, B.: Identification of electrical appliances via analysis of power consumption. In: 47th International Universities Power Engineering Conference (UPEC 2012), pp. 1–6 (2012)

A MAC Protocol for Underwater Sensors Networks

Rodrigo Santos[1]([✉]), Javier Orozco[1], Sergio F. Ochoa[2], Roc Messeguer[3], and Gabriel Eggly[1]

[1] Department of Electrical Engineering and Computers, IIIE,
UNS-CONICET, Bahía Blanca, Argentina
ierms@criba.edu.ar
[2] Computer Science Department, Universidad de Chile, Santiago, Chile
[3] Computer Science Department, Universidad Politecnica de Catalunya,
Barcelona, Spain

Abstract. Underwater sensor networks are becoming an important field of research, because of its everyday increasing application scope. Examples of their application areas are environmental and pollution monitoring (mainly oil spills), oceanographic data collection, support for submarine geo-localization, ocean sampling and early tsunamis alert. It is well-known the challenge that represents to perform underwater communications provided that radio signals are useless in this medium and a wired solution is too expensive. Therefore, the sensors in these network transmit their information using acoustic signals that propagate well under water. This data transmission type bring an opportunity, but also several challenges to the implementation of these networks, e.g., in terms of energy consumption, data transmission and signal interference. Few proposals are available to deal with the problem in this particular application scenario, and these proposals does not address properly the transmission of underwater acoustic signals. In order to help advance the knowledge in the design and implementation of these networks, this paper proposes a MAC protocol for acoustic communications between the nodes based on a self-organized time division multiple access mechanism. The proposal is still preliminary and it has only been evaluated in the laboratory; however, it represents a highly promising behavior that make us expect interesting results in real-world scenarios.

Keywords: Acoustic sensor networks · Collaborative systems · Opportunistic routing

1 Introduction

The ocean covers 71 percent of the Earth's surface and contains 97 percent of the planet water, yet more than 95 percent of the underwater world remains unexplored. UNESCO states that over 90 percent of the earth habitable space is within the ocean, and near 80 percent of all life is under the ocean surface.

© Springer International Publishing Switzerland 2015
J.M. García-Chamizo et al. (Eds.): UCAmI 2015, LNCS 9454, pp. 394–406, 2015.
DOI: 10.1007/978-3-319-26401-1_37

There are quite dramatic projections stating that by the year 2100 more than half of the marine species may stand on the brink of extinction [1]. This shows only some of the several reasons that we have to deploy underwater technology that help us study several phenomena that affect our lives and the health of our planet.

In this scenario, the underwater sensor networks could provide valuable information that helps us address some of these challenges [2]. However, underwater radio communications are practically unfeasible, specially in the ocean because radio signals suffers a strong attenuation, limiting the effective communication to a few meters. Acoustic signals instead are capable of traveling for long distances, depending on the power used for the transmission and the physical characteristics of the medium. Therefore the communication feasibility depends on several variables, such as the carrier communication frequency, point to point distance, the chemical composition of water, the topology of the seafloor, the temperature of the water, the depth of sensors placement and the spreading pattern.

Underwater acoustic sensors networks (UWASN) have several challenges that should be considered for a successful implementation. The first one is related to the lossy nature of the channel. Although acoustic signals can propagate well beneath the water, they suffer an important attenuation mainly produced by absorption; and this attenuation is proportional to the distance and the frequency of the signal. There are some other factors contributing to the attenuation, like the scattering and reverberation in the surface, because wind moves the reflection point in the surface. There is also reflection in vessels that may introduce Doppler effect in the signal. Moreover, the geometric spreading of the signal produces path loss in the transmission; regardless we are using spherical (that is common in deep water) and cylindrical spreading (that is more common in shallow water).

The second challenge refers to the nature of the acoustic signal used for transmitting the information. There are several man-made noises present in the ocean, and specially in the surf zone where it is usual to have a higher density, vessel traffic, sport activities and city noise. Another source of noise is provided by the environment itself; i.e., waves, winds, rains, animals and even seismic noise that may interfere with data transmission in the acoustic sensor network.

The third challenge is related to the multi-path characterization of the signals. Different signals may interfere between each other by means of the inter-symbol interference. The vertical links usually have little dispersion, so it is not common to have multi-path interference; however, in horizontal channels the spread may be significant and therefore different messages may interfere among them.

The fourth challenge to be addressed is the energy consumption. Underwater sensor networks are battery-powered, which also represents a mayor concern during its operation. The energy consumption during standby and data reception is low in commercial modems, but in data transmission the consumption depends on the distance that the signal should travel. The relationship between transmission power vs distance follows a quadratic function. One way to save the energy in these networks is by transmitting at a higher baud rates for short times, limiting the operating range. On the other hand, transmissions through long distances require high power and lower baud-rates; thus, high data volumes result incompatible with large distances under the power consumption point of view. Considering that in sensor networks the data volume is usually low, and assuming average ocean parameters, the speed of sound in the water is closed to 1.5 km/s, the carrier frequency is between 20 kHz and 70 kHz for distances larger than 1 km. The operating range to maintain sustainable communications at reasonable baud rate, and with low corrupted data rates, is limited to 2 Km point-to-point. The variance in the transmission times introduces uncertainty, therefore the round trip time for a message is usually pessimistically evaluated degrading the performance of the system.

There is a transversal component in these sensor networks that can be used to help address most of these challenges. This component is the medium access control (MAC) protocol used by the UWASN. Considering the needs and the challenges to implement underwater acoustic sensors networks, and the limitations that the current approaches for implementing MAC protocol for this type of networks, this paper proposes an extended medium access control protocol based on Time Division Multiple Access (TDMA), but specifically for UWASN. The transmission mechanism is inspired in the self-organized TDMA [3] and the ad-hoc self-organized TDMA [4]. However, its operation is simpler than the previous ones, involving only two phases for the configuration and operation. For the slot selection process it uses a simple carrier sense multiple access/collision avoidance (CSMA/CA) mechanism.

The rest of the paper is organized in the following way. In Sect. 2 a short review of previous work is presented. In Sect. 3 the proposed MAC protocol is presented. In Sect. 4 the evaluation process of this proposal is presented and discussed. Finally, in Sect. 5 we presents the conclusions and future work.

2   Related Work

This kind of networks has several aspects to consider, which are not yet defined, like the physical layer selection, link layer protocols, and network and transport layer protocols. The literature shows three main approaches to implement medium access control protocol (MAC): frequency division multiple-access (FDMA), carrier sense multiple access with collision avoidance (CSMA/CA) and time division multiple access (TDMA). The first one is not suitable for underwater acoustic transmission, due to the narrow bandwidth in underwater acoustic channels and the vulnerability of limited band systems to fading and multi-path. CSMA/CA has been proposed in previous work, but it is limited by the hidden station problem and the high propagation and variable delay. Long time periods are needed in each message transmission to guarantee that there has been no collisions degrading the overall performance. Finally, the TDMA schemes have problems with the synchronization, latency and unused bandwidth. However, for real-time transmissions it is the only option that can provide bounded delays, although it is necessary to leave several slots empty. In this section we discuss previous work mainly related to the medium access mechanism and its appropriateness for being used in underwater acoustic sensors networks.

In [5] the authors proposed the Multiple Access Collision Avoidance (MACA) protocol based on the use of short messages request to send (RTS) and clear to send (CTS), followed by the sequence of messages DATA and ACK. This mechanism has been successfully used in the Seaweb project [6]. Before sending data, the node should reserve the channel by issuing a RTS, and after that it has to wait for the CTS answer. Nearby stations also listen the request and wait for the answer. In the case that a neighbor station does not listen the CTS answer, it means there is no interference in the receiver, and that the transmission may proceed solving in this way the exposed problem. Any station, other than the original RTS sender, on hearing CTS will defer its transmission. In case of collisions of RTS messages, the nodes use a binary backoff algorithm to solve the conflict.

In [7], the authors extend the MACA protocol and named it MACA for wireless (MACAW). They propose a less aggressive backoff algorithm for the link layer introducing the sequence RTS-CTS-DATA-ACK. In lightly loaded scenarios this mechanism has less performance, but with high loads it has much better throughput and fairer allocation.

In [8] another MACA-based protocol is proposed. In this case, the Floor Acquisition Multiple Access protocol requires that every transmitting station should acquire the floor control (in a wireless channel), before sending any data packet. Both the sender and the receiver should perform the collision avoidance to guarantee the control of the channel.

In [9], the authors introduce the UW-MAC for acoustic underwater sensor networks. The MAC scheme is based on CDMA with a novel closed-loop distributed algorithm to set the optimal transmit power and code length to minimize the near-far effect. The algorithm compensates the multi-path effect by exploiting the time diversity in the underwater channel, thus achieving high channel reuse and low number of packet retransmissions. The protocol works both in deep and shallow water, and involving static or mobile nodes.

SO-TDMA [3] and ASO-TDMA [4] use a self organized TDMA scheme for the access control. However, these protocols were thought for VHF radio frequencies and they are used for the localization of vessels and ships in the ocean.

The UWSO-TDMA proposed in this paper is a simple mechanism that uses TDMA. In contrast to the other MAC protocols, this approach can be used for real-time communications, as it is possible to bound the transmission delay.

3   Description of the UWSO-TDMA Protocol

The proposed protocol is based on the predictability of TDMA, rather than on the probabilistic CSMA/CA approach. Time is divided in slots, where a message fully occupies one time slot. Like in SO-TDMA [3], UWSO-TDMA uses a structured access channel for slot assignment. The slots allocation is performed in a distributed way, where each station/node in the network chooses the best slot to transmit. This is a decentralized scheme where nodes are responsible for sharing the communication channel and the synchronization. In the case of the UWASN, GPS information is not available under the water, therefore the synchronization source is usually a sonobuoy anchored in the region that is in charge of synchronizing the clocks of the underwater nodes. The sonobuoy uses the UTC time for synchronizing the network.

Since acoustic signals are attenuated, not all the sensors listen to the sonobuoy synchronization slot. When a station is not within the sonobuoy transmission range, it is synchronized in a second phase by an already synchronized node. To do this, the frame is divided in m sub-frames (SF). Within the first sub-frame, SF_1, only the nodes listening to the sonobuoy can transmit. In SF_2, the nodes at two hops of the SB can transmit. Nodes in SF_2 are synchronized by nodes in SF_1. With this hierarchical distribution, nodes in SF_j are synchronized by nodes in SF_{j-1}. As nodes in SF_i with $i > 1$ are not in direct contact with the SB, their messages have to be aggregated by nodes in previous SF. Figure 1 shows the frame structure.

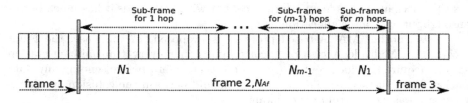

Fig. 1. Frame Structure (from [4])

The slot length is defined according to the data rate and message length. Based on these variables, the number of available slots in a frame are determined, N_{AF}. The number of slots in a sub-frame, N_k is a function of the nodes within that hop. Finally, the number of hops or sub-frames are defined according to the expected physical deployment of the UWASN.

3.1 Initialization

Figure 2 presents the general flowchart for the this phase. For ease of understanding, details on the slot selection process are not represented. In this phase the nodes scan one frame to locate idle time slots and check the existence of neighbor nodes. The sonobuoy transmits in the first slot of the frame. In that slot, this node sends the current time so nodes listening to this first slot can determine their distance to the sonobuoy. However, some nodes probably are out of the transmission radio of the sonobuoy; for these cases, the synchronization is made as explained before, through nodes in different sub-frames, SF_i.

Figure 3 presents an example with a possible distribution of nodes in a UWASN. The sonobuoy is noted as SB and it is the center of the red circle

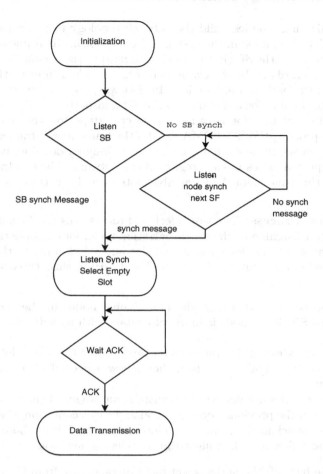

Fig. 2. Initialization Flowchart

that marks the communication range of the SB. As can be seen, two nodes may be in direct contact with the SB, but do not between them (e.g., nodes 1 and 2). Weather they are in direct contact or not, these nodes should select different slots within the first sub-frame to avoid both collisions and receiver collisions in the SB. In the next hop area, dotted red circle, there are 3 more nodes. Like in the previous case, even if they are at similar distance from the SB, that is within the second hop, they have different data paths. A message starting in node 5, may need to go through nodes 4 and 2 before reaching the SB. Instead, node 3 is within range of node 2, so messages beginning in node 3 pass through node 2 before reaching the SB. This example shows that even if nodes 3, 4 and 5 are within a distance of two communication radios from the SB, the amount of hops needed to reach such a node is different for each one.

During this phase, nodes build the network topology to determine the path towards the SB. Each node in the system selects a slot in the frame and informs its depth, distance to the SB (if it is within one hop) or the accumulated distance and the path towards it. In the example of Fig. 3, node 4 informs the distance to the SB and the path through node 2. In that way, node 5 can synchronize its clock and determine its own distance to the SB and path.

The selection of the slot may require several steps to avoid collisions. To facilitate this process, UWSO-TDMA divides the frame in sub-frames like in [4]. The amount of available slots in a sub-frame is a designer decision, based on the amount of expected nodes in each region of the network. The sub-frame should have at least the same amount of available slots as nodes within the area.

Slot Selection Process. The slot selection process uses a collision avoidance algorithm. After listening to the synchronization node, for example the SB, each node scans the sub-frame for an available slot and selects one. In the following frame, the nodes transmit in the selected slot. After this, three things may happen:

- There is no collision at all. In the next frame, nodes in the previous sub-frame or the SB (if the node is in direct contact with it) will acknowledge the selection.
- Two or more nodes within transmission range select the same slot. They will detect the collision and stop. Then, they follow a backoff algorithm to select another slot.
- Two or more nodes are not within transmission range, so they do not detect the collision in the previous nodes sub-frame. In this condition, the nodes will not receive the acknowledgment, therefore they assume that there has been a collision and follow a backoff algorithm to select a new slot.

During the backoff, the nodes select one slot randomly from the set of available ones in the sub-frame. As there is no master allocating the slots and to avoid a long selection process, sub-frames have more available slots than nodes in the area. The probability of two nodes selecting the same slot is equal to $1/n^2$, where n is the amount of idle slots in the sub-frame at the moment of the selection. As there is at least one available slot after all nodes have selected their own slot, the worst case is when two nodes compete for three slots. In this situation, the probability of collision is 0.11. If two slots are left idle, the probability decays to 0.06 and if three slots are left empty to 0.04.

The SB is in charge of reinitializing the network periodically. This process is repeated to shuffle the slot assignments and to facilitate the incorporation of new nodes. As frames are synchronized with the UTC and begins with the minute, the period is a designer decision based on the conditions of the UWASN. For example, in networks deployed in places with strong currents is probable that nodes even if anchored to the bottom are moved. The reinitialization procedure facilitates also the redefinition of the nodes in charged of aggregating the information from lower SF nodes.

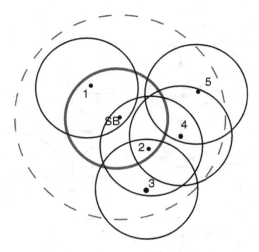

Fig. 3. Case 1: Deployment and transmission ranges

3.2   Data Transmission

Figure 4 shows the flowchart for the data transmission phase. In this phase, nodes transmit their data in the selected slot together with the distance to the SB and depth. As all nodes within range receive this information, they are able to keep an updated version of the network topology. As underwater transmission is prone to have data corruption, each message should be acknowledged after being received without corruption, by the synchronizing nodes in the previous sub-frames. If a message is not acknowledged, the sender retransmits it in the next frame. In the case a new message is generated, the information is aggregated or the old message is discarded, but this situation is flagged, so upstream nodes may notice the missing one. At the beginning of every frame, nodes wait for the synchronization message. If this message is not received with the acknowledgments of previous messages, the nodes in the sub-frame should assume that the synchronization node is out of work, and the backup synchronization node should be used if available. If there is not a backup, the node goes into the initialization phase.

   In the example presented in Fig. 3, the node 5 is the last node. Its messages have to go through nodes 4 and 2 to reach the SB. In this case, node 4 has to aggregate the information of node 5 in its own message and in the same way node 2 aggregates the information from nodes 4 and 5 in its own message. Figure 5 presents a case where more nodes are incorporated. In this case, the path from 6 to the SB is through node 1. However, as can be seen, the node 7 listens to nodes 5 and 6. Node 5 is in the third sub-frame (SF), but node 6 is in the second one. The aggregation process is made only by nodes in the previous SF. When there is more than one node in the previous SF that listens to the messages from lower SF nodes, only one node aggregates and forwards the information to the next SF. The other nodes keep a copy of the information as backup, in case there is a failure in the transmission. Even if the path with the shortest delay is

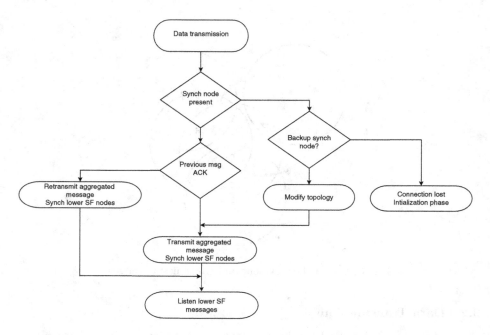

Fig. 4. Data transmission flowchart

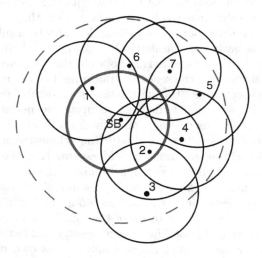

Fig. 5. Case 2: Deployment and transmission ranges

preferable, this scheme suppose the use of only one node as gateway to the next SF. The idea is that the first listened node in the SF is in charge of aggregating the information. As the slot allocation procedure is repeated in each periodic initialization phase, the nodes doing the aggregation are also changed.

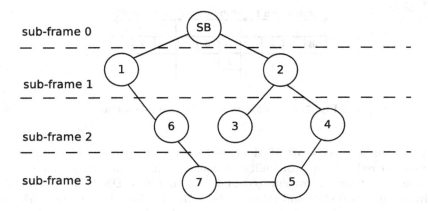

Fig. 6. Topology of the network in case 2

Figure 6 presents the topology of the UWASN represented in Fig. 5. The dotted lines represent the different sub-frames used in the transmission of messages. As can be seen, if node 6 disappears, the network will be reconfigured and node 7 will be in a new sub-frame behind node 5. In the same way, if node 4 is turned off, node 5 will send its messages through node 7.

3.3 Delay Management

The propagation speed of underwater acoustic signals is quite slow in relation to the amount of information that can be transferred through the air. In the case of encoding messages at 9600 bits/s, in the time required for the signal to cover 1.5 km (it is one second), the transmitter should send 1200 bytes. Usually, messages are much shorter, so they will require only a few milliseconds. This fact introduces an important synchronization problem between sources and destinations if acknowledgments are required for each message. The UWSO-TDMA solves this problem using slot identification and time stamps in every message. In this way, even if the round trip of a message requires an important delay, it can be handled.

4   Evaluation Process

In this section we evaluate the performance of the MAC proposal using the example introduced in the previous section. We compare the general behavior of our proposal with the one of the MACA-U protocol [10]. For this evaluation process we assume that each node has an acoustic range equal to 500 meters, the carrier frequency is set to 40 Khz [11] and the transmission data rate to 9600 bits/s. Each slot takes 167 ms for 160 bytes. Figure 7 shows the frame structure after the initialization phase for the network topology represented in Fig. 6.

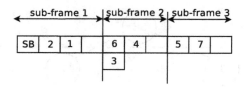

Fig. 7. Slot allocation in the example frame

As can be seen there are 10 slots used with 3 empty ones. The empty slots are used to reduce the probability of collisions in the selection slot process. The complete frame is transmitted in 1.67 s. In ASO-TDMA and SO-TDMA, the frame has 2650 slots and takes a whole minute. Nodes in the network have access to a GPS or UTC time, so they can synchronize their clocks and capture the beginning of the frames in the first instant of every minute. In the case of UWASN, only the sonobuoy has access to the UTC. Frames usually have less slots due the number of nodes are known.

Frames can start with different periodicity, for example every 10 s. In this case, the power demand (i.e., energy consumption) of the communication system in the node will be less than 20 %. After the initialization phase, a message from the farthest node (in our case, node 7), requires three frames to reach the SB or 30 s. The ACK message is issued in three steps. First, node 6 acknowledges the reception of the message to node 7 and in the next frame, then node 1 acknowledges node 6 in the following frame, and finally the SB acknowledges the reception of the message from node 1. In steady state it is possible to send a message every 10 s, receiving the acknowledgment in the following 10 s, and the general utilization ratio of the network is below 20 %.

In case of MACA-U protocol, the nodes can transmit whenever they have information available and they can lock the access to the acoustic channel, by issuing a RTS-CTS message with the next hop in the network. In this case, a timer is set with both, the time needed to send the message and the maximum delay for the message to reach the next node. Considering that the underwater acoustic signal propagates at 1.5 km/s, the time needed to reach the farthest possible node is equal to 0.333 s; therefore, the maximum round trip τ_{max} is equal to 0.667 s. The same time slot is kept for comparison purposes 0.167 s. In case node 7 has a message to send, it will send an RTS message and wait for $\tau_{max} + t_{slot} = 0.834$ s. If in this time this node receives a CTS message, then it gains access and transmits its message. So, the total time needed by node 7 to send its message to the *sonobuoy* is 3 s without collisions. However, node 7 may be delayed by collisions with nodes 5 and 6. In this case, and assuming only one collision with each one, the message from node 7 will only be transmitted to node 6 after 3 s. Node 6 can be delayed by collisions with node 1 and 7. Therefore, considering again only one collision with each one, the message needs another 3 s to reach node 1. In the last hop, node 1 may have collisions with nodes 6, 2 and the sonobuoy, and like in the previous cases, the message will be delayed for another 4 s. The end-to-end transmission time for a message originating in node 7 is the sum of the partial delays, i.e., 10 s.

This simple example shows that the complexity of a collision avoidance algorithm for transmission of information in networks with important delays may compromise its performance severely. Another important aspect is that the delay is not deterministic, showing great variations according to the network load. Instead, once the slot selection process is done, the TDMA approach guarantees a constant latency and transmission delay, making the message propagation predictable.

5   Conclusions and Future Work

In this paper we have proposed the UWSO-TDMA MAC protocol for underwater acoustic sensor networks. The mechanism is based on a TDMA protocol, but without including a master node or a fixed schedule for the nodes. In fact, each node selects the slot in which it will transmit in a distributed way. Time synchronization is kept through a sonobuoy that picks up the time from GPS or Galileo system. Nodes that are not within the sonobuoy transmission range, synchronize their clocks through retransmitting nodes. As the protocol is based on TDMA, transmission delay and latency are bounded, and the network can be used for transmitting messages with real-time constraints.

Although this proposal is still being evaluated, the preliminary results are encouraging. Addressing the data transmission in UWASN opens new opportunities for studying several environments that have been difficult to address for researchers. As part of the future work we intend to evaluate the performance of the proposed protocol in a real-world scenario: throughput, latency, delay against other protocols like MACA or MACAW. Depending on the obtained results we will determine specific opportunities and restrictions to use this proposal.

Acknowledgments. This work was partially supported by the European Community through the project Community Networks Testbed for the Future Internet (CONFINE): FP7-288535, and also by Spanish government under contract TIN2013-47245-C2-1-R.

References

1. UNESCO: Facts and figures on marine biodiversity
2. Xu, G., Shen, W., Wang, X.: Applications of wireless sensor networks in marine environment monitoring: a survey. Sensors **14**(9), 16932–16954 (2014)
3. ITU: M.1371: Technical characteristics for an automatic identification system using time-division multiple access in the VHF maritime mobile band
4. Yun, C., Lim, Y.K.: ASO-TDMA: ad-hoc self-organizing tdma protocol for shipborne ad-hoc networks. EURASIP J. Wirel. Commun. Netw. **2012**(1) (2012)
5. Karn, P.: MACA - a new channel access method for packet radio. In: Proceedings of the 9th Computer Networking Conference ARRL/CRRL Amateur Radio, pp. 134–140, September 1990

6. Rice, J., Creber, B., Fletcher, C., Baxley, P., Rogers, K., McDonald, K., Rees, D., Wolf, M., Merriam, S., Mehio, R., Proakis, J., Scussel, K., Porta, D., Baker, J., Hardiman, J., Green, D.: Evolution of seaweb underwater acoustic networking. In: OCEANS 2000 MTS/IEEE Conference and Exhibition, vol. 3. (2000), vol. 3, 2007–2017
7. Bharghavan, V., Demers, A., Shenker, S., Zhang, L.: Macaw: a media access protocol for wireless LAN's. SIGCOMM Comput. Commun. Rev. **24**(4), 212–225 (1994)
8. Fullmer, C.L., Garcia-Luna-Aceves, J.J.: Floor acquisition multiple access (FAMA) for packet-radio networks. SIGCOMM Comput. Commun. Rev. **25**(4), 262–273 (1995)
9. Pompili, D., Melodia, T., Akyildiz, I.: A CDMA-based medium access control for underwater acoustic sensor networks. IEEE Trans. Wirel. Commun. **8**(4), 1899–1909 (2009)
10. Ng, H.H., Soh, W.S., Motani, M.: MAca-u: a media access protocol for underwater acoustic networks. In: Global Telecommunications Conference, 2008, IEEE GLOBECOM 2008, pp. 1–5. IEEE, November 2008
11. EvoLogic: S2C M modem series

Monitoring and Control of Atmospheric and Substrate Parameters for Vegetable Crops

Germán-Aurelio Seguí-Miralles[✉], Alejandro Rico-Beviá,
Juan-Manuel García-Chamizo, and Francisco-Javier Ferrández-Pastor

Department of Computing Technology, University of Alicante,
P.O. Box 90, 03080 Alicante, Spain
germansegui@gmail.com

Abstract. This paper presents an ubiquitous system to control the atmosphere and substrate based on precision agriculture paradigm. The design we proposed consists of an embedded system, which integrates a reconfigurable FPGA module, a computational CPU module, and a power manager module. The embedded system is able to do environmental monitoring and control, and to manage the power supply of the FPGA and CPU modules, in order to decide which module supplies if the energy is not enough for both. We have assembled a first prototype in the laboratory, based on two independent and interconnected modules, in order to validate the processes modularly and also acquire all the necessary information to establish properly the requirements of the final design. After its implementation and experimentation, we have obtained satisfactory results.

Keywords: Precision agriculture · Hydroponic crop · Ubiquitous computing · Embedded system · Environmental monitoring and control

1 Introduction

Agriculture is an intrinsic human need, and has been evolved with him over time. This evolution gives us what currently is known as Precision Agriculture (PA), which is defined as a discipline that adapts common farming techniques to the specific conditions of each point of the crop, by applying different technologies (Micro-electro-mechanical Systems (MEMS), Wireless Sensor Networks (WSN), computer systems and enhanced machinery) and in order to obtain the greatest optimization and profitability [9].

These technologies can be implemented, among others, in indoor, outdoor and hydroponics crops; and its management is mainly divided into three stages [16]. The first one is called determination stage, wherein the crop type is identified and areas thereof are clustered based on their homogeneity. In this phase, sensors are the devices that analyse the characteristics of each area. The collected data is processed in the second analysis stage by computer systems, which establish procedures to apply in each area. Finally, the execution stage will be carried out by the advanced machinery.

© Springer International Publishing Switzerland 2015
J.M. García-Chamizo et al. (Eds.): UCAmI 2015, LNCS 9454, pp. 407–412, 2015.
DOI: 10.1007/978-3-319-26401-1_38

The right application of this method guarantees satisfactory results [15]. In the past few years, new trends have emerged in the agricultural sector. Thanks to developments in the field of WSN as well as miniaturization of the sensor boards, PA has started to emerge [3,5,17]. But even thought there has been considerable progresses in different technological areas, few of them are focused on the design and implementation of specialized low-cost systems for agricultural environments [12].

This paper makes an approach to this need and therefore it proposes a possible solution based on an heterogeneous [6] and scalable model able to acquire, process, store and monitor data from an hydroponic crop. This prototype is specialized in croplands automation maintenance, which will aim to control the conditions that determine the proper development of a crop, such as substrate and atmospheric temperature, luminance, atmospheric humidity, water pH level and EC [8]; and the actuators management which influence these factors, so that they will be able to recreate the optimal conditions for the crop development.

2   State of the Art

Sensors have traditionally been essential elements in industrial processes due to their ability to monitor and manipulate the physical parameters involved in the different production processes. Connectivity between them was done using traditional wired networks.

Currently continuous technological advances have spurred the development of devices with wireless communication capabilities, arranged at any location, getting smaller and smaller, autonomous, more powerful and with a more efficient battery consumption [4]; and which communicate the collected data to a centralized processing station. This is important since many network applications require hundreds or even thousand of sensor nodes, often deployed in remote and inaccessible areas. Therefore, a wireless sensor has not only a sensing component, but also on-board processing, communication, and storage capabilities. With these enhancements, a sensor node is often not only responsible for data collection but also for in-network analysis correlation, and fusion its own sensor data from other sensor nodes. When many sensors monitor large physical environments cooperatively, they form a WSN [10]. Sensor nodes communicate not only with each other but also with a base station, allowing them to disseminate their sensor data to remote processing, visualization, analysis and storage systems [7].

There are some applications based on the Internet of Things (IoT) paradigm that may be available on our smart phones and help in agricultural areas to control crops using a WSN. One of the most promising market segments in the future, is precisely the use of identifiable wireless devices in applications related to nature and environmental preservation [18].

The development of WSN applications in PA makes possible to increase efficiencies, productivity and profitability in many agricultural production systems, while it minimizes unintended impacts on wildlife and the environment.

The real time information obtained from the fields can provide a solid base for farmers to adjust strategies at any time. Instead of making decisions based in some hypothetical average conditions, which may not exist actually anywhere, a precision farming approach recognizes differences and adjusts management actions accordingly [11].

The combination of Wireless Smart Sensors (WSS), which are cheaper to implement than wired networks [2], with intelligent embedded systems and applying on this combination the technology of ubiquitous systems, [14] leads to the development of the design and implementation of low cost systems for monitoring and control agricultural environments, which due to its low cost, are optimized for implement in developing countries and areas which are difficult to access.

3   System Characterization and Embedded Control Architecture

The hydroponic monitoring and control system proposed in this paper collects environmental information such as luminance, atmospheric and substrate temperature, atmospheric humidity, EC and pH level which affect growth of crops through the WSN atmospheric and substrate sensors installed. The collected data is sent into a database, which stores suitable information that will be displayed on a web page.

System's structure integrates sensors, a database and a web server to collect environmental information, and to provide monitoring and various application services based on this information. It has 3 modules, the first one is a Field Programmable Gate Array (FPGA) [13], which is reconfigurable, due to rules can vary and reconfigure because of energetic supply and integrates control software. The second module is a CPU that will do processing, communication and storage functions and integrates the corresponding software in an embedded architecture with a processor, memory and communication interfaces (USB, Ethernet, Wifi, Blue-tooth) and the third module, a power manager that manage power supply of the previous modules, so that, the power manager will supply both modules when there is enough energy (i.e. during daylight hours) and will only supply FPGA module if is not possible to supply both of them.

As shown in Fig. 1, the prototype is composed of a physical layer, which consists of WSN sensors and solar cells to collect information of the environment, a middle layer, which supports communications between the physical layer and the application layer and sends the collected data from the physical layer to a database to provide data requested from the application layer, and an application layer, which is equipped with interfaces to support various services for the end user. The WSN sensors collect environmental information and this is sent regularly to the database. The web server fetches environmental data stored in the database to send it to a Graphical User Interface (GUI) at regular intervals, and users can monitor crop environment information via the GUI anywhere and at any time. In addition, in the GUI the user can view a chart with the average statistics of the atmospheric and substrate data (Fig. 2). Crop production could be increased by better understanding of the environmental properties of plantations and selecting crops suitable to the environment.

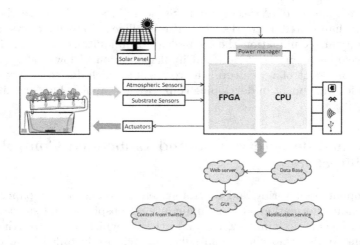

Fig. 1. Hydroponic monitoring, control and embedded system architectures

There is also a notification service in order to prevent adverse environmental conditions by notifying users in real time about changes in the environment and taking some measures against it, for example, activating the necessary actuators via the web page or user's Twitter account. These notifications are sent via Twitter, Email and an integrated voice alarm system. To enable or disable an actuator via Twitter, it is only needed to introduce the tweet: Actuator + ON/OFF. (e.g. Grow light ON).

4   Experimental Prototype

In order to validate the design described in the previous section, and capture the system energy needs, we have developed a low-cost prototype (Fig. 3) in DAI Lab laboratory [1] at the University of Alicante.

The prototype consists of an Arduino board, wherein control and actuators rules are validated, connected to a Raspberry Pi device, wherein the data processing, storage and communication are ratified, as well as web services and energy management. Both devices are powered from the electricity supply network and a solar panel, to evaluate the energy needs.

We have divided this first stage of the design in order to validate the processes modularly. From the results of this validation, will be established the requirements for the implementation of the embedded system described in this project (Fig. 1).

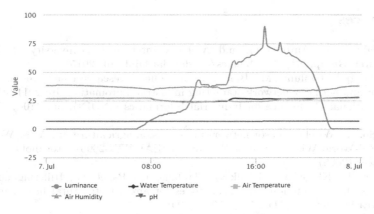

Fig. 2. Average statistics of the atmospheric and substrate data in one day (Color figure online)

Fig. 3. Developed prototype and crop growth

5   Conclusions

We have designed a specific system which accomplish the mentioned needs. Therefore we have developed a prototype which we realized several tests on, which have been found to be satisfactory.

As a consequence, it is justified to assess in detail how the system works. Therefore, the approach of this work continues, making the implementation in one embedded system (FPGA + CPU), instead of two independent modules, so that it can make a direct comparison between the first and second phase.

References

1. Dai-lab: Home Automation and Ambient Intelligence. University of Alicante Research Group. http://web.ua.es/en/dai/dai-lab.html (2015)
2. Åkerberg, J., Gidlund, M., Björkman, M.: Future research challenges in wireless sensor and actuator networks targeting industrial automation. In: 2011 9th IEEE International Conference on Industrial Informatics (INDIN), pp. 410–415. IEEE (2011)
3. Baggio, A.: Wireless sensor networks in precision agriculture. In: ACM Workshop on Real-World Wireless Sensor Networks (REALWSN 2005), Stockholm, Sweden. Citeseer (2005)
4. Becker, T., Kluge, M., Schalk, J., Tiplady, K., Paget, C., Hilleringmann, U., Otterpohl, T.: Autonomous sensor nodes for aircraft structural health monitoring. IEEE Sens. J. 9(11), 1589–1595 (2009)
5. Burrell, J., Brooke, T., Beckwith, R.: Vineyard computing: sensor networks in agricultural production. IEEE Pervasive Comput. 3(1), 38–45 (2004)
6. Chu, M., Haussecker, H., Zhao, F.: Scalable information-driven sensor querying and routing for ad hoc heterogeneous sensor networks. Int. J. High Perform. Comput. Appl. 16(3), 293–313 (2002)
7. Dargie, W.W., Poellabauer, C.: Fundamentals of Wireless Sensor Networks: Theory and Practice. Wiley, New York (2010)
8. El-Deeba, M.M., El-Awady, M.N., Hegazi, M.M., Abdel-Azeem, F.A., El-Bourdiny, M.M.: Engineering factors affecting hydroponics grass-fodder production. In: The 16th Annual Conference of the Misr Society of Ag. Eng., Agric. Eng. And Variables of the Present Epoch., vol. 25, pp. 1647–1666 (2009)
9. Gebbers, R., Adamchuk, V.I.: Precision agriculture and food security. Science 327(5967), 828–831 (2010)
10. Hu, J., Shen, L., Yang, Y., Lv, R.: Design and implementation of wireless sensor and actor network for precision agriculture. In: 2010 IEEE International Conference on Wireless Communications, Networking and Information Security (WCNIS), pp. 571–575. IEEE (2010)
11. Hwang, J., Shin, C., Yoe, H.: Study on an agricultural environment monitoring server system using wireless sensor networks. Sensors 10(12), 11189–11211 (2010)
12. McBratney, A., Whelan, B., Ancev, T., Bouma, J.: Future directions of precision agriculture. Precis. Agric. 6(1), 7–23 (2005)
13. Monmasson, E., Idkhajine, L., Naouar, M.W.: Fpga-based controllers. IEEE Ind. Electron. Mag. 5(1), 14–26 (2011)
14. Mostefaoui, S.K.: Advances in Ubiquitous Computing: Future Paradigms and Directions. IGI Global, Hershey (2008)
15. Mulla, D.J.: Twenty five years of remote sensing in precision agriculture: key advances and remaining knowledge gaps. Biosyst. Eng. 114(4), 358–371 (2013)
16. Zhang, N., Wang, M., Wang, N.: Precision agriculture - a worldwide overview. Comput. Electron. Agric. 36(2), 113–132 (2002)
17. Zhang, W., Kantor, G., Singh, S.: Demo abstract: integrated wireless sensor/actuator networks in an agricultural application. In: ACM SenSys. vol. 4 (2004)
18. Zhao, J.C., Zhang, J.F., Feng, Y., Guo, J.X.: The study and application of the iot technology in agriculture. In: 2010 3rd IEEE International Conference on Computer Science and Information Technology (ICCSIT), vol. 2, pp. 462–465. IEEE (2010)

An Integrated Framework for Enabling End-User Configuration of AmI Simulations for Open Wide Locations

Ramón Alcarria[1(✉)], Emilio Serrano[1], Jorge Gómez Sanz[2], and Alberto Fernández[3]

[1] Universidad Politécnica de Madrid, Madrid, Spain
ramon.alcarria@upm.es, emilioserra@fi.upm.es
[2] Universidad Complutense de Madrid, Madrid, Spain
jjgomez@ucm.es
[3] Universidad Rey Juan Carlos, Madrid, Spain
alberto.fernandez@urjc.es

Abstract. The deployment of AmI technologies in large facilities sets new challenges due to the difficulty to perform experiments in physical large settings, with high number of users. We propose a framework for such domain using simulations that combine social simulation techniques, specialized in assessing large population behaviors, along with experience in AmI systems simulations, specialized in considering sensor and actuator networks embedded in a physical environment. The framework will allow the configuration of simulation features and options according to user and device models defined by domain experts, as well as the interaction between the proposed simulator and a context generated by external sources (other simulators or AmI infrastructures). This paper also proposes the first steps towards an implementation of this architecture through contributions on known simulators.

Keywords: End-user configuration · Ambient intelligence · Simulation · Open wide locations

1 Introduction

Ambient Intelligence (AmI) environments [1] are ubiquitous computing environments where the interaction with the users is done in a transparent way in order to offer them proactive, adaptive and personalized services.

The design of these environments requires appropriate development tools to ensure inexpensive and repeatable experimentation. Experiments are performed mainly in facilities reproducing the physical environment where the AmI is to be deployed. The physical environment has participants that carry on their activities of daily living (ADL) assisted by, or monitored by, the AmI. The larger the physical environment is, the more complex, and expensive, is the experimentation. For instance, an essay in the Terminal 4 in Barajas Airport required 2000 actors [2].

Traditionally, AmI models users' behavior through their ADL. However, when larger groups of people are involved new collective behaviors arise. That is the case, for

© Springer International Publishing Switzerland 2015
J.M. García-Chamizo et al. (Eds.): UCAmI 2015, LNCS 9454, pp. 413–424, 2015.
DOI: 10.1007/978-3-319-26401-1_39

example, of panic during an evacuation [3] or the temptation to look at a point when enough people are looking at the same place [4]. Works on social simulation and mass psychology could be crucial to foresee expected behaviors of those large groups.

There is a need of convergence among (i) agent-based social simulation (ABSS), for modeling realistic human societies considering individuality and collective behavior, (ii) physical devices modeling, in which smart spaces support their world-view (sensors) and their action capacity (actuators) (currently, there are no reliable simulated models of these devices), and (iii) agreement technologies (AT), which enable intelligent behavior to improve the users' quality of life (managing resources, collaborating to reach shared goals, negotiating to resolve conflicts, handling properly conflicting information from different sources, etc.) and whose interaction with simulated entities has not been explored in the literature.

This paper presents a technological proposal for the combination of Social and AmI Simulation considering computer experimentation and its transference to the real environment. Section 2 reviews related work in AmI environments and end-user configuration of simulations. Section 3 explains how AmI simulations are performed. Section 4 describes the proposed architecture of our integrated framework and finally, Sects. 5 and 6 provide the first steps towards an implementation of this architecture and some conclusions.

2   Related Work

This section describes related work in AmI environments, taking into account their modeling and simulation and also the state of the art in the provision of tools for end-user configuration of simulation environments.

2.1   AmI Environments Modeling and Simulation

Deployment of large-scale AmI is a time-consuming and costly process. The logistical challenge of experimenting with thousands of small battery-powered nodes is the key factor that has greatly limited the development of this field. Simulation testbeds have been used in AmI and Internet of Things (IoT) literature to conduct, among others but specially, scalability research for AmI devices networks. Some of these simulation approaches are: WISEBED [5], w-iLab [6], Senslab [7], KanseiGeni [8], and TWIST [9].

To emulate and react to events produced by sensors, some simulators in the scope of AmI require human intervention to play the role of the user: Ubiwise [10], TATUS [11], UbiREAL [12], and OpenSim [13]. In this sense, the DAI Virtual Lab [14] is complemented with a living lab which allows researchers to continue their work in a physical environment. Furthermore, unlike the IoT simulators revised, these frameworks cope with the modeling of realistic environments and not only the wireless sensor networks. On the other hand, requiring human beings to emulate sensors events make impossible an automatic and rigorous testing and does not cope with the human cost of AmI experiments.

The social simulation in this scope can assist in the development of IoT systems by simulating artificial societies of users immersed into the intelligent environment and generating sensors events [15]. Although social simulation has been used for testing a number of closed systems, mainly in the emergency management scope, the general use of this technology for providing general AmI systems with automatic testing is still a novel field with few contributions such as UbikSim [16] and Phat [17] simulators.

Agreement Technologies (AT) [18] are especially interesting in AmI systems where agents compete for scarce resources (exits, lifts, escalators, parking places, parking payment machines, advertisement panels, security controls, etc.).

Related to AT for social simulation many works focus on autonomy, interaction, mobility and openness as key concepts of AT. AmI environments also contain those characteristics: high number of autonomous people, who enter, move around and leave a large installation, interacting with each other and with the environment (which consists of many devices with communication capabilities). *Semantic alignment* [19], *negotiation* [20], *argumentation, virtual organizations* [21], *trust and reputation* mechanisms [22] and other technologies are part of the ingredients for defining, specifying and verifying such systems.

2.2   End-User Configuration of Simulation Environments

Agent modeling [23] considers that, for each agent, its state, the resources it consumes and its behavior must be defined. There are a variety of approaches to design and implement agent-based models. North and Macal [24] discuss both design method-ologies and implementation environments in depth. Marsh and Hill [25] offer an initial methodology for defining agent behaviors in an application for unmanned autonomous vehicles.

Using configuration techniques for agent modeling was studied from the per-spective of individual-based modeling (IBM), on the basis that tools to facilitate cre-ation of populations are either too general, requiring the extensive knowledge of a computer language, or conversely restricted to very specific applications [26]. The authors of this study propose component programming for building executable user-defined tasks and for managing agent synchronization, results saving and the carrying out of simulation experiments. Other techniques such as spreadsheets (e.g. Microsoft Excel) offer the simplest approach to modeling. It is easier to develop models with spreadsheets than with many of the other tools, but the resulting models generally allow limited agent diversity, restrict agent behaviors, and have poor scalability compared to other approaches. Regarding composition techniques, different from spreadsheet applications, some authors [27] intend to build simulation and debugging tools allowing end-users to create, test the compositions and search for the causes of eventual errors. Nowadays, a service oriented approach [23] is followed to provide a way for modelers to identify which set of resources (e.g. files) constitute each model:

- These services can be in the form of a library offering an Application Programming Interface (API). Modelers create behavior models and constraints by making calls to the API functions allowing great flexibility in their models, such as in Repast [28], MASON [29] and Swarn [30].

- Services can also be provided in the form of IDE. This approach considers model construction as a model repository including a set of files defining one model in each file. This is the approach of NetLogo [31].

The inclusion of user-friendly interfaces to non-expert users in order to launch simulations is proposed for social simulator MASSIS [32], which incorporates a Drag & Drop AI design to specify the behavior of the agents that will take part in the simulation.

3   Simulation Process and Requirements

AmI simulations are often performed to check if a control system (a device or set of devices that manages and regulates the behavior of other systems in the AmI environment) correctly takes into account the context in which this control system will be executed. A simulation is performed and redefined multiple times to retrieve knowledge about users and devices in open wide locations. The process is described below:

1. Stakeholders meet to determine the specific problem to solve, capturing this information by field studies and/or other requirement acquisition techniques.
2. Analyzed information can be used to model what kinds of experiments are desirable for the particular problem and the type of situations considered. At this level social simulations would include hundreds or thousands of individuals.
3. With the social simulations, the work would focus on the control system and its communications. In both cases, new experiments might be needed.
   (a) The actions proposed by the control system would be applied on the simulation so as to affect the simulated actors and to product the expected effect. The system would be adjusted to deal with the different situations that might occur: necessity of repeating stimulus (without saturating the audience), unexpected problems with devices, etc.
   (b) Besides, communications among devices would be tested, assessing effectiveness and cost. Possible problems like bandwidth, transmission quality, etc. must be also validated by the control system.
4. The experiments are analyzed according to the dependent and independent domain knowledge. Moreover, the experiments would document the identification of new needs. When the experiments are successful, an exhaustive documentation is thus available about how the system is wanted to behave. The work carried out can be used to track the behavior in the real installation.
5. Regarding the deployment process of the control system in the real AmI environment we assume that the system tested against simulations would be the same to be installed in the AmI environment. Using a software-in-the-loop approach, we would ensure that the conditions of the control system in the simulation is the same or sufficiently similar to reality.
6. Once deployed, information collected during experiments can be used to determine whether current observation in the real AmI environment corresponds to a simulated scenario or whether it is necessary to launch a simulation with the current context in the real world so as to determine deviations with regards to experimentation and/or predict possible evolutions from the current situation.

This simulation process produces some requirements for the design and implementation of our framework.

Related to the characteristics of the environment to simulate we need to consider *both user's behavior and AmI device capabilities*. For example, movement in devices can be dictated by movement of people carrying those devices. Also, in a social simulation it is useful to know if persons that walk through a corridor should have enough WiFi coverage, or would detect a Bluetooth beacon that is broadcasting a signal in one of the surrounding rooms.

Some tools must be needed to *create experiments from previous ones*, by modifying functionalities or stimulus affecting simulated actors to produce expected effect. Experiment creation should be done by domain experts, who have the required experience to identify human and device behavior in knowledge bases but they also have little experience in software engineering. Thus, it is needed to *provide configuration and personalization tools easy to use* for domain experts and adequate to their skills.

Tools for *analyzing the results of the simulation* are extremely important to deal with the amount of data that is produced by the simulation. They should be able to process and facilitate the analysis by the experts. Moreover, once the control system is operating after deployment, those tools should also be used for analyzing and comparing current data against simulations so as to identify deviations and foresee future situations. For doing that, *performance data* must be generated by the simulator.

4 Architecture

In this work we propose an integrated framework for enabling end-user configuration of AmI simulations. The architecture is defined from two perspectives. The model perspective and the functional perspective. Both perspectives distinguish between reusable and non-reusable elements. Reusable elements are identified as commonalities that will constitute the reusable parts both in the information models and in the components. The non-reusable parts will, however, share some structure that allows telling in advance, for a different problem, which parts need to be known. Using this to our advantage, we will produce the elements that permit the developers to optimize the software and knowledge reuse across different domains.

The model perspective shows that the architecture is made of a number of models capturing essential aspects of the AmI system. Those models will be part visual specifications created with Domain Specific Languages and part raw data to feed simulations. The simulations will correspond to specific experiments where stakeholders, not only developers, evaluate the expected user behavior, the communications, or the AmI control system. If the experiments are satisfactory, the devised control system can be deployed to the target AmI hardware embedded in the real scenario. The data obtained from the different experiments is useful too and can be used to compare against the real performance to identify deviations.

Model and specifications contained in the model perspective of the architecture are presented in Fig. 1 and are described below:

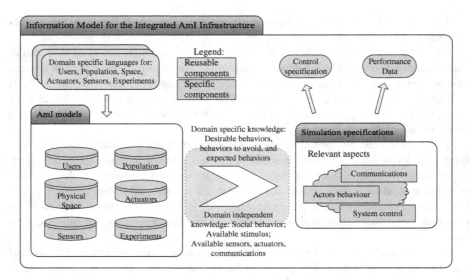

Fig. 1. Architecture showing the produced/processed information models

- **Domain Specific Languages (DSL).** They capture the knowledge to specify particular aspects of the AmI development. These DSLs will be described as meta-models, enabling the use of model-driven development for transformation of AmI models to simulation specifications, or production of executable code, which could be useful to refine the development of the control system.
- **AmI Models.** They gather relevant information about the operation parameters of the AmI to be developed. These models are created using raw data and domain specific languages. Considered models are *users*, *population* (describe individual and collective human behavior), *physical space*, *actuators*, *sensors* (describe the physical characteristics of the AmI environment) and, finally, the *experiments* model (describing what kind of scenarios are relevant to be studied and what results should be expected from them).
- **Simulation specifications.** The different AmI models will be transformed into simulations taking into account the available domain specific and domain independent knowledge. Domain independent knowledge will be taken from the scientific literature about human behavior, in particular, mass psychology. Domain specific knowledge will be derived from interviews with experts in the different experimentation domains as described in the simulation process of Sect. 3. There will be different specifications of simulations depending on the aspects to be addressed. It is foreseen to take into account: the population behavior, the communications, and the control system. Simulations addressing one or more of these aspects will be produced and evaluated by the developers. The required simulations will be described by the experiments model and will incorporate specific information, such as building blueprints or device limitations.

- **Control specification.** It is the specification of the control system satisfying the communication requirements of the AmI. It is also consistent with the different experiments defined so far.
- **Performance Data.** Information resulting as an input from the simulation that describes the performance of the AmI solution in the simulation environment. This data is compared against real data to identify deviations from the real world.

All of these models and specifications have to be produced or used by some functional elements which are described in the functional perspective of the architecture (Fig. 2). Functional components of the proposed architecture are described below.

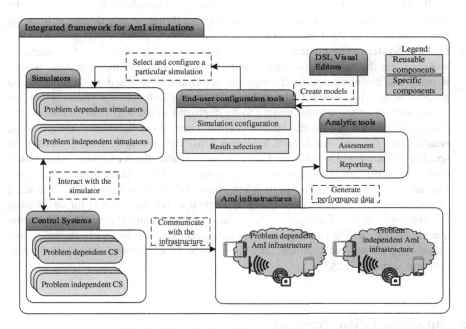

Fig. 2. Functional architecture of the system

- **DSL Visual Editors.** These editors are reusable across domains and permit the developer or any other stakeholder to describe specific aspects of the problem. These visual editors would be generated by using some end-user configuration tools. They are created from **Domain Specific Languages** specifications and produce **AmI models.**
- **End-user configuration tools.** They are particular applications to choose and select different models (users, populations, spaces, actuators, sensors), combine them, and prepare the different experiments that are going to be applied. Experts would facilitate end-users the task of creating those experiments by reusing existing information and allowing them to decide which information should be extracted from the simulation, for its later analysis. The result of applying these tools would be **simulation specifications.**

- **Simulators.** They are produced using as input **simulation specifications**. A collection of simulators can be produced from the different selection of AmI models made by the end-user configuration tool. Assuming there exist a collection of simulators that can be parameterized for the current problem, some code generation techniques from model-driven development allow us to produce the problem specific components the reusable simulation framework requires. This would allow reusing existing frameworks, such as UbikSim [16], PHAT [17] or MASSIS [32].
- **Analytic tools.** Produced performance data, either from the real world or from a simulation, is expected to be inherently vast and complex. Properly analyzing this information and infer correctness of the simulation or the real AmI performance is a challenging task. When the simulation is executed, the developer has to decide if the simulation runs according to the expectations, and if there is any deviation from the execution in a real AmI environment.
- **Control System.** The control system is a device or a set of devices that manages and regulates the behavior of other systems in the AmI environment. In other words, it perceives the environment through the information obtained from sensors and propose actions by using actuators. Typically, the final objective of the simulation is to test and refine the control system to be deployed in the real AmI infrastructure. Hence, the control system can be connected to either a simulation (which acts as an emulation of the real world) or to the target AmI. The control system, in addition to specific domain knowledge, uses *User*, *Population* and *Physical Space* AmI models during its reasoning process to make decisions and also to learn from simulations. This allows the systems to adapt to different user behaviors not modeled beforehand or not very precise. We propose using agreement technologies (AT) for developing this control system. AT allow services to have an intelligent behavior to improve the users' quality of life (managing resources, collaborating to reach shared goals, negotiating to resolve conflicts, handling properly conflicting information from different sources, etc.).

5 Implementation Proposal

This section describes the first initial prototypes in the implementation of the provided architecture. The UbikSim simulator has been employed to implement the users, population and physical space AmI models and also a problem dependent control system: control system for building evacuations in emergency situations.

In this implementation, the physical space is a three-dimensional model of a floor at the CeDInt-UPM [33], a Research Centre on Domotics and AmI. Population is simulated with two hundred users with an emergency in a random position, see Fig. 3. The simulated users employ the A* search algorithm to find the shortest path to the closest exit. The implemented emergency control system attempts to offer optimal escape routes considering aspects such as the simulated user's and emergency positions, and the available exits. The simulator was connected to a real AmI environment, an indoor location system developed by the Group on Virtual Reality (CeDInt-UPM) via web service as shown in Fig. 4 and a video available online [34].

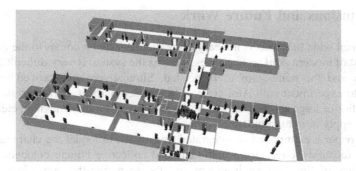

Fig. 3. Simulating an emergency by using UbikSim

Fig. 4. Emergency simulation execution   **Fig. 5.** UbikSim RESTful web service

The different components interact through a RESTful Web Service, see Fig. 5, and the implementation is free and open source code available online [35]. In this Figure it is possible to see one of the implemented end-user configuration tools, which allows end-users to include new participants in the simulation and to move their positions.

This work is in progress and still lacks sociological behaviors in the users' model, sensors, and actuators among others. However, even this simplistic implementation allows studying the effects of a number of what-if scenarios such as what happens if the fire is near an exit, or how to act if an exit is the closest to most of the rooms in the environment, or when the emergency plan produces crowds. Moreover, the UbikSim simulation environment the implementation relies on, allow researchers to easily model other physical and user AmI models.

6   Conclusions and Future Work

Building open wide locations is not easy, in particular when it comes to the design and deployment of modern AmI technologies. Testing the system is very difficult due to the complexity and the number of users needed. Simulations have proved to be very important to experiment with AmI systems before deployment. However, the inherent characteristics of large spaces (amount of devices, users, group behaviors, etc.) make it difficult to apply current simulation approaches.

In this paper we proposed an integrated framework to model the characteristics of open wide locations, considering individual and collective human behavior, physical characteristics of the AmI environment and the scenarios that are relevant for the experimentation.

Among all advantages of using simulation techniques, in this paper we focus in checking whether a control system correctly takes into account the context in which this control system will be executed. Based on the analysis of the simulation process we determine that it is needed to provide to domain experts some configuration and personalization tools in order to create and configure simulation experiments.

This requirement along with others such as the need to facilitate the deployment of the control system to the target AmI hardware embedded in the real scenario allows us to define an architecture proposal considering a model perspective and a functional perspective.

Finally, we present the initial prototypes towards the implementation of the architecture. We use the UbikSim simulator to develop the *users*, *population* and *physical space* AmI models, a control system for evacuations in emergency situations and some end-user configuration tools, which allows end-users to include new participants in the simulation and to move their positions.

In the future, we will continue the implementation of the architecture by defining the rest of the AmI models and some other problem dependent control systems. We plan to deploy these systems in three scenarios: A living lab for testing purposes, a faculty building to manage crowds of students for lectures and conferences and, finally, a monitoring and evacuation scenario in a well-known sports arena in Madrid.

Acknowledgements. This research work is supported by the Spanish Ministry of Economy and Competitiveness under the R&D projects CALISTA (TEC2012-32457), iHAS (grant TIN2012-36586C03-02), and ColosAAL (grant TIN2011-28335-C02-01); by the Spanish Ministry of Industry, Energy and Tourism under the R&D project BigMarket (TSI-100102-2013-80); and, by the Autonomous Region of Madrid through the program MOSI-AGIL-CM (grant S2013/ICE-3019), co-funded by EU Structural Funds FSE and FEDER.

References

1. Cook, D.J., Augusto, J.C., Jakkula, V.R.: Ambient intelligence: technologies, applications, and opportunities. Pervasive Mob. Comput. 5(4), 277–298 (2009)
2. Ruiz del Árbol, A.: Two thousand extras will test the new Barajas. Cinco Días, August 2005. (in Spanish)

3. Norwood, A.E.: Debunking the myth of panic. Psychiatry **68**(2), 114 (2005). (Interpersonal and Biological Processes)
4. Friesen, C.K., Kingstone, A.: The eyes have it!: reflexive orienting is triggered by nonpredictive gaze. Psychon. Bull. Rev. **5**, 490–495 (1998)
5. Chatzigiannakis, I., Fischer, S., Koninis, C., Mylonas, G., Pfisterer, D.: WISEBED: an open large-scale wireless sensor network testbed. In: Komninos, N. (ed.) SENSAPPEAL 2009. LNICST, vol. 29, pp. 68–87. Springer, Heidelberg (2010)
6. Bouckaert, S., Vandenberghe, W., Jooris, B., Moerman, I., Demeester, P.: The w-iLab.t testbed. In: Magedanz, T., Gavras, A., Thanh, N.H., Chase, J.S. (eds.) TridentCom 2010. LNICST, vol. 46, pp. 145–154. Springer, Heidelberg (2011)
7. Burin des Rosiers, C., Chelius, G., Fleury, E., Fraboulet, A., Gallais, A., Mitton, N., Noël, T.: SensLAB. In: Korakis, T., Li, H., Tran-Gia, P., Park, H.-S. (eds.) TridentCom 2011. LNICST, vol. 90, pp. 239–254. Springer, Heidelberg (2012)
8. Sridharan, M., Zeng, W., Leal, W., Ju, X., Ramnath R., Zhang, H., Arora, A.: Kanseigenie: software infrastructure for resource management and programmability of wireless sensor network fabrics. In: Next Generation Internet Architectures and Protocols. Cambridge University Press, Cambridge (2010)
9. Handziski, V., Köpke, A., Willig, A., Wolisz, A.: Twist: a scalable and reconfigurable testbed for wireless indoor experiments with sensor networks. In: REALMAN 2006 Proceedings of the 2nd International Workshop on Multi-hop Ad Hoc Networks: From Theory to Reality, pp. 63–70 (2006)
10. Barton, J., Vijayaraghavan, V.: Ubiwise: A Simulator for Ubiquitous Computing Systems Design. HP Labs, Palo Alto (2003)
11. O'Neill, E., Klepal, M., Lewis, D., O'Donnell, T., O'Sullivan, D., Pesch, D.: A testbed for evaluating human interaction with ubiquitous computing environments. In: Testbeds and Research Infrastructures for the Development of Networks and Communities, TRIDENTCOM 2005, Washington, DC, USA, pp. 60–69. IEEE Computer Society (2005)
12. Nishikawa, H., Yamamoto, S., Tamai, M., Nishigaki, K., Kitani, T., Shibata, N., Yasumoto, K., Ito, M.: UbiREAL: realistic smartspace simulator for systematic testing. In: Dourish, P., Friday, A. (eds.) UbiComp 2006. LNCS, vol. 4206, pp. 459–476. Springer, Heidelberg (2006)
13. Tang, L., Zhou, X., Becker, C., Yu, Z., Schiele, G.: Situation-based design: a rapid approach for pervasive application development. In: 9th International Conference on Ubiquitous Intelligence and Computing and 9th International Conference on Autonomic and Trusted Computing (UIC/ATC), pp. 128–135 (2012)
14. Nieto-Hidalgo, M., Ferrández-Pastor, F.J., García-Chamizo, J.M., Flórez-Revuelta, F.: DAI virtual lab: a virtual laboratory for testing ambient intelligence digital service. In: Proceedings of V Congreso Internacional de Diseño, Redes de Investigación y Tecnología para Todos, DRT4ALL, Madrid (2013)
15. Serrano, E., Botía, J.A.: Validating ambient intelligence based ubiquitous computing systems by means of artificial societies. Inf. Sci. **222**, 3–24 (2013)
16. UbikSim website. https://github.com/emilioserra/UbikSim/wiki
17. Campillo-Sanchez, P., Gómez-Sanz, J.J., Botía, J.A.: PHAT: physical human activity tester. In: Pan, J.-S., Polycarpou, M.M., Woźniak, M., de Carvalho, A.C.P.L.F., Quintián, H., Corchado, E. (eds.) HAIS 2013. LNCS, vol. 8073, pp. 41–50. Springer, Heidelberg (2013)
18. Ossowski, S. (ed.): Agreement Technologies. Law, Governance and Technology Series, vol. 8. Springer, Heidelberg (2013)
19. Euzenat, J., Shvaiko, P.: Ontology Matching. Springer, Heidelberg (2007)
20. Jennings, N.R., Faratin, P., Lomuscio, A.R., Parsons, S., Wooldridge, M.J., Sierra, C.: Automated negotiation: prospects, methods and challenges. Int. J. Group Decis. Negot. **10**(2), 199–215 (2001)

21. Ferber, J., Gutknecht, O., Michel, F.: From agents to organizations: an organizational view of multi-agent systems. In: Giorgini, P., Müller, J.P., Odell, J.J. (eds.) AOSE 2003. LNCS, vol. 2935, pp. 214–230. Springer, Heidelberg (2004)

22. Sierra, C., Debenham, J.: Trust and honour in information- based agency. In: Proceedings of the 5th International Conference on Autonomous Agents and Multi Agent Systems, pp. 1225–1232. ACM, New York (2006)

23. Macal, C.M., North, M.J.: Tutorial on agent-based modelling and simulation. J. Simul. **4**, 151–162 (2010)

24. North, M.J., Macal, C.M.: Managing Business Complexity: Discovering Strategic Solutions with Agent-Based Modeling and Simulation. Oxford University Press, Oxford (2007)

25. Marsh, W.E., Hill, R.R.: An initial agent behavior modeling and definition methodology as applied to unmanned aerial vehicle simulation. Int. J. of Simul. Process Model. **4**(2), 119–129 (2008)

26. Ginot, V., Le Page, C., Souissi, S.: A multi-agents architecture to enhance end-user individual-based modelling. Ecol. Model. **157**(1), 23–41 (2002)

27. Stav, E., Floch, J., Khan, M.U., Sætre, R.: Using meta-modelling for construction of an end-user development framework. In: Dittrich, Y., Burnett, M., Mørch, A., Redmiles, D. (eds.) IS-EUD 2013. LNCS, vol. 7897, pp. 72–87. Springer, Heidelberg (2013)

28. Repast Suite home page. http://repast.sourceforge.net/

29. GMU (George Mason University): MASON home page. http://cs.gmu.edu/~eclab/projects/mason/

30. SDG (Swarm Development Group): Swarm development group home page. http://savannah.nongnu.org/projects/swarm

31. NetLogo home page. http://ccl.northwestern.edu/netlogo/

32. Pax, R., Pavón, J.: Agent-based simulation of crowds in indoor scenarios. In: 9th International Symposium on Intelligent Distributed Computing (IDC 2015), Guimaraes, Portugal (2015)

33. CeDInt-UPM: Centro de Domótica integral – research centre for smart buildings and energy efficiency. http://www.cedint.upm.es/

34. GSI UPM: EscapeSim: ambient intelligence services with participatory simulations. https://www.youtube.com/watch?v=7ZHcpNjjO8c. Accessed February 2015

35. Serrano, E.: UbikSim web service. https://github.com/emilioserra/UbikSimWebService

Ambient Intelligence for Urban Areas

Architectural Figures for Urban Areas

Metaphorical Design of Virtual Museums and Laboratories: First Insights

Daniel Biella[1], Daniel Sacher[1], Benjamin Weyers[2],
Wolfram Luther[1(✉)], and Nelson Baloian[3]

[1] University of Duisburg, Essen, Germany
{daniel.biella,daniel.sacher,
wolfram.luther}@uni-due.de
[2] RWTH Aachen, Aachen, Germany
weyers@vr.rwth-aachen.de
[3] University of Chile, Santiago, Chile
nbaloian@dcc.uchile.cl

Abstract. This paper highlights and categorizes the rich metaphorical land-scape of the modern virtual museum and laboratory realizations recently applied in various leisure, information, presentation and education contexts. It also presents several technical resolutions, from desktop systems to CAVE installations.

Keywords: Metaphorical design · Virtual museum · User interface · Case studies

1 Introduction and Motivation

Digital heritage is an emerging research topic in the context of ambient intelligent space in urban areas. On the one hand, cultural heritage is one of major topics in research concerning urban history, where metaphors are present everywhere. On the other, virtual representations of cultural heritage not only form the content of interactive and collaborative virtual museums; they also often appear as applications of ambient intelligence in games and entertainment, especially if this type of content is embedded into real exhibitions.

Starting from existing exhibits or real world experimentation, research by Biella [1] concerns the modeling process of virtual museums and laboratories (VML) and focuses on the conception and creation of a virtual environment consisting of static and dynamic scene objects and acting characters in a navigable world. To build such a virtual world, developers and content specialists define tasks and goals using scientific theories, formal process models, and appropriate modeling languages and tools. They formulate requirements concerning conceptual design, the conceptual and perceptual model, and interfaces to support user interactions with the scene objects. A suitable metaphorical design has an important impact on the realization of such systems; metaphors concern localization, navigation, local or temporal neighborhood, interaction and organizational issues.

© Springer International Publishing Switzerland 2015
J.M. García-Chamizo et al. (Eds.): UCAmI 2015, LNCS 9454, pp. 427–438, 2015.
DOI: 10.1007/978-3-319-26401-1_40

This paper offers a short overview of the definition, types and uses of metaphors provided in earlier realizations. Lakoff and Johnsen [2] emphasize "that metaphor is pervasive in everyday life", that "most of our ordinary conceptual system is metaphorical in nature", and that "the essence of metaphor is understanding and experiencing one kind of thing in terms of another". Kuhn's and Blumenthal's tutorial notes [3] explain "that metaphors allow users to understand computational target domains in terms of familiar source domains", that "most common metaphors are spatial because space is central to perception and cognition", and that "metaphors provide a common ground for real and virtual activities". As stated in Biella [1], the metaphorical reference to physical places must also be completed by a reference to time scale. He concludes that spatial metaphors provide a basic understanding of objects in place and their relationship with one another and with their location, allowing the designer to define consistent actions with regard to the virtual objects and allowing users to move from one place to another and to interact intuitively with the objects. In addition to the spatial design elements, temporal metaphors provide meaningful representations of the domain "time scale" via geometric models such as lines, polygons or curves, and contextual metaphors create semantic frames and relationships in a virtual place linking the intended use and the behavior of the place with a consistent set of properties and actions.

The paper is structured as follows. Section 2 introduces related work and focuses on the impact of metaphorical design in various contexts. The discussion will show how these techniques can be embedded into the creation and visiting process of VMLs. Then we introduce a short classification and several new approaches for the use of metaphorical design in (non-)immersive VMLs (Sect. 3). In Sect. 4, an examination of several case studies demonstrates the feasibility of these concepts. Section 5 discusses our conclusions and presents future work.

2   Related Work

The metaphorical design in earlier work mostly focuses on icons as simple pictorial realizations of metaphors and their mapping. Each operation system supplier has published guidelines for icon design related to two-dimensional (2D) displays. These guidelines ensure that the form and appearance of the icons follow a standardized international design, independent of the intended world region and the cultural background of the user. The designer should use established concepts to ensure recognition, and consistency of meaning and interpretation. Nielsen [4] pointed out that simple metaphors with meaningful mappings between icon and represented action help users to bring the system feature and their mental model into accord. Icons in user interfaces have a conceptual aspect as well as a process-related aspect; van den Boomen [5] likens them to the head of Janus, with, "one side [facing] the user, who must be able to read, understand, and operate the icon; and the other [facing] software and machine processes" to be launched and controlled by the user. Therefore, we have to raise the question whether a metaphor can be at once conceptual and material, transferring a selection of qualities and quantities between various domains using natural and formal languages. This would be in accordance with Weyers [6], who shows that a user interface can be modeled as a three-layered architecture: (a) the physical representation, describing the outward appearance as set of interaction elements, (b) the system to be controlled, in the form of its system interface, and (c) the interaction logic, which models the flow of data between the two.

Spatial metaphors help people to navigate in a large hierarchy of places, rooms, floors, buildings, areas, cities and landscapes. Kuhn and Blumenthal [3] cite three levels of human spatial knowledge: *Landmarks* as salient points of reference in the environment, *routes* as paths for navigating between landmarks and *survey frames* as coherent network route layouts. The visualization of instances of this knowledge can be 1-, 2- or 3-dimensional and is generally scalable with several levels of detail. It is important to recognize that there are various types of reference frames, for example, *egocentric*, where the user is a part of a physical or virtual environment defined as a set of objects and a space in which the user moves and acts individually alongside other users, and *allocentric*, where local coordinate systems help the observer, who is often represented as an avatar, to locate an object in the visible neighborhood and to approach a location via a sequence of up-down, front-back and left-right movements (cf. Fig. 3).

Kuhn and Blumenthal [3] explain that *recognizing and identifying* are based on spatial relation schemata like neighborhood and directional link, *motion* on the path schemata, *organizing and ranking* on order schemata and *associating and aggregating* on near-far, link, path, and part-whole schemata.

In Lakoff and Johnsen [2] the authors describe several kinds of metaphors: "We use ontological metaphors to comprehend events, actions, activities, and states." Structural metaphors involve "structuring one kind of thing or experience in terms of another kind..."; "each structural metaphor has a consistent set of ontological metaphors as sub-parts." Metaphors that frame cooperation and interaction are discussed in several papers, such as [7]. Here, Barbieri and Paoli understand "a cooperation metaphor [as] a set of basic rules that describe the different modalities of interaction between users and between users and their environment". We prefer the term *collaboration pattern*, where the patterns include structured, spatial and ontological metaphors and frame activities that concern group structures and describe how to localize the avatars with respect to the users, to navigate and to communicate with the group members.

From the large number of papers dealing with interaction design, we will cite only a few that relate to VMLs. LaViola et al. [8, 9] discuss 3D user interfaces in immersive virtual environments and provide a framework for the design of new interaction metaphors. Whereas office applications run on PCs with standard input devices like keyboard and mouse and a two-dimensional output screen, post-WIMP (i.e., post-windows, -icons, -menus, -pointing) multimodal interaction, such as simultaneous speech and gesture input, using gloves or acting directly in a CAVE-like environment, provides a more natural way to communicate, select, manipulate or transform objects—often directly—without interfering metaphors. Moving or navigating is done via a *walk or fly* metaphor and special purpose metaphors make the user aware of complementary information or topics of interest. Geometric operations combining translation, rotation and scaling are executed with a *virtual hand* that acts within the immediate neighborhood. With selection and manipulation outside the area of reach in mind, the *ray-casting* metaphor metaphorically shoots a ray from the virtual hand into the scene to detect and select an object which can then be manipulated by means of an interactive elastic arm (GoGo) or, alternatively, users can *grow or shrink* themselves to achieve work on different scales.

To evaluate the metaphorical design, Hrimech et al. [10] present the results of an experimental study examining the impact of three 3D interaction metaphors (i.e., ray casting, GoGo and virtual hand) on the user experience in a semi-immersive collaborative virtual environment.

In conclusion, we want to emphasize the impact of successful metaphorical design as a principal vehicle of user understanding and familiarization with an unknown system from the beginning on. In the spirit of Lakoff and Johnsen [2], the designer has to conceptualize and to concretize the mapping used to transfer concepts concerning one ontological domain to another. We use our everyday experiences to interpret the metaphor and to launch or execute the correct activity.

3   Classifying and Using Metaphors in Virtual Environments

In most applications, the first contact with an unknown system occurs via standardized user interface icons. There are several style guides for shaping icons and selecting unambiguous symbols that are metaphors for underlying functions or activities; important sets of icons used in standard office applications are well known to the user. Icons refer to actions, functionalities or system offers; their pictures look like the intended feature. Landmarks and links help users to navigate and walk within the virtual environments or an application as well as to acquire information and execute the correct activity.

Metaphorical *spatial design* provides places where activities are carried out, paths leading to other places, and domains or semantic spaces consisting of several places linked by paths and separated from other domains by thresholds. Metaphorical *temporal design* allows the user to change from the (actual or historical) present to the past or the future. When conceiving a multidimensional metaphorical space, the designer must guarantee spatial and temporal consistency, which can be realized using an architectural floor plan with simple room icons and an ordered sequence of viewpoints along a path that can be reached by point and click actions.

3D single-user interaction can be roughly classified into navigation (viewpoint manipulation), object selection and manipulation, and application control. This approach was extended to *multi-hand* and *multi-user* metaphors for interaction and collaboration in many directions by Duval in [11], where the author introduces as an example two distant users seeking to apply a manipulation technique on a virtual plane defined by three points. One user acts within a CAVE-like environment; his head and two hands are tracked, and he uses his two hands to control 3D cursors; the second user works with a desktop system, a head-tracking unit and a 2D input device (such as a 2D mouse) for controlling a 3D ray.

Such co-manipulation is described (a) at the *conceptual* level using appropriate collaboration metaphors depending on the available technical environment, (b) at the *network* level by defining a communication model, shared workspaces with allocated tools and a synchronization mode, and (c) at the *presentation* level using convenient

3D graphics APIs for heterogeneous architectures including suitable input and output hardware and tracking systems.

Some emphasis is given to a new versatile *2D Pointer/3D Ray* metaphor dedicated to non-immersive or semi-immersive 3D interactions, which were tested in comparison with other solutions. Some of the 3D pointing and picking metaphors have already been defined and implemented in Java3D or 3D game engines (e.g., jMonkey, OGRE, Unity3D).

Camporesi and Kallmann [12] present another software framework for the development of immersive collaborative virtual reality applications, full-body character animation, real-time full-body tracking and interaction metaphors. The system is capable of retrieving information from platform-dependent devices, such as the motion-capture system OptiTrack, 5DT data-gloves, 3D-Connexion mice, etc. The 3D graphical user interface (GUI) manager includes primitives for distributed interactive widgets offering user perspective interaction with virtual objects via virtual pointers and hands.

Figure 1 describes classes of conceptual metaphors used in VMs: spatial or temporal metaphors; spatial or time-*relation metaphors; collections of simple icons used as structural metaphors to represent variou*s organizational forms in daily life; contextual metaphors such as a VML tour along a certain path (moving from viewpoint to viewpoint with a specific user interface), for example, a building floor hosting various historical replications and extensions of a key experiment in a virtual laboratory; and conceptual metaphors with their semantic frames for comprehending events, actions, activities and states that are accessible in a certain room or context. Some of these metaphors are included in the Virtual Museum and Cultural Object Exchange Format (ViMCOX) metadata standard. ViMCOX 1.1 provides the semantic structure of exhibitions and complete museums and includes features such as room and outdoor area design, interactions with artwork, path planning, and dissemination and presentation of content [13].

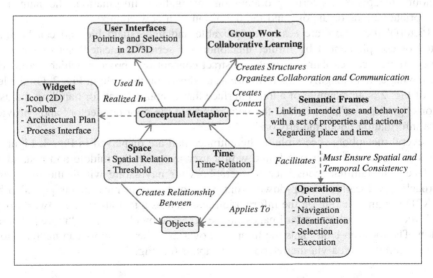

Fig. 1. Categorized conceptual metaphorical design in VMLs

ViMCOX's hierarchical structure allows the creation of exhibition areas: outdoor areas, buildings with floors, entrance halls and rooms—in arbitrary shapes—that can be linked directly as a floor plan or logically using metaphorical connectors.

Entrance hall, for instance, is a template-based conceptual metaphor with horizontal connectors to further rooms. A vertical connector between different entrance halls, rooms or levels can be an elevator or a staircase. *Viewpoints* are camera poses, marking points of interest; they are composed of location and view direction information. *Connectors* are elements that aid in navigation. *Thresholds* are horizontal connections/transitions between rooms or outdoor areas and may be doors, teleporters, gateways, or the like. From a technical point of view, connectors create links between remote 3D scenes like rooms or outdoor areas. To support the loading of custom connectors, we added this new attribute—the ability to specify a reference to a ViMCOX 1.1 object type—thus enabling curators to select an appropriate metaphoric connector for their architectural styles and exhibition contexts or themes. Metaphors like elevators, thresholds or intersection spaces can provide temporal coherence.

The main advantage of a stringent metaphorical design is to facilitate users' orientation and navigation, allowing them to access interesting viewpoints or to select and execute the right action in the virtual environment without switching between several screens and contexts or having to read explanatory text.

4   Use Cases

4.1   The Virtual Fleischhacker Museum

One of the most important problems in user interface design is the choice and consistent use of appropriate icons in order to support the interaction between user and application. The system designer has to choose a comprehensible set of icons as semiotic metaphors concerning orientation, navigation, information, the launch of appropriate actions or dialogs and the definition of a new context.

Pictorial metaphors are easily recognizable and understandable and can be integrated or complemented by further metaphors. A series or (nested) set of icons—a survey frame—can explain a complex abstract concept or a process, which avoids the user having to read lengthy texts or tutorials, as shown on the right in Fig. 2. On the left side of Fig. 2 is an example of a tour interface that contains icons for handling the user actions "go forward", "switch to the next room via the door connector" and "provide more information about the artwork".

Several metaphors accessible in the entrance hall are displayed in Fig. 3. Figure 4 shows an egocentric reference frame with a user avatar in the middle and a standard interface with familiar icons such as metaphors for navigating within the room and approaching a location via up-down, front-back, or left-right movements provided by the X3D plugin; clicking on the information icon causes a text about the artwork to be displayed, while further similar images can be accessed by clicking the "more pictures" button. The location icon loads the floor plan overlay, where visitors can navigate to a certain exhibition area via the teleporter metaphor (cf. Fig. 2).

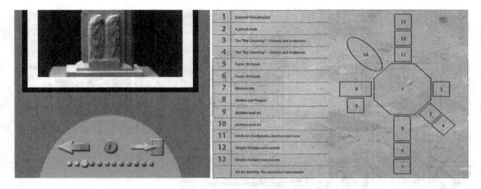

Fig. 2. Tour interface in Fleischhacker's VM on the left; architectural building metaphor on the right. The user moves via teleporter metaphor to one of the 13 rooms or to the outside area by pointing and clicking on the corresponding room names in the list

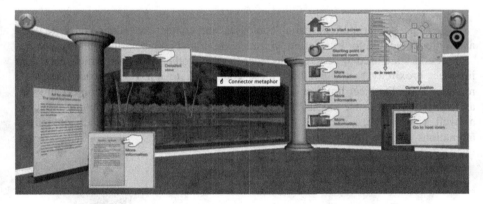

Fig. 3. The entrance hall with connectors to 13 rooms and the area with the tombstones. The user accesses the rooms via the point-and-click metaphor applied to one of the connectors, such as a door, threshold or window, to access the outdoor area. http://mw2013.Museumsandtheweb.com/paper/the-virtual-leopold-fleischhacker-museum/

Our Replicave2 software [14] provides an exhibition layout based on a spatial metaphorical framework design with navigation schemes. We use an octagonal entrance hall as part of the building metaphor, which provides access to the other exhibition areas. This metadata-based generative approach facilitates more flexible generation of exhibition spaces and enables automatic distribution of contents, metaphoric room connectors and camera viewpoints marking points of interest.

Sacher et al. [15] describe the realization of the virtual Fleischhacker museum in a Cave Automated Virtual Environment—a five-sided CAVE located in Aachen, Germany (aixCAVE). Alternatively, it is possible to use low-cost VR systems such as Google CardBoard, Oculus Rift or other tangible or multi-touch interfaces.

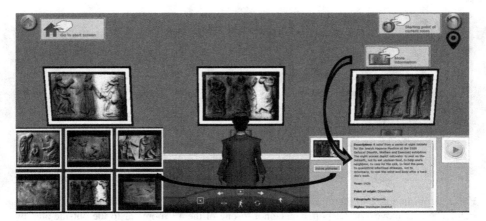

Fig. 4. Egocentric reference frame with a user avatar (seated, in the middle) and a standard interface with familiar navigation icons

The actual scenario offers spatial, contextual and content-related awareness to users and a great potential for interacting with the exhibit and collaborating on shared work.

QR codes are used to access audio recordings and other materials, which are placed in direct proximity to the exhibits; these codes link to our HTML-based metadata renderer and 3D-object browser (cf. Fig. 5). Furthermore, the digital object browser allows visitors to browse the 2D/3D exhibition items and their corresponding metadata as well as to rotate, zoom and pan the 3D reconstructions or to watch predefined animations.

Fig. 5. Users in a CAVE scanning QR codes in the Fleischhacker virtual museum

4.2 Virtual Museum for Replicated Scientific Laboratories and Experiments

In his thesis, Biella [1] describes the design and implementation of psychological key experiments in a virtual 3D environment using a new 3D virtual museum framework system. The environment is a building consisting of a ground floor with an entrance hall, media room and gallery, as well as several other floors devoted to selected key psychological experiments (See Fig. 6).

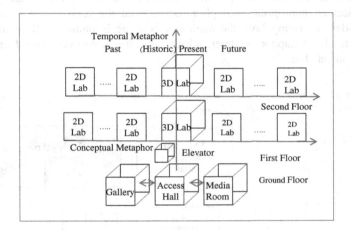

Fig. 6. Metaphorical design in Virtual Laboratories [1]

The temporal metaphor "elevator" provides access to the conceptual metaphor "floor"; each "floor" hosts a historical experiment reconstructed in a 3D laboratory and creates a consistent context: experiments that represent the same scientific theory are thus connected through a contextual metaphor. Moving left or right, the user can proceed to older and newer versions of the experiment visualized in 2D. The elevator serves as connector and the time spent to proceed to another floor allows for loading a new virtual world. The spatial design provides places where activities are carried out, paths for accessing other places, and domains or semantic spaces consisting of several places linked by paths and separated from other domains by thresholds.

The temporal design allows the user to change from historical present to past or future relative to the actual époque by walking through the floor and opening doors to related experiments. Conceiving a multidimensional metaphorical space, the designer is obliged to guarantee spatial and temporal consistency, which was realized through explicit access points to the elevator and the completely ordered space "floor".

4.3 Use Case in Daily Elder Care

Pinske et al. [16] propose a further step in UI development in ambient assisted living research that inverts the roles of technical system and user, that is, the system senses a human process and reports the state of task completion using metaphors. This concept views the user as being influenced by the system in a certain way, in contrast to the normal definition of HCI, where the human controls the system. A metaphor is modeled as a set of possible visual or acoustic symbols embedded in a certain context and a set of interpretations associated via IDs with appropriate contexts. Metaphors are grouped in MetaphorClass nodes in the XML representation. Class nodes correspond to event structures, mental events, emotions, and so forth and contain more specific MetaphorGroup nodes that subdivide the classes. Using simple sensors, the monitoring system scrutinizes the surrounding world and the human activities. The data gathered is used to select an appropriate metaphor model from the XML-based dataset and a context model describing how the metaphor is to be instantiated. Both models are transferred to the metaphor renderer, which generates a concrete visual or physical representation (cf. Fig. 7).

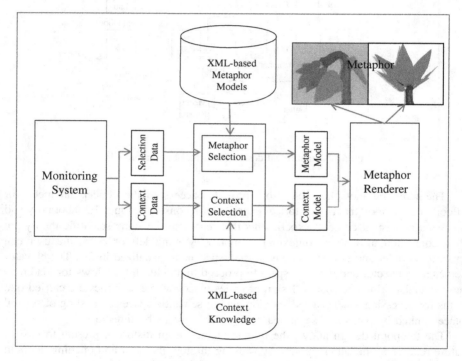

Fig. 7. Metaphor rendering system [16]

By using metaphors, undesirable behavior in elderly people is corrected without the need to confront the individuals directly with their mistakes. Instead, analogies are composed which are familiar to the individuals. The proposed metaphorical design was realized by Weber in his dissertation [17] as a mechanical motor-driven flower that blooms or droops depending on an individual's level of success in accomplishing his or her daily routine. This routine has been formerly identified through an automatic activity recognition system that was developed at the Fraunhofer-inHaus-Center in Duisburg. The main purpose of this metaphorical feedback is to indicate the extent to which the user's daily activities correspond to "normal behavior" in a simple, understandable way.

5   Outlook and Current Work

This paper demonstrates that the application of a stringent conceptual metaphorical design based on a metadata standard enables users to be familiar with an unknown system from the start, provides intuitive navigation, supports group building and various forms of interactions, and guarantees consistency in spatial layout and temporal order of action spaces. As stipulated in the ViMCOX standard, the Replicave2 3D-visualization framework provides template-based conceptual metaphors, which facilitates the ability to generate and arrange rooms and metaphorical connectors dynamically—depending on various construction parameters—and allows for the extensibility of the concept. Metaphorical design depends greatly on user interface design and degree of immersion, especially in multi-user scenarios.

Users' acceptance and the usability of a conceptual metaphorical design will be measured and evaluated by means of user questionnaires during a planned exhibition of Fleischhacker's estate in the Düsseldorf Memorial to the Victims of Persecution from November 2015 to February 2016. At this venue, we will also introduce and evaluate a gesture-based navigation approach utilizing Leap Motion VR Input device(s) and a one-screen projection of The Virtual Leopold Fleischhacker Museum.

The Leap Motion API (https://developer.leapmotion.com/documentation/csharp/api/Leap.Gesture.html) provides native support for dynamic gestures, which are similar to our touch-screen input as depicted in Fig. 3. The horizontal swipe gesture can be adapted for rotating the scene, by such means as mapping the velocity and direction of the performed gesture to the 3D scene's viewpoint-rotation around the Y-axis. The key tab gesture is suitable for forward/backward movement in the XZ-plane, where the movement direction is determined by the fingertip's motion direction. While QR codes are used to access exhibit-related metadata, the screen tap gesture—where the tip of a finger pokes forward—can be used to access this information, as well, or to navigate, for example, moving to another room by pointing to a door metaphor. A simple circular finger motion could trigger reset or reload the virtual museum. Our preliminary research has focused on dynamic gestures performed by a single user as mentioned above and has not yet considered interaction with the environment or with tangible objects or collaborative gestures.

References

1. Biella, D.: Replication of classical psychological experiments in virtual environments. Ph.D. thesis, University of Duisburg-Essen, Logos, Berlin (2006)
2. Lakoff, G., Johnsen, M.: Metaphors We Live By. The University of Chicago Press, London (2003)

3. Kuhn, W., Blumenthal, B.: Spatialization: spatial metaphors for user interfaces. In: CHI 1996 Conference Companion on Human Factors in Computing Systems, Tutorial Notes (1996)
4. Nielsen, J.: Icon classification: resemblance, reference, and arbitrary icons. http://www.nngroup.com/articles/classifying-icons/. Accessed 17 August 2014
5. van den Boomen, M.: Interfacing by iconic metaphors. Configurations **16**, 33–55 (2008). The Johns Hopkins University (2009)
6. Weyers, B.: Reconfiguration of user interface models for monitoring and control of human-computer systems. Ph.D. thesis, University of Duisburg-Essen, 2011, Dr. Hut Verlag (2012)
7. Barbieri, T., Paolini, P.: Cooperation metaphors for virtual museums. In: Proceedings of Museum&Web (2001). http://www.archimuse.com/mw2001/papers/barbieri/barbieri.html
8. LaViola Jr., J.J.: Interaction in virtual reality: categories and metaphors. In: van Dam, A., Forsberg, A., Laidlaw, D.H., LaViola Jr., J.J., Simpson, R.M. (eds.) Immersive VR for Scientific Visualization: A Progress Report. Computer Graphics and Applications, vol. 20, no. 6, pp. 26–52. IEEE Press, New York (2002)
9. Bowman, D.A., Kruijff, E., LaViola Jr., J.J., Poupyrev, I.: 3D User Interfaces: Theory and Practice, 3rd edn. Addison-Wesley, Reading (2011)
10. Hrimech, H., Alem, L., Merienne, F.: How 3D interaction metaphors affect user experience in collaborative virtual environment. Adv. Hum. –Comput. Interact. **2011**, 11. Article ID 172318 (2011)
11. Duval, T.: Models for Design, Implementation and Deployment of 3D Collaborative Virtual Environments. Université Rennes 1 (2012)
12. Camporesi, C., Kallmann, M.: A framework for immersive VR and full-body avatar interaction. In: Virtual Reality (VR), pp. 79–80. IEEE Press, New York (2013)
13. Biella, D., Luther, W., Sacher, D.: Schema migration into a web-based framework for generating VMs and laboratories. In: 18th International Conference on Virtual Systems and Multimedia (VSMM) 2012, pp. 307–314. IEEE Press, Milan (2012)
14. Sacher, D., Biella, D., Luther, W.: Towards a versatile metadata exchange format for digital museum collections. In: IEEE Proceedings 2013 Digital Heritage International Congress, Marseilles, France, vol. 2, pp. 29–136. IEEE Press, 28 October–1 November 2013
15. Sacher, D., Weyers, B., Kuhlen, T.W., Luther, W.: An integrative tool chain for collaborative virtual museums in immersive virtual environments. In: Baloian, N., Zorian, Y., Taslakian, P., Shoukouryan, S. (eds.) CRIWG 2015. LNCS, vol. 9334, pp. 86–94. Springer, Heidelberg (2015)
16. Pinske, D., Weyers, B., Luther, W., Stevens, T.: Metaphorical design of feedback interfaces in activity-aware ambient assisted-living applications. In: Bravo, J., Hervás, R., Rodríguez, M. (eds.) IWAAL 2012. LNCS, vol. 7657, pp. 151–158. Springer, Heidelberg (2012)
17. Weber, K.: A system for rating activities and monitoring behavior in ambient assisted living environments. Diploma thesis, University of Duisburg-Essen (2012). (in German)

Efficient Planning of Urban Public Transportation Networks

Nelson Baloian[1](✉), Jonathan Frez[2], José A. Pino[1],
and Gustavo Zurita[3]

[1] Department of Computer Science, Universidad de Chile, Santiago, Chile
{nbaloian, jpino}@dcc.uchile.cl
[2] Universidad Diego Portales, Santiago, Chile
jonathan.frez@mail.udp.cl
[3] Management Control and Information Systems Department,
Economics and Business Faculty, Universidad de Chile, Santiago, Chile
gzurita@fen.uchile.cl

Abstract. Planning efficient public transport is a key issue in modern cities. When planning a route for a bus or the line for a tram or subway it is necessary to consider the demand of the people for this service. In this work we presented a method to use existing crowdsourcing data (like Waze and OpenStreetMap) and cloud services (like Google Maps) to support a transportation network decision making process. The method is based the Dempster-Shafer Theory to model transportation demand and uses data from Waze to provide a congestion probability and data from OpenStreetMap to provide information about location of facilities such as shops, in order to predict where people may need to start or end their trip using public transportation means. The paper also presents an example about how to use this method with real data. The example shows how to analyze the current availability of public transportation stops in order to discover its weak points.

Keywords: Dempster-Shafer theory · Transportation networks · Smart cities

1 Introduction and Related Work

Cities are constantly growing. Their decision making problems are increasingly complex, and better methods to evaluate solutions are needed in order to support this growing [1].

Many decision problems are spatial. A typical problem is to define an area to support a certain requirement or service, e.g., a place for a new road, set an industrial area, locate a hospital. Besides, cities are constantly changing, and they have dynamic problems, like in public transportation services: the routes can be dynamically defined to cope with new requirements and constraints. Some of the decisions may be to find a place for a new bus station, define a route, define multiple routes, or even plan a full transportation network.

According to [2], a "smart city" is a city that monitors and integrates data and information of its critical infrastructures, including roads, bridges, tunnels, rails, subways, airports, seaports to better optimize its resources, and maximize services to its citizens.

© Springer International Publishing Switzerland 2015
J.M. García-Chamizo et al. (Eds.): UCAmI 2015, LNCS 9454, pp. 439–448, 2015.
DOI: 10.1007/978-3-319-26401-1_41

At same time, citizens are using information technologies (IT) to consume and provide data that can be used to support the decision making process of several cities requirements. Some of the IT used by citizens can be supported by Cloud Computing Services providing Software as a Service (SaaS). The SaaS model of Cloud Computing is often accessed by citizens from mobile applications and web interfaces [3]. Some of the SaaS services with spatial data properties are, e.g., Google Maps, OpenStreetMaps and Waze. These services provide geo-localized data in a graphical way, they are free, and they share a singular characteristic: they use Crowdsourcing data to provide data.

Here we report the use of services provided by Google Maps, OpenStreetMaps and Waze to develop a Spatial Decision Support System for transportation network planning, specifically for the Origin-Destination (OD) evaluation. The OD evaluation is done with the Dempster-Shafer theory [4]. This theory allows to model decisions based on uncertain and incomplete data, by studying the extent a hypothesis can be supported by data.

In [6], authors describe a user-friendly web-based spatial decision support system (wSDSS) aimed at generating optimized vehicle routes for multiple vehicle routing problems that involve serving the demand located along arcs of a transportation network. The wSDSS incorporates Google Maps (cartography and network data), a database, a heuristic and an ant-colony meta-heuristic developed by the authors to generate routes and detailed individual vehicle route maps. It accommodates realistic system specifics, such as vehicle capacity and shift time constraints, as well as network constraints such as one-way streets and prohibited turns. The wSDSS can be used for "what-if" analysis related to possible changes to input parameters such as vehicle capacity, maximum driving shift time, seasonal variations of demand, network modifications, and imposed arc orientations. The system was tested for urban trash collection in Coimbra, Portugal.

A crowdsourcing database is the OpenStreetMap project [7]. Worldwide, several volunteers are contributing information to this "free" geodatabase. In some cases this database exceeds proprietary ones by a 27 % [8], and for some authors [9] it is more complete than Google maps or Bing maps. OpenStreetmap data has been proposed to support traffic related decisions by developing traffic simulations [10], or solutions to achieve a new web-based trip optimization tool [11]. It has also been used to support transportation network planning [12]. Also, a spoken-dialogue prototype for pedestrian navigation in Stockholm by using various grounding strategies and based on OpenStreetMaps is described in [13]. Similarly, Jacob et al. [14] present a web-based campus guidance system for pedestrian navigation aimed at providing support for visitors. They developed an OpenStreetMap based system to generate short paths using both outdoor walkways and indoor corridors between various locations.

Another popular crowdsourcing geodatabase is being generated by Waze. Waze is a mobile GPS application that allows to measure and report traffic conditions and events, e.g., it automatically detects traffic jams, users can report accidents, weather effects on the roads, and other alerts. In the literature we did not find a decision support system using Waze data, maybe because it is hard to obtain. However, we found traffic condition analysis systems [15] based on real time data obtained from Waze.com using a WebCrawler, and an accidents data mining analysis proposal [16] based on the same real time data from Waze.com. In our work the data is obtained using the same technique: we developed a WebCrawler to reconstruct an historical database based on published data on waze.com.

We focus on spatial DSS using belief functions [17], in particular Dempster-Shafer theory (DST). The DST proposes to use sets of hypotheses regarding a variable (e.g. the temperatures at a location are between t1 and t2) associated with a probability of being correct. Using belief functions we can provide a "hypotheses support value" called belief. The belief can be assigned to a certain geographical area satisfying a hypotheses set.

2   The OD Route Problem

Regional transportation networks are composed of various transportation lines designed to cooperate and complement an urban scale transportation solution [18]. The planning of the paths or routes of a new transportation method is usually based on existing network data, volume predictions and the distribution in the network [19].

When a decision maker chooses a route, the travel time and time reliability are important factors under demand and supply uncertainty. When designing an urban route for a new transportation service, the choices must consider the behavior and reliability of the transportation network. Another factor is the OD traffic demand [21]. The OD describes the traffic demand between a particular OD during a time period.

A public transportation system is typically a complex network. In Santiago it includes bus stations and routes, subway stations and routes, shared taxi stations and routes. Each OD is composed of a start station and an ending station. A single OD can have multiple sub-OD in a single route. The design of a public transportation system is a task requiring analysis of the transportation demand, the traffic conditions of the possible routes for each OD, and the reliability of the OD. In order to define an OD route based on uncertain demand information, we propose to adapt belief maps [17]. This concept is based on the DST. A belief map allows to evaluate a geographical area generating a suitability evaluation on a set of hypotheses supporting a possible solution. For example, a map can show the belief degree of find people in each evaluated area. The hypotheses supporting this map can be "People go to commercial areas", or "People can be in schools".

3   Determining the OD Route

We propose a new concept called belief routes (BR). A BR can be used to evaluate demand hypotheses of an OD. A BR is composed of 3 basic elements: A set of hypotheses that defines a possible transportation demand of an OD; The Origin and Destination; The "polyline" or path of the route. Using this definition of BR, the decision maker can compare various paths satisfying the demands in each OD. Also, the decision maker can adjust the Origin or Destination. Another factor in the OD evaluation is the transportation and reliability time. In order to support both indicators we propose to combine the traffic information from Waze creating a belief value based on historical data. We call the result of this combination a Belief Congestion Route (BCR).

In order to explain the use of the BR and BCR in the decision making processes we are going to use a basic example: A single OD with two possible paths. In Figs. 1 and 2, two options are shown (A and B respectively). In this example route A is shorter than B, and the travel time is also shorter according to Google Directions API.

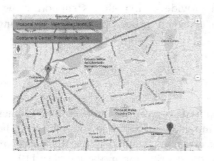

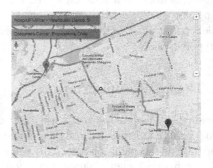

Fig. 1. Route A   **Fig. 2.** Route B

In Figs. 3 and 4, the transportation demand is represented by a BR, according to OpenStreetMap and the proposed hypothesis, route B has more demand than route A.

Fig. 3. Belief route A   **Fig. 4.** Belief route B

In Figs. 5 and 6 the BCR of both routes are shown. According to the Waze information for both paths, route A has more belief of having congestions or traffic jams which implies less reliability.

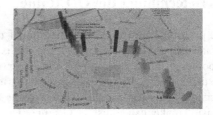

Fig. 5. Congestion route A   **Fig. 6.** Congestion route B

From this example we can note that route B has less congestion and more demand than route A. However route A is shorter and the decision will depend of what kind of OD the decision maker is looking for. In order to support the decision, the visual evaluation of the BR and BCR is not enough. An evaluation metrics framework is needed and it will be part of our future work.

4   An Application for Developing Belief Routes

We developed a prototype that allows its users to define an OD pair and it automatically provides the shortest route using the Google Route Service. It also allows the user to specify hypotheses for transportation demand modelling, after which it can generate two types of visualization: The demand Belief Route and the Congestion route (see Fig. 7). The platform provides Average Belief of the generated 3D visualization.

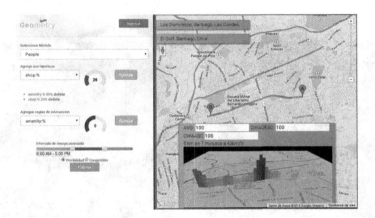

Fig. 7. Evaluation of an OD using the developed application

The application allows setting a transportation demand hypotheses set compatible with the Dempster-Shaffer Theory. It also allows including some model restrictions, for example: avoid schools. After the hypotheses are included, the application allows choosing the type of 3d map which will be generated and shown: BR or BCR.

5   Belief Routes in Real World

In order to test the proposed concept, we are going to use real data from a public transportation system. The testing method is simple: we use real data to evaluate an hypothesis set (used to build the BR), if the prediction generated by the hypothesis set "matches" with the real data we assume the hypotheses hold and thus the generated BRs are valid.

For the test we selected two different areas with high transportation activities in the city of Santiago de Chile. These areas were selected because one is representative for having many shops in the city center and the other is representative for a residential area with high population. Both areas have an important number of subway and bus stations. For these transportation methods we have the information about the time and location were people starts using each service. This was possible because the integrated public transportation system of Santiago (called "Transantiago") uses exclusively plastic cards with magnetic bands which should be pre-loaded with money as payment method. In this way, the system registers the point where every passenger started her trip. However, it does not register the point where it ends. Data were obtained from the Ministry of Transport.

Let's call "A" to the area in the city center, and B to an area that leads to residential areas with a high population. We first used the data for generating a heatmap coloring with intensity from 0 to 1 the areas where bus and subway stops are concentrated. The generated heatmaps showing the concentration of public transportation stops are shown on Fig. 8.

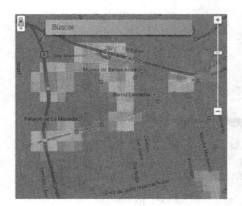 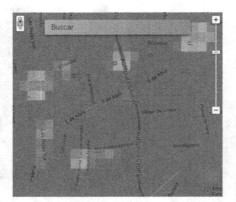

Fig. 8. Transportation network spatial distribution. Left: "A". Right: "B".

In a similar way, we used the data for generating a heatmap according to the number of people starting their trips at a certain bus or subway stop. The generated maps for both areas are shown in Fig. 9.

From Figs. 8 and 9 we can conclude that people concentrate their starting point at fewer stations than the available, which is something we would expect. This does not mean they are not using the other stations since they can be used to get off at them, but we cannot collet this data.

In order to generate scenarios which allow us to calculate belief routes which are usable for the travelers we have to propose hypotheses that generate scenarios according to the reality. This means, we should construct hypotheses that predict at least where people are going to start their trips with public transport. For this, we will propose two hypotheses which relate elements in the city with transportation needs for the people:

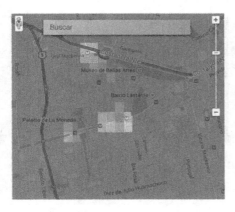 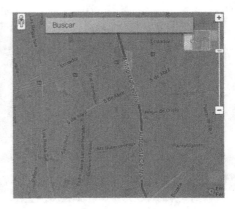

Fig. 9. Colored areas show spots where people start their trip using public transportation. Left: "A". Right: "B".

1. People start their trips using public transport means near "shops".
2. People start their trips using public transport means near "amenities".

Both terms, "shops" and "amenities", are standard tags for labelling geographical objects in OpenStreetMap. The definition of "amenity" covers "an assortment of community facilities including toilets, telephones, banks, pharmacies and schools."

The results of applying of both hypotheses to area "B" can be seen in Fig. 10. Comparing these scenarios with Fig. 9 right, we can note that shop places coincide in both maps with minimal differences. On the contrary, for amenities there is almost no match.

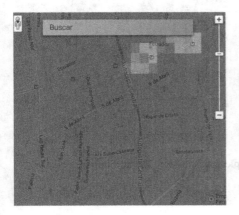 

Fig. 10. Belief map applying the hypotheses for "B" area separately. Left: Amenity places. Right: Shop Places.

From these results, we can conclude that the hypothesis that shop places generate trips starting in their near environment is a better predictor. (see Fig. 11).

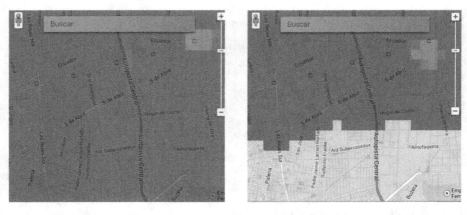

Fig. 11. Comparison at "B". Left: People concentration. Right: Shop Places.

When applying the "shops" hypothesis to the A area we find only some coincidence between the starting points and the shops. This is however explained by the fact that there is no bus and subway stations near some shops, as can be seen comparing the maps in Fig. 8 left, showing the stops, and Fig. 12 left showing the shops. In this way we can estimate a lack of proper public transportation stops in an area which according to the hypothesis should have a great demand of them.

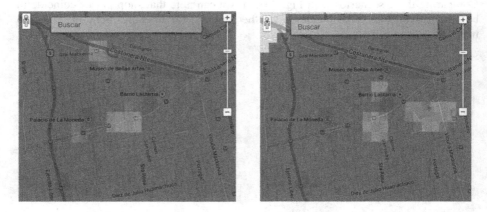

Fig. 12. Comparison at "A". Left: People concentration. Right: Shop Places.

6   Conclusions

In this work we presented a method to use existing crowdsourcing data to support a transportation network decision making process. The method uses the Dempster-Shafer Theory to provide a framework to model transportation demand based on the Open-StreetMap Data. The method also provide a simple way of use the Waze application data to provide a congestion probability value to each segment of a route.

In this work we propose that the use of croudsourcing data to build the transportation demand metric and the congestion probability it is possible to support a transportation network decision making process.

References

1. Heilig, G.K., World urbanization prospects the 2011 revision. United Nations, Department of Economic and Social Affairs (DESA), Population Division, Population Estimates and Projections Section, New York (2012)
2. Harrison, C., et al.: Foundations for smarter cities. IBM J. Res. Dev. **54**(4), 1–16 (2010)
3. Chourabi, H., et al. Understanding smart cities: an integrative framework. In: 45th Hawaii International Conference on System Science (HICSS), 2012. IEEE (2012)
4. Shafer, G.: A Mathematical Theory of Evidence, vol. 1. Princeton University Press, Princeton (1976)
5. Piro, G., et al.: Information centric services in Smart Cities. J. Syst. Softw. **88**, 169–188 (2014)
6. Santos, L., Coutinho-Rodrigues, J., Antunes, C.H.: A web spatial decision support system for vehicle routing using Google Maps. Decis. Support Syst. **51**(1), 1–9 (2011)
7. Haklay, M., Weber, P.: Openstreetmap: User-generated street maps. IEEE Pervasive Comput. **7**(4), 12–18 (2008)
8. Neis, P., Zielstra, D., Zipf, A.: The street network evolution of crowdsourced maps: OpenStreetMap in Germany 2007–2011. Future Internet **4**(1), 1–21 (2011)
9. Ciepłuch, B., et al.: Comparison of the accuracy of OpenStreetMap for Ireland with Google Maps and Bing Maps. In: Proceedings of the Ninth International Symposium on Spatial Accuracy Assessment in Natural Resources and Environmental Sciences. University of Leicester, 20–23 July 2010
10. Zilske, M., Neumann, A., Nagel, K.: OpenStreetMap for traffic simulation. In: Proceedings of the 1st European State of the Map–OpenStreetMap Conference (2011)
11. Klug, M. CS Transport-optimisation–a solution for web-based trip optimization basing on OpenStreetMap. In: 19th ITS World Congress (2012)
12. Joubert, J.W. Van Heerden, Q.: Large-scale multimodal transport modelling. Part 1: Demand generation (2013)
13. Boye, J., et al.: Walk this way: spatial grounding for city exploration. In: Mariani, J., Rosset, S., Garnier-Rizet, M., Devillers, L. (eds.) Natural Interaction with Robots, Knowbots and Smartphones, pp. 59–67. Springer, New York (2014)
14. Jacob, R., Zheng, J., Ciepłuch, B., Mooney, P., Winstanley, A.C.: Campus guidance system for international conferences based on OpenStreetMap. In: Carswell, J.D., Fotheringham, A. S., McArdle, G. (eds.) W2GIS 2009. LNCS, vol. 5886, pp. 187–198. Springer, Heidelberg (2009)
15. Silva, T.H., de Melo, P.O.S.V., Viana, A.C., Almeida, J.M., Salles, J., Loureiro, A.A.F.: Traffic condition is more than colored lines on a map: characterization of waze alerts. In: Jatowt, A., Lim, E.-P., Ding, Y., Miura, A., Tezuka, T., Dias, G., Tanaka, K., Flanagin, A., Dai, B.T. (eds.) SocInfo 2013. LNCS, vol. 8238, pp. 309–318. Springer, Heidelberg (2013)
16. Fire, M., et al.: Data mining opportunities in geosocial networks for improving road safety. In: IEEE 27th Convention of Electrical and Electronics Engineers in Israel (IEEEI) 2012. IEEE (2012)

17. Frez, J., et al.: Dealing with incomplete and uncertain context data in geographic information systems. In: Computer Supported Cooperative Work in Design (CSCWD), IEEE, Editor 2014, pp. 129–134. IEEE, Hsinchu, Taiwan (2014)
18. Yang, L., Wan, B.: A multimodal composite transportation network model and topological relationship building algorithm. In: International Conference on Environmental Science and Information Application Technology, 2009, ESIAT 2009. IEEE (2009)
19. Liu, S., et al.: Modeling and simulation on multi-mode transportation network. In: 2010 International Conference on Computer Application and System Modeling (ICCASM). IEEE (2010)
20. Xu, L., Gao, Z.: Bi-objective urban road transportation discrete network design problem under demand and supply uncertainty. In: IEEE International Conference on Automation and Logistics, 2008, ICAL 2008. IEEE (2008)
21. Castillo, E., et al.: The observability problem in traffic models: algebraic and topological methods. IEEE Trans. Intell. Transp. Syst. $9(2)$, 275–287 (2008)

An HTML Tool for Production of Interactive Stereoscopic Content

Alexey Chistyakov[1](✉) and Jordi Carrabina[1,2]

[1] Aitech S.L., Parc de Recerca UAB, 08193 Bellatera, Barcelona, Spain
`alexey.chistyakov@e-campus.uab.cat`
`http://www.uab.cat`, `http://www.aitech.es`
[2] Escola d'Enginyeria, Universitat Autónoma de Barcelona, CEPHIS,
08193 Bellatera, Barcelona, Spain
`jordi.carrabina@uab.cat`

Abstract. The benefits provided by the stereoscopic vision have been thoroughly studied for more than a century. The results of this research state that S3D, when properly implemented, enhances efficiency of different applications. At the same time, the market of 3D-enabled technologies is blooming, revealing new devices to the public. 3D cameras, TVs, projectors, monitors, and mobiles are becoming more and more affordable and are not considered as something exotic anymore. Yet this technology is far from being widely implemented. The scarcity of tools for production of such content along with the absence of proper guidelines establishing the rules for S3D depth implementation could be the main reason. With this work we present a tool for generation of interactive stereoscopic HTML compositions. We describe the tool's operation mode and expose results of the performance test.

Keywords: Stereoscopic · 3D · HTML · Human-computer interaction · User interface

1 Introduction

Since the discovery back in XIX century, stereoscopy advanced to a lot of different areas including some that nobody could have ever predicted. The comprehensive analysis of papers and experiments associated with the stereoscopic effect for the last 50 years shows that, in overwhelming majority of cases, usage of stereoscopic displays increases overall performance, if compared to conventional 2D displays, in various tasks [8]. It is known that the stereoscopic effect delivers better and more efficient gaming experience [18,21], and even increases the efficiency of number of medical applications [23]. This could be explained by the way the stereoscopic depth influences our perception of visual information.

As the human-computer interaction is our main research area, we are looking for ways how can HCI benefit from the stereoscopic effect. There are number of studies [1,3,4,24] exploring this influence and resulting to more or less the same encouraging conclusion: stereoscopy has a positive influence user experience

© Springer International Publishing Switzerland 2015
J.M. García-Chamizo et al. (Eds.): UCAmI 2015, LNCS 9454, pp. 449–459, 2015.
DOI: 10.1007/978-3-319-26401-1_42

and overall usability. But, despite relative simplicity of the concept behind the stereoscopic effect, nowadays there are few effective and easy-to-use tools to implement stereoscopic depth into user interfaces (UI).

We see the stereoscopic depth as a tool that allows user interface designers more efficient use of the 3rd dimension in graphical UIs (GUI). These stereoscopic depth planes could present a reliable solution for ambient intelligence system (AmIS) GUIs, which can be heavily cluttered with functionality, controls and, in case of augmented reality UIs, real life objects. Enhanced visual experience and naturalness of a visual image [11] along with a certain level of immersion [14] (if combined with other technological components: e.g. screen resolution, field of view, interaction model) generated by the stereoscopic effect could in turn lead to more natural interaction with the system. A proper approach to this problem could enhance user experience of a system and efficiency of its UI.

In our previous publication [2] we uncovered a 2D-to-3D conversion algorithm (the Algorithm) for HTML-compositions. We managed to update the Algorithm and built a framework, thereby excluding several important restrictions produced by in the initial version of the Algorithm. With this work we try to tackle the problem of introduction of the stereoscopic depth planes into GUIs by developing a tool for production of interactive stereoscopic compositions and validating whether the proposed technology can offer a reliable instrument for that purpose.

2   State of the Art

2.1   Stereoscopic Displays

Stereopsis is a depth perception mechanism that is being thoroughly researched since its discovery more than a century ago [10]. Our binocular vision is what makes this effect possible. Differences and similarities between two images on left and right retinas of two eyes are processed by brain into the information about relative distances and a depth structure of an observed environment. Stereoscopic displays try to follow the same basic principle: provide left and right eye of an observer with two different images, thus the illusion of depth is achieved. There are number of ways of producing such effect [9,16], but the overwhelming majority of them are two-view 3D displays, which all come to the simple idea of splitting so called stereo-pair into two separate images and deliver both images to respective retinas.

Nowadays the most used 3D displays are the *time-sequential two-view displays*. This technology uses interleaving of two images on the same display with a speed fast enough for the viewer not to notice the switching. The images are then filtered by glasses equipped with electronic shutter which delivers left or right image to a respective eye [6]. As of the date of hereby publication this technology is used on most of 3DTVs and 3D-enabled PC monitors available on the market. Thus we chose this type of 3D displays as our main target.

2.2   Platform

We have chosen HTML5 as our main development platform due to a number of features that can help us to build a proper stereo-pair and then provide the observer a way to interact with the output composition.

Though the standard is still in development [7], HTML5 is already in use for several years, supported by many different platforms, and it has one of the widest developer communities. Despite what is hidden under the abbreviation (*Hyper Text Markup Language*), as a standard HTML5 includes three different technologies: HTML, CSS (*Cascading Style Sheet*), and JavaScript. All three combined provide developers with a reliable environment to design and implement cross-platform, screen independent user interfaces.

Deserves mentioning that W3C has the Proposal of Special Extension for Stereoscopic 3D Support [5]. Soonbo H. et al. designed a set of requirements for HTML5 standard aimed specifically at handling stereoscopic content. The proposal contains HTML attributes and CSS properties that provide a possibility to introduce stereoscopic media into a prototype.

2.3   State of the Technology

Most of the tools for production of interactive stereoscopic HTML compositions are associated with WebGL technology [13]. WebGL is a Javascript API for rendering interactive 3D and 2D compositions using only HTML. WebGL elements can be seamlessly implemented into a user interface along with the rest of the HTML. There are several works showing successful implementation of this technology in different areas [12,15,25]. Nevertheless in order to achieve proper results WebGL requires expert knowledge of JavaScript and experience of work with 3D modeling. This problem is alleviated to some extent by a large number of WebGL frameworks, such as ThreeJS [22], even though it still can be considered as the main issue.

3   Method

We plan to use the benefits of all three HTML5 associated technologies. In order to increase the performance of the final application and reduce the time of development we decided to use jQuery [17], the JavaScript framework that was developed to do exactly that. The idea of using the WebGL for this task was declined due to (i) excessive functionality, (ii) complexity of the development process, (iii) lack of support by several targeted platforms, and (iv) overall irrelevancy to the task.

3.1   Conversion Algorithm

Based on the techniques behind the targeted stereoscopic displays and the requirements of HTML5 standard we designed the Algorithm of conversion of an input markup into a stereo-pair that preserves all the interactive features presented before the conversion. The Algorithm's operation mode can be divided into 4 main stages: (S1) cloning of the existing content and creating a side-by-side composition; (S2) detecting stereoscopic content, such as images, videos etc.; (S3) mirroring the interactions from one side to the other; and (S4) distributing user predefined markup elements along the depth axis (z-axis) the way the illusion of depth is achieved. At the same time, several challenges (see Table 1) had to be alleviated in order to achieve the desired result were defined.

Table 1. Main challenges to overcome during the 2D to 3D conversion process

HTML	(1) The specific of HTML as a language allows multiple variations of the code producing the same layout, all of this variations should be taken into account during the conversion process;
	(2) The output HTML should correspond to the W3C requirements all the violations should be predicted and eliminated
	(3) The invalid input HTML code that could sabotage the output result should be predicted and taken into account;
	(4) The tool needs to recognize the proposal for W3C requirements [5] aimed at handling the stereoscopic media content through respective *@media* queries.
CSS	(1) Multiple variations of style rules is allowed by the standard, such as (i) inline styling, (ii) styling through HTML's *styles* tag, (iii) styles inside inked *.css* file, (iv) using *@import* inside linked *.css* files. All the variations should be taken into account and processed;
	(2) Interaction related CSS pseudo classes, e.g. *:hover*, *:focus*, should be taken into account during the interaction mirroring stage of the conversion Algorithm;
	(3) During the shifting of the specified elements along the z-axis the rest of the HTML layout should not be disturbed.
JavaScript	(1) The tool should be easy to include on the page and require as minimum user input as possible;
	(2) The framework has to provide access to both original and clone elements at the same time during the programming of interactions with the output stereo-pair.

3.2 The Implementation

The final version of the tool (3DSjQ) exploits the Algorithm and successfully alleviates all the aforementioned challenges. During the operation, 3DSjQ recommended itself as a stable working easy-to-use tool. Due to the HTML in its core, the output composition can be viewed on 3D enabled projectors, TVs, PC monitors, tablets, smartphones, etc. The tool allows front-end developers to design all type of interactions supported on a client side and work with any type of user input devices, including basic ones, such as mouse, keyboard, touch

Fig. 1. Stereoscopic interfaces for the e-commerce application (top) and the stereoscopic video browser (bottom) created with 3DSjQ. User interface before conversion (left) and output stereo-pair after conversion (right).

screens, and more sophisticated like MS Kinect, Leap, and any other equipped with a corresponding API.

Since the first version presented earlier [2] 3DSjQ went through a number of optimization cycles and drastically advanced its functionality, features and stability. For comparison of features presented in both releases please refer to the Table 2.

Despite the great improvement in stability, the number of features and the fact that the latest version of the framework can predict invalid HTML code, 3DSjQ still has several restrictions to composition design and further HTML implementation caused by browser rendering issues and specifics of the Algorithm. For example, (i) it is strongly advised to maintain validity of the input code and its correspondence to the W3C requirements; (ii) all the interactions with the output stereo-pair should be specified after 3DSjQ was executed since all the javascript executed prior the tool was triggered could cause interaction fails; (iii) due to browser rendering issues some graphical stylings can look different from the input composition, thus visual properties of some elements need to be corrected correspondingly;

3.3 Operation

We designed 3DSjQ the way it requires only the basic knowledge of HTML and related technologies. The procedure of enabling the framework on the page similar to any other jQuery plugin: the *3DSjQ.js* file should be specified in a header

Table 2. 3DSjQ features

Feature	v.1.0
Files included in the package	1
Lines of code	1387
Size of the developer version, (kb)	29.8
Ability to set parameters of the stereoscopic environment[a]	Yes
Ability to convert already marked up prototypes	Yes
Framework of functions to manipulate the output	Yes
Prevention of code fails	Yes
Offline work	Yes[b]
Support of W3C requirements for stereo web [5]	Yes
- Stereoscopic videos support	Yes
- Stereoscopic images support	Yes
@media queriesic @media queries	Yes

[a] *stereo−pair arrangement (top-bottom, left-right), visual cues, depth budget, etc.*
[b] *most of the browsers*

of an HTML page to convert. Then, in order to start the conversion, one should launch the initiating function *go3DS elements, params)*, where *elements* is an array of elements to shift and *params* array of parameters of stereoscopic depth.

There are two ways of shifting a certain element away from a screen plane: (i) it can be specified within the parameters of the initiating function (see Listing 1.1), this way the element is going to be shifted right after the conversion has been executed, or (ii) with the *.shift()* function at any time after the conversion has been carried out (see Listing 1.2). This function, along with others completes the framework, which gives a possibility to distribute elements along z-axis.

```
    . . .
        <script type="text/javascript" src="jQuery.js"></script>
        <script type="text/javascript" src="3dsjq.js"></script>
        <script type="text/javascript">
            $(window).on({ load: function(){
                go3DS({ "#foo" : 3, "#foo:hover" : 5 });
            }});
        </script>
        </head>
    . . .
```

Listing 1.1. Basic initiation of the 3DSjQ, during which HTML element with *id="foo"* will be put 3 levels above the screen plane in a standby mode and 5 levels above when a *:hover* event is triggered.

```
$("#foo").shift(5);
$("#foo").parent().shift(3);
$("#foo").on({
    mouseenter: function(){
        $(this).parent().shift(3);
    }
});
```

Listing 1.2. Possible ways to shift elements away from a screen plane. From top to bottom: (i) shifting of the *#foo* element to a 5th level, (ii) shifting of a parent of the *#foo* to a 3rd level, (iii) shifting the parent the 3rd level when the *mouseenter* event was triggered.

4 Performance Evaluation

Each browser has specific properties and rendering capabilities which can affect the output markup. Moreover, operating system that is hosting the browser can also influence the rendering behavior. Thus, in order to evaluate the obtained tool in terms of performance and platform compatibility, we tested it on the most popular browsers (desktop and mobile) under the most popular operating systems [19,26] (see Table 3). We included in the research the following browsers according to its current market share: *Google Chrome* - 43.16 %, *Safari* - 13.8 %, *Internet Explorer* - 13.09 %, *Android Browser* - 6.99 %, *Opera* - 3.79 %. Other browsers were also tested, but they are not included into hereby research due to their low market share. As of operating systems, we included *Windows 7* - 33.9 %, *Android* - 20.67 %, *iOS* - 11.51 %, *Windows 8.1* - 9.26 %, *OS X* - 5.69 %. The displays that have been tested include: Samsung 3DTV with screen size of 1920x1080px, Samsung UD590 with 2560x1440px, Apple iPhone 5S - 1136 x 640px, LG G3 - 2560x1440px. It should be noted that a screen size, when requested by javascript and returned by a browser, is different depending on the display resolution, for example Apple iPhone's screen size is recognized as 320x568px. Thus, the aforementioned devices available at our disposal can be considered as a reference group for the currently the most used screen sizes [20]. We also added Tizen OS and PS4 System Software to the test. Though browsers hosted by those OS' can not be considered as popular, yet both platforms can benefit from stereo content due to their entertainment oriented purpose.

For the test purpose we created several responsive prototypes exploiting stereoscopic features provided by the 3DSjQ. The HTML markup of all the prototypes is done the way it can adapt its appearance to a current display screen size (also known as responsive). The prototype was developed on a desktop PC under Mac OS X 10.10.3 and tested on Google Chrome browser along the process, thus this browser-OS combination was used as a main reference.

Fig. 2. The initial HTML prototype (to the left) and the output stereo-pair (to the right) containing the stereoscopic image (courtesy of the NASA) as seen on Chrome Browser under Android OS

Fig. 3. Output stereo-pair as seen on Google Chrome under Mac OS X (top) and PS4 browser (bottom)

5   Results

As seen in Table 3 the framework performs flawlessly in terms of support of its features when tested under different operating systems. The final versions of the stereoscopic prototypes were compatible with almost all of the targeted platforms. Overall, the 3DSjQ was able to run on all the test devices with most of the visual features displayed correctly. Some browsers were unable to correctly render

Table 3. 3DSjQ browsers compatibility

	Chrome	Safari	IE	Android Browser	Opera	Other
Windows 7	✓	✓	x	–	✓	–
Android	✓	–	–	x	✓	–
Windows 8.1	✓	✓	✓	–	✓	–
iOS	✓	✓	–	–	✓	–
OS X	✓	✓	–	–	✓	–
Tizen	–	–	–	–	–	✓
PS4	–	–	–	–	–	✓

– - not applicable , ✓ - supported, x - not supported

the output composition due to incompatibility of the input HTML, though the framework performed as expected. The obtained results will be taken into consideration and will be useful for testing framework's fallback strategies.

6   Conclusion

With this work we proposed the tool for production of passive and interactive stereoscopic compositions which can be considered as a way to alleviate this problem and represents an effective instrument for developing S3D user interfaces for human-computer interaction research purposes. The framework was in a state of development for several years, and, as shown in this work, performs really well under all the most popular browser versions and operating systems. It allows developers to design complex interactions with a number of user input devices, such as keyboard, mouse, touch screens and many others that have a proper APIs. 3DSjQ can be used for production of stereoscopic user interfaces from scratch and as a conversion tool for already implemented HTML, which makes it one of a kind tool for front-end development of S3D applications.

7   Future Work and Discussion

Despite the outstanding technical performance, there is still work to be done to improve stability and overall functionality of the framework. This can include: (i) further update of the functionality, (ii) closer work with the stereoscopic web standards in order to support its features and contribute to the standard's development; (iii) find fallback strategies for browsers that can not support all the features provided by the HTML5; (iv) provide support for autostereoscopic displays. Taking into account the interaction related issues mentioned before, it is important to make a proper user evaluation of compositions built with the presented tool in order to substantiate the described approach.

We plan, and encourage other HCI researchers, to use this method to develop S3D stimuli for further research work on human interaction with S3D displays, which tend to become ubiquitous. It could help to establish guidelines and standards for efficient usage of the stereoscopic depth, test different S3D interaction paradigms, measure level of immersivenes and similar issues. In other words, find ways to design better UX and more efficient UIs.

Acknowledgments. Funded by the Catalan Government scholarship 2013-DI-030

References

1. Broy, N., Schneegass, S., Guo, M., Alt, F., Schmidt, A.: Evaluating stereoscopic 3D for automotive user interfaces in a real-world driving study. In: Proceedings of the 33rd Annual ACM Conference Extended Abstracts on Human Factors in Computing Systems - CHI EA 2015, pp. 1717–1722. ACM Press, New York, April 2015. http://dl.acm.org/citation.cfm?id=2702613.2732902
2. Chistyakov, A., González-Zúñiga, D., Carrabina, J.: Bringing the web closer: stereoscopic 3D web conversion. In: Collazos, C., Liborio, A., Rusu, C. (eds.) CLIHC 2013. LNCS, vol. 8278, pp. 22–25. Springer, Heidelberg (2013)
3. González-Zúñiga, D., Chistyakov, A., Orero, P., Carrabina, J.: Breaking the pattern: study on stereoscopic web perception. In: Urzaiz, G., Ochoa, S.F., Bravo, J., Chen, L.L., Oliveira, J. (eds.) UCAmI 2013. LNCS, vol. 8276, pp. 26–33. Springer, Heidelberg (2013)
4. Häkkilä, J., Posti, M., Koskenranta, O., Ventä-Olkkonen, L.: Design and evaluation of mobile phonebook application with stereoscopic 3D user interface. In: CHI 2013 Extended Abstracts on Human Factors in Computing Systems on - CHI EA 2013, p. 1389 (2013), http://dl.acm.org/citation.cfm?doid=2468356.2468604
5. Han, S., Lee, D.Y.: Extensions for Stereoscopic 3D support (2012). http://www.w3.org/2011/webtv/3dweb/3dweb_proposal_121130.html. Accessed 6 Jun 2015
6. Hartmann, W.J., Hikspoors, H.M.J.: Three-dimensional TV with cordless FLC spectacles. Inf. Disp. **3**(9), 15–17 (1987). http://dl.acm.org/citation.cfm?id=33861.33864
7. Hickson, I.: A vocabulary and associated APIs for HTML and XHTML (2012). http://www.w3.org/TR/html5/. Accessed 5 Jun 2015
8. Holliman, N.: 3D display systems. In: Handbook of Opto-electronics (2005). ISBN 0-7503-0646-7
9. Holliman, N.S., Dodgson, N.A., Favalora, G.E., Pockett, L.: Three-dimensional displays: a review and applications analysis. IEEE Trans. Broadcast. **57**(2), 362–371 (2011)
10. Howard, I.P.: Seeing in depth, Vol. 1: Basic mechanisms. University of Toronto Press (2002)
11. IJsselsteijn, W., de Ridder, H., Hamberg, R., Bouwhuis, D., Freeman, J.: Perceived depth and the feeling of presence in 3DTV. Displays **18**(4), 207–214 (1998)
12. Johnston, S., Renambot, L., Sauter, D.: Employing WebGL to develop interactive stereoscopic 3D content for use in biomedical visualization. In: Dolinsky, M., McDowall, I.E. (eds.) The Engineering Reality of Virtual Reality 2013, Proceedings of the SPIE, vol. 8649, p. 864–905, March 2013. http://adsabs.harvard.edu/abs/2013SPIE.8649E.05J
13. Khronos WebGL Working Group: WebGL - OpenGL ES 2.0 for the Web (2015). https://www.khronos.org/webgl/. Accessed 10 Jun 2015

14. McMahan, R.P., Gorton, D., Gresock, J., McConnell, W., Bowman, D.A.: Separating the effects of level of immersion and 3D interaction techniques. In: Proceedings of the ACM Symposium on Virtual Reality Software and Technology - VRST 2006, p. 108. ACM Press, New York, November 2006. http://dl.acm.org/citation. cfm?id=1180495.1180518
15. Nocent, O., Piotin, S., Benassarou, A., Jaisson, M., Lucas, L.: 3D displays and tracking devices for your browser: A plugin-free approach relying on web standards. In: Proceedings of the 2012 International Conference on 3D Imaging - IC3D 2012, pp. 1–8, December 2012. http://ieeexplore.ieee.org/lpdocs/epic03/wrapper.htm? arnumber=6615141
16. Pastoor, S., Wöpking, M.: 3-D displays: a review of current technologies. Displays 17(2), 100–110 (1997)
17. Resig, J.: jQuery (2006). https://jquery.com/. Accessed 5 June 2015
18. Schild, J., Bölicke, L., LaViola Jr., J.J., Masuch, M.: Creating and analyzing stereoscopic 3D graphical user interfaces in digital games. In: Proceedings of the SIGCHI Conference on Human Factors in Computing Systems - CHI 2013, p. 169. ACM Press, New York, April 2013. http://dl.acm.org/citation.cfm?id=2470654.2470678
19. StatCounter: StatCounter Global Stats - Browser, OS, Search Engine including Mobile Usage Share (2015). http://gs.statcounter.com/#all-browser-ww-monthly-201502-201502-bar. Accessed 8 Jun 2015
20. StatCounter: StatCounter Global Stats - Browser, OS, Search Engine including Mobile Usage Share (2015). http://gs.statcounter.com/#desktop+mobile+tablet-resolution-ww-monthly-201502-201502-bar. Accessed 8 Jun 2015
21. Takatalo, J., Kawai, T., Kaistinen, J., Nyman, G., Häkkinen, J.: User experience in 3D stereoscopic games. Media Psychol. 14(4), 387–414 (2011)
22. three.js: three.js - Javascript 3D library (2015). http://threejs.org/. Accessed 8 Jun 2015
23. Van Beurden, M., IJsselsteijn, W., Juola, J.: Effectiveness of stereoscopic displays in medicine: a review. 3D Rese. 3(1), 1–13 (2012)
24. Ventä-Olkkonen, L., Posti, M., Häkkilä, J.: How to Use 3D in Stereoscopic Mobile User Interfaces. In: Proceedings of International Conference on Making Sense of Converging Media - AcademicMindTrek 2013, pp. 39–42 (2013). http://dl.acm. org/citation.cfm?id=2523447
25. Wang, W., Dong, S., Wang, R., Cheng, Q., Zhang, J., Liu, Z.: Stereoscopic 3D Web: from idea to implementation. In: 2014 International Conference on Information Science, Electronics and Electrical Engineering, vol. 3, pp. 1440–1444. IEEE, April 2014. http://ieeexplore.ieee.org/articleDetails.jsp?arnumber=6946158
26. Zachte, E.: Wikimedia Traffic Analysis Report - Browsers e.a (2015). https://stats. wikimedia.org/archive/squid_reports/2015-02/SquidReportClients.htm. Accessed 8 Jun 2015

Opinion of the Patients About an Internet-Based Psychological Treatment Protocol

Alberto González-Robles[1(⊠)], Adriana Mira[1], Amanda Díaz[1],
Azucena García-Palacios[1,3], Antonio Riera[1], Rosa Baños[2,3],
and Cristina Botella[1,3]

[1] Universidad Jaume I, Castellon 12071, Spain
{vrobles,miraa,al294509,azucena,botella}@uji.es,
toni.riera82@gmail.com
[2] Universidad de Valencia, Valencia, Spain
banos@uv.es
[3] CIBER Fisiopatología de la Obesidad y Nutrición (CB06/03),
Instituto de Salud Carlos III, Madrid, Spain

Abstract. Emotional disorders (depression and anxiety disorders) are highly prevalent. Currently, there is evidence showing the efficacy of disorder-specific cognitive-behavior therapy for emotional disorders. However, high comorbidity rates among emotional disorders have led some researchers to shift the focus to treatment strategies that might be more widely effective across these diverse conditions (transdiagnostic approach). Another important line of research in the literature is Internet-based psychotherapy. An increasing number of meta-analyses have shown the efficacy and effectiveness of Internet-based cognitive-behavior treatment protocols for emotional disorders. Nevetherless, little is known about the acceptability (i.e. expectations and opinion of treatment) of these types of interventions. We have developed a transdiagnostic treatment protocol and have adapted it so that it can be applied over the Internet. The aim of this study is to describe the protocol and to present data about the acceptability of the online intervention by a sample of patients from a randomized controlled trial that we are currently conducting in Spanish public mental specialized care settings.

Keywords: Acceptability · Transdiagnostic · Internet · Computer-delivered psychotherapy

1 Introduction

Emotional disorders (ED) (anxiety and mood disorders) are among the most prevalent mental disorders, with lifetime prevalence rates of up to 29 % for anxiety disorders and 19 % for depressive disorders [1]. Nevertheless, despite these alarming data there is evidence showing that most people with ED (less than 50 %) do not receive adequate treatment [2]. These data strongly suggest that effective and efficient treatments are needed to address this important health problem.

© Springer International Publishing Switzerland 2015
J.M. García-Chamizo et al. (Eds.): UCAmI 2015, LNCS 9454, pp. 460–466, 2015.
DOI: 10.1007/978-3-319-26401-1_43

Currently, there is evidence attesting the effectiveness of cognitive-behavior treatments (CBT) targeting specific disorders [3–5]. However, several problems regarding disorder-specific protocols (e.g. high comorbidity rates among ED) has led some researchers to shift the focus to treatments that might be more widely effective across these diverse conditions (referred to as transdiagnostic treatments). Transdiagnostic treatments generally include treatments aimed at addressing different disorders with a single protocol. A growing body of research showing the efficacy and effectiveness of transdiagnostic treatments for depression and anxiety disorders has emerged in the past years [6]. An important line of research within the transdiagnostic approach is Barlow's theory of triple vulnerability, which emphasizes the underlying vulnerabilities that are common to the different ED and help to explain the comorbidity among these disorders [7]. Based on this theoretical framework, Barlow's team designed the Unified Protocol (UP), a transdiagnostic protocol for the treatment of ED [8]. The results obtained using this protocol in a traditional face-to-face format demonstrate its effectiveness [8].

Information and communication technologies (ICT), such as the Internet, may facilitate access by people for whom traditional therapy is not available [9]. The efficacy of Internet-based treatments for a variety of ED has been shown in previous research [10, 11]. Nevertheless, little emphasis has been placed in the acceptability of these interventions (e.g. expectations and opinion of treatment). It is important, however, to study the acceptability of these interventions since they are related to treatment outcomes [12], and can help to enhance the effectiveness of interventions [13]. Moreover, positive expectations are associated to better outcomes [13]. The existing studies do not assess acceptability directly and only offer indirect indicators of acceptability, such as take-up rates and patient drop-out rates [12]. Therefore, it is necessary to assess the acceptability of these interventions more directly.

We have developed a traditional transdiagnostic treatment protocol and an adaptation of this protocol that can be applied over the Internet. The aim of this study is to describe this protocol and to present data about the acceptability of this intervention by a Spanish sample of patients from public mental specialized care.

2   Method

2.1   Design

A two-armed simple-blinded randomized controlled trial (RCT) is currently being conducted. Participants are randomly allocated to one of two conditions: (a) Internet-based treatment protocol and (b) treatment as usual (TAU). For this paper, the data of the participants recruited and allocated to the Internet-based treatment protocol until now are used.

2.2   Sampling Procedure and Participant Characteristics

Participants are adult out-patients who attend Spanish public mental health centers to seek psychological and/or psychiatric treatment. They are recruited by psychiatrists and clinical psychologists working on these centers. Inclusion criteria are: (a) be 18 or older; (b) ability to understand and read Spanish; (c) access to Internet at home and having and an email address; (d) fulfill the DSM-IV criteria [14] for ED; and (e) providing written, informed consent. Exclusion criteria include: (a) suffering from a severe mental disorder (schizophrenia, bipolar disorder, and alcohol and/or substance dependence disorder); (b) high risk of suicide; (c) receiving another psychological treatment; and (d) the increase and or change in the pharmacological treatment (a decrease is accepted).

Demographic and Clinical Characteristics. The sample recruited until now consists of 21 adults (67 % women) (mean age: 38.71, SD: 11.34). Regarding marital status, 3 are single, 14 are married or with a partner and 4 separated or divorced. Regarding the study level, 6 have higher education, 7 have mid-level studies and 8 have basic studies. Each participant received a primary DSM-IV diagnostic (shown in Table 1).

Table 1. N for the different primary diagnosis given to participants

Diagnostic	N
Generalized anxiety disorder (GAD)	5
Major depression disorder (MDD)	4
Panic disorder (PD)	4
Agoraphobia (A)	3
Social anxiety disorder (SAD)	2
Dysthymic disorder (DD)	1
Obsessive-compulsive disorder (OCD)	1
Anxiety disorder not otherwise specified (ADNOS)	1

2.3   Intervention

The online protocol is delivered through a web platform (https://www.psicolo giaytecnologia.com/) designed by our research team. A team work made up of one computer engineer, one usability expert and four clinical psychologists worked in the design of the online protocol. The psychological treatment protocol was designed and manualized by the clinical psychologists and the usability expert, and then introduced in a web application by the computer engineer. The protocol includes 12 modules designed for the treatment of nine ED (MDD, DD, MDNOS, PD, A, SAD, GAD, ADNOS and OCD):

M1. Emotional disorders and emotion regulation. This module provides information about the role of emotion regulation in ED. *M2. Motivation for change.* The aim is to enhance motivation to engage in the program. *M3. Understanding the role of emotions.* This module provides information about the adaptive functions of emotions and the three-component model of emotions. *M4. The acceptance of emotional experiences.* This module aims to teach the patient the acceptance of emotional experiences. *M5. Practicing acceptance.* The objective is to increase awareness of physical sensations, thoughts, emotions and daily activities. *M6. Learning to be flexible.* It focuses on the importance of learning how to identify maladaptive ways of thinking and its role in the maintenance of emotional disorders. *M7. Practicing cognitive flexibility.* This module aims to teach the patients the ways maladaptive ways of thinking can be modified. *M8. Emotional avoidance.* This module aims to teach the patients the emotion avoidance strategies that contribute to the maintenance of emotional disorders. *M9. Emotion Driven Behaviors (EDBs).* The aim is to learn the concept of EDBs, and replace their own maladaptive EDBs with other more adaptive behaviors. *M10. Accepting and facing physical sensations.* The objectives are to teach the patients the role of physical sensations in the emotional response and train them in interoceptive exposure. *M11. Facing emotions in the contexts in which they occur.* The purpose is to help the patients to face the avoided situations that contribute to the maintenance of the problem. *M12. Relapse prevention.* This module aims to review the strategies learned and teach the patient how to cope with future high risk situations.

2.4   Measures

Mini International Neuropsychiatric Interview Version 5.0.0 (MINI) [15]. It is a short structured diagnostic psychiatric interview that yields key DSM-IV and ICD-10 diagnoses. The MINI can be administered in a short period of time, and clinical interviewers need only brief training.

Expectation of Treatment Scale (ETS) and Opinion of Treatment Scale (OTS). These questionnaires are adapted from Borkovec and Nau [16]. The content of the six items, rated on a scale from 0 to 10, cover how logical the treatment seemed, to what extent it could satisfy the patient, whether it could be used to treat other psychological problems, whether it could be recommended to a person with the same problem and its usefulness for the patient's problem. The expectation scale is applied once the treatment rationale has been explained. Its aim is to measure subjective patient expectations about this treatment. The opinion scale is administered when the patient has completed the treatment, and its aim is to assess satisfaction with this treatment. Our group has used this questionnaire in several research studies [17, 18].

Table 2. Mean and standard deviation for the items of the ETS (n = 21)

Item	Mean (SD)
1. How logical does the therapy offered to you seem?	7.43 (1.43)
2. How satisfied are you with the therapy offered to you?	7.43 (1.60)
3. How confident would you be in recommending this to a friend with the same problem?	7.67 (1.62)
4. How much do you think this treatment would be useful in improving other psychological problems?	7.62 (1.56)
5. How much do you think this treatment will be useful in reducing your symptoms?	7.38 (1.88)

3 Results

Results of expectations and opinion of treatment are shown in Tables 2 and 3, respectively. All participants completed the ETS and 6 out of 21 (those participants that have finished the intervention) completed as well the OTS.

Table 3. Mean and standard deviation for each item of the OTS (n = 6)

Item	Mean (SD)
1. How logical does the therapy offered to you seemed?	7.83 (1.17)
2. How satisfied are you with the therapy offered to you?	7.83 (1.17)
3. How confident would you be in recommending this to a friend with the same problem?	9.17 (.75)
4. How much do you think this treatment would be useful in improving other psychological problems?	8.33 (1.37)
5. How much do you think this treatment has been useful in reducing your symptoms?	8.50 (1.87)

4 Discussion and Conclusion

The results show all participants reported high scores in all items measuring treatment expectations (scores between 7.38 and 7.67): logic of the treatment, satisfaction with the treatment, recommendation of the treatment to other people with similar problems, usefulness of the treatment for other psychological problems and utility of the treatment for one's specific problem. After receiving the intervention, scores about treatment opinion improved in comparison to scores on treatment expectations (scores between 7.83 and 9.17). These results support the acceptability of this intervention, as measured by expectations and opinion of treatment, and are in line with systematic reviews indicating that computerized CBT treatments possess high levels of acceptability, positive expectations and high satisfaction with the treatment [12, 19].

Nevertheless, it is important to note that, as these data are preliminary, they should be interpreted with caution. Before drawing more solid conclusions it will be necessary to complete the recruitment to analyze data from the full sample of the RCT.

In conclusion, although the importance of studying the effectiveness of online interventions is currently out of doubt, it is also important to study its acceptability. Internet-based psychotherapy constitutes a new approach in the way treatment protocols are delivered, with important changes compared to traditional face-to-face therapy that may partly determine whether this way of deliver a psychotherapy is more or less well-accepted. Therefore, we consider research should focus in asking questions such as 'how can we improve Internet-based psychological treatments so as to enhance its acceptability among the population?' 'which features (e.g. content and usability features) should an Internet-based protocol possess to be successful in reducing symptomatology?'.

References

1. Kessler, R.C., Berglund, P., Demler, O., Jin, R., Walters, E.E.: Lifetime prevalence and age-of-onset distributions of DSM-IV disorders in the National comorbidity survey replication. Arch. Gen. Psychiatry **62**, 593–602 (2005)
2. Bebbington, P.E., Meltzer, H., Brugha, T.S., Farrell, M., Jenkins, R., Ceresa, C., Lewis, G.: Unequal access and unmet need: neurotic disorders and the use of primary care services. Psychol. Med. **30**(6), 1359–1367 (2000)
3. Antony, M.M., Stein, M.B.: Oxford Handbook of Anxiety and Related Disorders. Guilford Press, New York (2002)
4. Hollon, S.D., Ponniah, K.: A review of empirically supported psychological therapies for mood disorders in adults. Depress. Anxiety **27**(10), 891–932 (2010)
5. Nathan, P.E., Gorman, J.M.: A Guide to Treatments that Work, 3rd edn. Oxford University Press, New York (2007)
6. Newby, J.M., McKinnon, A., Kuyken, W., Gilbody, S., Dalgleish, T.: Systematic review and meta-analysis of trandiagnostic psychological treatments for anxiety and depressive disorders in adulthood. Clin. Psychol. Rev. **40**, 91–110 (2015)
7. Barlow, D.H., Allen, L.B., Choate, M.L.: Toward a unified treatment for emotional disorders. Behav. Ther. **35**, 205–230 (2004)
8. Farchione, T.J., Fairholme, C.P., Ellard, K.K., Boisseau, C.L., Thompson-Hollands, J., Carl, J.R., Gallagher, M.W., Barlow, D.H.: Unified protocol for transdiagnostic treatment of emotional disorders: a randomized controlled trial. Behav. Ther. **43**(3), 666–678 (2012)
9. Kazdin, A.E., Blase, S.L.: Rebooting psychotherapy research and practice to reduce the burden of mental ilness. Perspect. Psychol. Sci. **6**(1), 21–37 (2011)
10. Spek, V., Cuijpers, P., Nyklicek, I., Keyzer, J., Pop, V.: Internet-based cognitive behavior therapy for symptoms of depression and anxiety: a meta-analysis. Psychol. Med. **37**(3), 319–328 (2007)
11. Titov, N.: Internet-delivered psychotherapy for depression in adults. Curr. Opin. Psychiatry **24**, 18–23 (2011)
12. Kaltenthaler, E., Sutcliffe, P., Parry, G., Beverley, C., Rees, A., Ferriter, M.: The acceptability to patients of computerized cognitive behaviour therapy for depression: a systematic review. Psychol. Med. **38**(11), 1521–1530 (2008)
13. De Graaf, L.E., Huibers, M.J.H., Riper, H., Gerhards, S.A.H., Arntz, A.: Use and acceptability of unsupported online computerized cognitive behavioral therapy for depression and associations with clinical outcome. J. Affect. Dis. **116**(3), 227–231 (2009)
14. American Psychological Association: Diagnostic and Statistical Manual of Mental Disorders (4th edn Rev.). American Psychological Association, Washington, DC (2000)
15. Sheehan, D.V., Lecrubier, Y., Sheehan, K.H., Amorim, P., Janavs, J., Weiller, E., et al.: The Mini-International Neuropsychiatric Interview (M.I.N.I.): the development and validation of a structured diagnostic psychiatric interview for DSM-IV and ICD-10. J. Clin. Psychiatry **59** (20), 34–57 (1998)
16. Borkovec, T.D., Nau, S.D.: Credibility of analogue therapy rationales. J. Behav. Ther. Exp. Psychiatry **3**(4), 257–260 (1972)
17. Botella, C., Gallego, M.J., Garcia-Palacios, A., Baños, R.M., Quero, S., Alcañiz, M.: The acceptability of an internet-based self-help treatment for fear of public speaking. Br. J. Guid. Couns. **37**(3), 297–311 (2009)

18.
   Botella, C., García-Palacios, A., Villa, H., Baños, R.M., Quero, S., Alcañiz, M., et al.: Virtual reality exposure in the treatment of panic disorder and agoraphobia: a controlled study. Clin. Psychol. Psychother. **14**(3), 164–175 (2007)
19. Andrews, G., Cuijpers, P., Craske, M.G., McEvoy, P., Titov, N.: Computer therapy for the anxiety and depressive disorders is effective, acceptable and practical health care: a meta-analysis. PLoS ONE **5**, e13196 (2010)

A Cloud-Based Mobile System for Improving Vital Signs Monitoring During Hospital Transfers

Andrés Neyem[1], Guillermo Valenzuela[1(✉)], Nicolas Risso[1],
Juan S. Rojas-Riethmuller[1], José I. Benedetto[1], and Marie J. Carrillo[2]

[1] Computer Science Department,
Pontificia Universidad Católica de Chile, Santiago, Chile
{aneyem,gevalenz,narisso,jsrojasl,jibenede}@uc.cl
[2] Nursing School, Universidad Católica de Chile, Santiago, Chile
mcarrilb@uc.cl

Abstract. As the number of patients in hospitals constantly grows, the need for hospital transfers is directly affected. Hospital transfers can be required for several reasons but they are most commonly made when the diagnostic and therapeutic facilities required for a patient are not available locally. Transferring a critical patient between hospitals is commonly associated with risk of death and complications. At the same time, advances in wearable technologies and health applications offer new possibilities to support healthcare. This raises the question: How can we improve the monitoring of vital signs of transported patients through use of information technology and communication services? This paper presents a cloud-based mobile system to support decision-making in the transportation of patients in critical condition. The Rapid Emergency Medicine Score (REMS) scale was used as an outcome variable, being a useful scale to assess the risk profile of critical patients requiring transfers between hospitals. The platform is the result of research and development work performed during the last two years.

Keywords: Cloud-based mobile system · Mobile cloud computing · Rapid emergency medicine score · Cloud workspaces · Design guideline

1 Introduction

Healthcare services and transportation often need assistance with logistics and decision-making. Specifically, Inter-Hospital Transfers (IHTs), also known as inter-facility or secondary transfers, are needed when the diagnostic and therapeutic facilities required for a patient are not available locally [20]. Unfortunately, it is common for complications to arise during transportation. The decision of transporting a patient must be done after balancing the potential benefits of transportation and the risks involved. Among the factors that can elevate the risks are the patient's current medical status and the setting of the transfer. Although meticulous pre-transfer checks can be made to assess the risks, patients' vital signs may be subject to major variations while traveling [7].

© Springer International Publishing Switzerland 2015
J.M. García-Chamizo et al. (Eds.): UCAmI 2015, LNCS 9454, pp. 467–479, 2015.
DOI: 10.1007/978-3-319-26401-1_44

Chile's current emergency medical transport system is managed by SAMU (Emergency Medical Care Services initials in Spanish). It provides a central hub for first response vehicles and ambulances with or without a physician on board. However, most ambulances are not equipped with the proper equipment to remotely monitor the patient's vital signs while being transported. SAMU has had many problems with equipment on board their ambulances. The devices they use are very large and are not suited for emergency transports: some are very fragile while very few are capable of transmitting data to a server. Often sudden accelerations, stops and the constant vibration inherent of an IHT can significantly alter the measurements of the sensors and even break the equipment, resulting in huge monetary losses. SAMU also manages communications between vehicles and hospitals through radio channels, which pushes the responsibility of analyzing the patient's condition entirely on the personal on board and creates coordination difficulties for simultaneous transfers. Despite an increased interest in embedded devices, mobile applications and cloud platforms, there is still a gap between current vital sensor design used by SAMU and the actual requirements of the physicians and doctors monitoring the patient being transported.

This project tries to fill that gap by providing a low-power embedded solution capable of capturing some of the patient's vital signs, such as heart rate and oxygen saturation, and sending them to a smartphone using wireless connectivity. Patients' vital signs are monitored by embedded devices fitted with vital sensors. Outfitting patients with such devices enables the capturing and transmission of real-time vital sign data. This in turn allows for the construction of remote monitoring platforms and intelligent mobile applications. By centralizing this information in the cloud through the smartphones' cellular radio, offsite physicians can support paramedics in their decision-making process while simultaneously monitoring the patient's vital functions. This project aims to establish a risk assessment platform to be used to determine whether or not to transport a patient through SAMU and should provide many advantages over the current system.

The next section describes the current state of the art regarding m-health technologies. Section 3 describes the Rapid Emergency Medicine Score (REMS) research in Chile. Section 4 describes the status of information technology in medicine. Section 5 presents the proposed system and Sect. 6 presents conclusions and future work.

2 Related Work

The rapid growth of the mobile industry since the release of Apple's iOS in 2007 has seen the advent of several health related applications. This has given birth to some controversy of whether or not consumer mobile devices can actually be used for sensitive medical applications. The American Food and Drug Administration (FDA) has taken part in this debate and in February 2015 amended its definition of mobile medical device to include smartphones and tablets along with applications that meet certain requirements [12]. Yet long before that, several proof of concepts have been made available in academia revealing the potential medical applications of mobile platforms.

Remote patient monitoring is one such medical application. Scully et al. use the optical sensor of a smartphone, along with its flashlight, to monitor subtle skin color changes on the green band. This information has been proven to be tightly correlated with heart and breathing rates [19]. Chen et al. explore the usage of a ZigBee monitoring device to detect falls on elderly individuals, monitor in-door positioning and ECG, and routes that data through an ad-hoc network to reach the cloud [8]. Bourouis et al. make use of a mobile device to collect kinematic and physiological parameters of elderly patients via Bluetooth. This data is analyzed and sent to a server upon any relevant perceived change [3]. A similar architecture is presented in [22], although the collected information is further enriched by the patients' own status logging and social network messaging information. The data is later referred to a server via a SOAP API.

Mobile platforms have also played an important role in telemedicine. One such initiative is the AMBULANCE telemedicine system [17]. It featured a bio signal monitor hooked to a notebook computer with a modem. Its purpose was to enable real-time conferencing with a physician in the emergency ward from the moment an ambulance picked up a patient, as well as to provide him with real-time bio signals of the patient (ECG, heart rate, blood pressure and oxygen saturation). Similar technologies were later created to take advantage of the development of cellular networks [10, 13].

More recently, the integration of new and more accurate sensors into mobile devices has created new opportunities for developers to delve into the fields of wellness and fitness. Mobile applications based on these technologies help their users by giving real-time information and guiding. Wearable sensors also have the potential to influence their user's behavior. For example, daily activity monitoring can facilitate self-management practices and personalized care [9, 11]. New wearable technologies are becoming more accessible and increasingly accurate for patient care [4, 24]. Wearable devices can be easily used in health treatments as diagnostic tools and aid in managing several diseases [21]. Consequently, a vital-sign monitoring system enabled by wearable technologies can have a big impact on public health and health-care costs through disease prevention and cost reduction [2].

Our system is designed to take advantage of the latest APIs and consumer available mobile devices to create a low cost solution for vital sign monitoring in the specific environments of patient pickup and IHT. While many remote patient monitoring initiatives exist, these are mostly meant for static contexts and do not consider the mobility constraints of an ambulance. Others limit themselves at simple monitoring vital signs and do not perform any historical data analysis to proactively alert physicians of any irregularity. Our solution was specifically designed with these two goals in mind.

3   REMS as a Risk Assessment Tool for Critical Patients Requiring Ambulance Transfers

The Rapid Emergency Medicine Score (REMS) was created in 2004 and is one of the rapid evaluation scores that provide a measure of the mortality risk of a patient based on their clinical state, without the need for exams [7]. It evaluates six parameters: age of the patient, heart rate, respiratory rate, blood pressure, peripheral oxygen saturation, and score on the Glasgow Coma Scale. Each of these variables is given a score between 0–4, except for age, which is scored between 0–6. The REMS is calculated as the sum of the scores for each variable. The risk profile of the patient is classified as high risk (over 13 points), intermediate risk (between 6 and 13 points) or low risk (less than 6 points) [16].

Several studies have concluded that REMS is a useful tool for providing an accurate predictor of mortality risk and severity of a patient's condition [14]. To further illustrate this point, we also conducted our own study to verify the effectiveness of the REMS scale for evaluating the clinical state of patients undergoing secondary transfers between hospitals using SAMU. We know that IHTs of critical patients are associated with complications and carry a risk of death. We therefore expected to find a correlation between the REMS scale and these complications. For this study, 432 transfers of patients above 15 years of age were contemplated (95 % confidence). Cardiac arrests and increases in patients' REMS were considered as outcome variables.

The impact of a transfer was determined by measuring the patients' REMS both upon departure and arrival. The results showed that, in most cases, patients' risk profiles moved up a category. It was also possible to determine that REMS is one of the variables that can explain the presence of cardiac arrests by using a logistic regression analysis. From this we concluded that the higher the initial REMS, the greater the probability is for a cardiac arrest to occur during a transfer. That is to say, REMS is a predictor of cardiac arrests in patients.

Two follow-up studies later demonstrated that there is a significant association between the severity of the initial REMS and the occurrence of hospital mortality up to 24 h after the transfer [5, 6]. Therefore, when initiating a transfer of a patient with an intermediate or high REMS, constant evaluation must be maintained in order to identify potentially risky situations [7].

4 The Proposed Cloud-Based Mobile System

4.1 The Architecture of the Cloud-Based Mobile System

Cloud-based mobile applications that provide constant monitoring features and guidelines for healthcare, such as our solution, can be classified under the field of collaborative systems. These software applications can be particularly challenging to implement due to mobility-related limitations in both the frontend and backend [15]. Mobile frontend requirements are related to the intrinsic limitations of interacting with the device and are constant for most applications. On the other hand, requirements related to the application backend are very different and unique to monitoring and collaborative platforms. These include environmental (interoperability, heterogeneity, scalability, and availability), security (reliability and privacy), and performance (battery life, storage, and bandwidth) requirements.

In order to deal with these limitations, our solution augments the capabilities of the mobile devices by incorporating mobile cloud computing (MCC) principles. MCC architectures seek to leverage the capabilities of external resource rich nodes to improve performance and battery life [18]. As such, our solution uses a smartphone simply as a hub and display for wirelessly transmitted data of a variety of sensors; it later relays them to a server in charge of all the computer-intensive processing whenever a network connection is available. This enables the server to process and analyze incoming data in real-time in order to obtain statistics and contextual information without straining the battery of the mobile device [1].

Figure 1 shows the general architecture of the proposed system, separating functionality into three basic applications: (a) Cloud-based backend services for computational and data storage purposes, (b) Mobile and web applications that enhance collaboration and analysis between SAMU and medical teams, and (c) Embedded and mobile applications that aid vital-sign monitoring and improve communication within medical services.

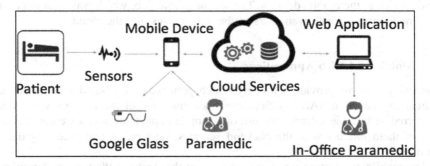

Fig. 1. General architecture of the proposed cloud-based mobile system

4.2 Mobile Backend as a Service

Backend services enable convenient, on-demand network access to a shared pool of computing resources or services that can be rapidly distributed with minimal management effort. These cloud-based backend services were used to gather data from multiple sensors and for providing access to this information to different users. Among the advantages of using the cloud to power mobile services are:

- On-demand self-service: the resources can be used and accessed at any time.
- Broad network access: the resources can be accessed over a network from multiple kinds of devices.
- Scalability: users can quickly acquire more resources from the cloud by scaling out.
- Processing power: permits reducing the computational time of complex tasks compared to devices with limited resources.
- Security and privacy: authentication and authorization can be centralized.

The service platform is built with the Ruby on Rails (RoR) framework. It exposes a RESTful web service through which to receive data and defines the protocols used by paramedics in case of emergency. Only authenticated users are allowed to interact with our web services, therefore ensuring the patient's medical data remains secure.

For storage purposes, our cloud service uses a MongoDB NoSQL database. This technology was selected over a relational database due to its higher scalability and better performance when handling large loads of concurrent write operations [23]. This paradigm fits very well with the intrinsically write-intensive characteristic of sensor data collection applications.

The RoR services and MongoDB instances are hosted on Heroku's cloud platform using one dyno, which is a lightweight Linux container that runs a single user-specified command. Namely, the components use the Platform as a Service solution, which allows us to manage the applications while avoiding the complexity of the infrastructure.

The backend service needs to share and distribute data to several users and several devices and platforms. To achieve this, two technologies were adopted. The first is the Google Cloud Messaging, which was used to send non-sensitive information from the cloud service to the mobile devices. The second is PubNub, which was used to provide real-time interaction with web users as the data arrives into the cloud.

4.3   Mobile and Web Applications

Monitoring systems provide a tool by which paramedics on board ambulances and medical regulators in SAMU offices can track the state of the patients while being transferred. It is achieved with the use of a mobile application and a web application. Both of them interact with the backend services for sending and receiving data in real-time.

The mobile application was built natively on the Android Platform and requires a device running Android 4.1 or higher. It provides a simple graphical user interface that enables paramedics to monitor the patient's vital signs over time through dynamic charts. These charts allow the paramedic to observe the tendency of the patient's REMS and its parameters, while a panel displays the current values of those parameters. The application also includes a list of protocols and guidelines to be applied when specific situations occur during the transfer.

The mobile application receives the data from the sensors by the use of a local Wi-Fi network. It then processes the data and updates the corresponding graphs. At the same time, the information is sent to the cloud service by the use of the mobile network. If the mobile network is unavailable, then the data is stored locally until a connection is reestablished. When this occurs, the data is sent on a last-come-first-serve basis.

This application also supports an optional Google Glass peripheral. During an emergency, the paramedics' attention must be centered on the patient and should have their hands free to attend him. With Google Glass, paramedics can focus their full attention on the patient while the relevant information is delivered directly in front of their eyes.

While the initial release of Google Glass into the consumer market has met with questionable results, we believe the current available version is mature enough to be of use in more specialized scenarios, such as medical support.

Figure 2 shows the mobile application user interface. Its layout is divided as follows: on the left side there is a list displaying the current values for REMS and its parameters. On the right side, there is a chart showing the tendency over time for REMS. It is possible to select one specific parameter from the left to observe its own tendency in the chart. At the top there is a list of checkboxes that allows the paramedics to select special conditions that a patient could have. Finally at the top right, it is possible to observe alerts that are generated when potential risky situations are detected.

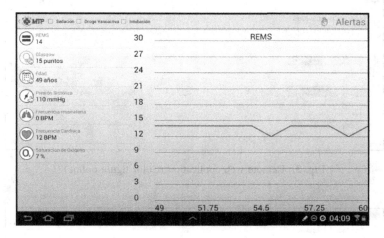

Fig. 2. Ambulance mobile application

As for the web application, its primary goal is to provide a remote real-time tracking of patients being transferred. It is mainly targeted towards medical regulators that can give remote assistance to the paramedics in case of emergency. With this information readily available, they are able to promptly order a re-transfer should the situation require it.

Medical data is provided graphically by charts that show the tendency of the clinical state of the patient (REMS and its parameters) for each active transfer. As the transfers are completed, the information disappears from the screen and is only visible to medical administrators. The technologies behind the application include RoR, AngularJS and common web technologies (HTML, CSS, and JavaScript). We used the Model-View-Controller design pattern for the backend services and the web application frontend.

The main layout of the web application is shown in Fig. 3. In the left side, there is a list of current transfers. When a transfer is selected, the tendency of REMS and its parameters is displayed in charts on the right side. When the parameter being observed is in its normal range, the data is shown in green, but when it is in dangerous values, it is displayed in red. Alerts generated by the mobile application are displayed at the top of this interface. They are removed when a paramedic attends it or when the condition of the patient returns to a normal state.

Given that a deterioration in the condition of the patient could lead to serious situations, it is important to be able to provide right directions to paramedics. One important decision is the change of the arrival hospital when the state of the patient requires it. In order to support this kind of decisions, the web application is capable of displaying a map that shows the location of the ambulance in real-time (Fig. 4).

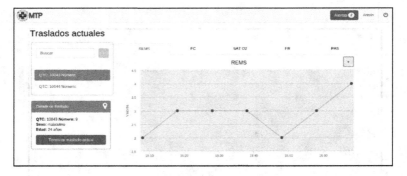

Fig. 3. Remote web application (Color figure online)

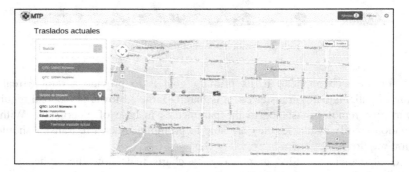

Fig. 4. Remote web application showing map with location of an ambulance

4.4 Embedded Devices

The embedded application is designed to enhance the process of collecting data from wearable vital sign sensor devices. The sensor platform is composed of two components, the sensor device itself and a mobile application focused on vital sign monitoring and communication with the cloud platform.

An Arduino Uno and an e-Health Sensor Shield v2.0 were used to support the acquisition of data from the corresponding sensors. In particular, an SPO2 sensor was used for reading pulse and blood oxygen levels, while an airflow sensor was used for calculating breathing rate. These sensors were connected to the e-Health Shield through a wired connection. The e-Health Shield was mounted on the Arduino Uno, which was programmed to receive data and send it through Wi-Fi to the mobile device using an XBee Shield and the RN-XV WiFly module.

It is important to stand out that one advantage of this platform over the equipment currently available on ambulances is the fact that, when a device stops working, it can be replaced without affecting the rest of the devices. This allows the system to continue working while the defective device is replaced.

Two important constraints were present with regards to the sensors. The first was the fact that no blood pressure sensor that could send data wirelessly was available at the time the prototype was built. For this reason, this data had to be entered manually into the mobile application. The second constraint was the fact that respiration rate is calculated from data provided by the airflow sensor. The system was built to receive data from this sensor every 50 ms in order to detect whether or not a patient was breathing and therefore calculate the respiratory rate. In order to avoid noise, a threshold for detecting new breaths needed to be defined.

Figure 5 shows pictures of the sensors (a) and the mobile device (b) in use during a simulated transfer. The Arduino is in the gray box shown in the first image, while the mobile device is in the hands of a paramedic shown in the second picture. The second picture also shows the current equipment available in ambulances for monitoring the patient's health state.

(a) Ambulance Embedded Sensors   (b) Ambulance Mobile Device

Fig. 5. Sensor platform and mobile device in use

5 Testing and Results

In order to test the system in a real environment, we performed a transfer of a simulated patient in an actual ambulance used for secondary transfers. Two paramedics were on board, while a third paramedic stayed at the office monitoring the transfer through the web application. Continuous communication was established in order to compare the information in the mobile device to the information in the web application.

The ambulance's path was approximately 6 km long, at points going behind hills in order to test the signal strength. The simulation called for an unconscious patient;

therefore, Glasgow was assigned a score of 4 on the REMS. The simulated patient was also under respiratory assistance, giving a score of 4 for respiration rate. Thus, the initial REMS was 8, assuming that all the other parameters were evaluated with a score of 0.

The sensors were connected to the patient during the journey. Blood pressure readings were taken every five minutes and were updated manually in the mobile device. With the data, it was possible to observe how the REMS changed due to variations in heart rate as well as changes in blood pressure.

In terms of the usability and performance of the system, the sensor platform performed favorably compared to the sensors available on the ambulance. In fact, the readings were almost the same throughout the journey. One negative aspect was the fact that the heart rate sensor occasionally lost connection due to the vibrations that occur during ambulance transfers. The connection was interrupted for about 5 s and was therefore not critical. According to paramedics, these disconnections also occur with the sensor platform currently available on ambulances.

On the other hand, the mobile application gave constant feedback on the state of the patient in REMS terms via charts. The information was successfully sent to the cloud in real time around 98 % of the time. The rest of the data was delivered with some delay due to the nature of mobile network signal. Nevertheless, since the downtime of the network was insignificant compared to its uptime, this was not considered an issue.

Another important aspect is the fact that the mobile application was capable of detecting disconnected sensors. When this occurred, the system assigned the worst possible score to REMS parameters, which was reflected as peaks in the REMS chart. The system also generated corresponding alerts, which prompted paramedics to check the devices. The web application allowed the observation and analysis of information about the transfer in real time without issues. The tendency of the parameters was displayed in charts, as well as the generated alerts.

6 Conclusions and Further Work

This paper presents a Cloud-based Mobile System as the best approach for implementing a risk assessment platform for critical patients requiring ambulance transfers. The infrastructure proposed has proved to perform very well in an actual setting. Requirements for the mobile platform include integration with embedded sensors and low fault tolerance during the transfers. This challenges developers to build more complex software solutions that are specific to these scenarios. An example of this is the addition of a local Wi-Fi network inside the ambulance to allow each sensor to properly communicate without depending on a constant Internet connection.

In terms of performance, the sensor platform was able to accurately read the required parameters with a low disconnection rate and rapid recovery when such disconnection errors occurred. The mobile application was able to receive the data at a fast rate, perform calculations, and send the data to the cloud without major problems. It was able to provide the data to the cloud in real time during approximately 98 % of the transfer.

The web application was able to show the information sent by the mobile device and update it in real time, allowing the paramedic to track the state of the patient efficiently while the transfer was made. Requirements for this component included the upkeep of several simultaneous ambulance transfers, each one sending data at a high transfer rate. Using a NoSQL database increased the performance of the application significantly.

In terms of usability, both the mobile and web applications provided the information in a way that was easy to read for paramedics, and they are expected to be useful for conducting future studies. With regard to the sensor platform, it was found that the sensor wires were rather short, and extending them can improve usability.

Further work includes more testing for new wireless sensors, which aims to improve the usability of the system. We expect to test the usability of the Google Glass application and compare it with the usability of the mobile application. The sensor platform used has a modular design, and adds the capacity incorporate different and newer sensors. With additional work we can make this system a component available in every ambulance and connect several emergency systems.

We believe that the evidence obtained from research data generated within real transfers can increase the quality, effectiveness and efficiency of decisions in patient care. Based on epidemiological needs and prevalence we identify a need to create risk profiles of patients treated at the health system, which would allow us to characterize risk groups and develop strategies aimed at preventing health problems and complications during transfers. A cloud service information built on top of predictive analysis solutions will quickly identify groups most at risk such as patients in extreme ages, generating new severity scales for such groups.

Acknowledgements. This work was partially supported by VRI-PUC Interdisciplinary Grant No. 03/2013, FONIS 2014 SA 12I2045 CONICYT, and SAMU. Finally, we would like to give special thanks to Mr. Claudio Jerez, CEO of TEVEUK Ltd.

References

1. Bahl, P., Han, R.Y., Li, L.E., Satyanarayanan, M.: Advancing the state of mobile cloud computing. In: Proceedings of the Third ACM Workshop on Mobile Cloud Computing and Services, pp. 21–28. ACM (2012)
2. Berkelman, R.L., Sullivan, P., Buehler, J.W., Detels, R., Beaglehole, R., Lansing, M., Gulliford, M., et al.: Public health surveillance. In: Oxford Textbook of Public Health, 5th edn. The Methods of Public Health, vol. 2, pp. 699–715. Oxford University Press, Oxford (2009)
3. Bourouis, A., Feham, M., Bouchachia, A.: Ubiquitous mobile health monitoring system for elderly (umhmse) (2011). arXiv preprint arXiv:1107.3695
4. Buyya, R., Yeo, C.S., Venugopal, S., Broberg, J., Brandic, I.: Cloud computing and emerging it platforms: vision, hype, and reality for delivering computing as the 5th utility. Future Gener. Comput. Syst. 25(6), 599–616 (2009)

5. Carrillo, B.M.J.: Deterioro fisiopatológico y mortalidad, de los pacientes adultos sometidos a traslado interhospitalario a Unidades de Paciente Crítico por móviles del Servicio de Atención Médica de Urgencia del área Metropolitana, Santiago de Chile. Ph.D. thesis, Universidad de Sao Pablo (2015)
6. Carrillo, B.M.J., Jerez, C., Cortéz, A.: Traslado interhospitalario samu área metropolitana: En búsqueda de una mejor calidad de atención. FONIS SA12I2045 (2014)
7. Carrillo, B.M.J., Urrutia S, M.T.: Perfil de riesgo de pacientes adultos sometidos a traslado secundario por móviles avanzados del sistema de atención médica de urgencia del Área metropolitana. Revista médica de Chile 140, 1297–1303 (October 2012)
8. Chen, S.K., Kao, T., Chan, C.T., Huang, C.N., Chiang, C.Y., Lai, C.Y., Tung, T.H., Wang, P.C.: A reliable transmission protocol for zigbee-based wireless patient monitoring. IEEE Trans. Inf. Technol. Biomed. 16(1), 6–16 (2012)
9. Chiauzzi, E., Rodarte, C., DasMahapatra, P.: Patient-centered activity monitoring in the self-management of chronic health conditions. BMC Med. 13(1), 77 (2015)
10. Chu, Y., Ganz, A.: A mobile teletrauma system using 3g networks. IEEE Trans. Inf. Technol. Biomed. 8(4), 456–462 (2004)
11. Dobkin, B.H., Dorsch, A.: The promise of mhealth daily activity monitoring and outcome assessments by wearable sensors. Neurorehabil. Neural Repair 25(9), 788–798 (2011)
12. Mobile Medical Applications: Guidance for Industry and Food and Drug Administration Staff. USA: Food and Drug Administration (2013)
13. Gállego, J.R., Hernández-Solana, Á., Canales, M., Lafuente, J., Valdovinos, A., Fernández-Navajas, J.: Performance analysis of multiplexed medical data transmission for mobile emergency care over the umts channel. IEEE Trans. Inf. Technol. Biomed. 9(1), 13–22 (2005)
14. Imhoff, B.F., Thompson, N.J., Hastings, M.A., Nazir, N., Moncure, M., Cannon, C.M.: Rapid emergency medicine score (rems) in the trauma population: a retrospective study. BMJ Open 4(5), e004738 (2014)
15. Neyem, A., Ochoa, S.F., Pino, J.A., Franco, R.D.: A reusable structural design for mobile collaborative applications. J. Syst. Softw. 85(3), 511–524 (2012)
16. Olsson, T., Lind, L.: Comparison of the rapid emergency medicine score and apache ii in nonsurgical emergency department patients. Acad. Emerg. Med. 10(10), 1040–1048 (2003)
17. Pavlopoulos, S., Kyriacou, E., Berler, A., Dembeyiotis, S., Koutsouris, D.: A novel emergency telemedicine system based on wireless communication technology-ambulance. IEEE Trans. Inf. Technol. Biomed. 2(4), 261–267 (1998)
18. Rahimi, M.R., Ren, J., Liu, C.H., Vasilakos, A.V., Venkatasubramanian, N.: Mobile cloud computing: a survey, state of art and future directions. Mobile Netw. Appl. 19(2), 133–143 (2014)
19. Scully, C.G., Lee, J., Meyer, J., Gorbach, A.M., Granquist-Fraser, D., Mendelson, Y., Chon, K.H.: Physiological parameter monitoring from optical recordings with a mobile phone. IEEE Trans. Biomed. Eng. 59(2), 303–306 (2012)
20. Sethi, D., Subramanian, S.: When place and time matter: how to conduct safe inter-hospital transfer of patients. Saudi J. Anaesth. 8(1), 104 (2014)
21. Son, D., Lee, J., Qiao, S., Ghaffari, R., Kim, J., Lee, J.E., Song, C., Kim, S.J., Lee, D.J., Jun, S.W., et al.: Multifunctional wearable devices for diagnosis and therapy of movement disorders. Nat. Nanotechnol. 9(5), 397–404 (2014)
22. Triantafyllidis, A.K., Koutkias, V.G., Chouvarda, I., Maglaveras, N.: A pervasive health system integrating patient monitoring, status logging, and social sharing. IEEE J. Biomed. Health Inform. 17(1), 30–37 (2013)

23. van der Veen, J.S., van der Waaij, B., Meijer, R.J.: Sensor data storage performance: Sql or nosql, physical or virtual. In: 2012 IEEE 5th International Conference on Cloud Computing (CLOUD), pp. 431–438. IEEE (2012)
24. Yang, C.C., Hsu, Y.L.: A review of accelerometry-based wearable motion detectors for physical activity monitoring. Sensors 10(8), 7772–7788 (2010)

Visual Exploration of Urban Dynamics Using Mobile Data

Eduardo Graells-Garrido[(✉)] and José García

Telefónica I+D, Av. Manuel Montt 1404, 3rd Floor, Santiago, Chile
eduardo.graells@mail.com, Joseantonio.garcia@telefonica.com
http://www.tidchile.cl

Abstract. In this paper we present methods to model citizen movement according to mobile network connectivity, and a set of visualization widgets to display and analyze the results of those methods. In particular, citizen movement is analyzed in terms of Origin/Destiny trips in workable days, as well as classification of city areas into dormitory, non-dormitory, and mixed. We demonstrate our proposal with a case study of the city of Santiago, Chile, and briefly discuss our results in terms of the design of Ambient Intelligence and Urban Design applications.

1 Introduction

Nowadays, urban population is growing more than ever. This must be considered when designing Ambient Intelligence and Urban Design applications, however, urban growth can be faster than the ability of urban planners and public policy makers to study the situation and to take action. Moreover, such activities are usually performed based on surveys, which, given the urban growth, are under the risk of becoming obsolete given how fast cities are changing.

In this paper, we present an on-going project to analyze and visualize the city considering citizen movement, modeled according to usage of mobile networks. In particular, we present methods to model movement, and then we present interactive visualization widgets to communicate how city areas are characterized according to commuting patterns. The display and communication of those patterns is helpful for decision-makers and public policy designers, not only because they visually expose patterns in the data, but also because the stream of information coming from mobile networks is continuous. This allows models like ours to be applied at arbitrary times, unlike surveys which are carried out every five or ten years in some places.

In our work, we propose how to analyze patterns and dynamics of urban movement by considering three different interactive visualization widgets: (1) a *continuous area cartogram* [8]; (2) a flow diagram without geographical context; and (3) a flow diagram with geographical context. These widgets are implemented in a data analysis tool which provides an interactive environment for data analysis and collaboration [11].

To test our methods and visualizations, we analyze citizen movement in *Santiago de Chile*, the capital of Chile, during two workable days in October 2014,

© Springer International Publishing Switzerland 2015
J.M. García-Chamizo et al. (Eds.): UCAmI 2015, LNCS 9454, pp. 480–491, 2015.
DOI: 10.1007/978-3-319-26401-1_45

and discuss potential insights that can be obtained from the interactive analysis of data. As results, we observe that by using mobile connectivity we are able to categorize districts in Santiago according to commuting behavior, as well as to display the geographic patterns behind this categorization and its dynamics. Furthermore, we observe that our models present similar results to other models of similar datasets of Santiago.

2 Mobility and Call Detail Records

In this section we explain how to aggregate and analyze citizen movement according to their connections to mobile antennas. When aggregating users we consider only those whose number of connections is reliable for analysis of regularity in their movement patterns. As this is a first stage of our on-going project, we focus on regular behavior to be able to detect irregular or unexpected events in future work. In particular, we analyze *Call Detail Records* (CDRs hereafter). CDRs are logged information from mobile transactions such as calls, SMS and Internet navigation. Each time a mobile phone establishes a communication with an antenna on the network, the communication meta-data is logged, providing attributes like phone number, call duration (if applicable), time-stamp, and so on. Although CDRs have low precision in comparison to GPS sensors (*e. g.*, those in mobile phones), they provide enough information to reliably model citizen movement patterns [2].

The analysis we perform is the generation of a trace of movement for each citizen, considering the corresponding CDRs in a given day. Note that the CDRs are generated with a non-uniform time frequency, because users usually do not use their mobile phones 100 % of the time. Then, we build a trace by interpolating linearly the positions of the corresponding antennas in consecutive records. Note that we do not follow walk-able connections in the interpolation. Instead, we study city zoning when analyzing movement. Specifically, we aggregate CDRs from people with specific commuting behavior from home to work and from work to home in specific time windows. In this way, we exploit the structure of regularity in movement, where we assume that the majority of citizens work during the day, and spend most of the time at the physical locations of their workplaces.

To define if a citizen is at work or at home, we proceed as follows:

1. Define time windows during the day that are likely to be related to home/work. For instance, to model home location, we consider two time windows: one in the range 6AM to 8AM, and one during 8PM to 10PM.
2. In all defined time windows, we model record weights using the exponential distribution:
$$f(x; \gamma) = \gamma e^{-\gamma x}.$$

where x is the position of the record in the time window, and the value of the parameter γ is determined according to the threshold given as confidence interval. If we consider a 95 % interval, then $f(N; \gamma) = 0.05$, having N as the number of records under consideration. Thus, the sum of weights for all records in a given time window is always 1.

3. For each mobile antenna a, we estimate $P(a_t)$ as the sum of the weights of its corresponding records in a specific time window t.

4. In order to determine the regularity of citizen behavior in the different time windows, we use an intersection metric converted to a distance. To calculate this distance, we define a as an antenna and $P(a_t)$ as its weight in the time window t. Then, the distance is defined as:

$$\mathrm{d}(t_1, t_2) = 1 - \sum_{a \in A} \min(P(a_{t_1}), P(a_{t_2})).$$

where A is the set of antennas. Thus, d is 1 when there is no overlap or similarity between distributions, and 0 when all distributions are equal. Empirically, we have found that a $d \leq 0.4$ is indicative of regularity. For instance, considering the time windows related to home locations (6AM to 8AM, and 8PM to 10PM), if the value of d is 0.4, then the citizen's home location is the weighted interpolation of the antennas he/she was connected to in those time windows.

Having these predicted home/work locations, it is possible to build an aggregated Origin-Destiny (OD hereafter) matrix where we consider source and target areas, which can be administrative locations as well as designated zonings.

3   The Case of Santiago, Chile

In this section we apply the methods defined in the previous section to see how transport in the city can be predicted and analyzed from CDR data. We focus on CDR data from Santiago, obtained from two working days of October 2014 from Telefónica.[1] Santiago is the capital of Chile and its largest city. It is a metropolitan area comprised of 37 municipalities. However, in transport surveys, up to 45 municipalities in the Metropolitan Region are considered. Its public transport system, Transantiago [7], integrates bus and metro systems (Fig. 1 Left displays the current metro network and planned extensions). In addition, there are private and shared cabs, as well as inter-communal trains. In the last survey from years 2012–2013[2], it was found that the rate of vehicles per home was 0.57, and that a total of 18,461,134 trips are performed on a regular work day (of those, 11,350,691 are motorized).

We applied our method to analyze citizen traces on the city as well as an OD matrix. First, we analyze the OD matrix, displayed on Fig. 2. It was estimated aggregating CDRs according to the corresponding municipalities of each antenna. At first sight it provides the following insights:

---

[1] For privacy and commercial concerns we do not disclose absolute numbers.

[2] http://www.sectra.gob.cl/Datos_e_Informacion_Espacial/Gran_Santiago/ encuestas_movilidad.html, visited on June 2015.

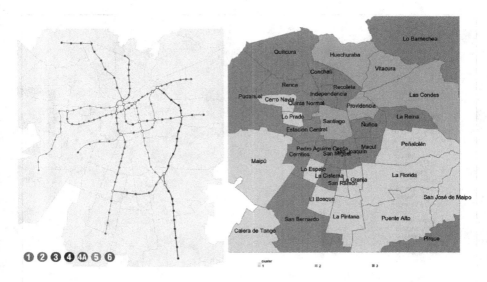

Fig. 1. Left: A map of Santiago with an overlay of the current and planned subway layout (planned lines are dotted). Source: Osmar Valdebenito, used with permission. Right: A map of Santiago showing land-use of municipalities according to a clustering algorithm. Source: Own elaboration (Color figure online).

– The top-3 originating locations are Maipú (9 % of the trips, 2nd in population size), Santiago (8.8 %, 7th in population) and Las Condes (7.7 %, 4th in population).
– The top-3 destinations are Santiago (24.4 %, 9th in Human Development Index –HDI–), Las Condes (14.7 %, 2nd in HDI) and Providencia (12.6 %, 4th in HDI).

We observe that top originating locations are related to population size, and destinations could be related to development. We do not perform a deep qualitative analysis of this, instead, we evaluate if our movement traces and OD matrix are coherent with physical world measures. The first evaluation is to compare our OD matrix with two other matrices: the one obtained from the OD Survey 2012–2013, and one estimated from public transport system usage through the analysis of smart card data [6]. To do so, we have estimated the Spearman rank-correlation of all source-target pairs of our dataset, and those of the two mentioned matrices. This correlation compares the ranks of two independent variables, and its values range between -1 (perfect opposite relation), 1 (perfect relation) and 0 (independence). This means that a value of 1 would mean that all OD pairs have the same rank. We have obtained the following correlations:

– Our matrix and Transantiago [6]: $\rho = 0.73$ ($p < 0.001$).
– Our matrix and OD Survey 2012–2013: $\rho = 0.70$ ($p < 0.001$).
– Reference: Transantiago and OD Survey 2012–2013: $\rho = 0.74$ ($p < 0.001$).

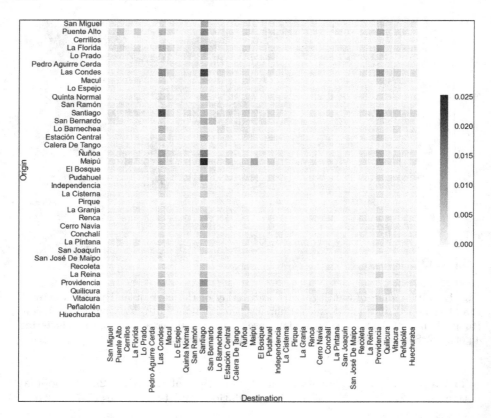

Fig. 2. Estimated OD matrix of municipalities for Santiago, Chile (Color figure online).

Thus, our predicted OD matrix for working days is highly correlated with other known OD matrices with the same focus. Note that a higher correlation between matrices is unlikely, because our matrix considers citizens who might not use public transportation with smart cards, and Transantiago's predicted matrix considers smart card data only.

In addition, with the purpose of identifying land-use, we aggregated the movement traces from the CDRs in municipalities. This allowed us to create a distribution per municipality according to the number of citizens in it during the day, including inhabitants, workers, students and commuters. We estimated a normalized cumulative density function (CDF) for each location, to be able to compare two different municipalities regardless of the total citizen count within them at a specific time. We used the CDFs to estimate a theoretical distance between municipalities using Manhattan distance, and built a distance matrix between locations. In this matrix we applied Agglomerative Clustering [12] to a distance matrix built from the district OD matrix.

There are at least two kinds of land-use: dormitory and non-dormitory. Dormitory municipalities are those whose primary use is to provide a home location

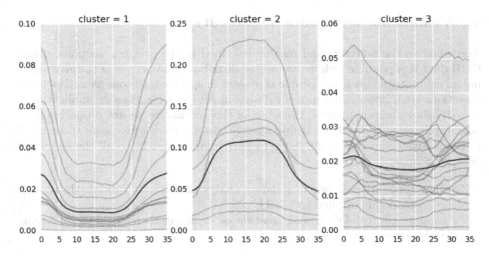

Fig. 3. Clusters obtained from the analysis of district dynamic population. The left cluster represents dormitory districts. The middle cluster represents non-dormitory districts. The right cluster represents mixed or transition districts.

for the working population, but that do not have industrial nor educational activity during a day. Thus, we experimented with two clusters, but results were not satisfactory, as there was too much disparity within each cluster. Then, we moved to the next level. Results with three clusters are displayed on Fig. 3. These results indicate the following:

- Cluster 1 (green in Fig. 1 Right) is about dormitory districts, which have a bigger population at the beginning and at the end of the day.
- Cluster 2 (orange in Fig. 1 Right) is about non-dormitory districts, with a dynamic population that grows during working hours.
- Cluster 3 (blue in Fig. 1 Right) presents a mixed situation, with several kinds of shapes that do not belong to Clusters 1 and 2.

By looking at Fig. 1, it is interesting to note that there is a geographic pattern in the clustering, even though the CDFs do not encode geographic information. Furthermore, by comparing the maps in Figure 1, there appears to be a relation between the presence of metro stations and the belonging group of each municipality: locations in the dormitory group (cluster 1) have metro stations and tend to be located in the south of the city, while locations in the mixed group (cluster 3) in general do not have any metro station and tend to be located on the north. Non-dormitory districts are coherent with the most common destinations for trips in our OD matrix, and their geographical closeness indicates that land-use is concentrated for non-dormitory activities. Whether this is a consequence of urban design or segregation is something that goes beyond the scope of this paper.

4   Visualizing Dynamics of the City

According to the methods and results described in the previous sections, using CDR data it is possible to have an on-line distribution of people in the city. Having an estimate of how much people is present in specific locations as well as their directions is an important input for design of Ambient Intelligence applications, as well as for decision-makers. However, in this section we do not propose a specific application. Instead, we define a set of *visualization widgets* [3] to be used in the analysis phase of urban data. In particular, we ought to fill the following design rationale:

- To allow application designers and data analysts to visually validate the results of urban modeling applied to CDRs.
- To support the validation and creation of explanatory hypothesis on urban dynamics by experts.

Following this rationale we have implemented three visualization widgets: a *cartogram*, a *flow diagram*, and a *graph over a map*. All of them have been implemented using the *d3.js* library [1]. In particular, we have implemented them having in mind compatibility with an interactive analysis tool named *IPython notebook* [9,11], by using a software library known as *matta*.[3] This library eases the implementation of interactive visualization widgets which can be used inside the IPython notebook. Additionally, the resulting widgets can be exported ("scaffolded" as described by the library) as Javascript libraries, enabling their use in Web-based applications aimed at exploration of urban data.

A Dynamic Shape of the City. The main purpose of this widget is to communicate the dynamic shape of the city. Typical maps are static in the sense that they display administrative borders and geographical features that do not change according to the data. Instead, this widget displays a *continuous area cartogram* [8] of the city[4]. This kid of cartogram is a visual representation of a geographic area where the shape of each area is distorted according to a specific variable. In our case, this variable is the fraction of citizens in each location at an specific time. This representation has been used before for mobile network connectivity analysis [10], and thus it is seen as helpful in our context.

Figure 4 displays two cartograms of Santiago using the movement trace from previous sections, at 6:30AM, where we expect that people is mostly at their home locations, and 1:30PM, where we expect that people is mostly at their work locations. Note that municipalities are colored according to the detected clusters in the previous section. In contrast with the traditional representation from Fig. 1, this image explains directly which cluster is non-dormitory. Additionally, this widget is interactive and animated. In the IPython notebook, users can

---

[3] http://github.com/carnby/matta.
[4] We use this implementation: https://github.com/shawnbot/d3-cartogram, visited on June 2015.

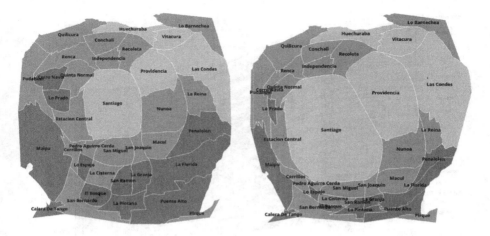

Fig. 4. Cartograms of municipalities of Santiago at 6:30 AM and 1:30 PM. Note that the orientation of the map is the same as in Fig. 1, with North at the top.

select specific times of the day (*e. g.*, every half hour), and the cartogram will update to reflect the new chosen time. This update is not static–the areas of the city are smoothly animated from the old state to new state. The animated transition, in addition to adding context to the change of the state as well as making it visually attractive, could improve graphical perception of changes [4].

In summary, with this widget it is possible to visualize how the city changes according to the movements of its citizens. The color coding used based on clustering results, helps to understand the geographic patterns of the city distribution.

Citizen Movement as Flow. When analyzing movement between districts and municipalities, sometimes the geographical context is not needed. Although the flow metaphor has been used before in maps, with applications such as the Flow Map Layout [13], the geography implicit in the visualization makes interpretation hard, not to mention potential cluttering of the image due to the fixed positions of sources and targets of the network. Thus, we propose to depict flow using Sankey diagrams. In these diagrams, the flow connecting nodes (*i. e.*, locations in our case) are represented with an arc that has a width with proportional size to the flow quantity (*i. e.*, fraction of citizens moving from one location to another).

Figure 5 displays a flow/Sankey diagram of the OD matrix. Flow is visualized from source nodes (municipalities) to target nodes (municipalities). Arcs between nodes can be colored according to any variable under consideration. In the figure, we used a categorical coding, where color indicates the estimated cluster (of the target location) from previous sections. We display only the top 50 % of OD pairs to avoid cluttering of the image and show the most representative OD pairs of the city. This percent of the OD pairs is customizable on the IPython notebook, as well as the color coding of edges. For instance, instead of target location cluster, it could be the source location's income level.

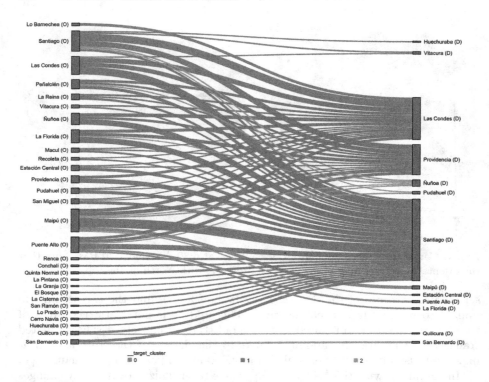

Fig. 5. Flow representation of the top 50 % most common trips in the OD Matrix (Color figure online).

Although this diagram does not include the geographical context, it allows experts to answer questions and validate OD pairs at the city level. In this way, an expert could validate land-use results, for instance, by checking if commuter clusters do not receive flow of passengers according to expectations during specific times of the day.

Citizen Movement with Geographical Context. Sometimes the geographical context *is* needed when analyzing flow in OD matrices. In contrast to previous widgets, where we focused on municipalities, we will display a zoning named "777", designed by the Direction of Metropolitan Transport in Santiago.[5] This zoning is more specific than municipalities, and each zone contains several bus stops and metro stations. Using this zoning we can estimate a more granular OD matrix, which we display using our graph of the map visualization widget on Fig. 6. The figure displays two different fractions of the OD matrix: on the left, it shows the destinations of the citizens who live in the Santiago municipality; on the right, it shows where people who works in Santiago comes from.

---

[5] Available in http://datos.gob.cl/datasets/ver/1655.

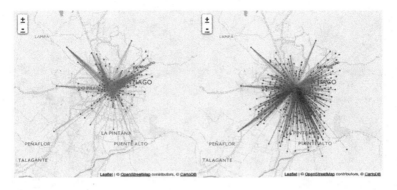

Fig. 6. Flow diagram of people commuting from/to Santiago.

In both cases, only the top 50 % of trips is displayed. Each black dot is the centroid of the corresponding 777 zone. The edges that connect different zones are colored according to source/target cluster of its corresponding municipality. In the left image, for people who lives in Santiago, we use the color of the target municipality; in the right, for people who works in Santiago, we use the color of their source (home) municipality.

Because the OD matrix does not estimate routes, source and target locations are connected through straight lines. Even though we are displaying only 50 % of the trips, as well as displaying more than one source/target municipality at the same time, the resulting graph is hard to interpret. To avoid this, we apply an algorithm named *edge bundling* [5], that identifies which edges are similar enough (*e. g.*, they start and end in nearby locations) to be bundled. Figure 7 Top displays the same graphs from Fig. 6, but with bundled edges. Figure 7 Bottom displays the corresponding target/source destinations for the *Puente Alto* municipality. Previously, we observed that working locations are concentrated on few municipalities, and with a widget like this one we can observe a more detailed distribution of that concentration. Even though the bundling does not represent routes, its proposed approximation gives insights:

- In terms of home locations, in the case of Puente Alto (the most populated municipality of the conurbation), its citizens commute through a long distance and following similar routes (similar enough to be bundled by the algorithm), while citizens from Santiago have a more diverse spread through the city, and their commuting distances are smaller.
- In terms of working locations, we observe that Santiago receives citizen from the entire city and from different kind of municipalities (dormitory and nondormitory, as well as mixed), while Puente Alto receives mostly people from nearby municipalities.

As with the previous widgets, this one allows users to explore the city by selecting source and target locations, as well as color coding of edges. We have highlighted specific insights but by no means the possibilities of the widget are limited to those.

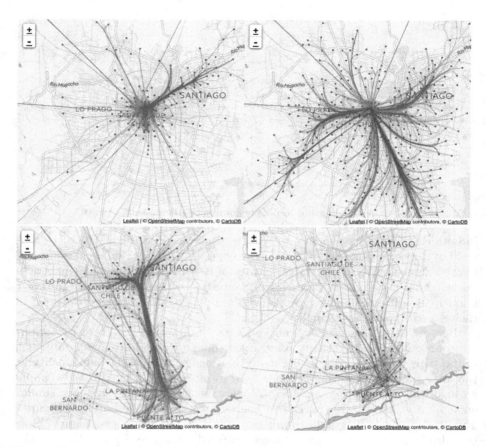

Fig. 7. Flow diagram (with edge-bundling) of people commuting from/to Santiago (top) and Puente Alto (bottom).

5   Discussion and Final Remarks

In this paper we present the current state of an on-going project to study and visually analyze citizen movement in Santiago, Chile. In the project we analyze aggregated information of connectivity with the mobile network of the city, in order to measure and understand citizen movement. We propose that such analyses should be communicated in a way that, first, surfaces the potential hidden patterns in movement; and, second, validates and quantifies current qualitative knowledge about a city (for instance, which districts are dormitory and which are not).

Our specific objective is to build Ambient Intelligence tools with the proposed visualization widgets, as well as to develop more of them. In our case study we presented specific insights obtained from each of them used individually, but we devise that a panel of experts can make use of our widgets in an exploratory tool with coordinated views between widgets [3]. We believe that such tools should be co-created with target users and urban planners, and as such, we think that a prototype/notebook [11] approach is more suitable than a straight application design.

For future work, we will work on the incorporation of qualitative information from census data to the clustering method. By doing so, we will be able to explain clustering results in deeper terms, as well as having more information that could be used to support human decision-making processes.

References

1. Bostock, M., Ogievetsky, V., Heer, J.: D3 data-driven documents. IEEE Trans. Visual Comput. Graphics **17**(12), 2301–2309 (2011)
2. Cuttone, A., Lehmann, S., Larsen, J.E.: Inferring human mobility from sparse low accuracy mobile sensing data. In: Proceedings of the 2014 ACM International Joint Conference on Pervasive and Ubiquitous Computing: Adjunct Publication, pp. 995–1004. ACM (2014)
3. Dork, M., Carpendale, S., Collins, C., Williamson, C.: Visgets: coordinated visualizations for web-based information exploration and discovery. IEEE Trans. Visual. Comput. Graphics **14**(6), 1205–1212 (2008)
4. Heer, J., Robertson, G.G.: Animated transitions in statistical data graphics. IEEE Trans. Visual. Comput. Graphics **13**(6), 1240–1247 (2007)
5. Holten, D., Van Wijk, J.J.: Force-directed edge bundling for graph visualization. In: Computer Graphics Forum, vol. 28. 3, pp. 983–990. Wiley Online Library (2009)
6. Munizaga, M., Devillaine, F., Navarrete, C., Silva, D.: Validating travel behavior estimated from smartcard data. Transp. Res. Part C Emerg. Technol. **44**, 70–79 (2014)
7. Muñoz, J.C., Gschwender, A.: Transantiago: a tale of two cities. Res. Transp. Econ. **22**(1), 45–53 (2008)
8. Oougenik, A.J., Niemeyer, D.R.: An algorithm to construct continuous area cartograms. Prof. Geogr. **37**(1), 75–81 (1985)
9. Pérez, F., Granger, B.E.: IPython: a system for interactive scientific computing. Comput. Sci. Eng. **9**(3), 21–29 (2007)
10. Salnikov, V., Schien, D., Youn, H., Lambiotte, R., Gastner, M.T.: The geography and carbon footprint of mobile phone use in Cote d'Ivoire. EPJ Data Sci. **3**(1), 1–15 (2014)
11. Shen, H., et al.: Interactive notebooks: sharing the code. Nature **515**(7525), 151–152 (2014)
12. Ward Jr., J.H.: Hierarchical grouping to optimize an objective function. J. Am. Stat. Assoc. **58**(301), 236–244 (1963)
13. Xiao, L., Yeh, R., Hanrahan, P.: Flow map layout. In: IEEE Symposium on Information Visualization INFOVIS 2005, pp. 219–224. IEEE (2005)

Video Game Script Design for Stability Assessment of Critical Physical Infrastructure Affected by Disasters

Roberto G. Aldunate[1], Oriel Herrera[2], and Marcos Levano[2(✉)]

[1] College of Applied Health Sciences, University of Illinois
at Urbana-Champaign, Urbana, IL, USA
aldunate@illinois.edu
[2] Escuela Ingeniería Informática, Universidad Catolica de Temuco,
Temuco, Chile
{oherrera,mlevano}@inf.uct.cl

Abstract. Effective and efficient assessment of structural stability of critical physical infrastructure affected by a disaster is a key task during disaster response. However, real world training of staff performing this task is an operationally complex and expensive activity. This work presents a framework for the development of video games to improve the training of structural engineers on this assessment task. Preliminary results suggest that the approach taken by this initiative is valid and promising.

Keywords: Critical physical infrastructure · Disaster response · Video game

1 Introduction

The response system activated when a natural disaster occurs, such as earthquakes, urban or rural fires, flooding, or volcanic eruptions, needs to be as much efficient and effective as possible. In this context, precise and quick early stability assessment of the critical physical infrastructure (CPI) is a crucial task on mitigating the impact of the disaster on the community.

One of the most recurrent problems occurring during early response to disasters, such as earthquakes, is the existence of incomplete information generating uncertainty on the decision makers and the non-lineal consequences of decisions [1–3], in general, and in CPI stability assessment, in particular. On the other hand, usually people with abundant experience on disasters response perform better decisions on tasks and situation assessments than people without such experience [4, 5], partially because their mental models to approach a disaster are not only based on traditional training, i.e., sequential plans and methods [6]. This suggests that if could reproduce a realistic disaster and the response to it, we could improve the performance of decision makers and CPI assessment actors.

Using video-game technology to support emergency response systems, in general, is not a new approach [9–11]. Nevertheless, literature review conducted by the researchers of this work did not reveal specific similar work on using video-game

J.M. García-Chamizo et al. (Eds.): UCAmI 2015, LNCS 9454, pp. 492–498, 2015.
DOI: 10.1007/978-3-319-26401-1_46

technology for stability assessment of CPI. The development of this capability is a joint goal for the Chilean Department of Transportation (MOP), through its Academia Office, the authors of this article, through Chilean research FONDEF Project CA13i10331 titled "Video Juegos Serios para toma de decisiones frente a desastres", and the Japan International Cooperation Agency (JICA). Research project CA13i10331 has amongst its goals to demonstrate that video game–based technology is a valid vehicle to achieve effective and efficient early stability assessment of CPI. This article describes a framework developed for this purpose and results in developing a simulator derived from it. The rest of this article is structured as follows. Next section presents the framework to develop simulations; after this, System Implementation and Results sections present a prototype and the evaluation performed by Academia Office from MOP. Lastly, concluding remarks are provided to the reader.

2 Script Design Framework

In this section, the main elements, and some of its relationships, which conform the video game/simulator under development in this project are described. It is not an exhaustive list of elements, but is sufficiently detailed to provide the reader an overview of the elements and their articulation which generate playability, interaction, or experience that the user/player faces (See Fig. 1).

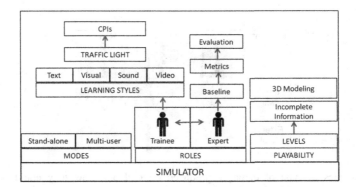

Fig. 1. Framework for the development of scripts for early assessment of CPI.

2.1 Simulation Modes

A simulation session may be stand-alone or multi-user. In the stand-alone mode, the trainee is able to navigate the critical physical infrastructure without other users in the session. All observations and descriptions the trainee conducts are definitive and without the possibility to receive feedback, while in the session, from other users or expert. On the other hand, in the multi-user mode, trainees may share their opinions about the condition of the structural stability of the critical physical infrastructure. Both modes involve a briefing session with expert(s) after their evaluation sessions are finished.

2.2 Roles

The simulator allows training of staff responsible for evaluating the infrastructure of buildings after an earthquake. At this stage two roles have been defined, which are:

- Evaluator (trainee): person being trained for early assessment of CPI.
- Expert (trainer): person that will evaluate the performance of the trainees, handing them the corresponding feedback. The expert sets the baseline for evaluation.

2.3 Playability

This principle deals with the need to build simulations that are immersive, usable, and realistic for the trainees.

2.4 Traffic Light Model

Early evaluation of structural stability of critical physical infrastructure in Chile is adopting a traffic light model widely used in the world [8]. This model signals search and rescue teams as well as shoring teams on the risk level related to the CPI. Green means safe to proceed; yellow means proceed with caution; and red means do not proceed (examples are shown in Fig. 2).

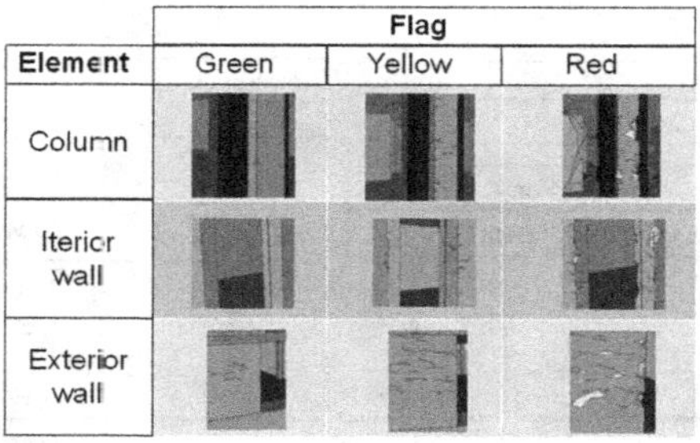

Element	Flag		
	Green	Yellow	Red
Column			
Iterior wall			
Exterior wall			

Fig. 2. Examples of type of damages produced on CPI and how they could possible be interpreted in the traffic light model.

2.5 Difficulty Level

Difficulty level is defined on two variables; magnitude and density. Magnitude refers to the impact of a decision, and density refers to the number of decisions (cognitive load) a user faces in a given period of time. The levels of difficulty for the script design process considers: (a) basic; low magnitude and density, (b) intermediate; low and medium magnitude and density, and (c) advanced; low, medium, and high magnitude and density may be encountered by the trainee.

2.6 Incomplete Information

The CPIs profiles are created with full information on features related with their stability. The system provides the system admin to select what information is available to the user. This enables the simulation experience to be both customizable to user's knowledge level and train users on stressful incomplete decision making processes.

2.7 Realistic 3D Modeling/Immersive Experience

The simulator considers real scenarios of different types of physical infrastructure, which have been designed with the necessary details to allow the player to live an immersive experience during the game.

2.8 Learning Style

The socio-cultural-technical characteristics of the target population to be trained determines how the learning process if conducted. In this case the simulation experience needs to generate a simulation environment that mimics the type of interaction the trainee will have with the affected CPI. Hence, learning styles [7] implemented in this initiative are: text mode, visual mode, sound mode, visual and sound mode, text and visual mode, and video mode.

2.9 Evaluation Metric

Communities can take different approaches in response to disasters, e.g.; some communities may want to put the urban area back to normal operations as soon as possible with a potential high cost, while others may prefer to control the cost of the response system and be able to delay until normality sets back onto the affected area. Hence, this work proposes a local expert-based metric. The local expert usually knows very well how the response system will approach disasters. This expert-based metric is established as a baseline, which is used to evaluate how well the trainee performs.

3 System Implementation

A prototype has been developed with the Academia Office from the Chilean Department of Transportation. Screenshots from the prototype are presented in Figs. 3 and 4. The trainee faces in this prototype the evaluation of several buildings affected by an earthquake of varying magnitude. The trainee may select the building and the magnitude of the earthquake. Once the earthquake occurs, the trainee may navigate the simulated scenario to conduct early and quick stability assessment of the affected building. As a result, the trainee eventually will end up classifying the structural stability of the affected CPI with the traffic model described previously.

Fig. 3. Evaluation form used by trainee.

Fig. 4. Screenshots from CPI's assessment prototype: (a) building model built with unity 3D and running on a web browser in a unity plug-in; (b) structural damage representation in 3D unity model.

Further work includes implementation of multi-user functionality, and development of replay capability for interaction debrief, among others.

4 Results

The system described in the previous section, which was developed from the framework presented in this article, was tested and evaluated by structural engineering experts (N = 2), general engineers and managers (N = 3), and researchers from other disciplines (N = 5), all of them related with the Academia Office from the Chilean Department of Transportation, who are participating in the development of standard procedures and capabilities for emergency response.

The evaluators/reviewers were given a demonstration on general concepts embraced by the simulator as well as details on navigation and usability aspects of it.

After that, they were allowed to interact and use the simulator at their own pace for a period of several days. After this they were interviewed on the following aspects: (a) functionality; how appropriate seems the tools for the purpose of developing a standard in engineers (and firefighters) involved in emergency response operations; (b) usability, how usable is the tool by experts and potentially future trainees; (c) simulation quality, how immersive is the 3D model/navigation and how realistic is the evaluation process in general; and (d) performance and online aspects. All aspects were graded on a 1-5 scale; where 1-very bad, 2-bad, 3-neutral, 4-good, and 5-very good. Figure 5 summarizes the evaluation conducted (averages).

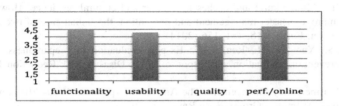

Fig. 5. Evaluation of video-game-based simulator conducted by academia office.

In general terms, it can be appreciated from Fig. 5 that the evaluation from Academia Office was very positive for the simulator built, which not only validates the approach of using video game technology for training and developing emergency response capabilities, but also opens an encouraging venue to improve emergency response systems.

5 Conclusions

This article describes the design of script for serious video games to be used as a tool for improving decision-making process on evaluating stability of critical physical infrastructure affected by disasters. The development of the script, the subsequent prototype, and the encouraging preliminary results, open a venue for exploring how technology like serious video games can better support operations and decisions during response to disasters.

Preliminary results are very positive and encouraging for the evaluation of trainees' assessment capabilities on structural stability of critical physical infrastructure. Results are also perceived by the Chilean Department of Transportation as an opportunity to change and improve the learning process involving the trainees to ultimately improve the performance of response systems activated when disasters affect critical physical infrastructure.

Acknowledgments. The authors want to acknowledge the support from the Chilean science and technology agency CONICYT, thought the FONDEF Project CA13i10331 titled "Video Juegos Serios para toma de decisiones frente a desastres".

References

1. Maki, N.: Disaster response to the 2011 Tohoku-Oki earthquake: national co-ordination, a common operational picture, and command and control in local governments. Earthq. Spectra **29**(S1), S369–S385 (2013)
2. Quarantelli, E.L.: Problematical aspects of the information/communication revolution for disaster planning and research: ten non-technical issues and questions. Disaster Prev. Manage. **6**(2), 94–106 (1997)
3. Seenivasan, M., Arularasu, M., Senthilkumar, K.M., Thirumalai, R.: Disaster prevention and control management in automation: a key role in safety engineering. Procedia Earth Planet. Sci. **11**, 557–565 (2015)
4. Barbara, L.: Multicultural approaches to disaster and cultural resilience. How to consider them to improve disaster management and prevention: the Italian case of two earthquakes. Procedia Econ. Finance **18**, 151–156 (2014)
5. Chou, J.-S., Yang, K.-H., Ren, T.-C.: Ex-post evaluation of preparedness education in disaster prevention, mitigation and response. Int. J. Disaster Risk Reduction **12**, 188–201 (2015)
6. Rubin, C.: Emergency Management: The American Experience 1900–2010, 2nd edn. CRC Press, Taylor & Francis Group, Boca Raton (2012)
7. Camacho, J.A., Chiappe Laverde, A., Lpez de Mesa, C.: Blended Learning y estilos de aprendizaje en estudiantes universitarios del área de la salud. Educación Médica Superior **26**(1), 27–44 (2002)
8. Tang, A., Wen, A.: An intelligent simulation system for earthquake disaster assessment. Comput. Geosci. **35**(5), 871–879 (2009)
9. Linehan, C., Lawson, S., Doughty, M., Kirman, B.: There's no 'I' in emergency management teams: designing and evaluating a serious game for training emergency managers in group decision making skills. In: Proceedings of the 39th Conference of the Society for the Advancement of Games and Simulations in Education and Training, Leeds, UK, pp. 20–27 (2009)
10. Crichton, M., Flin, R.: Training for emergency management: tactical decisión games. J. Haz. Mater. **88**, 255–266 (2001)
11. Haferkamp, N., Kraemer, N.C., Linehan, C., Schembri, M.: Training disaster communication by means of serious games in virtual environments. Entertainment Comput. **2**, 81–88 (2011)

Intelligent Management of Parking Lots in Urban Contexts

Juan A. Vera-Gomez[1], Alexis Quesada-Arencibia[2],
Carmelo R. García[2(✉)], Raúl Suárez-Moreno[1],
and Fernando Guerra-Hernández[1]

[1] Edosoft Factory, S.L., Las Palmas de Gran Canaria, Spain
{juan.vera, raul.suarez, fernando.guerra}
@edosoftfactory.com
[2] University Institute for Cybernetic Science and Technology, Universidad de
Las Palmas de Gran Canaria, Las Palmas de Gran Canaria, Spain
{aquesada, rgarcia}@dis.ulpgc.es

Abstract. How to manage the parking space in urban areas is explained in this work, assuming the aims of Smart City, presenting a realistic solution to this important problem. The proposed solution consists of an intelligent management system for on-street public parking based on wireless sensor network and cloud computing technologies.

Keywords: Intelligent transport systems · Parking management · Smart city · Wireless sensor network

1 Introduction

The solution to the problem of excessive traffic and its resulting consequences is an objective assumed by the developed and developing countries worldwide. This goal can be justified from different points of view: public health, environment, traffic safety and economy. According to Mahmud [1], the costs due to traffic problems are originated from different sources: time lost, extra travelled distance, extra energy consumption, vehicles operational costs and miscellaneous costs. In the specific case of parking searching in urban areas and according to Pineda [2], the cost produced by lost time and consumed resources in the cities of Madrid and Barcleona are about 347 M€ and 268 M€ respectively, and the extra costs by energy consumption are about 187 M€ and 145 M€ respectively. These amounts should be incremented due to environmental costs produced by MOX, PM2,5 and CO2 emissions, about 26 M€ and 20 M€ respectively.

A system model for an intelligent management of on-street parking lots in the context of smart city is presented in this contribution. The system aims are to produce a more efficient and ecological private transport, improving the parking spaces management in urban areas. The parking spaces management has been studied by several researches: for example MingKai [3] and Tang [4] propose cases of systems for the management of this type of spaces in off-street parking lots. However, the management of the on-street parking is challenge to face because this type of parking can provide

© Springer International Publishing Switzerland 2015
J.M. García-Chamizo et al. (Eds.): UCAmI 2015, LNCS 9454, pp. 499–504, 2015.
DOI: 10.1007/978-3-319-26401-1_47

more convenient access to destinations for drivers and occupies less land per space than off-street parking. This kind of management has been studied by Guo [5] that analyses how vehicles flow can be affected by the use of simulation techniques. Litman [6] proposes a good practices guide for the management of these spaces. Finally, Barone [7] proposes a model of architecture for parking management systems in the context of Smart City.

This work has been funded by AETySI – Competitividad I+D program of Spanish Ministry of Industry, Energy and Tourism with code TSI-020601-2012-47. This paper is structured as follows: the next section is dedicated to describe related works, the description of the proposed system is presented in Sect. 2, the tests performed are described in Sect. 3, and finally the main conclusions and future works are presented in Sect. 4.

2 System Description

This work permits the intelligent management and knowledge of the environment using the information and communication technologies. Its users will be informed about the available on-street parking using their mobile terminals, so this work can be considered a case of Internet of Thinks. From the point of view of transit agencies, the application of this system permits the information recollection in order to avoid the traffic vehicles seeking parking lot.

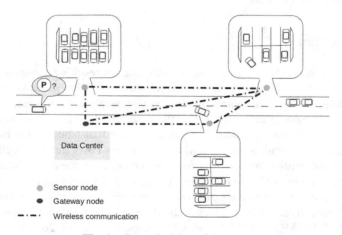

Fig. 1. General vision of the system

To monitor the available on-street parking lots, the system uses a low cost and low consumption wireless sensor network. Thus, a complex deployment is not necessary since no specific wired infrastructure is required in the zones where it is intended to deploy the sensors installation; Fig. 1 shows a general vision of the system. The platform permits the transport authorities to obtain information about the traffic density with the aim of managing the on-street parking lot spaces in a sustainable way. Other relevant aspect of the system architecture is the use of Cloud Computing and Virtualization Technologies.

Fig. 2. The sensor is installed in the middle of the speed bump (left). Physical deployment of the sensors in two speed bumps (right).

The system structure consists of a wireless sensor network installed in the entrance of parking spaces. Each sensor node produces asynchronously data related to the occupancy of each monitored parking space, transmitting these data using the wireless network. One of these nodes is the responsible to transmit these data to the Data Center for storing and managing; in the architecture this node is named Gateway Node. Once the data are processed, the information about vacancy on-street parking lots is provided to transport agencies and citizens.

Each sensor node is composed by a tiny infrared sensor of low cost and low power, SHARP 2Y0D02 [8], a radio module, CC2530, and an amplifier module, CC2591, both of Texas Instrument [9]. The on-chip system of the radio module has the 8051 microcontroller, a programmable 256 Kbytes Flash memory and 8 Kbytes RAM memory. The sensors were installed in a two small speed bumps, like those used for deterrent effect, installed at a minimum distance, system parameter D, see Fig. 2. With this configuration, when the two sensors simultaneously detect the presence of an object for a minimum time, system parameter T, then the system considers that a vehicle has passed. The sensors nodes send datagrams indicating the entrance or exit of vehicles in the monitored parking area. In addition, each sensor node must be able to interpret the datagrams received from the Data Center. To perform these basic actions, a Contiki operating system runs on each sensor nodes, being controlled by C programs. The development system used is Instant Contiki.

The Gateway Node is responsible to link the sensors nodes to the Data Centre. Using the 6LoWPAN protocol, this element receives the datagrams sent by sensor nodes and transmits them to the Data Center. Also, it performs the datagrams communication in the opposite direction, when the Data Center sends programming or status commands to the sensors nodes. The same software elements are used for programming this element.

The role of the Data Center is to control the sensor network and the management of the data obtained by them. Additionally, a web service is executed in this element to perform the control of the sensor network and to present the data produced by the sensors. A control software module, named Control Server, runs in this element for

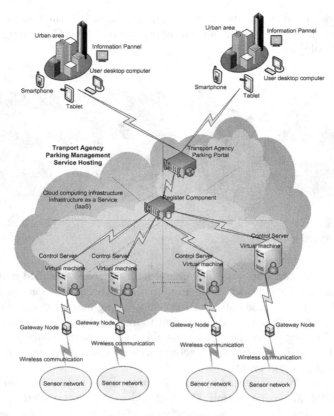

Fig. 3. System architecture

reading and sending datagrams to the wireless sensor network. Also, for data storing, a module, named Register Component, runs in the Data Center. This system architecture is presented in Fig. 3.

In many cases, transport agencies have responsibilities in different metropolitan areas of cities; therefore aspects related to scalability, flexibility, security and privacy should be considered especially. To fulfil these requirements, the Virtualization technology and Cloud Computing paradigm are used in the proposed architecture. Thus, the Data Center can be deployed as a hosting centre to provide parking management services to different metropolitan areas or even to private clients such as parking enterprises.

3 Tests

The proposed system has been implemented and tested in a real case; specifically it has worked at the parking of the Institute for Cybernetic Science and Technology of the University of Las Palmas de Gran Canaria, having this parking space a capacity for 10 cars. The tests were performed to verify the following aspects:

- Communication system used to control the wireless sensor network by the Gateway Node. The test carried out tried to check if the communications were performed correctly so that the status of sensor nodes of the network or when the sensors detected objects can be read or programmed.
- Correct detection of vehicles of different sizes. The goal of this test was to verify if vehicles of different lengths (from 2.6 m to 10 m), circulating at different speeds (from 20 km/hour to 50 km/hour, the speed limit in a garage is 20 km/hour) were correctly detected.
- False positives behaviour. This test was performed to check if the system generates false positives due to transit of objects that were not vehicles, like people or shopping cart.

With the first version of the system prototype we have checked that the communication system works properly, but not the vehicles detection with a high rate of false positives. The conclusion about this misbehaviour was that the sensor used in this first version of the prototype did not work properly. For this reason different sensors were tested, observing that infrared sensor SHARP 2Y0D02 behaved correctly. Testing vehicles of different lengths circulating at different speeds, the conclusions were: first, for a correct detection of the vehicle transit, the pair of sensors should be at a distance (system parameter D) of 1.6 meters, and second, these should simultaneously detect the presence of an object for a minimum time (system parameter T) of 0.123 s (worst case: a vehicle of 2.6 meters length, circulating at 50 km/hour).

4   Conclusions

In this contribution, a system for parking space management has been presented. This system uses a wireless sensor network to monitor automatically on-street parking lots in different areas of the city. The data produced by the sensors are transmitted to a Data Center that produce information about parking spaces availability for public authorities, transport agencies or citizen. The system permits a flexible management since it can monitor a specific parking zone or a set of parking areas. As a consequence of this characteristic, the system can work as a hosting system for parking management.

As future work, several lines of action arise. The first is to deploy the sensor network in Las Palmas de Gran Canaria City. A second line of future work would be to improve the configuration of the sensor network using the collected data. Finally, it is important to develop real time warning system for citizens about congested areas of traffic, recommending parking zones based on preferences or more frequent routes travelled by drivers.

References

1. Mahmud, K., Gope, K., Chowdhury, S.M.R.: Possible causes & solutions of traffic jam and their impact on the economy of Dhaka city. J. Manag. Sustain. 2, 112–135 (2012)
2. Pineda, M., Abadia, X.: Criterios de Movilidad, el estacionamiento urbano en superficie, Fundación RACC (2011)

3. Mingkai, C., Tianhai, C.: A parking guidance and information system based on wireless sensor network. In: 2011 IEEE International Conference on Information and Automation (ICIA), Shenzhen, China, pp. 601–605 (6–8 June 2011)
4. Tang, V.W.S., Yuan, Z., Jiannong, C.: An intelligent car park management system based on wireless sensor networks. In: 2006 1st International Symposium on Pervasive Computing and Applications, Urumqi, China, pp. 65–70 (3–5 August 2006)
5. Hongwei, G., Wuhong, W., Weiwei, G.: Micro-simulation study on the effect of on street parking on vehicular flow. In: 2012 15th International IEEE Conference on Intelligent Transportation Systems (ITSC), Anchorage, Alaska, AK, pp. 1840–1845 (16–19 September 2012)
6. Litman, T.: Parking management, comprehensive implementation guide. Victoria Transport Policy Institute, Victoria, BC, Can. (27 January 2015)
7. Barone, R.E., Giuffrè, T., Siniscalchi, S.M., et al.: Architecture for parking management in smart cities. IET Intell. Transp. Syst. **8**, 445–452 (2014)
8. SHARP: Distance Measuring Sensor Unit Digital output (80 cm) type. GP2Y0D02YJ0F datasheet (December 2006)
9. TEXAS INSTRUMENTS: CC2538 Powerful Wireless Microcontroller System-On-Chip for 2.4-GHz IEEE 802.15.4, 6LoWPAN, and ZigBee® Applications. CC2538 datasheet (April 2015)

Author Index

Printed in the United States
By Bookmasters